Franklin Smoke

FRANKLIN SMOKE

WOOD • FIRE • FOOD

AARON FRANKLIN
and
JORDAN MACKAY

Photographs by Wyatt McSpadden

Ten Speed Press
California | New York

Contents

Preface • 8

1
OUT OF THE ASHES
Smokehouses, Storms, and Sauces • **11**

2
THE HARDWARE
Smokers, Grills, and Firepits • **33**

3
THE WOODSHED
A Prime Ingredient and Other Fuels • **53**

4
THE WHOLE FIRE
Coals, Flames, and Smoke • **73**

5
WARMING UP
Essential Pantry Items, Tools, and Rubs, Spices, and Sauces • **93**

6
OPEN FIRES
Home Cooking on the Firepit and the Grill • **127**

7
SLOW SMOKE
A Return to Barbecue • **175**

Acknowledgments • 215
Index • 219

Preface

In 2021, Daniel Vaughn, *Texas Monthly*'s barbecue editor and a writer who continues to make a sizeable and underappreciated contribution to this country's food literature, penned a profound piece in that magazine. "After 411 joints tested," he wrote, "I can confidently report that our favorite smoked meat [brisket] is so reliably excellent in all parts of Texas that it no longer feels like an achievement. Texas brisket has peaked."

Vaughn notes that he's not complaining but rather marking this moment with appreciation, as in the past, "praiseworthy smoked brisket was the bovine equivalent of unobtainium for entire regions of Texas."

The piece was of particular meaning to people named Franklin and those associated with them because, as Vaughn wrote:

> I can tell you exactly when this path to excellence began: December 2009, when Aaron and Stacy Franklin started selling their smoked brisket in Austin.... Copycat joints—I won't name names because there are too many—started to pop up. Then Franklin wrote down all of his smoky secrets in *Franklin Barbecue: A Meat-Smoking Manifesto*, published in 2015. He had written an instruction manual and handed it to his competitors. When the most famous brisket cook the world has ever seen tells you exactly how to replicate his cash cow, enterprising pitmasters are going to do exactly that. Much of our current glut of superlative smoked brisket comes from barbecue joints that opened in the post-Franklin barbecue world . . . a whole lot of Texas brisket tastes like we're eating a cover song. Granted, it's a cover of the greatest barbecue tune ever written.

I quote at such length because the writing is good and perfectly explains the situation. In today's world, so rich with great barbecue, it's hard to imagine a time when truly tender, crusty brisket didn't really exist. I grew up in Austin in the 1980s and '90s and ate barbecued brisket mostly on special occasions. I don't remember ever being wowed by it.

In Aaron's decision to teach the world how to cook brisket just the way he does lies a certain contradiction: he remains somewhat competitive. Not with any single person or restaurant, but with the entire brisket-making establishment that he helped create. Aaron cares deeply—and he and Stacy work very hard—to ensure that the quality at Franklin Barbecue never dips. As he's seen other barbecue joints arise all over the state touting world-class brisket—and, as Vaughn notes, many of these pitmasters probably learned brisket technique from the book, while a few learned the craft directly from having worked at Franklin—he's taken it in stride and applauds new success stories, even as he doubles down on his restaurant's own efforts to remain top quality, which is no easy feat.

In a world where even top restaurants have trouble finding dishwashers and servers, recruiting people to work long hours tending fires in the Texas summer is even harder. Training them in the art of brisket (and other meats) is another story. Of course, Franklin Barbecue's success is not just about the quality of the brisket. All the food is good, but I maintain that the friendliness of the staff and the cheery hospitality customers receive there makes for an exceedingly satisfying experience worth repeatedly waiting in line for, which many people do. That spirit is in the restaurant's DNA and can't be taught in a book.

One thing about Texas in the era of Peak Brisket that's easy to overlook, yet can't be overstated, is that making and selling world-class brisket is never easy. Rather, it requires supreme effort, beginning with building or buying a costly, massive smoker and then devoting long, often thankless, nocturnal hours to cooking.

No matter who you are, it's a challenge to produce a great brisket once, let alone daily, and Aaron not only respects that, but applauds it. So even as sharing brisket-smoking technique has fostered new competition, Aaron recognizes the cost and effort required to produce good barbecue and create a sustainable business. For that, I know he wishes everyone the best.

Especially gratifying is that, in this digital world full of distraction and abstraction, so many people are taking up the challenge of slowing down and cooking with the elements. There are few slower "slow foods" than brisket, which we revisit in these pages. We also feature several other techniques that require the time and effort of building a fire, creating a strong coal bed, and then cooking slowly over it to get layers and layers of flavor and texture. As is Aaron's way, he's far more interested in technique than in the specific ingredients in sauces and seasonings, which he's more than happy to leave up to your own individual preferences.

Cooking anything—but especially large cuts of meat—with fire and smoke is one of the most challenging and gratifying culinary acts. So even in the era of Peak Brisket, where it's more available than ever before, we hope this book will inspire you to get outside, light a chimney, and fire up some deliciously slow food.

—Jordan Mackay

1

OUT OF THE ASHES

Smokehouses, Storms, and Sauces

When it rains, it burns. Is that a saying? Maybe not, but I feel that I can say it after the time I've had since I last reported from the pages of *Franklin Barbecue* and *Franklin Steak*. While I've enjoyed my share of laughs and fun, now that I reflect on it, I've also had a stretch of struggles, just as you—and the country as a whole—surely have.

My wife, Stacy, and I are very lucky to have an incredible staff and loyal, loving customers who help to sustain us during challenging times. Nevertheless, I can easily imagine watching a zany Netflix series (like the oh so many we've binge-watched lately) based on the totally unpredictable developments that have occurred at Franklin Barbecue over the last seven years or so, including a fire in the middle of a rainstorm and the storm that is the COVID-19 pandemic. Cue a trailer featuring the high jinks surrounding a popular barbecue joint in never-a-dull-moment Texas. (I *do* wonder who the director would get to play Stacy.)

In many ways, this book has emerged out of the ashes, so to speak, after everyone's normal way of life broke down during the pandemic. Like many of you may have experienced, I found myself with more time at home than I'd had since I was a child. At first, when none of us knew how long the pandemic was going to last, I headed into the backyard where my grills, smokers, and firepits live and started cooking for my family. I'm lucky to be able to say that this strange situation turned out to be positive for a number of reasons: it was a reminder of what I love doing, an outlet for my creativity, and a good excuse to spend time outdoors. Soon enough, I found myself on Zoom meetings, doing video cooking demos, and generally shifting to a distanced online world. When I checked in with my coauthor, Jordan, he was going through a lot of the same stuff: tons of cooking and sort of reveling in the free time and space we suddenly had while trying not to worry too much about what was going to happen to life as we knew it.

But before we go there, let's rewind a few years so I can catch you up.

In 2017, we had a fire—a big fire. In what could be described as almost biblical circumstances—a driving wind and rainstorm powered by a massive hurricane hundreds of miles away—our smokehouse went up in flames. If the last thing you read about us was in *Franklin Barbecue*, you might have in mind the cowboy-like romance of how I cooked barbecue under the stars, espresso in hand, eyeglasses reflecting the flickering of a half-dozen roaring wood fires.

Well, that situation didn't last for more than a few years. In fact, the cover of *Franklin Barbecue* was photographed on the freshly poured concrete slab of what would become our new smokehouse. The main reason for building the smokehouse was both practical and legal. We didn't own the vacant dirt lot on which we had been cooking. We rented it. But our operation was spread between two separate properties, which, it turns out, isn't technically very legal. We had to combine operations into one property, a shift we had tried to make countless times. In the end, that wasn't possible.

So, we built the smokehouse. Its unusual design—a two-story addition to the existing restaurant, with an industrial elevator to haul firewood and meats from ground-floor storage to a second-floor room packed with crackling barbecue pits—reflected the necessities of our unique property. It is built into a surprisingly steep hillside on the edge of a commercial block and is the only smokehouse I've ever seen located on the second floor of a building. On paper, I admit, this is a terrible idea. But up in the air was the only place to put it.

Property lines were not the sole reason to build it, however. The smokehouse was also an attempt to make life easier for me and the other cooks. This was all part of our effort to step up and act like a real, sustainable business versus a collection of pieces jury-rigged together. You see, when we first opened the brick-and-mortar restaurant, we cooked out of the back lot by necessity. The setup was very rustic,

OUT OF THE ASHES

making it feel as if we were still part food truck. While the restaurant that we took over had been a barbecue joint, the owner hadn't been cooking on offsets over live fire. Rather, he had two Southern Pride ovens, one he took and one he left behind. We had to cut out the back wall of the restaurant and get a slide truck in there to move that old oven out.

Late one night a few days before we were set to open, the inconvenient fact became clear that there was no place to put a couple of multi-thousand-pound barbecue pits. The only way we could set them up was to wheel the trailers right over. But that

was tricky because you can't have a door on one property, cross over to make food on a different property, and then cross back over to the original property to serve the hot food. Or at least you couldn't with our permits. That meant cooking in the back lot was a necessity. (And we rented that spot for $200 a month in, ahh, the old Austin of 2010.)

Two days before we opened, I cut a back door in the restaurant with a Sawzall to allow access to the vacant lot from our restaurant kitchen. Cutting through the metal on the side of the building was so dang loud. It was late at night, so Stacy was outside the wall with blankets trying to muffle the noise. Of course, at the time, most of the people sleeping in that neighborhood were the homeless or prostitutes and drug dealers—but we didn't want to wake them either!

There were no steps in the back lot, only gravel and dirt on the hillside—and it was slippery. When we had to add a new cooker to meet growing demand, I got railroad ties to terrace the hillside in order to fit more equipment. I'd be landscaping while cooking ribs. (Good thing a shovel is a multiuse tool.)

When we needed an office in our little shantytown, we added a trailer, which we still have. But, more important, we couldn't get a truck to unload firewood where we needed it, so it had to be hauled in. And there was no place to roll dollies, so briskets got dropped off on the front porch every day, and I had to pick them up and carry each box to the refrigerator. It was hard on the body and took a lot of time. I did the work because it was *our* business, but you can't expect to hire people for heavy loading when it's dark, dangerous, sometimes muddy or slippery, and completely brutal, physical labor.

I also hoped having a smokehouse that got us out of the rain, the wind, and the cold in winter would make our cooking more consistent. On the road to achieving that, though, the smokehouse made some aspects of our process *more* difficult. When I was cooking in the backyard, there was a little picnic table nearby where I could sit with my espresso. All the cookers were arranged so I could watch them at the same time—five or six at once. It was really convenient. Not so in the smokehouse. There was no vantage point from which you could see all the fires, so they had to be checked constantly. It took about a year, but we finally got our habits dialed in.

Back when I used to cook ribs, three degrees of temperature variability was my target. I might have one cooker at 278°F and the other at 275°F, burning really clean. That's not easy to do, and I was at the top of my game. When we moved into the smokehouse,

I had to relearn everything because all the radiant heat from the cookers got trapped in the room, making the ambient temperature hotter than it ever gets outside, even in the dog days of summer. And, of course, we had to extend the smokestacks enough to stick through the rooftop, which changed the dynamics of their draw. Plus, it was flippin' hot inside, just brutal—in the summer and in the winter.

Logistically, the smokehouse worked out great, and I was really happy with it, even if it slightly took away from the art of it all—but that's just me liking things as basic and as simple as possible. Altogether, it was a good thing. It made work less hard for people, which was the goal. (But the unintended consequence of *that* was that people didn't work *as* hard. Go figure.)

Now, the concept of building a wooden structure to hold several roaring fires might seem a little dubious. And, looking back, sure enough, it was.

The fire happened at around 5:00 a.m. on August 26. We close for about ten days every year in August to do maintenance and cleaning, and had saved up some money to put this amazing epoxy—the same stuff NASA uses—on the kitchen floor. I stayed at the closed restaurant while all the employees went on vacation. Then once we reopened, Stacy, our daughter, Vivian, and I took our vacation—the first time we had ever taken leave while the restaurant was open. I remember saying to the staff, "Alright, y'all, you got this! Don't mess it up. And don't call me unless the place is on fire." Talk about the dumbest thing I could possibly say.

Escaping Texas, we flew to Vermont, rented a car, drove to Montreal, and then headed down the Maine coast. We had a great time. On the night of the 25th, we were flying home from Portland, Maine. Hurricane Harvey, due to land that night on the Texas coast, was dominating the news. We were anxiously watching the TV, which was urgently broadcasting the news: "Texas Coast Braces for Harvey." Amazingly, our flight didn't get delayed. Nevertheless, with the reach of the coastal hurricane stretching all the way into Central Texas, we were warned that our flight might be a little dicey. Our approach was super-bumpy, and through the window I felt the clouds were blowing past at unnaturally fast rates. But we landed at 11:00 p.m. And after stopping for late-night tacos (of course!), we got home at midnight and poured ourselves into bed.

At 5:28 a.m., my phone started vibrating. The voice on the other end said, "Hey, the building's on fire!" I didn't freak out. I just said, "Okay, I'll be right there."

The fact is, I'd sorta been planning for this for a while. Like most kitchen people, I'm a prepper and had gamed a fire situation out in my mind. It seemed bound to happen one day. Hopefully it won't, I told myself, but if it does, I should definitely have my ducks in a row and not be caught off guard. So, I sat at the end of the bed for a second and collected my thoughts, then grabbed my shoes and slowly put them on, taking a deep breath. We'd been home for only six hours.

As I raced to the car, the weather was awful. The wind was howling, and sheets of rain were lashing the sides of my truck as I hit the highway in the pitch black of early morning. I got stuck at the interminable light at Twelfth Street with no other cars on the road, and I remember thinking, "Should I just run this?" Of course, I didn't, but from there I could already see the blue and red lights of the fire trucks reflecting off the clouds. Six or seven firehouses serviced the call, and the cops had arrived almost instantly. Everyone got there *so fast*. It makes me a little emotional just thinking about it.

At first, I didn't think it was going to be that bad—maybe just a wall or something. But when I arrived and found the whole street blocked off, cops and fire trucks everywhere, news vans already camped outside, the magnitude hit me. The cop at the roadblock just looked at me through my window, his expression downcast as he flagged me through saying, "Jeez, man, I'm so sorry." Everyone had their eyes on me as I walked up, eyeglasses dripping with rain. The devastation was shocking—walls burned out to the frames, ceilings crashed in, everything black and sooty. You wouldn't think that something could burn so heavy in a rainstorm. I went into the crowd and hugged the employees who were there. We were pretty shaken. Soon more employees, having seen the reports on the news, showed up.

Turns out the fire burned for just twenty-eight minutes, but, man, it did a lot of damage in that time. It started from Bethesda, the big, wood-burning rotisserie I had built. Due to the hurricane, that night had been really windy—windier than ever before. The smokehouse had screened-in windows but no storm covers. The wind came up from the ground floor, underneath the wood cage, and blew up through the elevator shaft to hit Bethesda's six-foot-long firebox. Our rib cook hadn't noticed that an ember had blown out of the firebox and tucked under a wall. It probably smoldered there for a few hours and, when more wind came through, the whole wall went up in flames all at once. Of course, at that point, the cook noticed and called 911. I'd installed some insulated heat shields and other things, but the wood in the walls had been heat-drying for a couple of years, making it extremely flammable. Later on, the firefighters told me it had gotten up to 1500°F in there.

In the end, we got real lucky because the outreach from our community was amazing. So many people called, texted, and emailed—we were flabbergasted. Someone from Europe saw the news on CNN and wrote in, completely worried and freaked out. Our restaurant burning down made international news? We couldn't believe it!

But, crucially, on that same day, the architect who'd helped design the smokehouse called, the framers reached out, the plumber checked in—everybody who had worked on the building. They said, "Hey, let us know when we can get started again." The general contractor said, "Tell me when, so I can clear my schedule." The city reached out almost immediately, and the permit guy that I'd dealt with on the first smokehouse said, "I can get this through pretty quick if you don't change much. I can resubmit the same plans and have a permit in your hand by the end of the week." It was like the plot of *The Blues Brothers*—we were getting the band back together!

The closure gave us a chance to make some improvements and take a much-needed break. Today, people note the unusual canted wall that juts out from the building at an angle far greater than 90 degrees. While, yes, that look does fit with my love of early modernist 1950s design, the reason for it is more practical. Let's just say that the smokehouse is something like 999.5 square feet. To go over a certain size would have pushed the project into an entirely different class of restaurant permitting, which would have been very difficult to navigate. The angled wall allowed us to fit in one more pit—a huge win for brisket capacity and for our ability to serve all our customers—with enough room for a cook to stand there and open the cooker door. We added steel window shutters so we can completely block the wind in case of another big storm. And we also changed the roofline—six feet on one side, four feet on another—and built a vent that allows the airflow to suck the radiant heat right out of the room.

To our great fortune, everything worked out. We maxed out every insurance policy—they all refused to renew our policies anyway—and began the rebuild. Construction lasted six months, but we were only closed for about three. When we first reopened, we were back to cooking outside. I had all new trailers built. We moved two of the cookers that we didn't like much from the smokehouse to use outside while we built two better replacements. Welcome, Mork and Mindy. Adios, Ciccone and MC5.

We reopened for business on the Tuesday of Thanksgiving week—a day that has mucho significance for us. It just happens that a lot of the same families come to the restaurant on that day every year. The amount of tears shed and number of hugs given as we walked up and down the line greeting people—talk about an emotional day. Who'd a thunk that barbecue could get people so worked up? That's when it dawned on me how much the restaurant means to so many people. And that's why we work so hard at what we do.

Lots of other stuff has happened in our little barbecue world since last I wrote. For a while, we had extra trailers in the parking lot to serve espresso and tacos. That was really cool. The coffee was primarily to cater to the people waiting in line for the restaurant, but people from all over the neighborhood ended up coming by too. And, not surprisingly, I drank my fair share. The taco truck was especially awesome because tacos are probably some of my favorite food. It was like a dream for me. We used brisket scraps, made our own delicious sauces, and even had eggs (which I don't like). The salsa was made with parsley (because I hate cilantro, a difficult situation down here in taco land). And the tacos were delicious. I loved it, and the truck was holding its own but, unfortunately, the pandemic shut it all down, and it didn't make the cut once we returned.

That said, today we have an awesome to-go trailer, which has been amazing for our business and our workflow. In true Franklin style, I bought a blank trailer and we customized it at the shop, adding prep and cutting stations, storage for to-go paraphernalia, a window, and so on. This operation is partly an evolution of a strategy to deal with the giant orders that often come from the head of the line. You see, the people who get in line early at the restaurant often come to place a huge order. But fulfilling those massive orders takes so much time, and it is agonizing to watch the faces of the rest of the folks who have been waiting almost as long and still have to sit by while we cut an insane amount of meat for just a handful of orders. So, we started diverting those big orders through the to-go trailer, which also services take-out orders and briskets for shipping. Right now, about half of our business goes through that trailer.

Having experience doing a solid to-go business and the fact that barbecue holds well for this kind of service were a real boon when the pandemic struck. As I said, I'm a prepper and don't like to be caught unaware. But the pandemic really caught me off guard! I don't keep up with the world of virology, and so I hadn't thought of this as a real possibility, much less gamed out situations if it did strike. Luckily, we had a leg up because we'd already started doing the to-go operation, which allowed us to transition quickly to pandemic conditions.

It was a Sunday in mid-March 2020. The South by Southwest conference had just been canceled, and an ominous feeling was settling over the world. No one was wearing masks in Austin yet, and it had become impossible to get people in our line to observe six feet of social distancing. So, Stacy and I just looked at each other and decided to close for dining and pivot to curbside service only. I don't know how Stacy did it, but within twenty-four hours, she had reconfigured the entire restaurant. We took out all the chairs and dining tables and moved in prep tables, coolers, and slicing stations. We brought in two computers, moved the telephone into the dining room, and figured out what we were going to offer, starting with minimum orders of three pounds. Stacy remade the website, figured out an ordering system, and photographed every item. By Monday, we had switched to curbside service. This was just a few days before the whole city shut down. Stacy has a photo of our sad, little darkened restaurant on a gray day in March with a sign out front reading

---

Dining Room Closed.

Curbside orders only. Franklinbbq.com.

We had no idea what to expect, but from the get-go, the curbside scene was *busy*. While Stacy, the brains of the operation, was inside directing the operation, I was outside managing traffic. Waiting cars started to back up, with the line stretching down the block. It was just like our usual lineup, only a car takes up a lot more space. Soon enough, the line was snaking down two blocks, curling around onto an arterial road, and even stretching onto the I-35 access road.

The city had to temporarily relocate a bus stop. I remember running around on foot, talking to people in cars on the access road, sounding ridiculous.

"Are you driving through or are you here for Franklin Barbecue?"

"I'm here for barbecue."

"Okay, head into this lane and just follow the car in front of you."

"Cool man. Hey, can I get a selfie with you?"

The pandemic was tough for everyone but it hit restaurants particularly hard. Yet, as things sort of stabilized, we realized that we could keep doing full to-go service, which kept us afloat during the long year and a half when we were closed for in-person dining. This allowed us to keep our heads above water, our workers employed, and our suppliers busy.

We even developed a healthy preorder business. Orders open six weeks in advance, exactly at midnight. You don't always have to plan that far ahead but should if it's Superbowl Sunday or Thanksgiving—all our orders sell out in about five minutes. However, if it's a Tuesday in the middle of winter, there's a good chance you could place an order only four days out. You still must order at least three days in advance so we can manage our quantities. After all, briskets take a half day to cook. And if people don't order it, we don't cook it.

We reopened the dining room to the public in the second year of the pandemic on, you guessed it, the Tuesday before Thanksgiving 2021. And, once again, just as when we opened after the fire in 2017, we saw many of the same people who make it a tradition to come on that day. Needless to say, it was another jubilant and emotional day.

• • •

I should also give y'all a heads-up about our new businesses. Some have been in the works for years, while others came about during the pandemic as ways of keeping us busy and challenged.

Over time, we had been getting tons of requests to ship our food, but due to capacity we were never able to satisfy that demand. During the pandemic, we were cooking less and were able to set some briskets aside to be chilled, shrink-wrapped, and shipped cross-country by Goldbelly or taken home by people who preordered them.

We're now starting to sell our sauces in bottles. I think our sauces are good, and we worked hard on them, but the idea of bottling occurred organically. It's not something we ever planned. And, indeed, it's been a very long process that Stacy has primarily directed.

We had been thinking about selling our bottled sauces, but the practicality it provided to our growing number of to-go customers made it a no-brainer. Once we began selling a ton of chilled, vacuum-sealed briskets—that people want to take on a plane or mail to friends—inserting an open pint of barbecue sauce became, well, messy. It sounds like a simple enough idea, but it suddenly became complex in execution. You can't just make sauce at a restaurant and put it into bottles. You have to use a certified manufacturer. And then once you get the sauce into a container, it must be shelf-stable and last for a certain amount of time. It also has to taste exactly the same as it does at the restaurant and live up to our standards of quality. That meant that the entire recipe had to be reformulated to account for all of this as well as increased production volume.

After many years of development in which we went through scores of recipe variations and tastings to ensure the bottled sauces tasted the same as the fresh ones, we were finally satisfied. (In fact, the new sauces are so good that we're using them in the restaurant now.) Then we had to figure out who was going to distribute the sauces, sell them, and where. Suddenly, a little idea that helped people who want to travel with a brisket became a brand-new business with a separate staff. Hopefully, these sauces will be coming to a store near you real soon because we're very proud of them and they taste good with *any* barbecue—not just ours. (By the way, we don't bottle our espresso sauce; it is only available at the restaurant. After years of trying, it turns out espresso is just too ephemeral to maintain consistency through bottling. Also, during the pandemic, as we honed our bottled sauces, I invented a new one: Spicy BBQ Sauce.)

We got rolling on another few businesses as well—charcoal, barbecue pits, rubs—which you can read about later in this book. These are items that we really wanted to have for ourselves and our friends and families and then thought maybe other people out there might also like to have them.

Well, that's a heck of an update. We're all breathing a little bit easier at Franklin Barbecue now. Who knows what the future will bring? No doubt its own share of calamity. But in the meantime, we have ever-greater confidence in our own abilities to cope and come through doing what we do best. And that's standing outside, tending a fire, and cooking up something good to eat, which is what the rest of this book is devoted to.

• • •

Franklin Smoke is a collection of ideas and recipes for using fire and smoke to cook everyday meals as well as a repository of dishes beyond barbecue that I've been preparing for years at special events and for family. A lot of what you'll find here is the kind of cooking Jordan and I do for ourselves and eat every day (surprise, it's not brisket!). We focus on getting the most out of a fire—in terms of process, flavor, and efficiency—over the entire life span of the coals, treating it not merely as a heat source but as an essential ingredient. We talk about smoking—and the offset cooker that I designed to get just the right touch of smoke flavor—and I detail my evolving thinking on smoking briskets. We break down some of the conceptual barriers that separate smoking and grilling, looking at the two as flip sides of the same coin: fire cooking. We offer techniques oriented toward the range of major cookers that most people have in their backyard. And we go deep into managing coal beds for different temperatures and durations to embrace a greater range of ingredients. As a result, I also include techniques for cooking some things that weren't included in my previous books, like vegetables, birds, fish and shellfish, and beef ribs. And, of course, meat plays a large role.

Along the way, you'll find ideas and some recipes for sides, sauces, and preparations and, as is expected, a detailed look at tools and equipment and serious talk about ideal setups. There is a bunch of recipes in here, too, but as usual, I don't distinguish between technique and recipe. I am way more into the former than the latter. I think if you figure out how to do something well—aka, learn the technique—then infinite recipes become available to you based on that knowledge. So, as always, do as I do and consider these recipes to be guidelines or formats to help you really learn the techniques.

2

THE HARDWARE

Smokers, Grills, and Firepits

Whether you're looking to smoke, grill, or do a little of both, you're going to need something to do it in. Given that myriad options exist in every category these days, selecting the right cooker is no easy task. The only question I probably get asked as often as "How do you know when to wrap a brisket?" is "What kind of smoker should I use?" And that question is almost unanswerable to me since I've cooked mostly on ones that I've built and used a few different styles here and there when I'm traveling. I've never tried too many of the hundreds of variations out there. That question is also one of the reasons—among others, as you'll see—that I decided to manufacture my own cookers. Now I have a surefire answer as to what I recommend.

Remember, you can always make a smoker out of a pit in the ground or a bunch of cinder blocks, and it'll cost you almost nothing. If you want to build a contraption big enough to smoke a whole hog and spend money on only a few big hunks of metal—steel bars, a steel plate for a lid, and maybe a burn barrel—you can do this on the cheap with a little bit of elbow grease. No, that pit will not be mobile, but if, say, you need to move houses, you could pretty easily disassemble it and build it again somewhere else. (Don't expect your grass to ever grow back. Sorry, Stacy!) And yes, this will live as a rather bulky structure in your backyard but, when it's not in use, it makes a fine surface on which to put your drink.

Similarly, instead of buying a fancy grill, you could always dump charcoal in a metal hotel pan, cover it with a cheap grate from a hardware store, and call it a grill—as my dad often did when I was a kid. Now, that's not going to give you any smoke unless you throw some wood chips on top, but it works for generating sizzle.

Likewise, you could spend money on a firepit (not to be confused with a barbecue "pit"), which I love, but remember that a firepit is just a convenient way to contain coals and fire, which could be made just as easily with a little indention in the ground surrounded by a circle of rocks.

You will not be surprised to learn that I believe the Texas-style offset smoker is the greatest device ever invented for cooking things with heat and smoke. While I am going to give some insight into how and why I developed my own smoker, your good use of this book is not at all contingent upon having one. And these techniques and recipes are certainly oriented toward offset cookers, but all the instructions can be applied or tailored to fit whatever type you have. And that includes the techniques of wood chopping and splitting, fire management, and cooking.

OFFSET SMOKERS

To avoid name confusion, I also use the word *pit* to mean a "smoker" or a "cooker," a relic from when folks roasted sides of beef or other large cuts over coals in a dugout trench in the ground. That's as rustic as it gets. To attain more control, enterprising cooks raised that pit off the ground, surrounded it with steel, moved the fire to one side, and exploited the remarkable phenomenon of airflow. Many people still call this a *pit* and some prefer to call it a *smoker*, but I often just refer to it as a *cooker*. So, I guess what I'm saying is that you can consider these terms interchangeable.

THE HARDWARE

The Franklin Pit

For a couple of years, I had been producing and selling my own cookers on a miniature scale, but that started to ramp up recently. The challenge of designing a small backyard pit—as opposed to the bigger, longer ones that I and my crew weld for professionals—came up when I was writing my first book. Given that the construction of pits was so central to the narrative of *Franklin Barbecue*, and because I prefer to do it myself rather than pay someone, I decided to detail the steps to building a cooker in your backyard, as I did with my first homemade pit.

The plan had been to downsize a Franklin Barbecue professional pit for home use. We made the big pits from old propane tanks. However, the day that we went looking for a suitable tank, none could be found in the usual places. Instead, we bought big hunks of steel pipe, which were thicker and heavier than a propane tank, and made a cooker that both worked and was even pretty neat looking. I lit it up once or twice but never had time to really refine it. Today, it occupies a nice pedestal in the YETI flagship store in downtown Austin.

As time passed, the thought of creating personal pits never left my mind, and I've been working on the design for about six years now. The actual shape and form of the smoker is not terribly different from the rustic prototype; but to create a product like this, I learned that we also had to design the production methods and materials, figure out the economics, and create suitable systems for packaging and delivery. It was more complicated than I ever imagined, which is why it took so long before we had anything to sell. For the first couple of years, I was never entirely happy with the quality. We had to learn about tooling, fixturing, and achieving a good fit and finish. I wanted the pits to be perfectly round, which required rolling our own steel. And it took time to learn how to lathe the little fittings for the casters.

Originally, the production shop was housed at our little property in Bastrop, a small town outside of Austin. But it was naive of us to mount a commercial operation there, as we didn't have enough space, there was no loading dock, and we had limited storage. I had been thinking that we could put out two cookers a week, enough to keep a couple of welders working steadily. But those economics didn't work out. And I realized that if we were going to do this, we couldn't half-ass it. It couldn't be a hobby; it had to be a real business. So, we bought land and built a large facility in Austin, but we've already outgrown it. We also found production facilities that are far better at making the cookers than we ever could be in terms of precision, craftsmanship, and efficiency. The first of these refined and polished pits went on sale right at the beginning of the pandemic.

I've been through so many revisions of the design and seen it assembled in different forms and by different teams that I can honestly say that this is the best version of an offset smoker I can imagine. Applying the language of car engines doesn't feel inappropriate. Once you get a fire going in the cooker and see how it starts drawing air in and pumping smoke out through the stack, you'll think it revs like a hemi. And then, once it's up to speed, you'll enjoy how it handles—how one properly selected and placed log, a slight reconfiguration of the coal bed, or a subtle adjustment of the firebox door will reflect shockingly quickly in the temperature.

At a svelte six hundred eighty pounds, the Franklin Pit is truly a rudimentary sort of device whose only moving parts are two doors and the wheels it rolls on. It has no electrical cord, no engine, no fans. It runs on wood (or charcoal)—not pellets—and it doesn't connect to your phone, watch, or the internet. It is primitive technology crafted with contemporary precision and NASA-level materials. Many qualities separate this pit from the kind you can buy for a couple of hundred bucks (like the offset I started on) or even more. First, what makes this pit not only hard to build but also hard to package and ship is the weight of its materials. Most inexpensive or mass-produced smokers are constructed from very thin metal, which has many drawbacks. With a fire crackling inside for hours, the cheap steel will quickly deteriorate. Ill-fitting doors and holes in the steel will negatively affect your cook and cause you to waste fuel.

For the Franklin Pit, we tested various thicknesses of high-quality American steel until we found the one that could withstand fire after fire without changing shape. That thickness assures heat retention at the levels we expect at the restaurant and offers such durability that you could hand this down to your children and grandchildren. Furthermore, in iteration after iteration, we tweaked the design to ensure incredible draw and airflow.

Our firebox is fairly big and double-walled. This allows a large enough fire to push sufficient heat through the cooker while giving you a measure of control. By locating the fire toward the front or back in the firebox, you can significantly raise or lower the amount of direct heat flowing through the cook chamber with the smoke. You can also use real logs in our firebox, not only charcoal and chunks or chips. I recommend cutting logs in nine- to ten-inch pieces; this thing is meant to run on wood.

THE HARDWARE

The door has the Franklin logo cut out of it, an intentional move to allow airflow and ensure that you never accidentally kill your fire. The door can be closed to slow down the fire a bit or opened wide to let air stampede through. But it's really meant to be closed, as the vents are a safeguard against running a dirty fire (one that is starved for oxygen and smolders).

The cook space on the grate inside is big enough to hold three medium-size briskets, enough food for thirty-plus people. Cooking just two briskets is ideal, but the third can be accommodated by placing it closer to the firebox (though I'd recommend setting an obstacle, like a log or a metal plate near the opening from firebox to cook chamber, to block some of the direct heat).

The passage between the firebox and the chamber contains a heat deflector plate that also serves to agitate the incoming stream of air, creating chaotic airflow that constantly bathes the meat in smoke on all sides.

The cooking grate comes out for cleaning with a wire brush and for oiling. The cook-chamber lid has been precisely engineered to open smoothly and handle easily. (It doesn't hermetically seal, however, because we want a little inefficiency there, this allows some variation to give space for delicate meats.) Of course, a Tel-Tru thermometer—the best!—is included. It sits two inches above the grate (the geographical center of most briskets) to measure the temperature the food is experiencing, rather than getting a reading from high above it. Also provided is a pan to fill with water and a shelf on which to place it inside the cook chamber to add humidity.

A grease drain and bucket underneath catch the drippings. Part of your post-cook ritual should be cleaning the pit while it's still warm and then wiping it down with oil. See Maintain Your Smoker on page 41 for tips on care. Remember to season the grates with oil, as well.

Inside, underneath the stack, is our proprietary (patent pending!) smoke collector, a complex design that is mounted on an ellipsoidal head. It directs and concentrates the airflow on the way out, like a guiding star, ultimately streamlining the chaotically moving smoke and air, focusing it around the meat before speeding it on its way.

The detachable smokestack is super-easy to affix: just stand it on its mooring and tighten the included bolts. The stack is a crucial part because it must be tall enough to have a meaningful impact. Air can't be pushed onto a fire efficiently—it must be

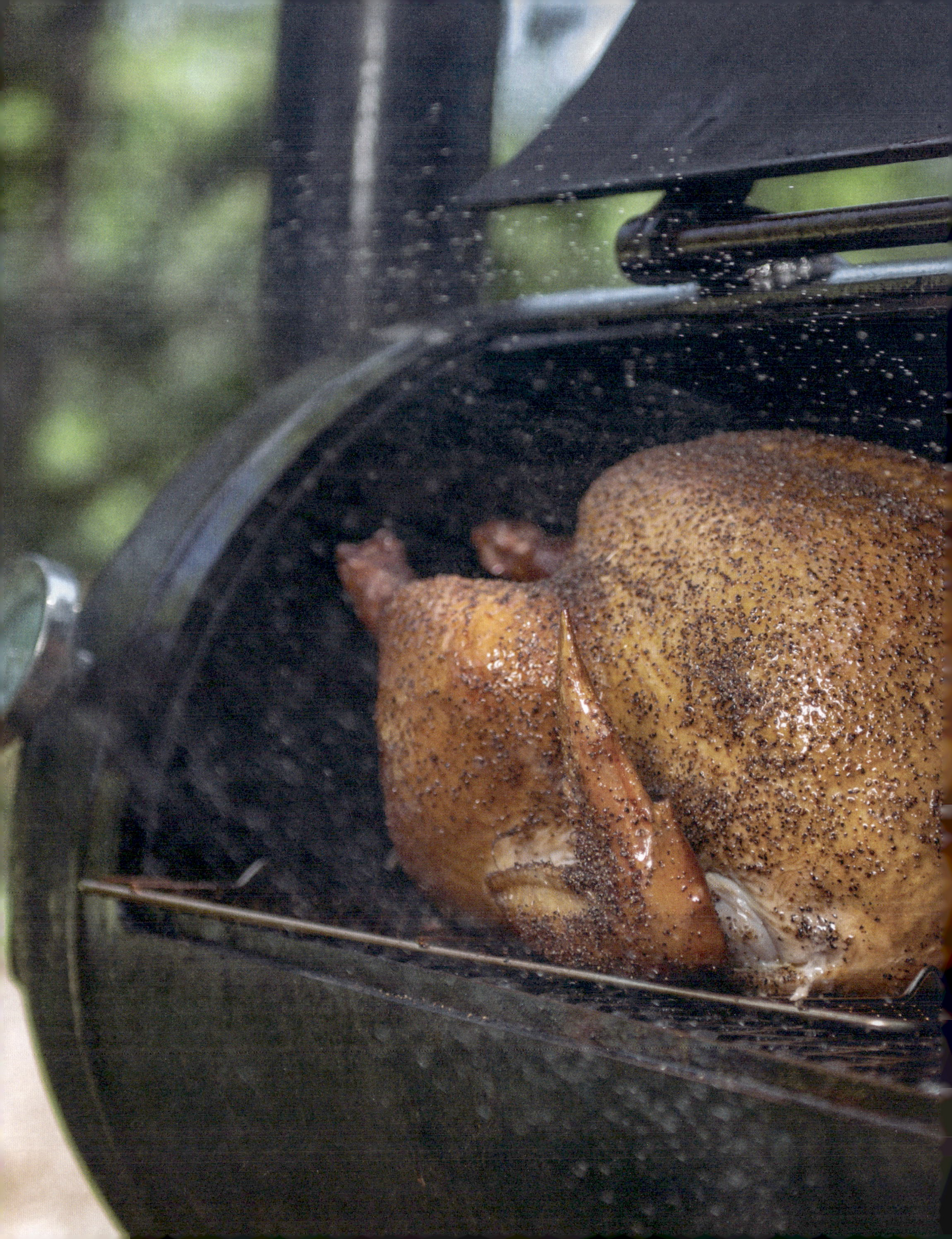

pulled. For that reason, we engineered the smokestack in reverse, starting with the stack and determining the ideal height and width to achieve perfect airflow. And, boy, does it draw, producing a powerful flow of clean smoke swirling in the chamber. Ultimately, forty-two inches turned out to be the magic number, which exactly mirrors the length of the cook chamber in a pleasing display of symmetry.

So, there you have the Franklin Pit as well as a mini-disquisition on the construction of offset smokers. No other kind of cooker smokes as consistently well, can be controlled so precisely with nothing but wood and airflow, and burns so cleanly with such sweet smoke as an offset. To be sure, there are other well-made offset smokers out there, so I encourage you to shop around for one that suits you. Or you can always build one yourself!

MAINTAIN YOUR SMOKER

> Although a well-made smoker is pretty much indestructible, nothing is sadder than one that has been left out to rust or forgotten for months and is caked with disgusting remnants of grease and food. I've cleaned out a few of those suckers in my day, and it's never fun. So make sure you periodically clean out your smoker on the inside—get rid of ash, coals, and grease that might have fallen into the bottom and brush off the grates. I take care of the outside of my cookers by rubbing them down periodically, when they're still warm, with leftover fat from cooking or even just some grapeseed oil. Do the same with the cook chamber grate. This not only keeps 'em looking nice and sharp but also protects them for the long haul.

GRILLS

If a modern-day pit barbecue is just a way of getting a hole off the ground, then a grill is just a method of lifting a cooking fire off the ground. A grill contains the fire, which gives you more control and means you don't have to stoop down while cooking (helpful for those of us with tired backs). With that in mind, I can say that we're definitely living in the golden age of the grill. You can find a million versions and pay as much or as little as you want, go no-frills or add all the bells and whistles.

Since this is a book about cooking over live coals, we're not going to talk about gas grills. While I don't personally use them, even I admit that they have some value if you're just looking to get a little char or some grill marks without any fuss or waiting. But I'm all about the fuss and waiting, often to the annoyance of my family!

In chapter 4, I talk about getting good smoke flavor from the grill, which is not always an easy thing. Charcoal doesn't provide much flavorful smoke on its own. Its action is more like that of a gas grill; the flavor comes from juices and fat dripping down from the ingredient to the heat source, vaporizing, and then rising back up to coat the food. This, on its own, is a distinctly sought-after and delicious flavor. So keep that in mind as you read about the various types of grills.

Kettle Grills

The standard kettle grill allows you to contain a charcoal bed, control the air feed from underneath, and trap heat and smoke with a big domed lid. Its geometry is brilliant, allowing you to have a small heat source in relation to a relatively large cooking area. It is inexpensive and easy to wheel around a deck or driveway. You could even keep a smaller one on an apartment balcony. While a kettle grill works well enough for straight grilling, it has some limitations.

One of those limits is flexibility. True two-zone cooking is compromised. When the cooking zone sits directly over the heat source, you don't have a lot of room to operate away from the heat (and some of the heat from the hot zone inevitably leaks over to the cool zone). A kettle grill is good for a sear and direct cooking but not ideal for more nuanced techniques.

The ability to smoke is also limited on this grill. The lid helps you contain heat and vapor, but a lot of that vapor is actually charcoal fumes, which are not the best. If you push all the coals to one side, you can create a makeshift two-zone setup and add some wood chips or chunks to create smoke, but the airflow isn't great. The vertical distance the smoke travels from the heat source to the top vent is short and direct and lacks proper pull—and the smoke from a smoldering fire is usually not very sweet—so it's hard to get a full, clean cook.

Finally, kettle grills are inexpensive because the metal used to make them is thin. On one hand, that makes them highly portable and affordable. On the other hand, that super-thin metal means it has a limited life span and just leaks heat, which makes it difficult to keep temperatures up for more than twenty to thirty minutes. During longer smokes or roasts, you must add new charcoal often, which is a pain and also slows the cook.

An old kettle grill can be useful for quick, hot cooks and as a place to burn down logs into a steady supply of wood coals that can then be transferred to any sort of cooker to which you don't want to add charcoal. A cheap kettle grill is a mighty handy thing, no doubt, but we can also do better.

PK Grills

I expounded on my affection for the PK (Portable Kitchen) Grill in my second book, *Franklin Steak*. In the intervening years, the company has released some exciting new models. My relationship with the company also progressed, as they allowed me to offer some tweaks and suggestions for their classic grill, which became a whole new model, the PK300AF.

PK is a brand from the early 1950s that had a loyal following until the company went through some trials and tribulations and eventually ceased production. One of those loyal followers rediscovered it in the mid-1980s and decided to resurrect the brand. I found it years ago and used it for all my grilling. I love not only the 1950s space-age look but the masterful construction and design. An oblong shape allows for true two-zone cooking. Four adjustable vents, two on top and two underneath, provide airflow control like no other charcoal grill has. The coal bed is positioned right up close to the grill, allowing for efficient use of charcoal and super-hot searing. And thick aluminum construction holds heat incredibly well (making it suitable for longer cooks) and conducts heat four times better than steel. It is also rust- and dent-resistant and will last for generations. On top of all this, it's not so heavy that one person can't lift it, it's easy to clean, and it's pretty darn portable. Creating a product that will outlive the buyer in our world of planned obsolescence might not be a business model that Wall Street sharks would approve of, but it's the kind of thing I love and support.

The PK is obviously great for grilling and the favorite of many steak cook-off champions in recent years because of its ability to create intense, direct heat. But it can also be used as a smoker, as its shape and vent design allow you to crudely mimic the action of an offset smoker.

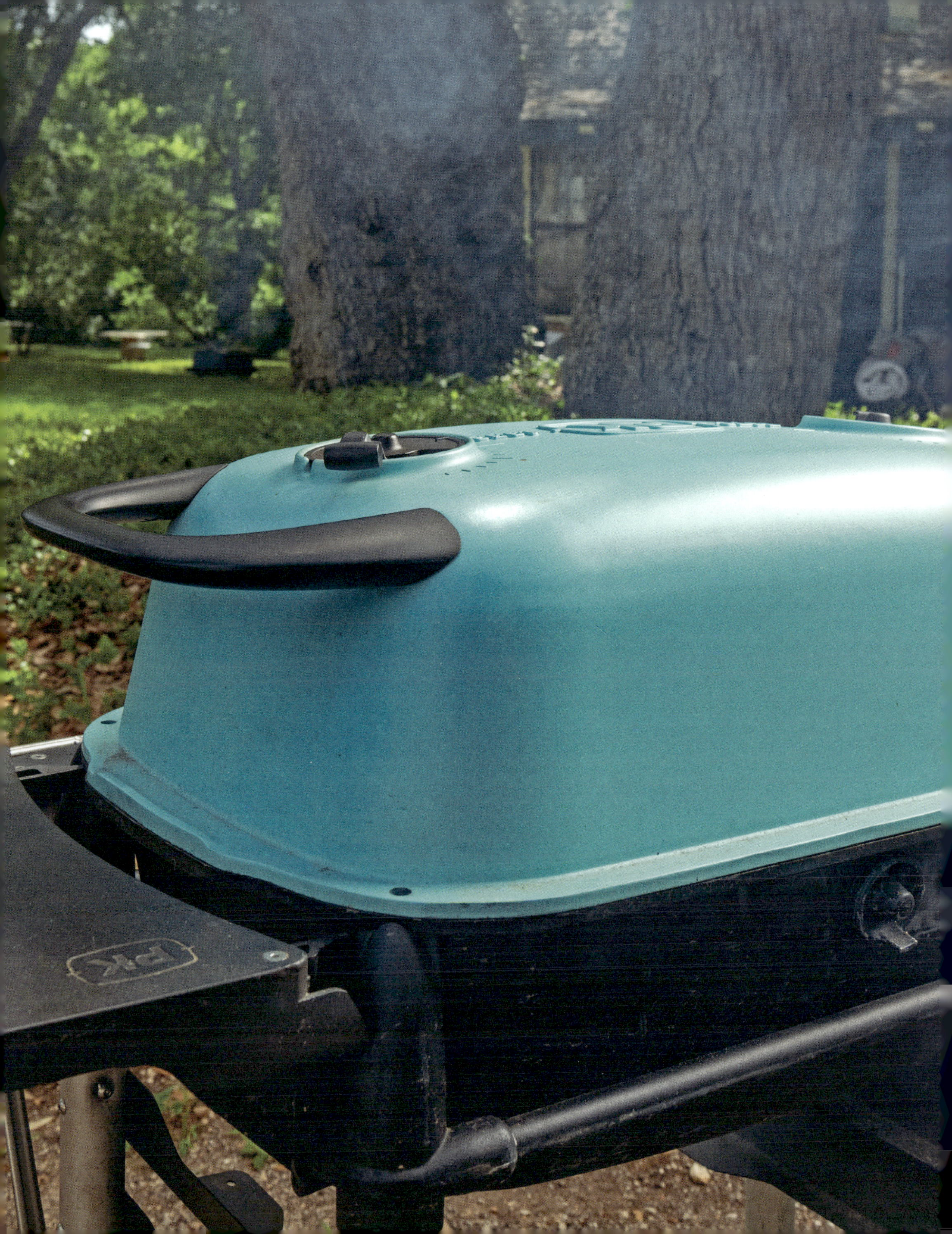

The PK model that I used for years and years is called the Original. I loved it so much that I touted it to anyone who asked (it's rare for me to "tout" anything) and recommended that all my grill-shopping friends consider it. Thanks to this unsolicited enthusiasm, the company brass and I ended up becoming friends, which is how a few of my ideas became incorporated into the PK300AF. The 300 indicates three hundred square inches of cook space, while the AF indicates . . . well, you get it.

The PK300AF is basically a redesigned Original with thoroughly considered new details and a few major additions—elements that, over years of cooking on it, I realized would make the experience just a little bit better. In fact, PK recently updated the Original model, too, incorporating several features such as radial top and bottom vents, which are more precise and easier to manipulate; a better hinge; an upgraded ash control system inside the cooker; a collapsible work surface; and an improved cart. The AF additions are practical and cosmetic, including a little rack on which to hang towels or tongs or whatever you want (they call it a "belly bar"); one more collapsible work surface, doubling the amount of space; and speed racks built right into the cart that hold standard-size sheet pans for added shelf space (the top one even gets warmth from the bottom of the grill). Finally, the PK300AF comes in the bright teal of Franklin Barbecue or in coal-black with teal flakes.

Although I've always clung to the Original model out of aesthetics and habit, the PK360, which PK calls its flagship model, is a great grill too. Its larger form factor provides an additional sixty square inches of grill space, which come in handy. The construction is super-solid, with two winged shelves for placing all your ingredients (and your beverage). And the knobs that PK created for controlling the air vents on the bottom are much more convenient to use than the knobs on the other models, which are located underneath.

The PKGO is a nifty little device that's way more than a hibachi. It's incredibly light, portable, and nice for all manner of single-zone grilling, but with its dual vents, lid, and shape, it actually offers two legit zones. It's also small enough to cart along in the trunk of your car, which is what I do on long, solo road trips.

Santa Maria–Style Grills

A Santa Maria is the type of grill that has a broad, flat surface to hold a thin layer of coals and a grill grate attached to chains and cranks that can be lowered up and down to the desired height above the heat.

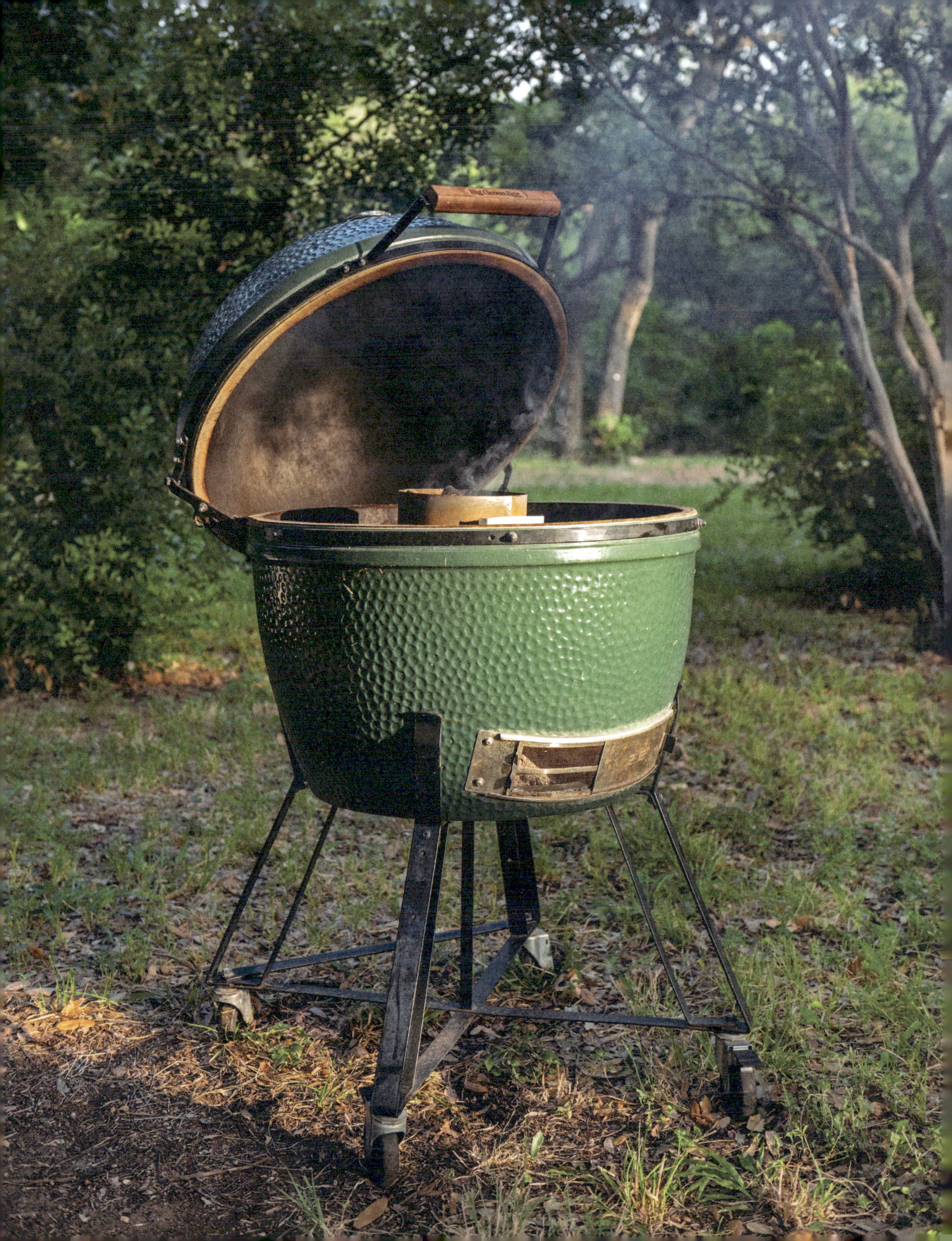

The ability to control the distance between the coals and grate allows for real delicacy and finesse in how you cook something. It's just elevated (pun intended) firepit cooking. You can take, say, a heavier piece of meat (like the tri-tip steak that people in Santa Maria, California, are famous for cooking) and sear it with some up-close heat before raising it to collect gentler heat and some smoke as it cooks all the way through with precision. The crank action allows you to easily replenish the hot coals, making it ideal for use in restaurants or for large gatherings when you've got waves of food to put out. Plus, it looks cool!

Kamado Grills

The ferocity of love, loyalty, and affection that people feel for their kamado grills never ceases to amaze me. Not that these tools aren't worthy of appreciation. It's just that the people who get into them, really get into them! The great appeal of a kamado, such as the Big Green Egg, lies in its versatility and ability to achieve and hold a steady temperature over a long period of time—two of the greatest challenges of cooking barbecue. Because of this, you can roast, bake, and do some degree of smoking on it.

Based on a Japanese design, these cookers are both heavy and bulky thanks to their thick, dense ceramic construction. That means once you put your kamado somewhere, you probably won't want (or be able) to move it. Due to the shape of the grill and the material, the coals are directly underneath the grate. Big Green Egg makes EGGcessories (as they call them), including one that allows you to sequester the coals on one side for a two-zone setup. That might shield food from direct heat but, when you close the lid, the oven-like effect can make it extremely hot inside. I think it works best to stabilize the temperature before grilling. That can take a long time, however, and if you start with too much heat in the first place, cooling down can take a while once this grill gets rolling. It's why practicing on your specific grill is so key. Big Green Egg also makes a heat-shielding plate, which is helpful for smoking. It sits directly underneath your food and forces the smoke up and around into the chamber while also deflecting some of the direct heat. You can get some reasonable smoke in this situation, though it doesn't provide the draw, convection, and clean smoke of a good offset smoker.

> **COLD EGGS**
>
> While Aaron and I were working on this book, I moved across country from California to the icy Northeast. It was my first real East Coast winter, and, despite what people from Wisconsin had told me about grilling year-round, it was definitely hard to get outside and get fires going when our driveway and yard were covered in ice and snow for weeks at a time. However, the few times that I was able to carve a little space to wheel a cooker out of the garage onto the drive, the Big Green Egg proved to be a good adversary against subfreezing temperatures. It heated up well and bravely held its warmth in the cold. **—Jordan**

FIREPITS

Firepits are like labradoodles—they're everywhere these days! Realtors love to photograph houses with a happy family laughing in front of a firepit as the flames and embers dance up into the night sky. Of course, nature's original firepit is as basic as the name suggests. Not only are they primordial (and naturally occurring, sometimes) but firepits, whether in a campsite or a backyard, connect us all. Campfires are the preindustrial televisions! They're nice for ambience, but I appreciate their utility as well. And now there's a new wave of high-end firepits that come with various attached cooking apparatuses that make them even more functional.

A number of years ago, I built a good-size firepit for my family, and we use it often. At the time, we lived in a house without a lot of backyard space, so it was nice to have a contained space for a fire on the back patio. Ours is quite large; made of solid steel, it is four feet in diameter and almost two feet high. The size allows for a very large fire and for five or six people to sit comfortably around it. Welded to the bottom and elevated a few inches above the ground is an external ring that runs around the circumference, serving as a handy footrest. After an hour or so, your toesies get nice and hot resting on the rail, even on the coldest nights. There's also a semicircular grate, which makes it perfect for campfire cooking. It's nothing fancy, but it provides a large surface on which to grill while offering full access to the fire itself to add logs and to push coals around.

Another use for a firepit is as a side fire to produce a ready supply of fresh wood coals that can then be used instead of charcoal in any grill.

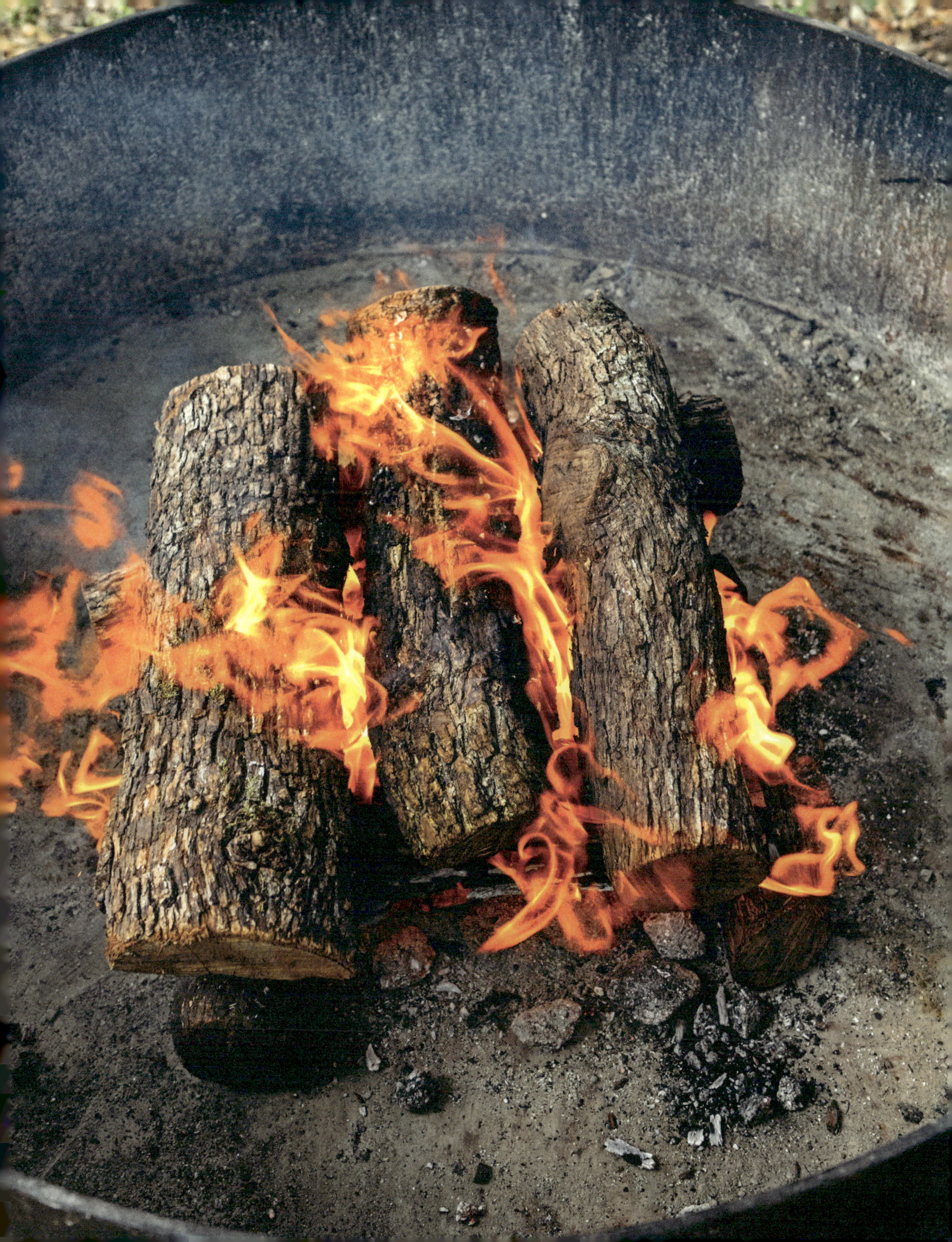

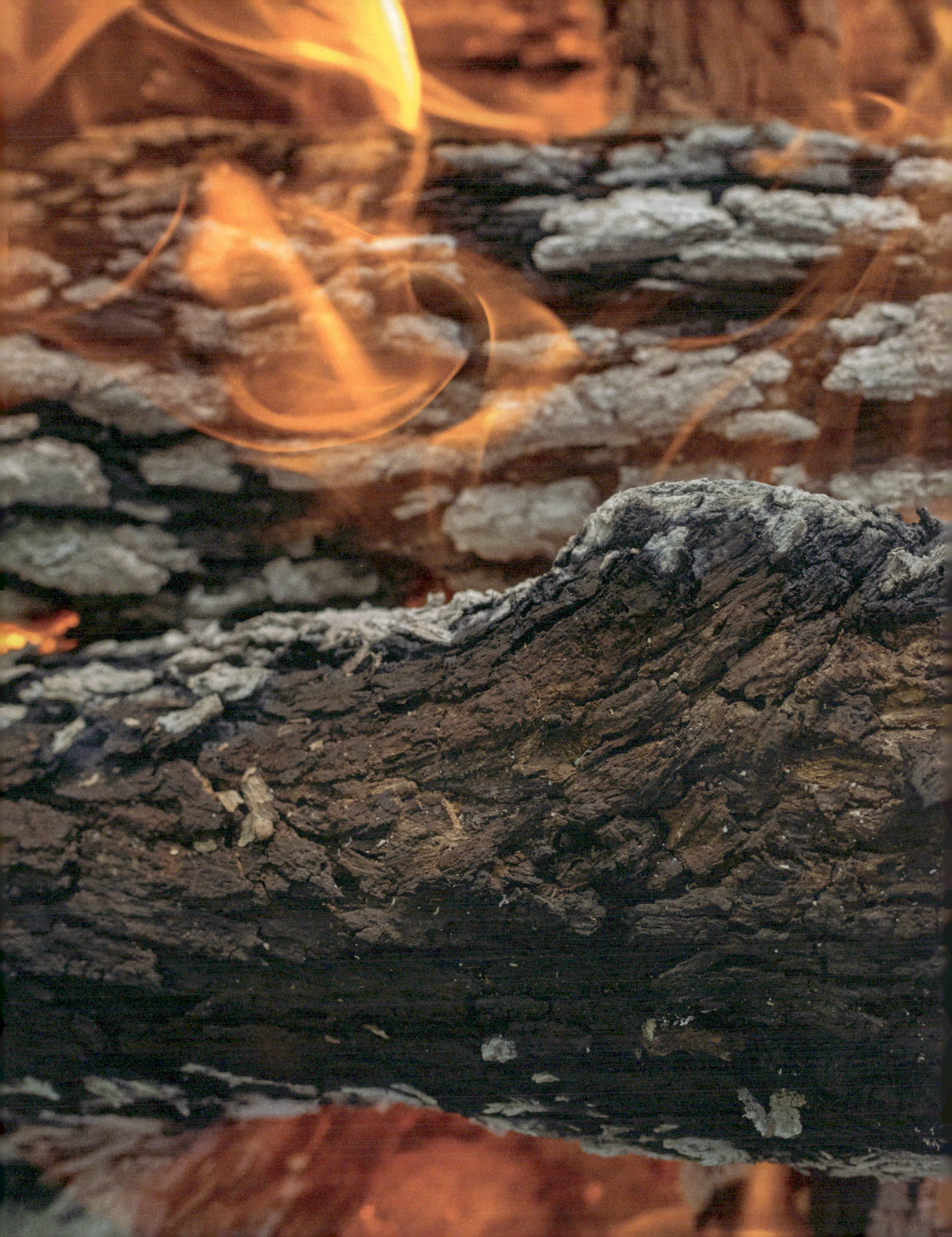

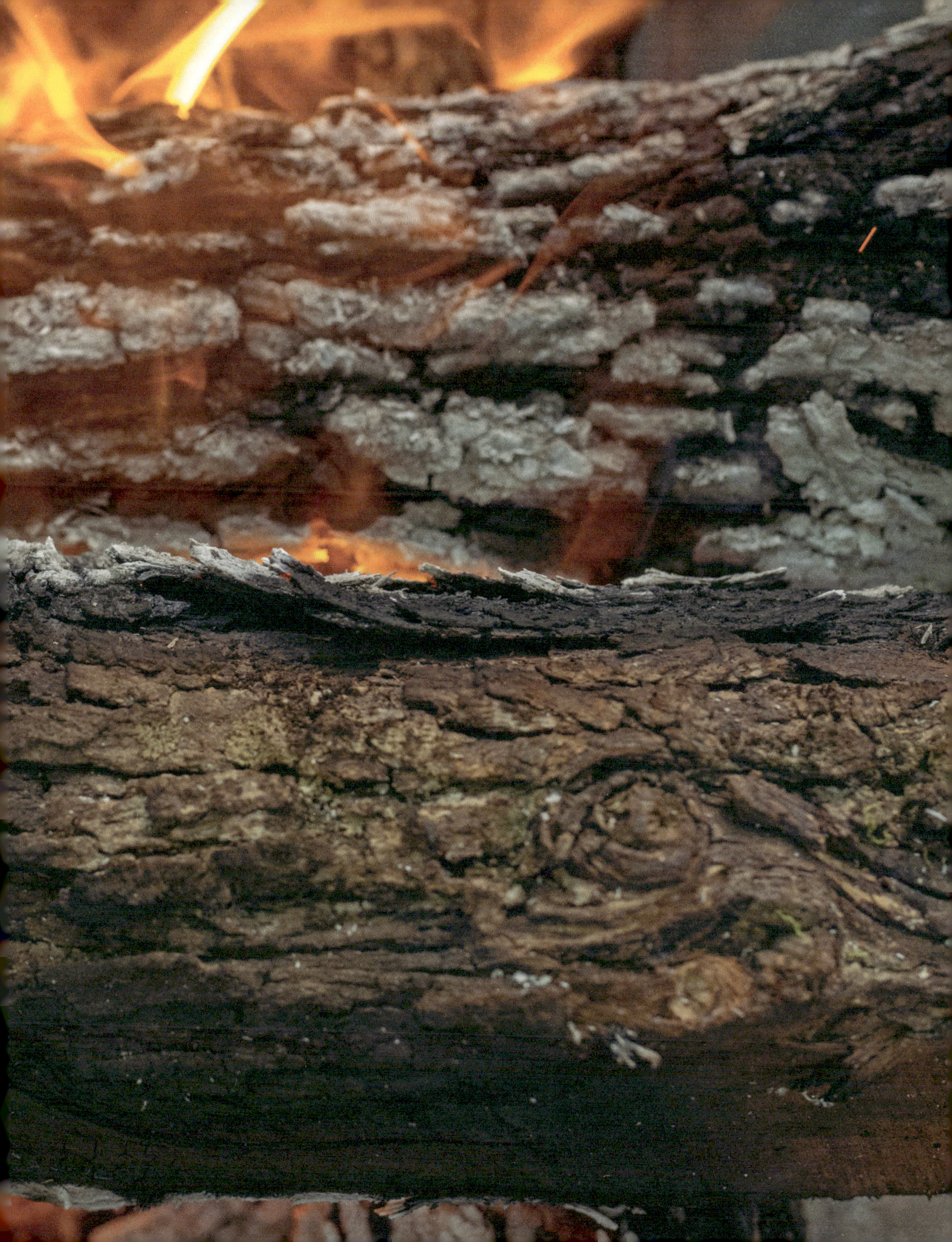

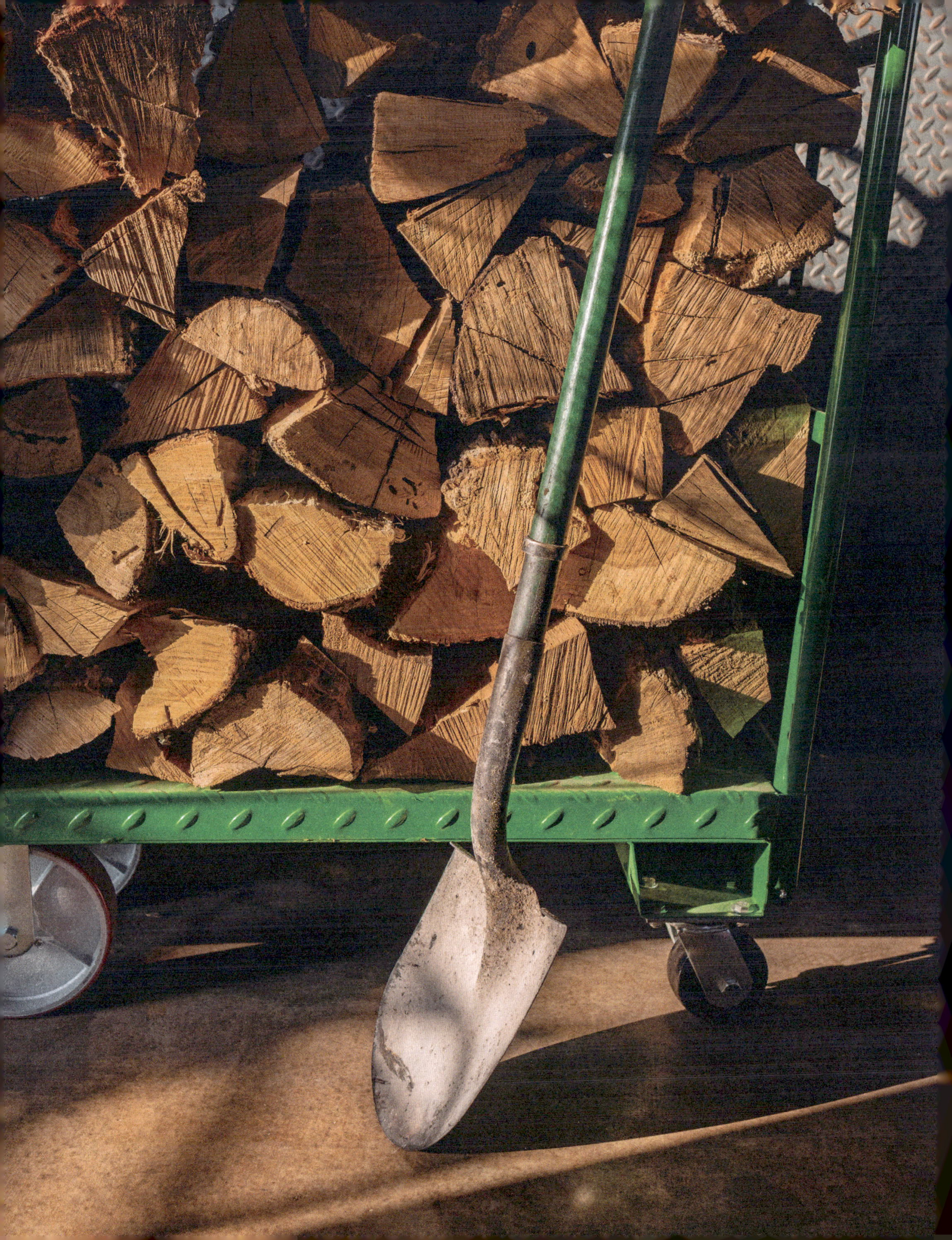

3

THE WOODSHED

A Prime Ingredient and Other Fuels

Where there's smoke, there may be fire. But where there's barbecue smoke, there better be wood. The soul of barbecue is wood. You could argue that it is barbecue's entire reason for being. Not to wax too poetic or anything, but wood is also what connects us to the land, to our natural environment, and to our own deep history as humans and animals. From a materials science point of view, wood is a truly incredible substance as well, designed by nature to be almost as strong, in certain cases, as stone or metal, yet also cuttable, penetrable, and burnable.

I still spend a fair bit of my time loading and unloading firewood from the back of my truck, whether I'm bringing home logs for a backyard cook, schlepping wood to an event, or setting off into nature for a camping trip. It never feels like a chore.

When it comes to cooking, wood is all the rage these days. In outdoor fire cooking, I consider wood to be the prime ingredient. And the quality of the wood is one of the most underappreciated aspects of smoking, which surprises me because wood provides a huge part of the food's flavor. The quality of the combustion of the wood has everything to do with how your food cooks and tastes. With that in mind, I suggest you pay attention to where your wood comes from and its size, consistency, and seasoning level. Of course, wood is a natural, organic product, so you can't expect perfect uniformity from one log to the other. But, in general, you want to have confidence in your supply and to pay attention to each piece you throw on the fire.

In addition to wood, I discuss charcoal in this chapter. Charcoal is valuable to me as a heat source, but I mostly use it in conjunction with wood. As the only true fundamentals of fire cooking, both these elements are worth understanding.

The amount of information—and opinions—about wood for barbecue has exploded in recent years. In some ways, I think the discussions have gotten out of hand. People who are just getting started with barbecue ask me all the time what I think about this or that kind of wood. And while I have had great experiences cooking on all sorts, I would be remiss not to admit that the vast majority of my cooking is done with the wood that is widely available in my area: good ol' Central Texas post oak. While I love post oak, I don't necessarily value it higher than any other kind of suitable barbecue wood. In other words, there's great worth in getting to know the primary wood in your area really well—how it cooks, how it tastes, how it feels. If you want to check out other woods, by all means, play around. But it's good to have a steady companion in barbecue. That said, there are a couple of rules you want to keep in mind.

HARDWOODS VERSUS SOFTWOODS

I like all kinds of wood for cooking as long as they are well seasoned and sourced. The only ironclad rule is that it be a hardwood. That is, don't use softwoods such as leftover IKEA furniture or pine or cedar or fir. Not only do softwoods go up like torches, but they're also commonly full of resins and compounds called terpenes. The smoke from these woods often smells pungently herbal and piney, and so will your food if you use them. Plus, these woods burn so hot and fast that it becomes difficult to control the fire.

Hardwoods, like oak, hickory, almond, pecan, and fruitwoods (apple, cherry, pear), all burn consistently and less wildly and have a deliciously savory smoke. Unlike the compounds of softwoods, the compounds of hardwoods include lignin and flavonoids, which break down through combustion into sweeter- and spicier-smelling smoke.

Just because wood is labeled "hardwood" doesn't always mean it's harder than a wood labeled "softwood." Balsa, for instance, which is often used in model-ship construction, is a very, very soft hardwood. Aspen and alder are both quite soft hardwoods too. On the other hand, southern pine is one of the heaviest, most durable softwoods.

While the terms *hardwood* and *softwood* stem from the descriptions that colonists gave to the woods they used for building, the difference between the two is more technical. Hardwoods have broad leaves, are angiosperms (reproduce by fruit and flower), and are often deciduous, which means they lose their leaves for a time each year. Softwoods, in contrast, are gymnosperms, meaning they reproduce by unencased seeds (not surrounded by a fruit or nut).

Practically speaking, the major differences relate to structure, grain, and content. Softwoods transport moisture, often in the form of resinous sap, through longer, tubelike ducts that make them feel softer when cut. Hardwoods move moisture through shorter, rounder pores of various diameters. When you cut into them, they feel much more solid. People often identify various woods by looking at magnified pictures of crosscuts to examine the pore structure.

Much as there's a measurement of the heat levels in chiles (the Scoville scale), there's a test for hardness in wood, known as the Janka hardness test. Although it sounds like a bar game and does involve shooting a metal ball, it's named for Austrian emigrant Gabriel Janka, a wood researcher who developed the test in 1906. It measures the amount of force needed to embed that steel ball halfway into a six-by-two-by-two-inch piece of wood.

The hardest woods are tropical hardwoods. Australian buloke (a species of appropriately named ironwood) takes the crown with a whopping 5,060 pounds-force (lbf). For reference, live oak checks in at 2,380, mesquite at 2,345, sugar maple at 1,450, and cherry at 995. My beloved post oak is a comfortable 1,350, similar to many other kinds of oak. By comparison, Douglas fir, a softwood, scores 660, while several pines are under 450. Janka measurements are more applicable to using wood as a building material than for barbecue, but it's still good to know something about the materials in your fire.

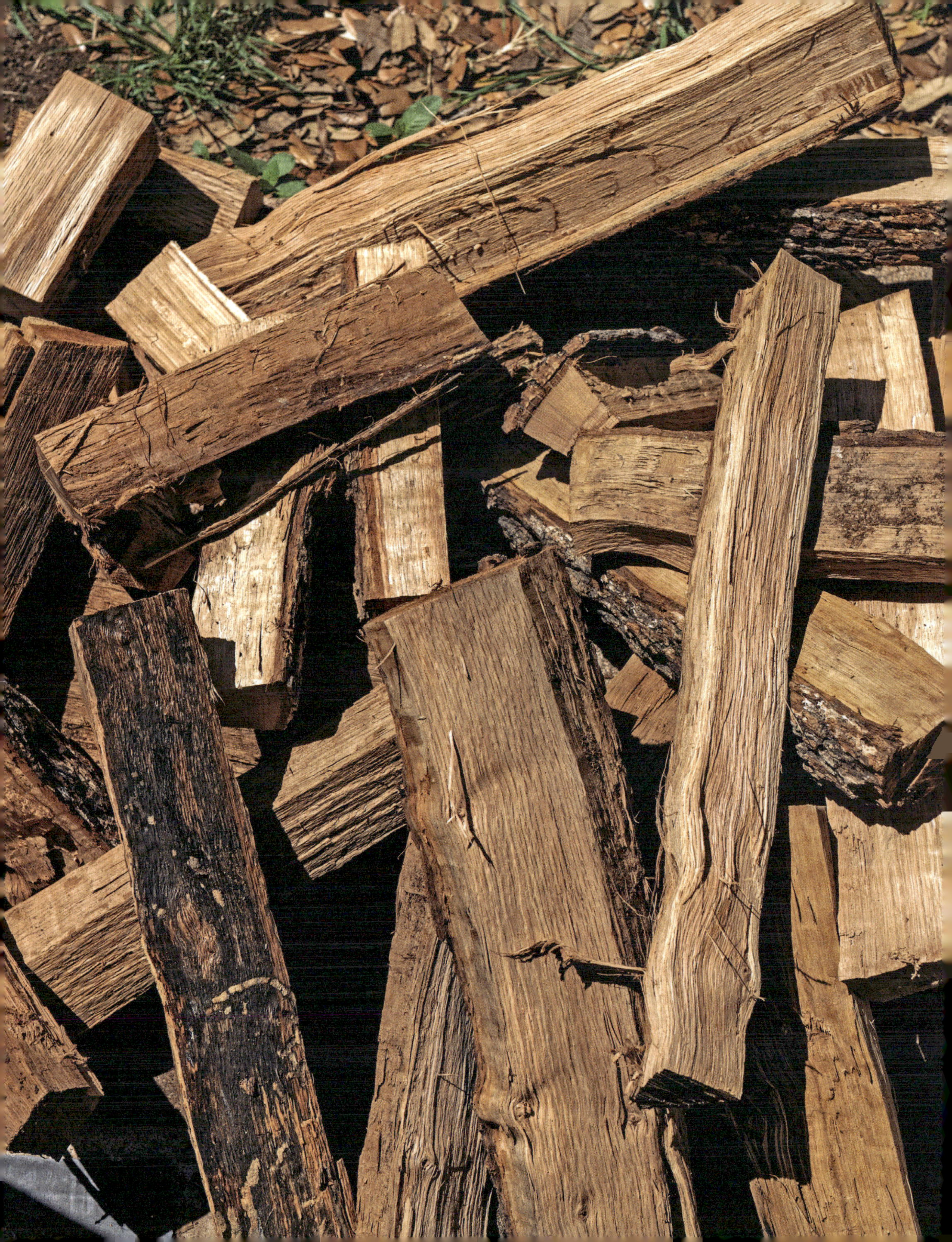

CHOOSE YOUR WOODS WISELY

Naturally, I'm 100 percent devoted to post oak, which burns sweet, hot, and clean. Of course, there are tons of other kinds of wood. You may read about people who choose certain types for various foods. And while that's all fine, I personally wouldn't fret about the kind of wood as long as it's a hardwood and it's well seasoned. There are differences, but you may not notice them unless you cook with one type all the time and then suddenly change. Your ability to deploy wood and fire is far more important than the flavor of each individual species of tree. That said, one thing I don't like to do at all is to mix woods on the same cook. To my mind, it muddies the palate.

A very useful article posted by the Forest Products Laboratory of the US Department of Agriculture notes that "the chemical composition of wood cannot be defined precisely for a given tree species or even for a given tree. Chemical composition varies with tree part (root, stem, or branch), type of wood (i.e., normal, tension, or compression), geographic location, climate, and soil conditions." So whether you're burning cherry or apple or maple, the flavor donated by a chunk or log depends less on the species and more on where it grew and what part of the tree it came from. If you're buying a box or bag of applewood chunks, you know what kind of wood it is (or at least, how it has been labeled), but you rarely know where it came from.

That's why I recommend you use what grows around you and you can get from a good local source. Post oak tends to give an even, mellow, and sweet flavor and burns quite well. Hickory burns as well as oak, but its flavor can be a bit more aggressive. I like the mild flavor of well-seasoned pecan and almond. And unlike many people, I'm not too put off by mesquite. While it can burn very hot and fast, almost like a softwood, and can have an aggressive flavor, I like the way it tastes on the grill when it's well seasoned, and it can give good flavor to a long smoke. Cherry is also quite distinctive, with a high-toned sweet, fruity aroma and a smoke that imparts a distinctive reddish hue to whatever's bathed in it, which makes it popular in competition barbecue.

'Tis the Season

Well-seasoned firewood is essential to a good smoke. Not every piece of wood in your fire has to be perfectly air-dried for two years—there is a time and place for denser logs. What you want to avoid is very green wood, aka wood from a tree that's been cut down recently. When I talk about green wood versus seasoned wood, what's really an issue is water content.

Unsurprisingly, the more water in a log, the worse it burns. That's because the heat from the fire must evaporate the water inside the wood before it can burn the remaining cellulose as a fuel source. Evaporating water—turning it from liquid to vapor—takes a great deal of energy. In fact, turning boiling water into steam takes five times the amount of energy required to bring that same amount of water from freezing to boiling. So, when your fire is trying to vaporize all that water, huge amounts of precious energy are being spent. This results in incomplete combustion, which creates heavy, wet smoke filled with creosote and other compounds that you definitely do not want to have clinging to your food. Have you ever eaten smoked food with a bitter aftertaste? That's bad smoke from a choked-off fire. Properly seasoned wood that is properly combusted solves that problem.

I don't use wood chips—or even wood chunks—but I still get asked whether they should be soaked before use. (The idea is that inundating the wood with water will keep it from bursting into flames when you put it on top of charcoal to get some smoke on your food.) I hope by now that you can anticipate my answer. This is a terrible idea for a couple of reasons. First, wet wood will always take energy out of your fire or your coals. Second, the quality of smoke from smoldering wet wood chips is not desirable. Indeed, it is what I usually call steam. Use dry wood.

It's shocking how much water can be carried within the cells of a piece of wood. Moisture content is measured as a percentage equal to the weight of the water in the wood divided by the dry weight of the wood times one hundred. You can technically have fresh pieces of wood with a moisture content of more than 100 percent when the water weighs more than the wood. Seriously, a very heavy piece of green firewood could contain a half gallon of water. You definitely don't want to try starting a fire with this wood, as it would be almost impossible to get it going.

One way to measure moisture content is with a moisture meter, a little battery-powered device with two pins you stick into a piece of wood, which can be bought inexpensively at a hardware store or online. The ideal moisture content for cooking wood is between 15 and 25 percent. A very hot coal bed in the firebox can absorb more water-laden logs, but keep in mind what you throw on there—even a raging fire will struggle when fed overly damp wood.

The easiest way to estimate moisture content in wood is with a version of the traditional touch test. The touch test won't give you an exact percentage, but it'll tell you enough about the log in question to be able to make a "seasoned" judgment (see Sensing Firewood, below).

Now, I haven't been the biggest fan of kiln-dried wood in the past, mostly because it was always dried to such a low moisture content that it burned too fast to cook effectively and had little flavor. Also, a lot of what's being sold as boxed firewood in local stores is pine or another softwood, so be careful. I wouldn't even use those in my fireplace, let alone my smoker. However, you can find some kiln-dried hardwood firewood that falls within the moderate-moisture-content sweet spot—again, between 15 and 25 percent—that works just fine in a smoker. This approach is more expensive than buying wood in bulk from a local supplier and then aging it yourself, but it works well enough. Also, I've found that kiln-dried chunks can work very well in small smokers or in conjunction with charcoal in a kettle grill, PK grill, or Big Green Egg.

SENSING FIREWOOD

Picking the perfect log to throw onto the fire is easy if you know what you're looking for. You will employ multiple senses while doing this.

TOUCH Pick up a few logs individually and compare their weight. If one is very heavy, as if made from stone, it's still green and contains a lot of moisture. That one's a candidate for more seasoning. If a log is really light or feels about average, it's likely well seasoned and you can use it with impunity—to start a fire from scratch or to keep a good fire truckin' along.

SIGHT Note the color of the log. Really well-seasoned wood turns gray. If you go to Lockhart, Texas, and check out the giant wood yard for big BBQ restaurants, like Kreuz or Smitty's, you'll find a lot of neatly stacked gray logs. You can tell that stuff has been sitting out for a couple of years and is really seasoned and dry. Also, well-seasoned wood tends to crack and shed its bark as it gets to a good place. If the wood still has a lot of color, be it yellowish orange, like fresh wood, or greenish, you know it's not seasoned enough. Fresh wood looks like a pristine log.

SOUND Tap two pieces of firewood together or tap the log in question against a stone. If you hear a heavy, muted clunk, you're probably holding a big, water-laden piece of improperly seasoned wood. If it offers a slightly resonant, hollow thump, it's good to go.

To season your own wood, stack it so the cut ends of the logs are facing out. The logs respirate, so to speak, through the pores bared at the cut ends—it's where moisture evaporates—so you want them exposed to as much airflow as possible. Likewise, unless it's raining directly on your woodpile, don't cover your wood with a tarp. Air movement is the key to evaporation, and if the logs are smothered underneath a big piece of plastic, they'll take much longer to season. The best woodpiles are stacked under roofed, open-sided sheds.

Log Size

When you buy firewood by the cord or some fraction of a cord, it tends to come in lengths of fourteen to eighteen inches. Sometimes you might get really fat logs or logs that are too long. Often the size of your logs needs to be altered—for your home fireplace and especially for cooking.

Every cooker has its preferred fire size. And every fire has its preferred wood size. Your job is to match wood to fire to cooker. For the Franklin Pit—and for most smaller offset smokers—logs in the nine- to ten-inch range fit perfectly into the firebox. While a standard-size log will technically fit into the twenty-four-inch-long firebox of a Franklin Pit, it's too big to burn effectively. Its bulk will restrict airflow and remove a lot of energy from the fire as it catches. And when it does start to burn, it's going to send your temps through the roof. Smaller logs are easy enough to fashion from the big ones. In fact, it's never a bad thing to keep some more modestly sized firewood on hand. It's good for getting fires started and for building smaller fires in, say, a kettle grill.

If you're cooking on a large firepit or in an indoor fireplace, you can certainly get away with full-size logs. The size of your cooker will clearly tell you what size wood you need. And be sure to have plenty of wood in the needed size to last through the length of your cook. You don't want to have to cut more once you've started cooking.

Experience and practice will teach you the best size log for your cooker. It becomes obvious rather quickly when, say, a log that's too big takes a long time to catch and, in the process, sucks the energy of your fire. Or when a log that's too small flames up immediately and disappears before it's made much of a contribution to the cook. A bit more questionable are logs that are just slightly too large and dense. They may catch quickly but then provide too big a boost of heat. You'll learn rapidly just

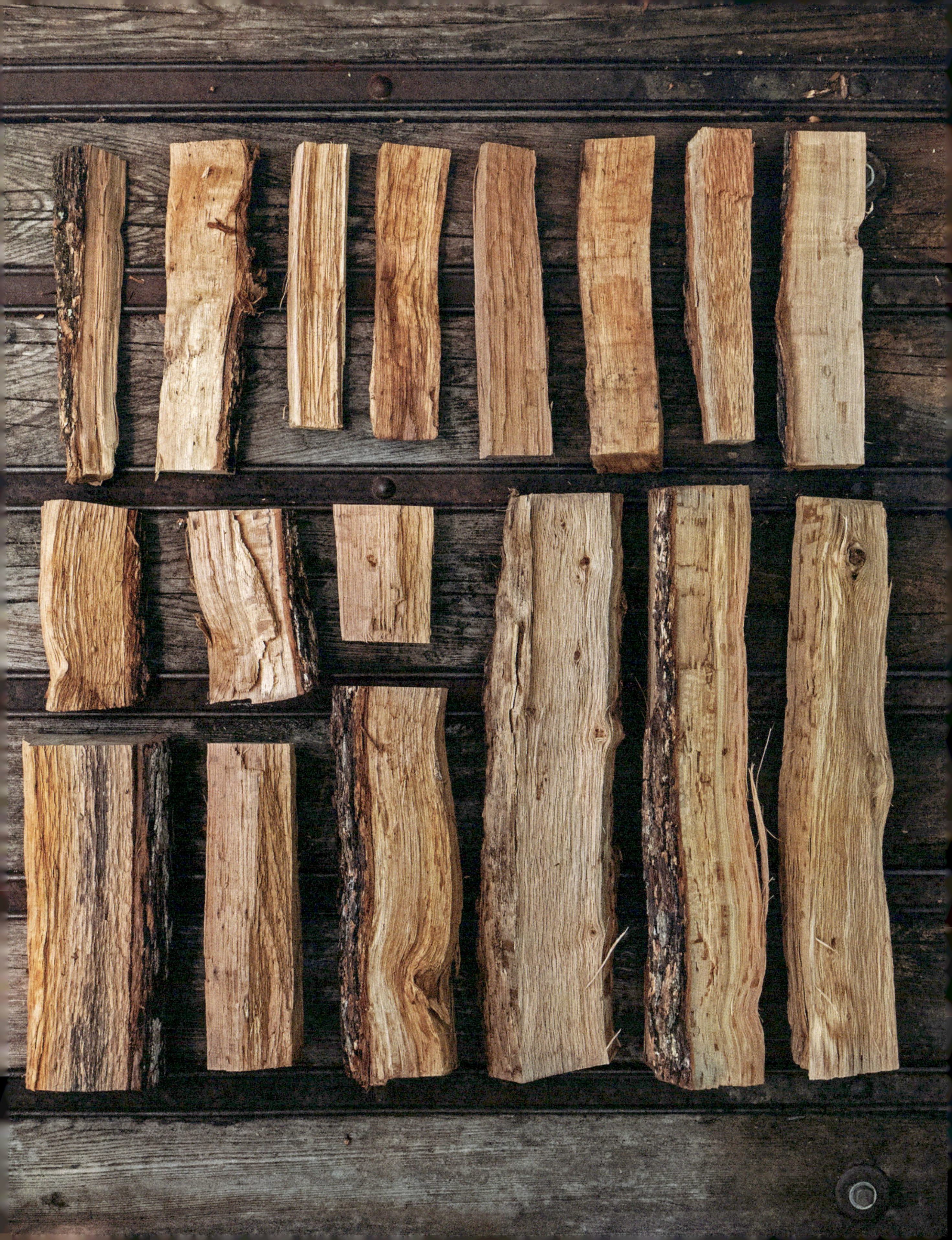

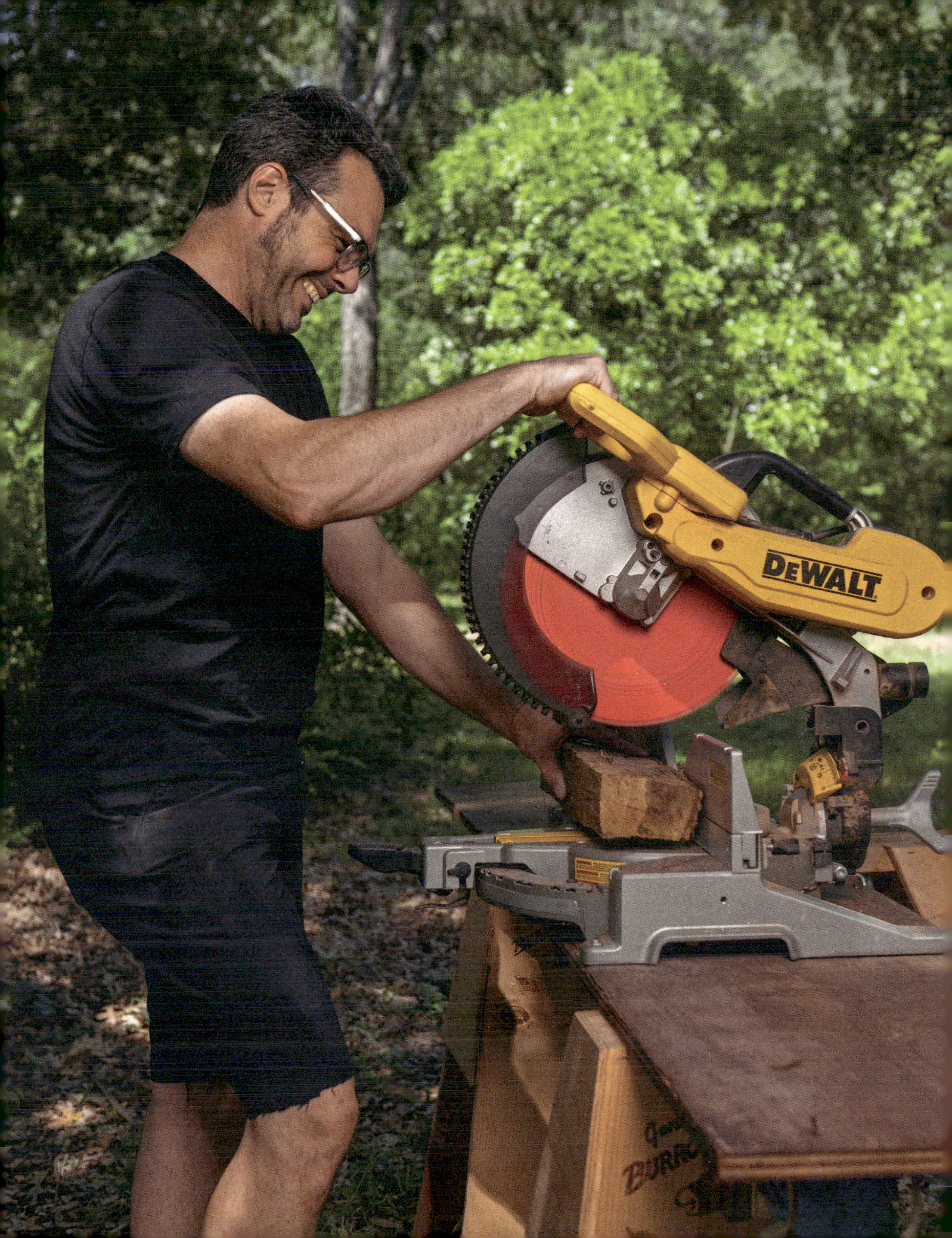
DeWALT

by watching the firebox and the thermometer to gauge the impact of each particular log. And remember, it's perfectly fine to pull a log off if it's giving too much heat or taking away from your fire.

WOOD TOOLS

Wood handling is an important part of cooking barbecue of any kind. If you're dealing with wood fires, though, wood management is more complex than just throwing another log onto the fire. Sometimes your wood needs to be resized, split, or splintered to maximize its benefits. Here are the tools you want to have around to get the most out of your fires.

WORK GLOVES It's always good to have a pair of these handy! Seriously, if you're like me and constantly hauling around firewood in the back of your truck, loading it here, unloading it there, you're going to want a pair of lightweight work gloves (canvas, Kevlar, or polyester will work) to avoid all those pesky splinters.

SAWS To trim my firewood down from eighteen inches to a more workable nine or ten inches, I use a chop saw (aka miter saw), but you can technically use any kind of saw you want or have. I have a chop saw mounted in my shed because I'm always building something or working on the house. It's really meant for cutting lumber or molding, but it works well for firewood too. It's the kind with a sharp-toothed saw wheel that spins on an arm you raise and lower to cut through the wood, which is anchored in place. It's really fast (and kind of dangerous, so remember to always work safely).

I saw each big log to about two-thirds of its length, or approximately ten inches. If you are using a chop saw, be sure to secure the log tightly between the saw's grips. Firewood doesn't have flush edges, like lumber, so be extra careful when bringing the sawblade down that it doesn't twist or catch the wood and toss it off somewhere or pull your hand in. Make fast, decisive motions when dropping the blade for the cut and raise it back up quickly.

If you don't have a mounted stationary saw, you can use a chainsaw or a reciprocating saw, like a Sawzall, which is often used for cutting tree branches. Just be sure you have a wood blade for your reciprocating saw (they have fewer teeth than blades intended for cutting metal). The main danger with all types of saws is kickback, so you must anchor your wood securely. (And, hey, if you want the exercise, a good old-fashioned handsaw works too!)

Trimming down your wood should obviously be done at the beginning of a cook. Cut as much as you think you'll need, because once you've opened that first beer or mixed that first cocktail, razor-sharp power tools have no place in your life.

MAUL Most firewood comes pre-split, but it's rarely the exact size you need. Matching the width of the wood to the size of your fire (and cooker) is as important as matching the length. Doing so is a knack that comes with both practice and intuition, but it's not as mysterious as it sounds. If you have a small or medium fire, it's easy to see that putting a massive log on it will destroy its momentum for the span of time it takes that log to catch (if it doesn't extinguish your fire altogether). So what do you do? You split a big, fat piece into two, three, or four smaller ones. I do this dozens of times a day using a maul.

If a sledgehammer and an axe had a kid, it would be a maul, which sports the blunt heaviness of the former and the general look and shape of the latter. Whereas axes are used to splinter and slice wood largely against the grain, a maul is used with the grain. It divides the wood where it wants to split naturally. Mauls come in all manner of weights, so choose one that you can swing and control without laboring (mine has an eight-pound head).

The maul can be used in two ways: you strike the wood directly with the V-shaped, axe-like edge to split it, or you use the dull, sledgehammer-like side in conjunction with a separate metal wedge. The wedge adds another step, but if you tap it into the grain of the wood where you want the split to occur and then pound it with the sledge, you achieve greater accuracy.

I skip that part, though, and just go directly into the wood. First, you need to find a good chopping block on which to stand the log on its end (or a solid patch of flat ground). Stand back an appropriate distance and distribute your weight across your shoulder-width-spread feet. Focus your eyes on a line of the grain that runs from the outside of the wood to the center. Raise the maul and bring it down decisively, keeping your eyes on the spot you want to hit. Don't try to swing it down hard. The point of the heavy head is to let gravity do most of the work for you. You should do some damage on the first swing, but if the log doesn't split all the way through, give it a second try, and even a third, in the same spot, and you'll hear that satisfying sound of cleaving wood fibers as the perfectly sized split falls to the ground.

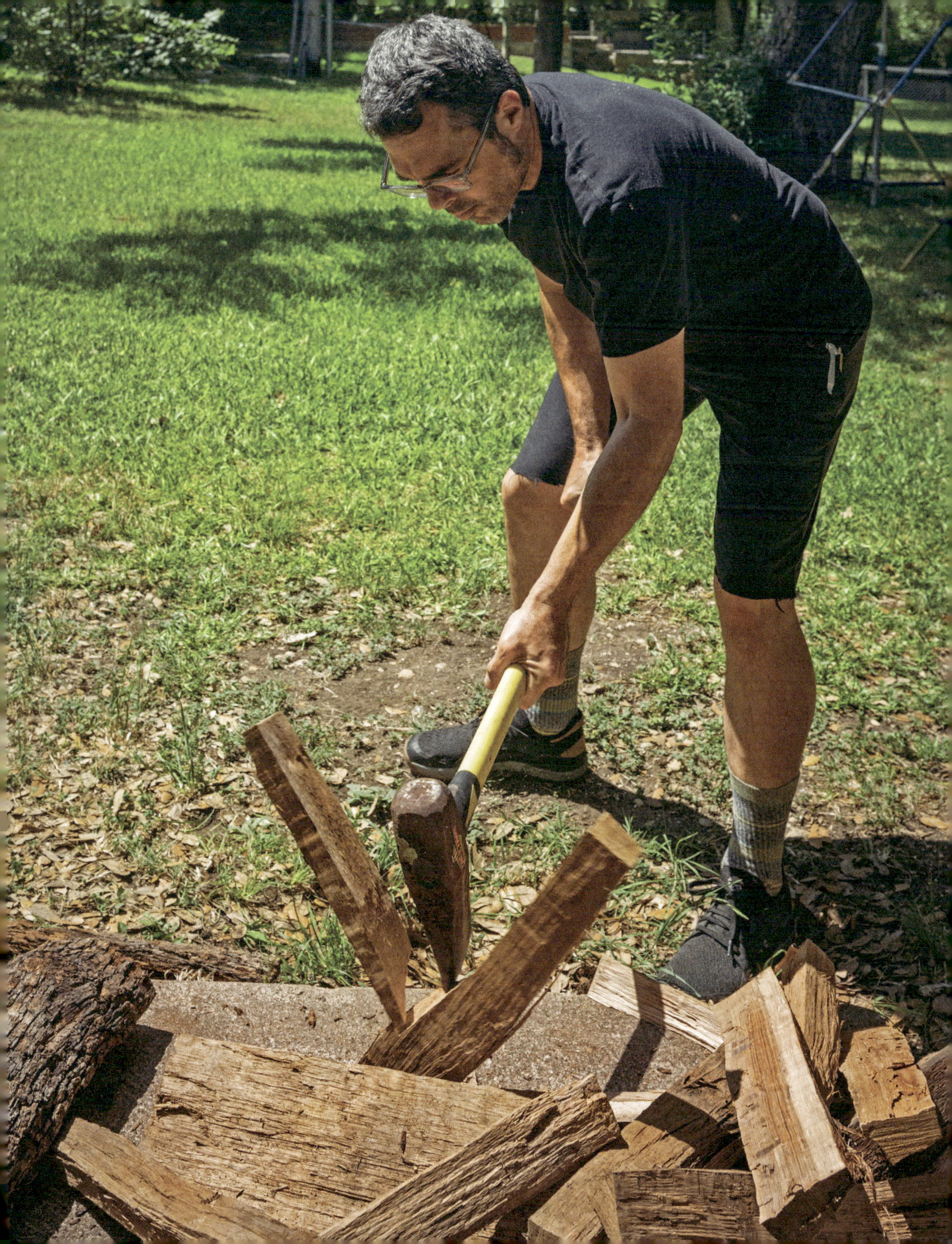

HATCHET Once you've created some smaller logs, you may also want to split off some kindling to help get your fire started. For this, a hatchet, the short-handled form of an axe, is a useful tool. Although it's not powerful enough to split a full-size log, it does offer the benefit of control, which is an important aspect of safety. Just place your little log on a stump or other flat surface. Make sure it can stand on its own end, as you never want to put your free hand on the log you're about to split. Then just make a decisive chop along the grain somewhere close to the edge of the log. You may have to hit it a couple of times to get a smaller sticklike piece seven to ten inches long and an inch or less in width. But with a little effort, it's not hard to generate the four or five pieces you need to get your fire started.

> **STORE-BOUGHT WOOD CHUNKS**
>
> As Aaron has mentioned, he's not a big fan of the bags of wood chunks you can buy at the store, but he lives a charmed life around a constant source of seasoned firewood. I've had good success getting flavorful smoke from store-bought kiln-dried wood chunks. While I disregard those labeled "cherry" or "hickory" (I usually opt for oak), when it's nestled atop a pile of thoroughly heated charcoal in a PK grill, a fat chunk of wood—even kiln-dried!—can give a good half hour of smoke. A moisture-meter reading on some wood chunks revealed 8 percent water content, which is a bit dry for optimal smoking. They are no substitute for a real wood fire and not a great solution for doing a long cook, like brisket, but for smaller things, they work quite well. —**Jordan**

CHARCOAL

Recently, I've had the adventure of helping to create our own brand of charcoal, and I've learned a lot. Since I've been cooking barbecue, I have to admit that I haven't been a big charcoal guy. Nothing, in my mind, can substitute for the coals achieved by burning down actual wood. However, now that I've been around charcoal more, I've softened a bit on its value.

Good charcoal sure is handy when you don't have time to build a full and proper coal bed out of wood or when you just need a quick, consistent form of intense heat. In fact, charcoal has a lot going for it, and humans have been making it and using it for more than thirty-eight thousand years. This is backed up in "The Art, Science, and

Technology of Charcoal Production," a 2003 paper by two experts in the study of renewable energy resources that observes, "As a renewable fuel, charcoal has many attractive features: it contains virtually no sulfur or mercury and is low in nitrogen and ash; it is highly reactive yet easy to store and handle." It becomes a lot easier to make choices about charcoal—briquettes or lump? mesquite or coconut?—when you understand a bit about where it came from.

Charcoal is nothing more than wood that has been cooked for days in a low-oxygen environment. Primitive humans learned that they could create charcoal by burying smoldering wood underground or covering it in a mound with heavy earth or clay. Modern humans do the same thing in industrial silos or burn chambers. The lack of oxygen keeps the wood from burning completely but generates enough heat to burn off most of the volatile compounds that existed in the original wood, including water, tar, hydrogen, methane, and more. What's left at the end are black chunks and fine powder made almost completely of carbon and some minerals and other impurities that don't burn away.

Charcoal ends up being about one-fourth the weight of the wood it was made from and burns far hotter when lit, thanks to the absence of all those volatiles. This makes it truly valuable as a heat source, though not at all valuable as a flavor source. All the organic and volatile compounds that were burned off during the production process are what makes woodsmoke aromatically compelling. Without that, you just have something that burns very hot, long, and (relatively) clean.

Depending on what kind of charcoal you're using, it may give off some fumes, sparks, and smoke when first lit. None of this is desirable for cooking, which I'm sure I don't need to tell you. But once it gets going, it burns very clean with little smoke and little impact on aromatics. What we taste as charcoal-grill flavor is very similar to the grill flavor from a gas grill. It's the ignition of the oils and juices—the fats, rubs, marinades, and so on—dripping from whatever you're cooking onto the heat source. Once they hit, they quickly vaporize and rise up to bathe the food in what amounts to a little smoky cloud of its own substance. The rest of the grill flavor comes from the Maillard reaction (browning)—represented by grill marks—that happens on the surface of the food thanks to heat and searing.

Briquettes versus Lump Charcoal

The big question on most people's minds when shopping for charcoal is whether to go for briquettes or lump. If you want to understand anything about charcoal, this is a good place to start. But before I say a word on the subject, I want to note that I'm speaking in general terms here. Every brand of charcoal is different, so it's hard to make definitive statements on this subject. That said, here's my general thinking on the matter of briquettes versus lump charcoal.

Charcoal briquettes are made from scrap wood and especially sawdust collected in giant quantities from such places as sawmills. At a charcoal plant, larger pieces of wood or foreign matter, like metal or rock, are separated out before the wood particles are dried and then carbonized (cooked until they are mostly just pure carbon). This carbon powder is then collected, potentially blended with other ingredients, dried, and stamped into briquettes. Those other ingredients may include anthracite coal (which helps the briquettes burn hotter and longer), limestone (which helps them turn white so you know when to start cooking), cornstarch (a binder), and nitrate (to speed up ignition). But I'm told by friends who know the industry that some of these additives are blended into the mix because wood is expensive, and it's cheaper to add external forms of coal than actual wood.

So if you don't like the sound of these additives in your fuel source—I don't—look for all-natural charcoal that has almost nothing added. This is exactly what I did and how I ultimately decided to make my own out of Texas post oak. To my knowledge, there's no other exclusive post oak charcoal out there. Our Franklin briquettes are made from nothing but post oak pieces, charcoal "fines" (the fine dust and other particles left from post oak handling), and a very small amount of vegetable starch as the binder, just as bread crumbs help to hold a meatball together. I've been nothing short of impressed with how hot and long they burn. And they don't leave much ash, which is a testament to the fact that there are no additives.

I have a number of positive things to say about all-natural charcoal briquettes. They're portable, effective, relatively inexpensive, and reliable. Serious grill cooks, such as those who compete in Steak Cookoff Association events, pretty much always use briquettes because they know exactly how much heat they'll be getting. They will actually measure out the precise number of briquettes into a chimney because they've pretty much calibrated the amount of heat that will be produced after a certain amount of time. (And most of them cook on PKs.)

While lump charcoal has often been prized as the more "natural" alternative to briquettes, now that we have all-natural briquettes, the differences between the two are fewer. Lump charcoal is, as it sounds, pieces of wood that have been carbonized whole, rather than broken down into dust and fine particles and then reassembled into briquettes. It has also been touted as contributing more flavor and burning hotter than briquettes, but I'm not sure about that either.

As any of you who regularly buy lump charcoal know, you are never sure what you're going to get in a bag. Sometimes it might be full of appealing chunks that resemble the pieces of wood they were before carbonization. Of course, the size is never consistent. Sometimes you'll have a ton of small shards, and other times you'll find pieces of former tree branches or roots that don't even fit in the chimney. Often, you'll find pieces of molding or joining wood that are clearly remnants from a furniture factory or some other production facility. In theory, this is a good thing, as we hope no useful wood goes to waste. But in practice, I'm a little skeptical that all the wood that goes into lump charcoal was carbonized in a raw, untreated state—and I certainly don't want chemicals in my charcoal. Furthering my doubt is the fact that I've found nails, pieces of wire, and other non-wood detritus in bags, suggesting that the producers aren't too strict in their processing.

As to whether lump charcoal offers more wood flavor, that's possible. You know when you light a chimney full of lump charcoal and it enters that phase of sparking and spitting out little embers for three or four minutes? Well, that's proof of an incomplete carbonization process. Little particles of leftover wood are getting heated and then exploding out of the charcoal as the water vaporizes. The preservation of some of the wood in the charcoal might provide a little woodsmoke character, but it's not bound to be much and is certainly no substitute for real wood.

Does it burn hotter? I've not found that to be the case, but it's hard to tell because of the randomness of the size and shape of lump charcoal pieces. If you filled one chimney full of briquettes and another full of lump charcoal, chances are the one full of briquettes would weigh more since they are uniform in shape and fill up the chimney more efficiently. More fuel weight means a more intense burn and a higher temperature.

Binchōtan

It's worth mentioning a special kind of charcoal from Japan (now also made in other countries) because it's pretty darn cool. Expensive but cool. This is the stuff you'd use to make yakitori in a konro grill—one of those narrow, boxlike tabletop grills meant for roasting skewers—because it burns hot and exceedingly clean with almost no smoke. It's the purest form of charcoal you can buy.

The skill of making binchōtan is a highly respected craft in Japan. It involves harvesting high-grade ubame oak—which is especially hard and has a fine grain—by hand from the particularly rugged forest terrain in which it grows. The wood is cut into long stalks taller than the average person, bundled, and then put into large kilns, in which a fire is built before the doors are sealed up with bricks and wet clay. An opening is left for air to enter, and there's an exhaust where steam and other vapors can escape. The total process takes about ten days, but what comes out are magical sticks comprising about 95 percent pure carbon (compared to the 50 to 70 percent you find in standard charcoal). When you tap two pieces together, they clang more like metal than wood.

Because of its purity, binchōtan is not as easy to light as standard charcoal. You can still place it in a chimney, but it might require a couple of refills of paper before it catches. Many people place their filled chimney over the flame of a gas burner for a few minutes to get it started. Even then, after it has caught, it still takes between twenty and forty minutes before it's glowing and fully heated.

Contrary to popular belief, binchōtan doesn't necessarily burn hotter than standard charcoal, but it definitely burns longer, often lasting for up to five hours and keeping a consistent temperature throughout. (Standard charcoal decreases in size and turns to ash in about thirty minutes.) If you're not going to use binchōtan for five hours—say, you don't own an izakaya—you can also submerge it in a bucket of water to cool it off. After it has cooled and dried, it can be used again just as effectively.

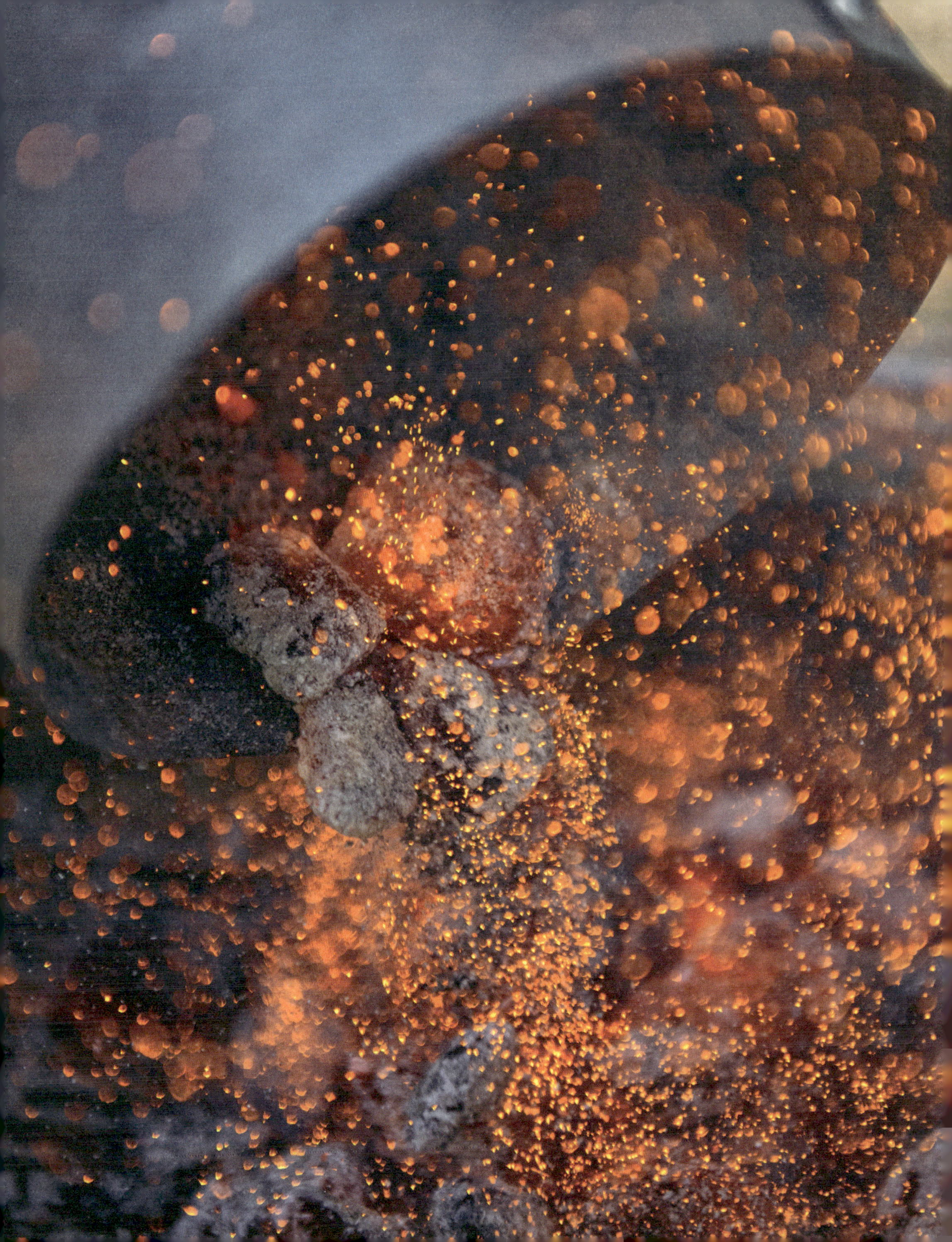

4

THE WHOLE FIRE

Coals, Flames, and Smoke

No matter how experienced you are in the kitchen, when cooking with wood, your most important job is to manage that fire. This is true whether you're maintaining a blaze in the firebox of an offset cooker or sustaining a coal bed on a grill to get just a flicker of smoke as you quickly cook some steaks. It takes a long time to get comfortable cooking with fire. Of course, cooking outdoors is appealing, except when it isn't—cold nights, hot nights, wet nights, late nights, snowy nights. But to gain meaningful experience, you have to do it regularly for a long time, as I did when we had our barbecue trailer and the restaurant. This means you will often be covered in grime and smell like smoke.

In a way, to cook with fire is to tend to its needs, to serve its interests so it will serve yours. After a while, live-fire cooking can get exhausting—even just a week or three, like when testing the recipes for this book. If you think about it, what makes modern cooking *modern* is the fact that you no longer have the burden of tightly managing your heat source. This has been true in every leap of cooking innovation, from the gas range to the electric stove to the microwave to sous vide. The evolution of cooking is about eliminating guesswork and removing some of the requirements of experience, feel, and intuition.

I've certainly made my share of mistakes in tending fires. I've used the wrong kind of wood, not enough of it, and too much of it. I've turned my back at the wrong time or missed the window when the coals are at their peak. There's always something to learn from these simple and universal errors.

This chapter is all about what I've learned from many years of staring into fires. I talk about essential tools, the stages of a fire, and the concept of using the *whole fire*: cooking different ingredients over the entire duration of a fire (from ignition to ash) to create a meal. Getting the most out of a fire (your principal ingredient) is not only efficient but also the greatest honor you can pay it.

I talk about lighting and maintaining the different kinds of fire you need for the various types of fire-related cooking in this book. The variability of fire makes recipes a little difficult to write, as your food may take more or less time to cook depending on the heat you generate.

And finally, I talk about smoke—how to attract it, collect it, and ultimately get the most out of it. Since it is the most important seasoning and a cooking method, taking smoke seriously is a hugely important aspect of the job.

THE STAGES OF FIRE

From the second a fire is lit to the moment it has truly gone out, you can chart its progression through separate but connected stages. Officially, the four stages of fire are ignition, growth, fully developed, and decay. (Too bad they couldn't find a single word for "fully developed"; it would sound a lot better.) But for the purposes of cooking, I look a little more granularly at fire, adding a couple more stages and using some slightly different terminology. My six stages of fire are ignition, white smoke, flame, coals, embers, and ash.

Understanding the stages of fire is important to cooking with the whole fire. Each embodies a unique dynamic of heat, flame, and smoke that can help you achieve nuanced and distinctive results in your cooking. In a fully blazing fire, all the stages are happening at the same time, which amounts to a chain reaction. (For this reason, some people consider the reaction itself to be another side of the fire triangle—fuel, heat, oxygen—and now call it the fire tetrahedron.) This chemical chain reaction occurs when each element acts on and enables the others, continuing the series of reactions without any additional external inputs. So, for instance, in a charcoal

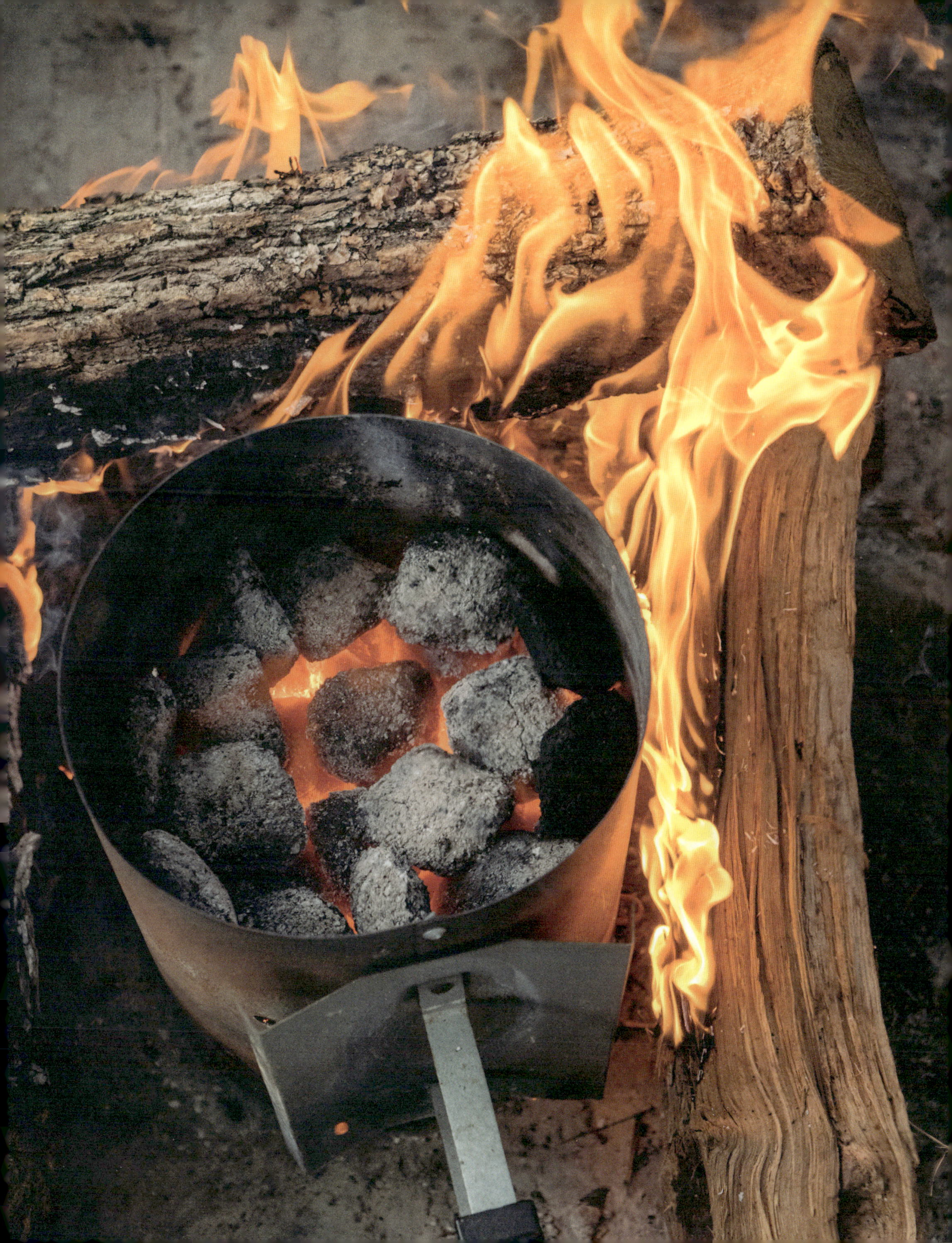

chimney, the heat generated by the burning of fuel contributes to the ignition of new fuel, or the departure of volatile gases draws in the oxygen to feed the fire.

IGNITION This is when the fire is just getting going. Or when, say, you've just lit the newspaper in a chimney to get the charcoal going. Be sure you have ample tinder with plenty of oxygen around it that is easily accessed by your spark.

WHITE SMOKE This stage, characterized by dehydration, begins after the wood or charcoal is ignited and heating but before it's fully burning. You'll recognize it by the billowing white smoke and steam—a mixture of water vapor, carbon dioxide, and volatile compounds. The water in the wood is literally boiling off, often leading to intense popping and the violent ejection of particles and sparks. As moisture dissipates, the fuel continues to warm.

FLAME Eventually, fire breaks out. You will see active and vigorous flames emanating from the wood. You may also have an intuitive sense of when the fire is thriving: there's a sound, a rhythm, a quickening to the noises it makes. It has a life of its own as it increases in heat, builds momentum. The smell of clean, sweet smoke starts to surround the fire. An aura of heat beckons us in (but not too close!). Make sure the fire has plenty of available fuel at this time because it's also stabilizing itself, producing the foundation of heat it needs to continue the chain reaction. The smoke, you'll notice, will no longer billow gray and white; it becomes more transparent, maybe with a light gray to blue tint. This is the ideal time for indirect cooking. You can cook over the flames also, but not too closely or intensely. Without focused attention, it's far too easy to burn things at this stage unless the distance is such that the tips of the flames only occasionally lick the food.

COALS For those who are cooking or even just seeking warmth, this is the sweet part of the fire, its lifeblood. The wood has lost its water and burned down into its constituent elements, which are slowly being disassembled by the heat and chemical reactions of the fire. These constituent parts, made of the carbon and hydrocarbons (lignin, hemicellulose, and cellulose) at the heart of wood, glow and radiate intense heat, but the volatile gases that create flames have for the most part burned off. This is the coal bed.

At this point, many chefs will rake off some coals to cook over, while leaving the rest as the heat source onto which they'll periodically throw fresh logs to keep it going. The consistent, dry, and intense flameless heat from the coals enables searing, caramelization, and smoking.

EMBERS If you don't refuel the fire, the coals will eventually begin to peter out. They'll develop a thin coating of ash and some white smoke may return. The ash slows the passive intrusion of oxygen, further dampening the fire. If you want to revive it, add some light fuel, blow to clear off the ash, and fan the flames or continue to blow. This environment offers some nice opportunities for gentle cooking.

ASH The fire is dead. No amount of oxygen or fuel will rekindle it without significant heat. Funny enough, this stage is harder to achieve than you might think, which is why forest fires get started when campers think they've extinguished their campfire. (To be clear, when this happens, the campfire was in the embers stage when it should have been cinders/ash.) Once you've combed through the ashes and cinders and found no pockets of residual heat, feel free to rake up the remains and deposit them in your ash bucket. Larger chunks can be reused in your next fire. Just add them after the fire is going or relight in the chimney.

COOKING WITH THE WHOLE FIRE

There's no reason to waste a good fire. Making fires at home is not something most of us do every day, so it's good to make the most of it when you have it. That's why I love using the whole fire when I cook, that is, from the earliest, spiking moments past ignition and white smoke all the way to the slow, smoldering coals.

What might this look like?

> Before you dump the coals, blister vegetables over a red-hot chimney, which focuses and concentrates the heat.
>
> Put a wok over the chimney and stir-fry on it!
>
> Then, if you're still on charcoal, grill.
>
> Or close the lid of your cooker and roast or smoke something (say, a chicken) with a two-zone setup.
>
> Add wood to a firepit and cook over it directly. Cook steaks or chops quickly over the flames while cooking a large roast off the coals.
>
> Finally, slow roast vegetables, like onions, squashes, or eggplants, in the coals and embers.

Consider the whole, malleable life of a fire when planning a meal. Even if you're not camping or out in the woods, think like you are. How would you prepare a meal if the fire was your only heat source? How would you efficiently combine searing, blackening, roasting, smoking, and grilling to get the most out of one blaze?

By the way, meals in which every single item comes off the fire can be rather intense. After all, smoke is an incredibly powerful flavor. So keep each meal balanced and remember that you can grill or smoke ingredients not only for the next meal but also for meals later in the week.

ESSENTIAL FIRE TOOLS

You don't need a lot of equipment to handle a fire, but in the interests of safety, cleanliness, and workflow, these are the tools I keep on hand.

ASH BUCKET Cleaning out ash is the unfortunate penance we all pay for the joys of outdoor cooking. Having a dedicated receptacle makes the job much easier. A simple galvanized bucket or can is easy to find at a hardware store. Ash is very heavy and dense, so look for one that's big enough to suit your cooker or firepit but not so big that you can't lift it. Also, make sure the bucket has a lid to keep the rain out so the bottom doesn't rust out. Let fresh ash sit in the bucket for at least a number of days before disposing, as you never know what's still smoldering. Down here in Texas, it's so hot that it may take more than a week for all of the coals to die out—and you don't want to start a dumpster fire.

CHIMNEY If you don't already use a chimney to light your charcoal, I don't know what to say. It's the easiest, cleanest, and most efficient way to start a cook. If you're going for a real outdoor-kitchen setup with a smoker, a grill, and even a firepit or side fire, I suggest that you invest in two chimneys because sometimes you need to get a second one started while the first one is already going. (Tip: To start a second chimney, put it right on top of the lit grill or even the first lit chimney.) Also, I recommend buying large chimneys. You'll find a number of smaller chimneys on hardware store shelves, but nothing's more annoying than not being able to spark up as much charcoal as you need. And if you need less than a large one holds, just fill it up halfway! Weber still makes the standard go-to chimney. It can get beat up pretty fast and doesn't always last more than a year, but it works well enough.

CLOSED-TOE SHOES You'll never see me in a pair of flip-flops or sandals around a fire, even in the summer, even if I'm playing the lead in a staging of *Julius Caesar*. (Won't catch me in a toga either!) I know plenty of people who exclusively sport sandals when the weather heats up. But hear me, friends, you want to wear closed-toe shoes during a cook. Ever try dumping a chimney full of hot coals with bare feet? Don't do it. Be safe and injury-free. Let's keep those toesies unburned!

FIREBRICKS These heavy fireproof bricks are useful to have around and can be deployed and redeployed depending on your needs. Put them on top of your grill grates and rest another grilling surface on top of the bricks to crudely mimic the action of a Santa Maria grill (see page 45). Stack them like LEGOs to build a makeshift konro grill for searing yakitori skewers. Lay them flat as a platform on which to set your charcoal chimney after dumping. So many uses! The only downside is their weight.

FIRE TONGS This is my preferred tool for finely manipulating logs in a firepit or firebox. I use extra long ones to reach into fireboxes and firepits from a safe distance. I often shift and rearrange the structure of my fires, and tongs are never far from my hand.

HOSE WITH A SPRAYER Hey, summer is hot and dry and only getting hotter and drier in many places. So I always keep a hose with a powerful nozzle nearby and set to on, just in case I need to hose something down quickly or to spritz the ground around my cooker before I go night-night.

SHOVEL A good old-fashioned shovel has been my number-one tool for as long as I've been cooking barbecue. Its uses are almost countless, but you'll mainly want one for manipulating and shaping your fire in the firebox. For a large, professional cooker like we use at the restaurant, any heavy-duty shovel will do. For a firebox the size of the one in the Franklin Pit, I recommend something smaller. You want a forty-eight-inch-long handle so you can reach all the way to the back of the firebox without having to stick your hands too close to the fire. Shovels are also essential for firepit cooking, which involves lots of shifting around of logs and coals. And if you've got a side fire going, you'll want a full-size shovel for transporting a load of coals from it to your cooker.

TROWEL I don't use one, but Jordan swears by this handy mini-shovel, particularly when configuring coals in a PK or kettle grill or even shifting things around in a Big Green Egg. They're inexpensive and come in different shapes and sizes. He recommends keeping a few around. And when you're not using them for cooking, they're great for repotting petunias.

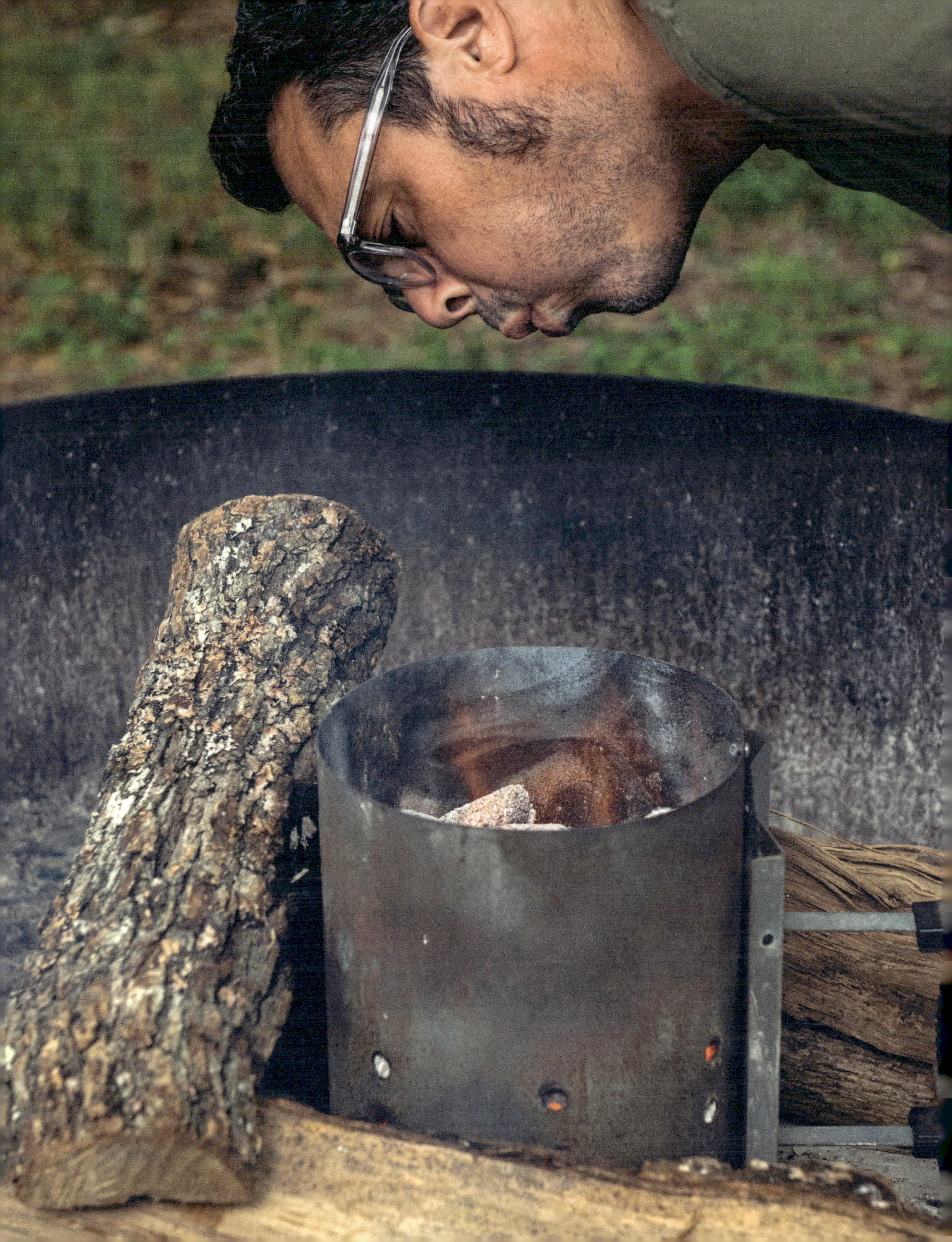

BUILDING FIRE

I used to be kind of orthodox about only lighting a fire with wood and a little piece of butcher paper dabbed with brisket fat or cooking oil. But I have to admit that, in my old age, I've softened a bit. Nowadays, I might start by lighting a few charcoal briquettes and letting them start the wood. And there's no getting around the fact that there are all kinds of idiot-proof thingamajigs available to help, like those little hockey pucks you light with a match that keep burning until your charcoal or kindling gets going. (Even I use those things when they're around, so yeah, definitely idiot-proof.)

However, I still use the log-cabin method to stack my logs in a square on top of one another, two or three logs high, depending on the size of the fire I'm building. (Two heavy logs on the bottom, lighter ones in the middle, and a heavy one on top; so, when the middle logs collapse, the heavy one drops in.) If I'm making a fire inside the small firebox of the Franklin Pit, I'll stack up about six mini-logs and drop in some hot charcoal. If I'm building a bigger fire in the firepit, I'll make the same structure but use full-size logs.

To create fire you need three things: fuel, heat, and oxygen. That's called the "fire triangle" because you can't have a fire without all three elements. The log cabin is an elegant and simple structure that ensures each of the three elements is present. The wood is obviously the fuel. In the middle of the log cabin's square, you place a little extra fuel—some kindling and tinder in the form of newspaper, wood shavings, or charcoal. The loose openings between the stacked logs allow oxygen to easily access the tinder and continue to supply the growing reaction.

Many people confuse fire for heat but, the fact is, fire is an ongoing chemical reaction whose effects we perceive as light and heat. If you want to put out a fire, remove one of the three elements (hence the lid on the ash can). Heat is introduced at the beginning in the form of a match, a lighter, or one of those thingamajigs, which is placed in the middle next to the tinder. (In the firepit, I often just light some charcoal in a chimney and either dump it into the middle of the log cabin or build the log cabin around my chimney and remove the chimney once the logs catch.) That should do the trick. Just wait a while and you'll have fire.

The triangle is important because if you're having trouble keeping your fire going, you know how to diagnose the problem. Are you lacking fuel, oxygen, or heat? The latter is the one element that many people have trouble with yet don't realize. If you overload your fire with fuel but don't have enough heat to cause the chemical reaction, you won't have fire. Also, remember that a log of firewood on its own isn't solely fuel. If it's green (carrying a lot of water), it contains a ton of anti-fuel, which makes it hard to generate enough heat. The temperature of your fuel has an impact too. Really cold wood takes longer to light (and removes energy from an already-lit fire). While I don't generally feel the need to pre-warm logs inside the firebox, in cold weather I will occasionally place a piece or two of wood on top of the firebox or on the perimeter of the firepit—especially if they're somewhat green—just so they are rarin' and ready to go when I throw them on.

CONTROLLING FIRE

You want to be the boss of your fire, not the other way around. Being in total control is a major requirement for successful cooking. It's very easy to let a fire get away from you in one way or another and end up cooking over insufficient heat or too much heat or with bad smoke. If this doesn't ruin your expensive ingredients, it will at least make them far less delicious than they should be and can be super-frustrating.

Luckily, you can control fire with surprising accuracy if you carefully consider what you're doing and *plan ahead*. That is, many of the adjustments you can make to a fire don't have instant results—they may take some time to develop. To stay on top of your game, you need to think a couple of moves ahead. What does this look like? Your approach isn't too different whether you're tending an offset cooker, a kamado, a live fire in a firepit, or coals in a grill.

If you need to lower the temperature in an offset cooker, close the firebox door a smidge (but never too much) to restrict airflow. Use your shovel to slide the coal bed back toward the firebox door, where it will leak some heat out the back side; this makes the heat less aggressive. If you need to raise the temperature quickly, push the coal bed forward toward the cook chamber or add a quick-burning piece of well-seasoned wood. If you need to bring the heat up over twenty minutes or so, add a larger piece of denser wood that will take a little while to get going but anchor the fire for another half hour or so.

Lowering the temperature in a Big Green Egg or kamado grill is one of the challenges of these cookers. But you can always close the vents a bit to minimize oxygen intake or open the lid periodically to let excess heat out until the whole thing dies down.

When tending an open fire in a firepit, the shovel is always your friend. I constantly shift logs and coals around depending on the needs of what I'm cooking. Pay attention to the direction of the breeze and expose your fire to it if you want a burst of heat. Conversely, shield the fire against the sides of the firepit if you want less flame. Throw on heavy wood to dampen a fire for a while (and have a place to move it off if you don't want a deluge of flame and heat).

To drop the intensity of the radiant heat on a grill, use tongs or a trowel to spread out the coals.

You got this—after all, you're just one more person following along after thirty-eight thousand years of people cooking over flames. Fire may seem intimidating, but if you have the right tools and ample space, you will be the one in control.

SIDE FIRES AND BURN BARRELS

One thing that you always need on a cook is a backup supply of fresh coals. That could be in the form of a chimney full of charcoal, lit and ready to go. But in the event you want to cook over only wood coals—my favorite way, but not always the most practical—you need a second supply of wood that's ready to go. One of the advantages of firepit cooking—especially if your firepit is big enough—is that you can always separate fresh coals from the larger fire and cook over them directly. But if you're cooking on a PK or kettle grill and you want fresh wood coals, the answer is a side fire.

One good reason to keep an old grill or firepit around, even if you don't use it much, is as a place to burn down a couple of logs so you're fully stocked with fresh wood coals as you need them. Then you can just shovel or bucket them over to your grill in the exact quantity needed for what you're cooking. Also, in cooler weather, it's a nice way to keep yourself warm!

Another alternative is what is commonly used in whole hog cooking: the burn barrel. This contraption is usually made from an old steel drum and a few pieces of rebar that have been driven through a foot or so above the bottom of the drum to create a matrix whose openings are not quite large enough to let a log fall through. A good-size opening—big enough to get a shovel in—is cut in the bottom of the barrel. After igniting a bunch of logs in the barrel, the fire quickly burns the wood and drops the coals down onto the ground (firebricks or another inflammable surface).

These can then be shoveled off and used. Keep adding wood as needed. In fact, this is a good place to use fairly green wood, as these barrels create a serious inferno (keep them away from anything burnable). It's the exact same principle often seen with wood grills at restaurants, where logs are stacked in a cage at the rear of the grill. The bottom logs on fire slowly drop their coals down to the surface, and the grill chef rakes them into use.

TIPS FOR SUCCESSFUL FIRE COOKS

These tips will help you manage your fire effortlessly so you can keep your attention focused on what you're cooking.

Set yourself up for success.

French chefs call it mise en place, roughly, "everything in its place." What it means, basically, is to be physically prepared. Have all of your tools ready and within easy reach. Think through your systems. Do you have a handy place to dump waste? If you need water, do you have access to it? How many different knives will you need and are they all within easy reach? With fire cooking, this means having all the firewood you need at the ready. It means having tongs, spray bottles, sheet pans, and towels at hand for when you need them.

Preheat, preheat.

Cooking on an apparatus that's not fully at the desired temperature is a surefire way to slow things down or cook poorly. For that reason, give your cooker or grill time to heat up, which often means starting earlier than dinnertime. Get your cooker going and allow it not only to reach the right temperature but to hold it for a good ten or fifteen minutes. This prep will make the rest of your cook so much better.

Patience pays off.

Along with the principle of preheating, having the patience to let your fire get to the proper stage is key. How many times have you dumped your chimney of charcoal too soon? You put your food on the grill and the temperature is *waaaay* too hot, so your food cooks too quickly and unevenly or flares up and burns. With all forms of fire, patience pays. Give yourself enough time to be sure the coal bed is at the right heat, it's not spiking too much, and it will last as long as you need it to.

Have backup ready.

Have the additional coals you may need at the ready to keep your fire controlled. Say you're cooking chicken pieces on the bone, and they're going to take longer than one chimney of charcoal is going to give you. Well, have a second chimney going for the moment you predict that to happen. I've had second chimneys going that I just allowed to burn out because didn't end up needing the coals. Yes, the charcoal was wasted, but better that than not having enough heat to finish the cook.

COOKING WITH SMOKE

Smoke, the inspiration for this book and one of the foundations of everything I've done professionally, is something with which I have a rather complex relationship these days. Perhaps because I've been around it almost continuously for many years now, I approach smoke with more apprehension than when I was just a bright-eyed fledgling looking to get that enticing smoky flavor onto brisket. These days, as my knowledge of smoke has grown, my approach has become quite a bit more nuanced, as has my taste for it.

Without question, smoke remains an alluring flavor for many people. However, it's also important to consider whether you're using good smoke or bad smoke and enough smoke or too much smoke. While the title of this book may suggest a full-throated endorsement of smoke culture, it's not that simple. I support a subtle, measured approach to smoke and want to talk about how to get good flavor and in just the right amount. I see smoke as a seasoning, and just as with any seasoning—salt, hot sauce, cilantro (yuck!)—moderation is key.

What Is Smoke?

A remarkable substance, smoke is a staggeringly complex mixture of gases, liquids, and solid particles that can range from visible specks of ash to microscopic molecules. The incomplete combustion of wood results in smoke, and the temperature of the fire dictates which particles are released and at what time. As wood is broken down during combustion, these components interact with ingredients in complex ways.

Research has shown that the visible part of smoke has the least (positive) impact on food. The vaporous or gaseous elements (invisible to the naked eye) are the most influential and desirable. The color of the resulting smoke can actually tell you something about its qualities. The hotter the fire, the smaller the particles. So if the wood went through complete combustion—requiring extraordinarily high temperatures—the by-products would be mostly carbon dioxide and water as well as some ash. Its "smoke" would be clear, as the particulate matter would be invisibly fine.

Poor combustion happens when there's not enough heat or oxygen and results in a large amount of very heavy particles, like tar and creosote—gross stuff. Those heavy particles absorb light and look sooty—black and gray in a viscerally unappealing way.

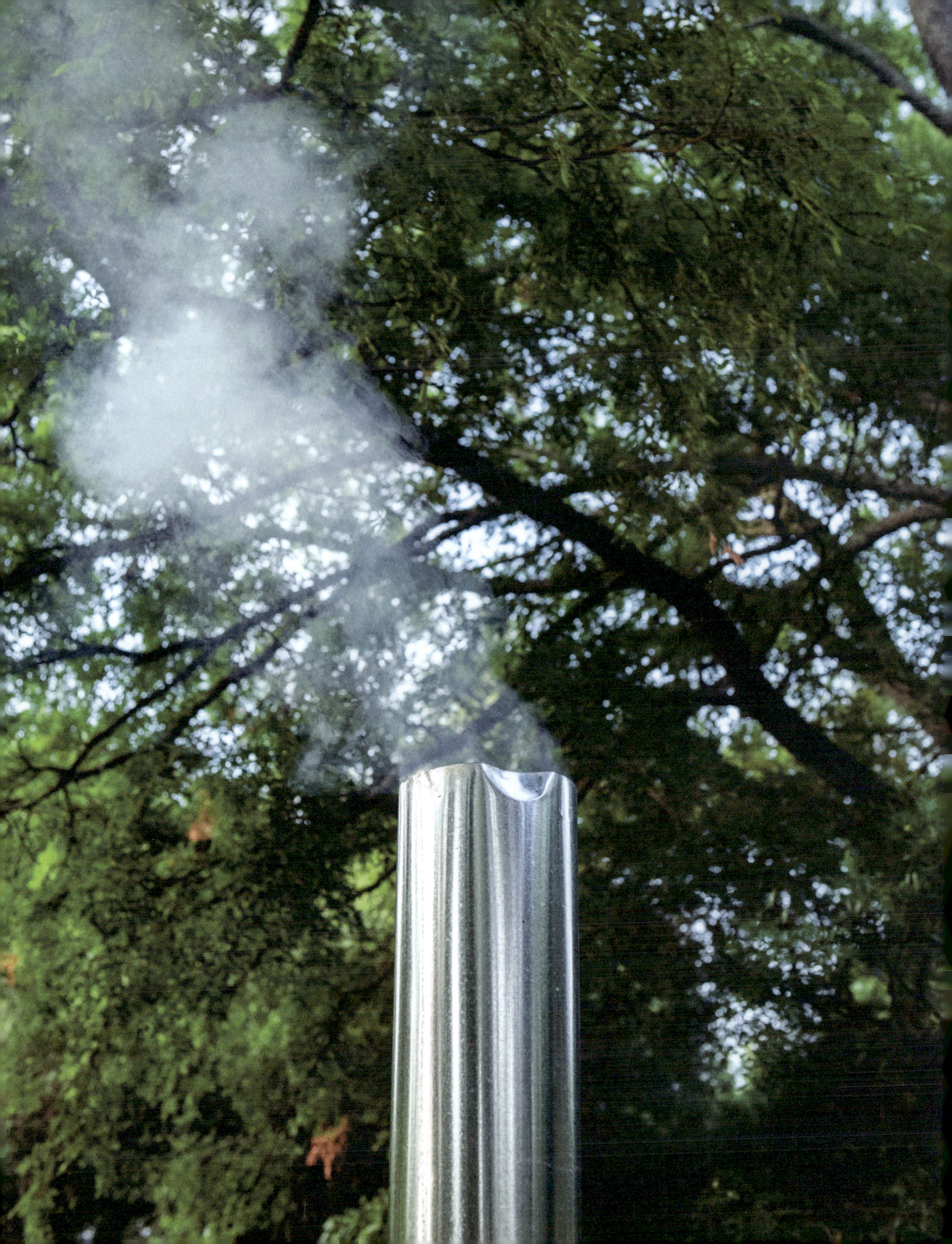

COLD SMOKING VERSUS HOT SMOKING

Primarily a method of food preservation, cold smoking can certainly be practiced at home, but you'll need both your smoke chamber to be far enough from the heat so the food doesn't cook and some sort of mechanism or setup that helps the airflow. Some methods of cold smoking suggest using the smoke from a cool or barely smoldering combustion, which, as you know, I think yields an undesirably dirty smoke.

Cold smoking is also tricky. It requires its ingredients to sit from several hours to several days at room temperature or slightly warmer. Furthermore, the low-acid environment of meat and the absence of oxygen create a dangerous breeding ground for bacteria, especially the spores that cause botulism. Because of this, cold-smoked meats are cured with sodium nitrate, which itself needs to be used with care. Long story short, if errors are made in temperature control, precise dosing of salt and preservatives, and other forms of food safety and storage, much can go wrong.

Hot smoking is much easier and requires no special equipment. It's as forgiving as it is delicious, and as long as you cook your meat to the proper internal temperature, you don't have to worry about getting sick. Unless you're really serious about cold smoking from a technical point of view, it's probably best left to the experts while you fire up your coals for a classic hot smoke.

White smoke is a little better, but smoke that looks faintly blue is the result of just the right amount of incomplete combustion. The fire is hot enough to break down the wood to finer particles that reflect the blue spectrum. This is the smoke that has the best flavor and the most nuanced impact on your food. It is created when your fire is between 600° and 750°F, which is where we aim to keep ours at the restaurant. It is also why I love the offset smoker, which supports the high temperatures that create such fine smoke in a moderate-size cooking space.

Carbonyls, which are released at lower temperatures when the wood compounds of cellulose and hemicellulose are being dismantled, primarily contribute to the browning of meat. At this stage, gasified acetic and formic acids add subtle hints of citric tartness and bitterness. At higher temperatures (around 600°F), lignin starts to break down, releasing phenols into the smoke. The phenols are what carry most of the flavors that we associate with smoke, both good (savory, smoky spice) and bad (medicinal and bitter).

One phenol, syringol, has the textbook flavor of smoke, while guaiacol (also present in oak wine barrels) offers toasty and spice notes, and vanillin imparts creamy sweetness. Phenols also have antimicrobial effects that sanitize meat, allowing it to be preserved for prolonged periods, yet another solid reason why you want to smoke with high combustion and aim for that fine blue smoke.

Attracting Smoke

Once you have your fire burning nice and hot and clean blue smoke is emanating from the stack, the next goal is to get your food in the best possible position to accumulate smoke. Although it seems like smoke gets into everything it touches, it actually just gets onto ingredients. Penetration doesn't reach very deep into the food, which is a good thing if you don't want too much smoke. Your taste buds do the work of merging the smoky flavor of the meat's exterior with the moist, meaty flavor of the interior.

Given that, it's important to attract plenty of smoke onto the outside of the meat. However, even in the very smoky environment of an offset cooker, smoke doesn't want to settle on the surface of the meat because of a very thin veneer of static air that surrounds objects. Known as the boundary layer, this is a concept most frequently used in the physics of turbulence (as with airplane wings). In our case, the boundary layer repulses smoke from the meat's surface.

To attract smoke, you want to keep the meat's exterior moist. Smoke particles move from warm to cool surfaces, and the constant evaporation that occurs on the surface of moist meat keeps it cooler than the surrounding air (even in the oven-like heat of a smoker), attracting the particles in smoke. Moisture also helps to trap the smoke particles when they do contact the meat. This is one reason why I periodically spray the exterior of the meat during a cook. (But be careful with that spray bottle. Excess wetting can remove smoke! The surface just needs to be a little damp.)

Finally, rubs also help, as the uneven surfaces they create flummox the boundary layer and attract smoke particles.

Delivering Smoke

Given the range of smoke's characteristics, it's important to get elements of each into the mix. Luckily, the chain reaction of the fire means that, to some degree, all of the qualities of smoke are available simultaneously: new wood starts to burn as old coals are exhausted. One of the benefits of having a strong fire and coal bed is that the smoky by-products of lower-temperature burning are minimized because newly introduced wood spends a much shorter time in that state before its lignin starts offering up those tasty phenols.

Still, it takes a good long while for smoke to accumulate enough phenols to get that complex, even, and tasteful flavor. Can you have too much smoke? In a word, yes! Every piece of food has its own smoke threshold, meaning the amount of smoke that tastes good on it. Something like a brisket, rich in gelatin and fat, can take a lot of smoke. But a chicken wants far less—just enough to add savory complexity to each bite.

Typically, you get a sense for how much smoke naturally wants to accrue by observing the surface of the meat. As the surface dries, it will stop attracting as much smoke. If you want more smoke, keep spraying and wetting the meat. At some point, however, this becomes a futile proposition, as the pellicle (a thin coating of proteins on the surface of the meat) will evaporate faster than you can keep it wet. By then you can be sure your food is plenty smoky, but I don't recommend even getting to that stage. Once you've reached a desired texture or color, you've probably gone far enough.

Throw too much smoke or stale smoke when there's not much airflow and you'll have something nasty and bitter. If you have a good temperature but not enough smoke—such as when your heat comes from charcoal but not enough wood—you'll just end up with roast beef. But when slow and steady wins the day, you'll have the perfect accretion that is the definition of good smoke.

REPELLING SMOKE—AVERT YOUR EYES!

While smoke is an appealing ingredient to our taste buds, it's not so appealing to the rest of our body, which is why it's important to get in the habit of only taking in the most minimal, unavoidable amount of smoke while cooking with fire. The number-one practice that I observe every time I open the smoker door is turning my head, closing my eyes, and holding my breath. Once it's been open for a second and the initial wave of smoke has rushed by me, I turn my head back and open my eyes to check out the meat, then maybe hit it with the spray bottle, all while holding my breath. After three to five seconds total, I close the smoker door and breathe sweet, fresh air!

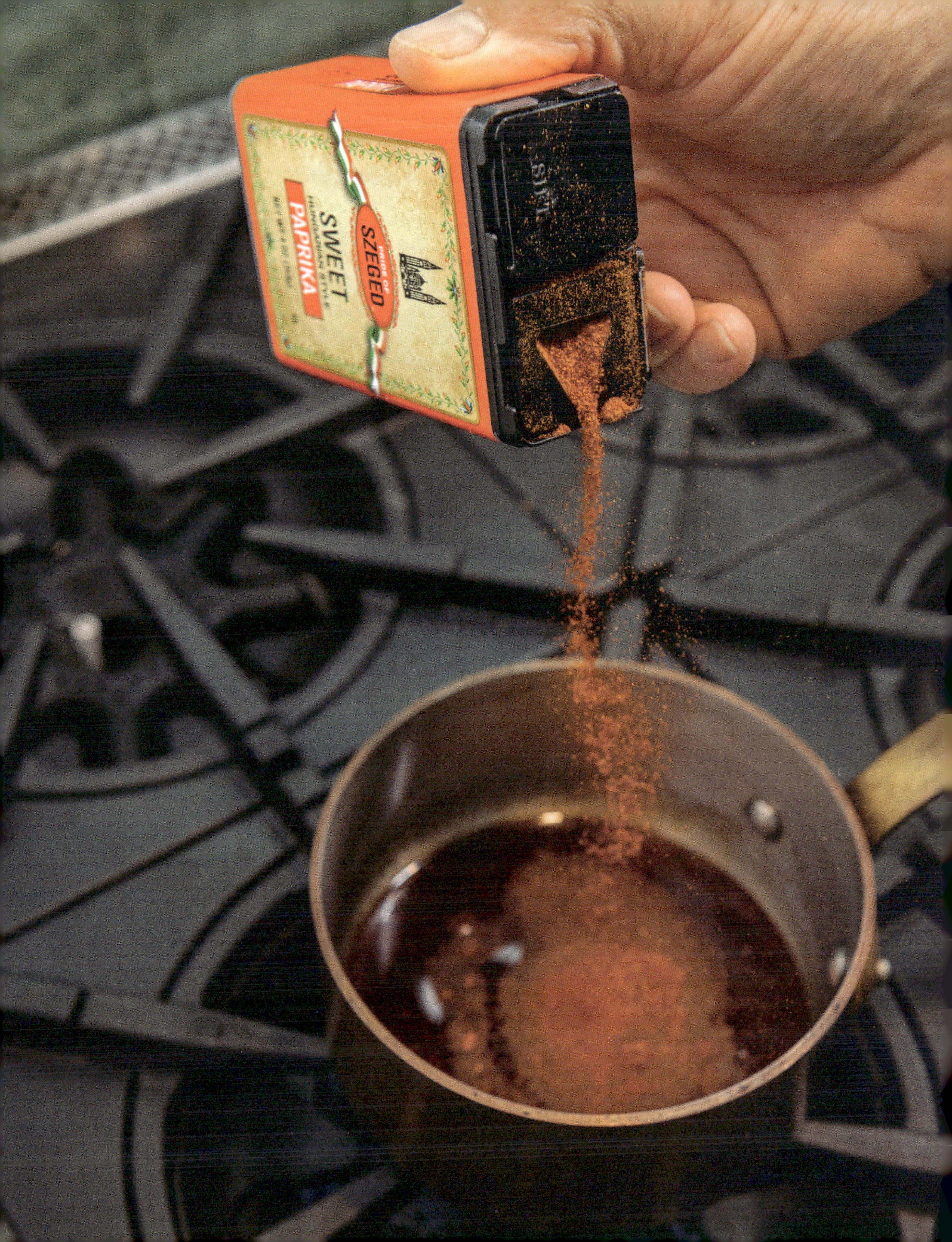
SZEGED
SWEET
PAPRIKA
SIFT

5

WARMING UP

Essential Pantry Items, Tools, and Rubs, Spices, and Sauces

Preparation is the foundation of good cooking and is especially important when working with fire and smoke. While the term *prep* applies to being well equipped with regard to tools and materials, it also refers to creating a schedule, getting your mind straight, and building flavor through process. When a meal is going to take upward of twelve hours to cook, you need to have a fair idea of the plot points ahead of time, especially if you've got a hungry family to feed or guests to serve. It may sound like a drag to sit down and sketch out in a notebook the timeline of a brisket cook, but you want to know that your food is going to be ready at the time it's needed—and when barbecuing at home, that's not always easy to accomplish.

Most of the dishes in this book call for dry brines, marination, air-drying, fermentations, tempering, and the like. These are all simple methods that can be done hours or days ahead, making the day of your dinner quicker and easier. Just because these crucial processes happen well in advance, they shouldn't be ignored or minimized. And just a tiny bit of early work can drastically improve the flavor and texture of your food and the way it cooks.

CREATING A COOKING TIMELINE

Whether I'm doing a short cook or a long one, I always plot a timeline to keep me on schedule. It is a form of temporal mise en place in which I outline a timed sequence of events from the beginning of a dish to the end, inclusive of everything from shopping and prepping to lighting fires and warming cookers to carryover cooking and resting. A timeline is a road map *and* an insurance plan if something gets off schedule or I get tired and mentally fuzzy. It allows me to trace back along my path to determine what I have or haven't done. When you start a cook on one day and finish it on another (or start so early in the morning that it feels like a different day by the time you serve the food), you'll be happy to have a written plan guiding you.

Since serving the food is what it's all about, that's where you start writing your timeline. Just as any restaurant kitchen has prep sheets for its cooks, you will fully plan out your menu and write down all the steps to cooking it, including making a list of the plates, platters, and tongs you need as well as all the ingredients for the cook. These are the puzzle pieces that must be assembled correctly for everything to go off without a hitch. For instance, if you're planning a brisket cook, you would ask yourself the following questions: How long will it take to cook that brisket? How long to trim it? At what time do I hope to wrap? How long will the carryover be? If I get behind, where can I make up time?

Begin with the moment you want to eat and work your way backward. So if you want to sit down to brisket with friends at 6:00 p.m., you might factor a two-hour rest (depending on conditions) starting at 4:00 p.m. That brisket would come off the cooker at 4:00 p.m., perhaps after a three-hour cooking window following wrapping. That means you'll wrap in the 1:00 p.m. range. Wrapping is often performed eight to nine hours after putting the brisket on. So, working back from 1:00 p.m., this means the brisket needs to be on the smoker at 4:00 a.m., which means you need to be up and firing up your smoker by 3:00 a.m. And that means trimming and rubbing it at 3:00 a.m., although I almost always trim it the night before and pull it out of the fridge to temper and rub when I get up. You should also probably factor an additional hour somewhere along the line as a safety net. For some extra guidance, I might jot down the projected temperatures that I want to hit at key points along the way, just as I watch for mile markers on a road trip.

WARMING UP

In the end, your timeline will look something like this:

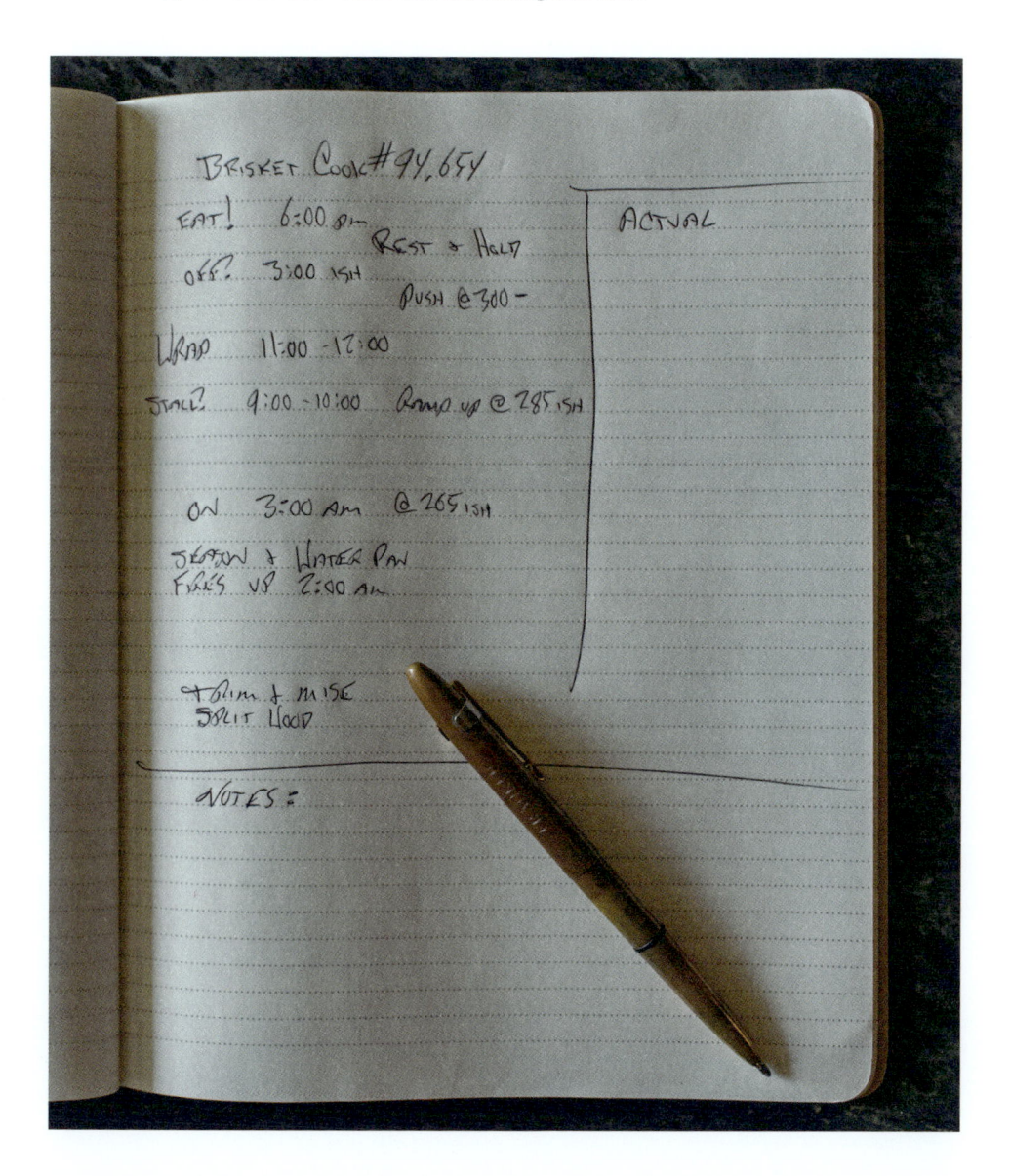

Doing a timeline for every dish—or, at least, every major one—may seem like an absurd amount of organization but, trust me, it really helps. If you get into the habit of doing this, you won't end up like Jordan, who often admits he should have lit the coals earlier as he and his wife, Christie, and their dinner guests sit down to dine at 9:30 p.m.

ESSENTIAL PANTRY ITEMS

To shore up your prep and prevent unexpected, time-consuming hiccups, like having to run to the store for more salt or oil, keep your pantry well and simply stocked. I don't use much in the way of spices or herbs. I like the flavor of the food to merge with the flavor of the fire—and leave it at that. As a result, my pantry is exceedingly basic, made up mostly of oils, vinegars, salts, lemons, garlic, fermented goods, and some spices. Here are my go-to items.

APPLE CIDER AND OTHER VINEGARS Apple cider vinegar is so central to my process that I buy it by the jug and keep a spray bottle of it on hand, whether I'm cooking in the smoker, on the firepit, or on the grill.

That said, I love the flavors of many different vinegars, so I keep red wine and white wine versions around, as well as sherry, balsamic, and especially rice.

BLACK PEPPER I use pre-ground 16-mesh (coarse) black pepper in our rubs and also keep a grinder handy (the incredible Männkitchen Pepper Cannon) for freshly ground black pepper.

CITRUS Acidity is key to making your dishes pop, so be sure your citrus bowl is always stocked with fresh lemons, oranges, and limes. I use the zest and peel of citrus in lots of dishes and preps. But, of course, the juice is also crucial. After you remove the zest from a citrus fruit, wrap up the fruit and keep it in the fridge so you can also use the juice later.

FERMENTED FOODS Sauerkraut, kimchi, and other naturally fermented foods are a constant around the house, as these condiments add instant complexity and contrast to whatever's coming off the fire.

GARLIC A miraculous little seasoning, fresh garlic not only can last unrefrigerated for weeks at a time (making it convenient to store) but it packs a huge punch, so use it in moderation. Yes, peeling garlic can be a chore, but pre-peeled cloves never have as much flavor as what you break off a whole head. If using it uncooked, tempering freshly minced garlic in vinegar or citrus juice for 10 to 15 minutes takes the edge off.

GRAPESEED OIL This is my oil of choice for most cooking needs because it has a high smoke point (good for cooking at very high temperatures) and neutral flavor. I keep it in restaurant-style squeeze bottles for mess-free delivery.

HOT SAUCE I love to make my own hot sauce, but I also keep bottles of other sauces around. Forever on my shelf are Crystal Hot Sauce and Yellowbird Jalapeño sauce (a delicious local product). I like these not just for the spice but also the acidity.

PICKLED ITEMS Continuing on the theme of acidity, it goes without saying that pickles of all shapes, sizes, and kinds play a huge role in my diet and in my pantry. They are great for garnishes, side dishes, condiments, and snacks.

SALT Kosher is my go-to cooking salt. The granule size and coarseness make it easy to handle when pinching and dusting and keep me from oversalting. Morton Coarse Kosher Salt is denser than Diamond Crystal Kosher Salt, so be sure you're calibrated to whichever one you're using.

For finishing salt, I use something along the lines of Maldon Sea Salt Flakes or Jacobsen Salt Co. Pure Flake Sea Salt. These are both beautiful, crunchy, mineral flakes that look and taste delicious, offering pleasant minerality and a soft, not-too-sharp flavor.

SPICES I don't keep a ton of spices around, but they tend to include chile powders, paprika, and other savory items that deliver a little kick. These also would include rubs and seasonings such as Lawry's, which I mention on page 110.

COOKING TOOLS

I love kitchen gadgets—utensils, knives, pots, pans, thermometers, scales—everything. My ever-expanding collection of kitchen equipment is the bane of Stacy's existence (well, one of the banes, at least). My excuse is that as a restaurant owner, cook, recipe developer, and constant answerer of questions, I need to be informed. But believe me, I get it when Stacy exclaims, "Maybe we don't need forty sheet pans at home."

Confoundingly, and to her point, I also believe that you need very little stuff for cooking. Some pieces of equipment can make your life easier and your cooking a little more refined and accurate, but you can also work around a lot of these gadgets if you don't have the space or the money . . . or you *do* have a significant other who deplores (kitchen) clutter.

So please view the following information through two lenses: (1) the things you *need* and (2) the things you might *want*. I try to make clear which items I put in which camp. But some tools—like smokers and grills, tongs and grates—are simply nonnegotiable.

CAST-IRON/CARBON-STEEL PANS Having durable and heat-resistant pans that you can throw on a fire or the coals are essential for all kinds of fire cooking. Sometimes you want to use the heat and a bit of the smoke generated by your fire while enjoying the ease of cooking in a pan. Also, even if you're cooking on a fire, you don't want every item to taste of the fire. The open-flame grill pan with perforations by Made In is very versatile. You get the best of both worlds—a sear from the steel plus the kiss of the fire—and it keeps your ingredients from falling into the coals.

CHAIR If you prepped well, you won't be scrambling around the whole time you're cooking. After all, barbecuing is supposed to be relaxing and enjoyable. You'll want to find moments here and there to take a load off, rest those dogs, and enjoy the outdoors while contemplating the weather, reading a magazine, or just daydreaming. So make sure you have a comfy outdoor chair, plus a few extras for a friend or two to relax in—everyone wants to sit by a fire.

COLD DRINKS AND ICE CHEST Don't mind if I do. An ice chest full of cold beverages is essential to your cook, unless it's a frigid midwinter evening. But let's imagine that, most of the time, the conditions are peachy, and you'll want refreshment whether you are quick-searing steaks or nursing a brisket for the long haul. My only caution: apply moderation. Be wary of the sneaky drinks, such as high-ABV beers, like IPAs, and especially well-made cocktails that magically disappear in seconds. This approach is, to a large degree, how I became a lager or pilsner or light ale guy over time. I love a crisp and refreshing beverage that has just enough alcohol to ease the passing of time without me forgetting something, making mistakes, or falling asleep—all of which can easily happen when you're planning to be up a good part of the night cooking for the next day.

A good ice chest is a cold drink's bestie, of course. I've been using YETI brand since it first came on the market, and to my mind, no chest offers a better combination of form-factor, insulating power, and lightweight mobility. YETI chests are expensive, however, and the fact is, any cooler will do—even a cheapie that's not the best quality—as long as you keep it filled with fresh ice.

COOK'S NOTEBOOK Keeping a notebook to record timelines (see page 94), recipe ideas, shopping lists, and everything that goes into a significant cook is essential. I never used to date my entries, which I regret now. Sometimes I look back on twelve years of recipes and the details of when and how I developed a certain method feel really valuable. So, as always, don't lose track of time.

FISH SPATULA No other spatula is thin enough to slide under a delicate skin to unstick it from a hot pan or grill surface without mangling the fish. But this is also a hardy enough tool to wonderfully flip all kinds of foods besides fish.

FLASHLIGHT I've got decent outside lighting for my setup, but there are times during a late-night cook when shadows get in the way. Having a good flashlight handy is always wise.

HEADLAMP

> I've never seen Aaron wear a headlamp, but my outdoor setup is not as refined, nor is my technique and timing as immaculate, and I often find myself finishing something in the dark that was meant to be done long before. For this reason, I find a headlamp to be invaluable. After a bit of shopping around, I chose the Nitecore NU25 for its brightness but especially for its wide field of illumination, which is helpful if you have a few things going on at the same time. —Jordan

FOIL Surely you already keep a good supply of aluminum foil around your house. I get the industrial-size rolls from a restaurant supply store. All the standard household uses apply, but foil can also be fashioned into a durable, malleable, heat-conducting cooking vessel. There's no better way to get the most out of your fire than to turn a piece of foil into a boat for fish or into an envelope in which to seal vegetables and other ingredients to steam away in their own juices.

GRILL/FRYER BASKET Most grill baskets are small, weak, and overpriced. That's why I go to a restaurant-supply store and buy fryer baskets of all shapes and sizes. For vegetables and smaller items that might easily slip through the bars of the grate, a tight-mesh grill basket is a really handy thing. It's not expensive, but it also doesn't last too long, so don't worry if you have to replace it once a year or so.

(EXTRA) GRILL GRATES The idea that the sooty black crust that forms on the grill grate adds "flavor" or "soul" each time you cook on it is not only a myth but also positively detrimental to your cook. The only flavors a dirty grate might add to your ingredient are burnt and carbonized along with a sooty, ashy color. That said, a used grate is hard to clean. If you're entertaining or just tired after a long day, you might not get to washing your grate until the next day (or, let's be real, the next week or . . . never). While it's worthwhile to put a little elbow grease into keeping those things bright and shiny, it's also okay to replace them once they get beyond recuperation.

KITCHEN SCALE I'm a big believer in the accuracy, simplicity, and scalability of measuring ingredients by weight, not volume, so a good kitchen scale, like the Ohaus, is a high-priority item. After all, a cup of brown sugar will have varying weights depending on how tightly it's packed. It's really easy to build recipes such as sauces and rubs on a scale. Just put a bowl on the scale and tare it, which returns the reading to zero. Add your first ingredient, tare the scale again to return to zero, add the next ingredient, tare again, and so on. This is a beautifully simple and supremely accurate way to cook!

KNIVES While it's true that any old knife will do most of the time as long as its decently sharp, there are certain pleasures and advantages in being a bit of a knife geek, which I am. I simply find pleasure in owning and caring for an exquisite, handmade tool that's been carefully considered and crafted to have a certain balance, weight, and action. When you use such a knife, you can feel all of these qualities: the way it accurately, cleanly, and effortlessly slices and how it feels connected to your body so you don't get sore. A good knife makes prepping and serving a joy, not a chore—like a jazz drummer having the right drumstick.

I'm on record for liking a mass-produced, machine-made Dexter Russell serrated knife for slicing brisket, and I stand by that. It's excellent at getting through supertender, jiggly brisket while keeping the meat and bark intact (if you do it right). I also use that knife for all kinds of other tasks, such as breaking down prime rib.

There is much ado about Japanese versus Western knives, and I think both traditions offer incredible products. Japanese knives are typically thinner, made of harder steel, and have a single bevel (sharpened on only one side), which allows them to slice more cleanly. They are better for precision work and pure slicing, the most common techniques used in much of Japanese cooking. Western-style knives,

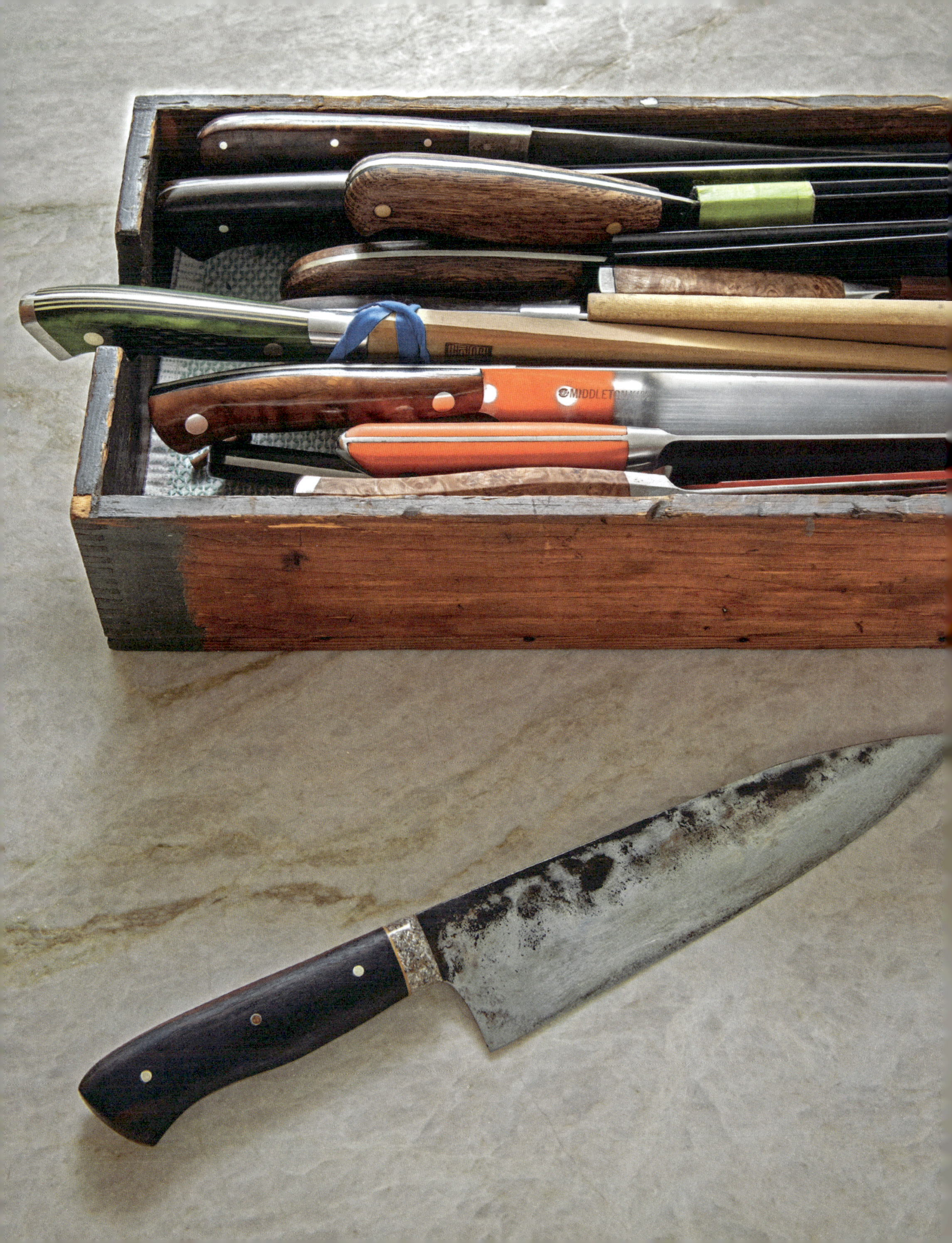
MIDDLETON

such as those made by Wüsthof or J. A. Henckels, are heavier, made of softer steel, and have two bevels (both sides are sharpened and come to a V-like point). This style is considered more versatile—it's a capable slicer, but it's also good for chopping, scraping, and crushing, which are more usual in Western cuisine. In a Western kitchen, it's common to have one or two all-purpose knives that can perform most tasks so you don't have to constantly switch blades. By contrast, Japanese cooks may constantly swap among a number of highly specialized tools.

Although you can find plenty of examples of pure styles, many manufacturers produce blades that blend or overlap the two traditions, such as Japanese-made Western chef's knives that apply the best of the Japanese craft to the Western double-beveled design. These hybrid knives are the kind that I use most often at home.

KNIFE SHARPENING

When my knives get a little dull, I sharpen them, and you should do the same. A sharp knife is a pleasing knife. When you have a high-quality blade, you need a quality sharpening protocol that takes sharpening shortcuts (like the inexpensive, little plastic tools) out of the equation.

First, you need a whetstone. While many sources say you need a wide range of grits, I keep just one stone with 1,000 grit on one side and 5,000 grit on the other. I bought a rubber holder from Korin, a knife shop in New York with an online store, to secure the stone to the countertop. I often ignore the instruction to soak the stone in water for thirty to sixty minutes before using, because I usually don't know an hour ahead of time that I'm going to want to sharpen a knife. Instead, I keep a bowl of warm water handy and repeatedly splash water on the stone as I run the knives across it. It is important to hit the right angle as you rub the blade on the steel, a skill that takes practice and attention. Don't forget to press down hard enough that you actually grind the metal.

For the most part, I sharpen on the 5,000-grit side of the stone only. It's a fine grain that is perfectly good for honing and maintaining the edge of a knife that's been well cared for. Occasionally, I may take a few swipes on the 1,000 grit if a knife really needs some help, but that's rare because I keep my knives in good condition. If I want a superfine edge, I'll finish it on a piece of printer paper. Some people use a leather strop, but paper works just fine. Many chefs use a steel, though I never do. If you keep your blades sharp, you really don't need to.

> **SOME OF MY FAVORITE KNIFE MAKERS**
>
> **CHUBO** Founded by an American, this company is a retailer and producer that commissions craftspeople across Japan to create blades while also curating a diverse selection of quality Japanese knives. Its website is very informative about the various styles of Japanese blades.
>
> **MAC** Much more affordable than Nenox and of amazing quality, MAC is a Japanese brand geared toward Western styles. However, the edge has a bit of a Japanese pitch to it, making it a more acute slicer than most Western-style blades.
>
> **MISONO** This is another terrific and less-expensive Japanese knifemaker. These sturdy, classically shaped knives (many incorporate excellent Swedish steel) really hold their edge. The ten-inch chef's knife in carbon steel is Jordan's main blade.
>
> **NENOX** These are my go-to knives. Nenox is a line of Western-style knives made by Nenohi in Japan. Unfortunately, they've become much more expensive than when I first bought them years ago—and they were expensive then. But they're amazing to work with. Their proprietary alloy of stainless steel is durable and keeps its edge but is soft enough to sharpen easily at home. The weight, balance, and feel of the knives are incredible. If you're awash in bitcoin money, consider these!
>
> **STEELPORT** These are very cool, exceptionally crafted knives made from American materials in one of my favorite cities, Portland, Oregon. Founded in 2020, STEELPORT is a fairly new company. The knives are not discernably Western or Japanese in style. They combine elements of many knife-making traditions in original and highly functional tools.

MOP The word *mop* applies to both the tool and the mixture of ingredients that the tool adds to the food. In this case, I'm talking about the tool, which is a mini-version of what a janitor may wield while cleaning a floor. You could use a spoon for the purpose of applying a (ingredient) mop, but it tends to be less thorough. You can make your own mop from an old towel or other absorptive fabric, or you can buy a dedicated tool.

It's possible to use a standard kitchen brush to apply a mop, as long as you use the brush as a mop and not a brush. That is, don't let the brush (tool) touch the meat because you don't want to rub any sauce off or disturb the bark. So use a mop to apply a mop, but if you use a brush, never brush!

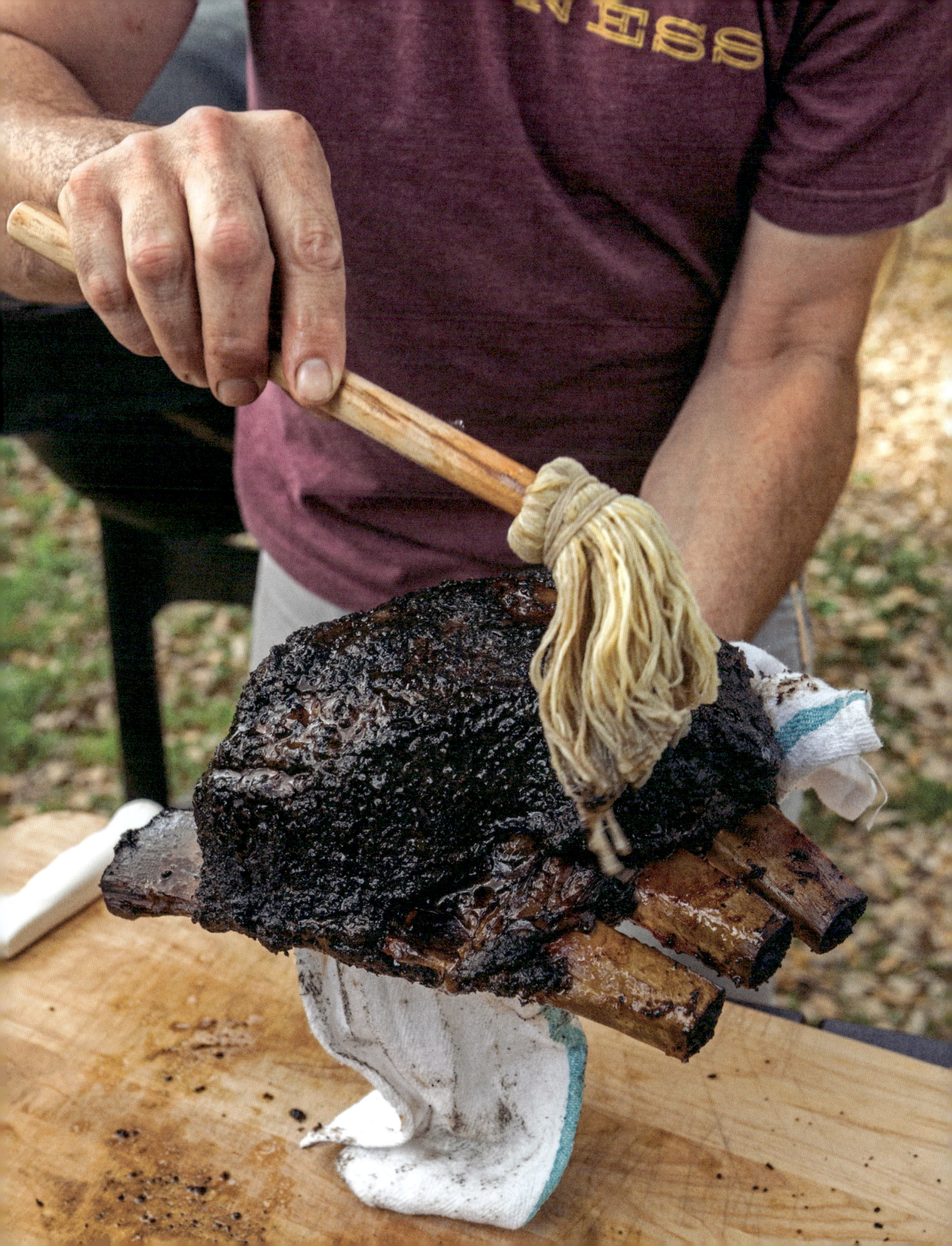

PEPPER GRINDER Black pepper and smoke were meant for each other. The crackling energy in black peppercorns echoes and intertwines with the snap and hiss of a live fire, so having a good pepper grinder is essential. For me, there is only one grinder to rule them all: the Männkitchen Pepper Cannon. Rarely does a tool rise above all others in its field but, as a fan of quality craft and design, I appreciate this object. Its build, versatility, and functionality are all exceptional. Yes, it's expensive, but if you grind a lot of pepper, and expect to do the same in the future, you'll appreciate the investment.

Note: In barbecue, black pepper interacts beautifully with fat, sinking in and almost merging to form the bark. However, on briskets, I don't use *freshly* ground pepper. I instead prefer a pre-ground pepper that has aged and mellowed a bit (see page 113).

RAGS AND TOWELS As with tongs and beer, so with rags and towels: you can never have too many. Wait, what? A piece of foldable cloth is a magical implement, good for everything from cleaning up spills to grabbing heavy slabs of meat to picking up hot irons or wiping off a knife. Just buy a pack of twenty-five. You can launder and reuse them until they fall apart, and if one gets soiled beyond repair, it's not a big deal to toss it.

SHEET PANS AND SIZZLE PLATTERS I keep stacks of full-, half-, and quarter-size sheet pans around to serve many functions: as a plate for drying out a steak in the fridge, to transport items between the kitchen and the outdoors, as a baffle in a smoker, and to receive freshly cooked items and their drippings. They are as tough as nails, both freezer- and oven-friendly, and very easy to clean.

The same can be said for sizzle platters, which are little steel or aluminum dishes that you may have seen in restaurant kitchens. These can be purchased inexpensively at a restaurant-supply store and serve much the same function as sheet pans. They're smaller but just as tough and will happily sit under a broiler. I've even been to sophisticated restaurants that serve food on them!

SPRAY BOTTLE This is not intended to cool you off on a hot day, but that could be pleasant unless it's filled with apple cider vinegar, as mine often is. I usually have a couple of spray bottles, one containing vinegar and the other water, within reach. Spraying your ingredient at the end of a smoke, before it's taken out or wrapped, moistens the exterior, extending the time the food can smoke and helping it cook to just the right moment without drying out.

THERMOMETER I'm an instant-read-thermometer junkie, especially the model called Thermapen, which I heartily endorse. It's the most expensive thermometer out there, but also the quickest, most accurate, best designed, and easiest to use. I always have at least two, if not three, on hand.

A good digital meat thermometer won't really help you determine when brisket or ribs are perfectly done, because doneness on those cuts is somewhat independent of temperature. But knowing internal temperatures provides useful information along the way. A thermometer is also invaluable for checking doneness on such shorter-cooking items as prime rib, tomahawks, pork steaks, poultry, and fish. The speed of the instant-read function is crucial because you only want to have the smoker door open for a very short time while cooking.

There are also ingenious options for checking temperature (connected via Wi-Fi to your phone or an external unit) where you never even have to open the smoker lid. For instance, we tried the popular MEATER device and liked how one end of the thermometer goes into the meat and the other end senses the ambient temperature around the meat. It also tracks the temperature readings and charts them over time for a quick record of your cook. Although the MEATER is very clever and useful, I am usually staring at fire, so pulling out my phone to open the app every time I need to check a temperature is highly inconvenient. And anyway, I think I'm set in my ways, enjoying the simplicity of an old-school (digital!) thermometer.

TONGS In an interview with *Bon Appétit* magazine, Marie Kondo, author of *The Life-Changing Magic of Tidying Up*, answered a query about keeping one's kitchen neat by saying, "Most people have too many tongs!" My response is "Can you ever have *enough* tongs?" (Stacy's response: "Do you really need all these tongs?")

But seriously, I use tongs constantly when I'm cooking outside. I have different sizes, from small ones for precision jobs to extra-long, heavy-duty ones. I use them to turn food but also to reach into a fire and grab a burning log. Indeed, on every cook, I have one pair for handling things inside the smoker or on the grill and another pair for going right into the firebox to arrange and rearrange the architecture of coals and logs.

I've found that the extra-long, heavy-duty tongs from a restaurant-supply store are pretty good. But, gee, wouldn't it be cool if someone made some great ones to their own specs? *(Hmmm . . . .)*

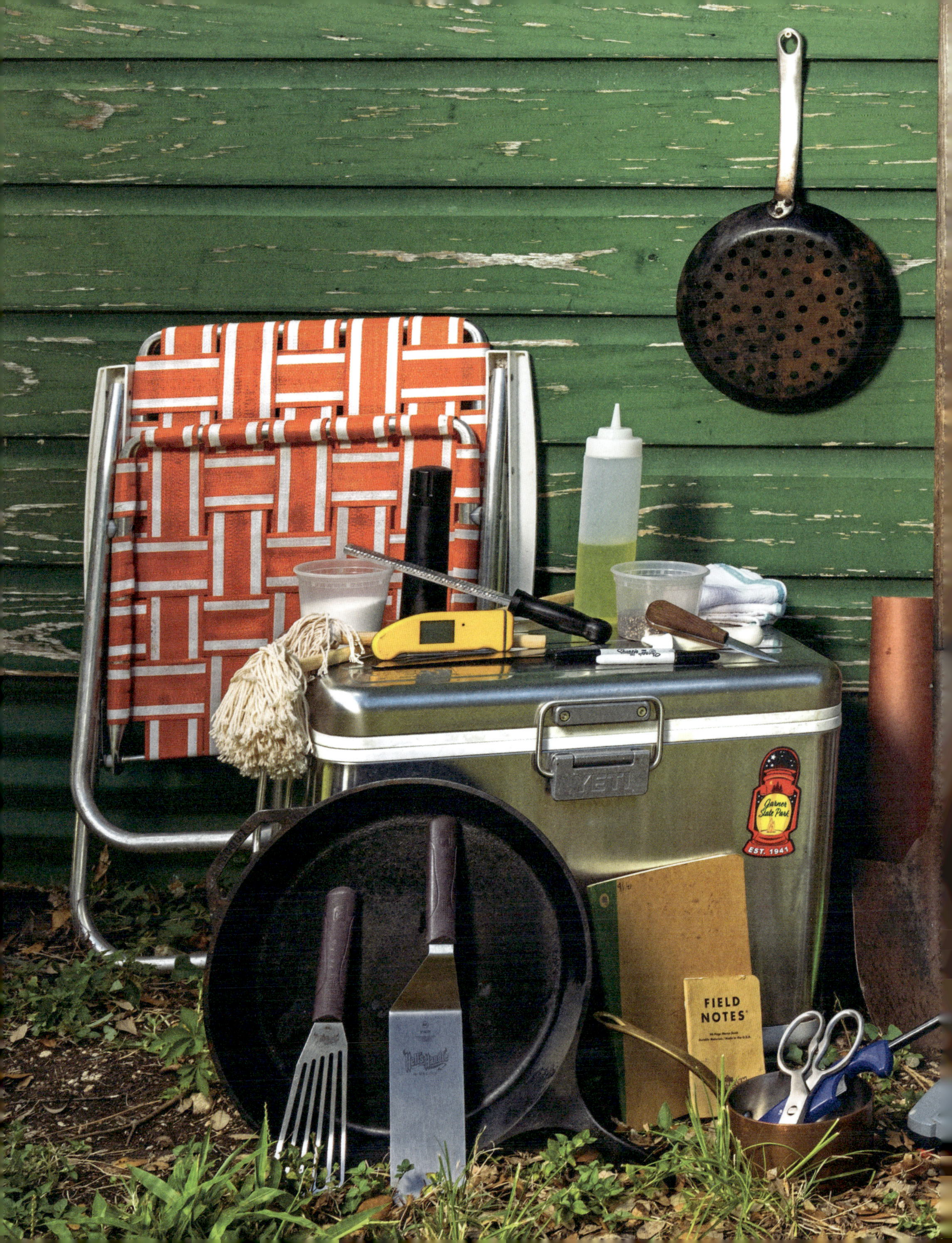
YETI
Garner State Park
EST. 1941
FIELD NOTES

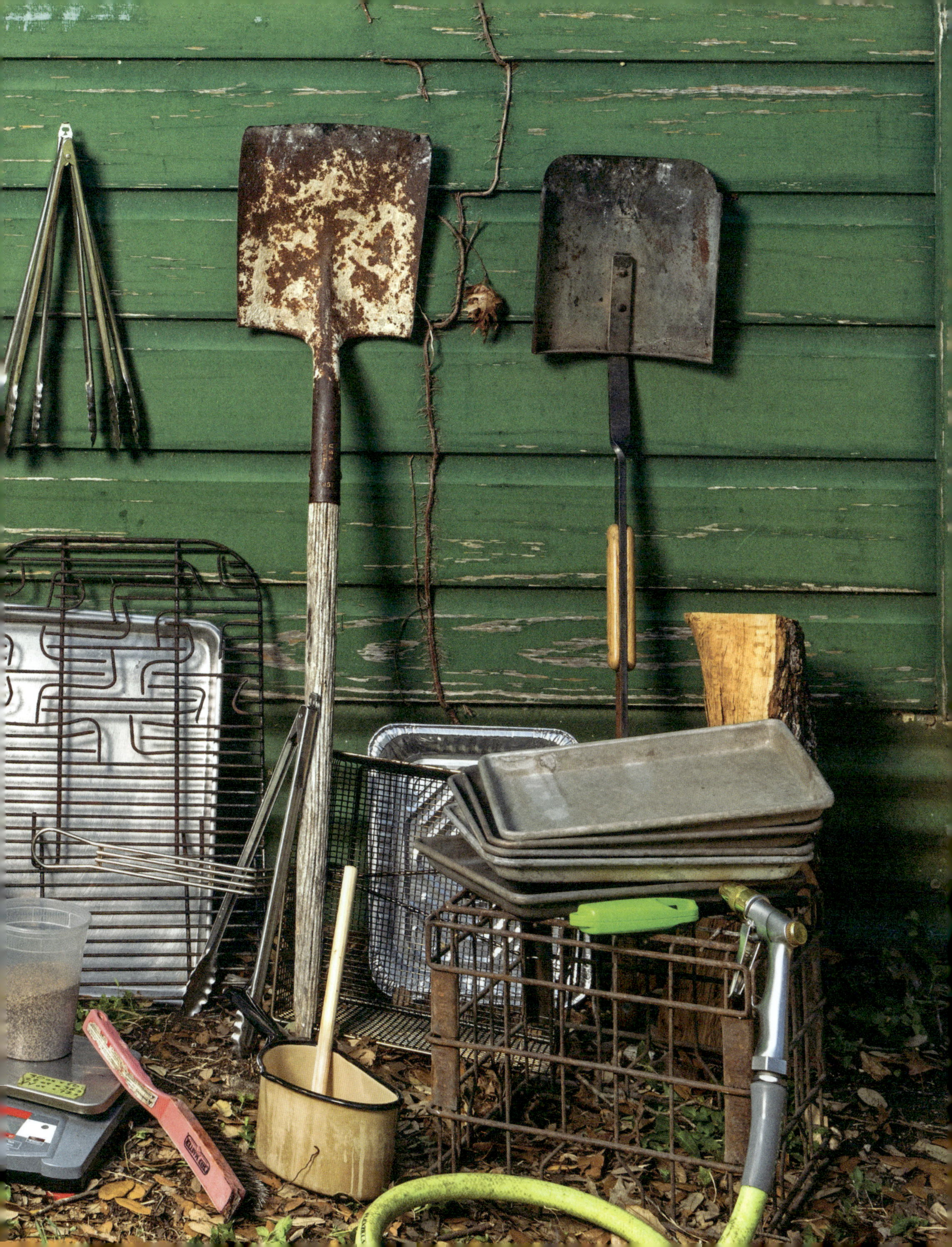

WORKTABLE When you're plotting out your outdoor kitchen, be it a bougie patio affair or a makeshift setup in the dirt around a campsite, do yourself a favor and plan for a table or other elevated, flat working area. Just as counter space always seems to be in short supply in a home kitchen, it's in even higher demand outdoors where ingredients are going on and off grills and tools, sauces, mops, sprays, seasonings, towels, drinks, kids' toys—you name it—are looking for a spot to rest. When I go camping, the first thing out of the truck is a folding table. I recommend you do the same and set up either a temporary or permanent work area at your house.

BUILDING FLAVOR

On weeknights, or even weekends, when you've been out all day and need to get dinner ready in a hurry, having a well-stocked cupboard of rubs, condiments, and sauces speeds the delivery of tasty, umami-rich meals. You can buy this stuff or you can make your own, customizing flavors and spice levels to your taste. The great thing is that they last a good long time, so a little effort up front can mean big time savings later on, not to mention the delicious satisfaction of having done it yourself.

Rubs

Fresh seasonings can be great, but it's super-handy to have spice rubs in the pantry, whether you're prepping for a long smoke or just want to add some hassle-free flavor to something you're about to grill. For this reason, Franklin now manufactures a few basic rubs. Our BBQ Spice Rub is our own (somewhat) less salty take on the iconic Lawry's Seasoned Salt. Our Steak Spice Rub is an umami bomb with universal applications that just bumps up the flavor of everything. And our Brisket Spice Rub, which is a mix of the classic salt and pepper I've always advocated, also makes a good foundation for your own additions.

When I'm first learning how to cook something or developing a new technique, I start with kosher salt as my sole seasoning. Then once I know that my process is solid, I build flavor from there. I truly believe that by the end of an hours-long smoke, what you ultimately want to taste is meat, smoke, salt, and pepper. But that doesn't mean I won't keep messing around with different spice blends for the rubs or new flavors for our slathers (like French's yellow mustard or hot sauce) with the hope that a little extra complexity might make our customers happier.

WARMING UP

The fifty-fifty combination of salt and pepper that we use is still unequivocally the best and most reliable seasoning for brisket, ribs, or whatever you want to smoke. It's our foundation. So if you're just starting your brisket game, begin with a basic salt-and-pepper rub and then, if you want to mess around with additional flavors, add a layer of something else, like all-purpose BBQ Spice Rub. (But take it easy on the sugar, as it burns at higher temperatures.)

On the following pages are my guidelines for assembling your own basic seasonings. I'm not exactly offering the recipes for the Franklin rubs, but I am giving you the general framework. Creating rubs at home gives you control of the ingredients, saves you a few bucks, and allows you to find the formulas that suit your own palate.

BBQ SPICE RUB

Lawry's Seasoned Salt is an American classic, and I've always appreciated it as such. In fact, when I was growing up, my dad put Lawry's on almost every steak he ever grilled, so it also has a taste of nostalgia for me. As you know, I'm a tinkerer, and I like to custom make things when possible, so following is a list of the most prominent ingredients (in order of volume) that go into our all-purpose BBQ Spice Rub. This is an homage to Lawry's—with a little less salt.

Use with: Practically everything, but notably on chicken, steaks, and chops, or mixed with salt and pepper for brisket, beef ribs, and baby back ribs. But you can really use it on anything you like, as it's that versatile.

Makes as much as you want

- Fine sea salt
- Garlic powder
- Onion powder
- Paprika
- Mustard powder
- Mushroom powder
- Celery powder
- Lemon powder
- Granulated sugar

Rubs such as this should be made to satisfy your own taste, which is why I don't offer volumes for each ingredient. You could make this à la minute to sprinkle on some chicken breasts you're about to cook up, or you could make a larger volume to last for a while. The base of most rubs is salt, garlic powder, and onion powder. I recommend starting with equal parts of those and adding in amounts of the other, more specialty flavors, like mushroom or mustard powders, in smaller quantities and to taste. Ultimately, combine all of the ingredients to taste and mix well. Store in an airtight container in the pantry for up to 3 months.

Variations: Other possible additions include vinegar powder, tomato powder (be careful, as it can burn), and Worcestershire powder.

WARMING UP

STEAK SPICE RUB

We created this rub to be an umami booster for almost anything you put it on—similar to old-style BBQ seasonings but without any MSG.

Use with: I sprinkle this rub on everything from steaks to pasta sauces; it delivers just that extra bump of deliciousness. For steaks, use this on larger cuts that cook at lower temperatures (like prime rib), as it can scorch at high temperatures.

Makes as much as you want

- Sea salt
- Garlic powder
- Onion powder
- Mushroom powder
- Tomato powder
- Mustard powder
- White pepper
- Granulated beef stock
- Worcestershire powder
- Mustard powder
- Celery powder

Again, start with the base of equal parts salt, garlic powder, and onion powder. Then add the other ingredients in smaller amounts to taste. In a bowl, combine all of the ingredients and mix well. Store in an airtight container in the pantry for up to 3 months.

Variations: Other possible additions include brewer's yeast, dehydrated parsley powder, and apple cider vinegar powder.

BRISKET SPICE RUB

A one-to-one ratio (by volume, not weight) of coarse salt and 16-mesh ground black pepper makes up our foundational brisket seasoning, but you can also use this mixture to start building any kind of rub you want.

Fermentations and Pickles

The only flavor as compelling as acidity in any dish is umami. Fermentation and pickling are two excellent ways to obtain both of these elements at the same time. If you don't already practice these simple ways of building flavor by making delicious condiments, you should definitely consider starting. These recipes require minimal labor and very little active prep. Time itself does most of the work, along with our little friends, the microbes.

SAUERKRAUT, TWO WAYS

I always have a jar or two of sauerkraut on hand. There's something about its tart flavor, prickly acidity, and fermented funkiness that takes the heaviness out of a rich smoked piece of meat. Best of all, it's very easy to make at home, which—without fail—yields a more complex, delicious, and healthful version than what comes in a can. (Canned sauerkraut undergoes pasteurization, which kills all the beneficial probiotics obtained during fermentation.)

Use with: Kraut is always good on a hot dog, of course, but it's wonderful served alongside Firepit Pork Shoulder "Steaks" (page 133) or Baby Back Ribs (page 199). Indeed, it's even good with Smoked Duck (page 207). Serve it chilled, or warm it up gently with some of the meat juices from the cutting board to give it a little extra heft.

Makes 1 quart

Equipment
- Kitchen scale
- Bowl
- Muddler (or some sort of implement such as a pestle or wooden spoon for pressing down hard)
- One 1-quart or two 1-pint widemouthed mason jars
- Rounded glass weights
- Fermentation lids (depending on number of jars)

Fermentation lids can be purchased online, where you'll find a number of brands, all of which work well. These are not required for making sauerkraut or any other fermented foods, but they do keep your ferment nice and neat. They are a type of air lock, allowing carbon dioxide to escape without letting oxygen in. This makes it harder for mold or other bacteria to grow on top of the kraut. Although almost anything that might grow there is harmless, it is neither appealing to look at nor to think about, so I discourage such growth by using the lids.

The glass weight—a thick, glass disc—can be placed on top of the cabbage at the end to keep it submerged in the brine.

SOPRANO SAUERKRAUT

You can make wonderful sauerkraut with nothing more than cabbage and salt, but I like to bump up the complexity and the high notes by adding a bit of garlic and ginger. You can really add any sort of additional seasoning you like. Caraway seeds are classic, but spicy chiles or dill would also be nice.

- 1 head green cabbage
- Kosher salt
- 2g piece fresh ginger, finely minced or grated on a Microplane
- 1 large garlic clove, finely minced or grated on a Microplane
- Distilled or spring water for topping if needed

Using a large chef's knife, halve and core the cabbage, then slice the halves into a thin julienne. A fine shred improves the fermentation dynamics.

Tare a bowl on the kitchen scale and then weigh the cabbage. Determine what 2.5 percent of the weight of the cabbage is and add that amount of salt. For instance, if you have 800g of cabbage, you'll add 20g of salt. (If you want a saltier kraut, feel free to up the percentage of salt. Keep in mind that anything more than 5 percent can be painfully salty, and the fermentation process may not work as well.)

Add the ginger and garlic to the bowl and, using your hands, thoroughly mix everything together. Pound the cabbage a bit with a muddler to speed the process of drawing out its liquid. Let the mixture sit for 30 minutes at moderate room temperature to allow the salt to draw moisture out of the cabbage. While the cabbage sits, sterilize the jar(s) by boiling them in a pot of water for 10 minutes, then (carefully) transfer them to a clean kitchen towel.

After 30 minutes, begin to fill the prepared jar(s) with the damp cabbage. After each addition, use the muddler to press on the cabbage, compacting it against the bottom of the jar. As you work your way up, you want the cabbage to be tightly and densely packed. Stop when the cabbage reaches 1 to 1½ inches from the rim of the jar. Pour in any liquid remaining in the bowl. As you pressed down on the cabbage, enough salt water should have naturally released from it to cover the contents of the jar. If you don't have quite enough, add a splash of distilled or spring water to submerge the cabbage completely.

Press the contents down with the glass weights and seal with the easy-fermenter lid(s). Set the jar(s) in an open container, such as a Tupperware bowl, to catch any liquid that overflows due to expansion during fermentation. Place your jar(s) and container in a dry, dark, room temperature spot.

Within a day or two, you should see tiny bubbles rising to the top when you tap the side of the jar(s). That means the fermentation has started. After 7 to 10 days, feel free to open the lid and taste. You should have a mild-flavored sauerkraut. For more intense earthy and funky flavors, let the sauerkraut go for more time, up to 3 weeks. When the kraut has achieved a flavor you like, suspend the fermentation by putting the whole jar in the refrigerator. The sauerkraut will keep in the fridge for up to 1 month.

FENNEL AND RADICCHIO KRAUT

This version of sauerkraut combines the refreshing bitterness of radicchio with the anise-flavored lift and added crunch of fennel. The purple cabbage and radicchio combine to turn the mixture a stunning deep purple.

- ½ head radicchio
- ½ head purple cabbage
- 1 fennel bulb
- ½ teaspoon fennel seeds
- Kosher salt
- Distilled or spring water for topping if needed

Using a large chef's knife, halve and core the radicchio and cabbage. Slice the halves into a thin julienne. With the knife, remove the stalks from the fennel bulb, then cut the bulb in half lengthwise and gently remove the core. Now slice it crosswise, matching the size and texture of the purple ingredients. Slice off several of the fennel fronds and peel off the tiny leaves. Mince the tiny leaves finely and reserve about ¼ cup.

Tare a large bowl on the kitchen scale, combine the vegetables in the bowl, add the fennel seeds, and then weigh the vegetables. Determine what 2.5 percent of the weight of the vegetables is and add that amount of salt. For instance, if you have 950g of vegetables, you'll add 24g of salt. (If you want a saltier kraut, feel free to up the percentage of salt. Keep in mind that anything more than 5 percent can be painfully salty, and the fermentation process may not work as well.)

Using your hands, thoroughly mix everything together. Pound the vegetables a bit with a muddler to speed the process of drawing out their liquid. Let the mixture sit for 30 minutes at moderate room temperature, continuing to allow the salt to draw moisture out of the vegetables. While the vegetables sit, sterilize the jar(s) by boiling them in a pot of water for 10 minutes, then (carefully) transfer them to a clean kitchen towel.

After 30 minutes, begin to fill the prepared jar(s) with the damp vegetables. After each addition, use the muddler to press on the vegetables, compacting them against the bottom of the jar. As you work your way up, you want the vegetables to be tightly and densely packed. Stop when the vegetables reach 1 to 1½ inches from the rim of the jar. Pour in any liquid remaining in the bowl. As you pressed down on the vegetables, enough salt water should have naturally released from them to cover the contents of the jar. If you don't have quite enough, add a splash of distilled or spring water to submerge the vegetables completely.

Press the contents down with the glass weights and seal with the easy-fermenter lid(s). Set the jar(s) in an open container, such as a Tupperware bowl, to catch any liquid that overflows due to expansion during fermentation. Place your jar(s) and container in a dry, dark, room temperature spot.

Within a day or two, you should see tiny bubbles rising to the top when you tap the side of the jar(s). That means the fermentation has started. After 7 to 10 days, feel free to open the lid and taste. You should have a mild-flavored sauerkraut. For more intense earthy and funky flavors, let the sauerkraut go for more time, up to 3 weeks. When the kraut has achieved a flavor you like, suspend the fermentation by putting the whole jar in the refrigerator. The sauerkraut will keep in the fridge for up to 1 month.

FERMENTED HOT SAUCE

Homemade hot sauce is a truly satisfying project that's also really tasty. Yes, there are tons of great hot sauces available on store shelves—more than ever before, it seems—but when hot chiles are in season in the summer, I like to buy them by the bushel and make sauce from my own combinations.

You can make a tasty hot sauce just by stewing chiles in vinegar and spices, then pureeing and straining the result into bottles. But fermenting the chiles first brings a complexity and umami that I find irresistible.

This recipe is for a basic chile hot sauce, but you can add other flavors and ingredients to your heart's content. Ferment your chiles with garlic or other vegetables, for instance. Or add fresh garlic post-fermentation before you puree. Put your chiles on the smoker or grill to add some of the flavor of the fire. Herbs and spices always have a place too. Fruits, like mangoes, pineapples, and berries, can also play a role. Add vinegar or mezcal to the puree for even more complexity. Getting creative with your sauces is half the fun.

Use with: All savory foods!

Makes 1 quart

Equipment
- 1-quart widemouthed mason jar
- Kitchen scale
- Rounded glass weight
- Fermentation lid
- Fine-mesh strainer
- Funnel (optional)
- Sauce bottles (optional)

If you already own the quart jar and lid described for fermenting sauerkraut (see page 115), you have all you need to ferment chiles for hot sauce. (Be sure to sterilize the jar before filling it, as you did for the kraut.) The strategy is slightly different, though, as you'll start with a brine. You'll also need a strainer and, if you want to be able to dash out the sauce onto your food, recycled sauce bottles.

BASIC PEPPER SAUCE

Use any kind of chiles you like or a mix of varieties. The fresher they are, the better. If you want a milder sauce, remove the seeds. The colors that your sauces achieve can be electric. Combine yellow, red, and orange varieties for brilliant shades, or stick with green chiles, like jalapeños and serranos, for an alluring green sauce. A standard brine for successful fermentation ranges from a 2 to 5 percent salt solution. I like mine on the less salty side, between 2 and 2.5 percent. (Salt can always be added later.) That's about 6g of salt for every 240g (1 cup) of water. Use your scale to make the calculations.

- Water, as needed
- 1 to 2 pounds organic chiles, stemmed
- Fine sea salt
- 2 garlic cloves
- White wine vinegar for pureeing (optional)

Estimate how much water you'll need to submerge the chiles once they are packed into the 1-quart jar. Tare a bowl on the kitchen scale, then weigh the water. Multiply the water weight by 0.02 for a 2 percent salt solution (or whatever percentage you wish) and add that amount of salt. Stir to dissolve.

Pack your stemmed chiles into the sterilized jar. You can cut them in half, but don't bother chopping as they'll be pureed anyway. Crush the garlic cloves and add to the mix.

Pour the salt brine into the jar, covering the chiles completely and leaving about 1 inch of headspace in the jar. Press the contents down with the glass weights so the chiles are completely submerged and give the jar a gentle shake or stir to work out any air bubbles. Seal the jar with the fermentation lid.

Store the jar in a dry, dark spot at moderate room temperature (anywhere from 65° to 80°F will ferment the chiles very evenly and thoroughly).

Within a day or two, you should see tiny bubbles rising to the top when you tap the side of the jar. That means fermentation has started.

After a week or two, feel free to open the jar and take a whiff. The fermentation funk will get stronger the longer you leave the chiles, so if you like just a light earthiness, consider taking them out now.

Once you've deemed your chiles ready, drain the contents of the jar through a fine-mesh strainer, capturing the brine in a bowl. Puree the contents in a blender or food processor with a little bit of the brine or any other liquid to taste. If you use water, it will dilute the flavor a little. Vinegar will give it that classic sharpness and also significantly slow down the ongoing fermentation process. A lot of vinegar will mostly kill the fermentation. If you want a completely shelf-stable sauce, boil it on the stovetop for about 10 minutes to kill the active bacteria. This process also changes the flavor a bit, making it a bit less intense and aromatic.

Strain the puree through the fine-mesh strainer into a bowl, reserving the solids. Now you can adjust the consistency to your liking. If your sauce is a little too thin, stir in some of the solid matter from the strainer. If it's too thick, strain it again to remove more of the solids. Your sauce should be thick enough to remain a mixed solution without separating too much but thin enough to dribble through the top of your sauce bottle. Simply store the sauce in the mason jar or use a funnel to fill your sauce bottles.

The sauce will keep in the fridge for up to 3 months.

PICKLED VEGGIES

Good ol' dill pickle slices are a classic condiment for Central Texas barbecue (as are raw onions), and you can guess why. The intense and unctuous flavor of long-smoked meats desperately needs something to cut it, and pickles have the piercing acidity and sharp flavor that both moderate the richness of the meat and refresh your palate for the next bite, just like a sip of wine or beer might do.

I find that pickles go with everything, and that's how we use them at the restaurant. They dress up a meal and can serve as either condiment or side dish. It's pretty much a core principle of Franklin Barbecue to have pickles at the ready, as we do at home with fermented hot sauces, sauerkrauts, and kimchi.

You can make fermented pickles by following the brine instructions given with the Basic Pepper Sauce (page 119). Those vegetables will indeed get very funky. But for everyday pickles, I preserve vegetables in a seasoned vinegar solution for a day or two—sometimes even a few hours is enough—to get the effect I want.

You will need a 1-quart mason jar with a lid and a rounded glass fermentation weight (or some other form of weight) to keep the pickles submerged. All sorts of vegetables can be pickled. I tend to favor carrots, fennel, onions, radishes, green beans, shallots, and cucumbers. As with hot sauces, you can create a multitude of flavors by adding spices, herbs, and garlic and by using flavored vinegars.

Here's my basic process, using fennel as the main ingredient. (By the way, pickled fennel made it onto the cover of *Franklin Steak*, but we forgot to include the recipe there. People email about this more often than you'd think. So here it is!)

Use with: Smoky, rich meats and rich, fatty fish.

Makes a scant 1 quart

- 1 cup / 230g rice vinegar
- ¼ cup / 200g granulated sugar
- 1 teaspoon / 4g kosher salt
- 1 large fennel bulb
- 10 black peppercorns

In a small saucepan over medium-high heat, combine the vinegar, sugar, and salt and warm through, stirring to dissolve the sugar. Do not allow the mixture to boil, as you don't want the liquid to reduce. Remove from the heat.

While the vinegar mixture is heating, prep the fennel by trimming off the stems and fronds from the bulb, then halving it lengthwise, removing the core and then thinly slicing crosswise on a mandoline or with a knife.

Put the peppercorns into a 1-quart jar and then pack the fennel on top. Pour the hot brine over the fennel and place a glass weight on top to keep it submerged. Leave the jar on the countertop with the lid set loosely on top until the brine cools to room temperature. Tighten the lid and refrigerate the fennel for at least 3 hours or up to 1 day before serving.

The veggies will keep in the fridge for up to 1 month.

Sauces

I'm a traditionalist at heart and truly revere the original folks who cooked barbecue and ran the small-town restaurants where it came into its own. Thus, I've always respected the fact that, traditionally, Central Texas barbecue has never employed sauces. Not only is this practice in tune with the sort of bare-bones, hardscrabble style of the people who settled this area and cooked their own version of barbecue, but it is truly the best way to show respect for the art of slow-smoking meat. Woodsmoke, itself, is a complex ingredient and a wonder to experience, with a little salt and pepper, as it interacts with the flavor of the meat.

That said, people love sauces. And by your third or fourth unadorned bite, a little bit of tang or acid, sweetness and spice definitely enlivens the palate. I like to serve my sauces on the side so people can indulge as much or as little as they like.

Over the years, I've come up with a number of sauces that I love. Most of these can be mixed and matched with any type of protein, so don't think that because I paired one sauce with a certain dish here it doesn't go just as well with something else. (And if you're looking for the recipes for our barbecue, espresso, and vinegar sauces, check out the *Franklin Barbecue* book.)

RYE BBQ SAUCE

I do like rye whiskey, I must admit. Hence, it has made it into various sauces I've thrown together over the years for dinners and events and all kinds of cooks. The basic idea is that rye and cherries go together really well (hey, Manhattan cocktail) and are even better when combined with black pepper and fatty meats. This recipe is a distillation of all those ideas. Pick your favorite not-very-sweet rye whiskey for this; I often use High West Double Rye. This is a pretty sweet sauce, so if it tastes too sweet to you, back off on the jam a bit.

Use with: BBQ chicken, pork ribs, and pork steaks.

Makes about 4 cups

- 1 cup / 320g cherry preserves
- 1 cup / 275g ketchup
- ½ cup / 115g apple cider vinegar
- 3 tablespoons / 20g freshly ground black pepper
- 2 tablespoons / 12g garlic powder
- 2 tablespoons / 12g onion powder
- ½ cup / 100g Worcestershire sauce
- 4 tablespoons / 65g tomato paste
- 2 tablespoons / 30g Dijon mustard
- 1 cup / 200g dry rye whiskey

In a medium saucepan over medium heat, combine the preserves, ketchup, and vinegar and warm through. Pour the hot liquid into a blender and puree until silky smooth. Pour the mixture into a 1-quart jar.

Add the pepper, garlic powder, onion powder, Worcestershire, tomato paste, and mustard to the jar and whisk until smooth. Let the sauce cool to room temperature, then add the whiskey and stir to combine. Taste and adjust any flavors as you like, then cap and refrigerate.

The sauce will keep in the fridge for up to 6 weeks, serve as soon as you can.

SPICY BBQ SAUCE

Most barbecue sauces are laden with spices but are rarely actually spicy. This one is—or at least it can be as spicy as you want it. The sweetness is balanced in the background, so you don't really notice it. The secret to a good spicy sauce is the spicy part, not the base, which makes preparing a sauce like this super-easy.

As a base, I simply use Franklin's standard barbecue sauce, or one that I think would take well to some spicing up, and augment from there. I like a Tex-Mex kind of sauce where the heat comes from Mexican chiles, but you could also mix up a version with Thai bird chiles, sriracha, or whatever you like. Because chiles vary in heat, flavor intensity, and water weight, this is a preparation that needs to be done by taste and to taste.

Use with: I love a tangy, sharp, spicy sauce with brisket, pork ribs, and, especially, chicken.

Makes as much as you want

- 1 cup / 100g jalapeño, serrano, habanero, and ancho chiles or a mix of your favorite hot chiles
- 2 cups / 450g your favorite barbecue sauce

In a blender or food processor, puree the chiles, adding a splash of water or vinegar if it needs extra liquid to form a puree. In a medium bowl, add the barbecue sauce and slowly add 1 to 2 tablespoons of the chile puree to start, stirring well to combine. Taste it right away, but also let it sit for about 15 minutes and then come back to retaste, as it can take a little while for the heat and flavors to integrate. For more chile pepper impact, add more puree incrementally until it gets to the right balance. If it was too much pepper to start, add a little more sauce to mellow it out.

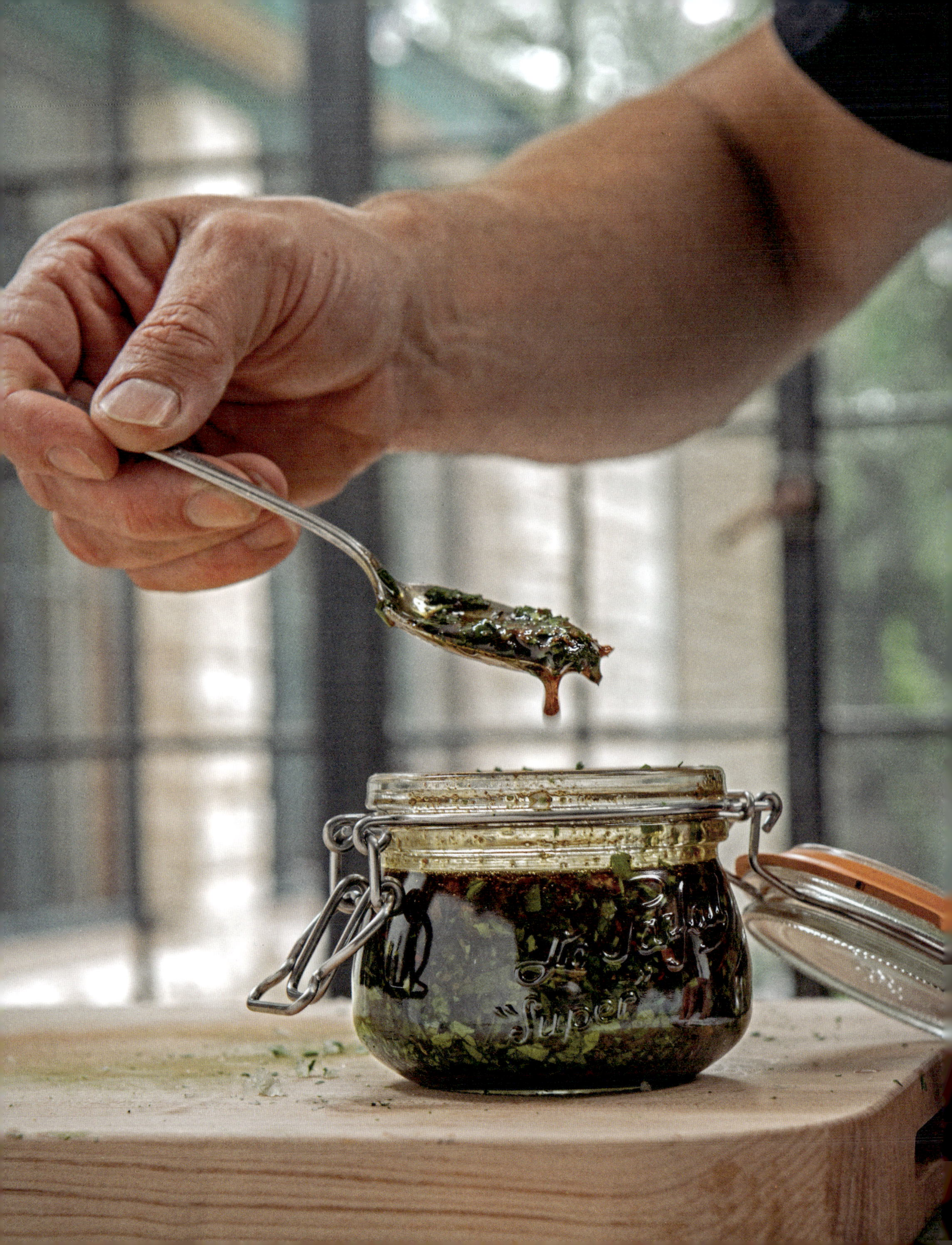
Super

RED CHIMICHURRI

I like sauces and condiments with versatility. After all, who wants to spend all of their time making a different sauce for every dish? That requires a lot of work and organization and results in too many sauces, which lead to muddled flavors. This chimichurri is the answer.

Use with: Almost every protein in this book, but it's especially delicious with Redfish on the Half Shell (page 147).

Makes 1 cup

- ½ cup / 115g grapeseed oil
- 1 tablespoon / 7g Hungarian sweet paprika
- 1 tablespoon / 9g Aleppo pepper flakes
- 1 teaspoon / 2.5g ground guajillo chile
- 6 garlic cloves, finely chopped
- 1 bunch flat-leaf parsley, leaves plucked and finely chopped
- 3 tablespoons / 20g finely chopped shallot
- ½ cup / 115g olive oil
- 4 tablespoons / 45g sherry vinegar
- Finely grated zest of 1 lemon
- 1 teaspoon / 4g kosher salt

In a small saucepan over low heat, combine the grapeseed oil, paprika, Aleppo pepper, and ground guajillo chile, stir to combine, and let infuse for about 30 minutes. Stir in the garlic and let it warm for 3 minutes. Remove the pan from the heat and allow the mixture to cool slightly.

In a medium bowl, combine the parsley, shallot, olive oil, vinegar, and lemon zest. Pour in the warm peppery oil and stir with a spoon. Adjust the salt, as needed, to taste.

Pour the chimichurri into a jar, let cool, cover, and refrigerate for 1 to 2 days to allow the flavors to develop before using.

The sauce will keep in the fridge for up to 2 weeks.

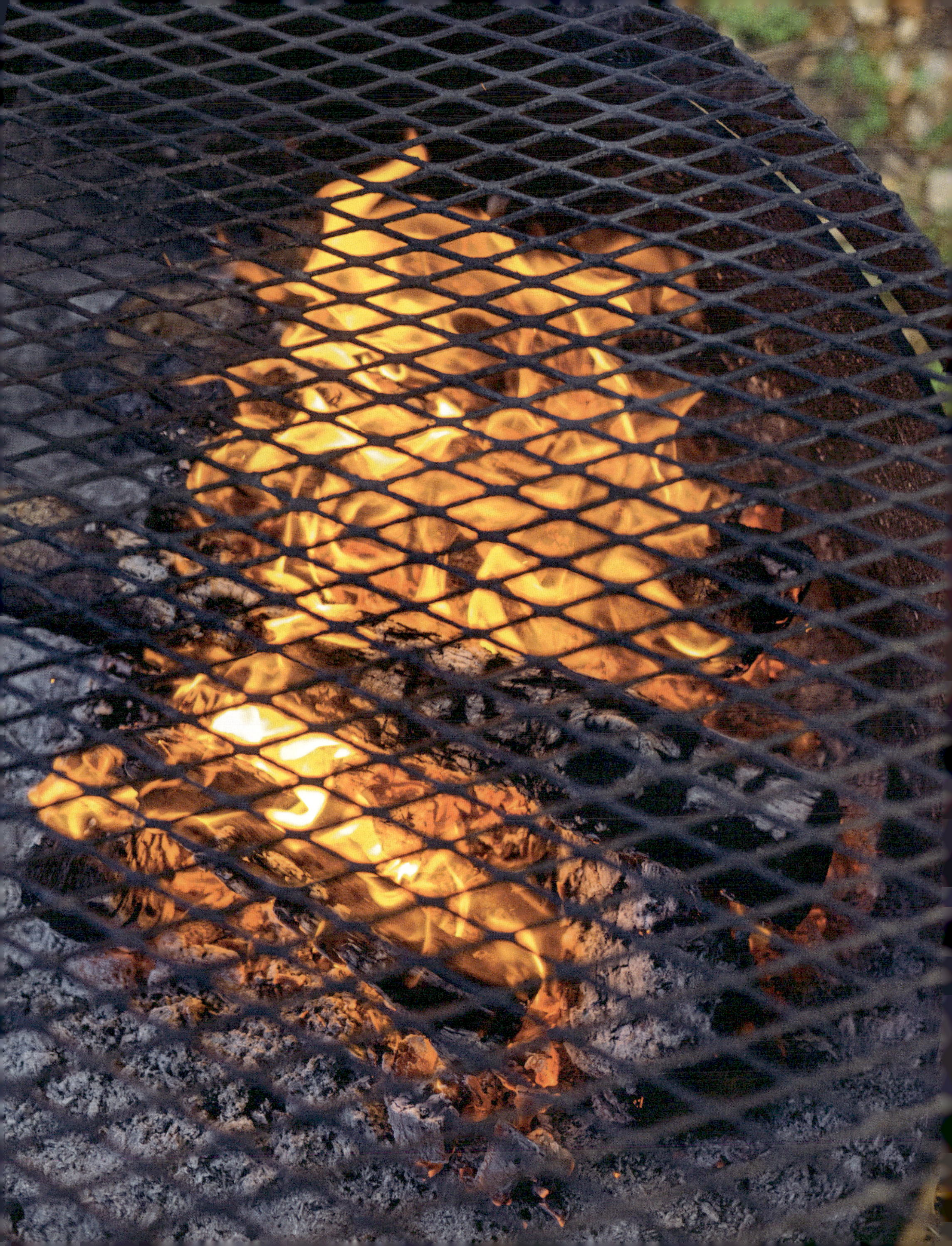

6

OPEN FIRES

Home Cooking on the Firepit and the Grill

There's almost nothing I like better than camping with my family. While we don't necessarily rough it, we love to get out of the city and into the hills and forests far from the noise of traffic, leaf blowers, and the surprisingly loud chatter of the spandex-clad cycling groups that pedal constantly past our Austin home.

Stacy likes to note that our camping meals aren't what you might expect on a typical camping trip. "It's not like we just open a can of biscuits or throw hot dogs on the grill," she says. However, cooking and eating a good meal in nature is one of the finest pleasures in life, so we eat well whether we're camping in a mountain forest or grilling on the firepit in our backyard.

This chapter is devoted to re-creating the often-primitive style of camping-trip cooking at home. The recipes require neither bells and whistles nor advanced techniques, but I do have some ideas that will enrich your meals, improve flavors, and take your campfire cooking to a satisfying place.

This is a good time to make use of the whole fire. After all, if you were fully out in nature, the fire is the only heat source you would have, so it makes sense to capitalize on every aspect of it. And while I love to coax all the energy, flavor, and nuance out of a fire, I don't always want to have the aggressive flavors of smoke or ash in every bite. Hence, some of the flavors I'm going for in this chapter are subtly smoky and some are not smoky at all. Good flavor and texture begin with prep, which is why many of these recipes include salting (dry brining) and drying out for a day or more before cooking.

I use different aspects of the fire to cook vegetables. You can char any tough green vegetables such as broccoli, brussels sprouts, or green beans over the hot flame of a chimney or in a roaring fire. I tend to like my vegetables rather undercooked, meaning I don't mind if they have a bit of crunch. Cooking larger vegetables directly in the coals is a surprisingly wonderful and low-effort way to fill the table.

As for proteins, there are a few things that I like to cook over direct and indirect heat on a firepit (pork steaks and côte de boeuf), as well as some hybrid smoking-grilling dishes on the PK grill (chicken and fish), which offers the best of both worlds. Finally, see the recipe for Jordan's Perfect Green Salad (page 169) for a simple and delicious accompaniment to every meal.

FIREPIT COOKING

The elements of firepit cooking are primitive: wood, flames, grill. The unbridled nature of fire often leads to extremes. If you are timid about cooking over open fire, you won't maximize the opportunities it presents. Don't content yourself with only hot dogs and s'mores or go all in when the flames are at their peak and either undercook or burn your food—or do both at the same time.

Firepit cooking rewards patience and nuance. Once you learn these skills, you can cook just about anything well. For that reason, I love to cook larger cuts of meat on the firepit. They can take a while—up to a few hours of careful tending—but when done well, they give you the best of cooking over hot coals: grill action and a bit of smoke at the same time.

Getting Started

First, have plenty of wood on hand that is sized to fit your firepit. If you've got a big, open area, full-size fire logs work fine. But if it's a smaller space, you'll want to split those logs and maybe cut them shorter so you can feed the fire without making it stumble. As with all of the cooking in this book, avoid softwoods, like pine and cedar, just as you would in your smoker. Oak, fruit and nut woods, and hickory are all excellent. For more on selecting wood, see chapter 3.

Obviously, don't build a fire—whether it's in your backyard or in a park somewhere—when it's dangerously hot, dry, or windy. Even in perfect weather, it's wise to have water at the ready from a live hose with a spray nozzle or a couple of full buckets in case the fire starts to get away from you. I also keep fire blankets on hand—one in the camper and a small one in my cooking kit.

The best firepit cooking is anchored by a strong coal bed, so when you finally start cooking, the fire is on its second or third round of logs (the initial logs having burned down to establish that bed).

If you have charcoal and a chimney, it's perfectly fine to start the fire that way, as the two generate quick and durable heat. I often place my prepped chimney in the center of the firepit and surround it with two or three stacked logs on three sides. I then light it and, after about twenty minutes, the heat and flame generated by the smoldering charcoal begin to escape the chimney and ignite the logs. This way, you get a jump on burning the wood while the charcoal provides an instant mini–coal bed to get you started.

After your first logs are going, dump and remove the chimney (place it somewhere safe) and use a long set of tongs to rearrange the logs in a log-cabin formation (see page 83) to encourage airflow and combustion. As those first logs start giving up some hot coals, add another log or two and wait. When those burn down, you should have an ample coal bed for cooking. After this, maintain the firepit so it has one or two burning logs and a good coal bed. This is how you always want your firepit set up for cooking.

The trick to cooking over a firepit is tending and managing the fire along with whatever you're cooking. It's a little more difficult to control a fire versus adjusting the flame of your gas stove's burner, but the general principle is the same. Only in this case, you adjust the logs and coals to produce the optimal heat and smoke you want.

To have precise control, use a pair of extra-long tongs to constantly move logs around and rustle up the coals. You can prepare a nice, flame-free coal bed to cook over while maintaining your gently burning logs on the side.

Prepping the Grate

For the recipes that follow, you need a good-size grate to cover the firepit. In the best of all worlds, it shouldn't cover the entire surface of the firepit (mine covers half) because you need to have access to the logs and coals. Make sure your grill is clean and give it a quick wipe with grapeseed oil before putting food on it.

Be sure to have a comfortable distance between the grate and the coals. You want it close enough to get plenty of heat but not so close that you can't escape the heat. It should also be high enough so the fat can drip down without creating flare-ups. A grate that is sixteen to eighteen inches above the coals should do the trick.

One of the beauties of firepit cooking is that you can achieve a hybrid of grilling and smoking. The fact that you're cooking over a ton of wood coals is significant—they provide the delicious smoke that you can't get from charcoal. But because the "smoke chamber" is simply the wide-open sky, foods can cook for a long time without taking on too much smoke.

In this chapter are a few things—both meat and vegetables—I love to cook on the grate and in the coals of the firepit. These are terrific ways to take full advantage of the whole fire.

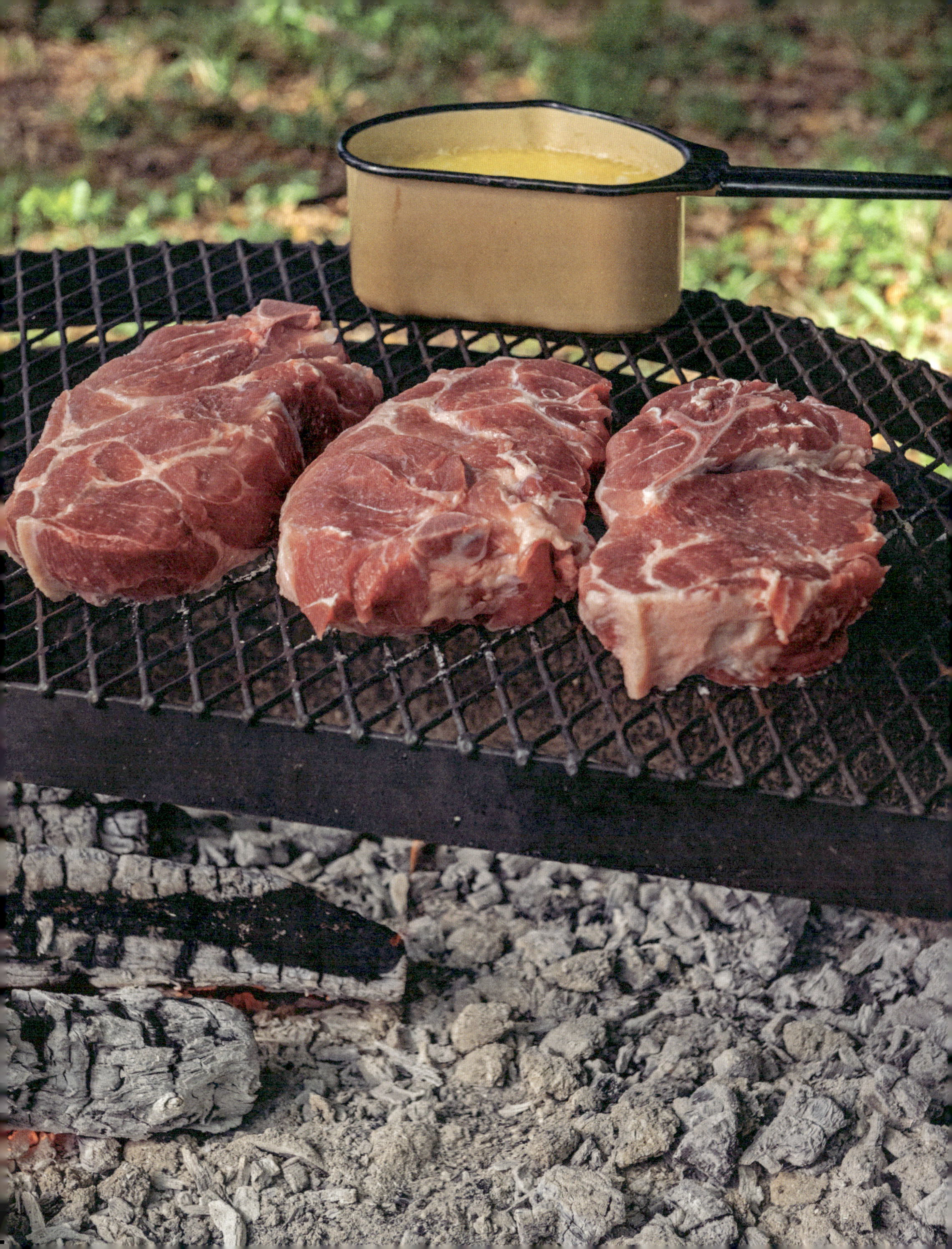

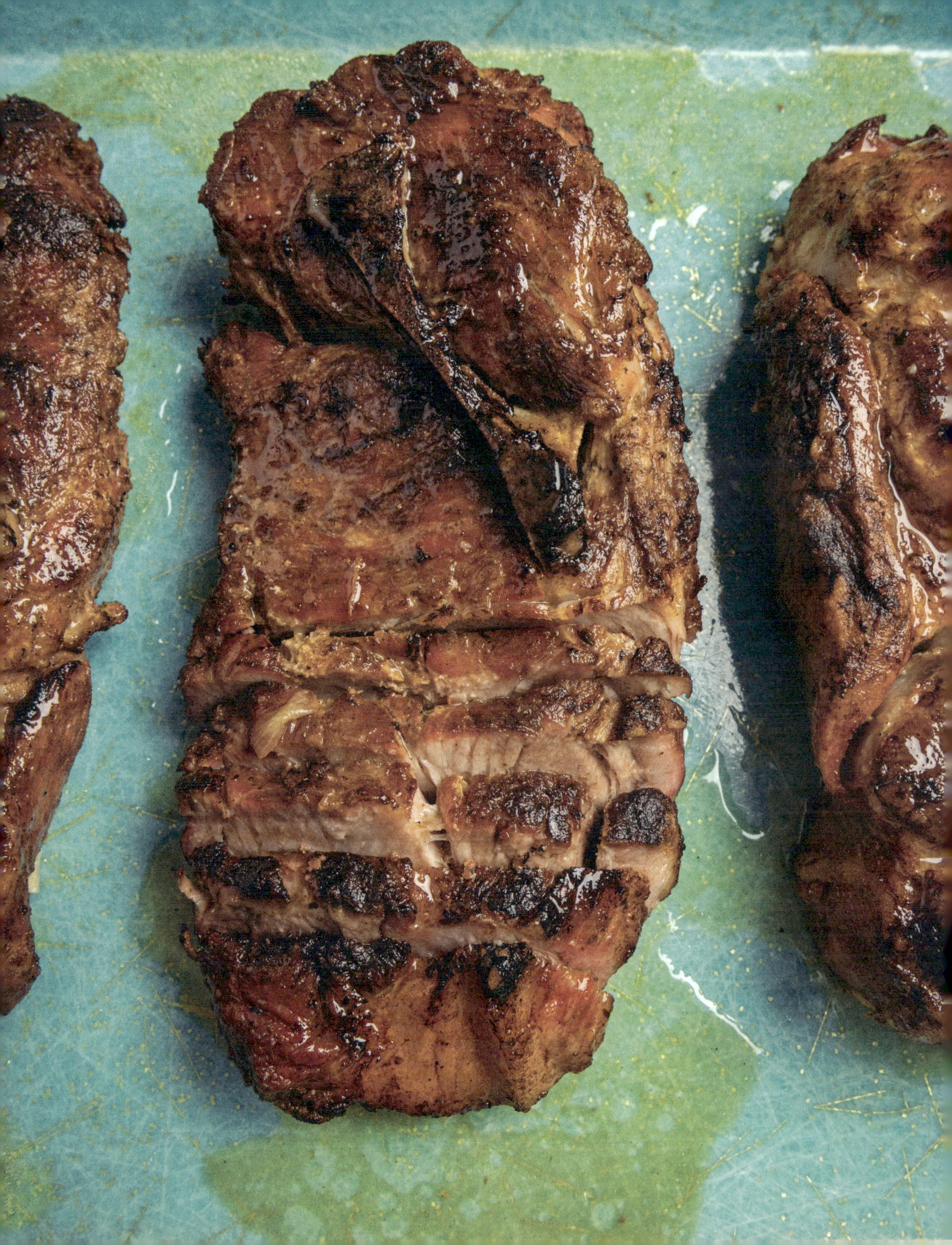

FIREPIT PORK SHOULDER "STEAKS"

This preparation of pork combines the dynamics of a slow cook with the fast grill, producing a flavor that hearkens to both. Pork steaks absorb the delicious effect of the grill as their drippings vaporize on the hot coals and subsequently rise up to perfume the meat. Yet they also pick up gentle smoke from the coals and burning wood.

While this pork is cooked like a steak or a chop, it is actually cut from the shoulder, aka the pork butt. As you know, the meat from the shoulder is much tougher than meat from the loin, where the chops are. Consequently, pork shoulder is usually cooked long and slow to break down the collagen and make the meat pull-apart tender. The goal for this approach to shoulder steaks is to cook them over direct heat, like a pork chop, but slowly and deliberately so they soften a bit over time. You're not looking for exceedingly tender, pulled-pork consistency here. But you're also going to cook well past medium-rare as you might do for a chop. The length of the cook allows the meat to pick up precious flavor from the fire.

Speaking of pork chops, they would be equally delicious cooked over the firepit and basted with the mop recipe listed here, but they are an entirely different muscle—from the loin, not the shoulder—which cooks quite fast, should be served at a lower internal temperature, and doesn't need all that time to break down tough muscle fiber. Cook thick-cut pork chops as you would a steak (though not as rare), but feel free to baste them with this mop for added flavor.

THE MEAT

I recommend using rich, well-marbled pork, as the fat content helps the meat hold up over a long cook. Definitely try to avoid modern, conventional pork, which has been purposely bred to be lean. I look for heritage breeds such as Berkshire or Red Wattle. There's even a ranch raising Ibérico pigs in Texas, the same breed that produces the world's greatest jamón in Spain.

Use a bone-in pork butt and ask your butcher to cut it into steaks two to three inches thick. You could also buy a whole shoulder (more affordable but also more work) and then break out the old bone saw, which I sometimes do much to Stacy's chagrin (not her favorite thing to find lying around the kitchen), and cut through the bone yourself. Most of the steaks from a pork butt will have a sliver of the blade bone in them. This is what you want. Boneless butts have to be butterflied to get the bone out and then are tied up in a round. This is fine for roasting a whole piece, but the steaks need to retain their structural integrity and thus must retain the bone.

THE MOP

A mop is necessary here to add pork-friendly flavors and to keep the meat moistened so it doesn't burn while it cooks for a good long while over the coals. The mop also provides additional fat that your pork might not have (even a well marbled heritage breed), augmenting the supply of vaporized juices as it drips onto the coals.

You can prepare the mop on the stovetop in advance and then warm it over the fire when it's time to use. Doing this advance prep makes it easy to cook these steaks at home or at a campsite.

Cook time: 3 to 4 hours

Makes 4 to 6 servings

- Kosher salt
- One 6- to 8-pound / 2700 to 3600g bone-in pork shoulder butt, cut into 2- to 3-inch-thick steaks

The Mop

- 1½ pounds / 350g unsalted butter
- ⅓ pound / 150g thick-cut bacon, in one piece, cut into chunks
- 3 cups / 690g apple cider vinegar
- Peel of 1 orange
- Peel and juice of 1 lemon
- 15 to 20 garlic cloves, smashed (use the larger amount if you favor garlic)
- ½ yellow onion, coarsely chopped
- Grapeseed oil for the grate

Liberally salt the steaks on both sides and set them on a baking sheet. Let the steaks air-dry, uncovered, in the refrigerator for at least 1 day or up to 2 days.

To make the mop: In a medium saucepan over low heat, combine the butter, bacon, vinegar, orange peel, lemon peel, lemon juice, garlic, and onion and warm until the butter melts, stirring occasionally. Keep the mop warm on the grate.

Build a firepit fire, burning down six to eight logs to create a nice coal bed, then maintain another couple of logs burning on the side to supply coals. When it's time to start cooking, clear the burning logs off the coal bed so you have just coals to cook over. The logs can continue to burn on the side. Because of the length of time that these steaks cook, they are best done over a medium- to low-heat coal bed with the grate set eighteen to twenty-four inches above the coals. Oil the grate.

Remove the steaks from the fridge and lay them on the grate. Don't temper the steaks, just put them on cold, as the first couple of hours are really about developing the exterior of the meat.

Since the steaks are going to cook in the open air for the next 1½ hours or so, set the fire to mellow and let 'em rip. Stand by with tongs and flip the steaks every now and then to develop a nice, rich crust. As the fire progresses, bring in fresh coals from the burning logs on the side and keep the meat moving so it never flames up. You want these steaks to be kissed by heat and the clouds of their own evaporations, not by flames.

After the first couple of flips, starting 15 to 20 minutes in or when you see the surface of the steaks beginning to dry out, start to mop to keep the surface moist. Gently drizzle the mop over the tops of the steaks. It will drip down and hiss in the coals, which is a good thing! Turn the steaks and mop the other side. Repeat this every 10 minutes or so as needed to keep the surface moist. Also, be careful with your mop—you need it to last the whole cook and then have some to put in the wrap, so go easy.

Now you're about 2 hours in. Much as with brisket, you need your crust to get a little crustier than you ultimately want it because it will be softened after you wrap. When you've built a great crust, it's time to wrap the steaks in aluminum foil. Have a foil sheet ready for each steak. Remove the steaks, place each one on a foil sheet, and pour a little bit of the mop over the top. Wrap each steak tightly in the foil and return the steaks to the fire for about 1 hour more.

Using a digital thermometer, test for doneness; the steaks are ready to remove from the heat when the thermometer inserted into the side of each at the middle reads about or just above 200°F. Allow the steaks to rest while you add some wood to replenish the coal bed. This could take 40 minutes to 1 hour.

Once your coals are back up and hot—or you're simply ready to eat—unwrap the steaks and put them back on the grate to sizzle up the surface and regain your crust. Save the juices retained in the foil to pour over the sliced meat.

Remove the steaks from the fire and, when cool enough to hold, it's time to slice and serve.

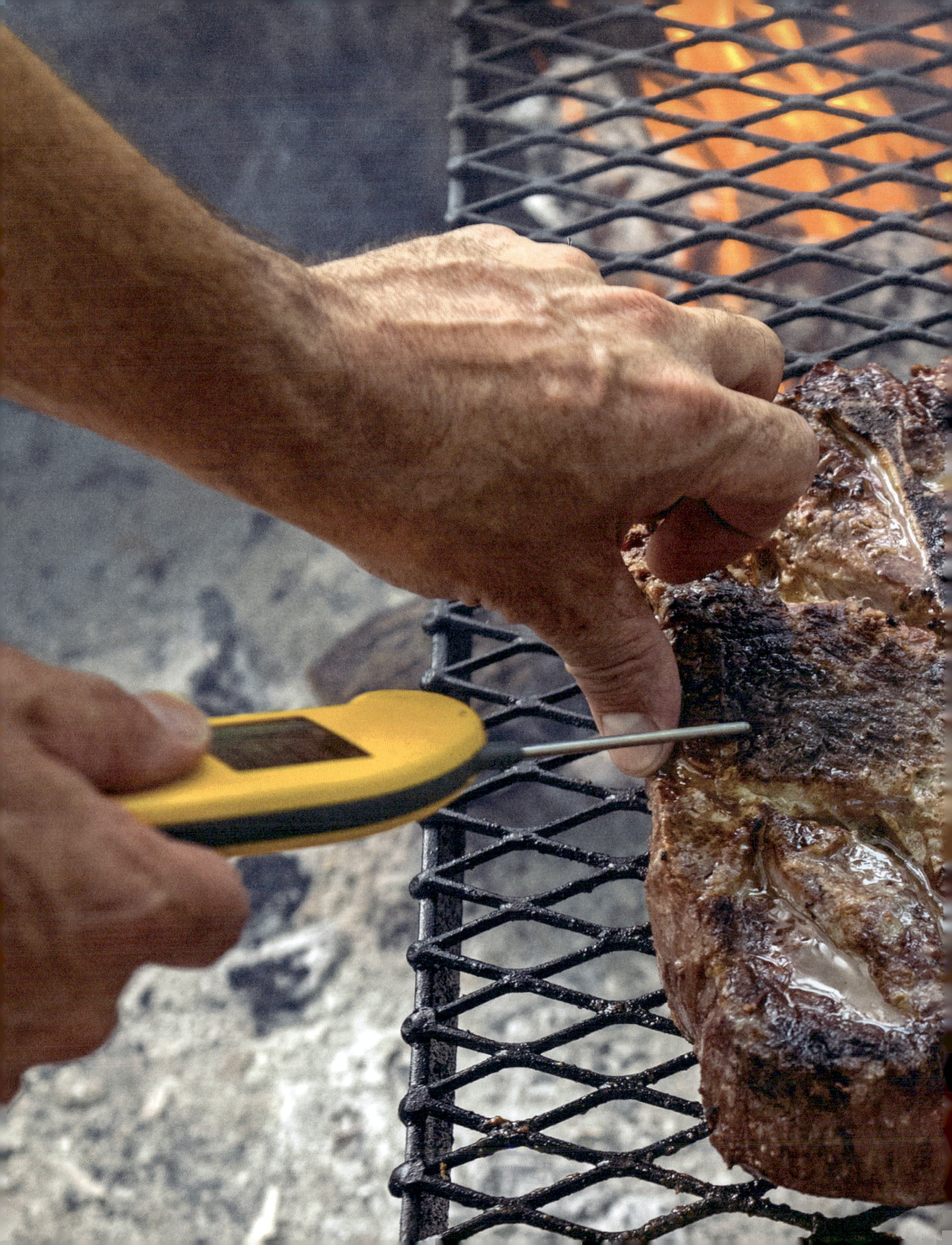

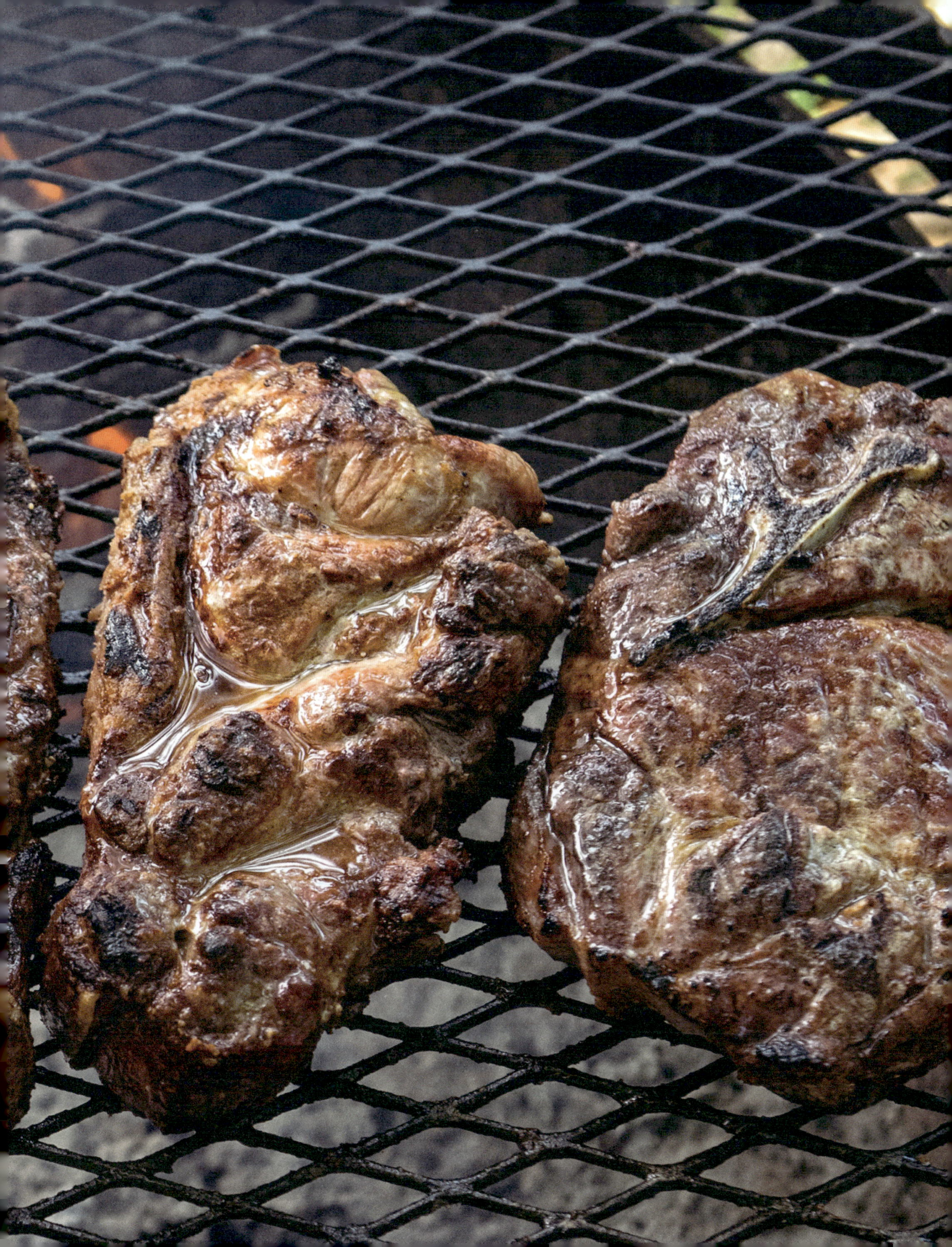

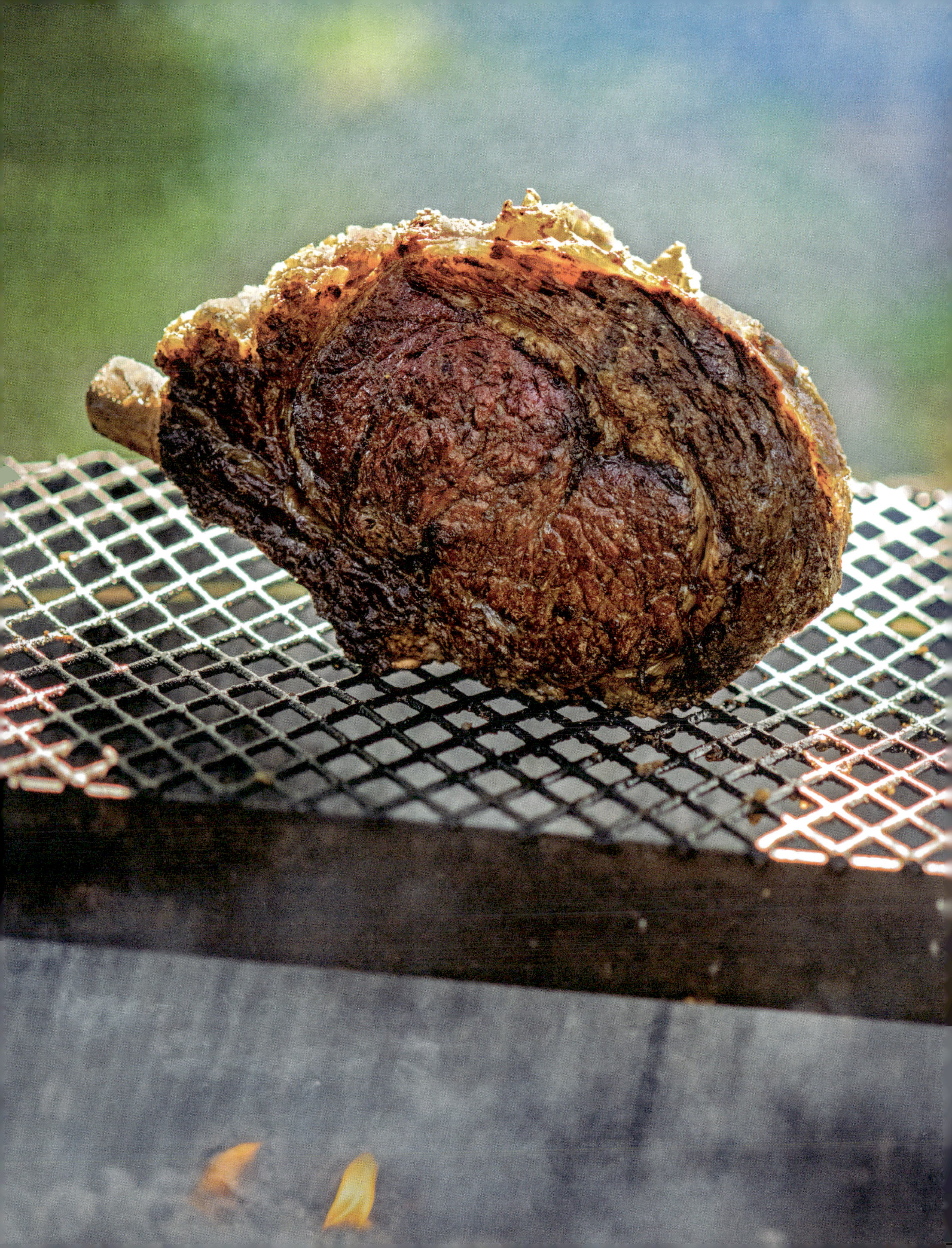

FIREPIT CÔTE DE BOEUF

A staple of French cookery, côte de boeuf is immensely versatile. The term basically refers to a bone-in rib-eye steak, as we call it here in the US when it's just one bone. It's typically cut thick in France and meant to feed two people. It could also be known as a (very short) standing rib roast. But rib roasts are usually cooked in the oven, and here I use a two-bone rib steak to create a sort of hybrid steak–prime rib dish. You could also use a thick-cut, single bone rib eye, but it would cook faster. The pleasures of prime rib roast and grilled steak converge in one piece of meat: plenty of tender interior meat is matched with a thick, crunchy crust that supplies the ideal contrast of smoke, salt, and caramelization. Plus, one big rib steak is plenty to feed two to four people, making for a lovely presentation that can be shared family-style.

Cook time: 2 to 3 hours

Serves 4 to 8

THE MEAT

Any good butcher can prepare a two-bone rib steak for you, though it's wise to order it a day or two in advance to make sure he or she can cut it to your preference. If the steak has an especially thick outer layer of fat, ask the butcher to trim some off to avoid flare-ups. You may also want to ask that the steak be tied with butcher's twine so it maintains its form during a fairly lengthy cook, though I usually skip this step. Prep involves little more than dry brining with salt.

Côte de boeuf is a natural for the firepit, which allows you to cook directly, indirectly, and with a bit of smoke—all from fresh wood coals. The thickness of the cut demands a relatively long cook and gives you lots of flavor from the fire. This is basically a low-pressure two- to three-hour cook—the kind of thing you do while waiting for friends on a Saturday afternoon. Ideally, cook it slowly to get even cooking throughout. But because it is steak, you can also cook over higher heat if you need to speed things up.

- Kosher salt
- 2 two-bone rib steaks, trimmed and tied
- Water, beef stock, or vinegar for spritzing
- Melted tallow or grapeseed oil for coating
- Horseradish Cream Sauce (recipe follows) for serving
- Grapeseed oil for the grate

Liberally salt the exterior of the steaks and set them on a baking sheet. Let the steaks air-dry, uncovered, in the refrigerator for 24 to 36 hours.

Build a firepit fire, burning down six to eight logs to create a nice coal bed, then maintain another couple of logs burning on the side to supply coals. When it's time to start cooking, clear the burning logs off the coal bed so you have just coals to cook over. The logs can continue to burn on the side. Because of the length of time that these steaks cook, they are best done over a medium- to low-heat coal bed with the grate set eighteen to twenty-four inches above the coals. Oil the grate.

While the first logs are cooking down, remove the meat from the fridge to temper it a bit before putting it on the fire.

Stand the steaks vertically on the bone on the grate. This heats up the bone and begins the process of slowly cooking the adjacent meat. After the bone is browned, turn the steaks onto a side and let them go from there. Don't turn the spinalis side (the rib-eye cap or muscle that runs along the outside of the steak, opposite the bone) to face the flames from the burning logs. The spinalis is the most tender and flavorful part of the rib eye. It will always cook past rare, but it's good to protect it from too much heat so it retains its moisture.

Keep the steaks over low to medium heat on the cooler areas of the grate. Move them around fairly frequently, flipping them at the same time. While you're flipping, also keep a spray bottle full of water handy to spritz the steaks, cool the sides, keep the crust from drying out too much, and prolong the cook. Slowly build a crust on the side facing the heat and then flip the steaks to let that side cool while the other side cooks. Do this repeatedly until a digital thermometer inserted into the side of each steak at the middle reads 110° to 112°F. At that moment, pull the steaks off the grate.

Allow the steaks to rest while you add some wood to replenish the coal bed until it is raging hot. After the steaks have rested no less than 30 minutes and for up to 1 hour—however long it takes to get the fire really hot again—gently coat the steaks in the tallow and throw them back on the grate for a couple of minutes on each side, until the crust gets nice and sizzling again. Remove the steaks from the heat.

When the steaks are cool enough to hold, it's time to slice and serve. Slice between the bones so you have two rib-eye steaks. Slice the meat off the bone, leaving the bone in place, thus retaining the shape of the original steak. Then cut across the steaks, fanning from the bone to obtain nice long strips. Arrange the slices on a platter and include the bones. Serve horseradish sauce alongside.

HORSERADISH CREAM SAUCE

Makes 1½ cups

- 1 cup / 240g sour cream
- ⅔ cup / 140g prepared horseradish
- 2 tablespoons / 28g champagne vinegar
- Grated zest of 1 lemon
- Fine sea salt

In a medium bowl, combine the sour cream, horseradish, vinegar, and lemon zest and mix well. Season with salt. Cover and chill for at least 1 hour before serving. The sauce will keep in the fridge for up to 2 weeks.

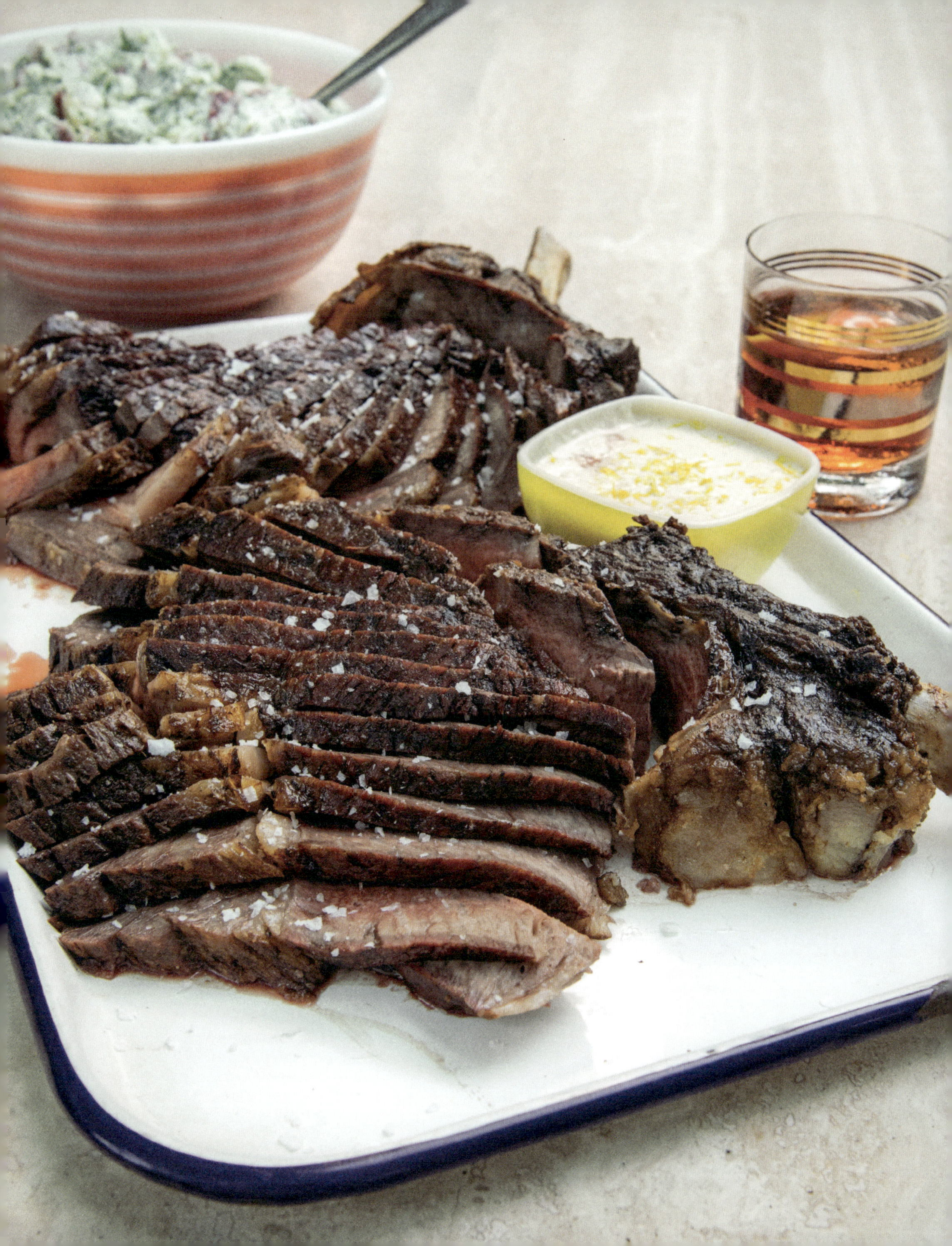

ADDING A HINT OF SMOKE

To get a whiff of smoke flavor when grilling with charcoal, add a little wood to the mix to combine the radiative heat of coals with the gentle complexity of woodsmoke.

In my second book, *Franklin Steak*, a framework was described in which a whole log is inserted lengthwise into the back half of a grill, dividing the grill into two zones. Named the Franklin Formation by Jordan, the half over the log is a cool zone, while the front half, containing lit charcoal, is a hot zone. The front edge of the log catches fire, creating some smoke and flames. This produces a sort of hybrid grilling and smoking situation.

In the interim, I have made some improvements to the original framework (although, honestly, it still works well). By putting the log in the back of the grill, you had to reach over hot coals any time you wanted to put anything on the cool zone. Lately, I've been playing around with wood lengths and placements and tried putting the log in different orientations (which Jordan jokingly named the "Franklin Reformation" and the "Franklin Reformation Variation Orientation"). Terminology aside, the following ideas are just different configurations of a good technique.

First, you want to cut the log to ten inches or so, which gives you much more flexibility. You can then insert the wood perpendicularly into the grill relative to the grill's length, set it at an angle, or position it parallel to the length in the middle, allowing hot coals to smolder it on two sides and creating a cooler zone in the center. Using a smaller log offers quite a bit more adaptability than the original formation—and provides the same benefits.

When choosing logs, I look for ones that are particularly dense and squarish in shape with no bark. I like these blocky logs because those with a wedge or a tip will catch fire on that end and burn too rapidly.

Whereas the cool zone of the original formation was rather long and narrow without much room to avoid the flaming edge of the log, this new version is both more comfortable and more adjustable. Like a slider on a mixing board, you can move the log in tighter to create a concentrated coal bed and large cool zone, or you can move it away from the charcoal to give the coal bed a wider birth, diminishing the intensity of its heat while maintaining a bit of smoke and a good-size cool zone. All in all, this is a much smarter configuration, and all that's required to add a hint of smoke is sawing down your firewood to the right size for your grill.

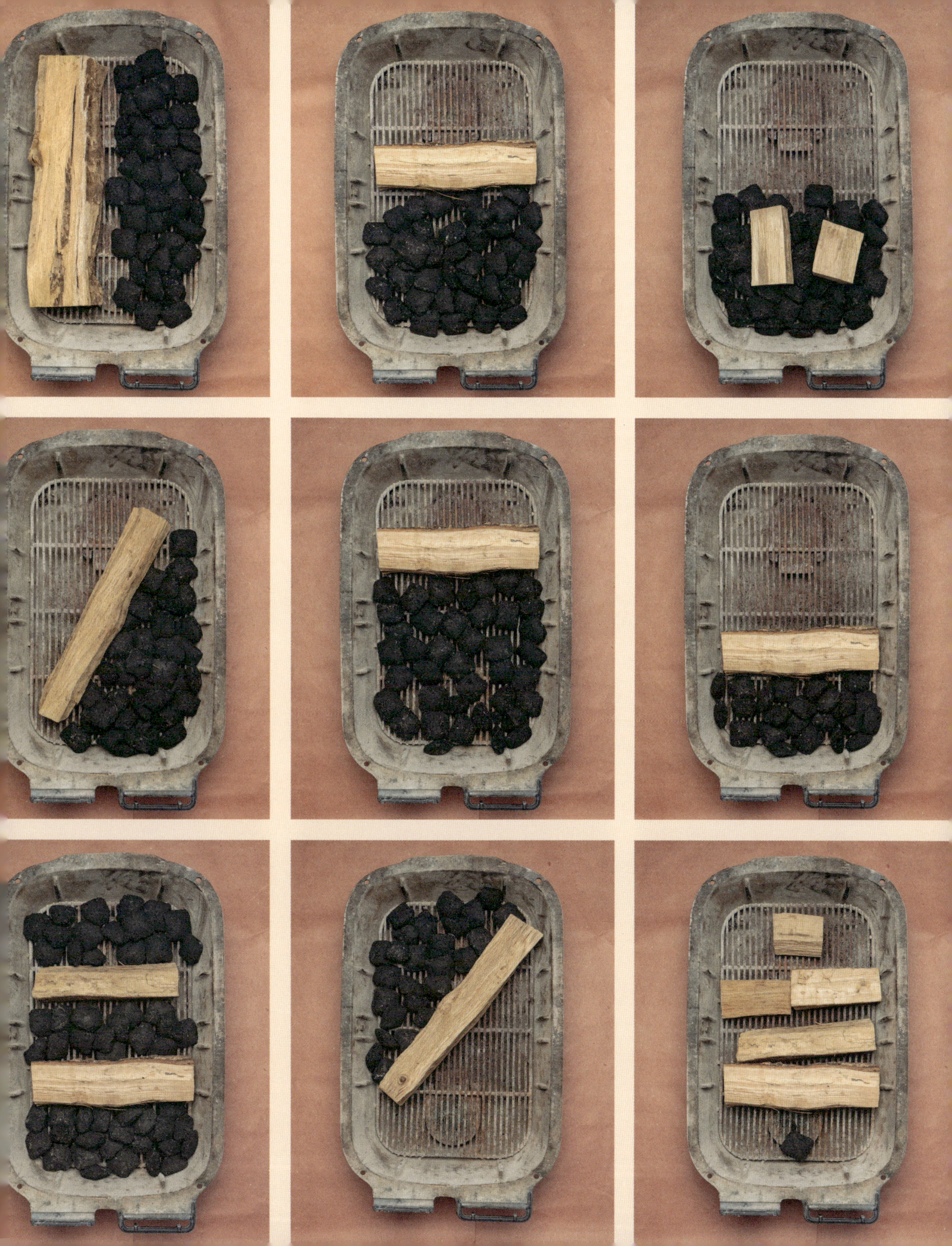

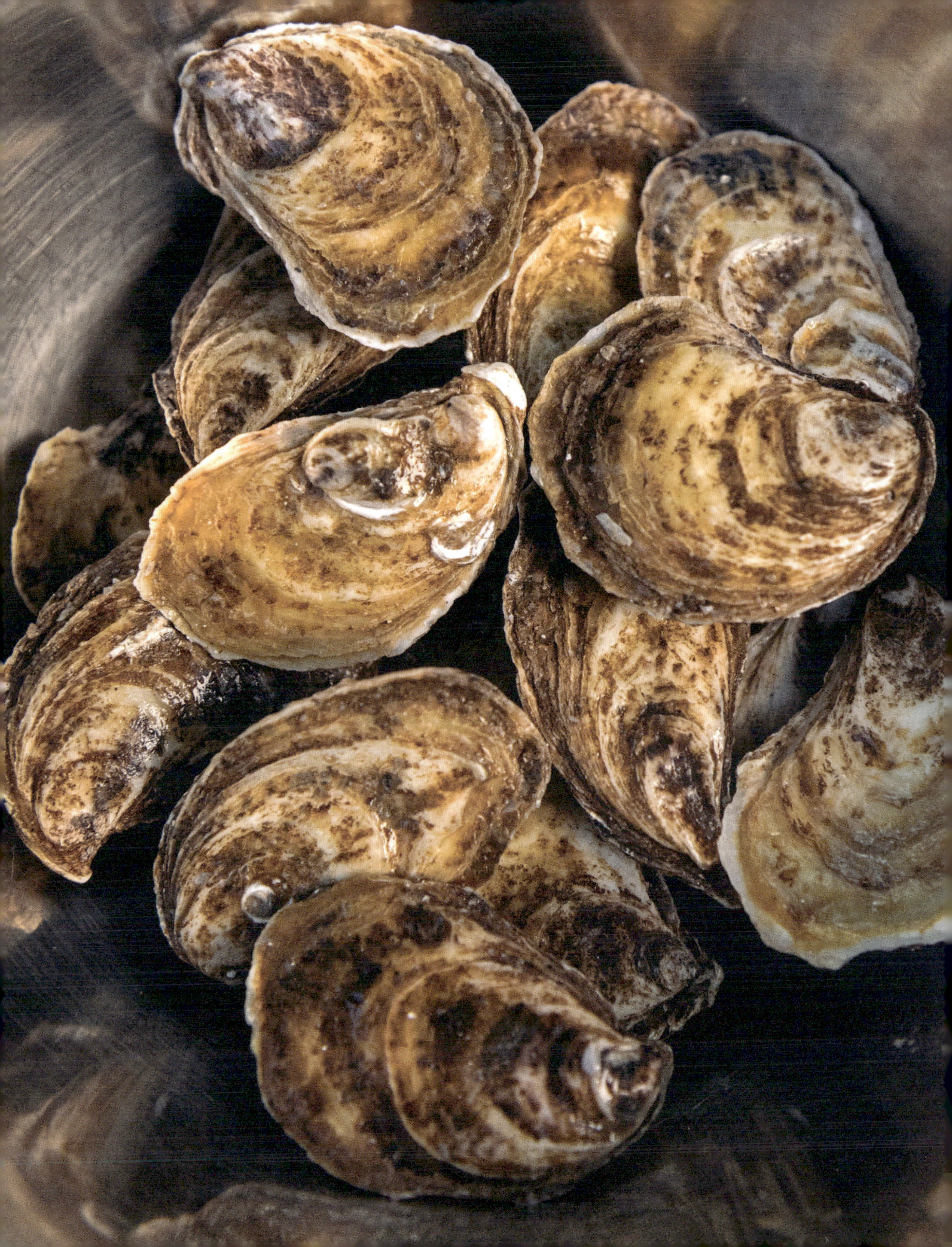

OUR FISHY FRIENDS

I'm not very good at cooking fish on the grill, which may be the reason I don't do it nearly as much as I could. Like everyone, I worry about all kinds of details particular to our fishy friends: the tiny bones that you have to remove from the raw fish, the cooked fish before you eat it, or your mouth after you've taken a bite; the scales that can slice and dice your fingers; and the skin that, no matter how hard you try, always seems to stick to the pan or the grill, mangling your fillet.

All that said, one thing is undeniable: fire-cooked fish done well is simply delicious. And certain fish love the kiss of the coals. Their flavors work almost as well as beef with a smooch of smoke. So, in recent times, I've set about to cooking fish and other sea delicacies on the grill, trying to replicate and even improve on the bites that I've had in the past.

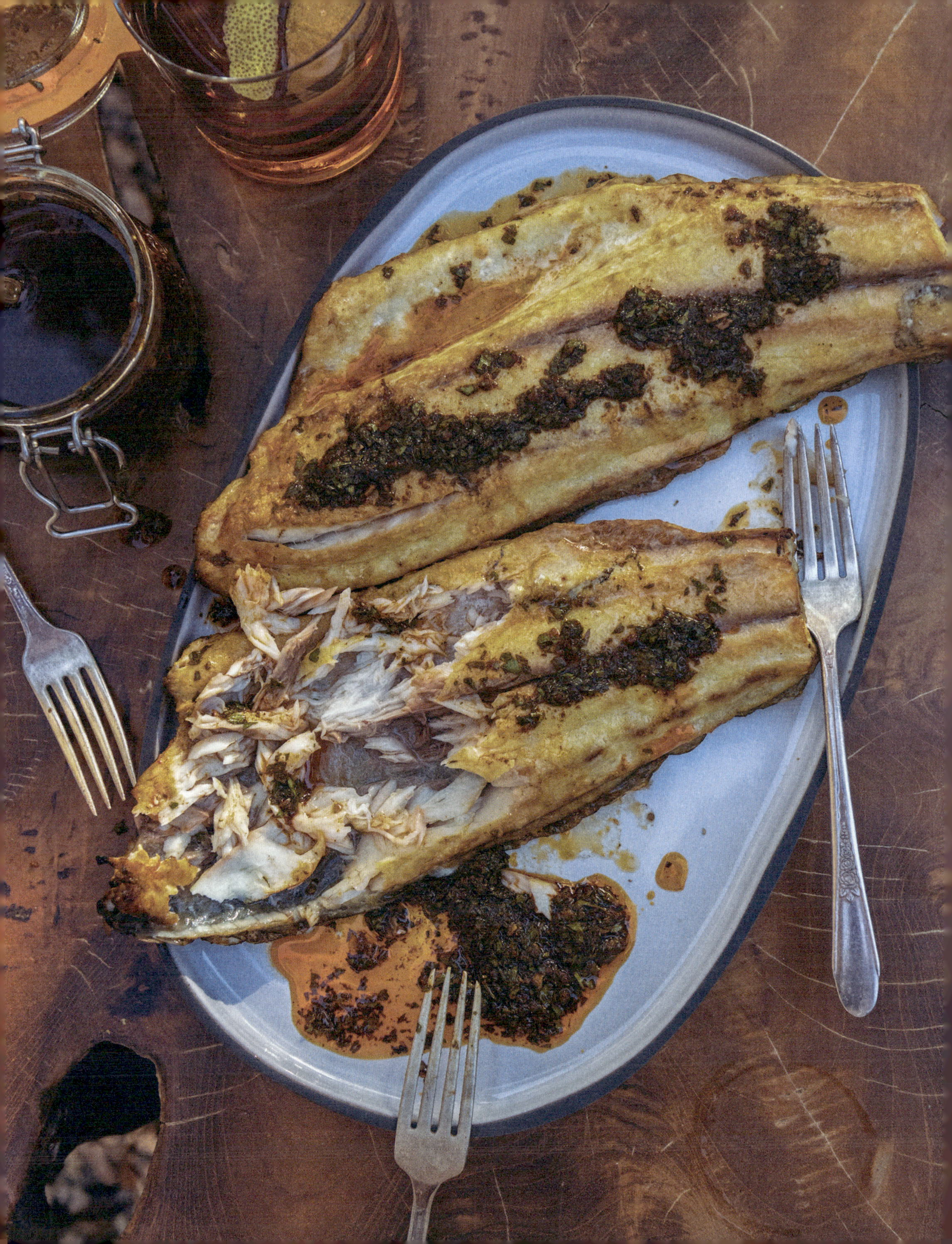

REDFISH ON THE HALF SHELL

I've been trying to master the technique of cooking fish "on the half shell" since having redfish served this way at an event a few years ago. In coastal Texas and eastward through Louisiana and the Carolinas, half-shell cooking—leaving the fish scales on—is famously practiced on redfish, also known as red drum. Redfish is popular among sport fishers for being a very wily prey; it doesn't stop fighting even once it's been brought to shore and subdued. Also, its scales are famously sharp and numerous, making it a dangerous thing to handle.

The idea behind half-shell cooking is so full of common sense that it's easy to underrate. When we buy fish at a store, the scales have almost always been already removed because they are difficult and messy to deal with at home. But scales also make the fish skin inedible. Of course, with this method, you can't eat the skin (and for those of us who love Japanese delicacies such as crispy salmon skin, this is a loss), but the hard barrier formed by the scales accomplishes three things: (1) it prevents the skin from sticking when it's cooked directly on a hot surface like a grill; (2) it prevents moisture loss to the base of the fillet, leaving a tender, flaky version of fish at its best; and (3) it prevents too much smoke from invading.

You can cook nearly any fish—cod, haddock, trout, salmon—this way with excellent results. In fact, I don't see myself messing around with skin in the future and will instead ask my fishmonger to leave the scales intact. This is a perfect grill for the family or small gatherings.

I've worked with the technique some and have a method for doing it. It involves covering the fillets with a large, preheated cast-iron pan so the top of the fish cooks in tandem with the underside. This method would work just as well on a firepit.

Cook time: 12 to 15 minutes

Serves 4 to 6

- 2-pound redfish fillet, with skin and scales intact
- Grapeseed oil for rubbing
- Kosher salt and freshly ground black pepper
- Red Chimichurri (page 125) for serving

Set the fish on a baking sheet and let air-dry, uncovered, in the refrigerator for 1 to 2 hours. This helps the top to brown during cooking.

In the meantime, get your charcoal chimney going to create a medium-hot coal bed in your grill—not blistering but also not about to die. If you like, add a log using the perpendicular Franklin Formation (see page 142) to generate a bit of smoke and subtly flavor the fish. (If you're using a PK grill, make sure the hinged side of the grate is over the coals, as you'll need to access them later.) You can also just use charcoal. Place a very large cast-iron skillet on the grate directly over the coal bed to preheat.

When your grill is ready, remove the fish from the fridge and rub the flesh side of the fillet with grapeseed oil, salt, and pepper. (Even though the scale side doesn't necessarily need it, I rub oil and salt on this side, too, to make doubly sure the skin doesn't stick to the grate.)

Oil the grate and lay your fillet, scale-side down, over the cool zone (not directly over the coals) so the thick end of the fillet lines up with the coal-facing side of the log.

Place the heated skillet over the fillet, making sure that one edge of the skillet also sits above some live coals. The idea is to funnel some of the heat and smoke from the coals and the log over the top of the fish. There's enough heat coming from below to cook the underside of the fish. Using tongs, grab about ten lumps of hot charcoal and place them on top of the skillet.

After about 10 minutes, carefully peek under the skillet to see how the fish is progressing. Using a fish spatula, pull the fish off the grill when a digital thermometer inserted into the thickest part of the fillet reads 135° to 140°F. When you pick up the skillet, drop the coals back into the grill.

Transfer the fillet to a platter, top with the chimichurri, and serve immediately.

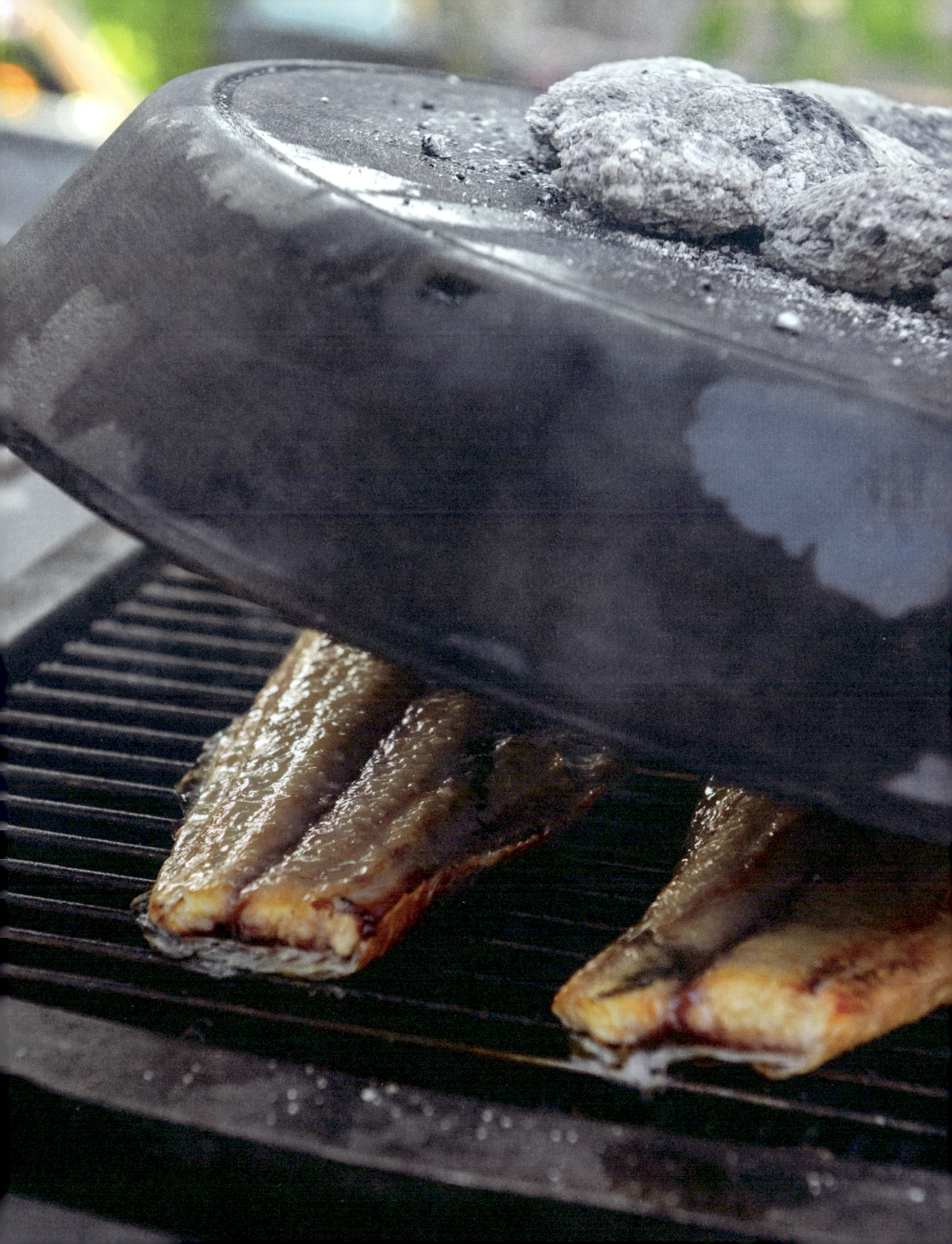

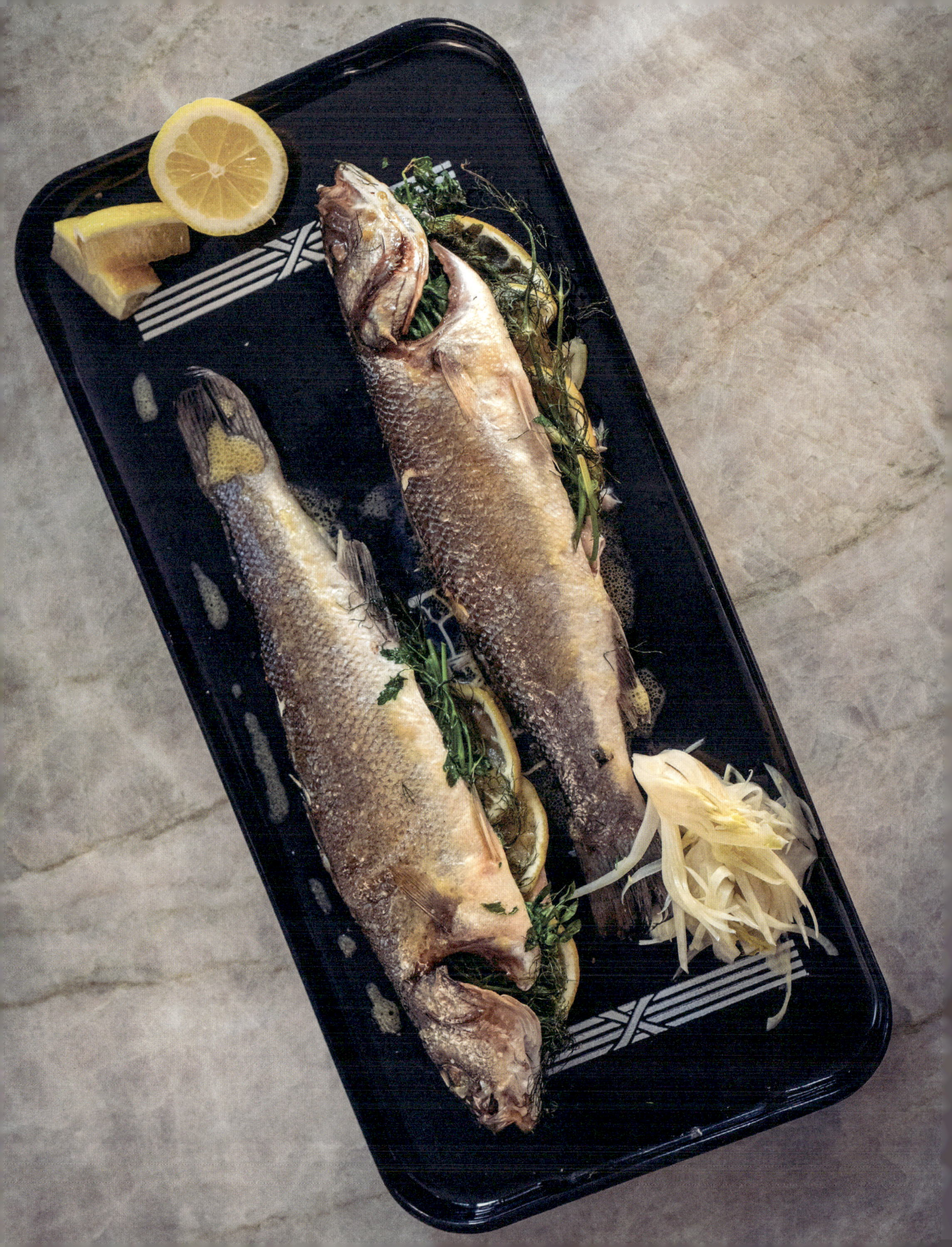

GRILLED, SMOKED WHOLE BRANZINO

Most good fishmongers have a nice supply of whole fish, but few people seem keen to buy and cook them. I was one of those people—until now.

There are great reasons to buy a whole, cleaned fish: you can see quite clearly that its integrity is intact; you get to enjoy all of its meat, from the cheeks to the belly; you don't have to remove the bones; it's very easy to cook; and it makes a nice shareable dinner for multiple people (depending on the size of the fish).

Leaving a fish intact helps it cook slowly and evenly on the grill. Of all the whole fish that I've grilled, I have consistently found that the well-known branzino, which is native to Mediterranean waters, is wonderful flavored with smoke from wood coals. You could also use trout, grouper, sea bream, or bass, but the buttery flavor of branzino combines deliciously with the sweet edge of the smoke.

When you purchase the fish, ask the fishmonger to leave the scales intact. Scaled fish tends to stick, even to the aluminum foil that I use for this method. The goal here is to get tender flesh, not crispy skin.

I love the classic preparation of fish stuffed with lemon slices, fennel, and parsley. While it may seem as though you need a special occasion to warrant cooking a whole fish, this is a no-fuss preparation that can be done quickly, inexpensively, and effortlessly on a summer weeknight. Deploying a piece of wood in the Franklin Formation (see page 142) provides just a kiss of smoke.

Cook time: 13 to 20 minutes

Serves 4

- 2 whole branzinos (about 12 ounces / 350g each), cleaned, with scales intact
- Grapeseed oil for rubbing
- Kosher salt
- Fronds from 1 fennel bulb (use the bulb to make pickled fennel)
- 1 lemon, thinly sliced, plus lemon wedges for serving
- 1 bunch flat-leaf parsley
- Pickled fennel (see page 120) for serving

In a large bowl, combine water and ice cubes to prepare an ice bath. Rinse the fish under cold running water (work carefully to avoid cutting yourself on the scales), then place it in the ice bath until you're ready to grill.

Ready a chimney half to three-fourths full of charcoal, then dump the charcoal into the grill bed. Using tongs, arrange a Franklin Formation with the log parallel to the length of the grill and in the middle so you can surround it on three sides with coals. You don't want the grill to be roaring hot, so use just a few pieces of charcoal on each side.

Remove the fish from the ice bath and carefully dry each one with a clean kitchen towel. Rub the fish all over with the grapeseed oil and very gently salt the flesh. Dividing them evenly, stuff the fennel fronds, lemon slices, and parsley inside the fish cavities.

Cut two squares of aluminum foil; you will lay each fish in a foil boat, so be sure the squares are big enough to accommodate the size of your fish. Fold each foil square in half. Using a sharp spike or the tip of a knife, poke six small holes in the center of the foil—the area that will be the boat's bottom.

Place a fish in the middle of the foil, spine near the holes, and fold the sides of the foil up into a little open-topped boat shape, pinching the ends together to form the bow and stern. (Technically, you could do this without foil, but the foil makes the fish easier to handle.)

Lay the foil boats on the grate directly over the log (the cool zone), with the fish spines facing in toward each other. Cook until the meat starts to firm up to the touch a little, 8 to 10 minutes. Flip each fish within its boat and cook for 5 to 10 minutes more. The length of time depends on how hot your grill is and the size of the fish. Remove the fish from the grill when the flesh appears flaky but still moist when tested with the tip of a knife or prong.

Transfer the fish to a large platter and serve with lemon wedges and pickled fennel.

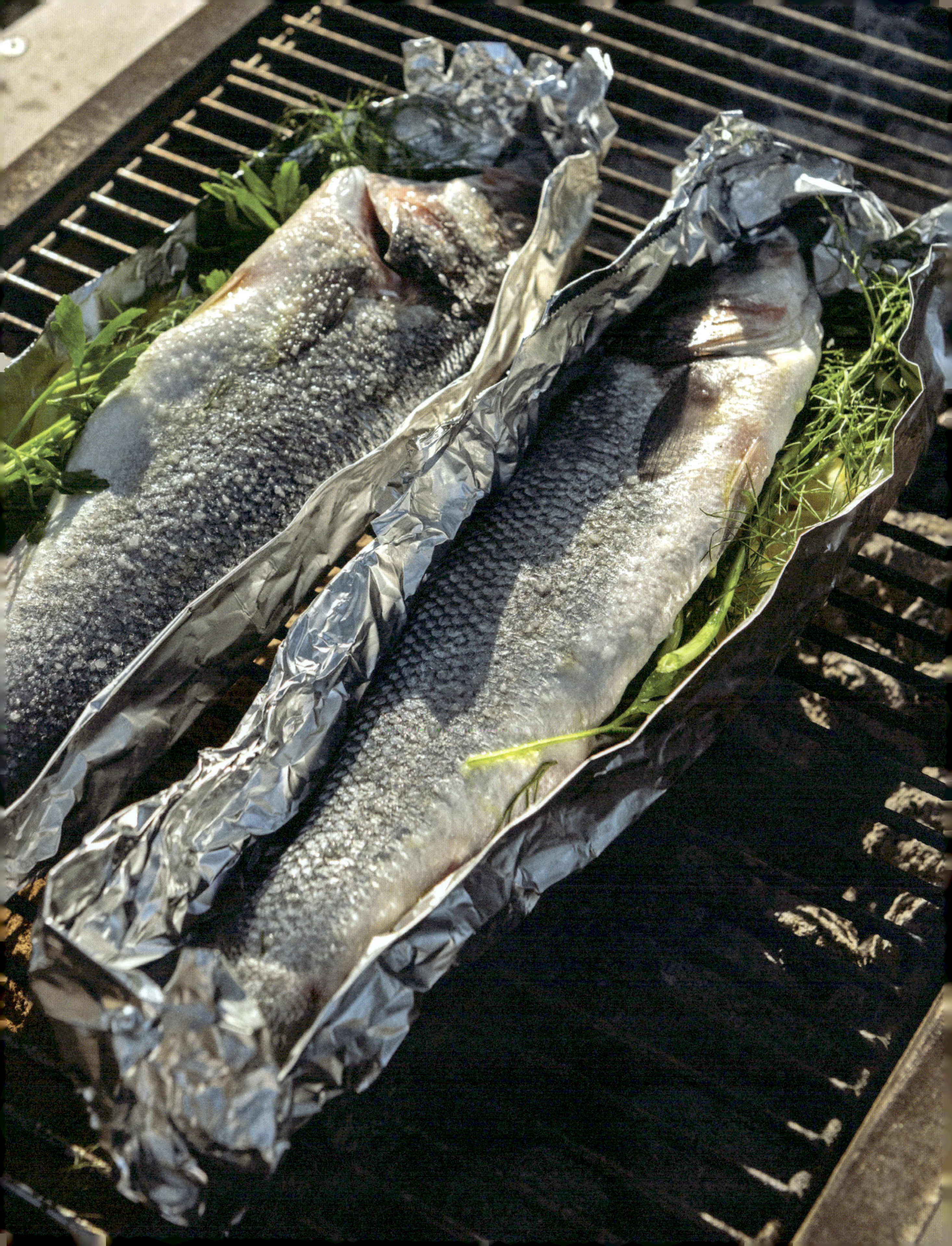

DEVISING AN OYSTER GRILL GRATE

When I couldn't find a grate specifically built for grilling oysters, I decided to fashion one myself! The idea was to make medium-size gaps in a grill grate so the "cup" of an oyster would fit snugly and not tip over and spill its juice while I'm gently cooking the oyster over hot coals. In this case, I modified a PK grate using bolt cutters and pliers. I made only seven slots, because by the time the oysters have cooked and then cooled enough to handle, they should be sloshed down and you should be getting a fresh round started.

OYSTERS WITH SHALLOT-CHIVE BUTTER

The act of buying and shucking oysters may seem like something that only happens at restaurants, but it turns out that shucking an oyster is only a minor challenge and becomes even less so the more often you do it. (I wouldn't want to do hundreds a night, but a dozen at home is no problem.) On top of that, oysters are an incredibly wholesome, hearty, and nutritious food that travels well. Delicious when served with wine, beer, and cocktails, oysters are a good change up if your home dining habits need some fresh ideas.

While I love the clean, crisp bite and salty rush of raw oysters, grilling them with a compound butter is revelatory. A little pat of butter placed on an oyster on the half shell quickly melts into the brine as the oyster gently cooks to tender perfection. The magic is in that mixture of butter and brine, which, in the confines of the shell, creates a tiny bit of buttery oyster bisque. Nothing could be simpler and more appealing.

The only challenge is to shuck the oysters and get them on the grill without spilling too much of their liquor. I do recommend shucking them first. Some people let the fire open the oysters for them—putting an unshucked oyster over the coals will eventually boil the oyster and release the adductor muscle that holds the shell closed. But, often as not, the brine boils and blasts the shell open, shattering some of the calcium and spilling the brine. You want a clean shuck and a gentle cook. Don't worry if you spill a little of the liquor when placing the oysters on the grill. As long as its shell is pretty level, the oyster will release more briny liquor as it cooks, providing plenty of liquid in the shell to mix with the butter.

Although you won't go through a whole stick of butter with only a dozen oysters, it's easier to make the compound butter in quantity, and it keeps well in the refrigerator for later use. Incidentally, feel free to riff on the compound butter mixture, as almost any herb or spice works. Even plain butter is delicious. Just be sure it's unsalted butter because the oyster brine itself contains plenty of sea salt. A splash of hot sauce is a wonderful way to finish off each oyster.

Cook time: 20 minutes (including making the compound butter)

Serves 2 to 6 depending on number of oysters

- ½ cup / 110g unsalted butter, at room temperature
- 2½ tablespoons / 8g finely minced fresh chives
- 1 tablespoon / 10g finely minced shallot
- 12 to 36 raw oysters in their shells
- Hot sauce (see page 97) for serving

In a small bowl, combine the butter, chives, and shallot and mix well. Spoon the butter in a uniform line down the center of a sheet of plastic wrap or aluminum foil. Fold one long side of the sheet over the butter and, using a straightedge (such as a ruler), press against the butter while pulling on the lower part of the sheet to force the butter into a uniform log about 1 inch in diameter. Wrap the butter in the plastic wrap or foil, twist the ends closed, and refrigerate to firm up. Leftover compound butter will keep in the fridge for up to 2 weeks.

Ready a chimney full of charcoal, then dump the charcoal into the grill bed and spread out the coals.

Shuck twelve of the oysters and gently set them on a platter. Remove the butter from the refrigerator and unwrap. Using a knife, cut off small slices of butter and place one atop each shucked oyster.

Gently place the oysters on the grate directly over hot coals. The liquor will start to simmer and melt the butter. When the butter has completely dissolved into the liquor, after 1 to 2 minutes, depending on the heat of your fire, use tongs or kitchen tweezers to remove the oysters from the heat and place them on a platter.

Allow the shells to cool enough to handle, then eat the oysters while still warm, topping each with a dash of hot sauce. Once you've slurped down a few, get started shucking the next dozen oysters for round two.

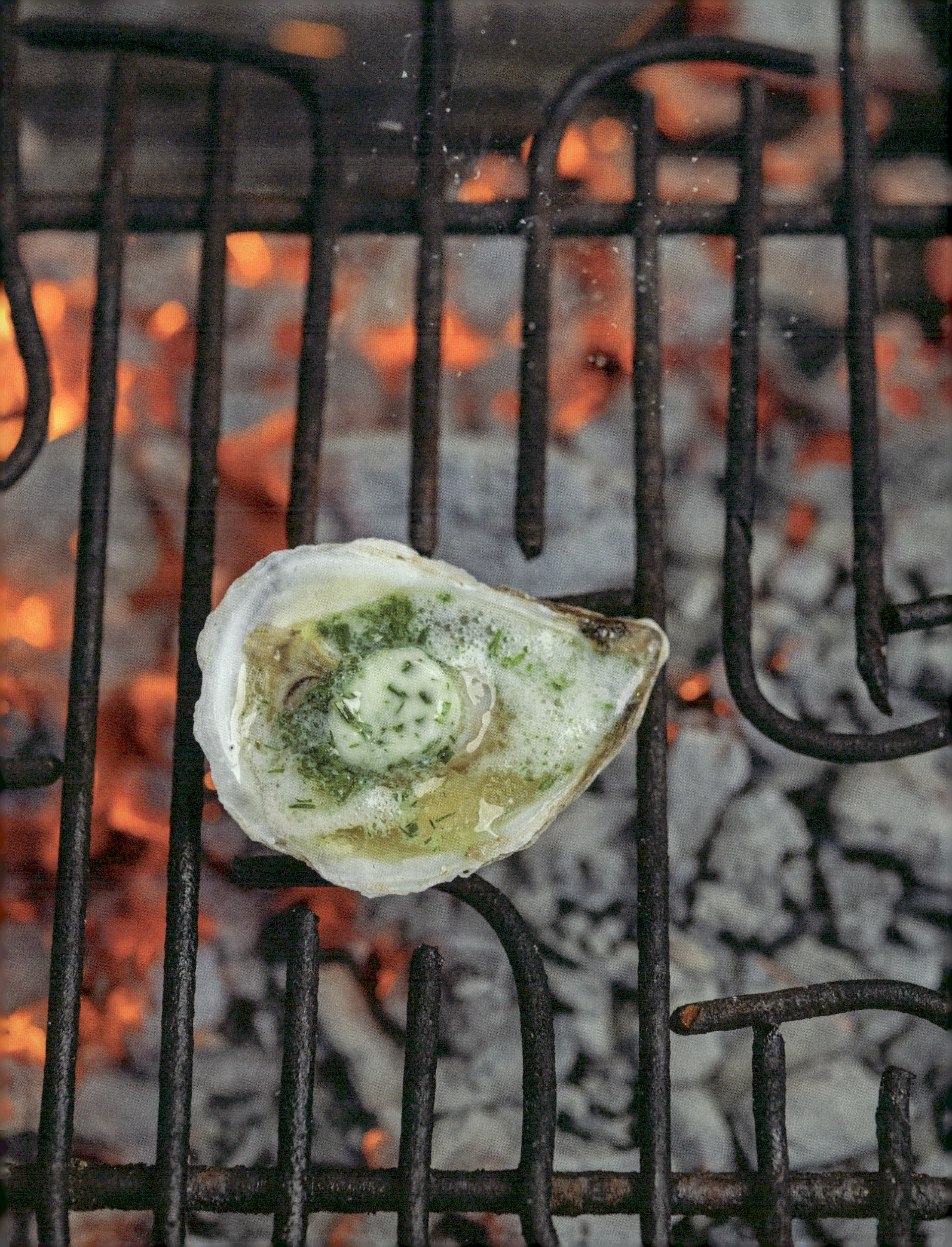

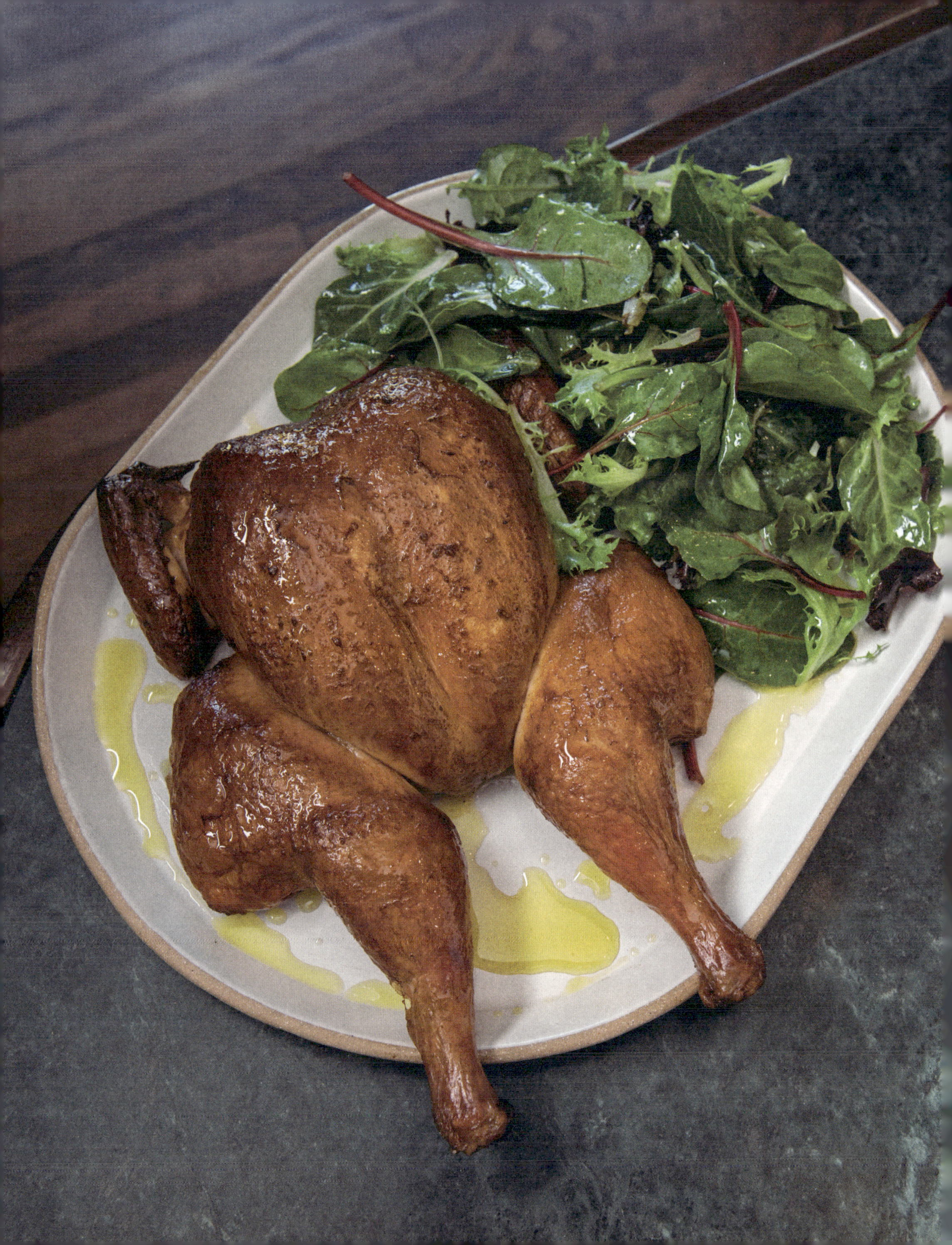

SMOKED CHICKEN

While working on this book, I discovered that Aaron never cooks with the lid of his PK grill closed, which I do all the time. Practically, this means that Aaron doesn't smoke foods on the PK, and I do. (All the other recipes for the grill in this chapter should be cooked without the lid.) This is probably because Aaron co-owns a restaurant that has a number of smokers and has at least one at home, while for the longest time I did not. And because of his preference for the perfect smoke that a fully burning fire creates, he's never even thought of smoking anything on the PK, which offers a more rustic, less efficient smoking environment but still works quite well for smaller items such as this chicken.

Every time that I serve a smoked chicken to guests, they all say, "Wow, I never thought of smoking chicken." Nothing seems more obvious to me, and, in fact, I can think of almost no more delicious way of cooking chicken. Smoking delivers not only beautiful golden brown skin with a ton of flavor but also incredibly tender, juicy meat. And the method could not be simpler. By the way, this method works equally well for quail, guinea fowl, Cornish game hens, or any other small- to medium-size bird with light-textured meat. It also produces wonderful boneless leg of lamb, pork roasts, and any other medium-size cut that will fit on the grill with the lid closed.

While you can easily do a whole intact chicken this way, I recommend spatchcocking (aka butterflying) it so it cooks more evenly and faster and thus doesn't take on too much smoke. Basting it with a vinegary mustard solution adds zest and character.

Basic spatchcocking is quite easy. You can make it more complicated if you decide to remove the wishbone and ribs, which requires a smidge of deft knifework. But I like to leave the ribs on to protect the breasts during cooking. Plus, they're much easier to remove when the bird is cooked. The wishbone is a little tricky to extract, so I usually just cut it out after the bird comes off the grill. As always, the chicken tastes and cooks better if it has been pre-salted and air-dried in the fridge for at least a day. —Jordan

Cook time: 50 to 80 minutes

Serves 4 to 6

- Kosher salt
- 1 whole chicken, 3 to 5 pounds, spatchcocked

The Mop

- ½ cup / 120g sherry vinegar
- ¼ cup / 55g unsalted butter
- 2 tablespoons / 30g Dijon mustard
- 1 tablespoon / 20g honey
- 1 tablespoon / 9g freshly ground black pepper
- ½ teaspoon / 3.5g kosher salt

Liberally salt the chicken all over and set it on a baking sheet. Let the chicken air-dry, uncovered, in the refrigerator for at least 24 hours or up to 72.

To make the mop: At some point before cooking the chicken (this can be done a day ahead of time, then refrigerated and reheated), in a small saucepan over low heat, combine the vinegar, butter, mustard, honey, pepper, and salt and warm through, stirring occasionally, until the butter melts and the mixture has formed a sauce.

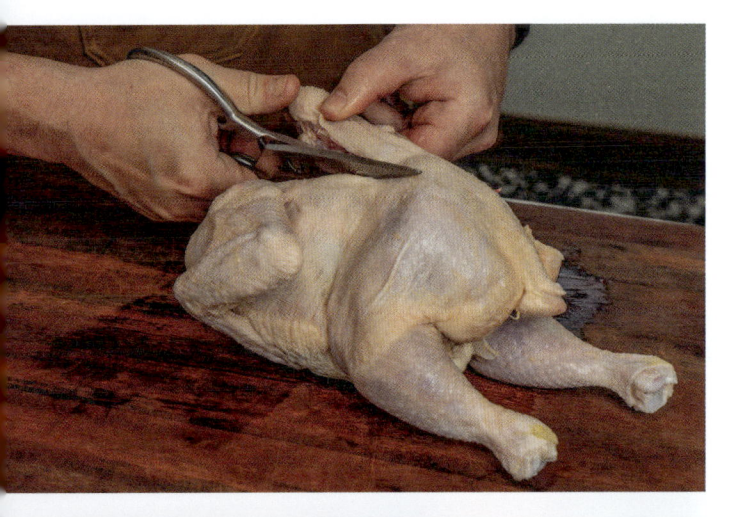

Remove the chicken from the fridge and allow it to temper on the counter.

Ready a chimney full of charcoal, then dump the chimney into one end of the grill bed. Using the Franklin Formation (see page 142), lay a log next to the coals to form the boundary of a two-zone setup, or alternatively, place a good-size wood chunk on the coals. Close the lid and allow the wood to start smoking. The temperature should be hot—somewhere between 400° and 450°F.

Lay the chicken, breast-side up, on the grate as far as possible from the heat, with the legs nearest to the heat. Close the lid and cook for 25 minutes.

Open the lid, lift the chicken (using tongs or pick it up with a kitchen towel in your hands), and place a quarter sheet pan under the chicken. The pan will capture your mop and let it combine with the chicken juices, evaporating them and steaming the underside of the bird. This is a good time for the first drizzle with the mop. Drizzle with the mop again after 15 minutes and a third time after another 15 minutes.

Now's a good time to gauge the temperature. Insert a digital thermometer into the center of the breast (you're looking for about 150°F) and then in the thickest part of the thigh, but not touching the bone (you want 175° to 180°F). It will probably require more cooking, so continue to baste every 10 to 15 minutes until it's done.

When the chicken is done, transfer it to a platter and let rest until cool enough to carve and serve.

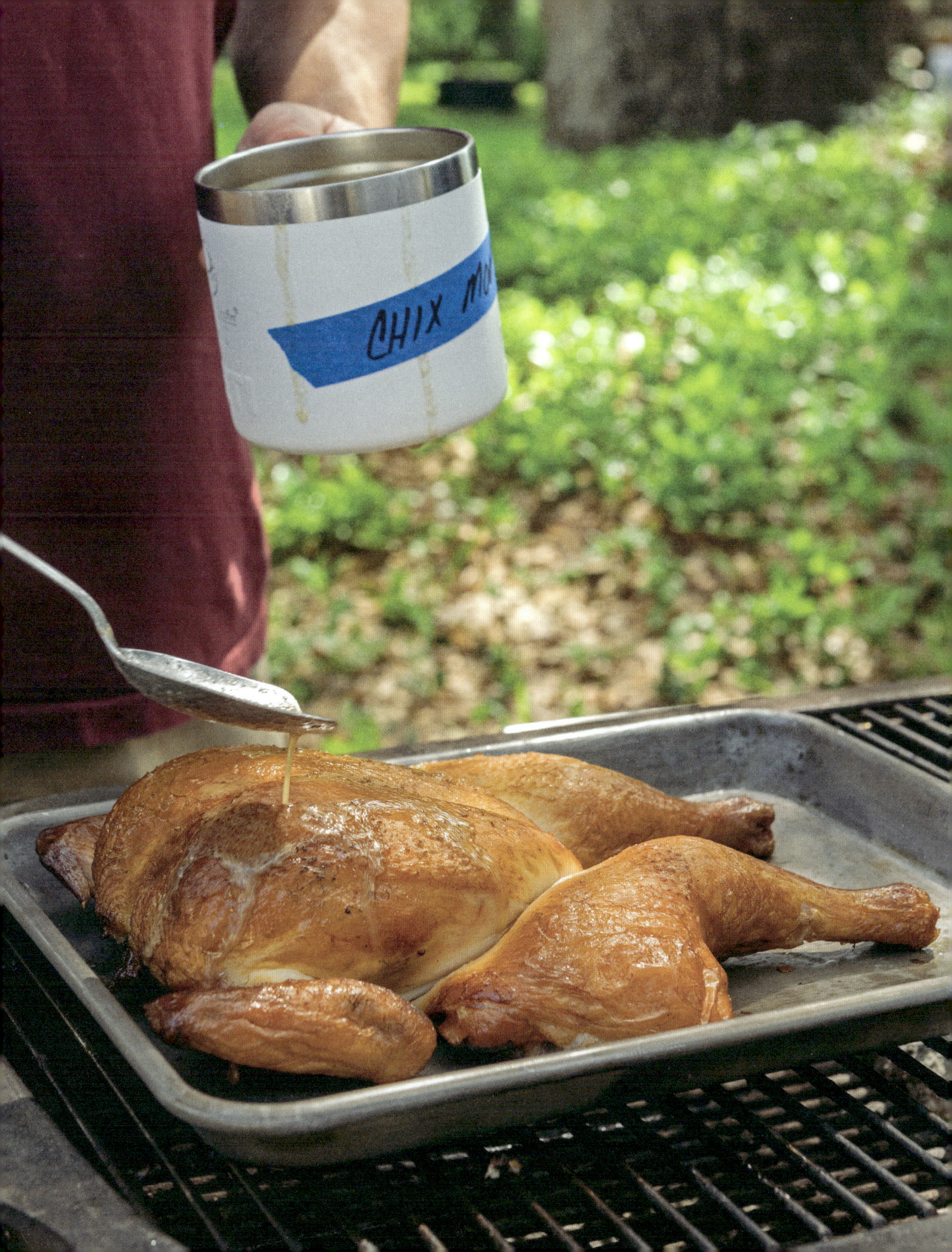
CHIX

VEGGIE SIDES AND MAINS

Vegetables are wonderful beings, and I love them a lot. As much as my career has been defined by the cooking of meat, my own eating life has always included a ton of veggies. And when I'm cooking out, it's often handy to cook my vegetables over the fire.

Firepit cooking allows you to cook several ways at the same time. While your pork or beef steaks are slowly cooking on the grate above the fire, you can pull aside some coals or burning logs to quickly prepare some appetizers or side dishes. Or you can cook sturdy vegetables right down in the coals.

These same simple techniques can easily be adapted for use in a charcoal grill too. Although the firepit conveys the added benefit of real woodsmoke, I don't want the vegetables to take on too much smoke, and most of the time they don't. A hint of smoke is nice on your vegetable accompaniment, but if you've already got smoky meats, too much might be overkill. Also, I'm not at all against cooking up these vegetables in the fire and making a giant spread for a meal unto itself!

GRILLED MUSHROOMS

Mushrooms are some of the easiest and most natural vegetables to cook on the fire, and they add an earthy, complex flavor to meals as a side dish, as a garnish to meat, or as a delicious meat substitute if you're feeding vegetarians. While they are light and seemingly flimsy, mushrooms are actually quite resistant to high heat and fire, giving them the ability to take on gentle grill or smoke notes.

Cultivated mushrooms available in bulk at good grocery stores tend to be fairly well cleaned and manicured. If you detect any soil or leftover matter from their growing medium, simply wipe it off with a damp towel and trim off the bottom of the stems. Never wash mushrooms under water, as their spongelike bodies will soak up the moisture and become damp and slimy.

The ideal mushrooms to grill are whole portobellos, large trumpet mushrooms, and, especially, clumps of maitake mushrooms, also known as hen of the woods. In nature, maitakes grow at the base of trees and reach sizes up to twenty pounds. But they're also easily cultivated, which is what you normally find at grocery stores. They grow in soft, feathery clumps that are more robust than they seem. You can pull apart the clusters into smaller bite-size strands or leave them attached in big clumps, as I do when roasting them over coals.

Cook time: 20 minutes

Serves 2 to 4

- 1 pound / 450g maitake, portobello, or trumpet mushrooms, wiped clean and trimmed as needed
- Grapeseed oil for brushing

Using fresh, hot wood coals in a firepit or glowing-red charcoal in a grill bed, spread out the coals so you have a wide area for grilling. You want fairly high heat, as mushrooms can take a lot as they cook down. Also, they absorb a lot of smoke flavor—almost too much at times—so fast cooking helps them not take on too much.

Put the mushrooms on a baking sheet and gently brush them with grapeseed oil.

Place the mushrooms directly on the grate over high heat and grill until tender, 10 to 15 minutes, depending on the heat of your fire. Maitakes take a bit longer; you want the edges to get a little crisp and begin to dry out. You'll be impressed with how much heat mushrooms can take.

Remove the mushrooms from the heat and serve immediately.

FIRE-KISSED BRUSSELS SPROUTS

I could eat brussels sprouts just about every day of the week, and I love doing them on the fire. The intense heat from the flames and coals tempers the bitterness of the sprouts while adding a layer of charry complexity. To finish, I toss in something a little sweet, like thinly sliced apples, pomegranate seeds, or halved grapes.

Brussels sprouts are convenient to cook on a fire that you already have going for a larger protein, and they roast equally well over the wood coals of an open firepit or the glowing charcoal in a grill. You want the brussels sprouts as cold as possible before putting them on the fire, so keep them in the refrigerator or on ice until just before cooking.

To cook down sprouts in the fire, you can use a perforated grill pan or even a cast-iron skillet, but I have had the best luck using an inexpensive metal fry basket purchased from a restaurant-supply store. The metal on these baskets tends to be heavy-duty, so they can take the intense heat and wear and tear.

You can use this method in a firepit over wood coals or over charcoal in a standard grill or even quickly over a charcoal chimney. And it works well for green beans, parcooked fingerling potatoes, cauliflower, broccoli, and any other sturdy, fibrous vegetable you might want to try. Their water content and fibrous character allow them to resist the heat of the fire long enough to pick up just enough charry taste to be delicious.

Cook time: 10 to 15 minutes

Serves 2 to 4 as a side dish

- 1 pound / 450g brussels sprouts, trimmed, halved, and well chilled
- Grapeseed oil for coating
- Kosher salt
- Juice and grated zest of 1 lemon
- 1 cup / 140g pomegranate seeds
- Apple cider vinegar for drizzling

Create an open bed of exposed coals. Then take two fresh logs and place them on the coals as a stand for the fry basket. Push the logs together tight enough to compact the charcoal so there are no major air gaps that could generate flames.

In a medium bowl, toss the brussels sprouts with just enough grapeseed oil to coat evenly and lightly and then season with salt.

Dump the brussels sprouts into a fry basket and reserve the bowl. Place the basket directly on the coals. Grasp the handle of the basket almost immediately and begin flicking your wrist to toss the sprouts gently so they don't become too charred. Continue tossing as the sprouts develop a lightly charred exterior. You want to prolong the cook as much as possible until it seems the sprouts are going to burn without ever getting to that point. You are cooking the exterior while keeping the interior crisp.

When the sprouts are ready, remove the basket from the fire and return the sprouts to the bowl. Add the lemon juice and mix well. Add the pomegranate seeds, lemon zest, and a drizzle of vinegar and mix.

Serve the sprouts immediately, as they get soggy quickly.

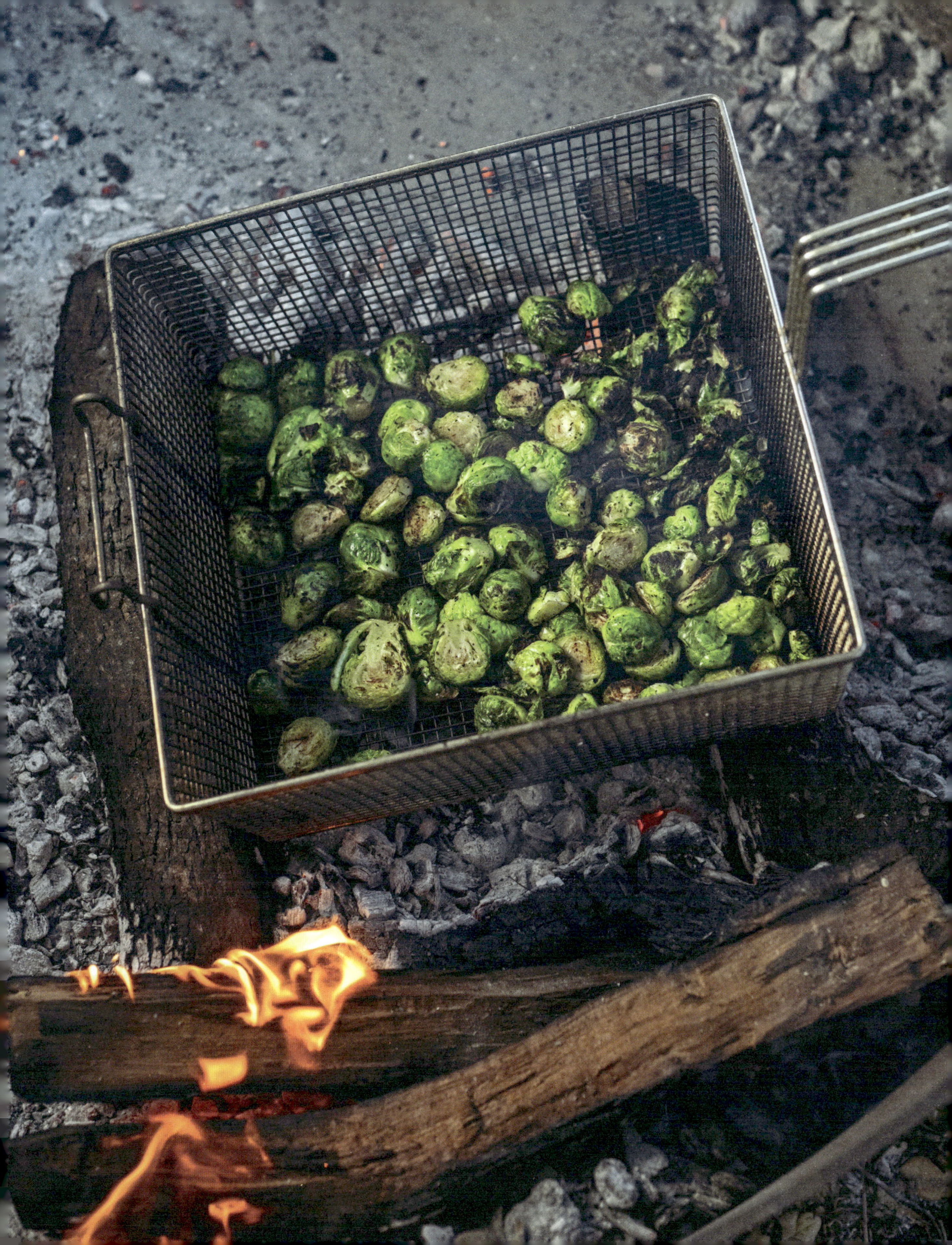

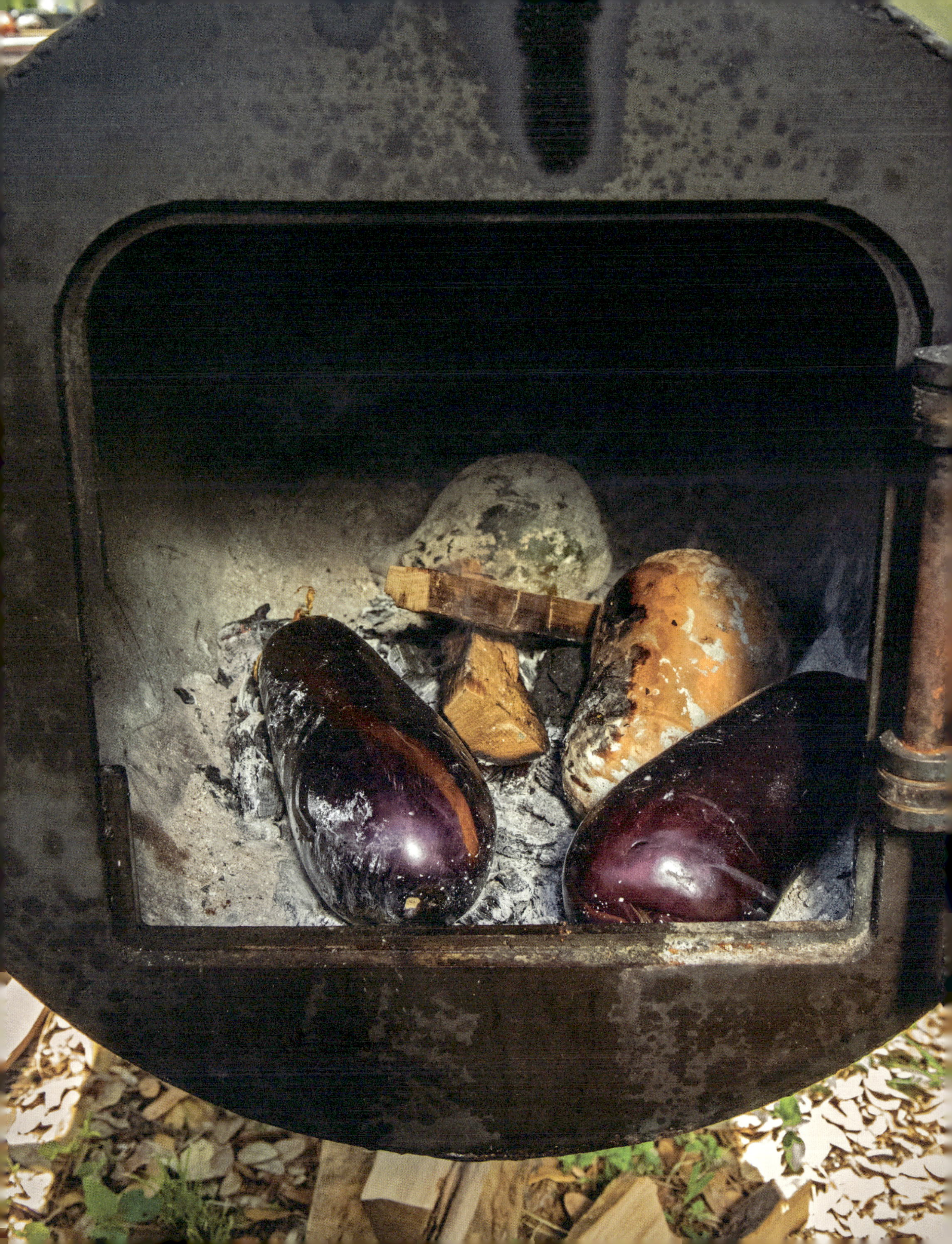

COAL-ROASTED VEGGIES

As long as you use the appropriate vegetables and take them off the fire at the right time, there's no easier way to cook vegetables than to put them directly on the coals. Instead of steaming them in a pot, they cook in their own juices, which concentrates their flavors.

Thin-skinned vegetables, like eggplants, definitely pick up some smoke, so be prepared for smoky baba ghanoush (the way it was meant to be). But thick-skinned vegetables, like gourds and squash, can take a lot of heat and will cook beautifully without getting particularly smoky. Onions and cabbages can be cooked without wrapping them in aluminum foil, and although their exterior will obviously blacken, you'll find a beautifully cooked interior when you remove the charred outer skin or leaves. They can also easily be wrapped in foil and steamed with full protection from the flames.

However you do it, the ability to cook vegetables on a fire that you've already got going to cook a major protein not only is poetic but also saves time, heat, labor, and steps (our kitchen is a fair distance from the backyard firepit, so roasting veggies in the oven while cooking outside requires a lot of schlepping and diverts attention). If you have a wood fireplace, and it's a cold winter night, you could even use that. You can also successfully cook eggplants on charcoal in a grill, but they'll lack the sweet flavor of woodsmoke. Whichever method you choose, you want hot, active coals.

SMOKY EGGPLANT BABA GHANOUSH

Cook time: 20 minutes

Serves 4 as an appetizer or side dish

- 2 medium globe eggplants
- 1 small garlic clove, finely chopped
- Extra-virgin olive oil for serving
- 1 lemon, halved
- Kosher salt
- Toasted bread slices or crackers for serving

Tuck the eggplants into the sides of the firepit, around the smoking coals. You can brush some coals on top of the eggplants too. Within 5 to 10 minutes, the eggplants will begin to shrivel and the skin will become crunchy. If you haven't covered them with coals, use tongs to turn the eggplants so the upward facing side goes into the coals. Try not to manipulate the eggplants too much, as you don't want to break the skin and release all the juice.

After about 20 minutes, the eggplants' skins should be shriveling and crisped. They should have cracked a little and will be lightly leaking juices into the coals. Using tongs, gently transfer them from the fire to a big bowl or platter and let them cool. They'll release a lot of liquid as they sit.

When the eggplants are cool enough to handle, cut them in half with a knife and use a spoon to scoop out all the flesh into a medium bowl. Remove any pieces of burned skin, as it will deliver an acrid taste. While the flesh is still warm, add the garlic. Then pour in a little olive oil, squeeze in the juice from a lemon half, season with salt, and mix until well combined. Taste and adjust with more olive oil, lemon juice, and salt as needed. Let sit for 5 to 10 minutes to allow the flavor of the garlic to mellow in the heat.

Serve the baba ghanoush warm, with toasted bread.

COAL-FIRED SQUASHES AND ONIONS

Cook time: 30 to 40 minutes

Makes as much as you want

- White, yellow, or red onions
- Acorn, butternut, or other winter squashes
- Extra-virgin olive oil for serving
- Unsalted butter for serving
- Flaky salt
- Fresh lemon juice for serving

Literally the easiest dish in the world to make, this involves nestling whole onions and squashes into the edge of the fire among the coals, then leaving them for 30 to 40 minutes. The onions will blacken and tenderize, which is how you know when to pull them out. The squashes will also carbonize on the outside, but a few pokes to gauge tenderness will tell you when they're done.

Let the onions cool on the outside before peeling. Serve as you wish. For instance, they're delicious as a side when cut in half and topped with a little butter and flaky salt. Likewise, allow the squash to cool enough to handle, then cut in half and scoop out and discard the seeds.

Serve the squash topped with a little olive oil, butter, salt, and lemon juice.

FIRE-STEAMED CABBAGE

Cook time: About 30 minutes

Serves 4 to 6 as a side dish

- 1 head red or purple cabbage
- Unsalted butter for topping
- Kosher salt and freshly ground black pepper
- 2 or 3 slices bacon (optional)

Cut the cabbage in half but don't core it. Lay the halves, flat-side down, on a cutting board and mold a piece of aluminum foil tightly around each piece, leaving a little extra foil for a lip (which makes for easy handling). Flip the halves so they are cut-side up. Top each half with a pat of butter and season with salt and pepper. Place the cabbage halves, foil-side down, in the hot, active coals.

If you have a grate that sits over the coals, roll the bacon slices, if using, together into a coil and place it on the grate directly over the cabbage so the delicious pork fat will drip down onto the slowly cooking cabbage.

The cabbage is ready when it appears soft and moist. This should take about 30 minutes, depending on the heat of your coals. Transfer the cabbage to a platter and serve immediately.

JORDAN'S PERFECT GREEN SALAD

One thing that I have in common with all of the Franklins (Aaron, Stacy, and their daughter, Vivian) is that hardly a day goes by that I don't eat a salad. Salads are everything that barbecue is not: fresh, raw, green, crunchy, acidic, and not too filling. When we're test cooking, I am often tasked with making a simple green salad for dinner because we need something wholesome and satisfying—even though the dressing is just oil and vinegar and salt.

There's not exactly a trick to my method, just a few things that I do always seem to provoke compliments. Here's my basic theory of salad, along with a couple of variations that use what you might have on hand or be inclined to eat on any given day.

THE KEYS TO A PERFECT GREEN SALAD
- **A mix of fresh, tender lettuces, washed and fully dried**
- **Very good extra-virgin olive oil**
- **Vinegars and citrus**
- **Salt and pepper**
- **Restraint**

Lettuces

I like to make a blend of two or more different varieties of lettuces, choosing from such types as butter lettuce, romaine, arugula, dandelion, and endive. Mostly, I love a little crunch. If you are starting with uncleaned lettuce, always wash and dry it fully using a salad spinner (something every kitchen should have). Wash and spin dry the leaves about 20 minutes ahead of dinner and let them chill in the fridge for the perfect condition. The leaves must be free of any dampness or the dressing will not adhere.

Very Good Extra-Virgin Olive Oil

Top-quality extra-virgin olive oil cannot be beat. It has a richness and complexity that you won't get from any other type of oil. I recommend that you splurge on a bottle from Italy that might set you back thirty dollars or more. It will last a long time if you use it sparingly. I use mine pretty much exclusively to finish proteins and for salad dressing.

Vinegars and Citrus

I use all kinds of vinegars, but my standard is the trio of red wine, white wine, and sherry vinegars, which I use interchangeably, depending on my mood. Occasionally I use balsamic vinegar, but it's somewhat sweet. You can also use fresh citrus juice in addition to or instead of vinegar. Sometimes I split this component of a dressing between the citric acid of a lemon and the acetic acid of vinegar, as each kind of acid imparts a slightly different tang, adding another dimension.

Salt and Pepper

It's easiest to add salt by the pinch. Be careful not to use too much, as you can always add more. Just a little bit brings out the flavors of the greens, oil, and vinegar. Too much obscures them. A couple quick twists of the pepper grinder should be sufficient. As with salt, you don't want too much.

Restraint

Even slightly overdressing it can make a salad vaguely off-putting. Too much vinegar and the acidity is too cutting. Too much oil and the salad is greasy. Too much dressing in general and the lettuces get soggy. Go as light as possible at the beginning and add a touch more dressing only if needed.

TECHNIQUE

When you have great lettuces, just a little oil and vinegar applied directly to the leaves can be enough. Most vinaigrettes call for oil and vinegar in a three-to-one ratio, but I find that less vinegar is preferable when you're using a great olive oil. I mix them together by feel, but you might start by trying a four-to-one or even five-to-one ratio.

Right before I serve the salad, I pour some olive oil on the lettuces. Use less than you think you need, then add just a light drizzle of vinegar and a pinch each of salt and pepper and gently toss together with freshly washed hands. Make sure every leaf gets coated with oil. If some didn't, add more oil. Taste a leaf and let your palate decide if the dressing is just right or if you need a few drops more of either oil or vinegar.

Variations

Premade vinaigrette: To make a vinaigrette ahead of time, follow the preceding principles, but combine the ingredients in a small bowl or jar with a healthy dollop of Dijon mustard (more than you think you might want), which allows the dressing to emulsify. Add a pinch of salt, an even smaller pinch of sugar, and a few twists from a pepper grinder, then whisk everything until the mixture has a nice, thick texture that will coat the leaves. Some of my other favorite additions include finely minced garlic, minced shallot, and fresh dill or tarragon, finely chopped.

Salad additions: Add whole leaves of fresh flat-leaf parsley, mint, or basil to your lettuce mix. They always lift a salad. Also, very fine slivers of onion contribute a nice little background jolt. If you're serving the salad in a wooden bowl, rub a clove of garlic onto the wood before adding the lettuces to give the perfect garlicky accent. A bit of crunch can also be nice: chopped radish, sliced cucumber, or chopped celery. Don't add more than one or two of these additional ingredients to a salad. A green salad should be almost invisible compared to the rest of the food—that is, until everyone remarks on how perfectly it is dressed.

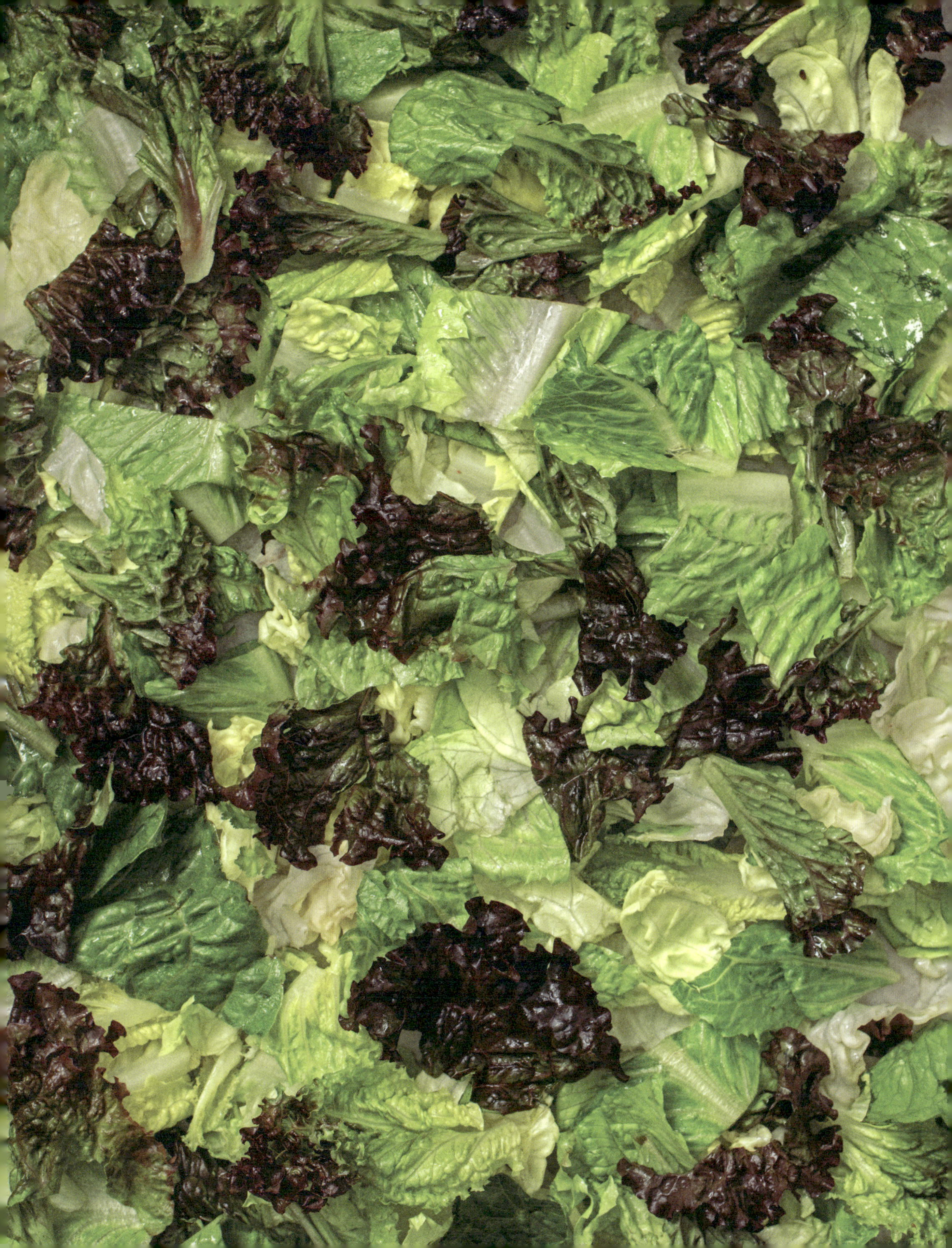

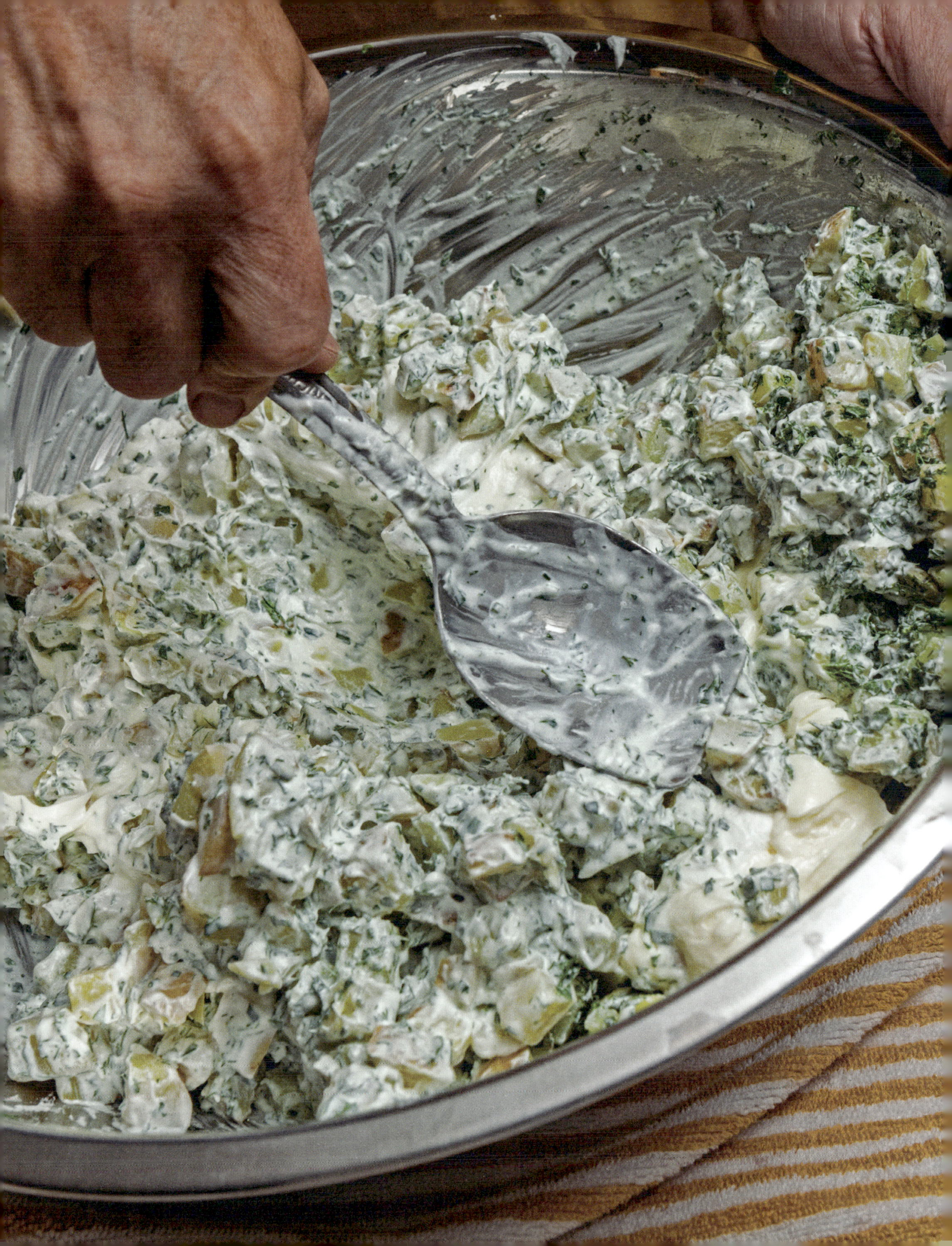

HERBY BUTTERMILK POTATO SALAD

I've been making this rich, creamy potato salad for years, as it goes great with just about anything, especially intensely grilled meats such as the Firepit Côte de Boeuf (page 139). The cool, slightly sour heaviness of the buttermilk and sour cream provide a soothing contrast to the smoky, crusty surface, and the herbs add some lift and zing. Best of all, it's really easy to make and to customize to your own taste. This is a large portion, but the leftovers keep well in the fridge for a few days, during which it will almost certainly get eaten.

Makes 3 to 4 quarts

- 6 pounds Yukon gold potatoes, diced into ½-inch cubes
- ¼ cup / 12g fresh dill, finely chopped
- ¼ cup / 12g fresh chives, finely sliced
- ½ cup / 30g fresh parsley, finely chopped
- 2 cups / 400g mayonnaise
- 2 cups / 480g sour cream
- ½ cup / 120g buttermilk
- 1 tablespoon / 20g kosher salt

Line a sheet tray with paper towels. Bring a large pot of heavily salted water to boil. Add the potatoes, turn the heat to low, and simmer them until close to tender, 10 to 12 minutes. Drain and then lay out the potatoes on the towel-lined sheet tray to cool. Do not refrigerate. Add the dill, chives, and parsley to a mixing bowl followed by the room temperature potatoes. Gently mix the herbs and potatoes. Next add the mayonnaise, sour cream, buttermilk, and salt. Fold in the liquid ingredients until all is well combined, then use the flat of a spoon to smash some of the potatoes.

Prepare the potato salad a day in advance, as the flavors marry and improve overnight.

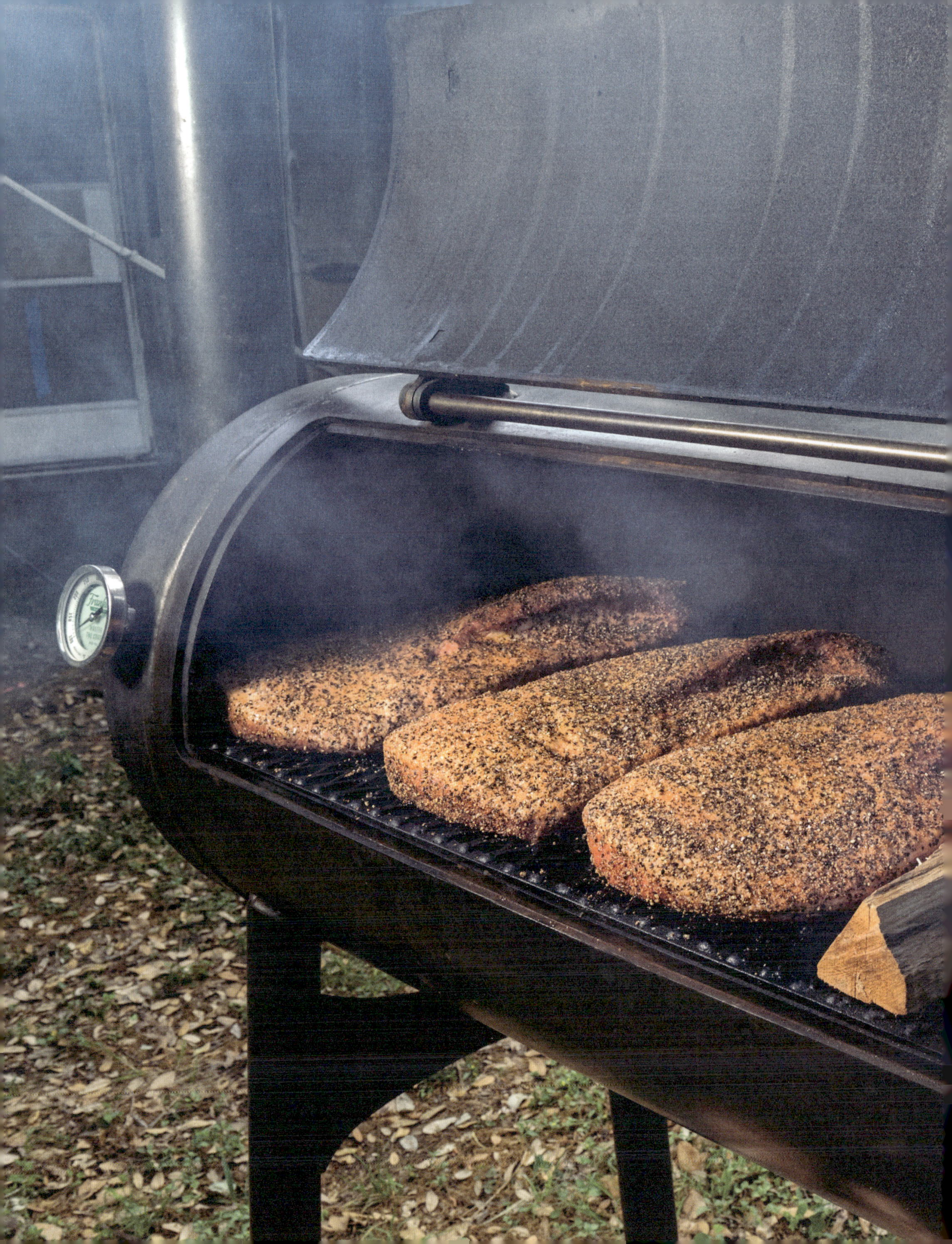

7

SLOW SMOKE
A Return to Barbecue

As both a food and a culture, barbecue is bigger now than probably at any time since the invention of gas and electric cooking. Everywhere I look, a new barbecue place has popped up, and I love that so many people are stepping up to the challenge of slow-smoking meat.

It never gets old. Each new hunk of meat, each day's weather, each smoker, and each piece of firewood presents a different set of circumstances to be figured out by the cook to achieve the best results. So, in a way, barbecue is a perpetual puzzle that keeps you sharp and thinking, just like a sudoku or crossword. Despite its puzzles, cooking barbecue provides ample time for peaceful rumination when you sit by as the fire slowly breaks down a piece of wood into the smoke that will curl around the meat on its way out of the stack.

This chapter is a return to that restful moment. At its heart is a new and refined brisket recipe that reflects our ever-evolving methods of smoking at the restaurant. This is how we cook our briskets today—and it yields even better results than when we published *Franklin Barbecue* in 2015. Some of the changes are subtle, but over the course of twelve hours, even subtle differences become significant. And when I say *brisket recipe*, I really mean an almost stream-of-consciousness narrative, since so many of the details are related to feel and observation.

In addition to brisket, I've included recipes for smoking duck, turkey, baby back ribs, prime rib, and beef ribs. The techniques are all similar, so the skill you develop in managing your smoker will serve you well going forward. The recipes are geared for a Texas-style offset smoker. In fact, I tested all of these recipes on the new Franklin Pit described in chapter 2. But, of course, you could easily do them on a bigger, more professional pit, or, if you don't have any of this equipment, the techniques and visual cues will work on any other kind of smoker or on a PK grill, Big Green Egg, or kettle-style grill rigged for smoking.

Have fun with the process. Great backyard barbecue has always been a mixture of relaxation and application, a chance to commune with your food, your yard, and yourself. As wise people say, the path is the goal; though, with smoking meat, the goal is also the goal, so enjoy your delicious barbecue.

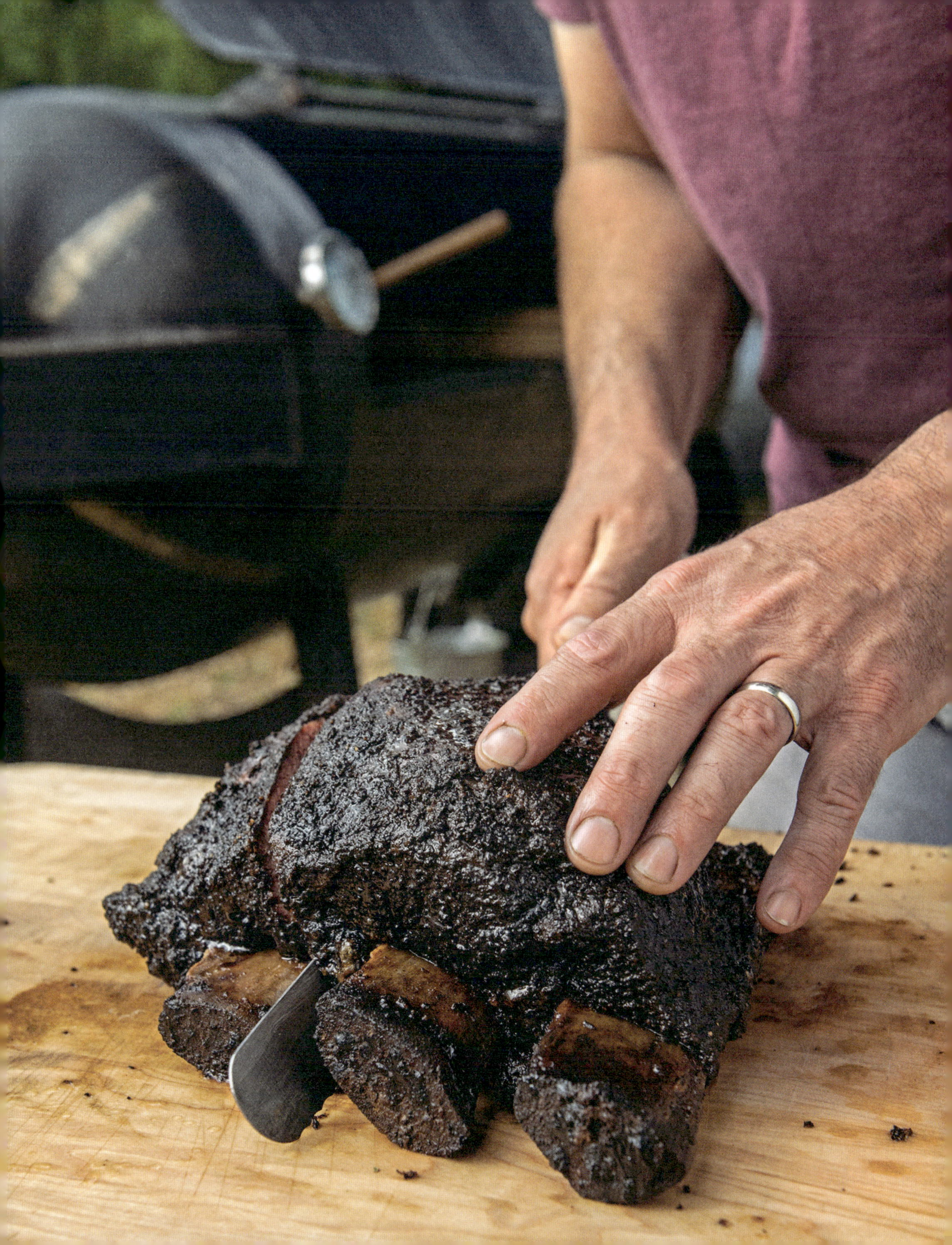

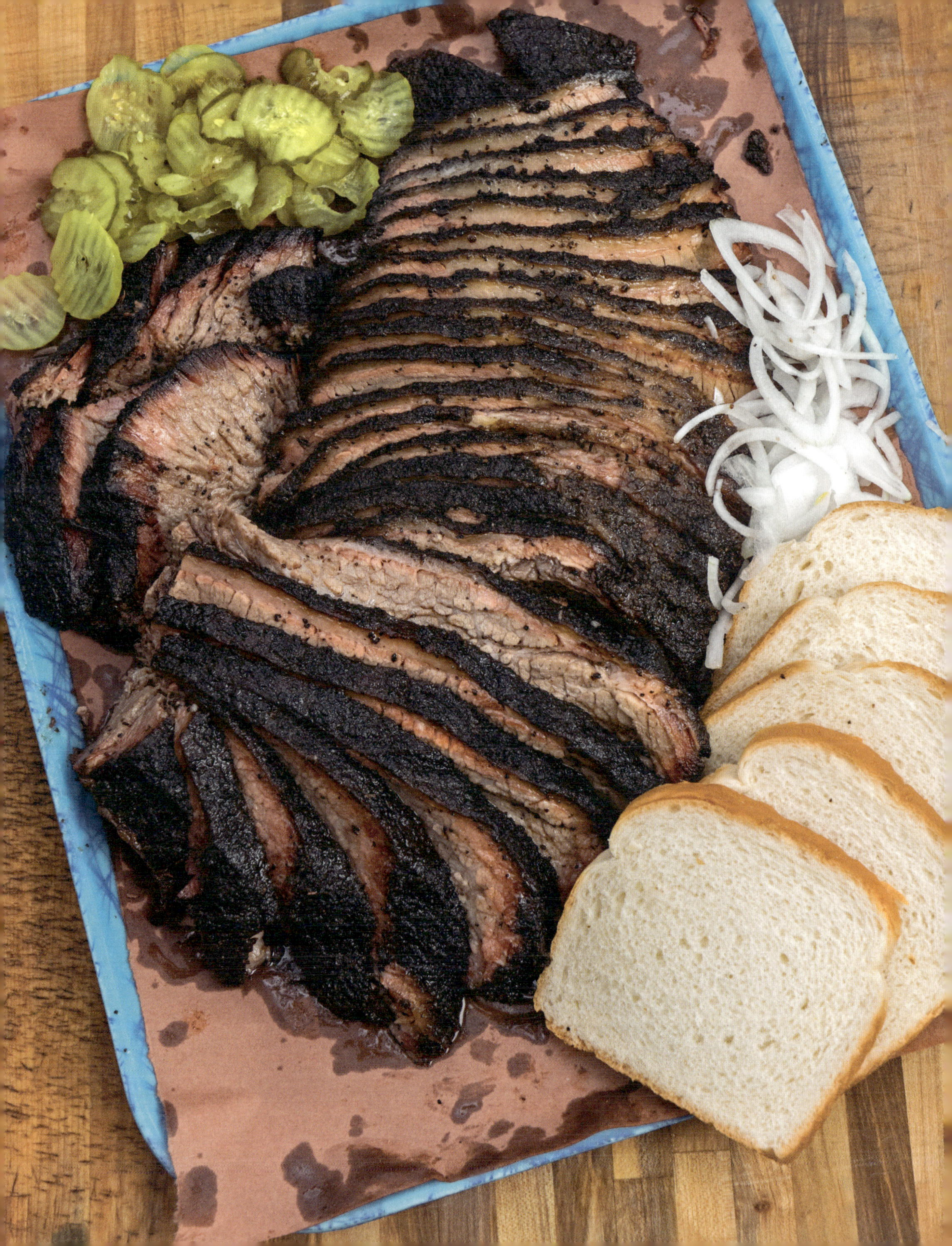

THE ULTIMATE BRISKET

The brisket recipe from *Franklin Barbecue* runs eleven pages, and—judging from the amount and intensity of feedback I've received over the years—it was really helpful to lots of folks. I truly don't have enough fingers to count the number of times someone has come up to me and said, "That brisket recipe changed my life!" I'm thrilled to have been able to help out, and people continue to ask me brisket questions often, even with the original, detailed recipe out there.

Every brisket that you smoke is a journey unto itself in which every step is filled with uncertainty, choice, and vagary—at least until you get comfortable with piloting this great big barge of meat. It's just one of those things where the investment of time and resources is so great that people are afraid of making mistakes and seek close guidance. That's hard to give when such elemental variables as wood, fire, smoke, and meat are involved, but here is, once again, my attempt to provide as much help in as much detail as possible—with the caveat that the best way to find answers to your questions is to cook a lot of briskets.

We never stop learning and growing—even at Franklin Barbecue. Over the years, I've evolved in my brisket thinking. Not that I've reinvented the beefy wheel or anything, but the technique we practice at the restaurant has shifted a bit and gotten tighter and more precise in certain ways. In fact, as the popularity of barbecue has grown around the country, brisket—which was traditionally a Texas thing—has become more widespread. Many people are looking at solutions for the inconvenient truth about brisket: that the length of time it takes to cook swallows up a day and pushes your levels of endurance and commitment. Today, approaches such as hot 'n' fast brisket, in which the meat is done in six hours as opposed to twelve hours, have become popular in barbecue circles. While I applaud anything that makes people happy, I don't think a brisket that I want to eat can be done in such a short time—at least not one with the qualities I consider to be important: sweetly smoky, peppery, and texturally rich bark; profoundly moist meat whose fat has rendered; a pliable texture that doesn't fall apart in the flat and melts in your mouth in the point; and even cooking throughout the meat.

Our brisket has always come out well, but over the years I've adjusted many of the specifications. I'll take you through them step by step. A number of these tweaks rely on good fire management, something we're all capable of doing if we practice and pay attention.

Basically, the idea with this revised brisket technique is instead of going hotter and quicker at the start, you want to ease into things. You don't have to go too low because a low temperature will make the cook go way too long, and you want to avoid a dirty fire at all costs. But you don't want to jump out of the gates at 275°F either.

The first problem you encounter with a hotter and faster technique—and I'm not even talking about the aforementioned hot 'n' fast approach that starts at 300°F—is that the brisket's edges dry out and moisture puddles up and concentrates in the middle, changing the cooking dynamic. The finesse in cooking a great brisket is in cooking the whole surface evenly because it inherently does not want to cook that way. If you look at a brisket, you'll see one part that's thin and lean and one part that's thick and fatty, and they don't cook at the same rate or have the same needs. The challenge is to accommodate this discrepancy in a way that allows all parts to come out beautifully.

PREPARING THE MEAT

Once you've completed your cooking lists, gather your tools, equipment, and ingredients.

- 1 whole (packer-cut) brisket
- Yellow mustard for slathering
- Coarse salt
- 16-mesh ground black pepper
- Apple cider vinegar for spritzing

Choosing Brisket

We cook around one hundred twenty Creekstone Farms prime-grade briskets every day at the restaurant. These are excellent pieces of meat and, when Creekstone is at its best, there are few operations that can compete. Theirs are well-tended Black Angus cattle that spend all but the last few months of their lives on grass before being finished on corn. I only buy briskets from cattle that have received no growth-promoting hormones. We pay a premium for these, but it's worth it without question—they cook better, taste better, and are happier animals. The cattle are slaughtered humanely in a facility designed by legendary scientist and animal behaviorist Temple Grandin in a way that preserves the integrity of the animal, its meat, and the workers. The brisket is fabricated—cut from the larger side of beef—to precise specifications that Creekstone and I worked on together. When you're cooking as many briskets per day as we do, consistency is paramount.

If you're a home cook who cooks brisket only occasionally, consistency is less important, but you still want to start with a good-quality cut. Evaluate the meat carefully before you cook it and consider its various characteristics. Namely, how fatty is it (intramuscular, subcutaneous, and external)? I'm always looking for as much internal marbling as possible. How was it raised (is it a grass-fed cow from a local farmers' market, which means the meat is likely leaner and tougher with much less fat, or was it finished conventionally at a feedlot)? I prefer grain-finished beef as opposed to grass-fed and grass-finished beef, which can sometimes come out too lean and grassy tasting after a long cook. As always, I recommend that you cook a packer-cut brisket, which is a whole brisket that includes the full muscle—both the point and the flat (see Brisket Terminology, opposite). A brisket in the 12- to 14-pound range is ideal.

Trimming

My trimming method hasn't really changed, but I want to reiterate that trimming is a very important step. It sets you up for success or failure during what is going to be a long cook.

When preparing to trim a whole brisket, take a second to look past its bulky, clumsy form and imagine the sleek, aerodynamic shape that exists inside of it. You want to whittle a Ferrari out of a big, dumb hunk of flesh. Imagine the smoke in the cooker smoothly flowing over and around the

> **BRISKET TERMINOLOGY**
>
> For the record and to get terminology clear, the *point* of the brisket is the thick, fatty half with a raised ridge, and the *flat* is the flat half that thinly tapers off. Also, when I refer to *forward* or *back* in the smoker, toward the smokestack is forward and toward the firebox is back. To me, the smoker is like a locomotive and the air comes in the rear, hits the fire, and pushes forward to the stack. I may be the only person who thinks of it like this, but now you know.

meat—like a car in a wind tunnel in an automobile ad. That's what you want to create here. The rub and the natural moisture of the brisket help to attract smoke, while a well-trimmed, fluid shape promotes even cooking.

I use a thin, slightly curved boning knife to trim because I like the precision and dexterity it provides. I trim more off the brisket than a lot of people do. What I mean is that I'm not afraid to cut away some strips containing a little meat if that's what I need to do to get the right shape. Mostly what I trim is fat, but sometimes there's lean in there. Nothing goes to waste, however; all those scraps go straight to the grinder for sausage. At home, I collect the trimmings and simmer them with water on the stovetop to create beef stock. My exact instructions for trimming a brisket are detailed in *Franklin Barbecue*, so have a look there if you want more information.

Tempering

You don't want to put a cold piece of meat in a hot cooker because the heat dries out the meat before it's thoroughly cooked. Food safety is always a concern, so I'm not telling you to leave a 31°F brisket out on the counter until it comes to room temperature (which would take forever, by the way). But letting it sit on the countertop for a couple of hours helps the meat temper a little, and, with brisket, a little goes a long way during a lengthy cook. (To be clear, it takes four hours for bacteria to begin to replicate after meat hits the temperature danger zone of 41° to 135°F, so I'm not suggesting conditions that will endanger you.)

Applying the Slather and Rub

Once you've got your brisket all nice and trimmed, it's time to get it ready for the cooker. This is a good time to apply a slather. A slather isn't mandatory, but it helps the rub adhere to the surface of the meat. You can use almost anything that wets the surface, from water to vinegar to hot sauce, but I like good ol' French's yellow mustard. Squeeze out just enough to coat the entire surface of the brisket. And while you might think such a strongly and distinctively flavored substance would affect the final flavor of the meat, amazingly, it does not. (Some old-timers swear by mayonnaise.) Perhaps it adds a little savory complexity, but whatever its impact is, you certainly won't recognize the flavor like you do on a ballpark hot dog.

Next, apply the rub. Alongside the requisite one-to-one ratio (by volume, not weight) of salt and pepper, use any flavors you want. The purpose of a rub is twofold. Salt and pepper are critical flavors for brisket. The salt allows you to taste the meat in all of its glory. The pepper basically fuses with the exterior layer of fat to form the bark, which in turn mellows the spiciness of the pepper and creates massive amounts of umami. The other function of a rub is to attract smoke, which it does thanks to its uneven surface. This is why we use coarsely ground pepper. But you can also add anything else you want—cayenne, garlic powder, paprika, or a seasoning mixture, like Lawry's Seasoned Salt. We try out different rubs at the restaurant from time to time. It's all good, so long as you also have plenty of salt and pepper

Firing Up the Smoker

At least 1 hour before you cook, get the offset cooker going. (If you're using a grill to smoke, it should take 15 to 20 minutes to warm up.) You want to have arrived at and held your desired temperature for a good 15 minutes before adding the meat. (This is also a good time to work out the needs of your particular fire, especially, for instance, if you're at an event using a weird smoker and unfamiliar wood.) You and your smoker want to find equilibrium relative to whatever climactic conditions you might be experiencing that day.

In this revised technique, I start off with a lower temperature than I did in the past, aiming for about 260°F to start. So bring your cooker up to 260°F and hold that temperature for at least 15 minutes before putting the meat on. Make sure you have a good coal bed and a clean fire. How can you tell? Take a whiff. If the fire smells good, the meat is probably going to taste good because we taste with our noses. It's always wise to lean into your temps. By that, I mean ease into new temperature levels rather than raising temps too fast, overshooting the mark, and having to scramble to bring them back down.

Also, make sure you put a full container of hot water inside the smoker, as it helps the brisket cook faster and more evenly. I add it when I build the fire.

MEAT'S ON: HOUR 0 TO HOURS 4 TO 5

It's time to put your brisket on the smoker. You want the point facing back toward the firebox, where the smoke is coming from, and the flat facing forward toward the smokestack. On our cookers, the sweet spot is close to the stack. This is where the heat is most even, the airflow most fluid, and where meats tend to cook the best. So we position our briskets as far away from the firebox as possible. If your brisket's flat is really thin, consider angling the cut with the flat closer to the door, where it will theoretically encounter slightly less heat and consequently cook more slowly. Your task now is to simply let the brisket hang out for a few hours. Keep the temperature even and maintain as clean a fire as possible. You can relax during this time, but never stop paying attention.

HOW TO FIT THREE BRISKETS ON A SMALLER SMOKER

If you're cooking on a Franklin Pit or a similarly small cooker and want to squeeze on a third whole brisket, here's what you can try. First, use smaller briskets from the left side of the cow, as their similar shape will allow them to fit together better. Place them at a diagonal and parallel to one another but not touching in the smoke chamber. Place a wedge-shaped piece of wood (hack one off a log) behind the briskets, positioning it with the thin end facing back toward the fire to deflect some of the heat that would otherwise hammer the rearmost brisket. But for the best results, stick to one or two briskets.

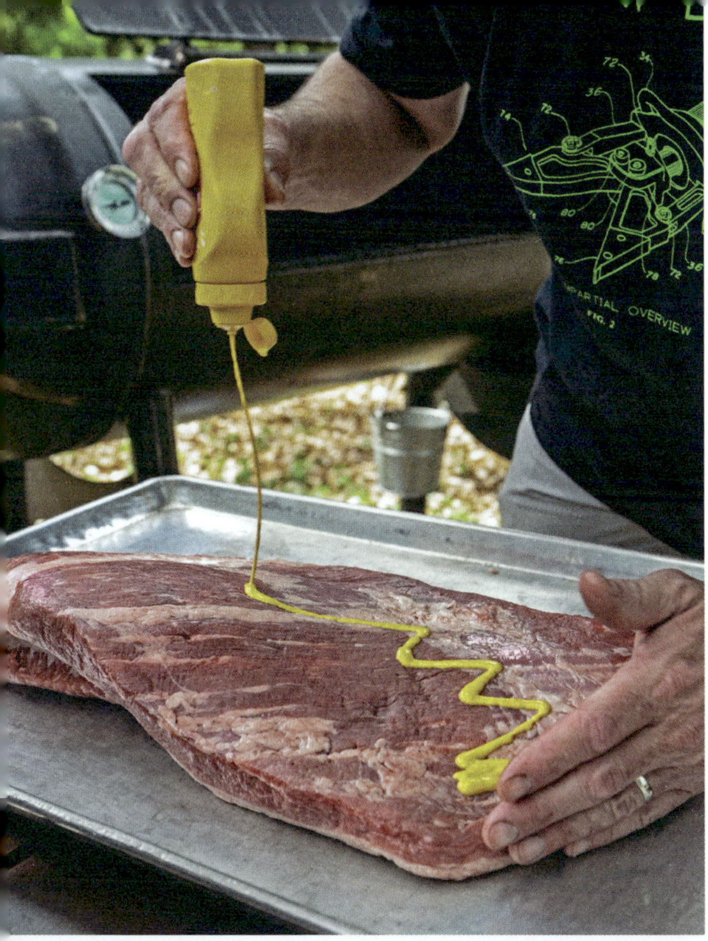
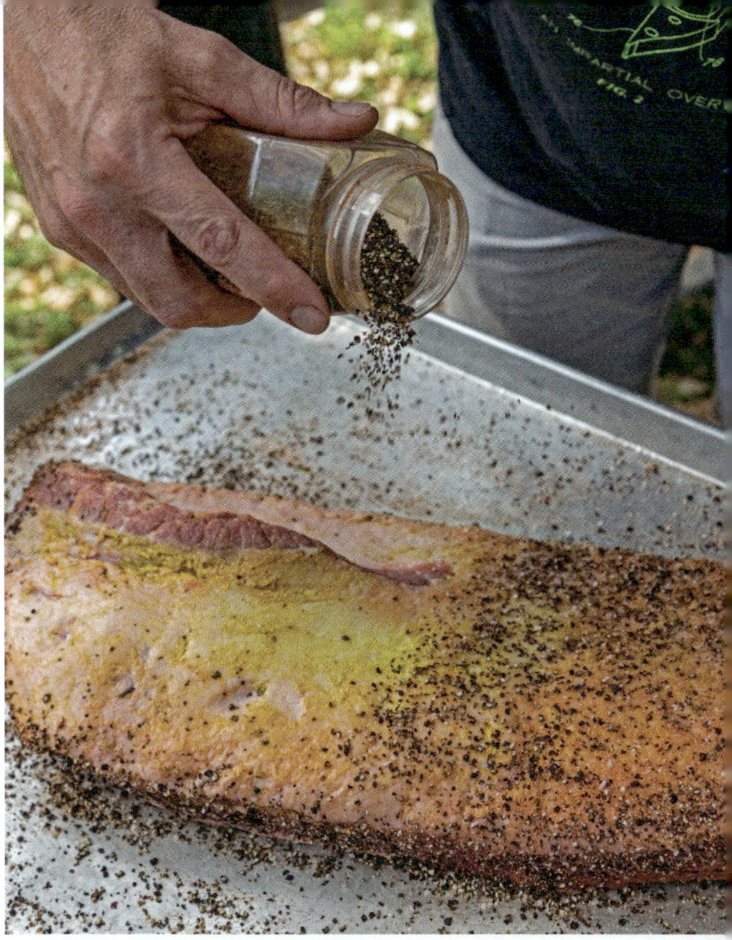
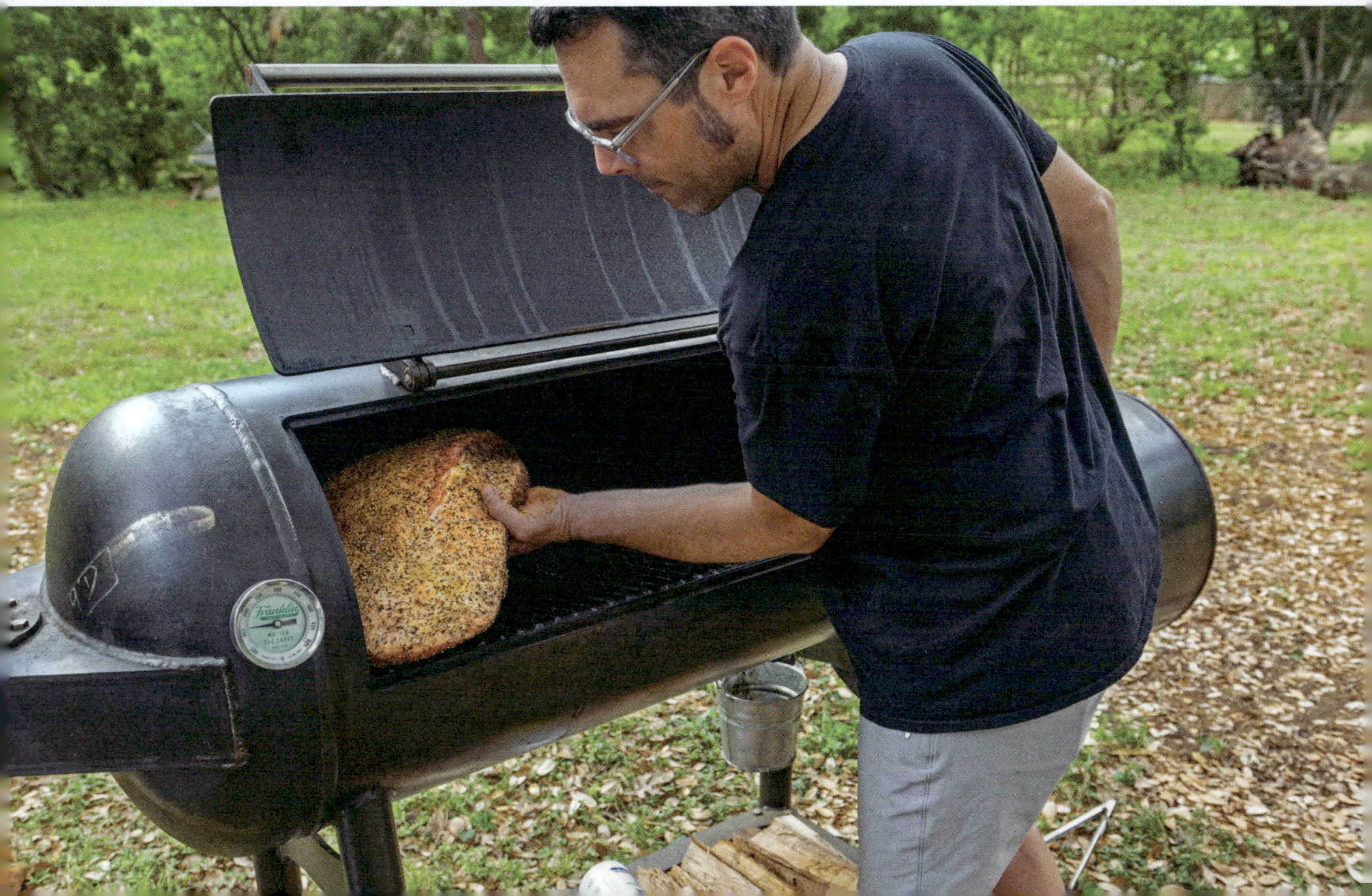

Maintaining Smoker Temps

If you're cooking on a Franklin Pit or another smaller-size cooker, you may find it maddeningly difficult to hold a certain temperature. There is no digital thermostat for you to just "set it and forget it." Don't get discouraged. Indeed, part of the magic of these surprisingly sensitive hunks of steel is the variation in temperature. While small cookers are more sensitive than big ones, this general oscillation of temperature also creates a wide range of compounds in the smoke, adding to the complexity of the brisket.

If you think of your goal as maintaining a temperature range that averages around 260°F, you'll be fine. Concentrate on burning a clean fire, which is determined by the color of the smoke coming out of the stack—mainly avoid anything gray and sooty—and keeping active flames in the firebox. After a while, you will start to get a sense of how much fuel you need in order to maintain certain temperatures. Also, you'll start to feel a rhythm that's like the percussive thud of a speedboat skipping across the waves. Each bump is the burst of heat you get from a new log. As that burst climaxes and begins to fade, add another little piece of wood to keep your boat rising back up again and again.

Cut and split your wood in small pieces (see page 60). If your pieces are too large, they may give your fire a big burst of energy that causes the temperature to spike too high. Smaller pieces allow for more precision, so, if needed, split your mini logs into even smaller pieces. These might feel like matchsticks to you, but feeding the fire small amounts of wood more frequently helps you maintain the pace and manage those gentle, rhythmic ups and downs. (This is true for any meat you cook on a smoker, not just brisket.)

Don't even open the smoker door for a peek during the first 3 hours. Your brisket will just be hanging out, gathering smoke. Between Hours 3 and 4, take a look and get your trigger finger ready to spritz.

Putting on the Spritz

The main reason for spritzing is damage mitigation. That is, you're slowing the drying of the brisket's ends while letting the middle cook. The midsection holds a lot of moisture that is constantly being wicked up and out of the flesh to the surface, where it evaporates. But at this time in the cook, there's more moisture than will evaporate naturally, so it can puddle up. This results in splotchiness on the exterior, which not only looks bad but also inhibits proper bark formation. Spritz on the parts that need cooling down so they keep pace with the midsection.

I use apple cider vinegar to spritz, but you could just as easily use water, wine, or orange juice. Perhaps the vinegar adds a little bit of acidity, though you don't taste it in the outcome. I guess I use vinegar out of habit and convenience because it's already in a spray bottle to use with ribs.

When you spritz, you don't want to cover the whole brisket. The goal is to hit certain parts accurately, so set your spray bottle to a fairly tight stream that expands to a couple of inches in diameter about 2 feet from the nozzle. The point of this precision spraying is to spray the ends, which dry out the soonest, without wetting the interior. Dry spots often occur at the end of both the point and the flat, along the sides if they're starting to harden, and at the crest of the little ridge on top of the point. Just keep these areas wet, creating the evaporation that cools them and slows down their cooking speed.

In this first part of the cook, you allow the brisket to gather smoke. You've prolonged the cook and evened out the surface dehydration through spritzing. It should all be going well. The surface is beginning to dry out as the bark starts to form. The color is changing, going from its original red and white to a deepening brown. The smoke smells sweet. I still think of the brisket as sort of hanging out at this point, but now it's time to really start cooking!

THE FIRST PUSH: HOURS 4 TO 5 TO HOURS 6 TO 7

In this phase, you will ramp up the temperature and gather momentum so that when the brisket hits the stall in Hours 8 to 9 and you eventually wrap, you'll be able to cruise right through. Much of the art of cooking brisket is knowing when to push into the higher register of the desired temperature range as you move up to the next temperature goal. You never want to suddenly jump to a new temperature; you want to ease into it smoothly by pushing.

In the period between Hours 4 and 6, it's time to ramp up the temperature. Add a little extra fuel to increase the size of your fire and create more heat, allowing the cooker to rise to 270° to 275°F. You're moving up in temperature range because smoke accumulation is becoming less important (the brisket got plenty of smoke in the first 3 hours). At this stage, rendering fat is critical, and that happens more efficiently at these higher temperatures. You are not just rendering the external fat that forms the bark, however. What you are really trying to do is melt the intramuscular fat in a measured but decisive way. This takes a long time.

The first push is the prelude to getting ready to wrap. You really want to nail that bark. The pellicle (surface) is starting to dry, and the color continues to darken. Pay attention to the pellicle as it dries; it will begin to look crunchy. Keep your spritz going every 30 to 45 minutes.

As the subcutaneous and internal seam fats start to render, push temperatures as high as you can without doing any damage. I'm talking 280° to 285°F. The sides of the brisket will start to sweat, and the ends will begin to pull up a little. The fat is beginning to melt and drip off the meat, but it's not going to render a ton because we're only pushing a little. Push but don't rush, and keep checking and spritzing every 30 to 45 minutes.

As you move deeper into the cook, make decisions by sight, smell, and observation. Although I offer a loose schedule here, there's no exact timeline, so your senses, not the clock, are your guide. Your goal is to wrap 8 to 9 hours after putting the meat on. So, say, by 6 hours in, you'll be pushing pretty strongly, in part because the brisket is going to hit the stall and you want to gather momentum so the expected stall doesn't become the unsurmountable stall. (I have witnessed this in the past. Briskets that refuse after many hours to get over the hump will, of course, eventually finish, but by then, you will likely have missed your window to serve the food, leaving everyone disappointed and hungry.)

If the thin side of the flat starts to curl up or if it appears like you could just snap it right off, your brisket is well on its way to being burnt. It takes experience to anticipate this, but using your senses to diagnose a problem is a big part of becoming an expert brisket cook.

Wrapping occurs during the stall, so you want to think to yourself, "I need to push these temps, because if I stay at this low temperature, I'm never going to break through the ceiling." Keep your fire revved and your coal bed strong.

THE STALL AND THE WRAP: HOURS 8 TO 9

By Hour 8, the brisket will look almost cooked on the outside, but it still has a fair way to go. You held steady at around 260°F for the first 5 hours or so and then pushed up to around 275°F. Moving into Hour 8, the internal temperature of the brisket is probably 160° to 175°F. As the brisket sweats and moisture begins to pool on top, pay attention to the condition of the bark. It's imperative to keep the bark in good shape. You want it to start to get dry but then bring it right back. As it dries out more and more, you'll notice that the effect of the spritzing lasts a shorter and shorter amount of time. As the spritzing starts to become less effective, you'll begin to get ready to wrap.

The stall occurs when the evaporation of the moisture being squeezed out cools the brisket faster than the fire can heat it. (It's the same dynamic by which our perspiration cools us on a hot day.)

TEMPERATURE CHANGES

> While I offer a rough temperature guide here, we change our cooking temps at the restaurant all the time, and they can vary by as much as 15° to 20°F, depending on the day. This is based on outside temperature and the briskets themselves, which do change in composition throughout the year. Just pay attention to the visual cues that I've given and adjust accordingly. You'll find your way after doing it a few times.

When this excess moisture is finally exhausted—at 7 to 9 hours into the cook—the meat begins its climb in temperature again. That's why this stage is called "the stall" and not "the end" or "the failure."

Leading up to the wrap you want the temperature to be solidly up around 285°F. Because you will be in the cooker spritzing and must open the door to take out the brisket, the smoker's temperature should be able to withstand all the activity.

Only experience can really tell you when it's time to wrap, but you know the brisket has entered the stall when its internal temperature has been hovering in the 160° to 165°F range and the bark is starting to dry out quite a bit. This is a good thing. The strategy here is to allow the bark to get a little bit crunchier than you want it to be, then wrap. Once the brisket is wrapped, the bark will remoisten in the steam of the package and ultimately become perfect.

Ideally, you wrap at the beginning of the latter half of the stall, but you've got a little bit of wiggle room to hover in that area if you need better bark. I like to wrap on the later side. You can sort of ride the wave and let the brisket hang out at a higher temperature to form better bark and then wrap. Or if you're in the stall and your bark is not quite right, you can back off your fire a bit and hang out in the back end of the stall before pushing out. If the temperature starts to go up and you haven't wrapped, you've gone too far. But don't wrap too early either. It's better to wrap on the back side of the stall than on the front side so you get as much bark development as possible before wrapping.

STALL OR NOTHING

Prior to recent times, when, you know, we didn't have science, the stall was the biggest mystery in barbecue. People were avidly watching the internal temperatures of their briskets when the seemingly impossible happened. After hours and hours of being in a hot smoker with its internal temperature gradually rising, the brisket's temperature would suddenly stop going up. Instead, it would flatline or even gradually drop a small amount. Then, apparently defying the ironclad laws of thermodynamics, it would remain this way for hours. It was spooky and added to the allure of briskets.

Naturally, home cooks panicked as this phase persisted. And when people panic, they tend to take dramatic action. Some pulled their briskets off the smoker, and, while the internal temperature might technically be "done" at 160° to 165°F according to USDA standards, when it was cut into, the brisket was anything but ready—the meat still tough as rope. Others built a huge fire to push the brisket out of this torpor, only to have to deal with out-of-control heat when the stall finally broke.

For a long time, even if professional barbecue cooks couldn't explain the evaporative cooling effect that was happening, they knew how to deal with it. And eventually science shined its revealing light inside the dark and smoky cooker and revealed the stall to be an obvious, if counterintuitive, occurrence.

Wrapping serves a few functions: (1) it keeps the brisket from taking on more smoke; (2) it concentrates the heat and discourages evaporation, which aids in breaking through the stall; (3) it helps the brisket retain moisture and fat; and finally, (4) during the endgame, it makes the cooked brisket much easier to handle and keeps the meat tightly cocooned throughout its lengthy resting stage.

Aluminum foil is the most popular wrap. However, I deliberately use butcher paper and have done so pretty much since the beginning. In a lot of ways, Franklin Barbecue has become synonymous with this technique. You can probably surmise some of the differences achieved by each material. Foil seals up the brisket somewhat hermetically, allowing little to no exchange with the outside environment. This locks in moisture but also encourages the meat to steam, which often results in a texture more like pot roast or corned beef and not the supple yet sliceable texture we think is ideal for brisket. (That said, if you don't have much fat to spare in a leaner brisket, foil is the better option.) To me, butcher paper is the ideal median between unwrapped and foil-wrapped. I truly appreciate the rustic nature of an unwrapped brisket, but that old-school method definitely results in meat that's drier to completely dried out and a bark that's more of a crunchy crust. When folded appropriately, butcher paper keeps the brisket tightly swaddled and allows some moisture to exit while retaining enough to keep the meat wonderfully moist.

On a table or countertop near the smoker, lay out the pieces of butcher paper you'll use to wrap the brisket (more details of the wrap are illustrated in *Franklin Barbecue*). There are two crucial points in this step: (1) Use enough paper to fold back over the bottom. That is, you need more than one layer of paper—my process uses three layers—so the bottom doesn't collapse when the package becomes filled with liquid and fat. (2) Wrap very tightly.

Spritzing the paper helps prevent it from taking moisture from the brisket. Wet it with anything you want—water, vinegar, or, better yet, melted fat. (Eventually the whole package will become saturated with fat anyway.) And don't ever wrap on a really cold table, as it will suck some of that hard-earned heat out of the meat.

Use a towel that you don't mind getting dirty to fetch the brisket from the smoker and take it over to your wrapping paper. Fold it quickly yet gently. Make it as tight as you can, then return the package to the smoker.

ENDGAME: HOURS 9 TO 12

With the brisket tightly wrapped in butcher paper, you can really start to push the temperature. Aiming for 300° to 310°F is a great target, but tread lightly because you can do a lot of damage at this point if you push too hard. Confoundingly, you can also mess up a perfectly great cook if you don't push hard enough. (Heck, if you want, you could even take the brisket out of the smoker and finish it in the oven, as temperature is the only important variable at this point. Younger me was firmly against doing this for reasons of orthodoxy, but older me really values a good night's sleep. Let circumstances dictate your actions. If you're having a good time outside and enjoying your fire and company, why not just keep it going?)

From here, you will continue cooking in the temperature range of 300° to 310°F for 3 to 4 hours. How long precisely? This is where it gets tricky because you can't see the meat anymore. If you haven't cooked thousands of briskets, this can be a daunting decision. Even I get rusty sometimes, and the same goes for our cooks at the restaurant. If someone has been off for three days, it often takes a day to get back the proper feel.

You can and should use a digital thermometer to gauge the internal temperature, which will be 175° to 180°F coming out of the stall. That will put you in the range, but it can't be your only metric because, as we learned during the stall, temperature doesn't equal doneness when it comes to brisket. The endgame is a race to break down the brisket's tough, fibrous collagen into soft, delicious gelatin before all the fat has been rendered out.

You want to try to take the brisket off the cooker in 12 hours. So if you wrapped at 8 to 8½ hours, you have 2 to 3 hours left to achieve the desired texture. This is subjective and requires experience, but eventually you will get a feel for how the fibers are breaking down and the fat is rendering.

Give the brisket a gentle little prod by placing a towel around the package and picking it up with your thumbs on top and your fingertips underneath. Press lightly with your fingers. Is it starting to feel tender or is it still hard as a rock? If it's the latter, increase the temperature a bit because you may be cooking too slowly. If you've fallen behind schedule (and are the gambling type), you could push your temperature to 325°F, but I would never go past that. You should only raise your temperature that high if you have enough moisture and fat in the package to keep the brisket from drying out (which you might surmise if you wrapped really early, as it wouldn't have evaporated as much). If you've got the moisture, you can push really hard. If it's not there, lay off and keep your temperature around 300°F, and let it run its course. If the brisket feels tender with a few tougher spots, you still have a little way to go. Check frequently and you'll feel those areas of tautness begin to recede. If the brisket is extremely pliant, you are getting close.

The Pull

One thing to keep in mind during the brisket's endgame—and when planning the whole cook—is that resting the brisket is part of the cooking process and pulling it off the heat is only done when you have a plan for its carryover. The heat that the brisket has accumulated for all these hours will carry over and continue the cooking even after you've pulled it. This is not a minor, post-cook situation that you can pay attention to by choice. You have to think about it and plan for it, as the carryover affects your decision on when to pull the brisket.

What are the climactic conditions of the brisket's resting place? Is it a hot summer day or a cold winter evening? Are you in the sun or in the shade? You must consider questions like these when you look into the future and try to guess how your brisket is going to carry over. If you think it has a lot of momentum—say, if you finished really hot at 315° to 325°F—pull it early to compensate. If it's going to begin a rapid cooldown—if it's smaller or finished at a lower temperature—let it go farther down the path in the smoker.

At some point, the brisket must come off the heat. This is when you discover whether you set yourself up for success on the front end and had enough fat render in a well-insulated package that didn't dry out the edges too badly. Doneness typically begins to occur when the internal temperature of the brisket is in the low range of 200°F. In *Franklin Barbecue*, I suggested that 203°F was my magic number. Today, I'll take anything up to 208°F or even 210°F in concert with the textural feel of the brisket as described previously.

To take the temperature of the brisket, pinch the stem of a digital thermometer between your thumb and a finger 1 to 1¼ inches from the tip (to ensure you don't puncture the bottom). Insert the thermometer through the wrap at a perpendicular angle into the middle height of the center of the brisket, as this is the last part to get tender. Or go in through the side, halfway up, and be sure you don't let any liquid spill out.

To pull the brisket, pick it up and set it on a baking sheet. You might want to put a little towel over it if, say, you're outdoors and the day is chilly or windy and you want to slow down the cooling. Keep it wrapped; you never unwrap a brisket until just before you're ready to serve it.

Rest in Peace

There's an art and a process to holding a brisket. (I once spoke at Texas A&M for an hour and a half just on holding, which is almost as long as you might hold a brisket that you've just cooked!) Many people cook their brisket well before they serve it because you never know how long it's going to take and you should always include an hour or two of wiggle room.

Once you've pulled the brisket, plan to let it rest for up to 3 hours in a warmish, room temperature environment. This span will vary depending on when you want to eat. Do not rush your brisket into a cooler or ice chest, as many people advocate. Most coolers have insulation, which might encourage the internal temperature of the brisket to climb too high, especially if it is large and has a lot of momentum or if you're resting several briskets next to one another. And definitely don't put your brisket directly into a warming oven for the same reason.

Use your digital thermometer to measure the internal temperature occasionally and get a sense of the brisket's rate of cooling. Just as you gauged the carryover potential while deciding when to pull the brisket, now you want to gauge where the internal temperature will settle down. The technique for checking temperature during rest is a little different from the method you used to determine the pull. Using the same hole in the butcher paper, test the middle of the brisket, then pull the thermometer out of the meat but not out of the package. Reinsert the thermometer and angle the probe to the left and then to the right to measure the temperature of both the flat and the point.

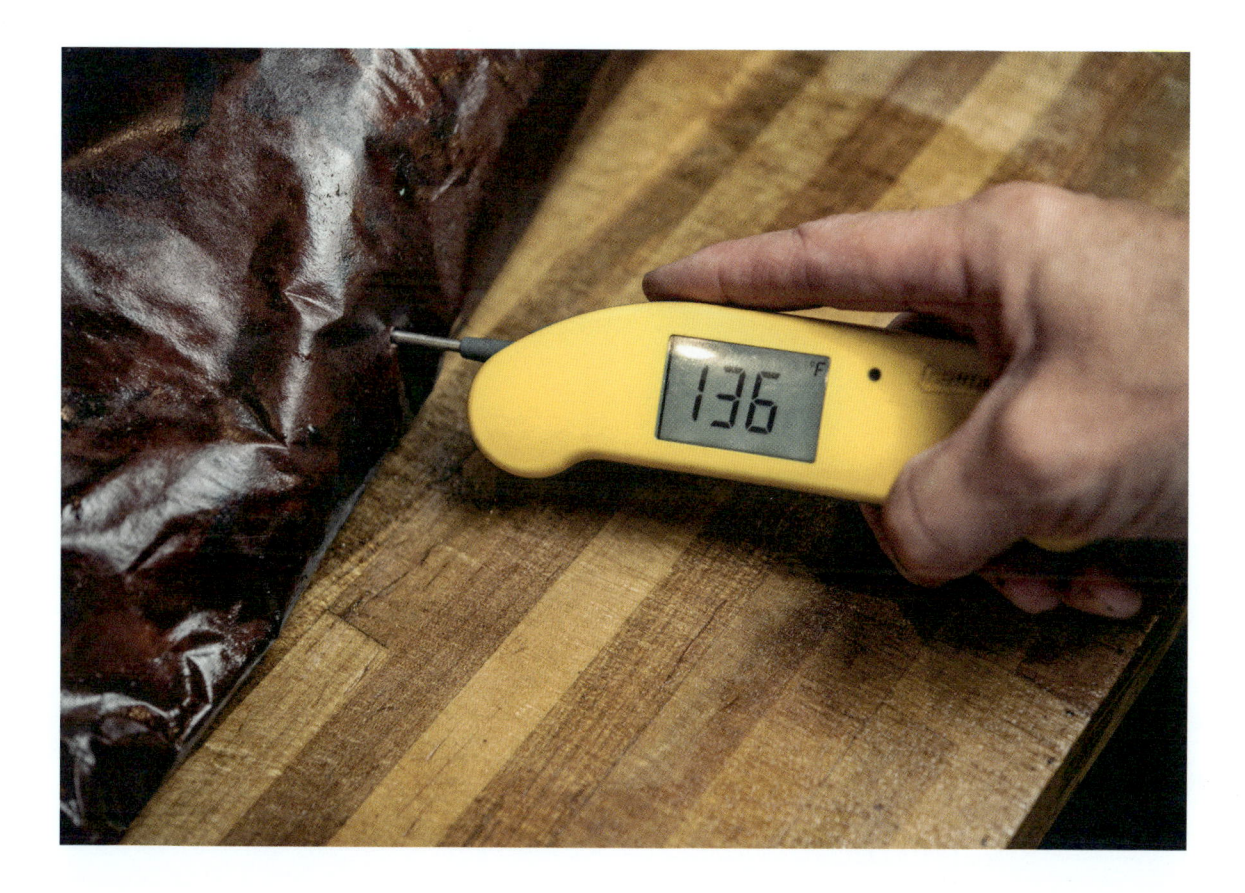

Monitor these temperatures. You are looking for something in the range of 140° to 150°F. If the temperature is descending really fast (go by instinct here, but it should descend quite gradually), you may want to put the brisket into a 140°F oven soon so it lands gradually, like an airplane. (Most ovens only go as low as 175°F, but you can finesse it by turning the oven on and off, much like you managed the heat when adding wood to the smoker. Bread proofing boxes also work well.) But if it's slowly cruising along on its descent, you can probably let it be until it gets much closer to 140°F. You just have to get a feel for it. You want to let it mellow and cool. The fats are still rendering, the collagen is still converting, and the muscles are still pushing out moisture. Once the brisket peaks and the temperature starts to descend, it relaxes. It reabsorbs some moisture and settles down while the flavors continue to meld.

When the brisket is in the range of 140°F, you can open and serve it or, if you want to hold it longer, put it into a 140°F oven for up to 2 hours. At this point, the brisket won't get any better, so serve it as soon as you can.

CARVING AND SERVING

Carving your brisket at any temperature warmer than 150°F will result in you burning your hand and the brisket falling apart. The meat pulls itself together while cooling and is much more pleasant to eat when you can cut full slices. (Also, please do not hold up a chunk of meat and squeeze out the juices to impress your friends. That only ruins what you worked so hard to cook!)

In brief, my method of carving brisket evolved out of the imperative to always cut across the grain. The trouble with carving a brisket all in one direction is that the point and the flat have differently oriented grains. So first I cut the brisket in half across the middle, right where the flat and the point meet, which you can easily determine because the point starts to bulge at that spot.

- To slice the flat: First, cut off the pointy tip. It's mostly bark and might be crispy, but it's usually delicious and you can slice it in half into two little nibbles. Then, making ¼-inch-thick slices—each against the grain with the same amount of fat, meat, and bark—begin to fan out the slices so you arrive uniformly at the horizontal bias where you first split the brisket.

- To slice the point: First, cut the whole thing in half lengthwise. Cut the leaner, tighter section against the grain into even fanned slices ⅜-inch thick. The other side isn't as servable because of all the fat. You might get a couple of slices of meat off of it, but we don't serve the rest to guests. It's very, very fatty. You can save that meat to make into stock, add to the beans recipe in *Franklin Barbecue*, give to your dog, or whatever you want.

There are lots of details and photographs of my carving method in *Franklin Barbecue*, so check that out if you want to learn more. Enjoy!

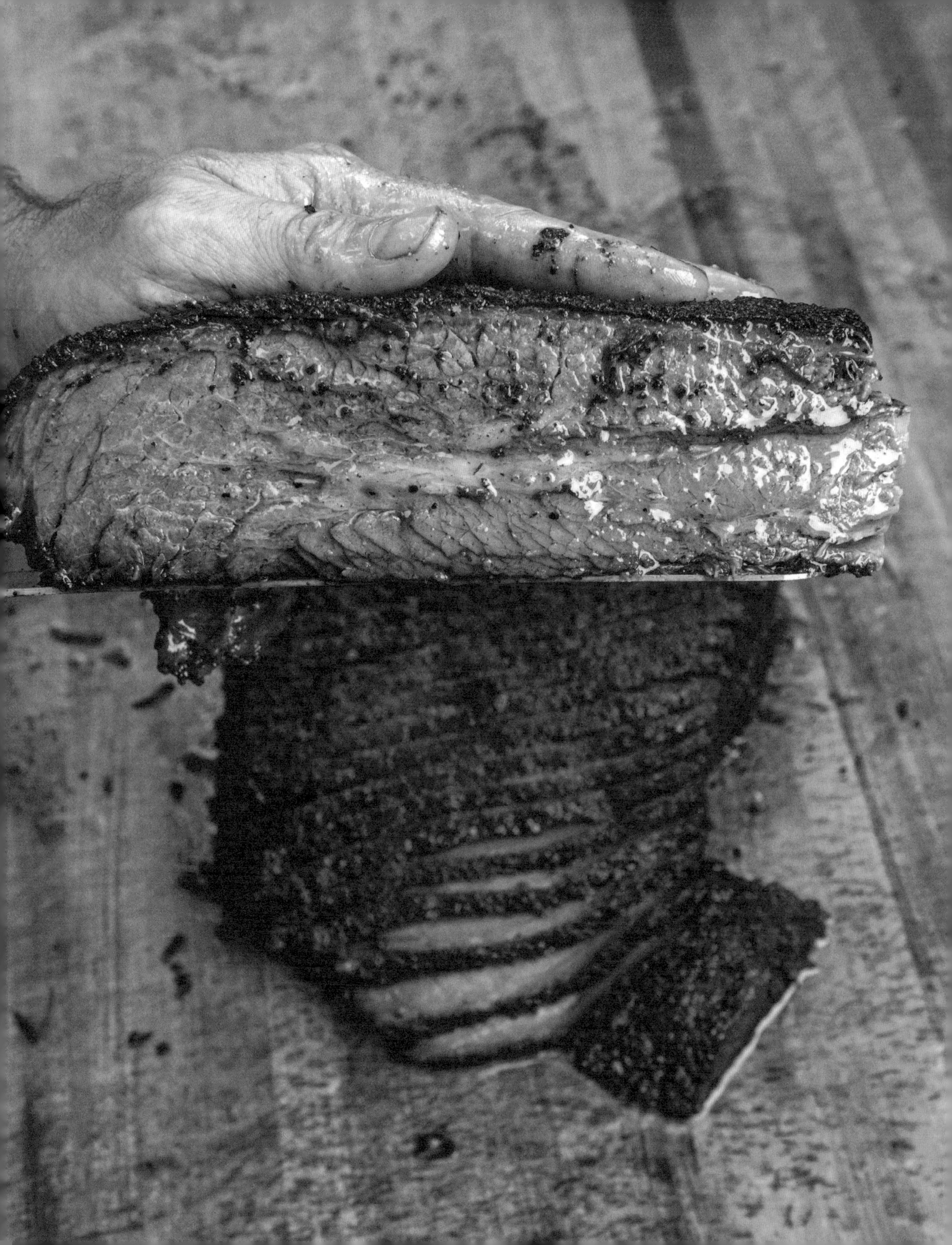

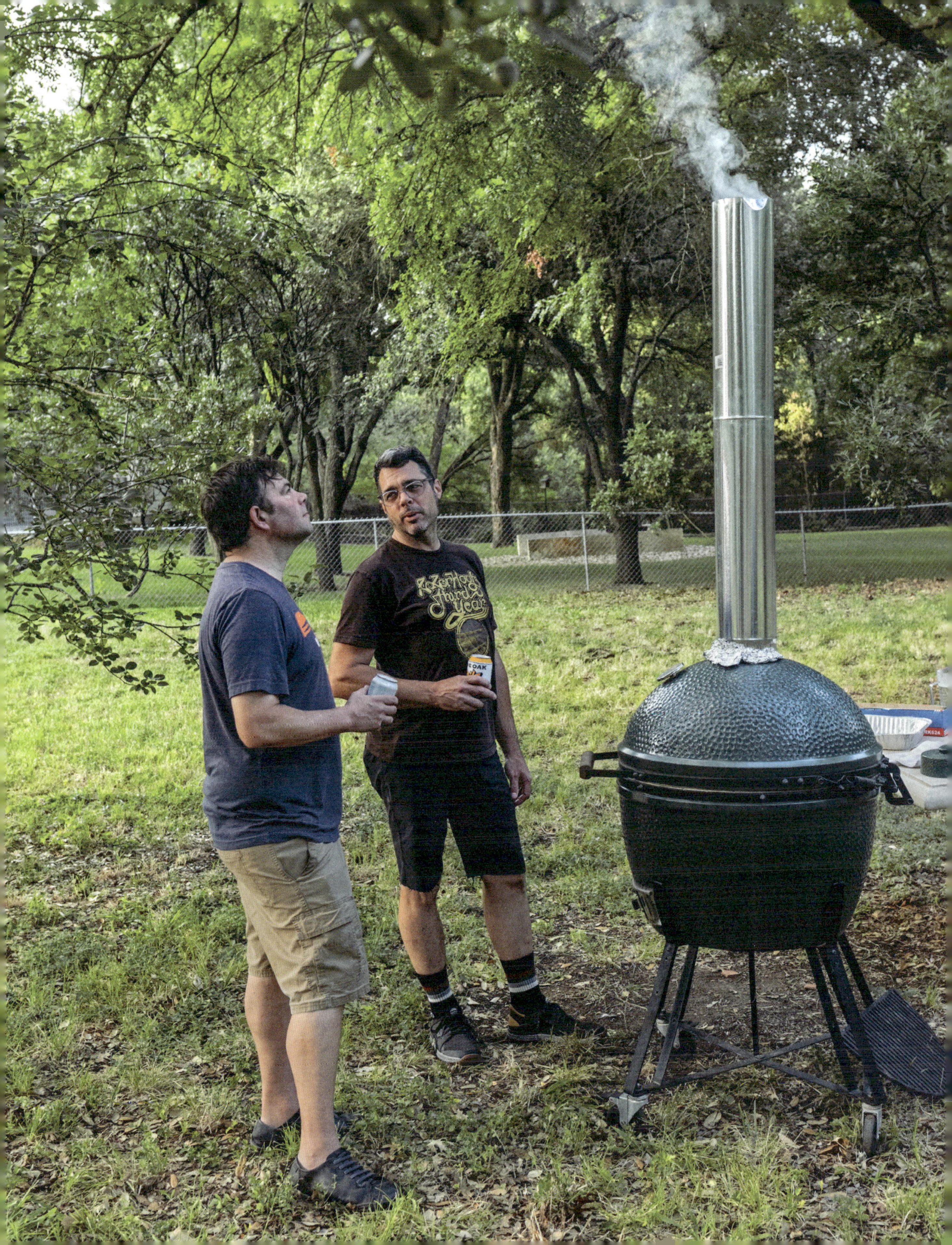

BIG GREEN EGG BRISKET

Forgive me if I vent a little. Or am I gushing? I'm honestly not sure. The question of whether or not you can produce great brisket on a Big Green Egg (BGE) has been a preoccupation of mine for a very long time. And in many ways, this question is a microcosm of my relationship with the BGE in full: I respect the heck out of it—and I truly admire and appreciate the company and the people who work there. I relish the quality of a BGE's every detail, just as I respect the people who sing its praises and are so enthusiastic about using it. And yet, I don't quite know how to get the most out of it for the way that I like to cook.

Allow me to explain. Many people have told me that they do great smoked brisket on the BGE. I've always been a bit baffled by that claim because the smoking dynamic of the BGE is so different from the offset cooker that I deem essential for making classic Central Texas BBQ. Yes, the BGE is a powerhouse and a revelation when it comes to maintaining stable temperatures, which is indeed an important aspect of smoking brisket. But the nature of the BGE's main heat source (charcoal, not burning wood), the composition of its smoke (made of smoldering, not burning, wood), and the difference in airflow (not as violently convective as an offset) are so different that I wondered how it could be done.

Over the years, I have questioned and conversed on the topic of brisket with every BGE diehard that I've met. To a one, they maintain that not only can it be done but it turns out great. I like people, and I trust (many of) them, so, while deep inside my bones I had my doubts, I also had faith in their virtue and have thus continued to exist in a state of belief that true Central Texas brisket can be done in a BGE.

Now, after many attempts and lots of pondering, I share with you my results. Also, let's remember that an attempt at brisket is not like attempting to grill a steak. We're talking a lot of hours here. It takes *work*. Cutting to the chase: Good brisket is indeed possible on the BGE, but it's not a Franklin brisket or even necessarily a classic Central Texas–style brisket. It's a BGE brisket, and that's not a bad thing. It has good flavor and a classic texture, but it doesn't taste or feel exactly the same as it does from an offset.

Following is the technique that I arrived at, which involves gentle modifications of the BGE to make it function more like a powerful smoker than a stable outdoor oven and grill. I won't go into as much detail as I did in The Ultimate Brisket (page 179) because there's a lot of crossover between the two. If you've got a BGE and want to try this, I suggest you read that recipe and sort of fuse the two in your mind. I've just presented the BGE highlights here.

THE MODS

For these modifications, I wanted to find simple solutions that could be accomplished easily and affordably with a visit to your local hardware store.

One thing that I have thought about for years and even suggested to a number of people but never tried myself is to attach a smokestack to the top of a BGE. This basic mod is meant to increase the draw of air through the egg and get fresher smoke pulling through as fast as possible. To do this, I bought and connected together two pieces of inexpensive galvanized-steel duct pipe, each six inches in diameter and two feet long, that I found in the HVAC section of my local hardware store. The top vent of my BGE was a bit smaller in diameter than the pipes, so I made a ring of crumpled aluminum foil and wrapped it around the interior of the pipe to get a tight fit. After the coals had started and were burning well, this makeshift stack helped the draw quite a bit. The only downside is that you have to take it off every time you open the lid. If I'd had more time and desire, I would have figured out how to attach it more permanently. But if you don't open the lid too often, it's not that inconvenient to just remove the stack and replace it after you've closed the lid.

My second mod was to use an angle grinder with a masonry blade to cut a crescent-shaped piece out of the smoke deflector plate—BGE calls it the convEGGtor plate—to give me a place to drop fresh wood chunks and/or hot wood coals into the egg. This is easier to do than it sounds and provided the access to the coals that I wanted. (In general, I think it's a handy modification—it doesn't change the internal dynamics very much and gives me a place to add wood and coals for longer smokes, no matter what I'm cooking. Shortly after I cut the plate, I cooked pizzas on the egg, and it was fine. Another solution is to buy two convEGGtor plates, one to modify and the other to leave as is.)

My final adaptation was to place three firebricks on top of the smoke deflector plate and then a half grate on top of the bricks. This was to get the brisket up a little higher in the cook chamber, where I hoped it would find more top heat to balance out the intensity of the heat from below, since the coals are located directly underneath the brisket. Also, hopefully the smoke would swirl and focus a little more before shooting up through the stack. Plus, the raised grate gave me a space to slide a drip pan under the meat.

With this setup, I burned charcoal and several post oak wood chunks in the bottom, as one would normally do to smoke something on the BGE. The only other casual technique that I employed was to prop the lid open slightly by sliding a pair of tongs in. Even with the lid slightly ajar, smoke did not escape through that opening, instead continuing strongly through the smokestack. The bit of extra air intake through the lid seemed to clean up the fire a fair bit and make for better-quality smoke.

It's important to measure the temperature of a BGE independently at grate level. The installed thermometer reads up at the top of the chamber, and I've often found it to be as much as 20° to 30°F higher than what I measure at grate level.

THE METHOD

With these mods in mind, you can, for the most part, follow The Ultimate Brisket recipe. All the basic temperatures and times will vary depending on the size and fat content of your brisket anyway.

Using charcoal and wood chunks, get the BGE fired up to 260°F (this is actually easier to do than in an offset). Put your brisket on at this temperature and let it ride for about 3 hours. You'll have to open the lid every 30 minutes or so to refresh the wood and coals. To have hot coals ready to put in, keep a chimney going next to the egg. When you take a few coals out of the chimney, dump fresh ones into it to keep it going. Now is when a side fire would also be helpful. You could just keep adding fresh coals.

The BGE is good at conserving moisture. However, if you smell fat starting to burn, feel free to add water to the drip pan.

After 3 to 4 hours, push the temperature up to 275°F or so and begin spritzing any edges where you see the bark drying out.

After 6 hours, turn the brisket because the bottom side gets hotter than the top side from the smoke deflector plate being heated directly from the coals. Now bump the temperature into the range of 285° to 290°F.

After about 8 hours, when the internal temperature is in the 160° to 165°F range, you should be entering the stall, and it's time to think about wrapping in butcher paper. Wrap the brisket and return it to the smoker.

At this point, if the brisket has a good deal of fat, you can raise the temperature to around 300°F. But if you're not confident that you have a really well-marbled piece, keep the temp at 285°F to be on the safe side. You could even put the brisket in the oven now if you don't feel like managing the fire anymore. But it's very easy to maintain temperature in a BGE, so you might as well leave it in. You can also remove the stack because the process is just about baking from now on.

Follow the instructions in The Ultimate Brisket recipe to measure the temperature properly and pull the brisket from the heat when the internal temp is between 205° and 208°F. Let the brisket rest until it cools to the 140°F range before you slice and serve it.

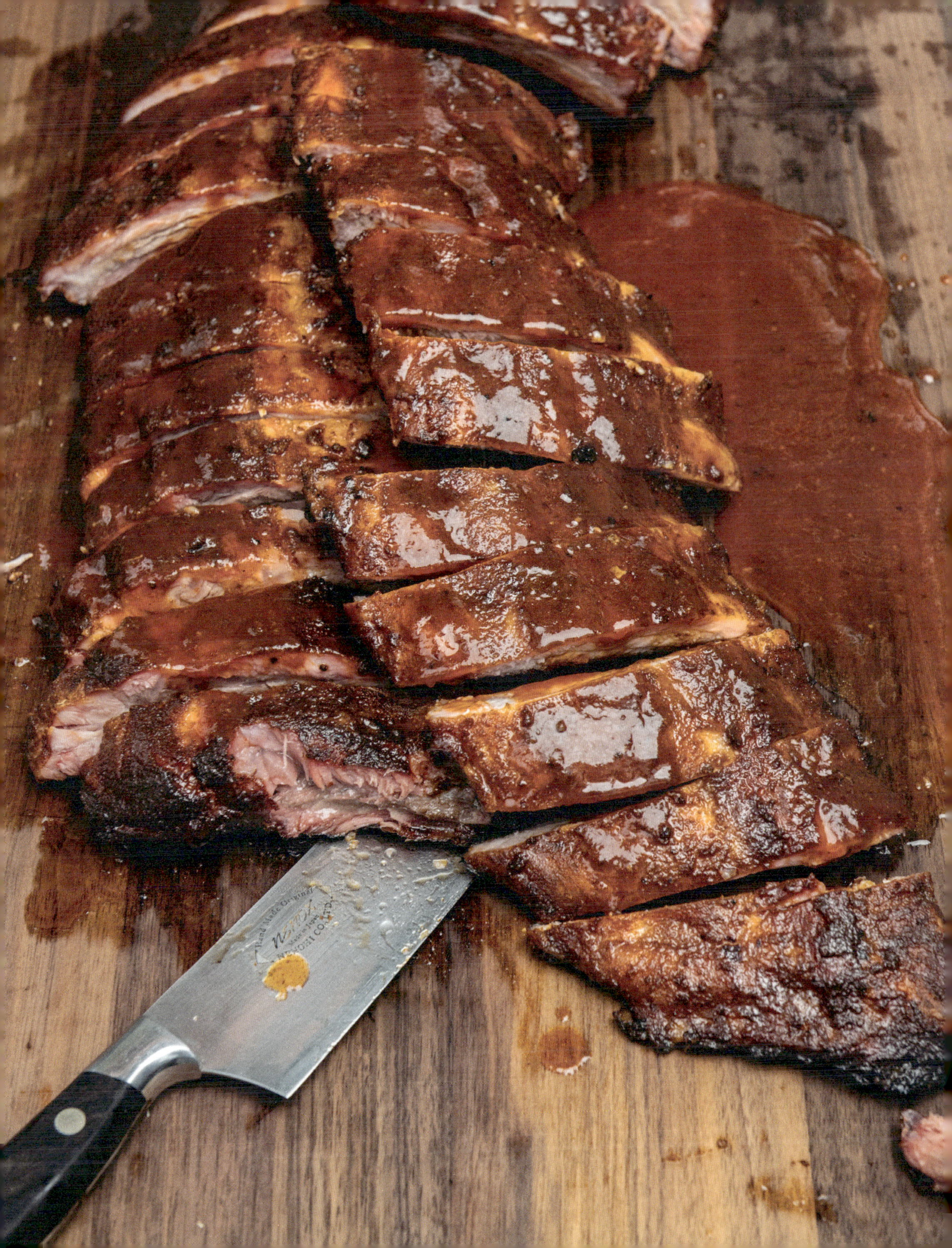

BABY BACK RIBS

Many people associate Texas barbecue solely with beef, but there's a large pork culture here too. At the restaurant, we've always served pulled pork, and pork ribs are one of our most popular items. But those are spareribs, which are different from the ubiquitous baby back ribs. I detail our sparerib method in *Franklin Barbecue*, but baby backs require a somewhat different method.

First and most important, baby back ribs do not come from baby pigs . . . nor does "baby got back." They're called *baby* because they're smaller than spareribs, even though they come from the same part of the rib cage. Baby backs are cut from the rib bones at the top of the pig near the backbone, where the bones have more of an arc. Cut farther down the bone, spareribs are bigger, straighter, more marbled, and meatier, which is why we favor them at the restaurant.

Because of their popularity, baby backs tend to be a bit more expensive than spareribs. A rack of baby backs weighs in the range of two pounds, half of which is bone. The other, meaty half can often be demolished by one person in a single sitting, making them a nice and tidy order. People love baby backs for their toothsomeness—when they offer a little resistance to the front teeth. (But that chewiness also makes me wonder if they've had ones that are properly tender.)

In general, the meat of baby backs is leaner than sparerib meat, which affects how they are cooked. I advocate going a bit hotter and faster than with spareribs because of this leanness. You don't want to exhaust the fat that baby backs do have over a long cook.

It's quite common to wrap baby backs tightly in aluminum foil. However, I stumbled on a technique of partial wrapping, and I like it. You make a foil boat to steam the underside while drying out the meaty top. The opening in the foil allows some of the liquid to evaporate, but enough moisture is retained to achieve optimum tenderness. The boat also allows the top to get perfectly colored without the whole rack drying out. The goal is for the meat to be plenty tender without completely falling apart. In other words, it should be resistant enough that your teeth still have something to do.

Cook time: 4 to 5 hours

Serves 4

- Two 2-pound racks baby back ribs
- Kosher salt
- BBQ Spice Rub (page 112) or your favorite rub
- Apple cider vinegar for spritzing
- 1 cup Rye BBQ Sauce (page 122) or your favorite BBQ sauce, warmed

Lay the rib racks, membrane-side up, on a large baking sheet. Salt the membrane side and then add the rub. Flip the racks and spread the rub on the meat side. Lightly spritz the vinegar over the rub on the meat side. Let the racks sit while you get your fire going in the smoker.

Fill a pan with water and place it in the cooker. Bring the temperature to around 300°F to start. Place the racks, meat-side up and perpendicular to the door, in the cook chamber close to the smokestack. Spritz the racks frequently with the vinegar to keep the surface moist but not too wet.

After about 2 hours, the ribs should be taking on a nice, tawny mahogany color. Now it's time to prepare the aluminum-foil wrap. Tear off two pieces of heavy-duty foil each 16 inches long and lay them on a table. Pour about ¼ cup of the warm sauce onto each piece of foil, extending it along the center. Using tongs, transfer each rib rack to a piece of foil, placing it on top of the sauce. Bring up the sides of the foil and wrap them tightly around the edges of the ribs, leaving the crest of the meat (a strip about ½ inch wide down the center of the rack) exposed. Make sure the package is tightly secured.

Spritz the crest of the meat with vinegar and then coat with the remaining sauce, dividing it evenly. Return the racks to the cooker and raise the temperature to 310°F. Cook for up to 2 hours more, with the meat exposed and spritzing if needed, until the ribs start to feel done. To test, using a toothpick, poke the meat side between the bones; if the toothpick slides in and out with ease, the ribs are tender and done.

Pull the two rack boats from the cooker and let the racks rest, still in their boats, until cool enough to handle. Slice between the ribs and transfer to a platter. Drizzle with the beautiful sauce in the bottom of the foil boats. Serve immediately.

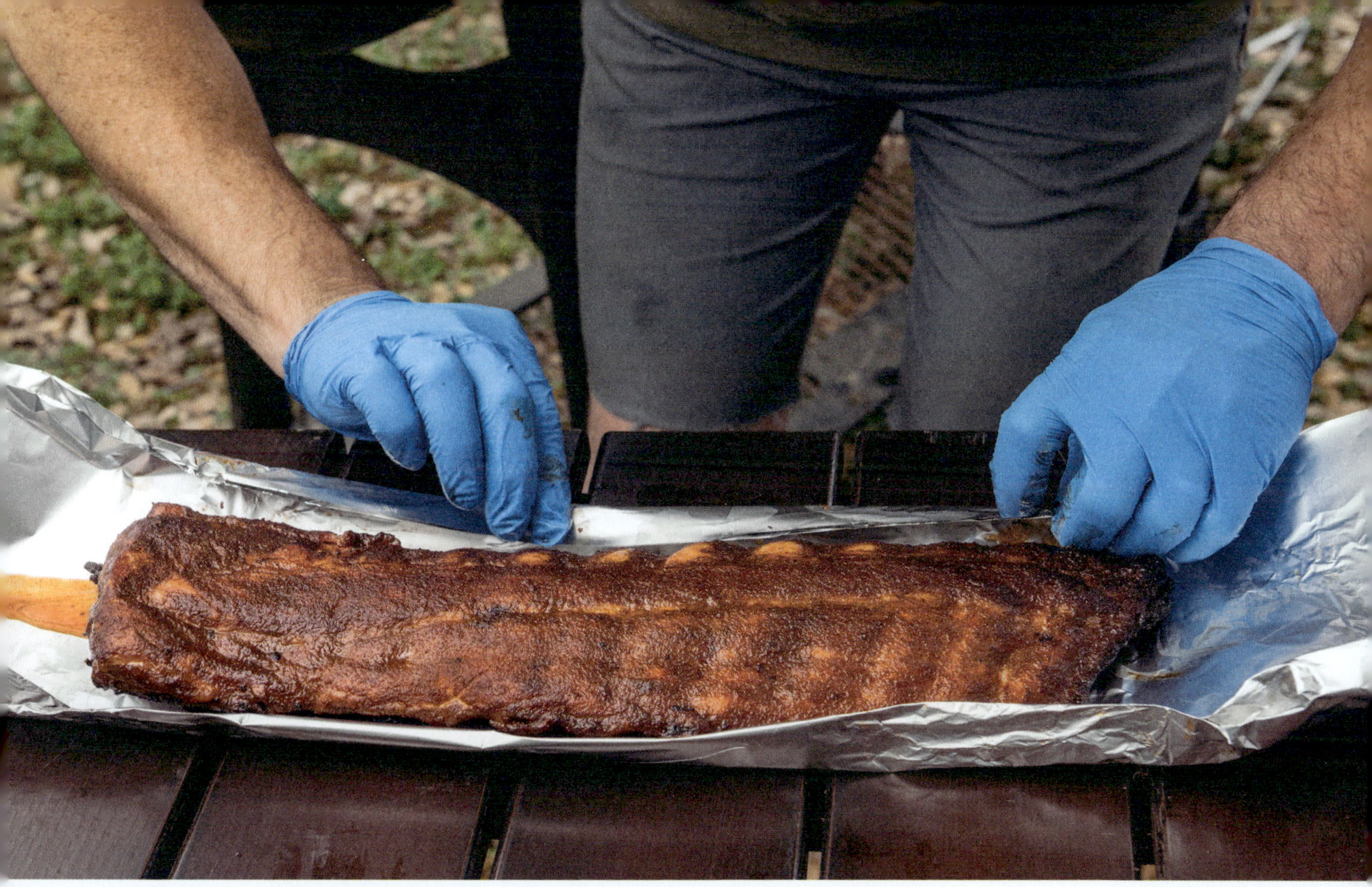
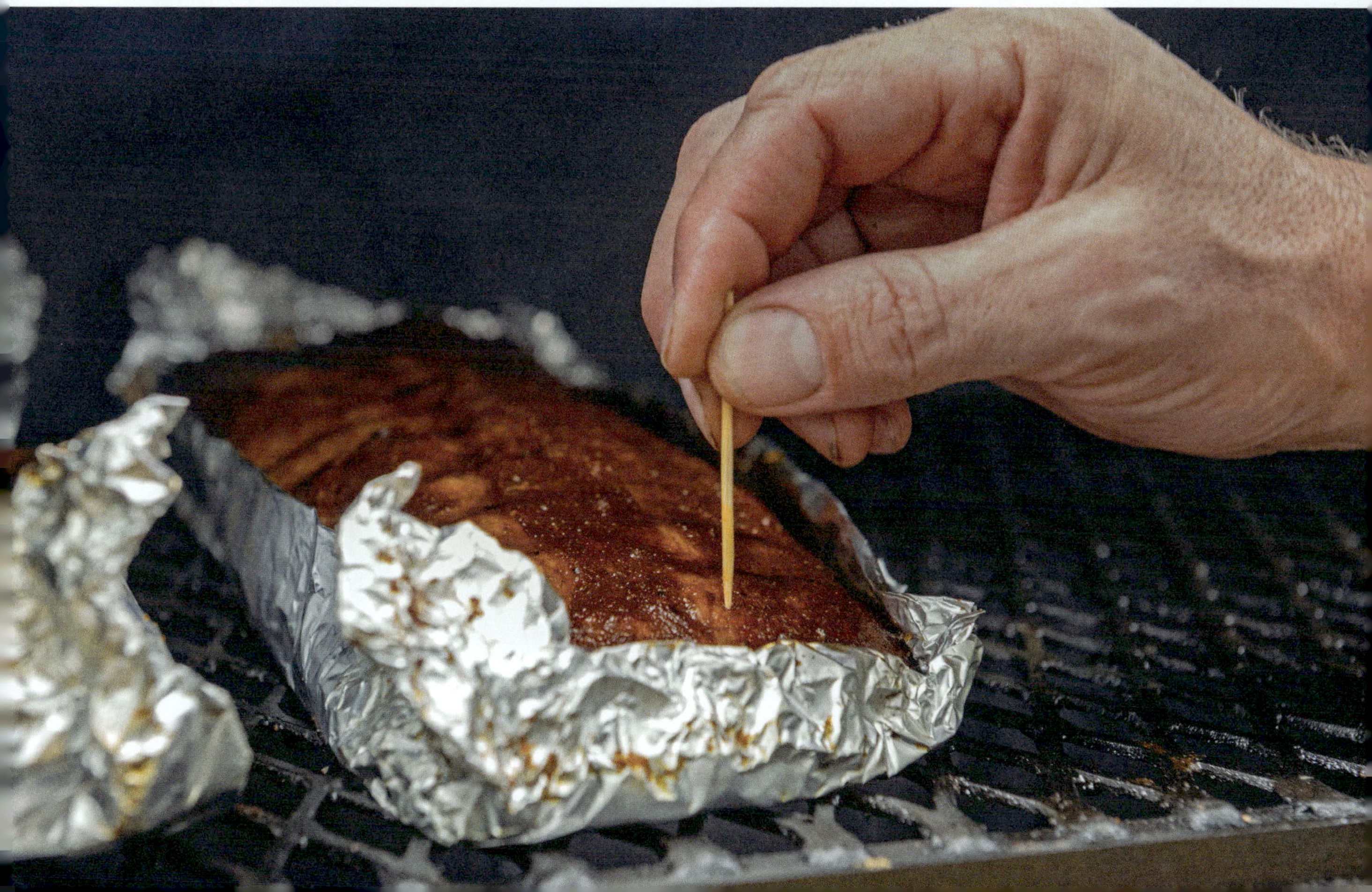

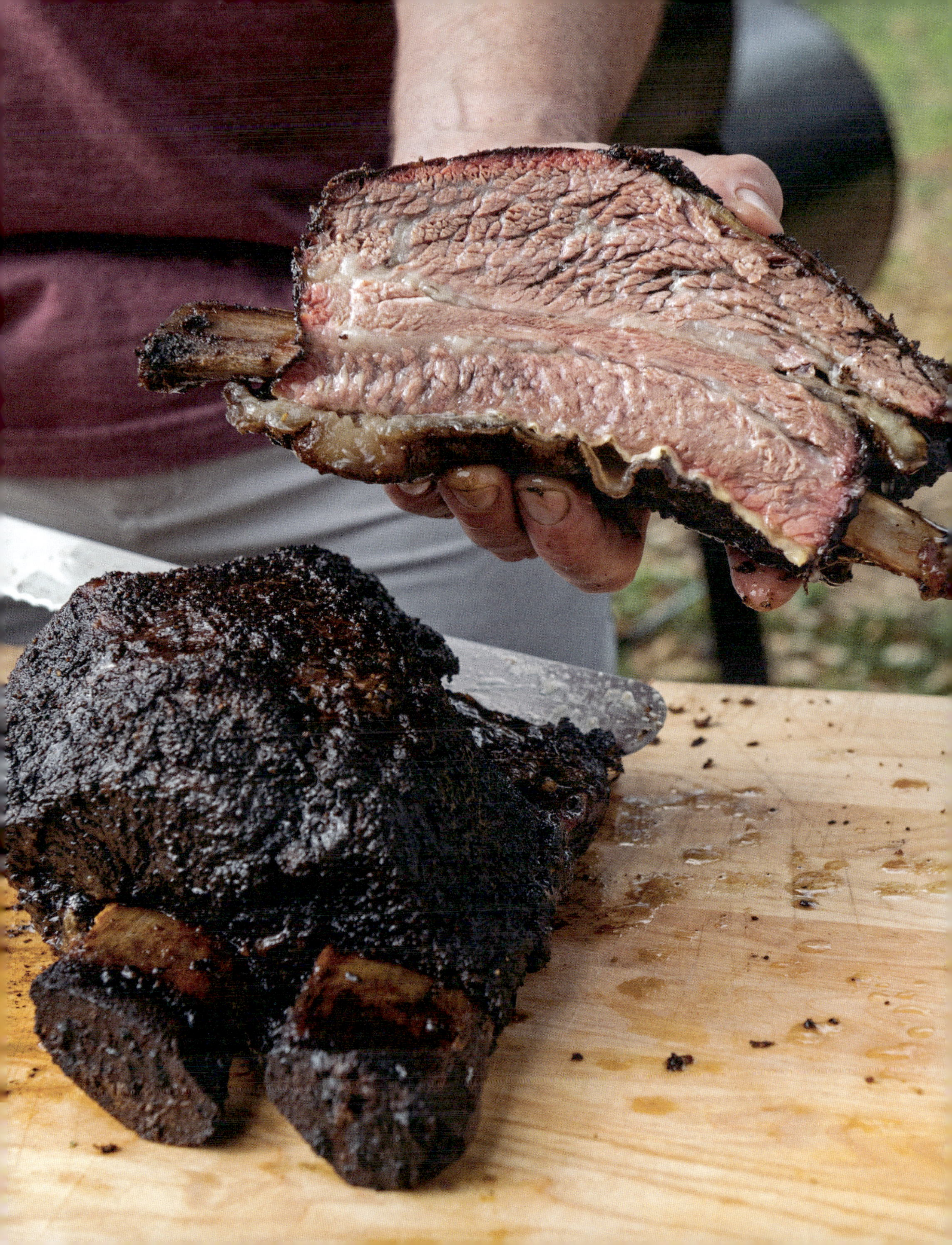

BEEF RIB

For some aficionados, the beef rib is the Texas barbecue pièce de résistance—yes, even over brisket—and I may be one of those people. In fact, the beef rib is probably the source of my favorite single bite in all of barbecue. From a rib that's been off the pit for just a little while and is still pretty darn hot, grab one of the top-front corners of the meat with your fingers and pull a little to loosen it. Continue to pull, twisting, and draw out the tender meat like a core sample. If you can slide out all the fibers of that little string in one piece, you have an excellent beef rib. It's so flippin' good!

On the whole, beef ribs are impressive and indulgent—big, solid, and on the bone. We use three-bone plate ribs cut from low on the rib cage, which provides a nice, thick bone that looks great. What exactly are the plate ribs? On a cow, part of the brisket muscle reaches underneath the rib cage and terminates between ribs five and six. For our beef ribs, we use the cuts from the next three ribs—six, seven, and eight. They're just the right size and come from the same animals that supply our briskets. If you can, get your plate ribs fresh, never frozen.

I like to do a slather on ribs because they're typically a lot drier than brisket once they are removed from their plastic wrapping (if that's how they came). I use a standard commercial hot sauce, such as Crystal Hot Sauce. You might think this flavor would be too intense, but, as with all slathers, by the time the rib is cooked, there's so much fatty richness and smoke that you can't taste the slather. My hope is that the additional acidity helps the rib taste just a tad more balanced. Ribs are so dense and rich that they can take a lot of seasoning. For the rub, I use our BBQ Spice Rub (page 112) or Lawry's Seasoned Salt mixed with freshly ground black pepper and kosher salt. Tallow—which you can render yourself from beef fat, buy from a good butcher or online, or simply save from a brisket cook—forms the basis of the mop, as it protects and drenches the gorgeous rib meat at the same time.

Be aware that this is an incredibly rich dish, and most people can only eat a few bites before moving on to less unctuous fare. At least that's how it is for me, so I don't center a meal around a beef rib. Instead, I offer it as a delectable bite alongside other meats.

A beef rib is easy to cook, and I have a method that I like for optimal deliciousness. At the restaurant, we do beef ribs only on Saturday and Sunday, billing them a weekend special. Unlike brisket, beef ribs never get wrapped and take about eight hours in the smoker. This is not exactly how we do them at the restaurant because that process is a bit more elaborate, but it makes maybe the best bite of rib I've ever had, so enjoy.

Cook time: 8 hours

Serves 6

- One 4-pound three-bone beef plate rib
- Crystal Hot Sauce or your favorite hot sauce for slathering
- BBQ Spice Rub (page 112) or your favorite rub
- Apple cider vinegar for spritzing

Tallow Mop
- 1 cup / 200g tallow (rendered beef fat)
- 1 cup / 240g apple cider vinegar
- ½ yellow onion, chopped
- 16 garlic cloves, crushed
- Few dashes Crystal Hot Sauce or your favorite hot sauce
- 1 squirt yellow mustard

Slather the entire rib with hot sauce, then lay it, bone-membrane-side up, on a baking sheet or sheet of aluminum foil. Apply the rub to the membrane side and then flip the rib and sprinkle additional rub on the top and sides. Let the rib sit while you get your fire going in the smoker.

Fill a pan with hot water and place it in the cooker. Bring the temperature to around 300°F to start. We start out hot because the amount of fat and bone mass can take the extra heat. Place the rib, meat-side up, in the cook chamber and let it rip.

To make the mop: Meanwhile, in a small saucepan, combine the tallow, vinegar, onion, garlic, hot sauce, and mustard; stir to mix; and keep warm in the smoker.

After 1 to 1½ hours, take a look. (I tend to check on beef ribs during the cook more often than I do brisket because I'm not worried about opening the smoker door too much and losing heat. It's already hot in there, plus the bone mass retains a lot of heat, protecting the meat.) Once you see any of the corners starting to dry out, begin to spritz frequently with vinegar. This needs to be done often to cool off the edges while waiting for the middle part to get hot. A beef rib will quickly get very crusty at this temperature, which is good, but you always want to spray it down. So you're constantly letting it get crusty and then spritzing it down; letting it go too far and then bringing it back. Keep the rib pretty wet on the edges.

About 4 hours in (roughly halfway through the 8-hour cooking time), when the exterior starts to dry out a bit, transition from spraying with vinegar to mopping with the mop. Whereas before you let the bark get crusty and then you wet it down to prolong the cook, now you want to coat the exterior with fat, which protects and strengthens the crust you've just built. This is especially important because you're not going to wrap the ribs, so you need to take extra care to ensure the bark has a rich, thick, crusty texture.

Mop the rib with the mop all across the top. Never touch the surface of the beef rib with the actual mop head. Just let the liquid drizzle down on top of and over the ribs. Do this every 30 minutes.

There's no temperature to tell you when the rib is done. It will have reached a "done" temperature in the range of 205° to 207°F, but you're looking for tenderness, and that assessment is accomplished by feel. Using the spike of a Thermapen or other digital thermometer, poke gently in a few places to gauge tenderness. You are looking for general softness, but there's one specific test that will tell you exactly when you've nailed it.

There are two membranes surrounding the bones on a beef rib. The obvious one covers the underside of the bone. Many people remove it before cooking, but I don't. There's another membrane above the bones and just between the finger meat (that runs between the bones) and the fatty meat (above the bones). This is the thin membrane that's important. At spots just between the bones, probe down through the top very gently with your spike and feel carefully for that second membrane. When it yields with only a tiny bit of resistance, the rib is done. Be careful not to poke all the way through to the bottom, which can

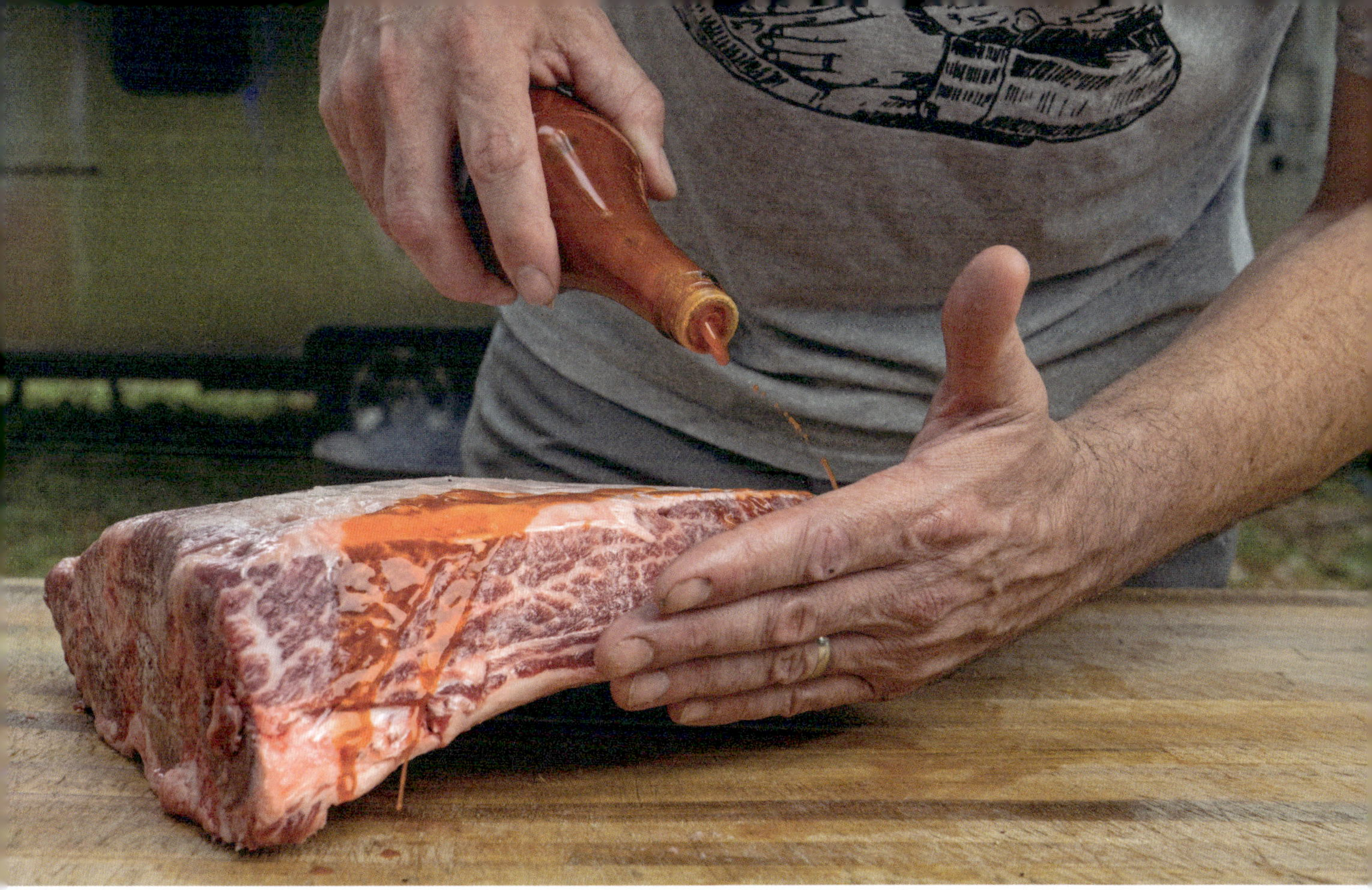

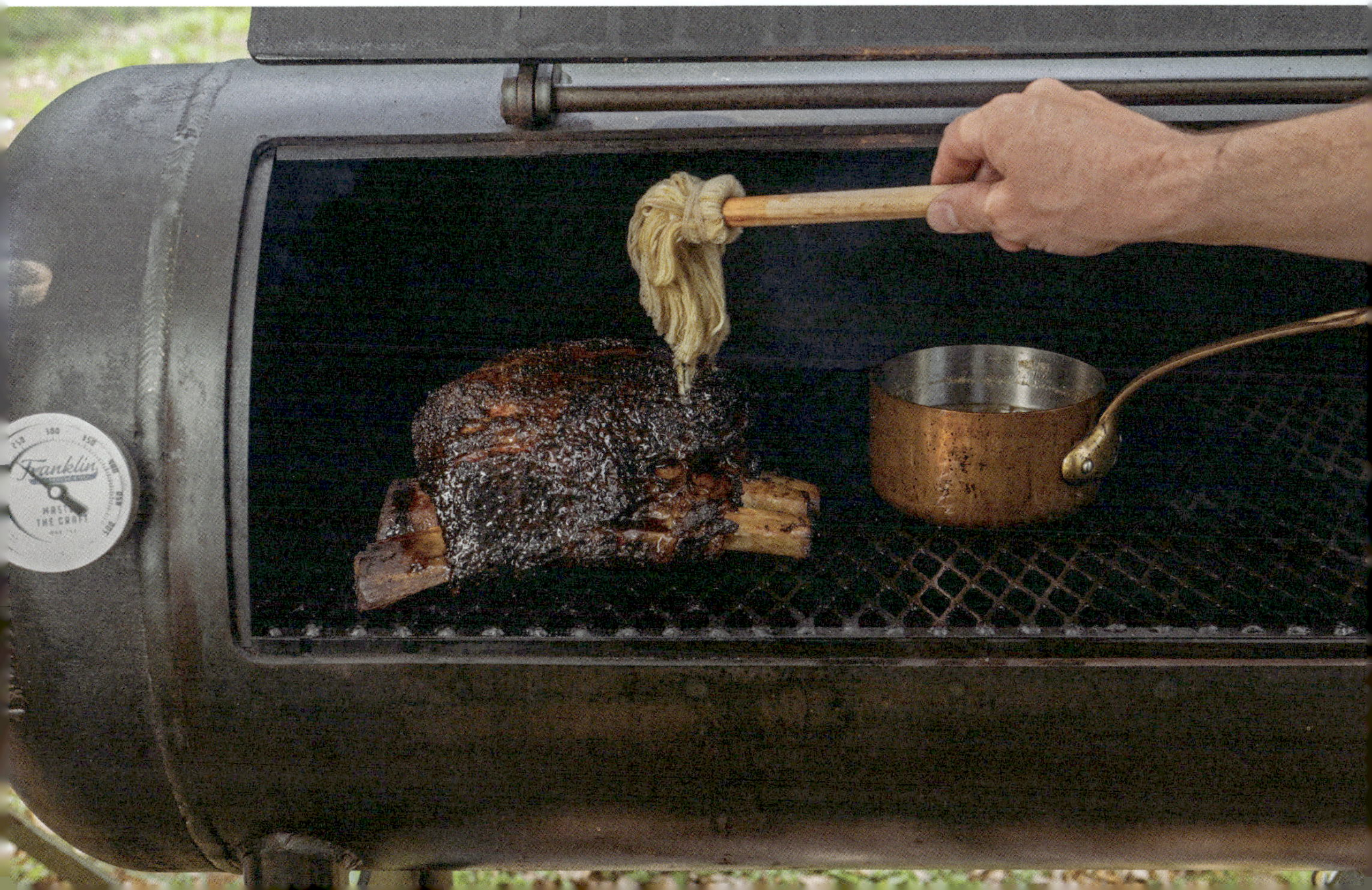
Franklin

cause a lot of moisture and fat to leak out. Because there's so much marbling on beef ribs, you have a very generous window here. It's hard to take a beef rib too far. Just don't miss that window because there's nothing sadder than a tough beef rib, which could happen if you don't cook it long or hot enough. You have to get a feel for it, but with practice, you'll get the hang of it.

When the rib is tender, transfer it to a baking sheet and let it rest until the internal temperature has lowered to 140°F.

Slice between the bones and serve immediately.

PRIME RIB

The process of cooking a prime rib in a smoker lies somewhere between cooking a beef rib (see page 203) and a côte de boeuf (see page 139). After all, the famed standing rib roast is just a larger bone-in hunk from which rib-eye steaks are cut.

To cook prime rib, salt it with kosher salt a day or two in advance and let it sit uncovered in the refrigerator. Get your smoker up to 250° to 275°F and put the roast in the cook chamber straight out of the fridge. Then let the temperature drop to around 225°F.

Let the roast cook, turning it occasionally, until you hit the desired internal temperature, about 120°F. This usually takes about 45 minutes per 1 pound of meat. As the roast starts to near that temperature, let the smoker temperature dip toward 200°F or even lower, until things line up. This inhibits massive carryover. Pull the roast at the temperature you desire, tent it with aluminum foil, and let it rest for only a few minutes to get that medium-rare texture, about 125°F.

With a very sharp knife, carve by first removing the bones in one neat slice (you can separate them later and give them to the bone lovers). Then simply slice the beef slab against the grain, perpendicular to the orientation of the bones, preserving the two end cuts for people who like more crust or slightly more done meat. Serve immediately with Horseradish Cream Sauce (page 140).

SMOKED DUCK

Even those who profess not to like duck will ravenously tear a smoked one apart after getting a taste of its crispy-crunchy, salty-sweet skin. Smoked duck is one of the most reliably delicious foods on Earth. This is a very straightforward preparation, and the smoking regimen is really easy. Using an offset cooker yields the best results and allows you to finish off the duck in direct heat in the firebox for extra-crispy skin. I've also had good success smoking duck on both the PK grill and the Big Green Egg.

There are several breeds of duck in the marketplace. The most common and popular is Pekin (aka Long Island duck), a white-feathered breed descended from the mallard. The Pekin has a mild flavor and decent fleshiness. Another common breed, the Muscovy, has more meat and a slightly more intense flavor and is also less fatty than the Pekin. If you cross a Muscovy male with a Pekin female, you get a moulard, which has more fat than the Muscovy and a nice broad breast. If you have trouble finding duck locally, you can order any of these from New York–based D'Artagnan (dartagnan.com). If you find a packaged duck at your grocery store, check its label to see if it has been brined. It is best if it hasn't been brined, but if it has, do not salt ahead of time.

There are only a few preparatory steps that help duck cook exceptionally well. The first is dry brining and prolonged air-drying. Duck has a lot of fat that renders out slowly, so having the skin as dry as possible helps. I recommend that you air-dry in a refrigerator for at least two days, but I have gone as long as four days with no problem.

Basting, mopping, or spritzing adds a lot of beautiful flavor. I use a solution of maple syrup, red wine vinegar, and soy sauce, with a little garlic, orange peel, thyme, and black peppercorns for zest.

And finally, let the duck temper at room temperature before cooking.

Cook time: 4 to 6 hours

Serves 4

- One 4- to 5-pound duck
- Kosher salt

The Mop

- 1 cup / 340g maple syrup
- ½ cup / 120g vinegar of your choice
- ¼ cup / 65g soy sauce
- 4 garlic cloves, crushed
- 6 black peppercorns
- 8 thyme sprigs
- 1 orange

- Grapeseed oil or rendered duck fat for coating
- Freshly ground black pepper

Trim any extra fat from around the neck and inside the body of the duck. Leave about 1 inch of neck skin. (You can render down the trim and use it to coat the duck before cooking if you like.) Using a needle, the tip of a knife, or the sharp tip of a Thermapen, gently prick the skin all over, taking care not to puncture the meat. Try to angle the needle horizontally to the skin.

Weigh the duck and then calculate 1.75 percent of that total. Measure that amount in kosher salt (it's 25 to 30g, or just over 1 teaspoon, of salt per 1 pound of meat). Sprinkle the salt all over the skin of the duck.

Place the duck on a drying rack on a baking sheet and refrigerate for at least 1 day, preferably 2 days, or up to 4 days. Flip the duck once a day to dry all sides.

Before cooking, remove the duck from the refrigerator and let it temper at room temperature for no more than 2 hours. It's important to start with a duck that's not cold.

To make the mop: Meanwhile, in a small saucepan, combine the maple syrup, vinegar, soy sauce, garlic, peppercorns, and thyme. Quarter the orange and squeeze in its juice. Remove the peel, add to the pan, and discard the spent flesh. Place the pan over medium-high heat and bring the mixture to a boil, stirring occasionally. Adjust the heat to maintain a gentle boil and cook until reduced by about one-third, about 15 minutes. Remove the pan from the heat and allow the mop to cool. Strain it through a fine-mesh strainer into a bowl and set aside.

Preheat the smoker to 250° to 275°F. Gently coat the skin of the duck with grapeseed oil and then lightly coat all over with pepper.

Place the duck, with its legs facing toward the fire, in the cook chamber. Smoke for 4 to 6 hours, mopping every 30 to 45 minutes, without brushing the skin and dislodging the pepper rub. Duck can be cooked to a range of doneness, but look for about 185°F in the thighs and legs and 165° to 175°F in the breast for this one. Shortening the smoking time and removing it at lower temperatures tends to result in very tough meat in the legs.

When the duck is done, remove it from the smoker and let rest for 15 to 30 minutes. Then, if desired, crisp up the skin before serving by using tongs or a spear to hold the duck in the firebox over the coals, gently turning it. The skin will eventually blister, so remove the duck before it burns. If you are not using an offset smoker, place the bird over the coals on a grill or in the broiler of an oven (but be careful here, as the skin will blister very, very quickly—in seconds).

Using a carving or chef's knife sharp enough that it won't ruin the skin, remove the legs and thighs, then gently slice the whole breast off the bone and cut into angled slices. Serve immediately.

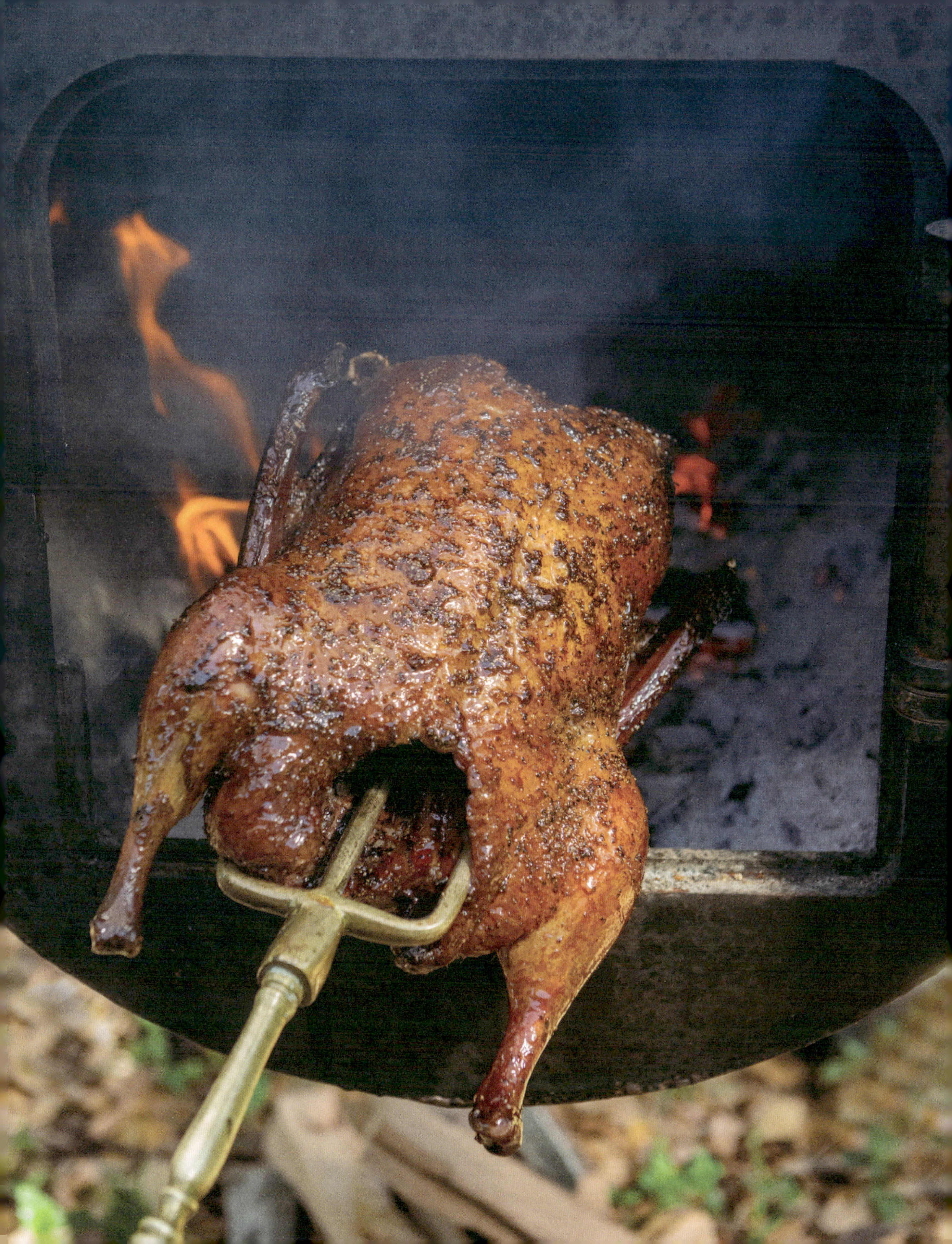

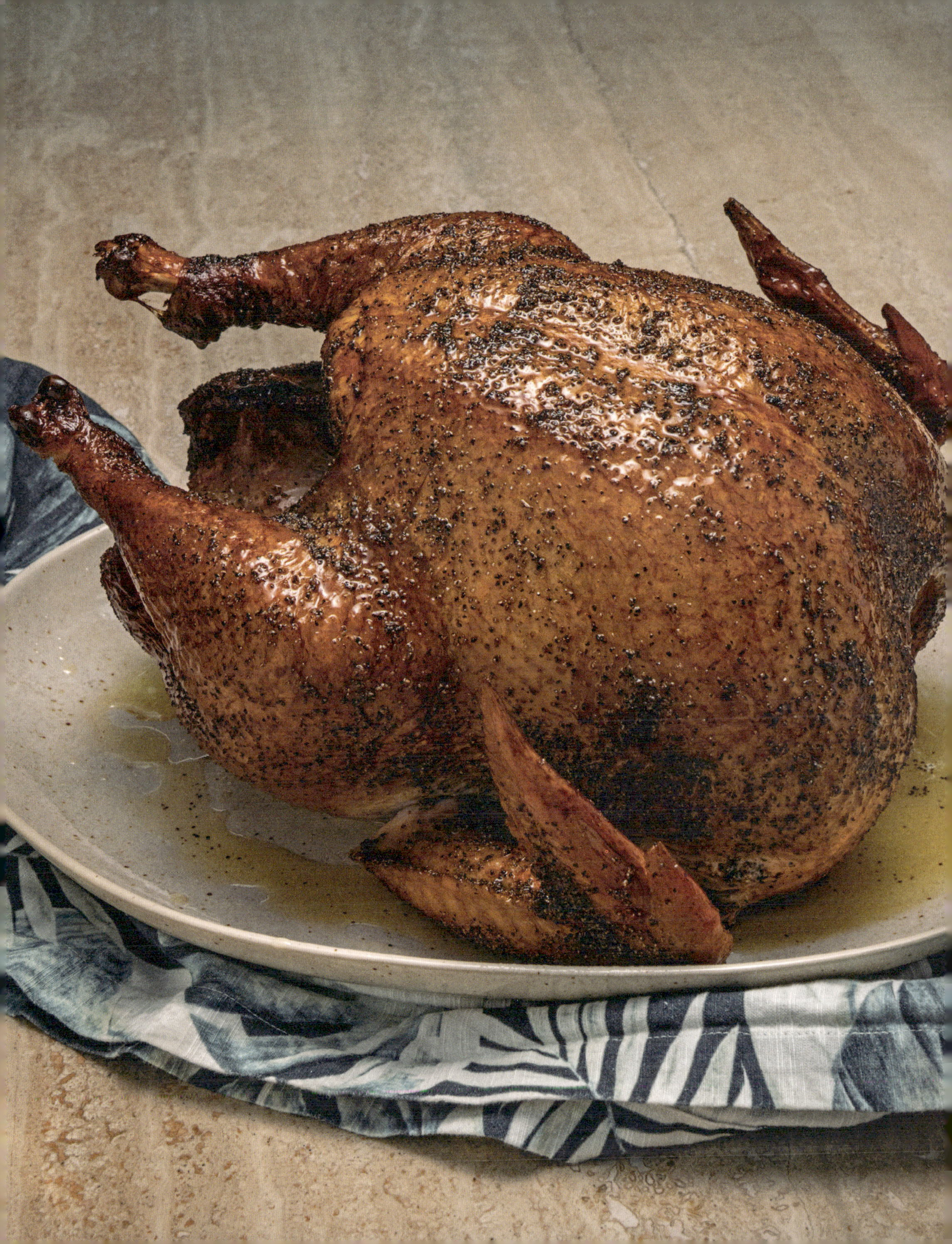

THANKSGIVING TURKEY

A couple of years ago, Stacy, Vivian, and I were visiting family for Thanksgiving, and I was tasked with cooking the turkey without a smoker. Faced with only an oven, I couldn't remember how to cook a turkey and had to search online videos for basic instructions! Of course, it came out just fine, but cooking a turkey in a smoker is clearly my second nature. I have smoked many, many Thanksgiving turkeys over the years, and they have all turned out delicious with this technique.

The key to this turkey is getting it well browned and then nailing the wrap. Unlike a brisket, which gets wrapped in butcher paper, the turkey is tightly wrapped in aluminum foil with lots of butter, which both enriches it and keeps the naturally lean bird from drying out. Because butter scorches and becomes unpleasantly dark and burnt tasting at high temperatures, I use an oil-butter blend, but you could also use ghee, or clarified butter. Because its milk solids are removed during the clarifying process, ghee has a much higher smoke point.

There are many options for buying turkeys these days, from the surprisingly affordable frozen specials at the grocery store to the shockingly expensive heritage birds that can cost well over a hundred bucks. I've had experience with both. Heritage breeds are an interesting proposition. As with heritage chickens, heritage turkeys are historic breeds developed over the last couple hundred years to promote various qualities: growth rate, life span, egg laying, and so on.

Today's commercial turkeys were bred to have more meat and to efficiently convert feed to that meat, though those traits have come at the cost of other qualities that make turkeys what they are, mating ability and egg fertility among them. Heritage turkeys have much more flavorful meat but less of it. That meat tends to be darker and tougher as well. And the birds are usually leaner. But if you like turkey with a deep, rich, more natural flavor, heritage is a good way to go. And the bones and carcass make incredible stock.

Although if you're looking to feed a large gathering, a well-grown commercial turkey is probably a better solution. They are not only less expensive and provide more meat but are easy to buy at most grocery stores. Their flavor, however, won't be as compelling as that of a heritage option.

This recipe is geared for a high-quality commercial bird. But, certainly, look for the best all-natural, unbrined turkey you can find. So many turkeys are brined these days, and I don't want to pay for added water.

- Unbrined turkey (whatever size you need, plan on between 20 and 30 minutes cook time per pound of turkey)
- Kosher salt
- Grapeseed oil for coating
- Freshly ground black pepper
- 1 pound / 450g oil-butter blend (such as SunGlow) or ghee (clarified butter), at cool room temperature

Weigh the turkey and then calculate 1.75 percent of that total. Measure that amount in kosher salt (it's about 8 to 10 grams, or just over 1 teaspoon, of salt per 1 pound of meat). Then sprinkle the salt evenly all over the skin of the turkey and in the cavity.

Place the turkey on a drying rack on a baking sheet and refrigerate for at least 1 day or up to 3 days.

Before cooking, remove the turkey from the refrigerator and let it temper at room temperature for up to 2 hours. It will cook much faster if not too cold.

Fill a pan with hot water and place it in the smoker. Preheat the smoker to 275°F. Gently coat the skin of the turkey with oil and then generously sprinkle with pepper. Place the turkey on the smoker's sweet spot—with mine, it's at the far end of the cook chamber, close to the smokestack—with the legs and body cavity facing toward the fire. (The dark meat of the legs and thighs can more easily handle the convective heat that courses through the smoker.)

Smoke the turkey until the skin has turned a deep golden brown, 2 to 3 hours—this is irrespective of weight, you're cooking for exterior doneness here, not specifically internal temperature. The goal is to get this deep brown shade by the time the internal temperature of the thickest part of the breast reaches about 130°F. Once the turkey has taken on all the color you want it to have, it's time to wrap with the oil-butter blend or clarified butter.

Lay out two large overlapped pieces of aluminum foil, shiny-side up, with a third long piece spread across them perpendicularly (see photos). Using a towel, gently lift the turkey out of the smoker without spilling any of the juices that have collected in the cavity and set it on the foil. Smear the oil-butter blend all over the exterior and inside the cavity of the turkey. You really want to pat it down, like you're a TSA agent. Now dust it with the pepper.

Now carefully flip the turkey breast-side down. Of course, it doesn't want to balance on the breast, so you'll have to rock it back and forth while gently bunching up the foil around it to create a little bunched-up nest that allows it to stand on its breast and retain all of its liquid. If you have a temperature probe with a wire, insert it into the thickest part of the breast and keep the wire within the wrap so it comes out the top. Otherwise, a probe such as a MEATER can be inserted poking upward. Wrap the whole bundle fully and as tightly as possible so the oil-butter blend is always in contact with the meat.

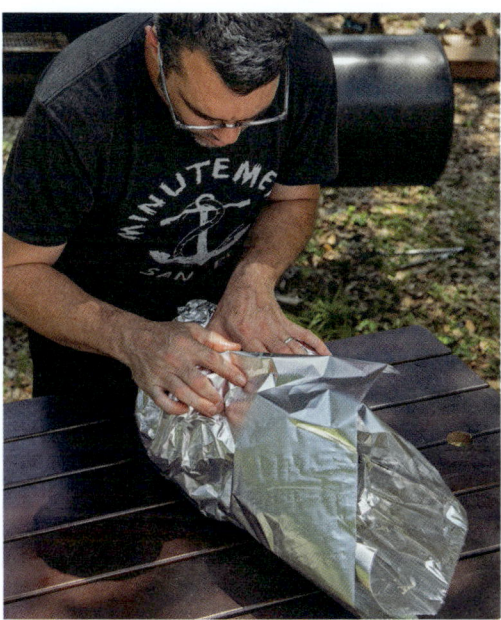

Place the whole package in a large foil baking pan; this way, if the foil wrapping tears, you won't lose all that buttery liquid. When you place the turkey in its pan back in the cooker, keep it oriented with the thighs facing the fire. Bump up the temperature to somewhere in the range of 300° to 325°F. Cook the turkey until the breast is at about 153°F and the thighs register between 175° and 180°F, anywhere from 1 to 2 hours, or until done. The thighs should be a lot hotter than the breast. You really don't want to unwrap the turkey, but if you need to unwrap it to get a good temperature reading, do it carefully so you don't get burned. Then, if necessary, carefully rewrap and put the turkey back into the cook chamber until it has finished cooking. (Don't let the buttery liquid pour out and travel down your pant leg and into your shoe, as I once did. Damn that hurt!) When the turkey has reached temperature, remove it from the smoker and let rest, fully wrapped, for 40 minutes to 1 hour.

Preheat the oven to 400°F or stoke up the heat in your offset smoker to that temperature. Unwrap the turkey and place it, breast-side up, on a baking sheet. Baste it with the buttery drippings, then slip into the oven or smoker for a few minutes to sizzle up the skin.

Transfer the turkey to a platter and carve. You'll have plenty of buttery liquid mixed with turkey juices pooled up at the bottom of the pan. Strain this and keep it warm; it's great stuff to spoon over the turkey.

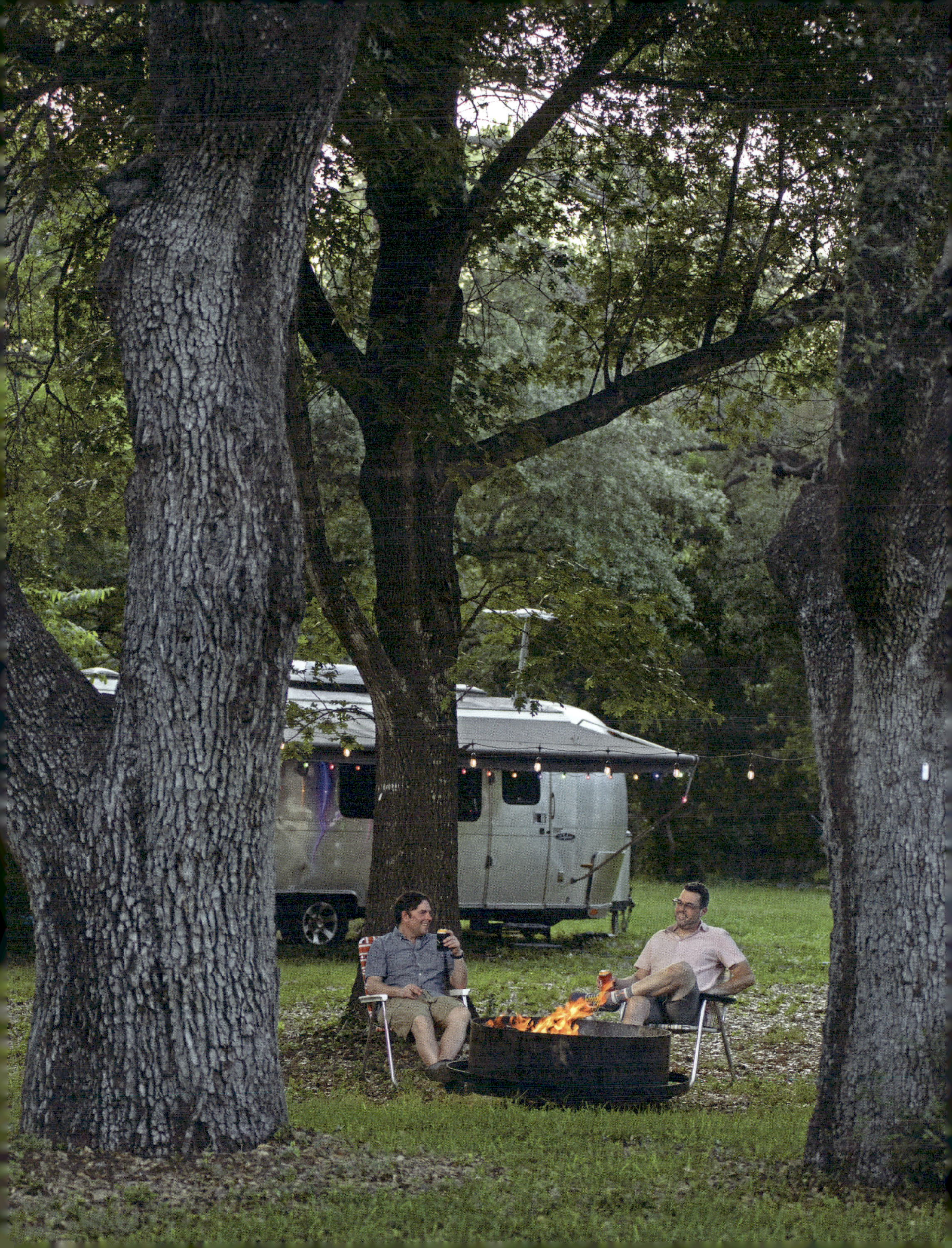

Acknowledgments

Many people contributed—sometimes unwittingly!—to the making of this book, which was in many ways the most difficult of the three we've written. Some of this can be chalked up to the general weirdness inflicted by the pandemic, some to timing—we ended up building a lot of fires and doing lots of cooking in very hot weather—and some to life, as we and our families both experienced moves during work on this book. In the end, though, it was a great experience that we thoroughly enjoyed.

The first person we must thank is Wyatt McSpadden, yes, for his transcendent photography, but also for his sparkling personality and overall Wyatt-tude. Equal parts curmudgeon and comedian, he's simply a joy to be around, and his very presence while we're cooking and setting up a shoot gives us the confidence that it's all going to be okay. Throw in the hilariousness of his buddy act with his able and knowledgeable assistant Will Phillips, and we were always laughing even during the strenuous moments. Thanks, Wyatt and Will (and Nancy too!).

Of great help during some of those moments was Ha Lam, an experienced photographer and editor herself. What a boon to have her assisting on several shoots. Of course, David Hale Smith—skier, fisher, literary agent—thanks for building the foundation of all this, with a hat tip to all the other folks at Inkwell.

We also want to offer deep and sincere gratitude to the good folks at Ten Speed Press, who are truly responsible for this book. Namely, Julie Bennett, our editor who did an amazing job on the text while also bringing the project to life and remaining calming and patient throughout. What a pleasure it was to get to work (for the third time!) with designer Betsy Stromberg, who understands these books better than we do. Thanks so much to copyeditor Sharon Silva for literally thinking of everything, and to Doug Ogan, for offering some very useful edits. Thanks to Kathy Brock, proofreader extraordinaire, who worked magic down to the last comma. And to the amazing associate editor Ashley Pierce, who was always there: abiding and guiding, editing, and holding it all together. And thanks to Allison Renzulli, Joey Lozada, and Kristin Casemore for getting the word out, as ever.

Several people and their companies supported us in various ways with product. Notably, Alfonso Terrazas from Creekstone, a company that continues to support us generously with some of the best product in the world. Likewise, Aaron wants to acknowledge Anthony Charles, who has helped out often and on short notice, when we really needed to find certain items. And Jake and Chip from Made In were more than generous in supplying us with whatever sort of kitchen equipment we might have needed or even just wanted to try.

In Austin, Aaron offers a sincere declaration of gratitude to the whole staff at Franklin Barbecue, who not only helped out in numerous ways on many occasions, but are just awesome in general and manage to maintain good attitudes even when it's 105 degrees out. Likewise the entire office staff supplied endless and thorough support. Matt Gase and Jared Harmeier do way more than just make the Franklin Pit business go; they helped out a ton on this book in little ways that are greatly appreciated.

We thank Terry and David from the Little Longhorn Saloon on Burnet Road for the morning beers, when we got a couple of photos and had a pleasantly relaxed moment after some long days of shooting.

Vivian Franklin, what can we say? She made a great assistant and was full of creativity and energy and never hesitated to get involved. The ever vigilant Honey Franklin didn't set too many Honey traps in the backyard, starting in 2022.

Stacy Franklin—there no words. People tend to give Aaron credit for everything, missing the fact that almost nothing in the extended Franklin multiverse would happen without her industriousness, guile, intelligence, good sense, hard work, and heart. Jordan agrees, but also notes the importance of her wickedly sharp sense of humor, easy laughter, and intuitive sense of when it's time to stop fretting, sit back, and have a glass of wine.

With deep gratitude, Jordan wants to thank the Franklins for making him feel like family, as he lived in the Airstream in their backyard for weeks on end during production of this book. He felt like a welcome hobo every morning as he stumbled out of the trees and into their kitchen, poured himself the excellent coffee Aaron made (shout-out Travis Kizer of Barrett's Coffee), and chatted with them as they began their day.

Finally, Jordan, as ever, thanks his wonderful wife, Christie, for allowing him to own five grills that clutter the garage and also letting him make frequent trips to Austin to dwell in a backyard. A quick wink as well to Stanley Fallot MacDuf, whose relentless desire to walk and play usefully pried Jordan away from his well-worn laptop several times a day.

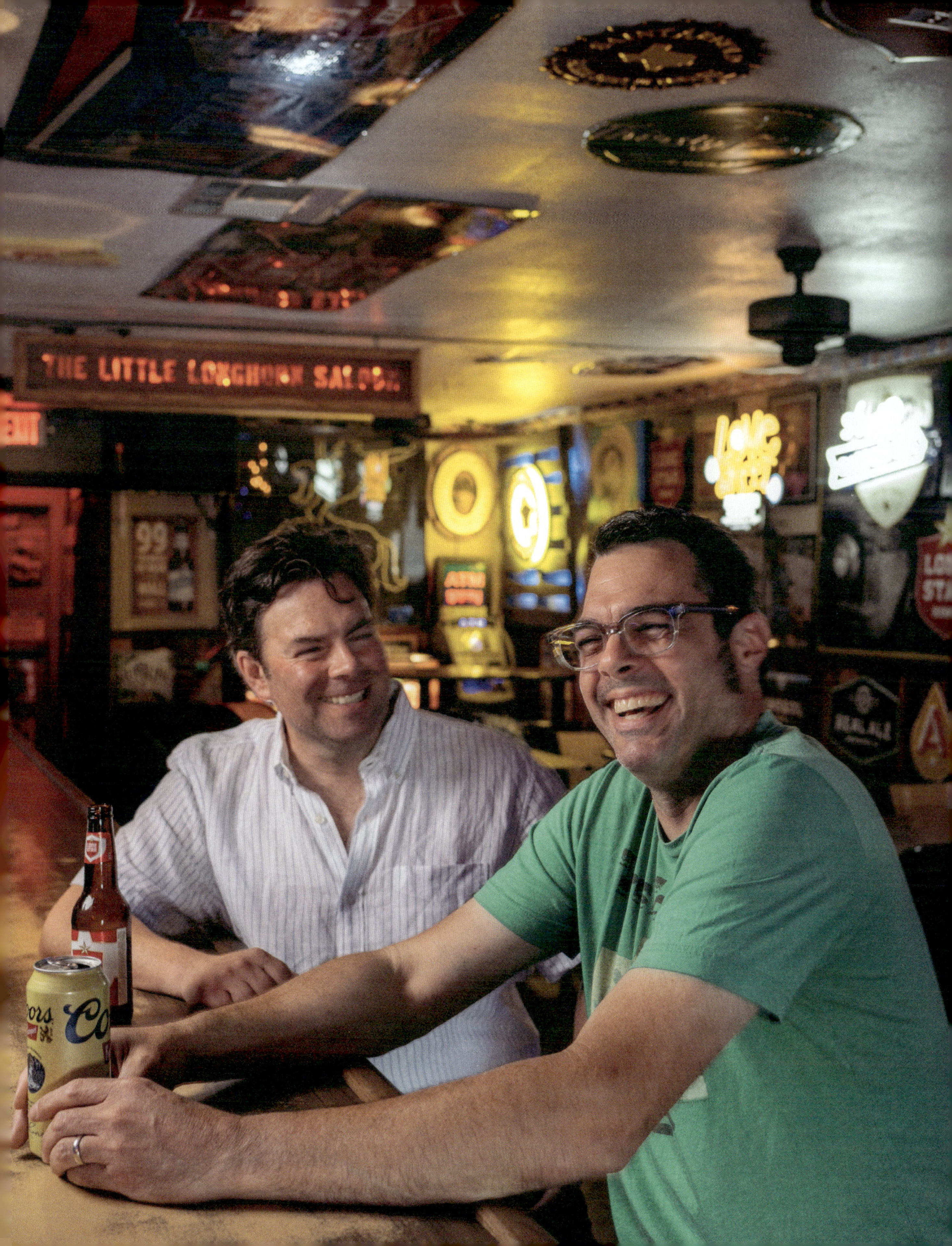
THE LITTLE LONGHORN SALOON

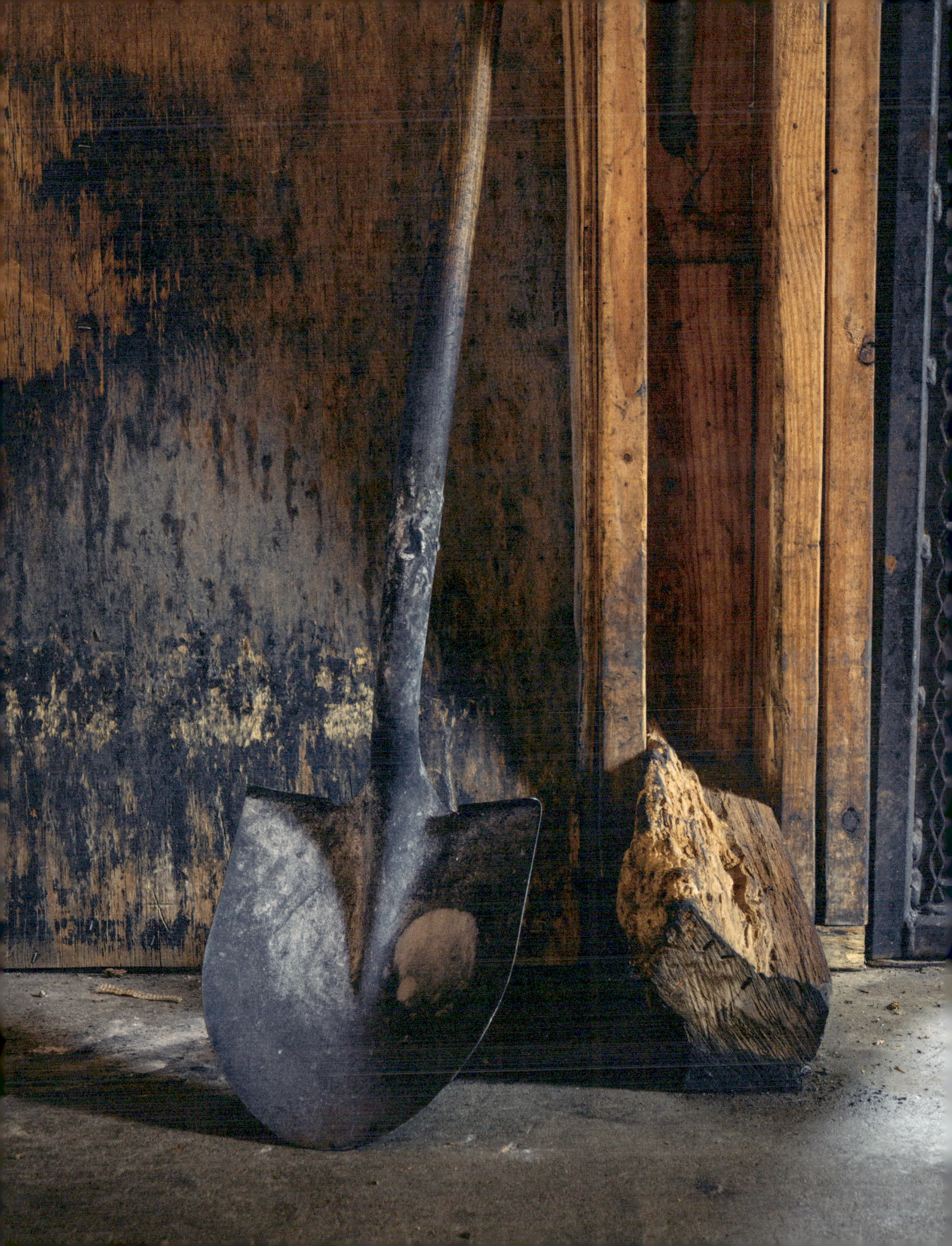

Index

A

apple cider vinegar, 96
ash buckets, 80

B

Baba Ghanoush, Smoky Eggplant, 167–68
Baby Back Ribs, 199–200
baskets, 100
beef
   Beef Rib, 203–6
   Big Green Egg Brisket, 195–97
   Brisket Spice Rub, 113
   Firepit Côte de Boeuf, 139–40
   prime rib, 206
   The Ultimate Brisket, 179–91
Big Green Egg (BGE), 47–48
   Big Green Egg Brisket, 195–97
binchōtan, 71
black pepper, 96, 106
Branzino, Grilled, Smoked Whole, 151–52
brisket
   Big Green Egg Brisket, 195–97
   Brisket Spice Rub, 113
   carving and serving, 192
   choosing, 180
   spritzing, 185
   tempering, 181
   terminology, 181
   trimming, 180–81
   The Ultimate Brisket, 179–91
Brussels Sprouts, Fire-Kissed, 164
burn barrels, 85–86
Butter, Shallot-Chive, 155

C

cabbage
   Fennel and Radicchio Kraut, 117
   Fire-Steamed Cabbage, 168
   Soprano Sauerkraut, 116
charcoal
   binchōtan, 71
   briquettes, 68–70
   lump, 70
   making, 67
   value of, 66–67, 68
cherries
   Rye BBQ Sauce, 122
Chicken, Smoked, 159–60
chiles
   Basic Pepper Sauce, 119
   Spicy BBQ Sauce, 123
Chimichurri, Red, 125
chimneys, 80
citrus, 96
cold smoking vs. hot smoking, 89
cooking tools, 98–110

D

duck
- buying, 207
- Smoked Duck, 207–8

E

Eggplant Baba Ghanoush, Smoky, 167–68

F

fennel
- Fennel and Radicchio Kraut, 117
- Grilled, Smoked Whole Branzino, 151–52

fermented foods, 96, 114. *See also* sauerkraut

fire
- building, 83–84
- controlling, 84–85
- cooking with whole, 74, 79, 86
- side, 85
- stages of, 74, 76–79
- tools, 80–81

firebricks, 81

firepits
- building, 34
- popularity of, 48
- tips for cooking with, 128–30
- using, 48

fish
- Grilled, Smoked Whole Branzino, 151–52
- Redfish on the Half Shell, 147–48

Franklin Barbecue
- bottled sauces business, 28–29
- pandemic and reopening, 26–28
- smokehouse fire and rebuilding, 12–23

The Franklin Pit, 37–39, 41, 60

G

garlic, 96
Grandin, Temple, 180
grapeseed oil, 96
grates, 101, 130, 154

grills
- gas, 42
- kamado, 47–48
- kettle, 42–43
- PK (Portable Kitchen), 43, 45
- popularity of, 41
- Santa Maria–style, 45, 47

H

hatchets, 66
Horseradish Cream Sauce, 140
hot sauce, 97, 118
hot smoking vs. cold smoking, 89

INDEX

J

Janka hardness test, 55

K

kamado grills, 47–48
kettle grills, 42–43
knives, 101, 103–4

L

lettuce
    Jordan's Perfect Green Salad, 169–70

M

mauls, 64
mops, 104
Mushrooms, Grilled, 163

O

offset smokers, 34, 37–39, 41
Onions, Coal-Fired Squashes and, 168
Oysters with Shallot-Chive Butter, 155–56

P

pans, 98, 106
pantry items, 96–97
pickles, 97, 114
    Pickled Vegetables, 120
PK (Portable Kitchen) Grills, 43, 45
pork
    Baby Back Ribs, 199–200
    Firepit Pork Shoulder "Steaks," 133–35
Potato Salad, Herby Buttermilk, 173
preparation, importance of, 93
prime rib, 206

R

Radicchio Kraut, Fennel and, 117
Redfish on the Half Shell, 147–48
ribs
    Baby Back Ribs, 199–200
    Beef Rib, 203–6
    prime, 206
rubs, 110–11
    BBQ Spice Rub, 112
    Brisket Spice Rub, 113
    Steak Spice Rub, 113
Rye BBQ Sauce, 122

S

salads
    Herby Buttermilk Potato Salad, 173
    Jordan's Perfect Green Salad, 169–70
salt, 97
Santa Maria–style grills, 45, 47
sauces, 121
    Basic Pepper Sauce, 119
    Horseradish Cream Sauce, 140
    hot, 97, 118
    Red Chimichurri, 125
    Rye BBQ Sauce, 122
    Spicy BBQ Sauce, 123
sauerkraut, 115
    Fennel and Radicchio Kraut, 117
    Soprano Sauerkraut, 116
saws, 63–64
Shallot-Chive Butter, 155
shovels, 81
smoke
    adding hint of, to charcoal grilling, 142
    attracting, 90
    color of, 87, 89
    components of, 87, 89–90
    cooking with, 87
    delivering, 90–91
    repelling, 91

smokers
    building, 33–34, 37
    The Franklin Pit, 37–39, 41
    maintaining, 41
    offset, 34, 37–39, 41
    terms for, 34
Soprano Sauerkraut, 116
spices, 97
Squashes and Onions, Coal-Fired, 168
steaks
    Firepit Côte de Boeuf, 139–40
    Firepit Pork Shoulder "Steaks," 133–35
    Steak Spice Rub, 113

T

Tallow Mop, 204
Thanksgiving Turkey, 211–13
thermometers, 107
timeline, creating, 94–95
tongs, 81, 107
tools
    cooking, 98–110
    fire, 80–81
    wood, 63–64, 66
trowels, 81
turkey
    buying, 211
    Thanksgiving Turkey, 211–13

V

vegetables
   coal-roasted, 167–68
   Pickled Vegetables, 120
   See also individual vegetables
vinegars, 96

W

wood
   chips, 58
   choosing, 57, 59
   chunks, store-bought, 66
   hard- vs. soft-, 54–55
   importance of, 53
   log size, 60, 63
   moisture content of, 58–59
   quality of, 53–54
   seasoned vs. green, 57–60
   tools, 63–64, 66
work gloves, 63

Ten Speed Press
An imprint of the Crown Publishing Group
A division of Penguin Random House LLC
1745 Broadway
New York, NY 10019
tenspeed.com
penguinrandomhouse.com

2025 Ten Speed Press /Publishers Trade Paperback Box Edition
Text copyright © 2023 by Aaron Franklin
Photographs copyright © 2023 by Wyatt McSpadden

Penguin Random House values and supports copyright. Copyright fuels creativity, encourages diverse voices, promotes free speech, and creates a vibrant culture. Thank you for buying an authorized edition of this book and for complying with copyright laws by not reproducing, scanning, or distributing any part of it in any form without permission. You are supporting writers and allowing Penguin Random House to continue to publish books for every reader. Please note that no part of this book may be used or reproduced in any manner for the purpose of training artificial intelligence technologies or systems.

Ten Speed Press and the Ten Speed Press colophon are registered trademarks of Penguin Random House LLC.

Typefaces: Hoefler & Co.'s Sentinel and Klim Type Foundry's National

Library of Congress Cataloging-in-Publication Data
Names: Franklin, Aaron, author. | Mackay, Jordan, author. | McSpadden, Wyatt, photographer.
Title: Franklin smoke : wood, fire, food / Aaron Franklin and Jordan Mackay; photography by Wyatt McSpadden.
Description: California : Ten Speed Press, [2023] | Includes index. |
Identifiers: LCCN 2022034856 (print) | LCCN 2022034857 (ebook) | ISBN 9781984860484 (hardcover) | ISBN 9781984860491 (ebook)
Subjects: LCSH: Smoking (Cooking)—Technique. | Barbecuing. | Outdoor cooking. | LCGFT: Cookbooks. Classification: LCC TX609 .F725 2023 (print) | LCC TX609 (ebook) | DDC 641.6/165—dc23/eng/20220803
LC record available at https://lccn.loc.gov/2022034856
LC ebook record available at https://lccn.loc.gov/2022034857

ISBN 978-1-9848-6048-4
Ebook ISBN 978-1-9848-6049-1
Box set ISBN 978-0-593-83963-8

Originally published in hardcover in the United States by Ten Speed Press, an imprint of the Crown Publishing Group, a division of Penguin Random House, LLC, in 2023.

Editor: Julie Bennett | Production editor: Ashley Pierce
Designer: Betsy Stromberg | Production designers: Mari Gill and Faith Hague | Production: Serena Sigona | Prepress color manager: Jane Chinn | Copyeditor: Sharon Silva | Proofreader: Kathy Brock | Indexer: Ken DellaPenta | Publicist: Kristin Casemore | Marketers: Joey Lozada and Allison Renzulli

Manufactured in China

10 9 8 7 6 5 4 3 2 1

The authorized representative in the EU for product safety and compliance is Penguin Random House Ireland, Morrison Chambers, 32 Nassau Street, Dublin D02 YH68, Ireland, https://eu-contact.penguin.ie.

Franklin Steak

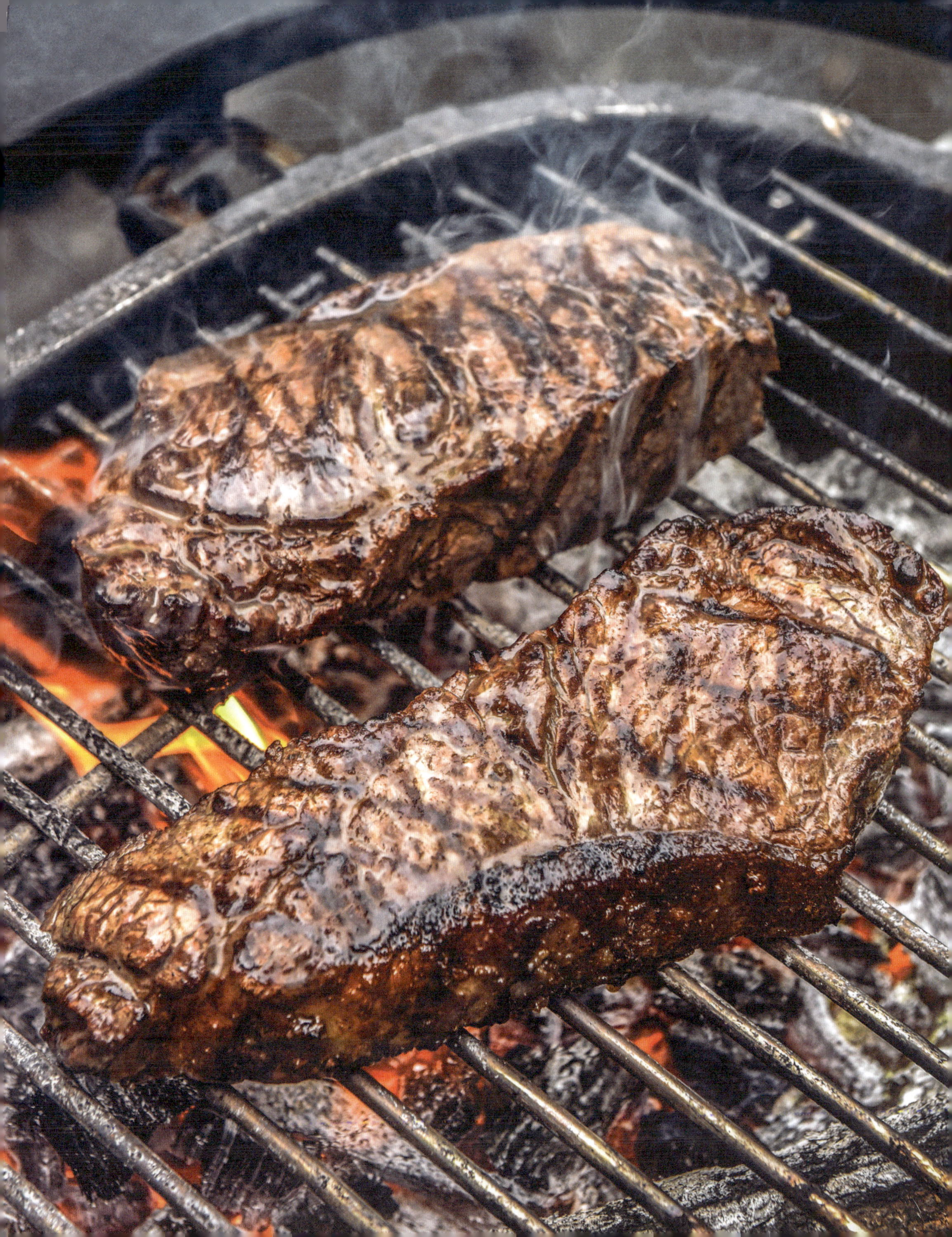

FRANKLIN STEAK

DRY-AGED • LIVE-FIRED • PURE BEEF

AARON FRANKLIN
and
JORDAN MACKAY

Photographs by Wyatt McSpadden
Illustrations by Bryan B. Butler

TEN SPEED PRESS
California | New York

Preface • vi

Introduction • 1

Part I
KNOW THY BEEF

CHAPTER 1
The Story of Beef
5

CHAPTER 2
Buying Steaks
29

CHAPTER 3
Steak Cuts
49

Part II
NEXT-LEVEL BEEF

CHAPTER 4
Dry Aging
81

CHAPTER 5
The Grill
99

CHAPTER 6
Fuel
121

Part III
STEAK PERFECTION

CHAPTER 7
Firing Up
141

CHAPTER 8
The Cook
153

CHAPTER 9
Sides, Sauces, and Drinks
175

Resources • 207

Acknowledgments • 208

Index • 211

How to Cook Steak • 214

Preface

Boy, do I ever love a good steak! And I eat a lot of it, which, along with beer, is how I managed to achieve this awesome bod. Nevertheless, since I'm known for Central Texas barbecue, many people will ask, why a book about steak? Well, I'm glad you asked. . . .

My love of steak goes back a long way. When I was a kid, it was a huge, really big deal if we ate steaks for dinner. My folks cooked and stuff, but not like we cook today. It was the 1970s and 1980s, you know, and Tuna Helper was standard pantry fare and pretty darn good. But steak night was an event. In Bryan, Texas, where I was born, my dad was actually a restaurant manager at a steak house. I'd guess my dad used a few tricks from that stint when he cooked for us.

In hindsight, my dad probably just put a bunch of Lawry's on steak. (That's all right by me, as I still put Lawry's on tons of stuff!) He'd always cook a T-bone, about an inch thick or something like that, on a grill with charcoal—nothing special or specific about it. His grill was likely just a shallow hotel pan with a grate on top of it. But those flavors—really salty and beefy—have always stuck with me.

I never really started cooking until I left home when I was eighteen. I moved to Austin to an area called West Campus, adjacent to the University of Texas, which was known for its ample frat and sorority houses and dozens and dozens of apartment buildings for student housing. Now, I wasn't a student, but I lived there anyway because it was cheap. I had an apartment with a small patio, and on that patio, a little Weber grill. Not really being a very good cook—never having cooked in a restaurant kitchen—I remember getting super-cheap grocery-store steaks and, at like four o'clock in the morning, firing up the grill and eating steaks with my roommate while watching the sun come up. We'd get the cheapest charcoal, the cheapest meat, and iodized salt packets from the taco stand for seasoning. It was absolutely the least expensive, foulest way to eat steak, but we still felt like kings. Nineteen years old, living on, like, twelve dollars a month, and drinking beer at six in the morning—that was a straight line from the way my dad cooked steaks, but I didn't know anything about charcoal or wood or grilling. Or meat, for that matter, especially the quality kind.

It was that same nostalgia that got me into barbecue. When I *really* got into barbecue, a bunch of lightbulbs started going off: what do I do with all these coals? I was around fire all the time and my relationship with fire and the nighttime is what got me into steak. If I have to sit there watching the fire for twelve hours, why not use the fire to feed myself something that would sustain me? I wasn't going to be eating barbecue because that's what I had to sell. But a steak was the quick, easy way to taste that beautiful union of beef and fire.

One of the most memorable steaks I ever ate was from Tom Perini of Perini Ranch in West Texas. While I was working on the PBS show *BBQ with Franklin*, we did a shoot at the ranch. Tom is a heck of a guy and a really talented chuck-wagon cook, which he started doing on the ranch in the 1970s, eventually going on to open a steak house in 1983. Later, at a live-fire event, our dish was loosely inspired by Perini: fifty tri-tips dipped in Cognac. We grilled the steaks over mesquite and let them cool down. Finally, we set up two PK Grills and got them raging hot (it felt like we were going to melt the bottoms out of them) and poured Cognac into a bucket. Yes, you read that right: a *bucket* of Cognac. We dipped the tri-tips in the Cognac and flambéed them on the grill—that's how we brought everything back up to temp. Man, what a great memory.

A person can eat only so much barbecue. I'm sure you understand: if, for your day job, you worked in a place that smelled powerfully of meat, fat, and smoke and then, when you went home, *you* smelled powerfully of meat, fat, and smoke, too! The smell of a grilled steak is always refreshing, bright, and less rich. While that fact might impact my hunger for barbecue, nothing ever seems to get in the way of my appetite for a good steak. I never get tired of it.

And that's part of the way this book happened. When Jordan and I were working on our first book, *Franklin Barbecue*, he noticed that dinner at my house very often ended up being steak. And over the course of many long nights outside on cooks, we spent a lot of time gazing at flames and hot coals and talking about grilling and meat. Without knowing it, we had started to plan a second book.

And what's more deserving of a book-length tribute than steak? It's as common in America (well, almost) as hamburgers and hot dogs, yet because it's so precious, cooking it is loaded with pressure not to screw it up. So we figured we might be able to lend folks a hand by helping them sharpen their steak skills and knowledge.

And that's all this book is meant to do. But along the way, we realized that most people don't have a great understanding of the modern beef industry, and I think it's important to know, as best as you can, where your beef comes from, be it the actual farm or at least a trusted supplier. Every year, I fire up the old truck and head up I-35 to Kansas to visit Creekstone Farms, which supplies our barbecue restaurant with excellent, all-natural briskets, and Loro, a new Austin restaurant I'm involved in, with bavettes and brisket. This is because I like to check in on where the beef is coming from and the people who manage it. It's a long drive every year but well worth it.

Then, it turns out, I have a lot of thoughts about wood, charcoal, and grills, too. People might think I just smoke meat all the time, but in fact, I grill just as much—for events, for parties, or just on a weeknight for me, my wife, Stacy, and my daughter, Vivian. Over time, I've developed some ideas about cooking steaks—different methods for different cuts and so on—that I thought might be useful to those of you out there who are as geeky as I am about live-fire cooking. And since Jordan travels around a lot writing about wine, he got some inspiration from other countries, especially Spain but Japan, France, and Sweden, too. All together, we thought we would make this book our so-called love letter to steak.

I hope you enjoy the book as much as I loved making it.

• **Aaron Franklin**

PREFACE

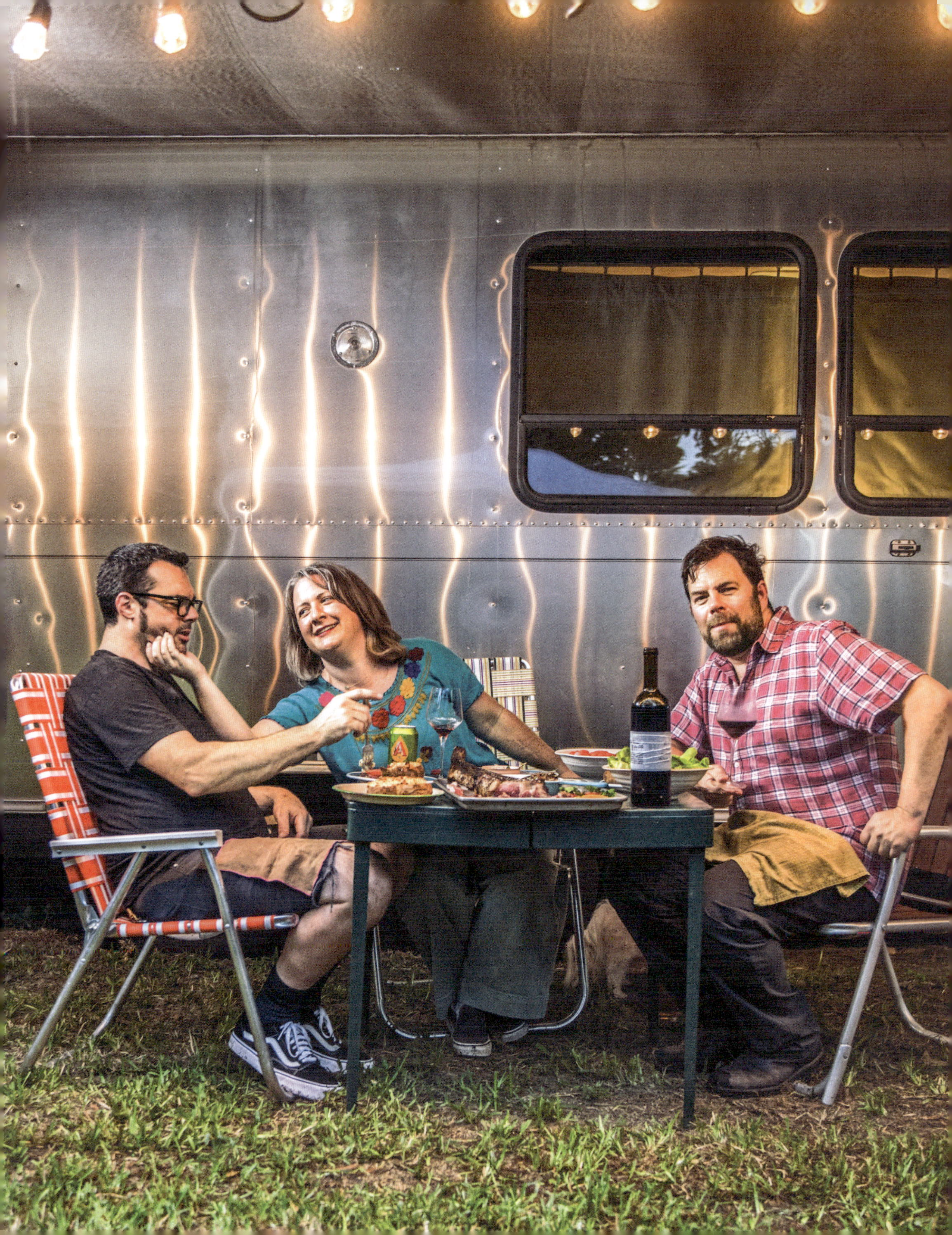

Introduction

In the past year, whenever we mentioned to someone that we were working on a book about steak, the unfailing response would be, "Steak? How can anyone write a whole book about steak?"

That's funny, as our sense has always been the opposite: "How can we ever meaningfully cover steak in just one book?"

But those two differing responses basically sum up the current state of steak in America and make a good case for why this book needs to exist. On the one hand, steak is among the simplest, most convenient, and most elemental of all foods. It is beef plus fire. Preparing steak requires very little in terms of money, thought, time, and equipment. But a *sublime* steak? That requires a fair bit of moola, consideration, patience, and accessories.

Clearly, then, this book is meant as a companion in the pursuit of sublime steak. And to get there, we believe you have to think through the meat from its source until it comes off the grill.

The first section of this book is all about beef. It will help you to know a little bit more about its history, the industry in general, breeds and feeds, and some of the core issues surrounding steak consumption today. We tell you how to find the best possible raw materials from the best purveyors—ranchers, butchers, and more. We talk about the wide and wonderful world of steak cuts, from the usual suspects, like porterhouse and T-bone, to the new wave of "butcher's cuts," like hanger and bavette. In the second section, we share some tips and tricks for taking your steaks to the next level, dry aging being the big one. (Spoiler alert: It's not that hard and, in fact, it's really fun to dry age at home.) Finally, we get into cooking steak—how to prep the meat, build an effective and flavor-delivering coal bed, and cook the steak to perfection. And to finish up, we offer a handful of ridiculously uncomplicated sides (because simple is best, in our opinion) and a few suggestions on what to drink. Along the way, we try to offer a limited global appreciation of delicious steak and some personal anecdotes of steaks past. Easy!

Hopefully, this information will help when you're trying to make choices about what kind of steak to buy and how to cook it. Of course, humbly, we answer the question above—How can you cover steak in just one volume?—with the admission that we can't. There are, inevitably, gaps here. For one, we would have loved to delve far deeper into the timely questions of cattle and environment, and the debate among those who think cattle are heavily responsible for destroying the environment and those who think cattle will be the ones to save it. So many fascinating issues surround the science behind grass and grain feeding, and we've barely scratched the surface. But just because we didn't include that topic here doesn't mean we're not interested.

Finally, a note to those savvy about cattle: Yes, we know that technically much of the steak we eat comes from steers. And we know the technical differences among heifers, steers, cows, bulls, and the like. For convenience and flow, though, we chose to use the familiar and eternal word *cow* when describing the sacred and venerable animal whose sacrifice graces us with steak. With that, happy cooking and may you never overcook your beef!

Part I

KNOW THY BEEF

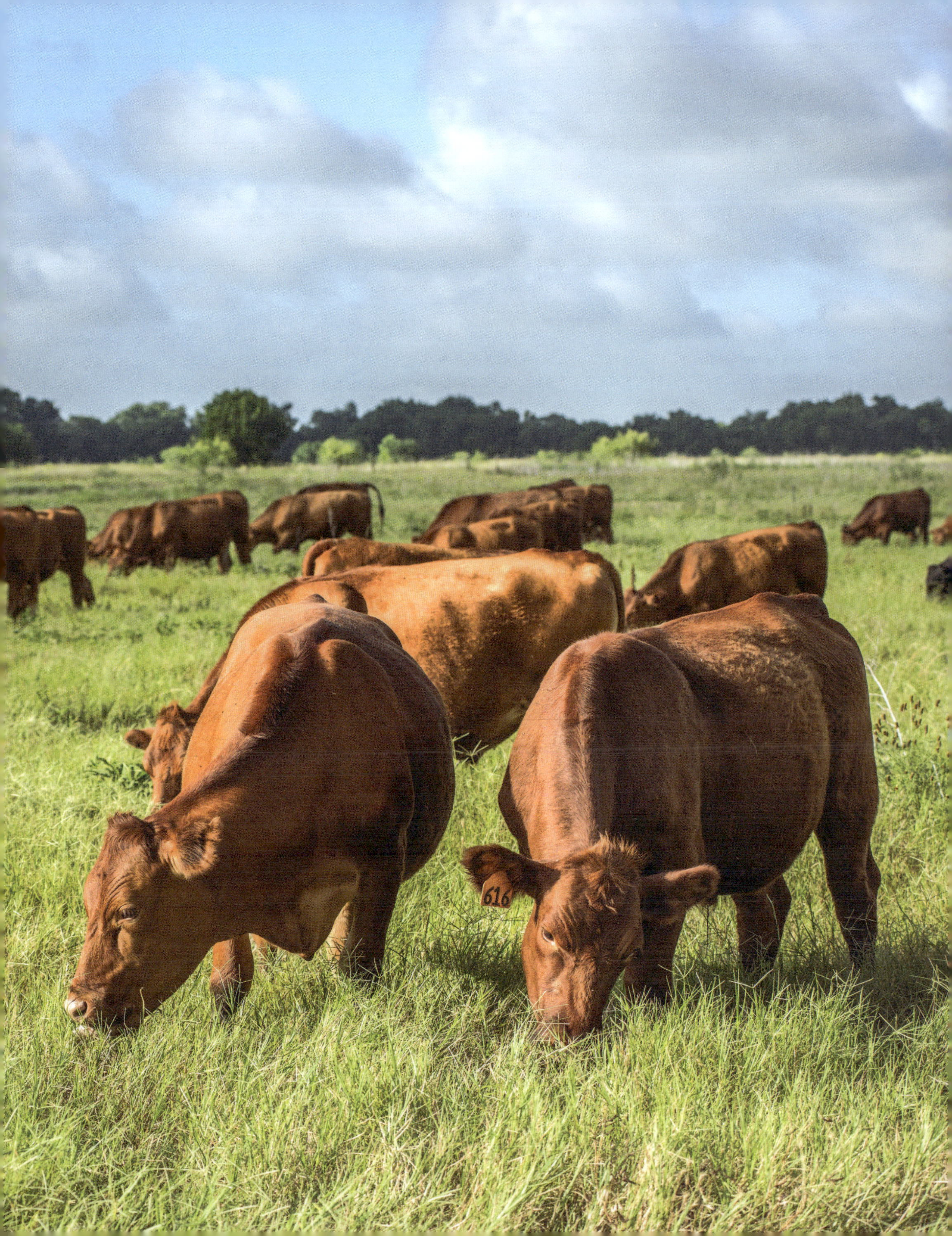
616

CHAPTER 1

The Story of Beef

It happens occasionally—to most of us. You're walking down the street, having a conversation, minding your own business, whatever. Suddenly you stop and lift your head. Nose to the air, you take a couple of quick inhalations. You can't help but twitch in the direction of an aroma so unmistakable and irresistible: a whiff of smoke, of gently burning oak, then that mixture of scents—savory, salty, smoky, and a bit sweet. It triggers something deep in your bones, flowing in your blood. Powerless to control your reaction, you stop in your tracks and spin your head, like a wolf on the prairie, to try and determine from which house that inimitable scent is coming. Someone is grilling steaks.

The fact that we completely freeze because of a primal, involuntary attraction to the smell of beef cooking over fire is understandable. People have been stopped dead in their tracks by the smell of beef for tens of thousands of years. Indeed, they've also likely been singing songs and telling stories about it. We know they painted pictures of beef. At least that's what the cave paintings at Lascaux in southwestern France (ca. 17,000 BCE), tell us. As do the cave paintings at Chauvet-Pont-d'Arc in France (ca. 30,000 BCE) and El Castillo in Spain (ca. 39,000 BCE) and the engraving at Abri Blanchard (ca. 38,000 BCE), not far from Lascaux. These are not line drawings of New York strips or ribeyes, of course, but images of wild cattle.

Cattle—wild and domestic—have been an essential part of human culture for thousands, probably hundreds of thousands and even a million, years. These animals have provided milk, meat, leather, labor, strength, transport. They've exponentially expanded—for better and worse—the capacity of what humans have been able to accomplish. We must marvel at them but also recognize that our love of and instinctive response to the smell of cooking beef is not some sort of quirk. It's hardly even a choice for most people. It's hardwired—something we're not powerless to refuse but certainly programmed to savor.

The enjoyment of steak, therefore, goes back a long way, intertwined inseparably into the early moments of human evolution. In a way, you could say steak (and beef in general) is part of what makes people *people*.

Early Steak

It's not necessary to know about the history of cattle when driving to the grocery store to pick up a couple of steaks to grill out back on a Saturday night. Yet it is interesting and somewhat profound to consider the earliest origins of beef. To know that, while on this errand, you are walking stride for stride with Grog and Thak as they stalked a wandering bull is a powerful notion (or at least an amusing one). Along with salt and pepper, sprinkle your steaks with meaning in a vast natural and historical context; it's good seasoning. Consider, friends, the aurochs.

Our ancient ancestors did more than merely consider the primogenitors of all modern cattle. They revered them. We know this because in those ancient cave paintings we see beautiful, skilled, sometimes full-size line drawings of these animals, which were about a third larger than modern cattle. One painting depicts a beast seventeen feet long, standing six feet tall at the shoulders, with fearsome curved horns. Aurochs were creatures to be reckoned with.

Tens of thousands of years later than the cave art, Julius Caesar, writing in his *Commentaries on the Gallic War* (when he headed into the wild lands north of Rome to make his fortune expanding the empire up into modern France, Germany, and Britain by conquering and pillaging the native tribes), would describe much of the exotic fauna he encountered. This included the wild aurochs—cattle had long been domesticated—which he described as "a little below the elephant in size, and of the appearance, color, and shape of a bull. Their strength and speed are extraordinary; they spare neither man nor wild beast that they have espied." He noted that the local tribes "take with much pains in pits and kill them. . . . But not even when taken very young can they be rendered familiar to men and tamed. The size, shape, and appearance of their horns differ much from the horns of our oxen. These they anxiously seek after, and bind at the tips with silver, and use as cups at their most sumptuous entertainments."

Julius Caesar's description is considered pretty accurate, especially if you consider he was likely comparing the aurochs's size to the relatively diminutive North African elephant (now extinct). The horns of an aurochs could reach three feet in length. You can imagine the difficulty Paleolithic humans would have had in bringing down one of these massive, dangerous animals, which likely weighed around two thousand pounds (compared to the one thousand pounds of beef cattle today). But you can also imagine how much those early people on their actual paleo diets must have savored the flavor of the steak dinners that came after.

Known as *Bos primigenius*, the aurochs evolved earlier than *Homo sapiens* did, with a history going back about 2 million years in India. Leading up to this in the Pliocene epoch (5.3 to 2.6 million years ago), global cooling (how refreshing) and drying from the warmer, wetter Miocene caused a retreat of forests and jungles and a vast expansion of grasslands and savannas. The shift in vegetation sparked the evolution of grazing animals, which came to the fore in this period. Following the Pliocene, the Pleistocene (at the tail end of which modern humans evolved) saw aurochs spread throughout much of the world, reaching Asia, the Middle East, and Africa. Popularly known as the Ice Age, the Pleistocene arrived in what is now Europe sometime around 270,000 years ago, not (relatively) long before the appearance of modern *Homo sapiens*, which

occurred about 200,000 years ago. *Homo erectus,* however, dates to at least 1.8 million years ago, and scientists have theorized that hunting and meat eating go back at least that far. That means human ancestors may have been eating steak for well over a million years, probably closer to two. Indeed, scientists now estimate that the earliest evidence of human ancestors cooking occurred around 1.9 million years ago, so perhaps steaks were some of the first things ever cooked. Perhaps cooking was invented for steaks!

Hunting giant, angry aurochs would have been unpleasant. It is much easier to select from a bunch of smaller, dumber, and tamer versions of the animals. Enter the domestication of cattle, which dates to as recently as 8500 BCE. Study of DNA suggests that all cattle today are descended from only about eighty animals, perhaps one small herd. No one knows exactly how an animal as fierce and enormous as the aurochs was domesticated, but the easiest scenario to imagine is that some babies were captured and raised away from the parents.

Domestication brings many changes. Both physical size and brain size diminish. With their movement, feeding, and reproduction now controlled by humans, animals become more docile and, well, not smart. They also generally change in physical appearance, developing colorations and marks that distinguish them from their wild relatives (think of the black and white blotches of Holstein cows—that did not occur in nature). Domesticated species lose some of their original strength, health, hardiness, and ability to cope with adversity.

All of this sounds sort of insidious when described so clinically. But it is true that the domestication of cattle has changed us even

THE STORY OF BEEF

AUROCHS REVIVAL

History's first recorded extinction was sadly the aurochs, in 1627, when the last one, a female, was killed in a forest in Poland by a nobleman. (They had survived that long because only the nobility were allowed to hunt in Poland at the time.) But on several occasions in the last hundred years, a surprising project has arisen: to revive the aurochs. We're not talking DNA suspended in a prehistoric drop of amber here (the DNA of the aurochs has already been sequenced), but resurrecting the animals themselves using the process of back breeding. This requires finding surviving cattle that retain some of the characteristics of the aurochs—size, shape and breadth of horns, color and markings, and the like—and breeding them together in a way to cause these genes to recombine and remain expressive. Scientists have even used cave paintings as one of their anatomical guides in this endeavor. The first attempt was made by two German zookeeper brothers in the 1920s. For them, success in restoring the aurochs would have been a potent example of a past of racial purity—of the power of Aryan eugenics. Fortunately, the cattle they produced bore some aurochs-like characteristics but were never taken too seriously.

In the last twenty years, however, new efforts have begun again with the far more noble purposes of "Rewilding Europe," as one of the several nongovernmental organizations working toward the goal is called. The reasons for restoring the aurochs are ecological. By some estimates, European farmers are abandoning their small farms at the rate of thousands of acres of agricultural land lost every year. Without the activity of large herbivores, unused land either reverts to forest or becomes barren because the soils have been ravaged by modern agriculture. The action of ruminants restores and protects grasslands, which become diverse natural habitats for numerous native animal and insect populations. Wolves have destroyed other herds of herbivores, but the aurochs-like cattle have been strong enough to suffer few losses.

Aurochs in Nature, 1889

as it has changed them. For instance, at one time, humans became lactose intolerant at the onset of adulthood. But over the millennia, this changed, as being able to digest milk protein and fat conferred some sort of evolutionary advantage on the people who could do that. Of course, domesticated cattle sped change in human culture in obvious ways, as well. The availability of strong oxen to help with work in the fields allowed the expansion of farming. Leather from cowhides became a hugely important substance with all sorts of applications, from shoes and clothes to shelter. Having a convenient source of nutrient-dense food available in the form of beef furthered almost all human endeavors. Cattle were the powerful engines of progress.

As the project of domestication itself evolved through controlled reproduction—a sort of fast-tracked evolution—people began shaping cattle to suit their specific needs. These take many familiar forms, such as physical strength, dairy, meat, or even an ornery temperament (which is bred into Spanish bullfighting bulls). Cattle have also been bred to exist in environments with different terrains, climates, and food sources. Over the centuries, this constant and selective breeding has given rise to a tremendous expanse of genetic diversity. These are the distinct breeds of cattle, which number somewhere around eight hundred.

However, in recent decades, globalization and technology have compelled people to focus on only certain breeds deemed more desirable than others, resulting in a winnowing that many expert observers consider dangerous. Hundreds of recognized cattle breeds, representing a valuable genetic resource of various types bred for specific environments, are threatened with extinction. As Valerie Porter points out in her book, *Cattle: A Handbook to the Breeds of the World*, "It is much easier to destroy such resources than to create them." The ability to produce great steaks is certainly considered a valuable genetic resource. After all, these cattle breeds have proliferated more than any other—all thanks to their superior ability to deliver that irresistible taste of beef.

The Taste of Beef

The flavor of beef is sui generis, prompting even the modestly curious to ask, what makes beef taste so beefy? When Jordan posed that question to Jerrad Legako, an assistant professor specializing in beef in the Department of Animal and Food Sciences at Texas Tech, the answer was surprising. "We don't have the full picture yet," says Legako.

We do know that even though raw meat is bland, it contains a vast pool of precursor compounds such as amino acids, reducing sugars, and fats. Cooking converts these into the aroma and flavor of beef, thanks to processes such as the Maillard reaction and lipid oxidation and the cascading series of interactions between them.

Legako notes that what we perceive on the tongue when eating cooked beef is related to umami—amino acids and small peptides. "And then in the aroma fraction, you find more of the sulfur-containing compounds," he says. "Lipids [fats] also play a big role, but they're tricky because a little lipid oxidation is attractive, but too much lipid breakdown becomes rancid tasting."

Most of beef's flavor emerges during cooking, when heat allows the amino acids to break down over time, layering their flavors. Sulfurous compounds come from the lean muscle.

At low levels, they're meaty, he notes, but at higher levels they can be revolting, like rotten eggs. Fat, too, plays a huge role. While the fat in marbling doesn't have a lot of flavor itself (for more on this, see page 41), Legako says, "it acts as a reservoir for the flavor compounds during cooking and delivers them across the mouth. We refer to some of these flavor compounds as lipophilic, meaning they have an affinity to fats and will more or less absorb into the fat and become available for taste."

If beef flavor can't be reduced to a single or even discrete set of compounds, where does it come from? What are the important influences on beef flavor? Basically the question is this: how do we find the tastiest steaks?

One beef expert we talked to said that the conventional wisdom in the beef industry is that three all-important elements contribute to the taste and culinary experience of beef: genetics, environment (feeding and lifestyle), and age. With a reasonable understanding of these, you can obtain an inkling of how a particular steak will taste.

Genetics

It didn't take long for the domesticated aurochs, accompanying migrating peoples, to start making its way from the site of its domestication in the Fertile Crescent to parts throughout the Old World. As the aurochs found its way into climates ranging from subtropical to subarctic, from desert to forest, from plains to mountains, it changed. In each place, people developed their own types of cattle, bred for environmental suitability. As those traits stabilized, breeding became even more specific.

The first types of cattle were bred for strength, to pull plows or timber or rocks. Later, cattle evolved traits beneficial for meat or milk production, but modern meat and dairy cattle are fairly recent developments, coming after horses and then tractors took over the heavy lifting of labor. Improvements in farming allowed the production of silage (wet hay or other feed compacted and stored anaerobically, whether in a silo or just a massive pile) for fattening cattle over winter. In time, cattle became a bankable food source, and the density of the calories and nutrition in meat drove the expansion of cities and other centers not based around farming.

When you visit meat producers today, you still hear a lot about genetics, as they are constantly looking to refine the gene pools of their herds, favoring some traits while discouraging others. Most of the traits they track meticulously are much more important to them than to the end consumer. These can be measurable, like yearling weight (how much the animal can be made to weigh after one year), calmness, or how easily and safely they give birth. Some traits, however, such as ribeye area, may very well matter to the end consumer.

These qualities beg the question, do different breeds produce different flavors? Are they like wine grapes, where Cabernet Sauvignon offers a completely different taste than Pinot Noir? Some steak houses and butcheries in Europe suggest the answer is yes, offering for sale, similar to a wine list, a variety of steaks with breed and place of origin listed on the menu.

In general, however, beef experts say no: beef flavor is largely beef flavor regardless of breed. What the animal ate and where it was raised are of much greater importance in determining flavor. Furthermore, almost all of the cattle we see—and eat—today are mixed breed. Just as mixed breed (mutt) dogs tend to be healthier and more resilient than purebred ones, so with cattle. DNA samples of most cattle will reveal a heritage of a number of different kinds of animals (even if some brands advertise a piece of steak as 100 percent one breed).

Nevertheless, breeds do remain important, as the breed itself may be inseparably intertwined with where the cattle are raised. For instance, in the southern United States, you find many cattle with strains of Brahman in them, which is a breed based on *Bos indicus*, the subspecies of cattle from India. Notable for the signature hump on its back, the Brahman was developed for its ability to tolerate heat and resistance to insects (and are not considered great eating).

Even if the specific breed of cattle is generally not crucial to the meat quality, there are exceptions, and we're going to be hearing more about breed in regard to steak in the United States in coming years. So here's a brief rundown of the major cattle breeds you'll find here and in other countries as they pertain to producing steaks.

ANGUS

The most prolific beef producer in the United States, Angus is described in *Cattle: A Handbook to the Breeds of the World* as "the mild-eyed breed which produces possibly the best beef in the world—lightly marbled, succulent, and tender . . . it remains a most economical breed to rear, able to thrive on rough grazing and to fatten on low cost rations." You can understand the popularity: it's a win-win for consumers and ranchers. A Scottish breed with roots going back to the mid-eighteenth century, the Aberdeen Angus was officially described in 1862. The first bulls came to the United States in 1873.

Despite the popularity and use of the name, what we eat today is not purebred Angus, as from the beginning and over the following generations, the breed has been intermixed countless times. To be certified Angus, either one parent or both grandparents have to have been Angus (but that doesn't mean purebred Aberdeen Angus). For instance, for a cow to be eligible for the Certified Angus Beef brand, the United States Department of Agriculture (USDA) definition states only that the live animal has to be "predominantly solid black." A litany of further carcass specifications define the quality necessary to make the grade— "modest or higher marbling, 10- to 16-inch ribeye area, no neck hump exceeding 2 inches (reduces *Bos indicus* influence)."

So really what's talked about with regard to Angus beef is Angus-type cattle. These are mostly black, stocky animals, though some white areas may be present. Red Angus can also be included, and the consensus is that the red color doesn't make a difference. Indeed, most high-quality brands, such as Creekstone Farms or 44 Farms, trumpet not just the fact that they sell Angus beef but also the quality of their own proprietary genetics.

WAGYU

The famous Wagyu from Japan seems destined to be the newest It breed, the Next Big Thing. Why? Because of its ability to marble. Wagyu can be a source of outstanding, high-end steaks. Travel around the United States and you'll find new Wagyu-focused cattle herds popping up all over.

In Japan, these are the cattle that produce those incredible, bizarre-looking steaks—steaks so marbled that they appear more white than pink. This kind of meat is a delicacy, is very expensive, and comes from purebred animals that are confined for their entire lives and fed only grain. Contrary to popular myth, they are not fed beer or massaged. We see very little of this high-level Japanese Wagyu beef in the States, as only tiny amounts are imported. American Wagyu cattle are neither bred nor raised to produce such extreme meat.

Wagyu, which simply means Japanese (*Wa*) beef (*gyu*), has a long and somewhat convoluted history. Some DNA evidence suggests genetic separation of the strain as far back as thirty-five thousand years ago. The animals were originally bred as pack animals, which is an important detail. Marbling—the ability to grow that intramuscular fat—is a trait that provides slow-twitch energy to the animal. Over the centuries, the Japanese emphasis on strength and endurance has led to beef of hedonistic juiciness. Wagyu cattle got an infusion of European genetics (Brown Swiss, Devon, Shorthorn, Simmental, Ayrshire) in the 1800s due to some imported cattle, but that was shut down again in 1910. Four distinct types of Wagyu exist in Japan: black, red (also known as brown), polled (hornless), and shorthorn. The latter two are found only in Japan. The first two, black and red, have been exported to other countries in extremely limited amounts.

The Japanese subtypes of Wagyu are distinct, as the rugged, mountainous nature of a country composed of islands has kept herds isolated from one another in separate pockets. While beef from Kobe is the most famous, the northern island of Hokkaido is also known for superior quality. And recent national competitions have been won by the Miyazaki region in the south, which today is regarded by many as home to Japan's best beef. Breeding is strictly regulated and registered, with every animal having papers and a lineage that can be traced over many generations.

Only a handful of Wagyu cattle have ever been imported to the United States, first in 1976 (two black and two red bulls) and not again until 1993 (two male and three female black) and 1994 (thirty-five animals, mixed black and red). Since then, Japan, zealously guarding the preciousness of its genetic resource, has not allowed any more out of the country. Significant numbers of Wagyu also exist in Australia, New Zealand, and Canada.

In the United States, Wagyu beef looks different for a number of reasons. One, the meat here predominantly comes from crossed animals—Wagyu that has been mixed with any number of other breeds, but mostly Angus type. These cattle simply don't have the genes to marble like the full-bred Japanese Wagyu, even if they are raised as the Japanese do. All consumers should be aware that when they buy a Wagyu steak in the United States, it has very little to do with Japan—just some traces in the cow's genetics.

Furthermore, the Japanese eat their beef only in tiny amounts, rarely if ever indulging in the comparatively enormous steaks we Americans like to eat. An American-style ribeye steak of A-5 marbling (the top-level grade in Japan) would be simply too rich to consume entirely.

Nevertheless, even mixed American Wagyu is usually good meat. The most prominent brands are Snake River Farms from Idaho, which produces from black Wagyu crosses, and HeartBrand Beef from Texas, which specializes in Akaushi crosses, a red Wagyu. Japanese beef experts agree that black Wagyu types marble better than red, but the Akaushi still produces

Angus

Wagyu

Holstein

Highland

Hereford

great steaks. Other outfits are also producing serious stuff. For instance, Fresh From OK, a local brand in Oklahoma, provides incredible pasture-raised Wagyu. First Light, based in New Zealand, is a farm cooperative with likewise superior meat, entirely grass fed on New Zealand's famously lush pasture. At the moment, First Light is imported only to the western United States.

The other notable trait of Wagyu is the high percentage of oleic acid in its fat, the kind of "healthy" fatty acid found in olive oil. Wagyu is also touted for having higher percentages of omega-3 fatty acids than standard breeds do. This is true, says Steve Smith, a professor at Texas A&M who specializes in beef fat. But while the concentration of omega-3 acids in Wagyu is higher than in conventional beef, it is still far lower than in fatty fish from cold waters. And despite the hype, omega-3 fatty acids have yet to be scientifically proven to be more important than other nutrients.

HOLSTEIN

Another "new" trend is meat from Holstein cattle, a breed primarily known as a dairy cow. It's not common knowledge, says Legako of Texas Tech, "but about 20 percent of our beef supply is Holstein. We've reduced our beef herd in the US significantly in the last few years due to

THE STORY OF BEEF

drought and other factors, and that's allowed the dairy industry to sell Holstein steers at a profit." Typically, Holstein steers wouldn't have had much value, as the females are the dairy engines. But Holsteins are predisposed to marble, he says, and have "a different muscle structure and fiber than traditional beef breeds, making them a positive in palatability." (This is how meat scientists talk about steak.)

There are some important fans of Holstein out there, notably Bryan and Katie Flannery of Flannery Beef (see page 33), who are aging and selling Prime-graded Holstein.

HIGHLAND

A great Scottish breed, Highland cattle are the shaggy, horned cattle you might occasionally see, especially in northern climates. Famous for being aloof and hardy, these cattle are from the rugged highlands of Scotland, where they could be left to wander and graze and largely take care of themselves. One of the oldest, purest breeds in Britain, Highlands can survive on sparse grazing and be productive in places other cattle could never endure.

"Temperament's a key thing for Highlands," says John McLaughlin, who raises excellent grass-fed Highland cattle at his family's eponymous farm in Michigan. "When they originated, the cattle were raised in close proximity to the children of their owners. You couldn't have an animal with these big horns killing your kids! So they were selected for temperament."

The other thing McLaughlin notes about Highlands is that they're slower-maturing animals. "It's more costly to raise them than other breeds, especially on grass," he says. "The typical Highland on a more grain-based diet will take at least twenty-four months, whereas the beef you're getting in the grocery store is probably thirteen or fourteen months old." But because of the age, the Highlands can have a lot of flavor, particularly those aged on grass, like McLaughlin's herd.

HEREFORD

The origin of this British breed can be traced back to draught animals used in Roman times. Over the millennia, the breed—notable for its red or orange coat and white head and belly—was converted into efficient beef cattle. Popular meat animals for centuries, Herefords today are prized for being muscular and quite enormous—males can get up to eighteen hundred pounds—and for their propensity to fill out admirably in the more valuable cut areas. Furthermore, they're considered vigorous and with good foraging ability, and they gain weight quickly.

Environment

As already noted, what a cow eats and how it was raised are considered far more important to its flavor than breed. "Temperament is tenderness," John McLaughlin is fond of saying. He's looking for and breeds well-tempered cattle, but their temperament also depends on how they're treated. Indeed, gentle and compassionate treatment of animals is vitally important across the board, but in the case of beef, it also has a crucial role to play in the meat's flavor and tenderness. An animal that is stressed or fearful releases hormones into its system that affect the flavor of its meat. Good farmers and ranchers know this and strive to see their animals treated well, as it's a moral issue that also directly affects their pocketbooks.

AG

**Kronobergsgatan 37
Stockholm, Sweden
tel: (+46) 8-410-61-00 • restaurangag.se**

One of the inspirations for this book, the remarkable Swedish steak house AG has taken steak to a new level of fetishization. It is housed on the second floor of an old industrial building—it used to be a silver factory, hence the name AG, the chemical symbol of silver—and the entrance brings you immediately face-to-face with the glass-walled dry-aging room in which numerous sides of beef are hanging.

AG was one of the first places to look at steak not just as beef, but as a vehicle for expressing characteristics of breed, place, and farmer. It typically carries dry-aged steaks from Sweden, Highland steaks from Scotland, and selected beef from Poland, which owners Johan Jureskog and Klas Ljungquist say is tragically overlooked as a beef-producing country. Its industry has yet to industrialize, they say, and thus the cattle live long, calm, pastoral lives on grass. The deep, beefy steaks those Polish cattle provide are worth traveling to Sweden for.

THE STORY OF BEEF

How cattle are fed is another huge discussion in the beef world these days. *Grass fed* and *grain fed* have become loaded terms that generate discussion and sometimes heated reactions. And while the focus of this book is on the flavor of beef, the issues surrounding how cattle are fed have implications far beyond the kitchen, into the realms of animal welfare, public safety, the environment, climate change, and more. It would be improper to pretend they don't exist and ignore them here. Yet hundreds of articles and books and a number of films have been made that look into the beef cattle industry in this country, so this section will simply summarize the main points of discussion in the hope that you will be inspired to look more deeply into these heady questions.

But before that, let's answer the big, simple question about flavor: which steak should you seek out, grass fed or grain fed?

Of course, everyone's taste is different. But in terms of flavor potential, the answer is grass fed. If you like beef with lots of complex, beefy savor, and flavor matters to you over tenderness, then there's no question that you should seek out the best grass-fed beef available. And it makes sense: A diet of forage—including grass, herbs, legumes, and forbs—simply incorporates a far greater diversity of nutrients than a diet of corn. The nutrients from forage make their way into the meat and fat of the animal and eventually express themselves as flavor.

Occasionally this flavor is even visible. You can see it in the yellow tint of the fat of a grass-fed cow that has lived long enough to bank the nutrients. The color comes from beta-carotene, a natural form of vitamin A and an antioxidant. Beta-carotene gives produce such as squashes, pumpkins, and carrots their signature yellow-orange colors but also occurs in the grasses and legumes that comprise a lot of pastureland. Fat soluble, it gets stored in the fat of grass-fed beef and is transferred to people who eat the meat.

Grain-fed beef, on the other hand, will have less flavor. This is preferable to those who shy away from strong flavors in their food. And for those who demand more flavor, dry aging of the meat can augment that to a degree. But grain-fed beef is also likely to be more tender, especially on the high end of Prime and in high-graded Japanese Wagyu. After all, cattle fattened on grain will move less than cattle that graze openly in a field. Reduced movement equates to less developed muscles and more tenderness. Furthermore, the kind of fat that creates marbling, which is deposited during the months the animals are on high rations of corn, is the kind of fat that melts at low temperatures, providing in the mouth the sensation of juiciness and silkiness.

But these days it's difficult to make beef choices in a vacuum, ignoring the social, ethical, economic, and environmental questions at the heart of this divide.

THE CASE FOR GRASS FED

"What I can tell you is this," says Dr. Allen Williams, "well-produced grass-fed beef far surpasses grain in flavor and quality. If you can seek out and find the right grass fed, it's far more memorable." That Williams says this is not surprising, considering he's one of the leading consultants on grass-fed beef on the continent, traveling all over North America to help ranchers get their soils and grasses to optimum condition

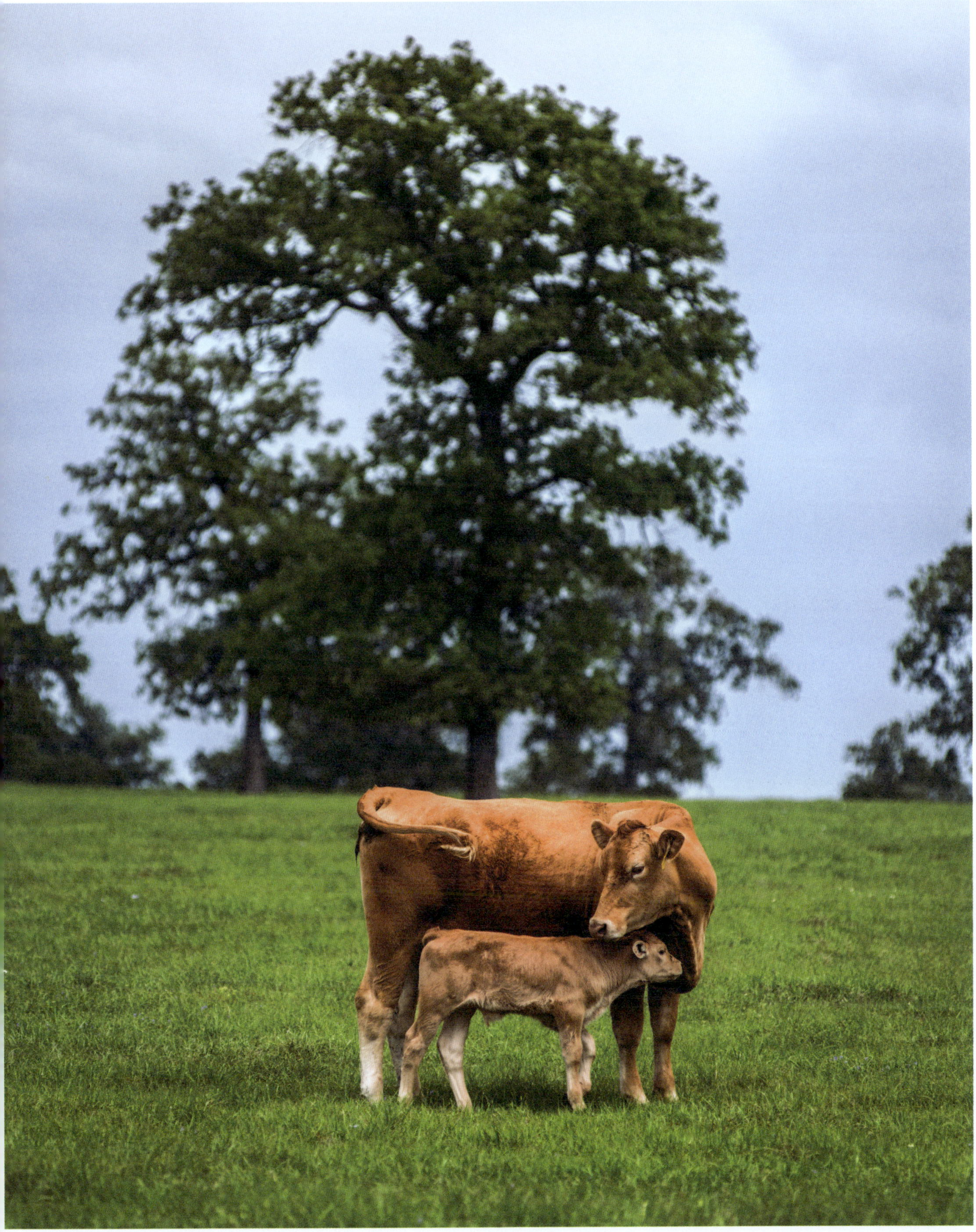

for grazing their animals. Grass is his life. But he also worked for a long time with grain-fed beef on his family's own ranch and once considered himself a proponent of it.

One of the challenges facing grass-fed beef as a category, however, is that not all of it is good. Indeed, it's depressingly easy to get a disappointing grass-fed steak these days, and grass-fed beef has gotten a bad rap because of that. And the stakes are high for the grass-fed movement (no cheap pun intended): one unsatisfactory experience of grass-fed beef apparently has the ability to turn people off it for life.

That drives Williams crazy. "Not all grain-fed beef is good," he says. "A lot of it is really bad, and people seem to forget that. No one ever says, 'I'm swearing off beef because that one steak I had was tough [or flavorless or off].' They keep buying it. So why do people put that onus on grass fed? They should be fair and judge their grain-fed beef just as honestly."

People aren't as tough on grain fed as they are on grass fed probably because the former fails less spectacularly. A bad piece of grain fed is likely to be . . . disappointing, forgettable. It may be flavorless or tough, and it may piss you off because you got ripped off, but it doesn't turn you off beef in general. A bad piece of grass-fed beef, however, may be pungently gamy or taste like liver *and* be as tough as nails. Being viscerally off-putting is what makes people say, "Ick, I never want to experience this again." That one individual steak shouldn't be an indictment of grass-fed beef, but, alas, it often is, for a number of reasons.

One, we've been trained to prefer bland grain-fed beef, which has set the palate for steak in America—tender and sweet. It tastes that way because the cow probably ate more than three thousand pounds of corn in five months. It takes just over two pounds of corn to make one pound of beef. And that's the same, familiar corn that sweetens most American processed foods.

Also, not all grass fed is the same. Good grass-fed beef requires a real program and real intention. Ranchers need to know how to graze their cattle, to pay attention to what they are eating. They need to harvest them at the right time. A lot of what passes as grass-fed beef in farmers' markets or roadside stands may simply be from scrawny old dairy cows that were never intended to be great beef. Or perhaps it is cheater grass-fed beef, in which the cattle are confined on a feedlot and just fed concentrated grass pellets, which are legal under the term.

Along the way from birth to slaughter are lots of places for grass-fed beef to go south. Jordan got clued in to this by observing the evolution of Long Meadow Ranch, a farm-to-table operation and wine producer in Napa Valley.

Jordan was excited when he learned the owners had the ambitious program of raising their own herd of Highland cattle for beef to serve at their restaurant in St. Helena and to sell at the farmers' market. But the first time he tried it, the flavor wasn't great and the steak was tough. Apparently they recognized this too and were already working to change the program. They started by interbreeding Angus with their pure Highland cattle to try for better-marbled beef. And they put the cattle on richer pastures and also upgraded their selection process for slaughter. Before that, their guy had sort of indiscriminately been choosing animals when the restaurant was running out of beef, paying little attention to the state of the cattle. Now, they've learned that they need to be harvesting seasonally in late spring or late fall, when the grass is green and the cattle are on richer forage. They needed a better eye for selecting individual animals who were at their peak. When the grass dries out in the summer, the cattle actually lose fat because they need as much or more energy to digest the dried grass as they get from eating it. The Long Meadow beef sold at the market and at its restaurant Farmstead is now delicious and getting even better. (They're even opening a butcher shop adjacent to the restaurant.)

Mainstream grass-fed beef has to improve across the board. And another reason to support grass-fed beef and help drive its improvement is that it's beef in accordance with nature. Pastures are where cattle are supposed to be—and this lifestyle is better for them and better for the world. Indeed, there's a great pleasure in marveling at the coevolutionary miracle of nature that is the relationship between cows and grass. It's one of those beautiful examples of symbiosis from which all beings profit.

Ruminants—be they cattle, buffalo, sheep, or elk—both support and feed off the grasses. They protect grasslands by keeping trees and brambles from encroaching, and they fertilize the ground with their manure and urine, spread grass seed, and plant the seed in the soil with their hooves. Grasses grow back stronger than before after being munched on; they evolved to resist the grazing of ruminants. In turn, the cattle get an endless lunch, for they evolved to do something most mammals can't: digest cellulose. The most abundant organic molecule on the planet, cellulose—an organic structural component of wood, grass, leaves, and the like—is created by plants using the sun's energy.

Other organisms win in this relationship, too. Grasslands regenerate themselves after grazing (if they are not overgrazed). As they grow, grasses shed their roots, depositing carbon into the soil, and then regrow even more and deeper roots. In turn, this subterranean environment provides home to the thriving community of bacteria and fungi that support countless other organisms by breaking down the organic matter of plants into humus while simultaneously feeding essential minerals from the ground to the roots of the plants. As this soil becomes deeper and more alive, it pulls more carbon out of the air and sequesters it, creating new pathways to store water in the process.

A growing movement of farmers and scientists see cattle and other ruminants as crucial to rebuilding soils worldwide that are being lost to erosion and desertification thanks to deforestation and industrial agriculture. Although some critics say that ruminants are a major cause of climate change, others posit the problem as being that too few of them feed on grass anymore, promoting carbon sequestration.

Humans thrive from the cow-grass relationship, too. We need the sun's energy to live but can't get it directly from light. Eating meat is one way to harvest that energy. Basically, when we dine on beef, we are consuming grass and other plants, some of the most plentiful substances on Earth. Raising meat on grass can be sensible ecologically as well. Yes, vegetable and grain crops can also provide energy, but they don't grow well everywhere. Much of the land on which cattle graze is too stony, arid, and hilly to grow crops profitably without major inputs such as irrigation and fertilizer. But grasses grow in much thinner soils than crops, and the action of ruminants helps soils store water (requiring no irrigation) and fix nitrogen (obviating fertilizer). When it all works as it's supposed to, it's a virtuous circle.

Betsy Ross on her ranch outside of Austin, Texas

Indeed, the great deep soils that turned the American Midwest into an agricultural powerhouse were achieved thanks to passage of the bison over grasslands for thousands of years.

To get a sense of how right this feels, go out and visit an enlightened grass-fed operation like Betsy Ross's, just outside of Austin, Texas. There, her herd of Devon cattle graze on a brilliant spread of pastureland—flowering plants, wild herbs, grasses, weeds, and thistles. Ross practices what's called holistic management. Like most people who observe this, she'd consider herself more a grass farmer than a cattle rancher. Scratch that, they consider themselves soil farmers, as grass and cattle are really just parts of an ecosystem that builds soil. And that soil is what keeps the ecology in balance, supplies water when it's scarce, and keeps the climate stable. The cattle, busy munching away and not at all afraid of the humans standing amid them, seem happy. The meadow is robust and full of life. It just seems good.

"When we started this in 1992, the prevailing wisdom was that we couldn't do this," says Ross, a spry woman of seventy-eight. "The prevailing wisdom said you couldn't raise them for their lifetime on grass without supplementing. At that time, the cost of carrying a cow through the winter was $513, so you had to sell for more than that to break even. Now it's up to about $750. We don't spend nearly that because we're powered by the sun, not chemicals. We spend that money on people here."

Ross looks at herself as a steward of a system that can manage itself. "We don't feed minerals, we let the weeds bring the minerals up. It's a harmony. It's a symphony. Sometimes the animal itself is the dominating figure, other times the grass is, other times the insects, other times the water. Grass-fed beef is an experience not just about raising beef. Hopefully you feel good; there's a different energy here."

She's right. And when you eat her beef, you get a different feeling. It tastes different from conventional beef. She gave some to Jordan, and he served it to a bunch of friends along with some steaks from other producers. It was one of the favorites of the group and elicited an unusual comment. One diner said, "It's so mineral—like eating an oyster. It doesn't taste like an oyster," she added, but noted that you get a rush from a sensation of minerals surging into your body.

That wasn't an overstatement. Grass-fed beef is significantly higher than grain fed in beta-carotene, selenium, potassium, magnesium, zinc, and more. And there's that fatty acid profile: grass fed is higher in healthy conjugated linoleic acid.

So, grass-fed beef is better for humans, cattle, microbes, and the health of the entire planet. What's not to like? Ah, yes, the flavor of that beef. That's where it becomes incumbent on the ranchers themselves to make this work. They must be aware of the necessity of having truly delicious grass-fed beef to offer. It means making sure the cattle's diet of grass and silage is rich and diverse. This requires only harvesting it when the beef is full and marbled, which generally means an older animal. But we diners should also open our minds to a product with a slightly different flavor than what we're used to. Also, we must remember that grass-fed beef is an agricultural, not an industrial, product, and is therefore as prone to variation as the produce we find in the store. But the more we support the good grass-fed producers with our dollars, the greater the incentive for others to join the cause and up their game.

THE TRUTH ABOUT GRAIN FED

Arguments supporting grain feeding of cattle are far slimmer than the very brief summary of the benefits of grass feeding just offered. Grain feeding might produce some qualities of beef that we like, but quite simply its existence represents the opposite of a harmonious natural system. After all, feeding cattle massive amounts of corn perverts what Mother Nature intended for ruminants. Instead, it represents a solution to the man-made political, economic, and industrial problems of overproduction of corn. As Michael Pollan lays out in *The Omnivore's Dilemma*, the roots of this problem, which are deep and convoluted, involve the shift to producing industrially made, petroleum-based chemical fertilizers in order to use up the vast surplus of ammonium nitrate, a key ingredient in explosives, left over after World War II. New hybrid strains of corn (which grow faster and with higher yields than heritage breeds) required the huge amounts of soil nitrogen only these fertilizers could supply. Suddenly, corn farmers could produce exponentially more corn per acre than had ever been possible in history.

Starting in the 1950s and surging in the 1970s, issues relating to politics, economics, and food security pushed farmers to overproduce corn. Despite the resolution of these issues, production has remained ridiculously high, which theoretically should drive down the price and cause farmers to cut production. But because, for political reasons, politicians have continually supported farmers with direct payments, there has been no incentive to slow cultivation. In short, the corn market is artificially supported by tax dollars.

Something had to be done with all that corn, and the idea was hit upon to use its calories systematically to fatten the country's cattle, fundamentally changing the traditional life cycle of the cow. It's not new to supplement a cow's diet with grain, but it is new to only or primarily feed cattle grain for a good chunk of their lives.

Whereas in the past a beef cow's life would have been largely spent on pasture, now they spend only the first five or six months on pasture before heading to feedlots. Here's where the race to fatten them as quickly and as cheaply as possible begins until they make a decent weight and head off to slaughter. This whole system has been much documented, so it won't be belabored here. But you should probably know that much of the cattle raised to produce industrial beef have been given antibiotics to stave off infections caused by confinement in overcrowded living quarters and by problems associated with a corn diet. Cows can tolerate eating corn as long as it is accompanied with the right percentage of roughage. Too much corn causes fatal bloating and painful acidosis. Hormones and other chemicals are also given to speed growth. Today, cattle are being specifically bred to better tolerate a corn diet (salmon are too). A balance of grass in the diet can alleviate these issues, but it will also slow down the fattening.

Corn feeding does fatten the animals quickly and causes them to marble well. That greater marbling (see page 41) is the driving force of the government's beef-grading system is simply a reinforcement of this perverse economy. Cementing the system, in just seventy years, the American taste for beef has become the sweet, tender meat produced by feeding cattle corn.

The typical American beef cow will spend its first five or six months on grass with its mother in what are known as cow-calf operations. These are mostly small, family-run farms, and there are hundreds of thousands of such operations across the country. They are the idyllic places where young cattle do what they're supposed to do. Indeed, cattle are routinely trucked all over the country to places grasses grow best to complete this stage of life and then shipped back for the next. When they reach five or six hundred pounds, they're transitioned for life in the feedlot.

Not all feedlots are the wretched, filth-strewn cow megacities that have been (rightfully) demonized. Some are much more humane, clean, well-kept places. Pollution from decomposing manure and runoff are serious environmental problems, however. Nevertheless, the feedlot is where the cattle put on their next five hundred to seven hundred pounds as quickly as possible. When they reach the correct weight and form, they are sold back to the beef processors. Most beef cattle are slaughtered between thirteen and eighteen months. It could take a grass-fed animal another year to make it to the twelve-hundred-pound weight preferred at slaughter. That's another year or more of not profiting on the animal. And 85 percent of all beef comes from the big four processors: Cargill, National, JBS, and Tyson.

The arguments in favor of this system basically amount to this: If we didn't have the ability to grow these massive amounts of corn (and soybeans) we wouldn't be able to feed all of the people on the planet. Technically, concentrating beef cattle on feedlots could preserve the land needed to graze them for better uses. Raising cattle does require considerable land and time. As a food source, the current system may be faster and cheaper. What those costs would be without subsidized corn, however, are up for debate. Some estimates suggest a 33 percent increase in price, but it would probably be a lot more.

The best argument for grain-fed beef is that people really like it. And, no question, there is some exceptional grain-fed beef out there, brands such as Creekstone and HeartBrand. But at what cost do we maintain this system?

GRAIN FINISHING

Not all grain finishing is the same. It's not hard to find beef marketed as grass fed but grain finished. In basic terms, that means very little. It could describe cattle that spent six months on a corn diet in a concentrated feedlot. Or it could be used for pastured animals that spent their last month on a diet supplemented with a mixture of non-corn grains—millet, rye, oats—grown organically on the very farm where they were raised. Many ranchers believe such a way of finishing the cattle gives them a little extra marbling and perhaps tones down any edgy flavors the beef might have gained from time on grass. Grain finishing of this type may sweeten and soften the meat, making it more palatable, but the longer the time off grass, the greater the reduction of healthy compounds and fatty acids.

Age

The one piece of the beef flavor puzzle that goes missing in this country is the factor of age. Meat from older animals has more flavor. If you want proof, go to Spain. Here in the United States, producers pride themselves on the quickness they can get a cow to slaughter, the younger the better. If they can be harvesting cattle at twelve months, they are really making money. In Spain, people celebrate how old the cow is.

Jordan experienced this firsthand on a trip to Spain. He was in the town of Ávila, just randomly at a meat restaurant on the outskirts of town. This place specialized in beef, so he ordered a ribeye. It was lunch. When the beef came out and was set in front of him, his saliva glands instantly started firing. No steak he'd ever had smelled so beefy. First bite, he couldn't believe what he was tasting. It was a deep, rich, savory sensation of beef he'd never experienced before. He found himself thinking, "Maybe Spain has the best-tasting beef in the world." That steak became one of the inspirations for this book. It came from a steer about six years old. Was it tender? He can't remember. That didn't even matter because it tasted so damn good.

Older animals always have more intense flavor than younger ones. It's true in chickens and it's true in cattle. Sadly, for reasons of economics, in the United States our industries are incentivized to harvest animals as young as possible, meaning that flavor is greatly diminished. We eat a lot of incredibly bland meat, hardly ever experiencing what true chicken flavor or real beef flavor is all about.

True flavor comes from animals that have lived life. A steer's work, its movement, and its diet are what create flavor. The longer it's had to live, to move, and to eat a variety of foods, the more savory and beefy it's going to become. Wagyu cattle, for instance, are slower maturing. This means that it takes them longer to get to slaughter weight. It makes the meat more expensive but also explains some of its enhanced flavor. Age also accounts for some of the flavor advantages of good grass-fed beef. Because grass-fed cattle take longer to reach a decent slaughtering weight, they not only move more in their lives, building more flavorful muscles, but also spend more time putting on weight. Consequently, grass-fed beef usually has more flavor.

The gastronomic argument against older cattle usually has to do with tenderness. In some studies, many Americans have stated a preference for tenderness over flavor. So long as the steak is juicy and melts in your mouth, people don't seem to care that it's bland. When a cow lives only fourteen months and is fed corn for almost half that time, it's had little chance to develop flavor but it will likely be tender. But for those who love flavor and don't mind a little chewiness, there are few choices.

The limiting factor for raising older animals, of course, is cost. No rancher wants to pay to feed a cow an extra six months or a year or four. It's expensive and risky (more opportunities for the cow to get sick or injured), and at this point, there's not a market where the cost of the steak can be high enough to recoup that investment.

But in other countries that market exists. In Spain, farmers will take dairy cows who have retired from producing milk after four or five years and put them back on the pasture for another few years. Now, you're getting a cow that is eight years old. Or there's the madness of chef José Gordón of El Capricho (see page 62), who buys oxen at three years old and pastures them on his ranch (at great expense) in León Province until they're ready, usually between eight and twelve years of age. This might be the most flavorful steak in the world.

Of course, we have older cattle in the United States, and they do get slaughtered—just not for steaks. Indeed, one of the little-known facts about hamburgers is that one reason they're so beefy and delicious is because much of their meat comes from older cows whose steaks would be too old to get a grade of Prime or even Choice. This instantly downgrades them into the category of cheap meat, so—no matter how flavorful—they usually go into hamburger. This is great for the nation's hamburgers, but, if handled with more care and intention, older beef could be used more profitably and perhaps satisfy people in other ways.

While Spain is the king of old cows, things may be changing in favor of older beef in other countries. High-end food scenes in Europe are catching on to the deliciousness of steaks from older cattle, and Spain can provide only so many (older cattle are a diminishing resource). However, the new taste for highly flavored meat from old cows may spark other countries to convert part of their industries to conserving and reconditioning older cattle.

Will Americans ever develop such a taste? Glenn Elzinga, of Alderspring Ranch in Idaho, is doubtful. "In Spain or France, those people can tolerate an incredible amount of flavor, but Americans are on Nebraska corn-fed beef since 1950," he says. "Even people who are food people are not ready for the intensity of flavor development after thirty-six months. I can eat that intense steak off our grass. That is an intense steak. But I serve up this incredible steak to people, and they can't handle it. They'll say it's too beefy. We have an American clientele who are steak lovers but have never really experienced flavor of that intensity, and as a result, it's a no sale."

But perhaps a high-end market could be developed for a small number of people who love the taste of beef and are willing to pay extra to support older cattle. In California, a top-end meat supplier called Cream Co. is experimenting with just this—putting retired dairy cattle onto pasture for a time to recover and develop more fat. At a tasting in Austin with Cliff Pollard, Cream Co.'s founder, we tried some of this steak, and it was outstandingly flavorful and not at all tough. Not quite at the level of Spanish beef, but highly encouraging. It doesn't seem ridiculous to think that such a market could develop in the United States.

The Upshot

In the interest of flavor and eating experience, what is the hypothetical best steak you could buy? It would be from a grass-fed, grass-finished animal at least five years of age. Right now, that steak doesn't exist in the United States. So beyond that, in the realm of choice, what should you look for?

Some good-tasting corn-fed beef is out there, but it's few and far between. Most of it—and the vast majority of beef in this country—comes out of a system that does not produce much good meat and is also negative in terms of animal welfare, public health, and the global environment.

Grass fed is the right way to go for reasons of health, social responsibility, and—at its best—taste. But finding great grass-fed beef isn't always easy. The best thing to do is locate a great source and support that producer. It will likely be more expensive and harder to source. If that's worth it to you, then consider the idea of eating less but higher-quality steak.

THE HOLY GRAIL OF AMERICAN BEEF?

They call it "grass-fed gold." Just as we were finishing the book, we made a steak discovery that could be a game changer in the United States—at least for those of us who want fuller-flavored, well-marbled grass-fed beef. Most people think that's impossible, but it's not. It simply requires older cattle—cattle that no one was committed to keeping around and feeding until now. Enter Carter Country Meats, a family-owned ranch and beef business in Wyoming. For the first time, they are marketing dry-aged beef from five- to ten-year-old cattle that have grazed on nothing but mountain pasture their entire lives (save the winters, when they are fed home-grown and fermented silage). The beef is exquisite, with a deep, beefy savor, long-lingering flavor, and a remarkable degree of tenderness. And it came about mostly by accident.

RC Carter and family manage a cow-calf operation on forty-five thousand acres of mountain pasture in the Bighorn Range and an additional four hundred square miles of rangeland in southern Wyoming. They maintain a large herd of cattle throughout the year, including cows from five to ten years of age that have gone dry and stopped becoming pregnant. The typical fate of these animals is to be sold on the commodity market, where they fetch sixty cents a pound (or about nine hundred dollars an animal). "That's not a lucrative profession," says RC. "The commodity guys have convinced everybody that these cows aren't worth anything. They usually try to discount you because they're so old." RC wouldn't have known any better himself, but he happened to see *Steak Revolution*, a 2014 French documentary that included José Gordón of Spain's El Capricho (see page 62) talking about turning his older oxen into some of the best steaks in the world.

RC got an idea. He gathered his dad and brother and they drove down to southern Wyoming to check out their cattle. "There are wild horses roaming and antelope and our cows, just purely on open grassy range. We spent a week gathering up all of these cows [as they now do annually], and some of them were superfat. Having eaten grass all summer long, they looked like finished beef." The Carters took nine of them. Shockingly (to them), 30 percent graded Prime. "They were considered throwaway cows," says RC, "but it turns out they're better than the younger animals anyway—hands-down. If I sold them commodity, I might get nine hundred dollars a cow, but that same animal I can sell to Nate for four thousand dollars."

Nate is Nate Singer, a talented butcher who runs Black Belly, a great shop in Boulder, Colorado. Having grown up in Wyoming, Nate knew the Carters and he also knew good beef (his dad is a butcher with a restaurant in Cody). Now, in addition to holding down his job at Black Belly, he serves as an ambassador and agent for Carter Country's beef program. "I'll never forget those first animals we harvested," says Nate. "Their meat was gorgeous, their fat a deep yellow color. They were the most beautiful animals. 'Grass-fed gold' is what we called it."

Nate says that the biggest problem with selling older cows is dry aging. Older grass-fed animals (and there aren't older grain-fed ones because no one will pay to feed them corn for more than a few months) will have more developed muscles, so they need some dry aging for tenderness. But dry aging has been next to impossible to come by for older cattle because of the thirty-month rule.

What's the thirty-month rule? That's the rule the USDA imposed that says cattle slaughtered over the (rather arbitrary) age of thirty months need to have their spinal column (and certain other parts) separated from the carcass before the meat leaves the slaughterhouse, to prevent mad cow disease. Whether that's reasonable or even necessary is a whole other argument, but it's the law. Because of this rule, slaughterhouses are loathe to process older animals because they require a special run, with thorough cleaning of equipment before going back to conventional younger cattle, which make up almost all their business. Furthermore, beef wholesalers don't want to age the meat, because in losing the spine bones a valuable form of protection from dehydration is gone. And finally, there's a bias against older animals in the USDA grading protocol, meaning they can't grade high on the commercial scale no matter how marbled the meat. Basically, the entire system is rigged against older cattle.

"When you think about raising grass-fed beef," Nate says, "well at thirty months of age, the animal is like a fifteen-year-old kid—they're skinny, hyper, and nuts. But when they get older, they start to marble and hold fat on their carcasses. By the time they're five to six years old, they're starting to pack it on, this beautiful golden-tinged fat." As for the expense most ranchers face when keeping animals past the typical twenty-four to thirty months, well that's where the Carter family's access to forty thousand acres and twenty-seven natural springs comes in. "It's why we've got to conserve these old ranches and land," continues RC. "This is beautiful cattle country that grows its own resources in grass and water. It's the opposite of a feedlot that's a drain on resources."

Nate and RC were able to work a deal with a local slaughterhouse to harvest their older cows once every two weeks and then hang the whole carcasses anywhere from fourteen to forty days, depending on space. The spines are removed just before the meat is shipped. Nate may age some other cuts longer in his shop, but there are no porterhouses or T-bones (because the spine has been removed). They hope to create some greater slaughterhouse flexibility in the future to expand their offerings.

Eating older cattle is an answer to many of the beef industry's annoying problems. The meat tastes exponentially better. It's from untreated, 100 percent grass-fed cattle that live a bountiful life as they were meant to live, while regenerating open rangeland and consuming only naturally occurring resources. Ranchers make more money and carnivores can have a better experience. Much like California's Cream Co. (see page 25), which is revitalizing older dairy cows on grass before sale, it's a win-win-win for all involved. Now if only the entire industry would get involved, we would have a real steak revolution.

THE STORY OF BEEF

The iconic Prause Meat Market in La Grange, Texas

CHAPTER 2

Buying Steaks

Figuring out how and where to get the best steaks can be a dizzying experience. Well, it can also be a darn simple experience. One thing's for sure: finding the best steaks becomes more and more complicated and more confusing the farther away from the actual producer you get. In Texas, Aaron is lucky to have access to Dai Due, Lee's, and Salt & Time (more on Salt & Time in the next chapter). In California, Jordan has Olivier's, 4505 Meats, Clove and Hoof, and the Fatted Calf. The most common ways we Americans find steaks these days are via three main methods: straight from the rancher or farmer, from a butcher or other curator, and through some sort of branded program (or just from your local grocery store). Each has its pros and cons, always involving that all-important connection to the source.

The farther you get from the ranch, the more the quality of the beef declines. And when there's no way of determining the source or even who's selling the meat or where it's from, it's hard to make any guarantees about quality or provenance. It's hard to find guarantees no matter what, but the best bets always rely on some degree of trust.

Straight from the Farm

If you've read chapter 1, you know the care and work that goes into raising high-quality beef cows. One way to guarantee your beef is the best it can be is to get it directly from the source, that is, the rancher who raised the cow. This could be someone in your area from whom you can buy locally at the farmers' market or even at his or her own farmstead, or this could be done from across the country thanks to the miracle of interstate shipping.

Despite the dominance of national grocers like Whole Foods, Costco, and Kroger, buying locally from the person who actually raised the animals is increasingly easy, as many farmers and ranchers have developed casual direct-to-consumer programs and achieved loyal followings. Every state has ample opportunities to buy meat this way. And it's fun to shop locally, too. If you're on a road trip, buying a steak is a pleasant way to start a conversation with a native and sample the local beef *terroir*. It's hard to resist getting a piece of grass-fed beef when driving through the lush, emerald valleys of Vermont, The Green Mountain State. That's equally true if you're cruising through Central Texas and see groups of mighty longhorns glaring at you from a pasture or if you are traveling past a wildflower-strewn meadow in Wisconsin where plump cattle are grazing.

Of course, local beef isn't always a hit. When you're a tourist, you never really know what you're going to get. For instance, Jordan actually was that tourist, and after seeing all those lush Vermont pastures, he just *had* to find some delicious local grass-fed steaks. Unfortunately, what he located was an example of "bad" grass-fed beef, meaning that it was lean, tough, and tasted more like liver than loin. It spoke of a farmer who probably raised cattle primarily for dairy and not meat and didn't really know how to or care to finish his beef properly. Disappointing!

But when you find a tried-and-true local producer of good quality, there's almost nothing better. If you've got freezer space, you can buy a quarter of a cow (about one hundred pounds) or more at one time, saving money on a per-pound basis while making the life of the farmer easier. Many folks go in on such a deal as a group, sharing an entire animal. Of course, you're going to get more than just steaks if you go this route. But even though this is a steak book, we highly encourage you to learn what to do with all the rest of the animal!

But given that steaks are a luxury item, the idea of buying the best you can find from a producer in another state and spending a bit on shipping isn't so far-fetched. After all, without a second thought, we purchase everything from Nerf Official N-Strike Elite Strongarm Blasters to high-waist yoga pants (both recent best sellers on Amazon) through the mail these days. Why not meat? In fact, there's a long tradition of sending frozen meat by mail, just as there is boxes of grapefruits or pears. Omaha Steaks started shipping to front doors in 1952.

One concern with mail-order meat, besides the sometimes extravagant cost of shipping, is the environmental costs of packaging materials, which even in our more eco-conscious age are still often Styrofoam and gel packs. Some outfits are counteracting this standard, however, like Alderspring Ranch of Idaho, whose packaging is recyclable and also returnable. Alderspring includes a prepaid return label in every shipment and offers a five-dollar rebate on your next order if you send the box back.

Beyond that generous and responsible recycling program (and the fact that the company eats the estimated ten-dollar cost of returns), Alderspring is a prime example of what you can get by ordering directly from a farm. If you're interested in grass-fed beef of the highest quality, this is the place. Alderspring is a family-run ranch located in remote May, Idaho, in the Pahsimeroi Valley. They have about eight hundred acres of grassland in the valley, but more important, in the summer, they saddle up their horses and take the cattle into the mountains the old-fashioned way, leaving them on seventy square miles of mountain meadow and pasture. "We basically follow the snow line up the mountain," says founder Glenn Elzinga. In the summer, the cattle eat a rich and diverse diet based on hundreds of native plant species growing on untouched, virgin soils. During this time, the cattle walk around and get to choose what they want to munch on. The beef is dry aged for tenderization for a couple of weeks and is then shipped out.

It's American Angus beef like no other, and you can get it delivered to your door—one of the amazing aspects of being alive today.

Butchers and Curators

The very best butchers are just a half step further from the source. Old-fashioned whole-animal butchery is being revived as a craft and a business, a stark contrast from industrial butchers who get their beef parts in boxes and are merely responsible for separating them into steaks (if even that). In contrast, the new crop of throwback butchers buy entire carcasses and use their ingenuity and the superior sharpness of their knives not only to create great steaks but also all manner of other beef products, too.

In the case of a superior butchery like Austin's Salt & Time (see page 50), a lot of the steaks (and other meats) come directly from single farms and ranches. The butchers have visited these producers, or at least had long, probing conversations, and are fluent in the nature of the beef, the breed, and the conditions in which the cattle are raised.

SOME OF OUR FAVORITE REGIONAL PURVEYORS

In the next chapter, we talk with Ben Runkle and Bryan Butler, our friends and the owner-operators of Salt & Time in Austin, Texas. But if you're not lucky enough to live in Austin, fear not; there are great artisanal butcher shops and meat purveyors across the country. Some ship by mail and some you've just got to be there for. Here are a few of our favorites.

Olivier's, San Francisco, California

All butchers have their own unique approaches and specialties. Olivier Cordier is a passionate and voluble Frenchman who offers high-quality beef sold in the classic French cuts: *côte de boeuf, entrecôte, faux-filet, onglet*, and more. He dry ages his beef in the American style, sometimes for very long periods of time, inviting customers to reserve cuts of 60-, 120-, and 200-day dry-aged beef months in advance.

MEAT IS YUMMY

When it comes to sourcing, however, Olivier won't divulge where his beef comes from. In the Bay Area, where diners cynically joke about how restaurant menus tout the farms on which each morsel of food was grown, such a response is at first a bit shocking. But in such a competitive marketplace, Olivier figures if he literally gives away the farm, someone will try to horn in on his source or that source will cut him out, using his patronage as a stepping-stone to becoming a stand-alone brand. In this case, you just have to trust him . . . an easy thing to do after you cook up one of his steaks.

Flannery Beef, San Rafael, California

In a large space whirring with refrigeration and perpetual fans, in an anonymous industrial park, operates a butchery that has become internationally renowned for the quality of its beef. Bryan Flannery used to run a retail butcher shop but gave it up as his mail-order business took off. The spread of Flannery's fame predates social media and has largely been due to word of mouth. His steaks have been buoyed by landing on the tables of some truly influential diners. For years, one of Flannery's most high-profile clients has been Robert Parker, the world's most prominent wine critic. In his newsletter, Parker often chronicles his always epic meals, occasionally writing things like, "The 55-day dry-aged Private Reserve Sirloin Strips from Bryan Flannery were, as usual, unreal. If this guy is not the best and most consistent purveyor of high-quality American beef, I would be interested in knowing who is."

Like Olivier Cordier, Flannery doesn't detail the sources of his beef, just listing California, Midwestern, and Montana (for Wagyu). The point is that Flannery Beef is the trusted source, and to that end, all of the meat they buy is chosen and regraded by Bryan and his daughter, Katie, his business partner and successor. "We buy Prime beef," says Katie, "but it happens all the time that we get meat delivered [on which] we have to downgrade the rating. Our standards are more exacting." The Flannerys also age their beef, usually a minimum of thirty days, but work with individual customers and will age to specified lengths of time.

Crowd Cow, Seattle, Washington

Joe Heitzeberg and his cofounder, Ethan Lowry, came at their business thinking like consumers. A lifelong steak lover, Joe notes how steak has been regarded—and still is—as a commodity; you never know where it's from or who raised it. But, he points out, coffee and chocolate were like that too, yet those products have become decommoditized. Today, you can buy single-origin, fair-trade, farm-specific versions of both from a dizzying number of global places. Joe and Ethan wondered why steak, such a special food, couldn't be seen in the same light. At some point, a friend happened to mention to Joe that he was buying mind-blowing beef directly from a farm. The purchasing required a fair bit of coordination (arranging multiple people to contribute toward the cost of shares in a whole cow) as well as freezer space for maybe a hundred or more pounds of beef.

So, in the digital spirit of the times, Ethan and Joe hit on the idea of crowdfunding a cow—same way that random people might crowdfund a project on Kickstarter—allowing a larger number of people to buy a smaller amount of superior beef. In short order, after visiting some ranches and constructing a website, Crowd

BATEAU

1040 East Union Street
Seattle, Washington
tel: (206) 900-8699 • restaurantbateau.com

One can have no greater respect for a restaurant than one that reveres the cow so much that it commits to a program of raising its own beef, as well as butchering, aging, cooking, and serving it. Very, very few restaurateurs are willing to take on such a labor- and capital-intensive operation. When they do (such as at Spain's El Capricho, see page 62), their restaurants deserve our attention and support.

This is not difficult to offer Seattle restaurant maven Renee Erickson, whose other triumphs include the Walrus and the Carpenter, an oyster bar. The concept is simple: Erickson, along with chef Taylor Thornhill and talented butcher Tom Coss, brings in whole beef carcasses (some of which they've raised themselves, some of which are raised by trusted small ranchers) and turns them into dry-aged goodness. On a big chalkboard in the dining room, the dozens of steaks are listed first by ranch and length of aging and then by particular cut. Coss is resourceful with the animals, producing many obscure cuts, such as Jacob's Ladder, Merlan, Oyster, Ball Tip, and more—as well as the old standbys. Each carcass offers only a limited number of cuts, and each cut is listed by weight and price. When one is purchased, a staff member takes a long pool cue–like pole with a piece of white chalk at the end and crosses it off, so everyone gets a fair shot at what's remaining. All of the steaks are grass fed and grass finished.

The room is casual but elegant. Cooked in cast-iron pans and butter basted, steaks are given a long rest, after which they are picked up in a hot pan and reflashed for service. They are served with a choice of three different, pungent compound butters: bone marrow, preserved lemon and brown butter, and anchovy.

A hallmark of Erickson's restaurants is her exquisite taste in everything from interior design to cocktails, and this is on full display at Bateau. The wine list is moderate in length but well chosen, and the seasonal sides are pitch-perfect, with gorgeous green salads, vibrant tomatoes, and foraged-mushroom fricassees. You may think salmon when visiting Seattle, but don't sleep on the steak.

Cow launched, selling its first cow out in a day. The spirit of Crowd Cow is now as much about exploring the rancher and the ranch as it is about just selling delicious beef; Joe and Ethan want to show that in beef, as in wine and chocolate, there is *terroir*. The two founders have even put out a book, *Craft Beef: A Revolution in Small Farms and Big Flavors*, chronicling their philosophy and tales of beef sourcing.

Indeed, the sourcing side of the job has become the most compelling part of it: Joe and Ethan have become steak hunters, that is, they now travel around the country and the world in search of the tastiest, most ethically raised, distinctive beef. On their site you can purchase shares of cows (as much or as little as you want, and when the order fills up, the cow "tips" and the meat will be harvested and sent out) from everywhere from Washington State to California, Montana, Missouri, and Pennsylvania.

Crowd Cow has even broken open Japan, where, among its several super-marbled triumphs, it has found the ultimate cult beef: olive-fed Kuroge Washu-breed Wagyu from a tiny corner of the country, the only place in the region where imported olive trees were planted. The beef is extraordinary. Joe shared one of the first samples with us, which we and a few of our steak-obsessed friends cooked up in Jordan's mom's backyard in Austin, along with a bunch of different steaks from other producers. With an oleic acid content of 65 percent (for reference, olive oil itself tends to run 55 to 83 percent) and bursting with juice, the steak's featherlight fat belied its richness. It simply melted in the mouth, leaving a light, nutty flavor and disappearing with a resonant smack of umami.

Marketed Meat: The Truths and Myths of Branded Beef

Branding cattle with a hot iron is (rightly) seen as cruel these days and is hardly practiced. But what's called "branded beef," well, that's one of the biggest trends in the world of beef in the last twenty years. Simply put, it's just beef with a name, be it Creekstone or Niman Ranch. That name could stand for something like a real place or stringent standards, or it could be totally made-up and functionally meaningless. The simple act of putting a brand name on meat is a form of marketing. It suggests to the buyer that this beef stands for something, implying some aspect of quality that, if the brand is purchased again, will remain consistent. That suggested quality might be tenderness (Tyson's Tender Promise) or environmental and animal welfare (Publix's GreenWise).

In many cases, the brand does stand for something, as every branded beef program proclaims its own standards, based on things like locality, aging, genetics, and grade. To become certified in the United States, the program must be accepted and monitored by the USDA, which verifies that the claims of the brand are backed in every carcass. Not all brands are USDA certified, meaning that those that are not are held only by their own standards. American Branded Beef programs tend to fall into three major categories: breed specific, place specific, and company specific.

BREED SPECIFIC

Breed-specific programs focus on one particular breed. Most famous of them all, Certified Angus Beef (CAB for short, founded in 1978) promises that all of its meat comes from Angus cattle. There's also a Certified Hereford Beef program for that breed and even a Certified Texas Longhorn Beef program. HeartBrand sells Akaushi cattle, a subset of Japanese Wagyu. In each of these cases, the genetics of the cattle used in the program are maintained and considered central to the quality of the beef.

Today, many, many brands peddle the ever-popular Angus breed, including Niman Ranch and Creekstone. In addition to the guarantee of breed, some of these brands support further standards, such as vegetarian diet, no hormones or antibiotics, and humane treatment. With the certification in 1978 of CAB, the general thought about branded programs would be that they were based on breed. But a decade later, the USDA began approving brands based on qualities other than breed.

PLACE SPECIFIC

Other brands are based on place, often launched by a coalition of like-minded ranchers to leverage teamwork and size to compete better in a brutal market. Oregon Country Beef is a good example. This brand doesn't claim to be USDA certified, but it is non-GMO verified and GAP certified (a nonprofit that promotes animal welfare) by third parties.

While we don't have designation of origin—another type of brand, in its own way—for beef in the United States, other countries do. The most famous in the beef origin world is arguably Kobe beef, a special kind of beef from Wagyu cattle that can only come from the Kobe region of Japan. Over the years, misuse of the name Kobe beef has been a constant problem for those protecting the brand. Merchants in the United States have repeatedly sold beef as Kobe that wasn't from the region or even from Japan. (If you're offered Kobe beef at a restaurant, be skeptical, exceedingly little real Kobe beef comes into this country, and it is tightly controlled.) Other famous beef designations of origin lie in the European Union, such as Spain's Carne de Ávila, France's Boeuf charolais du Bourbonnais, and the United Kingdom's Scotch beef.

COMPANY SPECIFIC

New categories of branded beef were based on a single company. For instance, Cargill, one of the country's big four beef companies, introduced its Sterling Silver program, becoming the second USDA-approved brand after CAB. Cargill differentiates its Sterling Silver beef not by breed but by a promise of marbling and maturity.

Then, of course, there are the grocery store brands—those weird labels you find in big grocery store chains that vaguely sound like something significant but that you've never seen anywhere else. They try to stand out against generic beef, though they may not be much better. A good example would be Safeway's Rancher's Reserve, which began in 2001 and was Select grade beef supplied by Cargill. The claim of Rancher's Reserve was tenderness because, as a Safeway executive explained in a 2006 article in *Beef* magazine, "Every focus group we conducted indicated the most important aspect of beef-eating satisfaction was tenderness."

The power of branding allowed Rancher's Reserve to fetch a higher price than normal Select-grade commodity beef. And it worked splendidly. In only a few years, Rancher's Reserve was moving a similar amount of tonnage as the vaunted Certified Angus Beef. However, the tenderness

MIYACHIKU

**1401-255 Shinbeppucho Maehama
Miyazaki 880-0834, Miyazaki Prefecture, Japan
tel: (+81) 985-28-2914 • rest.miyachiku.jp/miyachiku**

In the United States, the most famous high-end beef from Japan may be Kobe, but in Japan the beef that has been winning awards and that many consider the country's most decadent is from the region of Miyazaki, located on the southeastern coast of the southern island of Kyushu. While this area is flush with water from rivers and an abundant coastline, it's the nearby mountains where the black Wagyu cattle are bred that are of importance to us. These grain-fed animals produce some of the most marbled, tender, and tasty meat in the world.

Several restaurants in Miyazaki serve this beef, but none does so with the care and integrity of Miyachiku. The style here is teppanyaki, meaning the beef is cooked on a flattop. This is where Benihana's shtick came from, but in Miyachiku and the other area restaurants, you simply sit at a counter built around the cooktop while the chef cooks small cubes of this expensive, rarefied beef in front of you. The meat is served in only small portions because any more would be almost indecently filling. And to the side, in fat rendered from the steak, the chef cooks vegetables and mushrooms, which are also served in small bites. Every now and then, the chef pours a few drops of alcohol onto the meat and sets it aflame to get a seared crust.

All in all, it's a far cry from the lusty, carnal American steak experience. But in its precision, restraint, and pinpointed pleasure, it's very Japanese. When you have those small bites and the steak literally melts in your mouth, almost disappearing into a wisp of profoundly beefy essence, you understand why they do it this way.

BUYING STEAKS

BAD BEEF AND BEEF SAFETY

Everyone should know bad beef when they see it . . . or rather smell it. If you're wondering whether to cook a piece of meat on the edge, go with your, er, gut. But we'll lay it out for you, as bad beef is both unpleasant and potentially unsafe. Most beef spoilage comes via bacteria introduced at processing, as the meat of a living animal is typically microbe-free. But once the animal is killed, bacteria from the hide or processing facility can get in there. Indicators the meat has spoiled are a slimy surface and the aroma of rotten eggs, which occurs because the bacteria is breaking down protein molecules and releasing sulfur compounds. Also, the surface tension of the meat will have disappeared; rather than be resilient to the touch, it will feel flaccid and dead. "Most of these [bacteria] are harmless but unpleasant," notes Harold McGee, but it's best to avoid the experience.

If you've got beef in a Cryovac bag, it's undergoing what is called "wet aging" (see page 86). The amount of time meat is wet aged is much shorter than for dry aging, as the moist environment (even in a really cold refrigerator) is a happy one for bacteria. Wet aging should not go on for more than three weeks. Whatever the beef gains in tenderization will be finished by then, and there are no flavor gains to be had. Indeed, the beef will start to deteriorate. In working on this book, we tasted some Cryovac-aged meat that had been bagged for somewhere between thirty-five and forty-two days. It didn't make us sick or anything, but its texture lost some integrity, and the flavor had a touch of funk that was nothing like the delicious taste of dry-aged beef. For safety and taste, don't keep unfrozen meat in Cryovac bags for more than twenty-one days in the refrigerator.

---

standard for Select beef was difficult to maintain, both accurately and consistently. The only reliable test of tenderness, Safeway meat scientists found, took forty minutes to process, making it unrealistic, so they came up with their own rating system that presumably worked faster but was less reliable. The brand was retired in 2015, as Safeway recast its image with upgraded meats and produce overall. Safeway simply started selling USDA Choice-graded meat, a higher-level product.

Branded beef is something to be aware of, and USDA-certified brands actually involve a third-party guarantee (in this case, the government) that you're getting something that lives up to certain standards beyond the USDA grades. You can look them up on the USDA website to learn what criteria are being imposed. However, plenty of brands—notably grocery store versions—are little more than names attached to beef to make it seem more specific or significant than it is.

Grade School

The grading of beef can seem both incredibly simple and contentiously complex, and your relationship to it depends on how far down the rabbit hole you want to go.

If you want to remain on the surface, there are only three USDA quality grades you'll ever confront: Prime, Choice, and Select. Categories below Select exist, but you won't deal with them for steaks.

Grading is done by the US Department of Agriculture, a service paid for by the meat packer or producer; companies can opt to sell their beef ungraded. (That's not the same as uninspected. The USDA inspects facilities as part of its taxpayer-funded mandate.) Many slaughterhouses—especially the biggest ones—employ full-time USDA agents who grade every carcass as it passes through.

Beef is graded to create an estimate of the satisfaction consumers can expect from a piece of meat. This is done visually by the evaluation of marbling, the amount and distribution of intramuscular fat (see page 41 for more on that) between the twelfth and thirteenth ribs. From that glimpse at a tiny part of the cow, a grade is given to the entire carcass.

In the simple worldview, Prime is the best, accounting for about 5 percent of all graded beef, according to the USDA, which describes Prime beef as having "slightly abundant to abundant marbling and is generally sold in hotels and restaurants."

Second best and accounting for around 70 percent of all graded beef, Choice is "high quality, but has less marbling than Prime." Both grades are "well-suited for broiling, roasting, or grilling."

Third best is Select, noted by the USDA as "normally leaner than Prime or Choice. It is fairly tender, but because it has less marbling, it may not have as much juiciness or flavor. Select beef can be great on the grill, and is also good for marinating and braising." Select is about 20 percent of graded beef, with the balance falling into five lower categories that sound more like punishments than anything you'd want to cook: Standard, Commercial, Utility, Cutter, and Canner.

(The truth about Select is that grocery chains often create their private brands of beef in order to avoid customers having to see "Select" on a label. Generally, if any beef grades high enough to earn a Prime or Choice grade, it will be marketed under that designation.)

There you have it. That's the simple version. But you don't have to be Sherlock Holmes to reckon it might be *too* simple. And indeed it is.

Prime Suspect

As the USDA wrote in the just-noted definition, Prime beef is unusual enough that it generally goes straight to high-end hotels and restaurants. It's true that it's still pretty hard to find Prime-rated beef at your average grocery store, hence the rise and cachet of the steak house: the meat you could get there used to be substantially better than what you could cook at home and worth going out for. But you'll notice we're using the past tense there. In the age of the gourmet grocery store, top-level beef gets disseminated much more evenly. Furthermore, the mail-order business has grown hugely in the last twenty years. (Today, the best way for steak houses to add value is by dry aging, which is covered in chapter 4.)

But how do we know Prime-rated beef is all it's cracked up to be? The short answer is we don't. That shouldn't be all that surprising, now that we know grading is done by the eye test of a fallible human.

"In my father's day," says butcher Bryan Flannery, "probably 20 percent of the cattle raised was classified as Prime. That was in the full-blown corn phase." (Here, Bryan is referring to the then common practice of feeding cattle corn

BUYING STEAKS

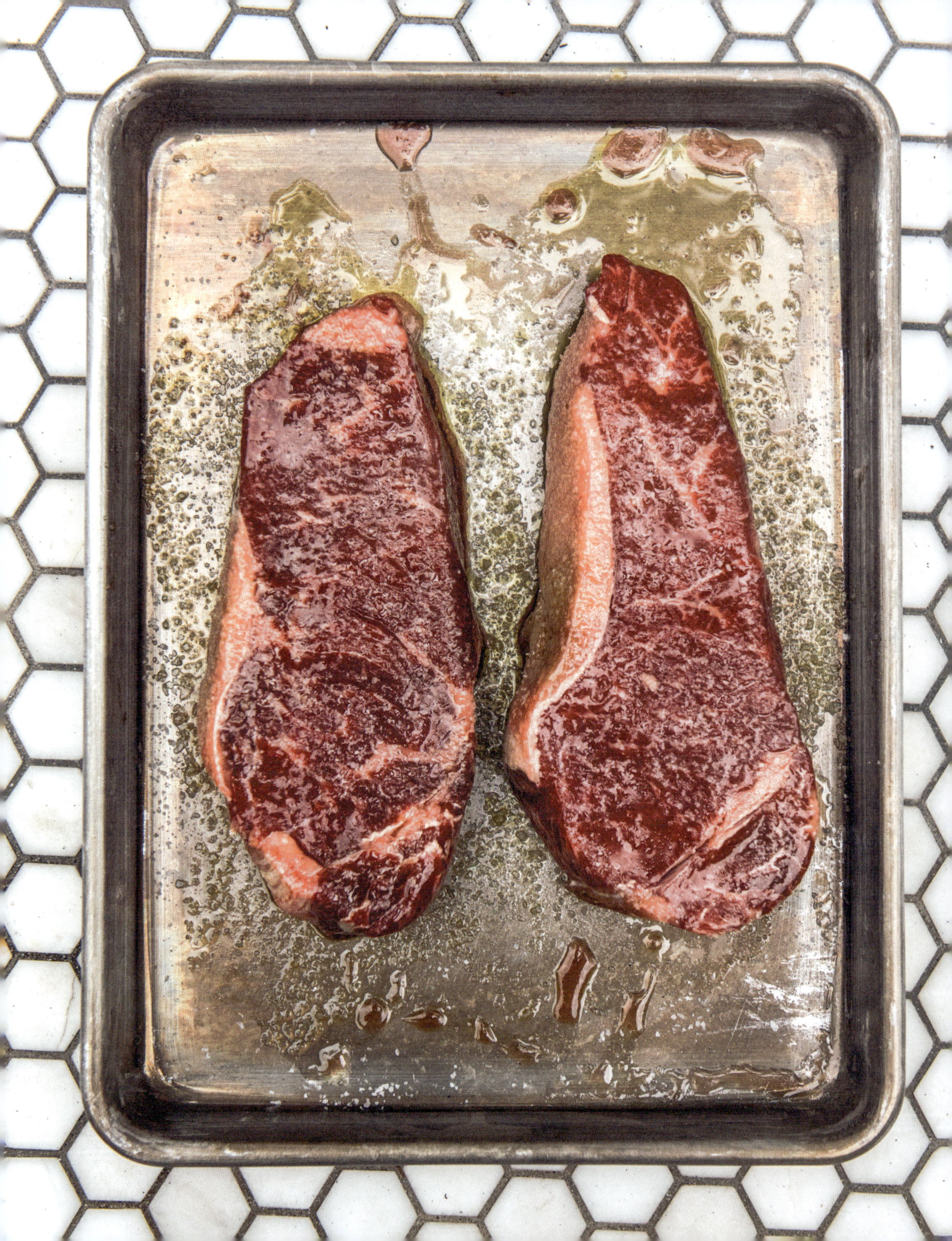

diets that made them fat, which is still the primary diet today. But in the 1960s and 1970s, he says, the cattle came from many fewer places and were in general much more consistent.) "But about ten years ago it was down to about 2 percent." That's a precipitous drop, fueled by a number of factors. First, market demand was down. Fat was the enemy in the 1980s and 1990s, and the country wasn't calling for well-marbled meat. (This also marks the ascent of chicken in the American diet, which has taken a huge swath of market share from beef in the last thirty years.) To combat this fear of fat, in 1987, and for the third time since creating grading, the USDA lowered the marbling standard for Prime, eating into the category that was once Choice. It also changed the name of the third-tier category from Good to the suave-sounding Select. (We think there should be a grade called "Meh.")

While industry conventional wisdom has Prime grading up in recent years to 3.5 percent or even higher, Flannery is suspect of those numbers. "I think that right now, in my experience, it's probably down to 1 percent. We order Prime-rated beef all the time and end up downgrading it because it doesn't meet our standards of Prime. Probably 15 percent of what we buy as Prime we don't sell as such. And we can't return that. We take the loss. If the government slaps Prime on a piece of beef, there's no recourse."

So, if the reported supply of Prime-graded beef has almost doubled in the last twenty years, but someone like Bryan Flannery, who orders only Prime beef, attests it's lower than he can remember, what gives? It seems the Prime grade has slid down the sliding scale. "A lot of meat graded today as Prime wouldn't have qualified in the past," Flannery says. "And I understand. If the inspector is looking at one thousand head and has in his mind that twenty to thirty of them need to be Prime rated to fall into the accepted percentage, he's going to grade them Prime, even if they might only barely qualify or not qualify on traditional standards."

If you can't trust the grading system, how can you know whether or not your meat is up to par? The easiest way, of course, is to find a trusted source, like Flannery, who you know can vouch for the quality of his or her product. But what if it is not just the grading system and the Prime conspiracy that are the problem? What if it's the *criteria* by which we've been taught to grade beef that's actually bunk? As you'll discover when you're reading this book, there are lots of things we like to be contrarian about (tempering, resting . . . just wait, you'll see). But perhaps the biggest and most controversial one is the question of *marbling*.

The Truth about Marbling

All this fuss over grading really comes down to marbling—to intramuscular fat. Not the big lips of fat that cling to the exterior of muscles and divide them from one another, but those little rivulets and wisps of white that disperse out into the lean red meat like veins in a leaf. That's the marbling we can see. It also exists as microscopic little cells of juicy goodness that melt as the steak is cooked and explode in our mouths when we burst them with our teeth.

"Fat is flavor" is one of those memorable aphorisms for meat, much like "location, location, location" is to real estate. We've been told over and over that marbling is the key to everything. It causes the burst of juiciness we love in moist steak, and it carries—no, it embodies!—the deepest, most savory flavors. It is simply the essence of great steak. This is why Japanese Kobe beef, which shows more marbling than lean meat, is considered the world's greatest steak delicacy. As Mark Schatzker writes in his book *Steak*, "Sensory evaluations have proven the supremacy of marbling time and again. American meat scientists believe in marbling the way American physicists believe in atoms and American biologists believe in cells."

But is marbling *truly* the key to steak? *Is* fat flavor? There are reasons to doubt these assertions, reasons you don't need scientists to prove. Well, do as Schatzker suggests: take a big bite of fat. Does it taste like beefy delicious steak? No, it doesn't taste like much of anything. Now, the external fat does have a different composition than the intramuscular fat, but not *that* different. Even when you do have a big, juicy bite of liquefied marbling, say in a bite of real Japanese highly marbled Wagyu, the sensation you get from the liquid is not that of overpowering beef essence. (If you want to get scientific about it, it's the flavor of soft, slightly nutty oleic acid.) Jordan has tasted what he (and many others) consider the beefiest-tasting steaks in the world, the ones from eight- to twelve-year-old oxen in Spain that have been grass fed and have been active their whole lives. The meat is not at all what we'd consider "heavily marbled," yet there's no denying its beefy flavor.

We're sorry, but we've all had Prime and Choice steaks that have very little flavor, despite an abundance of juicy, unctuous fat. Perhaps the cow was fattened up exceptionally fast; plied with hormones, antibiotics, and beta-agonists; and then harvested at twelve months of age. It may have fat, but it simply won't have as much flavor as an animal that was on pasture for most of its life, lived drug-free, and was harvested at twenty to thirty months.

None of this empirical evidence seems to support the idea that fat is flavor. More likely, it seems reasonable to assume that flavor comes from both muscle *and* fat. The genetics of the cow, what the cow ate, and how it lived all matter. We know that grass and a diverse forage show up as flavor in both the milk and the meat of a cow. Animals that move more in their lifetime develop not only more toughness in their muscles but also more flavor. Age contributes to flavor, too: the longer the cow lives, the more phytonutrients and beta-carotenes and other compounds get stored away in the muscles and the fats. And finally, how the animal was treated affects the flavor. Cattle that are stressed or fearful tend to have off flavors. If you really want steak with great flavor, you have to seek out meat of character—not just graded Prime.

Other Steak Labels and What They Mean

Producers love to plaster their meats with labels and certifications. From various labels, you can learn whether the steaks came from animals that were raised on open grassland, fed organic food, raised free of chemical additives, and treated humanely—allegedly. Of course, as with many food terms these days, these labels often mean less than you might think. Here's a brief guide to them.

GRASS FED

It may be the most meaningful movement happening in the steak world these days, but when it comes to the label, "grass-fed beef" doesn't

BERN'S STEAK HOUSE

1208 South Howard Avenue
Tampa, Florida
tel: (813) 251-2421 • bernssteakhouse.com

Of all the old-school steak houses in America, Bern's, improbably located in Tampa, Florida, is king. Founded in 1956, it offers the decadent clubbiness of the classic steak house but with a baroque eccentricity that distinguishes it from the far-too-common soulless, corporate steak temple. For instance, the restaurant is a vast, multichambered, warren-like space, with each of its windowless dining rooms uniquely appointed with one-of-a-kind decorations that range from oil paintings to classical busts to images of European vineyards.

Although the décor may be quite theatrical, the food is highly serious, with a DIY spirit that reaches into every corner of the kitchen. Bern's not only operates a farm that grows some of the produce on offer but also roasts its own coffee, cellars its own cheese, buys its spices whole and grinds them, and, yes, ages and cuts to order every steak.

All of the steak served is Prime and aged five to eight weeks. Ordering it can be a little daunting, however, as the specificity on the menu is reminiscent of a spreadsheet. Filet mignon, Chateaubriand, strip sirloin, Delmonico (ribeye), porterhouse, and T-bone are all offered in at least four options based on width and weight that correspond to recommendations for number of people served and proper doneness. You can even choose from eight different degrees of doneness, such as very rare (no crust), very rare (with crust), rare (cold center), and so on. It's a complicated but loving and respectful testament to the supreme value of steak. Take some time to explore the steak section of the Bern's website—it's remarkable.

There's much more to the menu and the quality of offerings at Bern's than can be covered here, but we'd be remiss not to mention the wine program, which boasts the largest restaurant cellar in the world, harboring around seven hundred thousand bottles, and a remarkable two hundred wines offered by the glass. Because Bern's long ago bought not by the case but by the pallet (fifty-six cases), huge supplies of high-quality wines dating back to the 1960s and 1970s remain, not to mention rarities from the eighteenth and nineteenth centuries.

Tampa may not be a destination for most people, but if you find yourself in Florida—or even in the southeastern United States—it's worth a detour for a great steak dinner and a fine bottle of wine.

BUYING STEAKS

have a lot of meaning. In 2016, the USDA's Agricultural Marketing Service dropped any official definitions of the term *grass fed* from its regulations. The USDA website still defines the grass-fed standard as requiring "ruminant animals be fed only grass and forage, with the exception of milk consumed prior to weaning . . . cannot be fed grain or grain by-products and must have continuous access to pasture during the growing season." However, this term is not rigorously enforced or inspected. That is, producers who want to label their product as officially grass fed and earn the "USDA Process Verified" tag have only to submit $108 and documentation stating their animals are fed solely on grass and they'll receive the label. No inspection is required.

The upshot • Real grass-fed producers complain all the time that many ranchers simply cheat the system—they have the grass-fed label, yet don't feed their animals only grass. Furthermore, there's consternation that other producers don't actually graze their animals, but instead confine them to a feedlot and give them concentrated grass pellets that contain none of the wholesomeness or diversity of true, well-managed pasture. Plus, this label focuses only on diet and doesn't take into account whether or not the animals were fed hormones or antibiotics or how they were treated. In essence, the USDA's grass-fed label is toothless.

Fortunately, much more rigorous and serious third-party grass-fed certifiers exist who actually do annual audits of producers. The gold standard among them is the American Grassfed Association. If you see the circular, green "American Grassfed" logo on a product, the cows were fed only forage, were raised on pasture and not in confinement, and were never treated with hormones or antibiotics. Another organization is the Oregon-based A Greener World, whose "Certified Grassfed by AGW" label also requires documentation and annual audits of both farms and plants (if applicable) and goes as far as requiring forage testing for the nutrition of the feed.

ORGANIC

The organic seal from the USDA is quite thorough. For meat, it requires that the animals were raised on certified organic land—meaning it's been free of most synthetic fertilizers and pesticides for at least three years—have year-round access to pasture (although they don't necessarily have to be grass fed), were fed 100 percent organic feed and forage (which can include grain), and were not administered antibiotics or hormones. This is regulated by documentation and an annual audit from a USDA inspector.

The upshot • Although this says nothing about grass fed, and the list of allowed organic and synthetic substances within the organic designation is incredibly long and full of all sorts of chemicals, this is the most highly regulated and demanding of the USDA labels.

PASTURE RAISED

The USDA doesn't conduct third-party "Pasture Raised" certification, but it does have to approve any product that bears this label. In this case, pasture raised, or variants like "pasture grown" or "meadow raised," refers only to the living conditions of the animals and not to what they were fed. The USDA requires meats bearing these labels to come from animals that had a minimum of 120 days a year of continuous free

HOW TO CHOOSE A STEAK IN THE STORE

The meat case of a good grocery store can be a tempting place or a minefield. A good way to increase your chances of having a decent steak for dinner is choosing the right piece of meat. Unfortunately, the clerks behind the counters are less likely to be able to offer good guidance as they may once have been. Grocery store beef these days is often cut at a central processing facility and delivered to the stores, meaning the counter people just lay it out without needing to know anything about the cuts. Here are a few tips to take out some of the guesswork.

- **Take your time and really inspect the cuts on offer.** Every piece of steak is different, so it pays to make sure each one is great. You wouldn't buy an expensive pair of pants without first trying them on, would you?

- **Choose the freshest steaks.** All the meat in the supermarket looks red. This is because special packaging is used that allows the myoglobin in the meat to combine with oxygen to "bloom," or turn a bright, attractive shade of red. (Incidentally, harder-working muscles like chuck or flank contain more myoglobin and will thus appear redder than rib and loin steaks.) However, if you detect brown or gray on the steaks, it means the iron in the myoglobin is oxidizing. That's not necessarily a sign of spoilage, but rather just a steak that's been sitting around longer.

- **Go for thicker steaks.** Even if the outside shows more oxidation, a thicker steak will have a greater proportion of fresh, unexposed meat.

- **Prepackaged or under glass?** Not always, but usually, grocers put their best meat in the case. The case generally holds a better selection of cuts as well.

- **Do look for fat.** The whole point of our marbling screed was that marbling is not the *sole* source of flavor in a steak, but it *is* a good indication of what will turn juicy and sweet. Exterior fat, while you don't want to pay for too much of it, can help the steak cook more evenly and slowly.

- **Avoid connective tissue.** Look for steaks that have large, single muscles or muscle groups. When you can see several individual muscles in a piece of beef being offered as a steak, pass up the cut. The connective tissue separating the muscles will toughen during fast cooking, making large parts of the steak inedible.

- **Avoid the fancy store-created brand names.** This is how stores have learned to sell lower-grade meat. Go for well-marbled, upper Choice for the best quality-to-price ratio.

BUYING STEAKS

access to the outdoors. This is "desk regulated," meaning that these labels only require the submission of documentation.

The upshot • Given that the labels only require access to "the outdoors" (whatever that exactly means) for only about four months of the year and that the access is not physically verified by a compliance agent, these labels can be considered essentially meaningless. Any farmer serious enough about pasturing his or her animals and wanting to communicate that to the general public would seek more stringent certification than what the USDA provides.

RAISED WITHOUT HORMONES OR ANTIBIOTICS

Products bearing this USDA certification can have no antibiotics or any added hormones—ever. The USDA certifies these labels by reviewing documentation sent in by the producer. No in-person audits are made.

The upshot • Concerns about giving cattle antibiotics, the widespread use of which is considered very likely to contribute to the rise of antibiotic-resistant bacteria and create dangers of superbugs that can't be controlled, or added hormones, whose negative effects on health have not been substantiated (though they're banned in Europe), are legitimate. These labels are helpful, but, once again, enforcement is light, and it's generally up to the producer to stand by the claims. The best way to ensure the absence of hormones and antibiotics in your beef is to buy organically certified meat or to research the producer yourself.

"PRODUCT OF THE USA"

In 2015, Congress repealed the Country of Origin Labeling law (COOL, for short) that required beef labels to state where the animal was born, raised, and slaughtered.

Industry groups who lobbied against COOL (and won) said that tracking, labeling, and verifying the movement of beef wasted a billion dollars a year for an industry that's already tight. The anti-COOL forces also said that there's no regulation against meat companies offering that information voluntarily, and customers can vote with their dollars by supporting the companies that do.

But now, without COOL, imported beef can misleadingly but legally bear a "Product of the USA" mark if it's been processed in this country. So, a side of beef raised in Australia but processed and packed at a facility in Kansas can be called American beef, which is outrageous.

Luckily, the USDA seems to think it's a serious enough question to revisit the issue. They were scheduled to open up the topic for debate starting in August 2018. We shall see what they decide.

In the meantime, be wary of beef that is being heavily promoted as a US product. As with someone who doth protest too much, it may not be from here at all. And there's really no way to know.

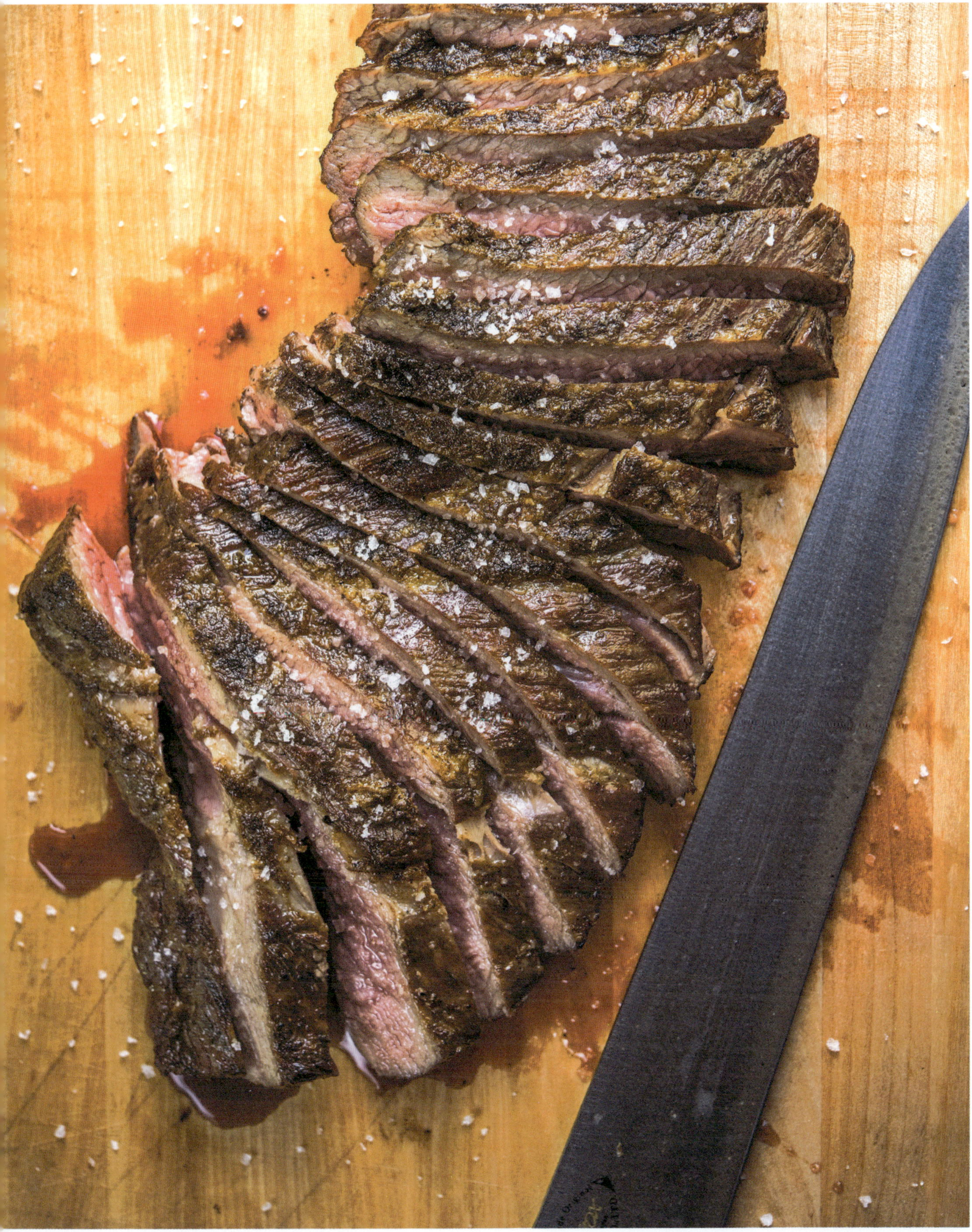

Bryan Butler of Salt & Time in Austin, Texas

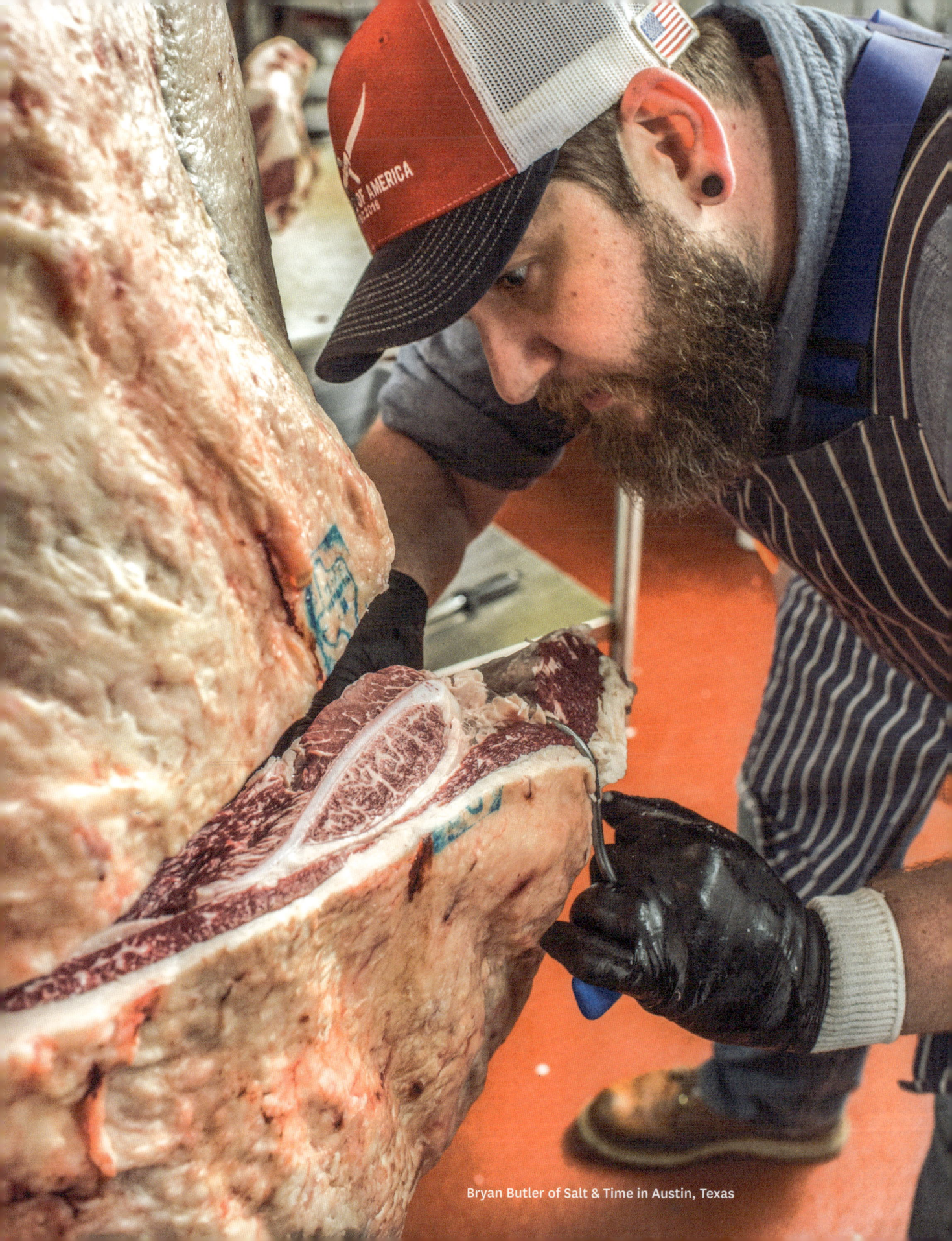

CHAPTER 3

Steak Cuts

Recalling some of the steaks we've bought in the past can be a little cringe inducing. Aaron flashes back to the commodity briskets he bought for ninety-nine cents a pound at H-E-B when learning how to barbecue. When he was broke all the time, he, like most people, ate cheap commodity steaks—you know, the ones in those plastic-wrapped Styrofoam trays in the grocery store cooler. That meat could be from anywhere. For Jordan, it's similar, but he remembers buying really cheap chuck and flank meat and thinking he could cook it like steaks. It would always smell really great when it hit the pan, but then you had to chew a piece for five minutes to get it down. Jordan and his roommates would study up on the Heimlich maneuver when they bought beef, just in case.

Hey, we've all been there: who among us hasn't bought that cheap, dull gray slab of organic matter sealed beneath a shiny layer of plastic wrap on top of some flimsy polystyrene foam back? But when the beef craving strikes, there are better ways to indulge it.

In the previous section, we talked about what makes for good beef, but we didn't specifically talk about all the other kinds of decisions necessary to get steak on the table: What individual cut do you want? How do you want it cooked? Where should the meat come from? Should it be fresh or aged? What should you do with it?

To secure the tastiest steak, you need a good provider. You need a place where you have choices and where you can ask for more information about the meat you're buying and about what to do with it once you've got it. Does that sound like Costco, Walmart, or Kroger? Not at all. Even at many high-end grocers like Whole Foods, it's almost impossible to find anyone who can tell you anything about the meat or give sound advice on how to prepare it.

That's not how it used to be. Before the massive scaling and industrialization of groceries, every local store had a butcher, and the good butchers could tell you all you needed to know to get dinner on the table that night.

Luckily, the tradition of the local butcher is coming back. Many cities now have one or more small, artisanal butcher shops where whole carcasses are broken down and the meats are handled with care and experience. (Shout-outs to some awesome butcheries across the United States: McCann's Local Meats in Rochester, New York; Clove & Hoof in Oakland, California; Taylor's Market in Sacramento, California; Purely Meat Co. and Butcher and Larder in Chicago; Porter Road in Nashville, Tennessee; the Organic Butcher of McLean, Virginia; Fleisher's and the Meat Hook in New York City; Gwen Butcher Shop in Los Angeles; and Chop Butchery & Charcuterie in Portland, Oregon.) Austin is very lucky to have a few such shops. The most ambitious among them is Salt & Time, a butcher shop and *salumeria* opened by two friends on the east side of town in 2013.

Many good butchers exist across the country now, but it is hard to imagine two who are more talented, thoughtful, driven, and passionate than business partners Ben Runkle and Bryan Butler. Aaron remembers Bryan when he was just a butcher about town working at the Wheatsville Co-op on Guadalupe, though they didn't really meet until Aaron started going in as a customer. Jordan first encountered them as a customer too, but quickly introduced himself as he was so impressed by their commitment to local producers. They have a badass restaurant attached to their shop, incredibly sourced and butchered meats, and some of the tastiest charcuterie in the country. This is why we asked them to be a part of this book to help us talk about steak cuts: where they come from, how to choose them, and what to do with them.

A Good Butchery

A massive, long-bearded hulk of a man, S&T's Bryan Butler is the partner who breaks down the whole carcasses (Ben has the skills, but as a wizard of charcuterie, he's happy to defer to Bryan's passion and prodigious talent for whole-animal butchery.) Despite his years of training and his enthusiasm for the art, Bryan had considered getting out of the business on several occasions. As Ben observes, "I really

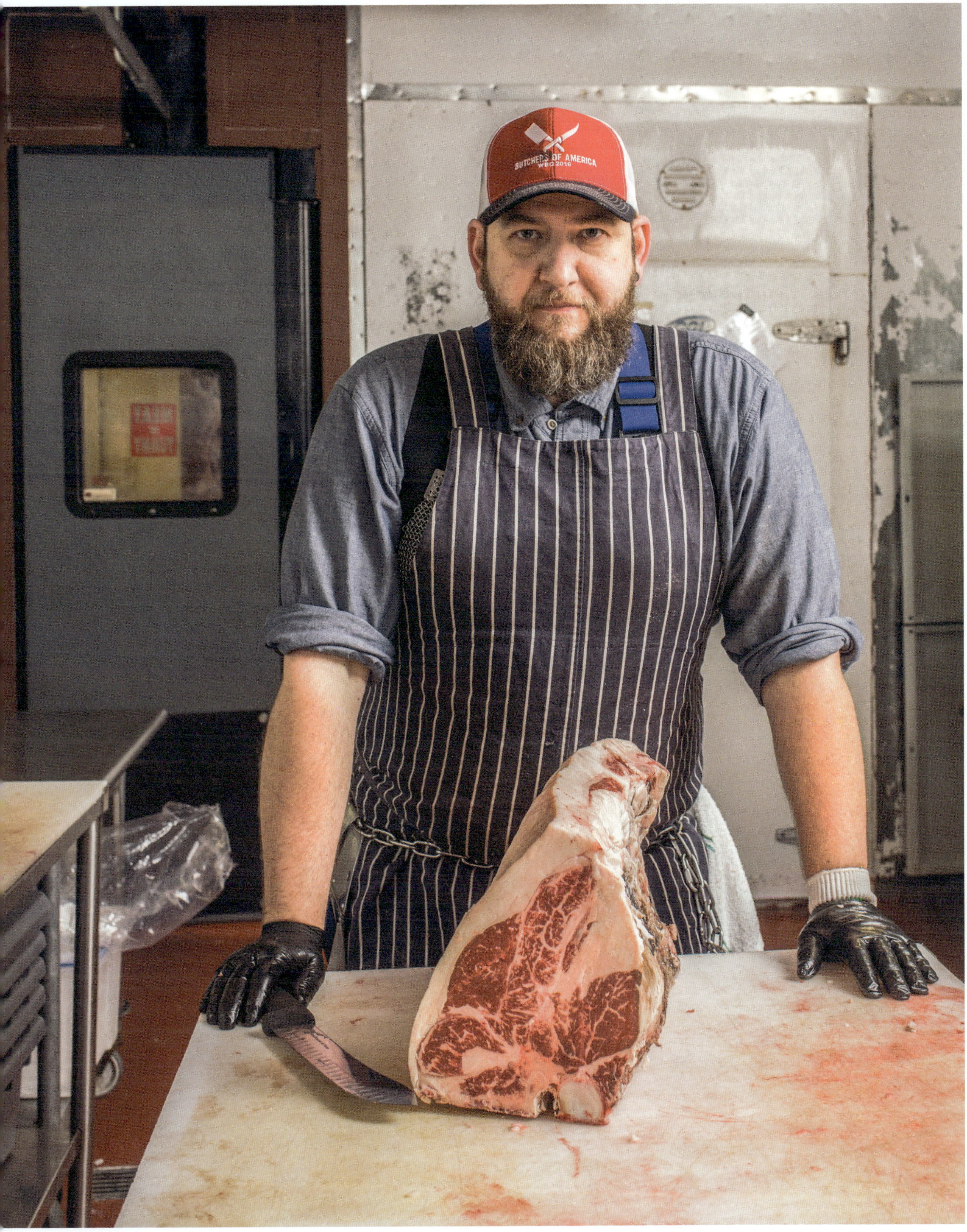
BUTCHERS OF AMERICA
WBC 2016

think Bryan's career arc is like what happened to butchery in America in a nutshell."

In 1996, straight out of high school and seeking a trade, Bryan went to a formal two-year program for whole-animal butchery, meat-market management, costing—the works. His was the last graduating class, as the school then shut down due to low enrollment (remember, this was well before the craft-butchery boom of the last few years). Bryan found work at some small mom-and-pop places, all of which were struggling just to stay open against the onslaught of cheap meat sold by the likes of Walmart, where he would ultimately end up employed for a short run. There he faced the horrors of working from (excuse the pun) inside the belly of that monster, a dehumanizing experience. Bryan quit and found work with smaller, independent grocers, before joining Ben at S&T.

Today, Ben and Bryan are inundated with people who want to learn how to butcher, as a wave of new-school butcheries became one of the more compelling food trends of the last decade. Butchery was almost completely lost as a skill, as assembly-line, low-wage meatpacking plants dominated. It was a trade maintained by only a handful of obscure folks scattered throughout the country who, like Bryan, lacked career opportunities and considered abandoning the profession. When this new wave came around—thanks to the slow food movement, a new reverence for artisanship, and a growing love and appreciation of fine cooking at home—enough customers were willing to spend more money for better meat.

As Ben says, "As a personal consumer of meat, there's a number of qualities I consider in the question of whether I want to buy it, and cheap is nowhere on my list. Obviously, value matters, but cheap is not the same as value. When you're talking about something as complicated with as many factors that affect how it tastes and what it does to your body and what it does to the world around it, cheap is not the way to go about thinking about good meat."

Today, the small, artisanal butcher shop still represents an economically challenging model—Walmart and Costco haven't gone anywhere—but as the interest in quality, well-raised meats continues to rise, craft butcheries will remain our country's small, ecumenical temples to meat that matters.

Speaking of the skills, in 2018, Bryan was part of the first-ever United States team to compete in the World Butchery Challenge, an international competition that pits teams of butchers in a timed contest of breaking down a variety of whole animals (to be precise, three and a quarter hours to do a side of beef, a side of pork, a whole lamb, and five chickens). They must produce salable, beautiful cuts, and create a slew of preparations, from patés to sausages, and products while being judged on cleanliness, appearance, professionalism, and efficiency.

The American team, which finished sixth (a satisfying result, considering it was their first go-round), received an interesting comment from one of the judges at the end. Noting their paltry amount of waste afterward (which was dwarfed by the amount of waste produced by rival teams), the judge said incredulously, "That's all your waste?" Bryan's American team had offered in their presentation some thrifty things that clever American butchers do (like creating a bougie pet food from scraps, or packaging and selling bones for home chefs). So impressed were the judges that they mentioned they might look for ways to emphasize thrift in the future.

Thrift is an essential aspect of the butcher's art. It's an important quality in and of itself, but it's also the whetstone that keeps a butcher sharp. A butcher's main job is to buy a carcass and figure out the best way to get the most money out of it. Each animal is a complicated mass of muscle, tendon, bone, and fat that can be taken apart in almost infinite ways. It's the knowledge, skill, and desire of each butcher that determines how much he or she gets out of each carcass. A skilled one can produce a panoply of steaks and other cuts, as well as enticing preparations (pâté, tartare, terrine, sausage) made from trim or less exciting cuts. If the butcher is lazy or lacks vision, he or she can cut up the obvious steaks, grind the not-so-obvious stuff into hamburger meat, and waste all the rest.

Salt & Time is a butcher shop that goes the extra mile, but this isn't just an endorsement of two men. It is recognition of the hardworking artisanal butchers trying to get a foothold everywhere. Ben and Bryan know all of the cuts and are deft with the knife in preparing them. They buy whole carcasses directly from farmers, almost always from places they have visited so they can speak to the way the animals are raised. And they both have a great touch in the kitchen, an underrated skill for a butcher, to whom the most common question asked is probably, "How would you recommend cooking this?" But most of all, they understand bovine bone and muscle structure: they know every cut, from the renowned to the obscure. Following, we're going to go over our favorites with them.

Bryan Butler (left) and Ben Runkle (right)

STEAK CUTS

BEN AND BRYAN'S TEN BUTCHER SHOP STEAK COMMANDMENTS

1. **Do ask: "Where is the meat from?"** • If you're going to go out of your way to go to a butcher shop instead of a grocery store, you should be able to know that. Not every place is going to be local, but the person behind the counter should know a good bit about the supply chain and where the shop's beef is coming from. We take a lot of pride in our sourcing and believe any steak—any meat, really—is all the more enjoyable if you know something about it. So go ahead and ask us about the farm, what the cow was fed, anything.

2. **Don't ask: "Is that cut any good?"** • People come in and don't seem to have much confidence in us or even in their own taste. We don't carry bad meat. And in our opinion, every cut can be good if the meat itself is good, if the animal is raised with integrity.

3. **The most expensive cuts are not necessarily "the best."** • If you're going to go to a butcher shop, don't get hung up on ribeyes and strips. Ask us what our favorite steaks are or which ones we love to turn customers on to. One of the biggest differentiations between a real butcher shop and a grocery store is that at a butcher shop you have all of these other options. Even if the ribeyes at our place are a lot more expensive because they're super high-end, we probably have three or four cuts you might like better than the anonymous grocery store meat.

4. **Look beyond grade.** • A lot of people ask, "Do you have Prime?" without really knowing what that means. They assume it means something about more wholesome or more natural, whereas it has a pretty narrow definition. Furthermore, USDA Prime and Choice are not the only measures of quality in beef. Not all beef is even graded. Marbling is important, but other factors can influence tenderness and flavor, and we always select our beef for those things. So if it doesn't say Prime on the card, don't be put off.

5. **Know your portion sizes.** • Before coming in, you should have a rough idea of how much meat you want. When we ask people how much they want of a particular cut or tell them how much it weighs, they usually have no sense of how much to buy. But there's a big difference between a three-ounce piece and an eight-ounce piece. We can help only so much, so it's good if you have some idea of how much you want per person.

6. **Ask our opinions about how certain steaks are best cooked.** • On one end there are people who overcook their steaks to medium-well or well, but on the other end, there are people who undercook some cuts because of, say, the machismo of cooking it as rare as you can. Not every cut benefits from that; some cuts are better cooked a little further to render the fat or to break down the connective tissue. Tell us how you like to eat your steak, and we can tell you which cuts are best that way.

FRANKLIN STEAK

7. **Tell us what you want to make, and we'll sell you the right cut.** • We butcher, but we also cook. So if we know what you're making, we can help you out with the right meat. It may not always be exactly what's written in the recipe. For instance, if the recipe asks for a pound of lean-end brisket, well, we're not going to just trim a pound off and leave the other ten pounds unsold. But we can steer you to any number of cuts that will work just as well, if not better, for the dish.

8. **Be adventurous.** • There are lots of delicious cuts and techniques that go beyond steak. Steaks never disappoint, but knowing how to use the rest of the animal is important, too, not to mention usually economical and delicious. So instead of just defaulting to the standard, let us help you discover new cuts and techniques.

9. **Don't forget to ask about bones and fat.** • Two things that tend to set the professional kitchen apart from the home kitchen are cooking technique and pan sauces. For instance, cooking in animal fat rather than vegetable oil and the depth of flavor that adds. You can always ask us for a little extra beef fat to season your pan or grill for cooking your steak. We sell stock, but if you want to make your own, ask for some bones to make a stock for a nice, thick pan sauce. You can make a steak that much better by using the fat and stock from the same animal.

10. **Feel free to make requests.** • If you don't see it in the case, it doesn't mean we don't have it. As with most small butcher shops, our display space is limited, and we often have a number of interesting things in back. Just ask!

STEAK CUTS

Know Your Steaks

If you've never bothered to consider it, here's something obvious: steak—and meat in general—is the muscle of an animal. Steaks are simply what we call the fast-cooking portions. All steak cuts—whether everyday or esoteric—come pretty much from the middle of the cow. By contrast, meat from the front and back legs and their attendant muscle groups in the chest and haunches is better served by slow cooking, because those muscles are tougher (after all, they do literally tons of work moving around the bulk of a thousand-pound animal).

A cow uses the middle of its body far less for movement. Rather, the muscles there protect and reinforce vital body parts and structures, like the spine, the heart, the rumen, and the other organs. Because the muscles are less strained in contraction and extension, the muscle tissue will be softer and less sinewy. Softer tissue means you can cook the meat faster without sacrificing tenderness, hence steak. Knowing a bit about the individual steak cuts, where on the anatomy they come from, and their use to the animal only makes things easier when deciding how to cook them.

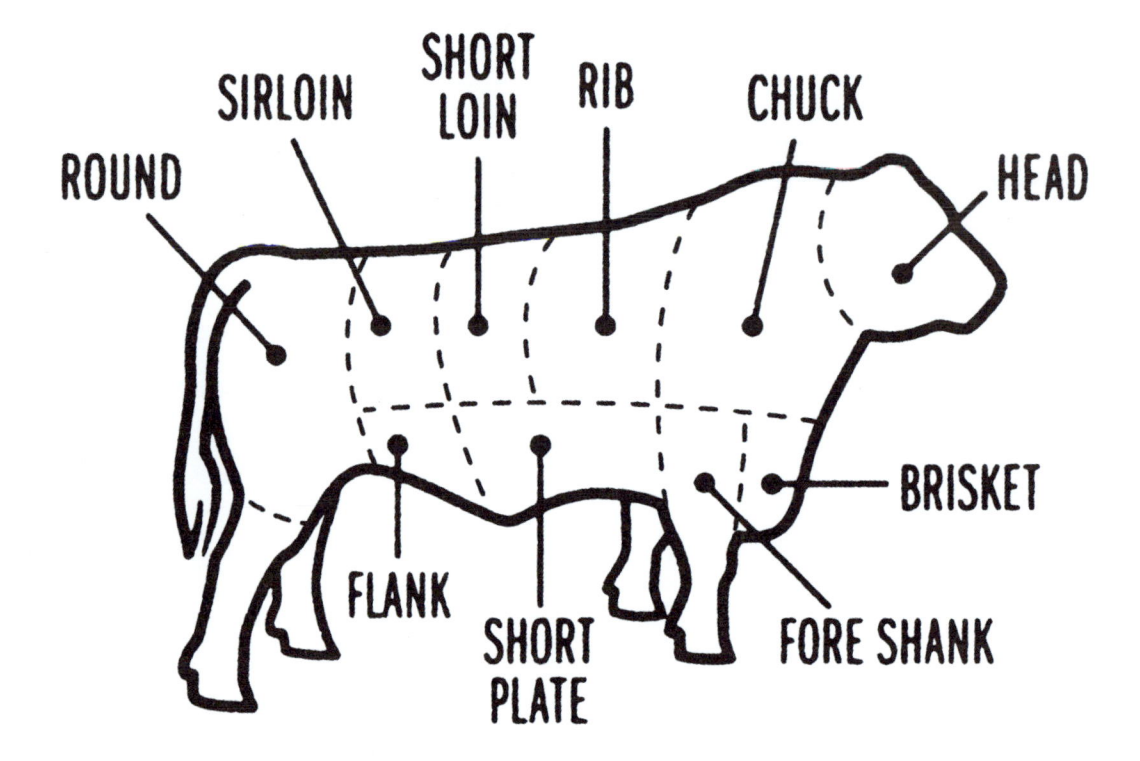

In American butchery, a side of beef (half of a cow split lengthwise right down the middle), which may be six feet (or more) long and weigh several hundreds of pounds, is subdivided into seven more manageable sections, broken down according to bone structure. These are called primals, and there are seven of them. Starting at the head and topside of the animal, the primals are chuck, rib, loin, and round. Starting at the head and underside, they are brisket (the pectorals), plate, and flank. Given the length of the spine and rib cage of the animal, divisions between the rib-containing primals are made by counting ribs. Saw and knife in hand, the butcher will count five ribs from the front of the rib cage to separate the chuck from the rib section, between the fifth and sixth ribs. The top of the ribs (rib primal) near the spine will be separated from the bottom section (plate primal) ten to twelve inches from the spine, sawing crosswise straight through the ribs. The hindquarter is separated from the forequarter between the twelfth and thirteenth ribs. The loin and sirloin are removed from the round (the leg and haunch), and the flank, which is the underside, is separated from the loin and ribs up top.

The steaks that we'll be focusing on here come from the middle sections: the **rib**, **loin** and **sirloin**, **plate**, and **flank**. All of the other meat is (usually) too tough to cook like a steak.

KNOW YOUR STEAK LINGO

Chine or chine bone • The vertebral column; in some rib roasts, this may be left on. For most steaks, butchers remove it.

Chuck steak • Any steak cut from the beef chuck primal. Some may have more specific titles—e.g., the flat iron—but sometimes these steaks are just generically called chuck steaks.

Côte de boeuf • the French term for a thick-cut bone-in ribeye; usually serves two.

Cowboy steak • A chined, bone-in ribeye with a short, Frenched rib bone.

Culotte steak • A flavorful steak from the sirloin cap, also known in Brazil as the *picanha*.

Dark cutter • Term for when the lean muscle has a dark appearance, typically caused by stress to the animal prior to slaughter. Also, when plural, the name of Aaron's new band!

Delmonico steak • Over the generations it's had a bit of a shifty meaning, but generally acknowledged today as boneless ribeye steak.

Dry aging • The process of aging meat in closely controlled cold temperatures for a period of days or weeks to increase tenderness and flavor.

Filet mignon • A thick-cut piece of the tenderloin without any fat or connective tissue.

Frenching • The process of removing all remaining meat and connective tissue from a bone until it looks clean, slick, and white.

Marbling • Intramuscular fat, or the white streaks inside the lean, red meat.

Pepper steak • Preparation in which steak is rubbed with coarsely ground black pepper, from the French *steak au poivre*.

Primal cuts • The seven major subsections of a side of beef in American butchery. Separating these are the first cuts a butcher makes on a carcass.

Subprimal • The next division after primals. For instance, the loin primal can be divided into short loin and sirloin.

Tomahawk steak • A chined, bone-in ribeye with a long, Frenched rib bone.

STEAK CUTS

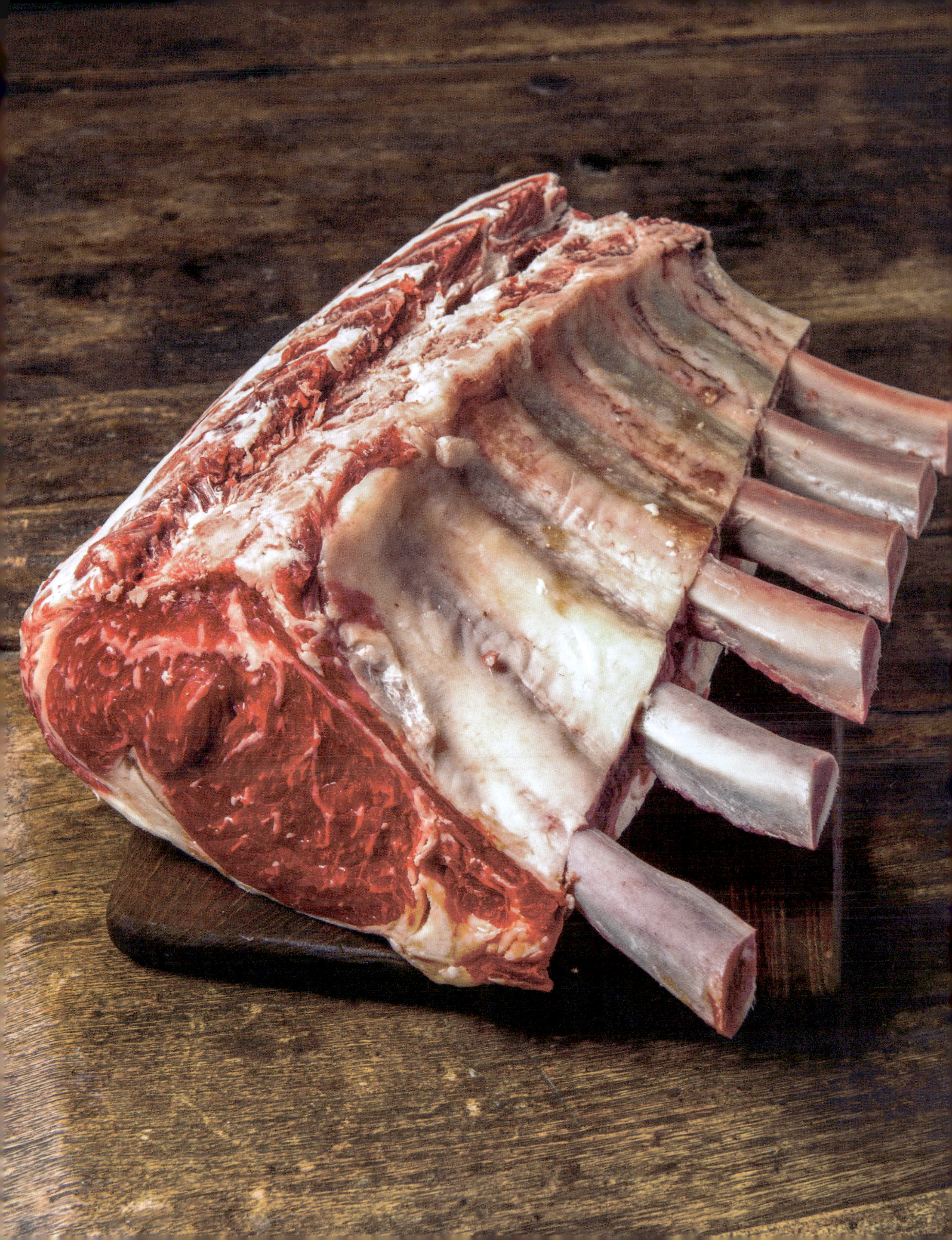

THE RIB STEAKS

The rib primal offers some of the most tender, marbled, and flavorful meat on the entire animal. This is, of course, the source of the rib roast; of, when subdivided, the ribeye steak—what old-timers call the Delmonico—and of the French thick, bone-in *côte de boeuf*. The entire rib primal, rib bones and backbone and all, is known in the meat trade as the 103 (all cuts have a processing number). It's a massive and impressive cut that often gets dry aged as a whole, as we do in the home-aging fridge. Depending on how or whether the meat is taken off the bones and how much of the rib bones is left on, you get a variety of different steaks.

When the rib roast is kept in one big piece, it's known as prime rib, a popular special-occasion or holiday cut. It's an impressive hunk of beef, but because it is roasted whole and served in thin slices, it is not a steak. Therefore, unlike a steak, the emphasis is the internal meat, not the crust. The standing rib roast, on end with all the bones sticking out, is an equally majestic sight.

"This 103 is one of the most labor-intensive areas," says Bryan, as he turns it on his table. "During the holidays, I do a dozen or more of them, which involves frenching the bones. (Frenching is when all the meat and sinew is peeled off the bones, leaving them bright, white, and clean.) Over the years, I've adopted more of a culinary approach to frenching. Most cut around the bone and scrape it lightly. I put in a little more time and get it completely clean," he says, tugging all the interior membrane from the bone, like peeling a tube sock off a foot. "The reason why is if you rush it, there will be dry little bits on the bone, and we want that stark white alabaster bone. It just looks more appealing that way."

Ribeye

Prime rib is nice, but we prefer this long roast when it's been divided into individual steaks, called ribeyes, simply because when you cook individual steaks, you have exponentially more surface area to turn into a beautifully browned Maillardian crust (that is, the crispy, tasty exterior of a well-seared steak, explored further on page 154).

If you take the meat off the bone as a whole, you get a boneless rib roast or, when cut crosswise into steaks, boneless ribeye steaks. The butcher may choose to leave some amount of the rib bone intact. If a short section of the rib bone is left and cleaned, you get the cowboy steak. And if the entire length of rib remains, meat removed, you get the famously long-handled tomahawk steak.

Despite its immense popularity, the rib steak can be a little challenging to cook and to eat because it's not just a single muscle like the loin, but rather a collection of four muscles connected by a little tender sinew and fat. The muscles are the ribeye, the heart of the steak also called the *longissimus dorsi*; the ribeye cap, aka the *spinalis dorsi*; the *complexus*; and the tail, which is just a little tip, often removed.

When cooking a ribeye, the fat and sinew between these four muscles render, occasionally making a ribeye something of a floppy mess—or it can even fall apart. Also, because the grains of these muscles run at slightly different angles, you need to take special care to make sure you're always cutting against the grain. This isn't usually a problem because

STEAK CUTS

American ribeyes aren't so big, which means you can simply slice in one direction across the steak and easily remain perpendicular or some transverse angle to the meat's grain. But if the steak happens to be huge....

The tastiest and most tender and juicy piece of the cow is the ribeye cap, or *spinalis dorsi*. Somehow, this muscle has the most intense beefy flavor of any part. It's possible to deconstruct the rib roast not as steaks, but as individual muscles (creating ribeye fillets that look like large tenderloins), and thus preserving the *spinalis* as an entire steak unto itself rather than just the outside ring of a ribeye steak. But that's so impossibly decadent and selfish to deprive the rest of the ribeye steak of its best part that almost no one ever does it. But if someone did, we'd hope for a call.

Best way to cook • Depending on whether they are thin or thick, bone in or bone out, ribeyes warrant different approaches. Thick-cut, bone-in *côte de boeuf* (the French love to serve this cut for two people) needs to cook hot to gain the sear and then to spend a little time in ambient heat to get the proper internal temperature. Reverse searing works great. In contrast, thin, boneless cuts do well in a cast-iron skillet just on top of the stove. Remember that fat slows down the cooking, so this marbled cut can be forgiving, allowing flexibility in the searing of the outside, because the inside will unavoidably take longer.

Opposite page: Aaron trims a chined, bone-in ribeye, leaving the bone long to create a "tomahawk steak." This cut is great on the grill, and you can even use the bone as a handle to flip the steak!

BONE IN OR BONELESS?

One of the eternal questions when buying steaks is whether you want them bone in or boneless. It's a tough question mainly because people don't really know what the bone is good for and it seems like one more thing to stress about. But believe us, it's not. The answer is always bone in.

The reason for this is not, however, the one you most commonly hear, which is that the bone provides flavor by somehow infusing the meat. Rather, the bone provides structure and insulation to the steak, meaning that it can affect the rate of cooking (usually the impact is slowing it down, making it easier to get even cooking). Different bones have different densities. The lighter the bone, curiously, the better an insulator it is; rib bones are lighter than leg bones, for instance. That's because the lower-density bones contain more air, which is a poor conductor of heat. So, for steak purposes, the bone will heat up more slowly than the meat and fat around it, slowing down the cooking.

This is a good thing, leaving a small streak of rarer meat at the bone, which a lot of people like. Just remember to measure the internal temperature of large steaks away from the bone, as closer to the bone will likely read ten to fifteen degrees lower than the rest of the meat. That is to say, if you get the meat adjacent to the bone to a perfect medium-rare, the rest will be well overcooked.

The other advantage of cooking on the bone: someone (or some dog) gets to chew on all that delicious meat.

STEAK CUTS

EL CAPRICHO

Parade de la Vega
Jiménez de Jamuz, León, Spain
tel: (+34) 987-66-42-24 • bodegaelcapricho.com

Some people like to slice their own steak. They want the whole slab of meat on the plate in front of them to enjoy the primal experience more fully. But if you're hungrily awaiting the delivery of your steak in the dim crypt that is the dining room of El Capricho, that won't be an option.

It's difficult not to call El Capricho the greatest steak house in the world simply because above all else, it is an act of passion. The fact that the destination is in the middle of a bleak nowhere, three hours northwest of Madrid, makes it all the more remarkable.

Every year, chef-owner José Gordón scours northern Spain and Portugal for high-quality, three-year-old oxen—two-thousand-pound beasts with giant, fearsome horns—that he brings to his sprawling ranch, where they are condemned to a gentle, roaming life of leisure. They feed on pasture—much of it wild thyme and lavender—and have grain supplement available, but only if they desire to eat it. He visits his oxen twice a day, inspecting their health and bestowing affection, and starting when they reach age eight, he begins to select individuals who are ready for sacrifice, as he says. They may become as old as fifteen before their time comes. After sacrifice, he ages the meat for 120 days before serving it in his grand, subterranean restaurant. This is the ideal steak: pasture-raised, older animal, lengthily dry aged.

Coming from giant, older oxen, the ribeye steaks he serves are enormous—around five pounds, bone in. They are grilled in the Basque way, reverse seared (see page 165) over hot charcoal with healthy handfuls of coarse salt, and then sliced at the table. The deep, transcendent beefiness of these steaks is almost indescribable, but savoring one of them is probably the most primal, resonant beef experience anywhere. Given that Gordón is responsible for the whole animal—not just the ribeyes—the rest of the menu is an ode to the remainder of the beast.

Start with a plate of *cecina*—this is nonnegotiable—thin slices of Castilian cured beef that has been salted and aged for at least eight years. It's like Spain's famous *jamón ibérico*, but with the depth and richness of beef. Don't miss the beef tongue, which has been brined, smoked, cured, and boiled before being served in thick medallions at the table. A crunchy, bracing watercress salad, simply dressed with olive oil, balsamic vinegar, and salt, is all you need with the steak, except for a good bottle of wine, and El Capricho has an excellent and well-priced list.

When the main event, the steak, comes to the table, the first thing you'll notice is that the mighty rib steaks are two to three times larger than anything you've ever had before. Indeed, they're bigger than your entire plate. So it's easier for everyone if chef Gordón or one of the servers slices the meat at the table, which is what they do on a little stand they bring to the table when the steak arrives. Gordón shows up with his long, curved breaking knife (a butcher's tool for breaking down carcasses) and carefully but quickly cuts the meat. Instead of just cutting across the grain of the ribeye in one direction, however, he treats each of the constituent muscles individually. The ribeye gets sliced on its own and arranged on the platter. Then he shifts and cuts the *complexus* at a slightly different angle to slice it as perpendicular to the grain as possible. Next comes the tip, which he cuts into little morsels. After that, he takes the whole long *spinalis dorsi* (ribeye cap) and first slices it lengthwise into two plump strips and then slices it across into bite-size chunks, allowing everyone to get an equal piece. Finally, he takes the fat that separates each muscle, cuts it into manageable bites, and leaves it in a little pile. "Don't forget to taste the fat," he reminds diners in his broken English. "A lot of flavor in there."

If you love steak—and because you're reading this book you probably do—it is incumbent on you to make the pilgrimage to this otherworldly temple of steak.

STEAK CUTS

Porterhouse

THE LOIN STEAKS

Moving from the head of the cow toward the rear, after the rib primal comes the loin, separated from the rib between the twelfth and thirteenth ribs. The muscles in the loin connect the front and back of the animal and support it, but they aren't responsible for direct movement, hence the tenderness of these cuts. Indeed, before the current fashionability of the ribeye, these were the most celebrated and desired cuts of steak: T-bone, porterhouse, and tenderloin.

T-Bone and Porterhouse

To understand these cuts, let's talk a little bit about cow anatomy. In the loin, we're still working at the top of the cow, right along the edge with the muscles that protect and surround the spine. When a cow is split into two sides of beef, the spine is cut through the middle. The spinal cord is surrounded by bones that spur in each direction—up and down and to the left and right. If you think of it in cross section, it looks like a plus sign, with the intersection of the two lines being the spinal cord. The top quadrants (the northwest and northeast) are filled with the *longissimus dorsi* muscle, which extends toward the head into the rib primal as the "eye" of the ribeye, though here it is called the strip. The lower quadrants (southwest and southeast) are occupied by the tenderloin muscle, or *psoas major* for you Latin speakers. You can see how these important muscles protect the all-important spinal cord but don't do much work of their own. So as you split the carcass in half vertically, you get two halves, each with a T-shaped bone running through it. This is the bone that gives the T-bone its name.

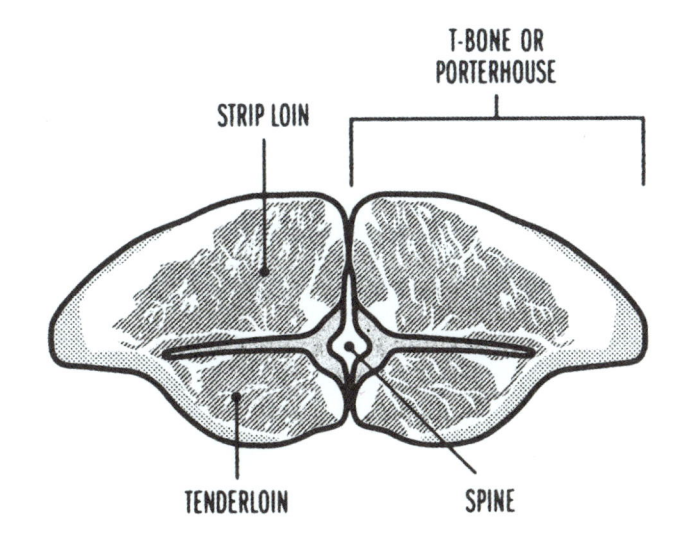

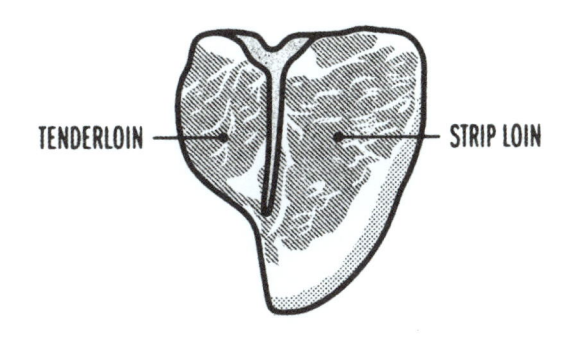

It's also the same bone that defines the porterhouse. The T-bone and porterhouse are just names for steaks taken from different ends of this bone segment. These cuts are renowned because they contain meat both from the tenderloin, prized for its namesake tenderness, and from the strip, prized for its strong beefy flavor.

So what's the difference between T-bone and porterhouse? The tenderloin muscle has a severe taper—imagine a baseball bat—starting from a point near the rib and enlarging in diameter as it heads toward the rear of the cow. At its most severely tapered end, when its diameter is, say, only as big as a quarter or even less,

STEAK CUTS

it's too small to enjoy as its own steak, so it's left on the spinal bone, with a portion of the strip on the other side of the bone. When the portion of the tenderloin is just a smidge—less than an inch and a quarter in diameter—you're looking at a T-bone steak. As the tenderloin increases in diameter heading back toward the rear, the overall steak becomes larger and more luxurious, offering a sizable portion of both tenderloin and strip. That's a porterhouse, which some consider the greatest of all cuts. In Italy, this is the famed *bistecca fiorentina*. Not only do you get both tenderloin and strip on the same cut, but you also get substantial portions of both.

Best way to cook • The T-bone is usually a thinly cut steak, and it's best taken right from the refrigerator and thrown onto high heat to get a good sear and a medium-rare interior. Porterhouses are thick-cut, luxuriant steaks. Because of this, some attention must be paid to getting the interior to medium-rare as well as the outside well browned. Try the reverse sear (see page 165): Start slow, cook to doneness, rest, and then finally, sear really hot. The meat closest to the bone will be the rarest, but part of the pleasure of the cut is having different shades of doneness on the plate. After the steak has rested, cut both sides off the bone, then slice them and present them with the bone.

Tenderloin (aka Filet Mignon)

Of course, you can take the tenderloin off the bone as a complete muscle. As just noted, it will be long and tube shaped, with a narrow section at one end expanding to a much thicker, baseball bat–like opposite end. We see this cut sold whole more commonly with pork—the famous pork loin. With beef, butchers usually slice individual round steaks from this tubular muscle. Prized for their soft texture and mild flavor, these steaks are called tenderloins and are the most tender cut of the whole animal. The other names for this cut are filet mignon and Chateaubriand. The former usually describes the narrow rounds, while the latter is reserved for the plump, larger end and is sometimes offered as a steak for two. (Bern's, the venerated steak house of Tampa [see page 43], cooks the filet mignon and Chateaubriand differently: The filet mignon is broiled with the grain running up and down, perpendicular to the heat, so it cooks faster. The Chateaubriand is cut from the thick end of the tenderloin and cooked with the grain

Tenderloin

FRANKLIN STEAK

parallel to the heat, so it cooks slower and allows the development of a significant crust.)

Oh, and what about the really narrow end that's too small to be served as a steak? Well, that end can be cut up into smaller pieces for kebabs or finely diced for tartare.

Tenderloins are generally rather lean, soft, and, again, mildly flavored. These qualities used to make them popular among a certain dainty set. But in today's world of macho meat, the fillet has fallen in esteem, probably equal to and opposite of the rising popularity of the ribeye. Aaron, on the other hand, is a true believer. For him, it all comes down to texture. People regularly assume fattier meat is better meat, but it's not always true. It's also the quality of the fat, and in the tenderloin, there's no heavy marbling; instead, all of it is well integrated. There's a reason this cut is called the tenderloin: it eats like butter. And speaking of butter, Aaron always augments his tenderloins with some. In the pan, he adds a tablespoon or two and bastes it over the top while the tenderloin is cooking. On the grill, he'll often take a stick of butter and rub it on the warm steak as it cooks to help build the crust, a technique he picked up from his dad.

Best way to cook • Given its leanness and relative delicacy, this cut is best cooked in a heavy-bottomed pan on the stove top or an outdoor grill. Tenderloins don't have a lot of interior fat, meaning they cook quickly. A pan gives you more flexibility and greater control. Plus, add butter as Aaron does and do a little pan basting at the end, which helps make up for the lack of fat in the steak (also consider adding herbs and garlic to the butter to boost the flavor of this mild-tasting cut).

Strip

If you remove the whole tenderloin in one piece, you're left with a bone with the *longissimus dorsi*, or "strip" muscle, attached. Butchers have a choice here. They'll often remove the entire strip loin in one piece from the bone and then cross-cut the loin into boneless steaks of a desired thickness. These are called boneless strips or New York strips. They may also be called Kansas City strips. People argue about whether there's a difference between the two. One side says there's no difference, that the cut was called the Kansas City strip until Delmonico's restaurant in New York decided it would be more attractive to customers if it was called the New York strip.

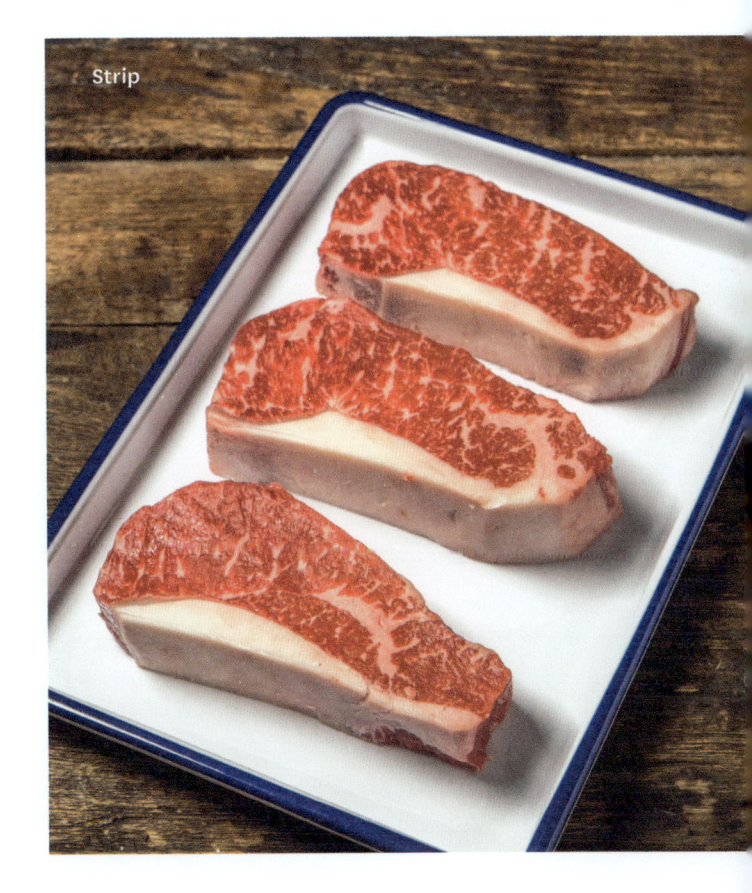

Strip

STEAK CUTS

67

Some say, however, that there is a slight difference. The Kansas City comes with a small portion of the bone attached and perhaps a bit of tail fat at the pointy end of the steak. These can also just be called bone-in New York strips, however. No matter the name, this is a flavorful, luxurious steak that has a tight grain, not too much fat, and a lot of flavor. If it's possible that one of the most iconic of all steaks could be underappreciated today, the New York strip is it.

Best way to cook • Most strips are thin enough that cooking them conventionally on a medium-hot grill or stove-top griddle should allow the formation of a nice crust without over- or under-cooking the exterior. Medium-rare is the goal. These are great as individual steaks: they're not too big, feeding one person generously.

THE BUTCHER'S CUTS

Some people call them "off cuts" or "new-school cuts," but the term *butcher's cuts* seems the most apt. These steaks are some of the most flavorful, affordable, and satisfying cuts from the entire animal, yet because of their appearance, lack of mind-blowing tenderness, or unimpressive marbling, they are overlooked and unappreciated by the masses. So if they didn't sell, these were the pieces the butchers took home for themselves (or, perhaps more accurately, if the butchers never put them out for sale, they could always take them home).

In some ways, the steaks that follow are fundamentally different from the luxe cuts we've just discussed. The famous steaks—ribeye, strip,

---

THE DIFFERENCE BETWEEN THE RIBEYE AND THE STRIP

Okay, so the two most luxuriant and reigning celebrities of the steak world come from opposite ends of one muscle, the *longissimus dorsi*. So what makes these two steaks different?

Let's start with looks. The ribeye is a rounder steak with a rounder shape. Remember, it incorporates parts of other muscles, too, the *spinalis* and the *complexus* for two. These muscles are part of the ribeye steak as a whole and are separated from one another by seams of fat and membrane. The strip steak, on the other hand, is just one muscle, and its shape is narrower, a little more wedge-like and pointed.

Flavorwise, both are potent and beefy, with the edge in beefiness and depth of flavor going to the strip steak. Marbling, however, usually falls in the other direction, with ribeyes tending to be fattier and juicier than strips, though sometimes they also contain big, annoying interior clumps of fat where the different muscles are connected. Texturewise, the ribeye is usually the more tender and juicy, while the tighter grain of the strip can give it more chew, which to some of us is not a bad thing. Price? Usually similar, with the ribeye, due to its current popularity, maybe slightly more expensive.

So, head-to-head, which should you choose? It is hard to award an advantage. The ribeye does have the *spinalis*, the greatest cut on the steak, but it can also be somewhat of a mess and contains big pockets of fat. On the other hand, the strip is less flashy but more solid. For our money, advantage strip.

porterhouse, tenderloin—are all long, tubular muscles near the spine from which the individual steaks are cut thickly and across the grain of the whole. These butcher's cuts are all thin and relatively flat and long. Called thin meats, they have long, coarse muscle fibers that run in one direction, and you can usually see that grain. The steaks are cut with the grain, though to eat them, you must cut them across the grain to make them chewable and tender.

People who favor tenderloins say they love the texture, but Ben Runkle takes a slightly contrarian view. "People actually love the *absence* of texture. We've been taught to value the lack of texture as silkiness—the idea that having to chew a little bit is a sign of inferiority." Indeed, the more tender the steak, the more quickly it goes down, and the faster and more of it you eat. Mainstream Americans seem to like that. But think of the advantages of a little extra chewiness: more tooth means more chewing, with each bite releasing more juice, more flavor.

So these aren't thick-cut luxe steaks but rather thinner, grainier steaks with a huge amount of flavor, a satisfying amount of chew, and prices that reward the thrifty.

Hanger

For a long time, no one in the United States but the butchers knew about the hanger steak. Then, about twenty years ago, it started to appear on menus at restaurants. Even then, it didn't become a widely known cut until recently. But now the secret is out. The hanger is one of the most fully and uniquely flavored steaks on the whole cow, and it's still relatively cheap for such a rich, savory cut. Shaped like a long tube or almost like a baguette, it's easily cooked and sliced.

It's an unusual piece, as there is only one hanger per animal, as opposed to all of the other muscles, of which there are two symmetrically oriented on both sides of beef. It's called the hanger because it actually hangs off the inside of the carcass when the carcass is hung. According to Bryan, it hangs predominantly on the left side and is difficult to remove from the carcass. "It hangs inside the gut, so if you pierce the stomach or anything [else] when removing it, it becomes immediately contaminated," he says. "To remove it you almost have to climb into the carcass like a tauntaun." (That's a reference from *The Empire Strikes Back*, if you're wondering.) "You can't do that until the cow is eviscerated, then you reach up into the cavity with a knife and cut it freehand

Hanger

STEAK CUTS

without being able to look at it. It takes real skill, and we realize it's something you should pay a little money for because if the butcher messes it up, it just goes to trim."

Bryan also notes that the aorta runs right through it, which is a big reason why there's such a strong mineral and iron-like flavor: it has blood pumping through it at all times. If you like full flavor at a good price, this is the cut for you.

Best way to cook • A dense piece of meat, the hanger cooks well over medium heat to a solid medium-rare. Too rare and the meat is tough to chew. Too well done and it becomes notably stringy and tough. The smoke and char of the grill are wonderful complements to the intense, bloody flavor of this cut.

Bavette

Aaron's favorite cut, the bottom sirloin flap (aka flap meat) is perhaps the greatest of the so-called butcher's cuts. But much more poetic is its French name, *bavette*, which means "bib" and describes the broad, flat shape of the steak. The bavette is, along with the hanger, the apex of the flavor and price ratio, though its taste is a little more conventionally beefy and its texture a little more tender. Aaron will take a well-cooked bavette over a ribeye most days. That's because it's not as rich, which he likes, and the flavor's usually stronger.

Bavette comes from just below the sirloin and adjacent to the flank. "I call this area the onion of the cow," says Bryan, "because it's in the belly of the animal and inside of here you keep peeling off all these great cuts—flank steak, bavette, and it's near the skirt."

The bavette is really just a flap muscle that supports other muscles on the side of the cow. It doesn't do a tremendous amount of work, and thus remains relatively tender. It's not highly marbled, but nevertheless filled with flavor, and its grain is quite wide and slack. This is the quintessential bistro steak.

If you have a whole bavette flap, one end will be tapered and thinner than the thick, heavy end. You can cut it (with the grain) into individual steaks or cook it as a big whole. If you opt to cut, be aware that the thinner ends will cook faster.

Best way to cook • Bavette cooked on the stove top is good, especially if it's been divided into small steaks, shaped sort of like those tall strips of salmon. But when cooked in larger pieces,

Bavette

it's great on the grill over a medium-hot fire. The density of the meat means it cooks rather slowly, and it's essential to bring it to medium-rare or medium, as a really rare bavette is too chewy. It will form a big crust—sometimes almost too crusty and dry—so make sure you have enough heat to cook the interior without leaving the steak on the fire too long.

Flat Iron

We're now going to talk about an area of the cow we haven't touched on before, as it is not known for producing steaks: the chuck. Otherwise known as the shoulder clod, the chuck is a big, heavily worked muscle that does a lot of lifting and supporting—not exactly a recipe for tender meat that you can cook quickly. But that was before the "discovery" of the flat iron steak.

"Before the flat iron," says Bryan, "the chuck was generally taken as a whole piece, the seven-bone roast, etc. Or [it was] used for ground beef." But a couple of meat scientists at universities in Nebraska and Florida changed that. Working under funding from a national beef trade organization specifically dedicated to finding new ways to increase the value of a cow, the two searched through thirty-nine different muscles of the chuck and round (rear of the cow) in 144 carcasses (meaning over fifty-six hundred muscles tested in all) for tenderness and flavor. They eventually discovered the flat iron, a muscle in the shoulder blade that had previously been consigned to ground beef or stew meat because of the presence of a brutally tough tendon running through it. The scientists showed that if a butcher takes the time to remove the silver skin and then the connective tissue in the middle of the muscle delicately, he or she can end up with two neatly shaped flat (but not thin) slabs of rectangular meat.

Turns out this meat rates as the second most tender in the entire cow (after the tenderloin). And for the price, which is way under that of the tenderloin, and the flavor, which is way over, the flat iron is a fantastic deal. In England, the flat iron is known as the butler's steak; in France, it's called the *paleron*; and in Australia, it's the oyster blade.

It's best to have a good butcher remove the seam for you. Jordan recently was at someone's house and got tasked with cooking the steak, a flat iron from Costco. The butcher there (or wherever) had done a terrible job trimming out

Flat Iron

STEAK CUTS

the tendon, so it took Jordan another fifteen minutes to find and remove all the sinew, and the steak still looked rough. A good butcher can clean it up in just a few minutes.

Best way to cook • This tender steak is exceptionally forgiving. The rather fine grain and decent marbling mean that you can cook it rare, though it's at its best between rare and medium-rare. The neat, rectangular shape makes it easy to handle. A dense muscle, it can take a lot of high heat, making it great on a wood-fired grill, but it also cooks up with an exceptional crust in a pan. One flat iron is usually enough to feed three, or even four, people, especially if you've got a number of tasty side dishes.

Skirt

The skirt is one of the most confusing steaks of all because it's not actually singular. There are two skirts, and they're different. The inside skirt is called that because it lies inside the body cavity, where its job is to compress the abdomen. The outside skirt is attached to the diaphragm, which it moves. Both are long, thin, and ribbon-like, with the inside skirt being about 30 percent wider. "Any of those diaphragm muscles do work," Bryan explains. "They expand and contract millions and millions of times [over the life of the animal]. That's how they get flavor."

But the two skirts are not created equal. "Of the two skirts on the carcass, the outside is the one you want," says Bryan. "It's much more tender than the inside." Both have flavor, but the outside skirt, in addition to being more tender, has even more flavor. Although these are usually very cheap cuts, the outside skirt of a cow that's been raised well can have significant marbling.

Best way to cook • Best used for fajitas or stir-fries, the inside skirt inevitably needs marinating or some other form of tenderization (pounding, perhaps) to make it easier to eat. At Salt & Time, after marinating, the inside skirt often gets rolled into a pinwheel, tied with a string, and sold as spiral rounds, which can be cooked like steaks, but "only if it's high-quality meat," cautions Bryan. "Also, it should get some mechanical tenderizing, lots actually—like a mallet or meat tenderizer device. Most skirts sold at grocery stores come tenderized already. [And] a good marinade with high acid helps." After cooking the pinwheel, just unwind the meat and cut it into thin, easily chewable slices (though the meat will still be chewy). The outside skirt, if it is high quality, doesn't need special treatment. It can be cooked simply as a steak, though it shows best when cooked medium-rare to medium on the grill.

Flank

Another flat, broad steak, the flank comes from the belly of the animal, where, as part of the abdomen, it does quite a bit of work. "Flank steak can be tough," says Bryan, "but if you get a good marbled one, it's delicious." The flank is notable for the distinctly coarse grain running down its length. Judge a good one by looking for telltale white marbling generously dispersed through the grain. Although it can be tough, the flank's got good flavor, and precise cooking makes it extremely easy to eat. If it's lean or tough, just slice it more thinly than you normally would for serving.

Best way to cook • The flank's big flavor and obvious grain take especially well to grilling, as the licks of fire and smoke penetrate into the heart of the meat. As long as you don't cook it past medium-rare, it's rewarding. Flank steaks are cheap and great for parties, as they cook quickly and consistently. Just don't forget to slice them thinly for serving—and only across the grain.

Tri-Tip

Some may debate whether the thick, dense tri-tip is fairly dubbed a steak, as it takes quite a while to cook, sort of like an outdoor roast (and it's almost always cooked outdoors). But conventional wisdom generally hails this large piece as a steak because you can cook the whole thing slowly over direct

Flank

heat. "Underrated," says Bryan. "It's a hybrid between a steak and a roast."

The tri-tip is so called because of its somewhat triangular shape, though it also looks a bit like that arrowhead-shaped Star Fleet insignia from *Star Trek*. The muscle is right in between the bavette and the ball-tip roast in the lower sirloin of the cow, so it's thicker than most steaks and usually very lean, requiring careful cooking. The cut became popular in the 1950s in California, the state with which it's still most closely associated, and it's the signature of Santa Maria (a town on California's Central Coast) "barbecue." Barbecue is in quotation marks here because Santa Maria style calls

STEAK CUTS

for cooking the tri-tip on big grills that can be hoisted up and down over a coal bed to adjust heat exposure, rather than slow smoking over many hours. The meat is usually rubbed with some sort of spice mixture. While it's a big, heavy cut, resist the urge to divide a whole tri-tip into smaller pieces. It cooks most easily as a whole, so just plan to feed six to eight people with a good-size one.

Best way to cook • The reason Santa Maria cooks use a height-adjustable grill for the tri-tip is because it should not be cooked too fast. You have to go fairly slowly to give the outside heat time to penetrate to the middle of the steak. Reverse searing (see page 165) works well. The grain of the meat shifts a little across the steak, so pay attention when slicing and shift directions along with the meat to ensure you slice against the grain.

Tri-tip

THE DIFFERENCE BETWEEN AMERICAN AND CONTINENTAL BUTCHERY

If you go into a butchery in France or into, say, the shop of a good French butcher in America, such as Olivier's in San Francisco, you may see a number of little steaks you've never seen before. At Olivier's, odd muscles that hang from the racks in the back of the cooler are offered at inexpensive prices. These cuts symbolize the stylistic differences between French-style and American-style butchery.

If you wanted to boil it down to its essence, the classic American way is to use a band saw and the European way, also known as "seam butchery," is to use a number of different knives. The American method prizes efficiency and speed but is cruder. The approach is to slice through whole clusters of muscles in one cut, with each muscle separated by fascia. The result is a hodgepodge of different muscles and a lot of gristle. For instance, "Americans will render a square chuck," says Bryan, referring to the act of cutting out a big, cube-shaped hunk of the one-hundred-pound shoulder clod (chuck) regardless of individual muscles. "This cuts through the flat iron, cuts through the mock tender, cuts through the clod and the chuck eye." In contrast, he says, "The French tradition maximizes the profit by separating each individual muscle—tracing the seams and membranes. For butchers, it's a point of pride to be able to pull these muscles cleanly, follow the seam, and not cut into the muscle."

One of the challenges of seam butchery, of course, is that butchers end up with all of these very small, obscure micromuscles—such as the *gousse d'ail* (garlic clove), *l'araignée* (spider), *poire* (pear), *surprise*, and *merlan* that hang at Olivier's—that are hard to put on a restaurant menu because you're only going to get one or two per side and each one is only an ounce or two of meat. Ben Runkle points out that the cruder American method of just breaking down the side of beef into larger chunks while paying no heed to individual muscles is probably a reflection of burger and fast-food culture. "If you're grinding most of it up, why spend the time to isolate individual muscles?"

At Salt & Time or Olivier's or any good butcher shop, the approach is usually seam butchery. "Our philosophy is that we don't want to grind up good cuts into ground beef," Ben says. "And we don't need to, because as skilled butchers, we end up with enough trim. If you're fabricating beautiful steaks, you're going to end up with a couple of pounds of trim for every ten pounds of steak. But if you're selling how many billions of burgers, you need a lot of ground beef."

STEAK CUTS

CHEAT SHEET
Some of Our Favorite Cooking Approaches

In part 3, we'll dive deep into the mechanics of how to cook a steak perfectly. There is, of course, no single path to perfection, and no one way to cook a steak. But now that you have a sense of all of the different cuts out there, we want to get you thinking about some nice ways to cook each of them. Again, this is not meant to be the final word for any of these cuts. They are just some approaches that have served us well in the past.

CUT	IDEAS FOR HOW TO COOK
Bone-in ribeye	While good in a pan, it's always better on the fire, which doesn't need to be too scorching, as a thick-cut bone-in ribeye needs time to cook the interior to medium-rare. That bone holds the thing together, and if it's long like a tomahawk cut, it gives the option of using it like a handle if you want it to go right onto the coals.
Boneless ribeye	Boneless ribeyes are great for the pan. Without the bone to hold the different muscle groups together, these steaks can get floppy on the grill and leak fat into the fire, creating flare-ups. In the pan, they develop a perfect crust, too. Plus, they're delicious all the way from rare through to medium.
T-bone	Thin-cut weekday steaks work great in a hot pan, as they take just a few minutes to cook. But a searing fire gives a great crust and keeps the interior pink.
Porterhouse	The bone-in wonder steak, the porterhouse is meant for the grill. Cook the fillet side to medium-rare and the sirloin side will be fine. Remember, the meat near the bone will be a little rarer in order for the center of each side to be perfect, but that's part of the pleasure.
Tenderloin	The tenderloin likes to be babied in a pan over medium heat, with a good dose of butter in the pan to add back a little of the fat that's inherently missing from the cut. Tenderloins are best on the rare side of medium-rare, as the meat is so silky.
Strip	All-around crowd-pleasers, strips (whether you call 'em New York or Kansas City) are especially good on the grill, as their deep beefy flavor loves a dash of wood smoke. Always aim for medium-rare on this one.

CUT	IDEAS FOR HOW TO COOK
Hanger	The hanger delivers big flavor from a big muscle that runs close to the internal organs. Pan cooking tends to take too long and can result in stringy meat if the water can't escape fast enough. It is best on a hot grill, cooked to solid medium-rare. Too rare and it's tough.
Bavette	Works in a pan, but is better on the drier environment of the grill. The open grain releases a lot of water, which can cause steaming in the pan, making it hard to form a thick crust. On the grill, you get a great crust. Cook to solid medium-rare.
Flat iron	Great on the grill or in a pan, and forgiving on either side of medium-rare. The flavor really comes out in the cooking, though, so don't go too rare.
Skirt	Inside skirts need marinating or tenderizing and are best cut thinly for fajitas or stir-fries. Outside skirts have excellent flavor and can be cooked fast as a steak but still like marinades. Best cooked superfast on the grill.
Flank	Great, inexpensive cut with lots of flavor. Won't wow you with tenderness, but loves some smoke from the grill. Don't overcook or it's too tender. Just fast sear it to medium-rare.

STEAK CUTS

Part II

NEXT-LEVEL BEEF

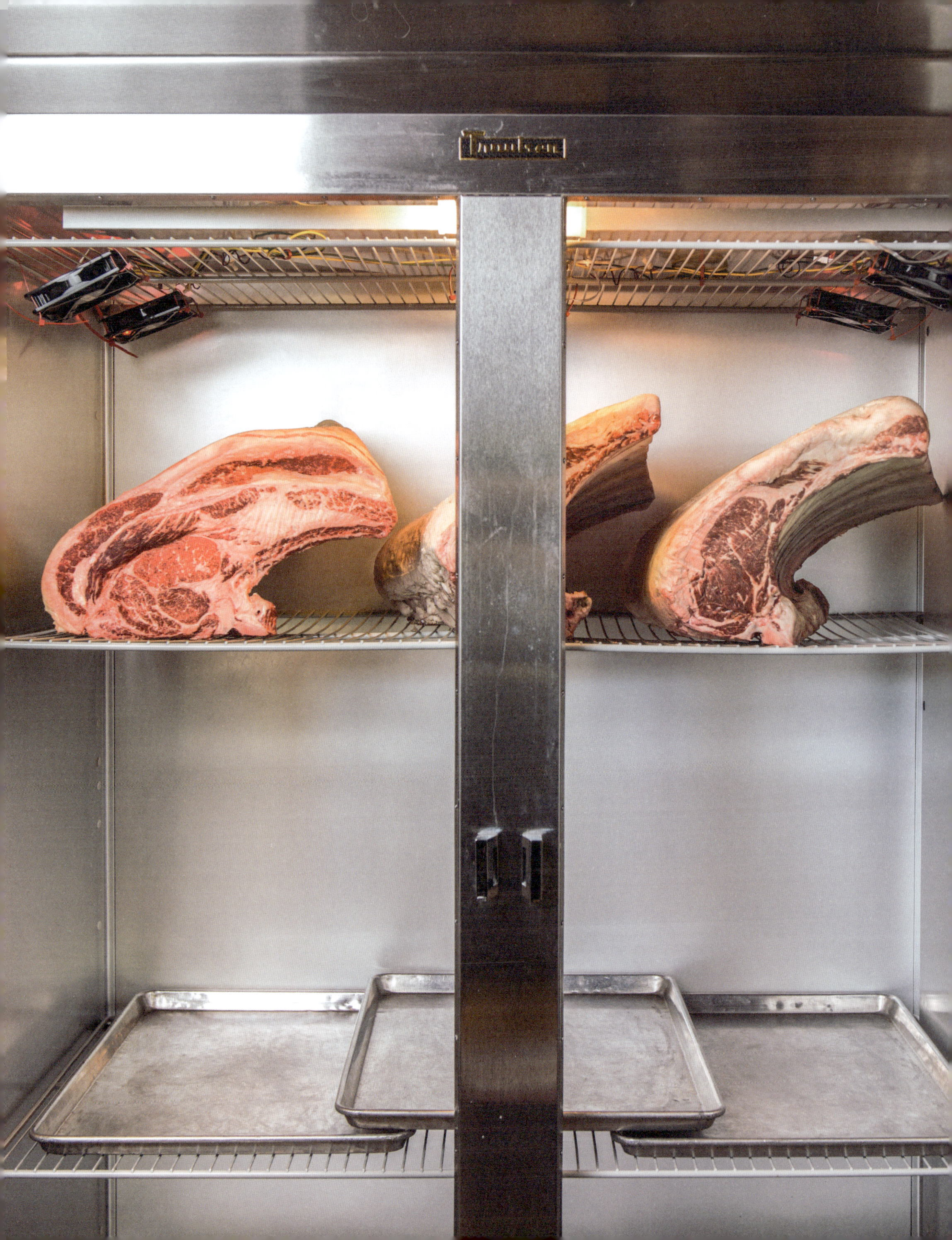

CHAPTER 4

Dry Aging

The term "old meat" does not sound appetizing. But "dry-aged meat"? Well, that's different. Now we're in the realm of finely aged wine or a cheese served at the peak of ripeness.

No bigger trend exists in steak these days than dry aging. What used to be a rare, dark art has now become a mainstream dark art. What used to be a rumored delicacy and difficult-to-find product has become popular—and by consequence less difficult to find. And its popularity is no surprise. When you can transform an ordinary, delicious piece of steak into something that retains all original deliciousness but becomes even more tender, more complex, more savory, why wouldn't you do it?

Aaron had his eyes opened to the wonders of dry-aged steak a few years ago at John Tesar's Dallas restaurant Knife (see page 84). Tesar gave Aaron a tasting that ranged from a 45-day steak all the way to over 200 days. Man, that was some beefy, beefy beef. He'd never had anything like it. Some of the older stuff was almost too funky and intense, but the midrange had just the right amount of gaminess. Jordan's first memorable encounter came in Spain, where a 120-day dry-aged rib cut blew him away (see page 62). Afterward, he had to find more beef like that. Years later, he can still remember the taste.

Because finding great dry-aged beef isn't always easy, in this chapter, we're going to tell you exactly how and why it works and how to do it. Neither of us had any experience aging steak before writing this book, but lots of conversation and advice from friends showed that it's definitely something you can do at home. But before we get into that, we want to offer a few words on the differences between "old meat" and dry-aged majesty from someone who knows.

"I inherited a dry-age program at this facility from the people we bought it from," says John Kosmidis, chief operating officer of Prime Foods Distributor, an important New York–based beef supplier to such esteemed steak houses as the high-end chain Smith & Wollensky. "Our predecessors had built a new establishment for dry aging with all the modern tools. But although they had a successful business and were highly regarded for their dry-age program, when we took over, I and my partners hated it. We thought the beef was terrible. We would look at each other and say, 'Is everyone here brainwashed?'"

Kosmidis and his partners realized the answer was yes. "The brainwashing had gone up the chain from the producers to the processors to the further processors to Michelin-starred chefs to the media to the end consumer," he says. "Everybody accepted something that if found in any other product would get you fired. But if you put it [spoilage] on the beef, it was prime dry-aged product. We thought that was so wrong."

What Kosmidis is describing happened several years ago, when he and his partners founded the business. But it also describes something about dry-aged beef. If it doesn't taste good to you, something is probably wrong. The tolerance for dry-aged chicanery in this world is great, as beef can get weird if it's not properly aged. People might eat it anyway, find it off or too funky, and then say they don't like dry-aged beef. Kosmidis sees this as the result of bad and irresponsible practices. "Other packers post photos of their dry-aging rooms [on social media], and we just shake our heads," says Kosmidis. "They have meat piled up on meat, on racks that obviously haven't been cleaned or moved in years, [and] there's no air circulation. If you have mold growing because of bad conditions, your beef will be different colors. It can have purple, yellow, green, peach fuzz and hair. It's not aging. It's rotting."

Kosmidis et al. decided to fix the situation. But for the art of dry aging, there's no manual, no textbook, not even any real experts or scientists. You can't just hire a dry-aging wizard from the Internet to come in and fix your program. You have to start from the ground up. Over the next few years, the group revamped their procedure time and time again, spending millions in the process. They learned they had to pay attention not only to their aging conditions but also to their suppliers: how the meat was brought to them (full carcass or Cryovaced), how it was

APL

1680 Vine Street
Los Angeles, California
tel: (323) 416-1280 • aplrestaurant.com

Nothing made us happier than the 2018 opening of Adam Perry Lang's long-awaited, long-toiled-over Hollywood steak house APL. No other accomplished American chef has ever been as associated with steak as Lang. Along with a Michelin three-star background at Guy Savoy in Paris and Daniel in New York and some respectable barbecue chops (Aaron has made custom smokers for him), Adam has serious steak credentials. More than anyone, he's responsible for the surge of dry aging across the country, an art form he mastered at programs he created at Robert's in New York and Carnevino in Las Vegas.

His beautiful new restaurant at the corner of Hollywood and Vine fulfills the dream of doing it for himself. The achievement here is purity: incredible steaks, done simply and perfectly. To that end, Lang is involved in every step of the process. He built a one-thousand-square-foot dry-aging room under the restaurant and tracks all of the meat himself. Everything is butchered on the premises (at the time of writing, by Lang himself) and cooked in a high-powered broiler. Every aspect of the experience has been considered, down to the steak knives, which Lang makes himself, having learned to forge and shape steel for this purpose (the knives are listed at nine hundred fifty dollars on the menu, the lowest cost of a felony in California; he's serious about people not stealing them).

The menu is impressively simple: dry-aged steaks with a couple of sauces, as well as some classic sides, a lovely fish selection, a few pastas, and some starters. It's rather minimalist, putting all of the focus back on the quality of the meat, which is impressive. The aging is done just long enough to create that savory, funky bite, but never gets in the way of the carefully sourced, deeply beefy steak.

DRY AGING

KNIFE

5300 E. Mockingbird Lane
Dallas, Texas
tel: (214) 443-9339 • knifedallas.com

In his previous incarnation at Spoon, chef John Tesar was known for fish. That makes his reinvention as a master of meat all the more remarkable, especially because in no time his steak became some of the very best in the country. Tesar is known as a skilled technician who can cook anything, so his touch with simple, dumb steak is impressive. Here, it's really the quality of the beef he chooses and the flavors he coaxes out of his dry-aging room that make eating steak at Knife worth a diversion.

The lengthy, diverse menu is well executed across the board (don't skip the bacon-crusted bone marrow and caviar), but the steak menu—divided into New School, Old School, and Exotic—is the place to mine. The New School category lists such butcher's cuts as the flat iron, culotte (sirloin cap), and skirt, all grilled over red oak. These all come from 44 Farms, an Angus ranch between Dallas and Austin that serves as Tesar's main supplier and muse. Old School cuts include ribeye, filet mignon, and such. The Exotic menu comes from the dry-aging room and features 240-day and 110-day steaks, among others. Tesar has become known for pushing the dry aging to new distances, and sometimes he'll have the odd 360-day pieces back there. Meat sources in the aging cellar also include HeartBrand and Creekstone. A variety of sauces—béarnaise, au poivre, Bordelaise, *chimichurri*, and *salsa verde*—are available on request.

fabricated, how long since its slaughter date. They learned they had to pay attention to their refrigerated rooms: how much new meat was going into the same room as meat that had been there for a week or two. They had to clean. They had to have air circulation and rotate the meats. "It was the school of hard knocks," Kosmidis says. "Trial and error. We took notes. We learned from our mistakes and paid for all of them." But today, their steaks set the standard for dry-aged perfection.

Nowadays, Prime Foods keeps something like seven thousand subprimals of beef in its massive aging program. To be that large and precise is an achievement, and the lessons are well learned. And it turns out that all of the professionals who are dry aging meat for sale to customers or at their restaurants voiced the same refrain as Kosmidis: you have to learn by doing.

"We're still learning as we go along," says Bryan Flannery, who runs the famed Flannery Beef with his daughter, Katie, in Northern California (see page 33). "We've got a system we like right now, but it's changed over the years as we've grown and changed and learned more about the aging process." For the Flannerys, getting enough air movement and making sure it was reaching every corner of their dry-aging room was key.

"You've got to figure out what works for you," adds chef Adam Perry Lang, the reigning king of restaurant dry aging, from the vast room underneath his new APL Restaurant in Hollywood (see page 83). Lang can largely be credited for popularizing (or repopularizing—after all, hanging beef for tenderization has been around for centuries) the dry-aging trend, as he's done in New York, Las Vegas, and now at APL, his signature, personal spot. "There's no manual for this. No teacher," he continues. "But when you determine what you like in an aged piece of beef, it just takes time and experimentation to learn how to make it happen."

That's true in the restaurant and commercial realm, but it's also possible in the home. It's an undertaking, to be sure, but if you're a serious and passionate steak lover with a little extra room in your place, it might be worthwhile.

What Is Dry Aging?

Dry aging is a complex but natural process that's essentially an early-stage degradation of meat in which chemical processes alter its fundamental nature, making it more tender and more flavorful. As great food scientist and writer Harold McGee wrote in an essay in the bygone food journal *Lucky Peach* (issue #2), raw meats don't have much flavor in their natural state, which is why we cook, season, and transform them.

"But sometimes we can get our food to make itself more delicious," he says, "by treating it in a way that creates favorable conditions for the enzymes that are already in the food to work together in a certain fashion. Enzymes are molecules that exist in foods—and in microbes intimately involved with food—that can transform those basic, bland building blocks. They're nanocooks—the true molecular cooks. Dry aging, ripening, and fermentation are all processes that take advantage of enzymes to make foods delicious before cooking."

Every meat ages, but none quite as well as beef. As *Modernist Cuisine*, the incredible multivolume tome on the science of cooking, explains, "For reasons having to do with the relative activity of enzymes in different muscle-fiber types, red meat generally matures more slowly than white meat. Large animals require more time than smaller animals. And meat from younger animals ages faster than the meat of their more mature kin." Fish see almost no benefit from aging, chickens for only a handful of days, and pork and lamb for a week or so. But beef? Beef needs two or three weeks to tenderize properly. Flavor development usually starts at anywhere from twenty-eight to forty-five days and can be taken into the hundreds of days.

This process has been around for centuries and likely longer, as there's a thin line between intentionally aging meat and just trying to keep it from spoiling until your clan can finish it all. Of course, people have known how to preserve meat with smoke and salt for tens of thousands of years. But in the nineteenth century, McGee writes, beef and lamb would be hung at room temperature until the exterior flesh actually rotted. This result was desirable, probably because of the gains in tenderization and flavor, but also for matters of practicality, as the lack of refrigeration meant that a side of beef simply aged until it was fully consumed. Of course, we don't desire rot today, but by controlling the simple variables of time, temperature, humidity, and airflow, we can guide the aging process to transform meat into something truly stupendous.

So what's going on here? After slaughter, naturally occurring enzymes in the meat go to work. When the animal was alive, those enzymes were controlled by the living cells. But after the cells die, the enzymes are uninhibited and go to work on other compounds in the organism. They break down larger, flavorless molecules and chop them into smaller bits we can taste. In particular, they start to chop up fats, proteins, and a carbohydrate called glycogen into sugars, amino acids, and fatty acids. One of those amino acids rendered is glutamate, aka umami. And umami is, well, everything—or at least a primary reason savory things are so delicious.

Dry aging also forces beef to lose moisture. It's not much but significant, as the remaining juices and tissue become more concentrated. Evaporation further concentrates the newly created enzymatic sugars and umami-boosting protein compounds. It makes beef beefier and, on cooking, creates even greater Maillardian cascades (remember, Maillard is the set of reactions that occur when the surface of the meat is browned during cooking). It's an orgy of flavor, thanks to microbes that have been let off the leash.

WET AGING? MEH...

Inevitably, all the talk of dry aging brings up the topic of wet aging. This is when beef is Cryovaced and kept in the plastic bag for a few weeks, sitting in its own juices. Some people claim it is not only as effective but also more efficient than dry aging. After all, if it's the enzymes that are acting, can't they do so in a bag without any of the moisture loss that occurs during dry aging? The answer is yes, and it turns out that wet aging in a sealed bag does yield the same gains in tenderizing after about fourteen days. However, there appear to be no attendant flavor gains. In fact, after more than about four weeks maximum, research has shown tasters find wet-aged meat to be "flat" and "metallic." Indeed, dry aging in a windblown cellar seems vaguely healthful. Who would want to be smothered in a wet plastic bag for weeks?

The other great benefit of aging is tenderization. A couple of enzymes called calpains and cathepsins sever the bonds in certain proteins, weakening connective tissues and reducing pressure, resulting in more tender, silky meat that's also juicier because the relaxed meat has squeezed out less moisture during cooking. It's a win, win, win—more flavorful, more complex, more tender.

The Challenges of Aging Beef

So if aging beef is so great, why isn't everyone doing it all the time? There are a number of factors. On the commercial scale, dry aging takes time. And time equals money. If you have to lay out a lot of cash for beef you're not going to sell for weeks or months, you're taking on a big negative on your books for a significant amount of time, not to mention running an aging cellar requires space (additional rent), climate control (higher bills), and attendance (more labor costs). There's also risk. What if something goes wrong? It could mean tens of thousands of dollars or more in losses. As long as people aren't demanding it, as long as they're satisfied with a simple, conventional unaged steak, why bother?

For the home dry ager—which you could become—the challenges are analogous. You need room for an extra refrigerator and to be able to afford the bills of running it full time. You need humidity gauges and wind-force producers to have the confidence that the meat is not going bad on you. You need to have a source where you can buy a large subprimal of meat. And most of all, you need patience.

DRY AGING

How and Why to Age Beef at Home

Despite all the previous talk about the dry-aging school of hard knocks, it's not that hard to age beef at home. And indeed, if you're a steak lover, eat it regularly, and have a spacious abode, all the reasons in the world implore you to do this. After all, in most places, it's difficult if not impossible to buy dry-aged meat to cook at home. Restaurants may have it, but they don't sell at retail. And if you can find such places, dry-aged meat is expensive—not just the meat but also the shipping if it's coming from a seller outside of your area. That said, dry aging beef is a commitment, so you have to really want it. On the other hand, as complicated and edgy as dry aging sounds—it's really neither.

1. CREATE A DRY-AGING FRIDGE AND TRICK IT OUT

Beef aging can only occur in a highly controlled environment, which means temperature control is imperative. Maintaining a sufficiently low temperature without freezing is what decides the difference between aging and rotting. It's the low temperature that keeps the spoilage bacteria at bay while allowing the enzymes to do their work. If there's too much heat and moisture, the bacteria go crazy, and you've got a big hunk of rotting meat on your hands. A proper aging fridge should give you at least two feet across, though three feet is better, and about five feet of height, enough for two or three separate racks. The point of having a large enough fridge is that if you're going to age large subprimals (big pieces of meat containing several steaks that you'll slice off yourself), you need to have a couple going at any one time so you don't run out and have to start from scratch and wait months every time you want an aged steak. Also, this is not a fridge into which you're going to throw some extra bunches of celery and leftover risotto. If you want to be serious about dry aging, only beef goes in here.

Any sort of fridge will work as long as its reliable and has adjustable racks. Commercial refrigerators with glass doors are cool because you can see the meat transform (in slow motion) before your very eyes. But it's certainly not necessary. Aaron bought a Traulsen two-door fridge from a restaurant supply store (he needed it anyway) and put it in his home garage (with plans to move it to a new facility later). But you don't necessarily need restaurant-grade equipment. A good-quality used fridge purchased on craigslist will do the trick as long as it's consistent and reliable. Whatever you buy, after you get it home, thoroughly scrub down the interior with water and bleach to disinfect it. Once the whole thing—top, bottom, sides, and racks—is wiped down, it's fine to start decking it out.

2. BUY SOME FANS

Besides the proper-size fridge itself, you need to account for humidity and airflow. Of the two, airflow is the more important. Without constant air movement, the air stagnates and moisture hovers, creating a ripe environment for bacteria and mold to propagate. They love a moist and somewhat warm environment. As you dry out that exterior layer of beef, it forms a bulwark, preventing the interior from losing moisture. So air movement is a hero: it stifles bad bacterial growth and protects the juicy interior of the steak.

You'll need at least one fan, but two or more are better. As Kosmidis said about his professional dry-aging cellar, "Every piece of meat is getting

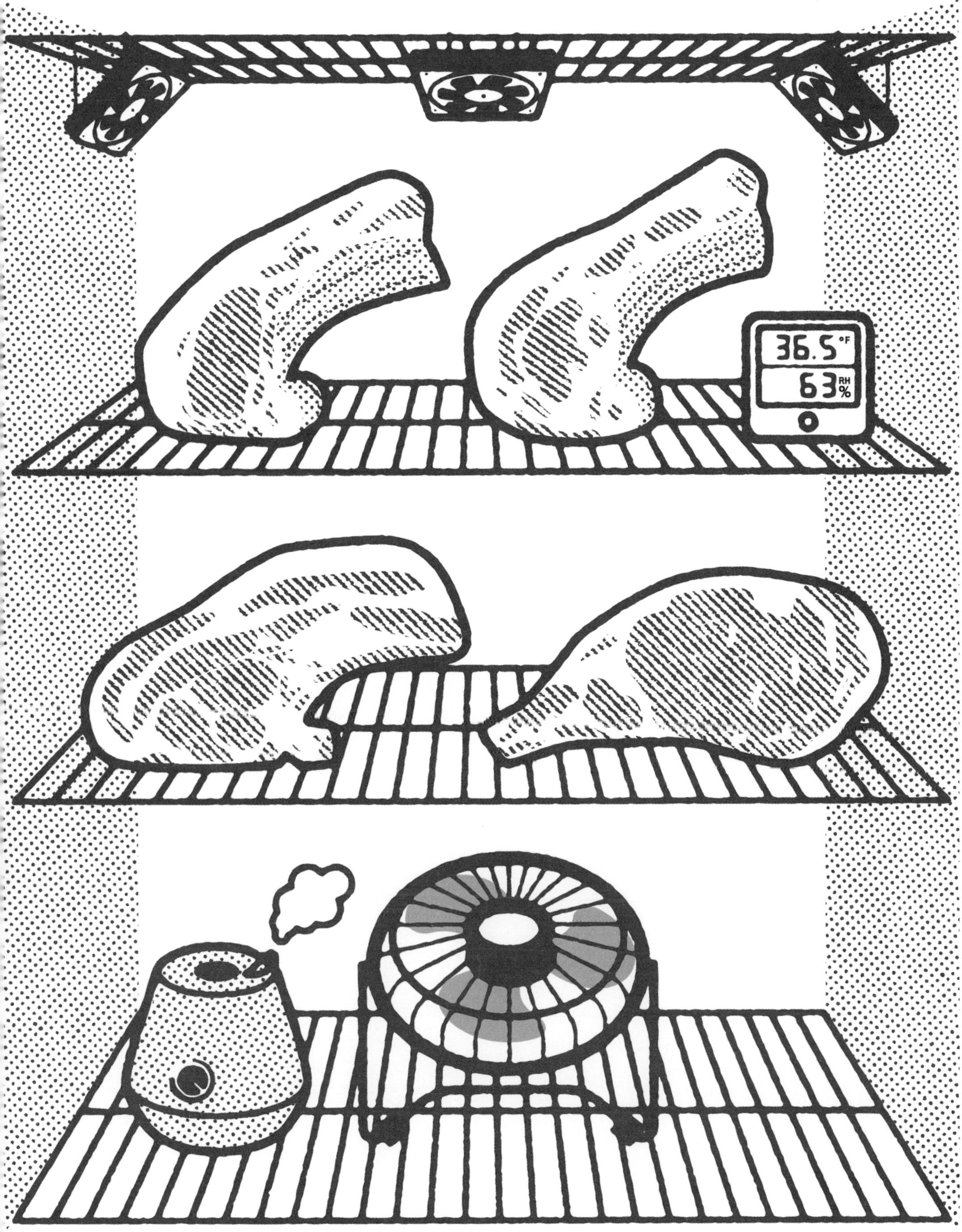

36.5 °F
63 RH %

hit by air from at least eight different directions." That's overkill for the home setup, but good circulation is key, not unlike the dynamics inside a barbecue smoker. To get maximum air movement in a small space, Aaron set up several small but powerful fans to create an array. He bought a few small twelve-volt CPU cooling fans at a computer store, wired them in parallel, connected them to a power source, and then hung them from wires at the top of the refrigerator. But now he says that was overkill and he wouldn't bother going to that much trouble again. It's cheaper and easier just to get two or three small Vornado or other desk or room fans and point them from different directions at the meat. The result is a swirling chaos of air that ensures moisture is swept away. Professionals talk about necessary wind velocity in measurements of linear feet per second, but without getting so geeky, this setup has worked well for meat that's been steadily aging for months.

3. HUMIDITY AND TEMPERATURE

Humidity is a concern in dry aging, though it is not as big a deal for the home dry ager as for the people working on a commercial scale. The crucial aspect of humidity is making sure it's not too high. Too moist an environment and bacteria will grow, so drier is better. But the drier it is, the more moisture evaporates from the meat, causing the meat to lose weight. Indeed, after a standard forty-five to sixty days of dry aging, a rib rack of beef can lose up to 30 percent of its weight in water. So large meat packers—people who sell meat by the pound—typically like to keep the humidity as high as possible to retain water weight without courting microbes.

For those interested foremost in quality, however, that shouldn't be a concern. Kosmidis says, "We experimented constantly. At first, we were at high humidity, around 80 percent. In the beginning, we accepted the thinking that if you're dry aging, your first priority should not be to minimize your yield loss but to produce a proper product regardless of loss."

The figures generally cited as necessary for maintaining a safe environment are 70 to 80 percent humidity. If you have a restaurant with a giant room full of aging meat with fresh, wet meat being introduced on a weekly basis, managing humidity to maintain sterile levels becomes more of a challenge. But in a typical refrigerator, staying below 80 percent humidity is not a problem.

Home refrigerators are programmed to be dry: to condense humidity and then dispose of the water periodically. This is because the frequent opening of a refrigerator door introduces humidity into the environment, which makes fridges less efficient because it takes more energy to cool humid air. That means if you have a fridge dedicated to meat aging and you're rarely opening the door, it's going to dry out in there, to the tune of humidity levels in the 30 percent range.

Very low humidity doesn't appear to be a severe problem in aging meat. You might think that low humidity will cause the meat to eventually shrivel up and dry out, but luckily it doesn't seem to work that way—at least not over the few weeks or months most people will age their meat. Rather, and amazingly, dry-aged meat is usually quite juicy. Scientists debate why this is so, but some have referred to the exterior drying of the meat as basically closing off the channels through which water contacts the air, sealing moisture in.

Temperature in a refrigerator generally takes care of itself. Standard temperatures for aging beef run between 34°F and 39°F. This is generally easy to maintain, especially if you keep the door closed all the time.

Aaron added a humidifier to keep his dry-aging fridge from getting too dry and set the temperature at 38°F. He also added a basic sensor, easily purchased at any hardware store, to monitor the humidity and temperature. After just a few days, the rig stabilized in a range at which it seems comfortable: 36°F to 38°F and 60 to 64 percent humidity. The beef happily aged for months.

4. BUY SOME BIG HUNKS OF MEAT

Aging individual steaks doesn't work. Sure, you can let them sit out in the refrigerator for a few days, but these loners will dry out before any of the significant chemical changes from aging take place. If you left that steak in the fridge for, say, twenty-eight days, by the time you trimmed off the rock-hard, dried outer shell, you'd have nothing left to cook. Thus, aging has to be done on bigger pieces, large enough that you can trim off that crusty pellicle and still have plenty of delicious, juicy meat. So what cuts, er, make the cut?

First of all, you want well-marbled cuts with bones and fat caps, so this factors out most steak cuts. Pieces like skirt, flank, bavette, and even tenderloin are all too small and lack bones and much exterior fat. Also, you want high-quality meat that has been handled well since it was fabricated (the meat industry's term for cut). It should be fresh, pristine meat that hasn't been punctured or opened up in any way. This all ensures the integrity of the interior of the meat, as the exterior pellicle that develops during dry aging will all be trimmed away.

Bones and fat caps are essential for a few reasons. First and foremost is that they lie on the exterior and protect the meat. As the enzymatic aging occurs within the meat, these components are slowing the loss of moisture from the exterior. But there's also a flavor component to the fat.

A good deal of that "funk" people love about dry-aged meat, that somewhat gamy, mushroomy, cheesy, nutty aroma that layers on the irresistible umami, is dependent on fat. As *Modernist Cuisine* notes, "The oxidation of fat and other susceptible molecules also contributes to the aroma of dry-aged meat. In the case of meats high in saturated fats, beef being the prime example, the aroma can be pleasantly nutty, with mild cheesy notes. Indeed, it is the combination of concentration and oxidation that further enhances the flavor of meat as it continues to dry age beyond the point at which enzymatic tenderization has come to a halt."

The upshot of this is that tenderizing is accomplished within about two weeks. Further aging is for flavor, and a healthy fat cap and lots of marbling provide that. The most profound expressions of the aged flavor occur on the perimeter of the steak; the interior will taste less intense. Perhaps this is because the interior meat isn't exposed to oxygen and thus the fat doesn't oxidize. But it does mean that as much of the outer part of the steak as possible should be left on while cooking. You may take off most of the fat cap, but consider leaving on some of the fatty scraps. And definitely keep the bone. All of these parts—especially the rib-cap muscle, or *spinalis dorsi*, which takes on the most intense aged flavor of any part—will contribute flavor and aroma to the final, delicious steak.

So with their processing numbers and a brief description, here are the large cuts that offer

DRY AGING

Long bone 103 rib

maximum efficiency, return, and character for dry aging.

- First, you can do an entire **rib primal**, known affectionately as a **103**. It's the works: ribs six through twelve, with chine and blade bones intact, covered with a fat cap and "lifter" meat (the latter, also known as blade meat, is made up of thin muscles, often removed, that line the extended rib bones). The 103 is what you see in the home aging fridge in Austin (pictured on page 80). Its cousin, the long bone 103 rib, is pictured at left. It meets all the criteria but is incredibly heavy and unwieldy—not an easy carry from the fridge to the countertop. Also, when it comes time to cut steaks off of it, cutting through the chine is a lot of work.

- The **107** is a smaller version of the 103, with blade and chine bone removed and rib bones shortened; everything else is intact.

- The **109A** has even more rib bone removed as well as some of the exterior "lifter" meat that's always removed on ribeye steaks, making it a nice and tidy package. This is an excellent cut to age because the bone and fat cap protect the meat during drying.

- The **109 Export** is similar to the 109A, but the fat cap is removed. Along with the 109A, this is the easiest big rib cut to age because of its size and ease of handling. However, the missing fat cap is a downside, as the fat protects the outer layer of meat, which in this case is the precious *spinalis*. Without the fat, the *spinalis* will dry out.

- The **112A** is a boneless rib roast and will still age well, but it's better with the bone. If you have less space and aren't planning to age for too long, the smaller package of the 112A can be handy. But in general and for longer aging, you want to age on the bone, as it protects the meat from moisture loss.

- The **loin primal** ages well, too. Remember, this is the area that has both the tenderloin and the strip loin on either side of the T-bone. In this case, most people age only the strip, as it is better marbled than the tenderloin and thus develops more flavor. Recommended for aging are the **175**, which is the bone-in strip loin, and the **180**, which is boneless. Again, if you have the choice, go bone in.

When it comes to sourcing your meat this should be obvious: try not to buy anything that's been previously frozen. If you have the ability to procure primals and subprimals that haven't been Cryovaced, do that, as the freshness of the beef is an asset. However, if the meat's been in plastic for just a short time, it's okay. What you want to avoid is meat that has wet aged for more than a week or so, as the degradation that occurred inside the plastic doesn't translate well to the dry-aging environment. The meat will tend to dry out without much flavor development. The way to source these cuts is by talking to a butcher at a specialized shop or a good grocery store. These large cuts won't be offered at the counter, but the butcher should be happy to get them for you from his or her supplier or at least connect you directly to the supplier.

5. STORE YOUR MEAT

When you put the beef in the dry-aging refrigerator, make sure it sits on standard wire shelves (as in Metro shelves) that allow air to pass through them. Remember, the idea is for air to be blowing on all sides of the meat at all times. Make sure there's five or six inches between cuts of meat, as the evaporating water needs some place to go and fresh air needs to circulate freely around the cuts. Every week or so, shift the angle or position of the meat just to even things out.

DRY AGING

6. WAIT AND MONITOR YOUR PROGRESS

Okay, you have your fridge plugged in and chilling. You've set up an array of three or more fans and have cold air blowing like mad throughout the fridge. You've purchased your beef and placed it on one or more shelves in the fridge. What's next? Now is the easy part: you just wait. But for how long?

How long you age your beef is entirely up to you. But here's a handy guide to the general cutoffs. Remember, every animal is different, however, so every piece of meat is different. Also, differences in temperature and humidity can have a profound effect on the rate of these chemical transformations. There is no precise accounting for any of this. And even if you're getting a piece of meat cut from a fresh carcass that has never seen the inside of a bag, the likelihood is that the meat is already at least a week old. Cooling, processing, and transportation all take a certain amount of time, so it's almost surely not "fresh" meat that you're getting.

In the first 14 days of aging, you'll start to experience tenderization of the meat, but no flavor change. From 14 to 21 days, the meat will continue to tenderize, but that process should technically end around the three-week mark. From 21 to 28 days, you may get the first hint of an evolution of flavor, though not much. The advent of that dry-aging funk only starts to kick in after 28 days, when it should become noticeable the moment you open the fridge door and take a whiff. Flavor development will continue indefinitely and then becomes a matter of taste. At 45 days, you might get that telltale whiff of blue cheese that some people talk about, though in our experience, it's more of a gamy, mushroomy quality. Many people consider 45 days of aging a sweet spot; some people think of it as just the beginning. It's not unusual to find meat sellers taking steaks to 60, or even 90, days. You can expect quite a bit of funk after 90 days. And flavor keeps developing, albeit more slowly. Nowadays, chefs are taking aging to ever more distant extremes, up to 220 or 360 days—and sometimes up to 400 days. A butcher in Paris even sells vintage steaks that are over a decade old, though it sounds like he uses a special freezing technique (ice-cold air is blown at high velocity over the meat), so it's not quite the same.

In general, you may have diminishing returns from aging more than 60 to 90 days, and we don't recommend going beyond that. The meat will just dry out and become hard and crusty. You'll have to cut the dried parts off, as they become basically petrified and harder to eat. Over time, that dried pellicle will simply increase and you'll lose more and more meat. At 60 days you can have both great flavor and great tenderness.

7. FINISHING

Whew, you've made it to the end of your journey and successfully aged a large chunk of beef. It smells funky-delicious, and the exterior meat has dried and turned a glorious color of dark reddish brown. Now it's time to slice off a couple of steaks to taste the results.

Pull the big piece from the fridge and set it on a clean cutting surface. Have a very sharp slicing knife handy. If there's any bone like the chine (spine) bone on your piece, also have ready a saw—we recommend the twenty-two-inch Weston butcher saw—as you can't slice through a heavy beef bone with a knife. Then decide how thick you want your steaks and slice them off cleanly. It's all basic, no matter what subprimal you're using. Just visualize the kind of steak you want and cut through the bone. Now, if there's still a lot of meat left on the piece, it can be returned to the refrigerator to continue aging. Or you can just plan to consume the rest over the next week, keeping it in your kitchen fridge.

After you've got the steaks, you'll want to clean them up a by removing the hardened exterior crust. Do this carefully, and not too generously, as you want to keep as much good meat and fat as possible. If you cut too deeply into the steaks, you'll discover meat that's as bright and fresh and red as you'd find in a grocery store meat counter. Instead of going that far, just remove the driest bits, as the rest cooks beautifully, softening in the pan (or on the coals) as the fat around it melts and wets it. These will be some of the tastiest, meatiest bites you'll have.

DON'T SCRAP THOSE SCRAPS!

After you've trimmed your steaks, you'll find a little pile of trimmings sitting on the cutting board. Given however many weeks you dedicated to aging the meat to perfection, don't you dare throw those bits away. That's valuable stuff right there! There are a number of things you can do with the scraps. For the fat, you can render it down into a liquid and baste or spray the meat with it during and after cooking, as you would with butter. This way, you're simply dressing this delectable meat with some of its most flavorful bits. Any shards of meat bark you slice off can be saved along with the bones and turned into deep, savory, rich stock, which could then be reduced again to make an aged-beef demi-glace for aged beef.

LET'S GROW MOLD TOGETHER

You can't talk dry aging without bringing up the subject of mold. A good cellar with great air movement and moderate humidity should grow little to no mold as the beef ages. However, for long periods, even at low temperatures and moderate humidity, some species of mold will eventually form on the exterior of the beef. Is it something to be afraid of?

In an email, Harold McGee agrees that the meat's own enzymes are key, but microbes play a role, too. "I do think that the changes in flavor and texture are mainly due to the meat's own chemistry," he writes, "but there is evidence from dry-cured hams that surface microbes can affect the external muscles. What we easily see is the molds, but there are yeasts and bacteria in there as well, and apparently their *Gemisch* of enzymes can penetrate to some extent. Of course, hams are aged for months to years, so that effect may not be relevant to dry-aged beef.... I haven't found any real research on this."

The most common molds are harmless and even beneficial. As a 2016 paper published in the *Journal of Animal Science Technology* noted, several molds can appear on the surface. "*Thamnidium,* which is the most desirable, appears as pale gray patches called 'whiskers' on the fatty parts of aged beef. These organisms are important because their enzymes are able to penetrate into the meat. In fact, *Thamnidium* releases proteases and creates collagenolytic enzymes which break down the muscle and connective tissues. As a result, these actions bring about tenderness and taste in the dry-aged beef."

In general, a little mold is natural and will get trimmed off before cooking. The dried crust of the meat protects the interior meat from mold-based spoilage. And beef will also usually be seared at a very high temperature for several minutes, making it difficult for any microbial life to survive. The mold in all the best dry-aging cellars we've seen has taken the shape of a sort of white film, similar to the mold you'll find on the exterior of a salami. It always gets trimmed off and the interior meat is fine.

Exterior mold is not usually dangerous. But if there are openings in the meat into which surface microbes could have entered and found a moist environment, throw away that piece. Likewise, if the beef has developed slime or off-colored molds or any sort of bad aroma, throw it away.

To try to preempt the mold question, some people have taken to introducing a tried and proven mold at the beginning through innoculation. Adam Perry Lang brought out some aged meat to inoculate his Las Vegas dry-aging room at Carnevino and then again when he built APL, his palace in Los Angeles. John Tesar got some scraps from Adam to inoculate his dry-aging room at Knife. Even so, Tesar's steaks taste different from Perry Lang's, suggesting that the source of the meat is far more important than whatever culture grows on the outside. But even cellar mold can have a proud provenance. To do this for your home dry-aging fridge, simply find your favorite dry ager of steak and ask for some scraps and fat trimmings. Take those scraps and leave them in your own fridge for a couple of weeks, then toss them. If it works, you'll have introduced a microbial culture that will thrive and take up residence. We didn't do this for our first dry-aging runs and the beef was fine. Indeed, it didn't develop much mold at all. But in future cycles, we're going to inoculate. After all, better the mold you know than the mold you don't.

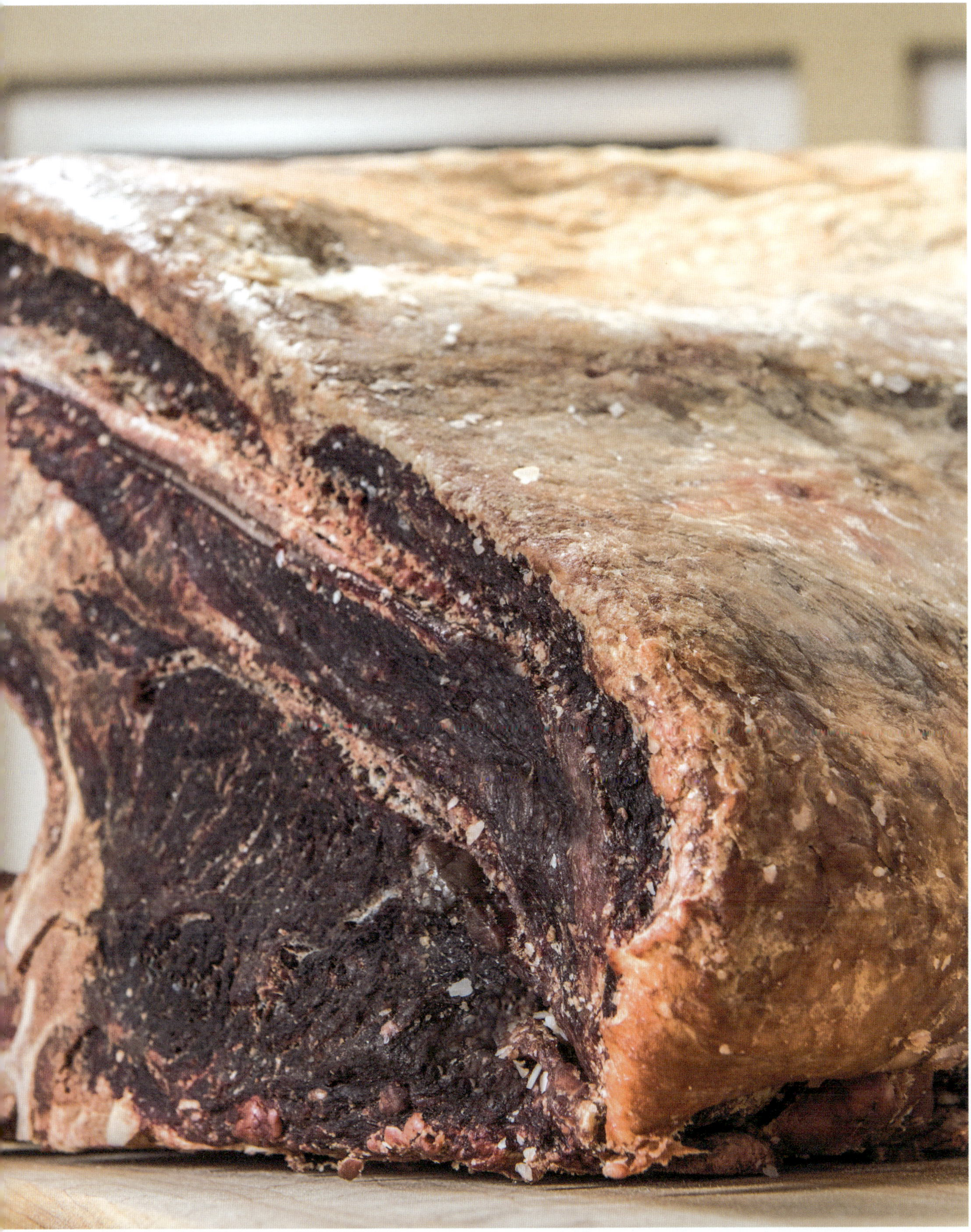

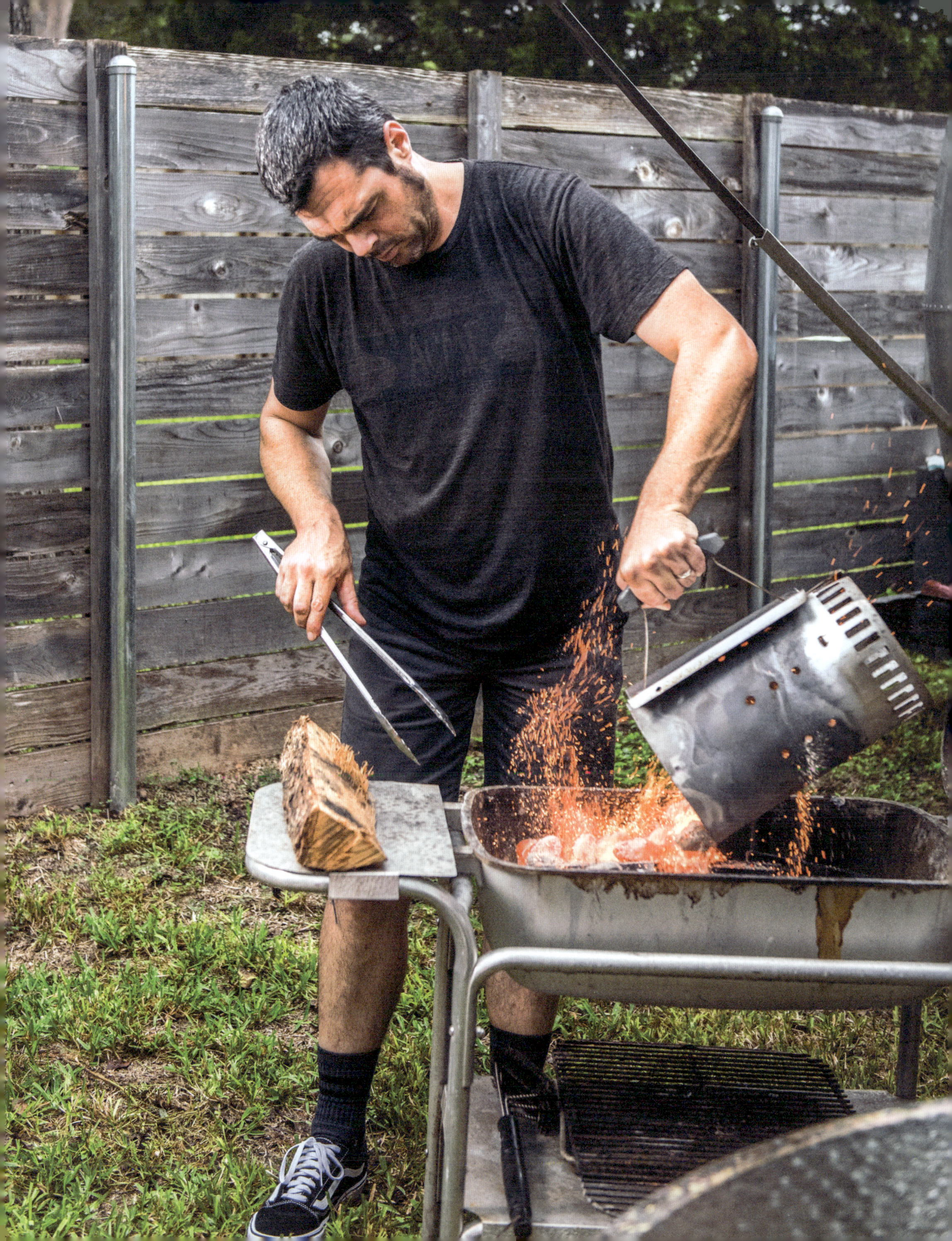

CHAPTER 5

The Grill

There's a saying in the steak business: show me how you cook a steak, and I'll tell you who you are. Well, actually, there isn't. But there could be. How people like to cook their steaks is a very personal thing. And it is more than just about cast iron versus grill. Are you a techie or a Luddite? Do you like to tinker or do you like things neatly prepackaged for success? Are you a stickler for family tradition or a free DIY spirit? Steak tells all.

When it comes to cooking spaghetti or making an omelet, few options exist. But a steak, though a simple food, offers many ways to get it to the table, each with its own set of advantages and challenges. Steak eternally provokes curiosity. "How do you cook a steak?" is cocktail banter that rarely fails to incite discussion—at least in carnivore circles. And for those who care, the answers are always telling. Many folks just default to the old Weber grill on the back patio, while others throw a cast-iron pan into a super-heated oven to get it ready for a stove-top sear. Tech-minded people get out a plastic bag and start heating up a bin filled with water to sous vide the cuts.

And unlike noodles or omelets, with steak, each cooking method leaves an impression on the meat. A finished steak is as much a product of how it was cooked as what was cooked. And this is why it's a personal matter. As an expression, your steak-cooking rig is not unlike your car. Are you a hot rod or a Prius or a Mercedes SUV?

In this chapter, we're going to look at the various kinds of cookers and methods most commonly used today to get a steak from raw to medium-rare (hopefully) and offer some thoughts on each. Now, this book is mostly about cooking with fire, so we're going to focus on that. But we'd be remiss if we didn't mention other energy sources, like gas and electricity, before we get to wood and charcoal. And just maybe we can learn something about ourselves in the process.

Stove-Top Cooking: Indoor and Classic

The classic method will never go out of style, whether your stove is gas or electric (hopefully the former). With a good pan, this is one of the best techniques to get a thick and dense crust on the steak, which is always desirable. The magical browning potential of a cast-iron pan is only one of the attractions of stove-top cooking. The fact that it's an indoor method means you can do it any time, including in the middle of winter or at 2:00 a.m. if the craving for a late-night steak hits (as it does).

The drawbacks to this method are ancillary—more like inconveniences. For one, cooking a steak in hot fat for several minutes generates smoke, which, even when employing a consumer-grade stove hood, will fill a house or apartment with thick, gray clouds and likely set off the smoke alarm. This is something you don't want occurring at, say, 2:00 a.m., as happened to Jordan one night after the bars closed and he and a couple of friends found themselves at his house and hungry. His (formerly) sleeping wife, Christie, had some choice (or were they prime?) words after being piercingly jolted from sleep by an alarm to find a massively beefy cloud of smoke, a heavily steaky aroma (not her favorite), and a few drunk dudes.

Also, cooking this way generates a lot of sizzle, and it's common to find the stove and anything within a three-foot radius (and sometimes far beyond) of it splattered with a sheen of steak grease. Some people think this is a bad thing, such as, again, one's spouse! Stacy Franklin has been known to comment sarcastically after indoor steak cooking about the veneer of grease that somehow coats kitchen cabinets even all the way across the room. It's easy to clean up but not so attractive if it sits around a day, attracting lint and dog hair.

Those people are the ones who worry the relative lack of heat generated by most conventional home stoves is a serious limitation. They may go to such lengths as preheating a pan in a 500°F oven for thirty minutes before pulling it out with a heavily oven-mittened hand and putting it on the stove top over an equally high flame. This attempt at high heat ensures that you're cooking at 500°F, though that's still far below the broilers most steakhouses use, which cook on both sides at temperatures between 800°F and 1200°F. And, yes, this method is almost guaranteed to set off any home smoke alarm.

Although some cooks believe the average home stove's inability to generate higher heat is a drawback, that might not be so. A lot of people cook their steaks too hot, overcooking the exterior while undercooking the interior. If you're cooking a two-inch-thick rib steak with a bone, you won't be able to finish it on the stove top anyway. You'll want to brown the outside and then finish it in the oven until your desired internal temperature has been reached. In this case, superhigh heat doesn't really help that much. The same browning can be achieved at lower temperatures.

Another advantage of the cast-iron pan is the transparency of flavor. Say you've got a piece of well-aged steak whose intense beefiness you want to highlight as cleanly as possible. In this case, you may not want to cook it over coals and layer smoky flavor on top of the hard-earned savor of good dry aging. Thus cast iron over a flame (be it from live fire on a grill or your gas range) is the best bet, using just some neutral oil or tallow in the pan to give the most transparent version of the steak. Conversely, if you've got a relatively mild cut like a tenderloin without any age on it, doing it in a pan allows you to pan baste it with butter, garlic, herbs, or any other sort of aromatic, "cooking in" the seasoning, so to speak.

To cook on the stove, any pan will work, but the heavier the better. Heavier pans retain more heat from preheating, which lets them deliver it to a big slab of meat without cooling down too much. You also want a large skillet, so the meat is not crowded by the sides of the pan. Moisture from the meat needs to be able to escape rapidly during cooking to get that nicely browned crust; in a crowded or tight pan, the steam hangs about and steams the meat. One of the problems with most cookware, especially the fairly crude category of cast iron, is the microscopic unevenness of the pan, leading to differences in diffusivity on the surface, or hot spots and cooler ones. One way to circumvent this is to move the steak around while you cook it and to flip it frequently. Another is Aaron's method.

Aaron uses two pans. He places a large, square, flat griddle (no grill grooves) directly on the burner and on top of that he sets his cast-iron skillet. Then he heats them both up simultaneously for at least twenty minutes. The griddle underneath serves to double the thickness of the metal being heated (making it similar to a *plancha* or French top you'll see at a restaurant), which compensates for the unevenness of a single pan. It also doubles the heat-holding capacity of the metal, meaning that when he drops the steak on it, there's much more thermal mass to transfer the heat to the steak. This gives the steak a good wallop of heat at the beginning and prevents the cast iron from losing too much heat to the steak. Plus, the pan makes a quick recovery, powering the steak through the rest of the cooking. If the steak then has to go into the oven, he keeps it in the top pan and leaves the underlying griddle on the stove to cool.

WHEN TO USE THE OVEN

For thick steaks, the oven is your friend. We need the stove top to build the all-important crust, but if your steak is more than an inch or an inch and a half thick and you want it medium-rare at the center, you'll probably need to finish the steak in the oven. In there, the ambient heat will now keep the cooking going until the interior of the steak comes to temp, but the browning of the exterior will come to a halt so the steak doesn't burn. Determine if the steak needs to finish in the oven by checking the temperature with a meat thermometer. For thick steaks that came straight out of the fridge, the interior might still be at 70°F or 80°F by the time the crust is finished, so make sure the oven is turned on to 250°F or so before you start searing the steak on the stove top. You can go straight into the oven with the pan you're already cooking the steak in. Or if you want cooking on the exterior to slow down, move the steak onto a different ovenproof pan.

Gas Grills: Charmless Convenience

Yes, yes, gas grills are handy, but we still find ourselves indifferent to them. Why? Well, they're the Prius of grills. They're effective and efficient at their job, but there's also something soulless and clinical about them. Car analogies aside, among tools people love, the gas grill tends to rate way down on the list, falling somewhere between a (nonriding) lawn mower and a

> ### A NOTE ON HEAVY PANS
>
> Cast-iron pans are great, but they are not the only skillets you can use. Anything thick bottomed and heavy will do the job. The reason you want something heavy and dense is that it retains a ton of heat, so when you put the cool steak into the hot pan, the pan will take only a slight dip in temperature before recovering and continuing to cook the meat. The great thing about cast iron and carbon steel is that these metals love the fat in the steak and actually bind it to the metal, creating a lovely thin, almost nonstick sheen.

washing machine. It earns your grudging respect by getting the job done, but it's not a treasured tool that you scheme how to take with you when the waters rise.

The advantages of gas grills all have to do with practicality. Without a doubt, they are convenient, as they effortlessly fire up at the flip of a switch. You can be grilling in ten minutes. This is perfect for getting a solid dinner on the table in a timely fashion on those nights when you don't have time to light a proper fire or when you have a dozen screaming kids hungry for hot dogs. (*Timely* is the key word in the above sentence, as the goal is to avoid what Jordan's mother-in-law, Linda, terms "martini meat," otherwise known as horrendously overcooked meat due to a surfeit of predinner gin cocktails that, in addition to resulting in sloppy grillwork, tend to slow everything down until the cooking occurs in the dark, another potential pitfall.)

Gas grills also afford the same kind of control that a gas burner does on a stove, as you can

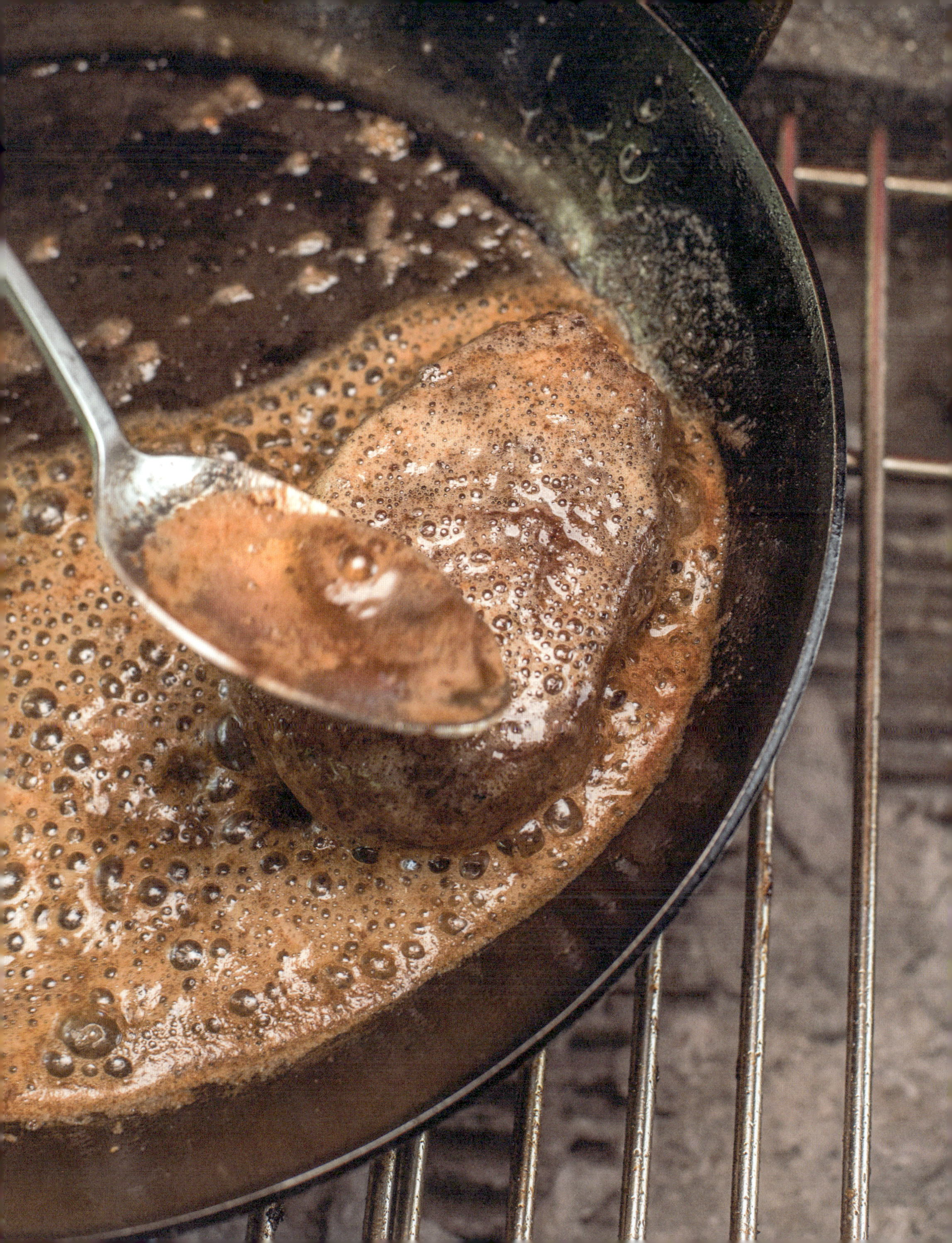

raise or lower the heat just by turning a knob. This allows a level of precision cooking hard to attain with live fire. Cleaning gas grills is a breeze, too. Rather than have to shovel out piles of ash from the depths of a sooty pit, you can just remove the heating plates and grills and scrub them under a hose with soapy steel wool on a sunny day.

The downsides of gas grills are nothing more than crucial counterarguments to a couple of the previous points. Yes, turning a gas flame up and down provides precision, but there's no real skill involved in that. It's as basic and intuitive as turning the volume up and down on your car radio. Learning to use live fire properly is an art and a skill that cooking on a gas grill will never provide. Also, what you don't get on a gas grill is smoke or any of the flavor that comes from a real fire. For many, the taste of the fire is part of the primal appeal of steak. Lastly, gas grills tend not to get as hot as wood or charcoal grills, which can present a challenge if you want that fast, deep sear.

Sous Vide Equipment: Steak by Spock

A long time ago, people had to relieve themselves outside. Then there were rusticities like outhouses and chamber pots. Modern plumbing arrived and we had toilets in the house flushed by pulling a chain. Next, a little handle was introduced. Today they flush themselves. And then there are Japanese toilets, with blow dryers, seat heating, and more. Are these better ways or just different, foolproof, equipment-driven changes?

The same could be asked about sous vide. Sous vide steaks are a modern phenomenon, and the tech bros and gals have flocked to this technique because it involves gadgets and some general smug sense of "hacking" or "disrupting" traditional cooking methods. As gas grilling took the effort out of grilling, sous vide takes the guesswork out of gas grilling. Now, don't get us wrong, we like a good gadget. Aaron loves his digital moisture meter for randomly checking the water content of post oak logs; Jordan is attached to his Sony digital voice recorder. And the sous vide method makes sense in some situations. But much like gas grilling, it's a results-based approach, not process based. And as much as we love a good result, we love it that much more when it's the product of a process in which we've been deeply engaged.

For the uninitiated, here's the deal with sous vide. It's essentially a reversal of the traditional method for cooking steak, accomplished with the precision of technology. It begins by cooking the inside, and the finishing touch is cooking the outside.

The term *sous vide* is French and means "under vacuum." This refers not to the actual cooking, but to the fact that it involves food (in this case steak) in a vacuum-sealed plastic bag, which prevents moisture loss and oxidation. The bag is then submerged into a heated water bath, which is kept at a precise temperature through the use of an immersion circulator, a device once found only in laboratories but now sold at (not inconsiderable) retail prices for the home chef. This nifty gadget circulates the water, warming it to the precisely desired temperature. Over time, thanks to thermodynamics, the meat comes to the same temperature as the water—your desired internal temperature.

For steak, sous vide has been a game changer. Say you want a medium-rare steak. You set the water-bath temperature for 130°F, or just under.

Then you bag your steak and drop it into the water for at least forty-five minutes to an hour or more (depending on the thickness). When the steak is done, it will be sopping wet and look unpalatably gray and unappetizing. Throw away the bag, dry the steak off, and then slap it into a superhot pan to sear the outside until it's nice and brown and crisp. That's it. The inside remains medium-rare while the outside develops a quick, attractive crust.

There's a ton of upside to this. For one, perfect doneness is guaranteed to the exact temperature desired by the chef. The searing at the end happens fast enough that it doesn't alter the internal temperature of the meat. No method is more precise. If overcooking the meat is a profound fear, this is the way for you.

You can see why this can be an excellent idea for restaurants. First, precision is more crucial in a restaurant than in a home-cooked meal. If you overcook a steak at home, shame on you, and you'll probably hear about it from your spouse. Yet at the end of the day, you just suck it up and eat the overdone meat. But if that happens at a restaurant, the steak goes back to the kitchen and the restaurant eats the cost. The customer has had a stressful and unpleasant experience in having to send back food, and the restaurant loses money. The other factor for restaurants is speed and convenience. Rather than figuring out the timing on how to get a thick-cut steak cooked and rested (which can take twenty to thirty minutes when cooking conventionally) on the table the moment you're ready for it, restaurants can now just have steaks prepped in a water bath. When the order comes in, the meat is pretty much done, needing only that final sear, which takes but a minute. A home chef can benefit from this method, too. You can simply set the steak to cook for an hour while you prepare the side dishes.

So does sous vide have any drawbacks? Of course! First, there's the cost of the equipment. A decent water circulator for the amateur chef runs $130 to $200. You need to have plastic bags, too. And all of this for something you could just as easily cook in a pan you already own. Then there's the notion of juiciness and texture. Sous vide steak in a bag can be kept in a bath for hours and hours without its temperature getting too high. Technically, you could put the meat in the bath before you leave for work and finish it when you get home. However, the texture of the meat starts to break down after more than an hour or so in the water. It gets mushy, losing its chew. It also loses its juices into the bag, not on the plate. Therefore, mushy *and* dry steak is a possibility if the sous vide is not done with maximum integrity and timing. We've had steaks like this at restaurants, and it's not pleasant.

Even when done well, sous vide steak is fairly obvious. The transition zone in the steak from the outer, seared crust to the internal meat is very thin. One of the pleasures, we've found, of grilled or griddled steak is that spectrum of doneness you get from inside to out: the crunchy, dried exterior crust with a thin band of well-done meat inside leading all the way to a rare or medium-rare center creates a complex textural experience. This is diminished with sous vide.

The plastic bags are another drawback. The vast majority are not reused. Instead, they get thrown in the trash and potentially end up as part of the massive floating garbage island in the Pacific. Why waste plastic when you don't have to? And lastly, clinically preparing steak in a plastic bag in a water bath misses out on the old-fashioned analog pleasures of cooking. You don't get to

THE GRILL

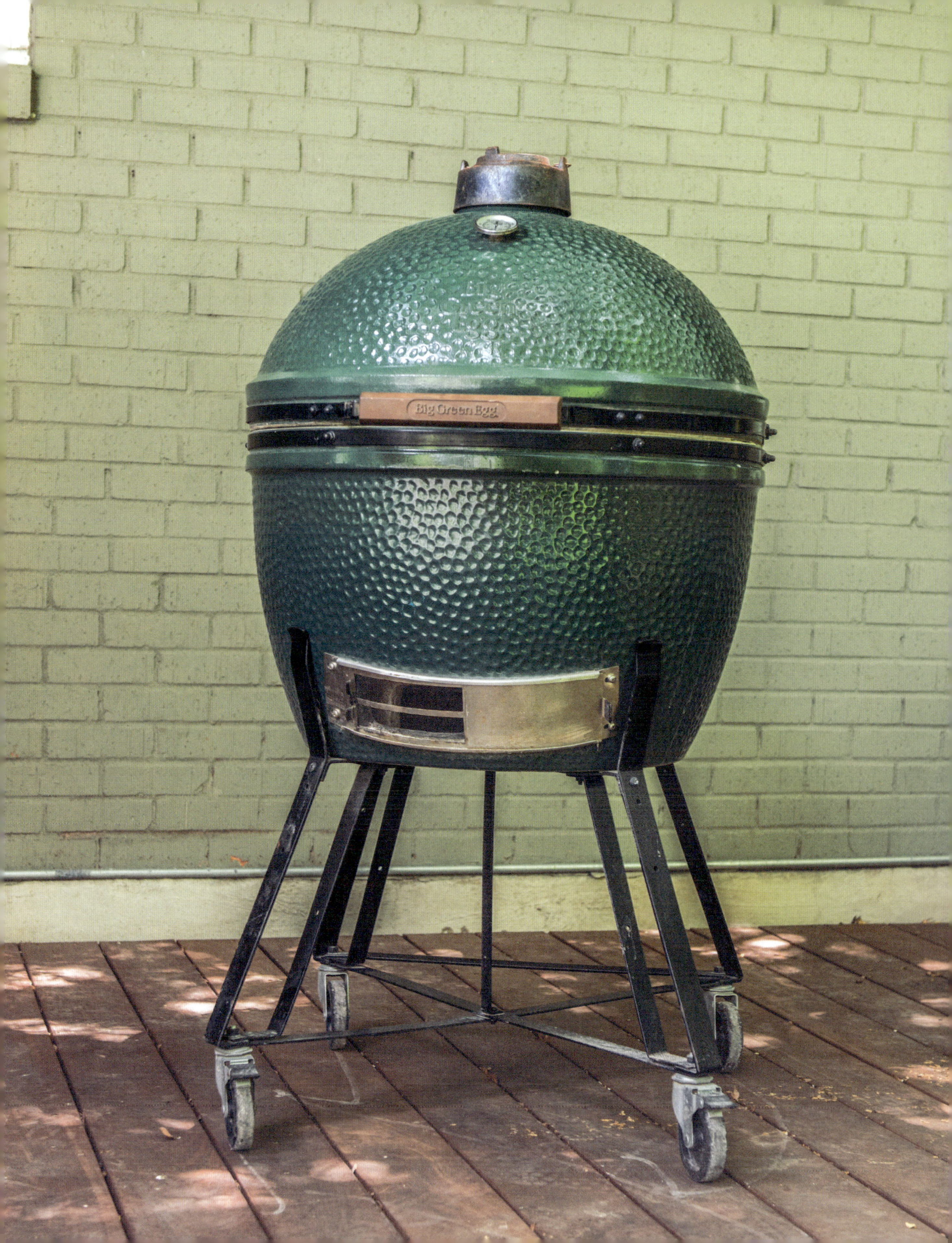
Big Green Egg

work on your skills in cooking the steaks to perfect doneness. You also miss out on many of the smells and sounds of cooking, which impact your perceptions of the flavor, driving hunger and anticipation.

Kamado Cookers: Hot and Heavy!

The luxury SUVs of outdoor cooking, those oval-shaped ceramic cookers known by the ubiquitous brand Big Green Egg (BGE) have been the biggest trend in outdoor cooking for the last ten years or so. The BGE and other brands are examples of kamado cookers, a style that originated in the Far East thousands of years ago. These ovoid cookers are tiled on the outside, have thick, smooth ceramic interiors, and lids that hinge near the top and open like a Fabergé egg. Air intake comes in through the bottom. These grills have become badges of the bourgeois, essential possessions for the suburban backyard set. And all that's a good thing. Kamado-style cookers are excellent devices for cooking many things. Unfortunately, steak is not one of them.

Yes, kamados, which are heated by placing charcoal in the bottom, can sear steaks beautifully at the incredibly high temperatures they are capable of reaching (800°F to 900°F), but cooking the steaks evenly and gently is the problem. Because of their thick ceramic walls, these cookers hold heat especially well, getting very hot and maintaining the temperature easily for a long time. That's a great feature in an oven but not necessarily in a grill. Thus, the kamado "grills" work best for processes with long cook times, where holding a consistent temperature is the name of the game, such as roasting, smoking, and baking.

Kamado cookers are awesome, rock solid, almost indestructible pieces of equipment and do any backyard proud. For smoking briskets and ribs or roasting chickens and pork shoulders, they're amazing. If you want to bake a loaf of bread in the dead of summer without turning on the oven, the BGE is for you. Spareribs? No problem. Even pizza! But the challenges in cooking *steaks* on a kamado are legion. For one, the circular shape of a kamado (especially the smaller models) makes it difficult to have a two-zone setup in which hot coals are placed on only one-half of the grill (see page 147). Especially important for cooking thicker cuts of meat, a two-zone configuration permits you to sear the outside of the meat directly over the coals, but then move the meat off the coals to a warm but not scorching spot where it can cook more slowly, allowing the inside to come up to temperature. In a conventional round grill like a Weber kettle, this is easy to do, as its thin walls don't retain a lot of heat, clearly dividing the hot and cool sides and enabling real contrast. In a kamado, the radiant heat can be so great that even in a two-zone setup, the cool side will still be really hot.

Heat in general can be a challenge in these ovoid cookers. While they have a remarkable ability to hold lower temperatures for long periods, arriving at those desired temperatures can be difficult. Experience has shown us that one of the key skills in using a kamado is to keep it from getting too hot. Once you overload it with even just a little excess charcoal, it can get too hot to use optimally. And kamados take forever to cool down, especially in warm weather. (In cold climates and in winter, however, they can be great assets in outdoor cooking.) Grilling well-marbled steaks in such heat over live coals can cause a lot of fat to render and ignite

THE GRILL

immediately, creating a flare-up fest and plenty of bitterly charred, overdone meat.

Lastly, kamados are expensive. The smallest Big Green Egg costs four hundred dollars without accessories, and its grill only measures ten inches in diameter, big enough for one good-size ribeye or porterhouse cooked in a single zone. The extra-large Big Green Egg, which has a grill measuring twenty-nine inches, costs around two thousand dollars.

Good Old-Fashioned Charcoal Grill: The Answer We've Been Waiting For

The charcoal grill is an even more ancient technology than the three-thousand-year-old kamado. After all, a grill can technically be as simple as a hole in the ground with a cooking grate over it. Or you can make one at home by putting hot coals in a metal pot and covering it with a cooking surface. A charcoal grill can be improvised out of almost anything that won't burn or melt.

If you value flavor and experience over convenience and speed, a charcoal grill is the choice you make. Learning to master hot coals and manipulating their intensity to your advantage is both a challenge and a pleasure—and an important life skill! But getting really good at charcoal grilling is not easy. You have to practice often to get good. And it requires paying attention throughout the process, from lighting the coals to shaping your coal bed all the way to cooking. The required mental presence and observation can be tough to achieve if, say, you only grill when you have company over to distract you (and watch out for those martinis!).

The only other drawbacks are a lack of precision and, of course, cleaning out the ash. Charcoal grills are unfortunately a bit dirty to maintain.

Even if you can charcoal grill for free using a hole in the ground, better options are not very expensive. The stubby, ground-bound Weber Smokey Joe will get the job done for only thirty-five dollars, and if you prefer to tend the steaks while standing up, the original Weber kettle grill sells for about one hundred dollars. While nothing special, the kettle has a good design and is easy to use, relatively easy to clean, and fairly durable. And with its some 360 square inches of grill space, it's plenty big to cook for a good-size party and to set up for two-zone cooking.

Of course, you can always ascend up the price and quality scale from there. The Char-Broil Kettleman ($150) has a more intricate design, a hinged lid like a kamado, and fancier "TRU-infrared" grates, whose thicker steel and tighter configuration are touted as transferring more heat to the meat while reducing flare-ups.

From there, things get pricier, mostly because the grills themselves are given more elaborate mountings (inset into various carts with countertops) and accessories (like gas-powered ignitions to light the charcoal), timers, and other accoutrements.

A not-too-common subset of charcoal or wood grills is the Santa Maria grill, also known sometimes as an Argentine or Tuscan grill. These setups feature a large metal container open on the top and often a couple of feet deep, which holds wood that's slowly smoldering down into coals. A couple of rods are attached vertically up from the wood container. They house a cable or chain that attaches to the big cast-iron grill. By use of a wheel-like hand crank, the grill can

Stove top

Weber

Kamado

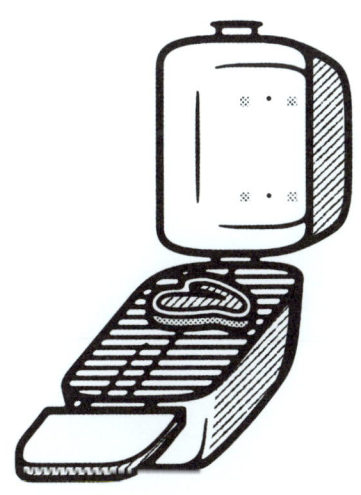

PK

Santa Maria

Chimney

be raised or lowered. This allows the cook to find the perfect distance for the meat above the ever-changing fire. Also, the whole grill can be easily raised when more fuel needs to be added to the fire. The Santa Maria is especially good for larger steak cuts that need a little more time. Tri-tip is the classic example of a steak that can cook with direct heat but needs to have some distance from the fire in order to cook all the way through. Big, chunky bone-in or double-bone ribeyes would also be good candidates.

Hibachi: Easy There, Little Guy!

While the Big Green Egg is a symbol of the modern upscale backyard, how much fire do you really need to cook a steak well? The Japanese answered this question long ago and continue to do so today with their itty-bitty grill we call a hibachi, which they're more likely to refer to as *konro* or *shichirin*.

But since we're Americans, we're just going to hold on to our local jargon. Hibachis are small tabletop boxes or containers resembling flower pots that hold coals and emit heat. In Japan, they have little mesh grates to hold the food or no grate at all when they are meant to cook yakitori skewers of meat, fish, and vegetables laid over the coals. Cute as they may seem, these little powerhouses pack a punch: they're efficient, portable, and versatile, too. Whether you have a tiny studio apartment or a sprawling suburban compound, you may want to consider a hibachi as an efficient everyday solution to low-hassle grilling. One of Jordan's fondest childhood food memories was when he stayed with his grandparents in Seattle, and on warm summer nights, his grandfather fired up a little hibachi on the deck to sizzle one or two steaks for a casual dinner at the round kitchen table.

To grill something like a thin steak (or a couple burgers or fish or chicken breasts) that will only meet the fire for a few minutes, why build a big coal bed and waste a lot of energy when you don't have to? At times like those, the hibachi is a great solution. Just light eight to ten briquettes in a chimney, dump them into the little cooker, and grill away.

Of course, the hibachi's strengths are also its weaknesses. If you need to grill a lot of things over a long period, the hibachi is not your answer. Because it has no cover or lid, long roasting and smoking are out; it can only do open-air grilling. Likewise, two-zone setups are practically impossible in such a small setting. But for efficient one hitters, hibachis can't be beat.

We have a feeling a hibachi renaissance is on the horizon, as society begins to retreat from the giant, charcoal-hungry Webers and kamados and endeavors to cook ever more efficiently. This is why we played around with building a hibachi and why, to our great surprise as we worked on the book, we found that out favorite grill maker, PK (see facing page), is working on its own hibachi version.

OUR CHOICE FOR GRILLING: THE PK GRILL

If you're looking for the ideal charcoal steak grill—incredibly versatile, highly portable, easy cleanup—that will last your entire life and beyond, there's only one choice. Meet the PK Grill. Two of these live in the backyard of Aaron's house and are used pretty much every time a meal is cooked at home. They're not only easy to use but also among the most intuitive grills you'll ever encounter. When you're cooking on one, you feel in the presence of something unique—you feel equipped with a secret tool that no one knows about. And the PK story—about how these near-perfect backyard cookers came to be, developed a following, and then were cast into the ash bin of history only to be rediscovered and resurrected in the early 2000s—makes the experience of owning one all the more special. PK is that trusty classic car that you've kept running for years, learned to tune up yourself, and is a joy to take out in the neighborhood (maybe not too much on the highway, though).

continued

THE GRILL

OUR CHOICE FOR GRILLING: THE PK GRILL, CONTINUED

In the mid-1980s, at a garage sale, Little Rock, Arkansas, lawyer Paul James stumbled across an odd, puffy, box-like grill with a silvery cast and rounded corners. He instantly recognized it as the same kind of grill one of his mentors used to cook on way back during James's early days out of law school, which brought back fond memories of good times and good food. He also recalled the reverence his mentor had for the grill, so James bought it, took it home, and started cooking on it. Immediately apparent was that, despite decades of age, it still worked like a dream. The curious appearance and remarkable performance of the grill incited query after query from friends and guests. After some research, James discovered that these odd little grills hadn't been made in years. But in their heyday, they had been manufactured right there in Little Rock.

A little more digging taught him that the full history of the PK goes back to Texas (appropriate for something that makes great barbecue). In 1952, Hilton Meigs, a Beaumont designer, inventor, businessman, local character, and barbecue lover, set out to design the perfect, transportable barbecue pit. He wanted it to be durable, rustproof, and lightweight, yet also able to hold both high and steady temperatures and be easy to use. Meigs chose cast aluminum because it's lighter than steel (the standard material for backyard cookers) and conducts heat better. He called it the Portable Kitchen.

Meigs started to sell his grills, first across Texas (out of his car) and later in greater numbers across the South. Everywhere he went, he won new devotees. In 1958, he sold the business to another man, who moved the business to Little Rock. This was fortuitous, as bauxite, the primary component of aluminum, was a primary resource of Arkansas. The business took off, with the cookers developing a cult following and selling in the tens of thousands in the 1960s. But times change, and in the 1970s and 1980s, gas grills started to edge out pricey little boutique charcoal grills, and cheap, thin steel displaced the more intricate cast aluminum. The PK brand changed hands a couple of more times but eventually went out of production.

James also learned that the intellectual property and brand currently belonged to the Char-Broil company of Columbus, Georgia. Char-Broil had no plans to resuscitate the PK, so James was able to acquire the rights and intellectual property. Over the next several years, he, working with his sister Martha, brought the PK back into production and it began its slow climb back onto the scene. Compared to the big players, it's still a tiny, boutique company. But in 2014, James took on some partners, veterans from the tech world, to help take PK to a new level. That's where things stand now, as PK picks up new devotees every day. To use one is to love it. Let's look at why.

PK makes two styles of grill, the original and the 360. The latter has more bells and whistles and is a little larger, but the basic concept is the same. We mentioned the cast aluminum. Again, it's an excellent conductor of heat, lightweight, and rustproof. That's why a PK will serve a family over generations. Of course, never breaking down or tarnishing might not be the best business model, compared to something that's going to rust out and need replacement after five or ten years. But integrity is part of the plan. "Our entire team loves being involved in a thing that doesn't end up in landfill," says Scott Moody, one of the new PK partners. "I take a lot of pride that I help make a thing that somebody can buy, use forever, and then hand off to their kids, and it's never going to go into a garbage heap."

The design is poetically simple. The two halves of the shell fit together to make a box-shaped clamshell. One end cleverly interlocks to form a hinge, allowing the top to be lifted, but there's no pin or hasp keeping them together. You can even put each half in the dishwasher.

These are handy conveniences. The real brilliance is in the design for cooking. The oblong—instead of round—shape makes it perfect for two-zone cooking, as the hot area and cold area can be clearly defined and separated with enough space to make both zones effective. Rounded corners instead of angular ones allow air to move more fluidly. Interior convective currents and airflow are determined by four easy-to-operate vents, two on the top and two on the bottom. Using these wide open, you can flood the chamber with air to reach high temperatures perfect for grilling. Opening and closing them in combination permits the creation of convective heat for roasting and smoking. That's right—one simple cooker on which you can grill, roast, or smoke. It's simple and ingenious. Conveniently, one end of the grate is hinged, which means more coals can be added during long cooks without having to remove any food on the grill.

When it comes to steak, the PK is literally unsurpassed. A few years ago, it was organically adopted by some of the top competitors in the Steak Cookoff Association and has since taken that scene by storm. In March 2015, Scott Moody gave a couple of PKs to some of the finalists in a cook-off, who took them home and just kept cooking on them. By October of that year, according to Moody, six of the ten finalists were using them. The following year, that number was eight or nine out of ten. "And now it's like our grill is the go-to kit for competitive steak cooking. Anybody that cooks competitive steaks cooks on a PK Grill because they feel that's the only way you can compete."

What makes the PK so good for steak? Mainly, it's the aluminum. Aluminum conducts heat about four times more efficiently than steel. It gets superhot inside. Another advantage is the relatively shallow base. Compared to a Weber kettle and kamados, the coals rest quite high and close to the grates. This allows the meat to absorb maximal heat directly from the coals for a great sear, but without heating the entire chamber too much (for two-zone effectiveness).

When it comes to cost, the PK (about $380 for the original) is more expensive than a base-model Weber kettle. But when you think about the performance, versatility, and unequaled durability, the cost is more than justified. And on top of that, you'll develop a real love for this little grill. And who would put a price on love?

THE GRILL

Experimental Build: The Hybrid Hibachi

Given Aaron's experience in welding his own tools, we thought we'd experiment with building a small, supercharged steak cooker for the handy backyard open-fire enthusiast. The idea was to take the efficiencies and small footprint of a hibachi and trick it out with some of the features of other kinds of grills.

Disclaimer • This hybrid hibachi (HH), made of 5⁄16-inch steel, is heavy. The density of its material allows it to hold and radiate its heat more intensely and for longer than a traditional model. It also has the added functionality of grates you can raise and lower, like a Santa Maria grill. Thus, you can make a hot fire but still cook more delicately on it by raising the grates high above the flame. And like a fancy restaurant hearth, it's got a wood cage to keep a steady supply of wood coals going, as opposed to a traditional hibachi, which uses some kind of charcoal for fuel rather than more flavorful and aromatic wood coals.

When it comes to fueling our HH, you need fairly small chunks of wood in the cage, and it helps to mix in some charcoal to keep things burning in this confined space. Just keep an eye out for small coals that can slip out through the sides of the cage.

Altogether, this proved a phenomenal little hybrid hibachi. Not much charcoal was required to get it up to screaming-hot temperatures, and it really responded when we added binchōtan charcoal (see page 126) for a long and even burn. You can certainly give these instructions to a steel worker or welder, or if you have basic welding skills, do it yourself.

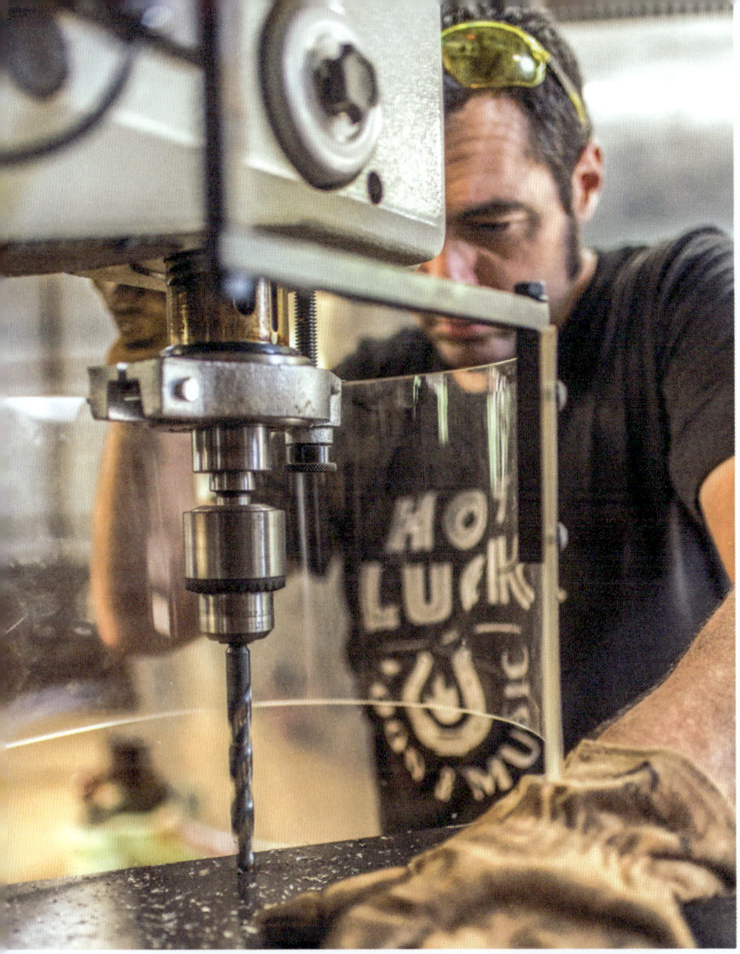

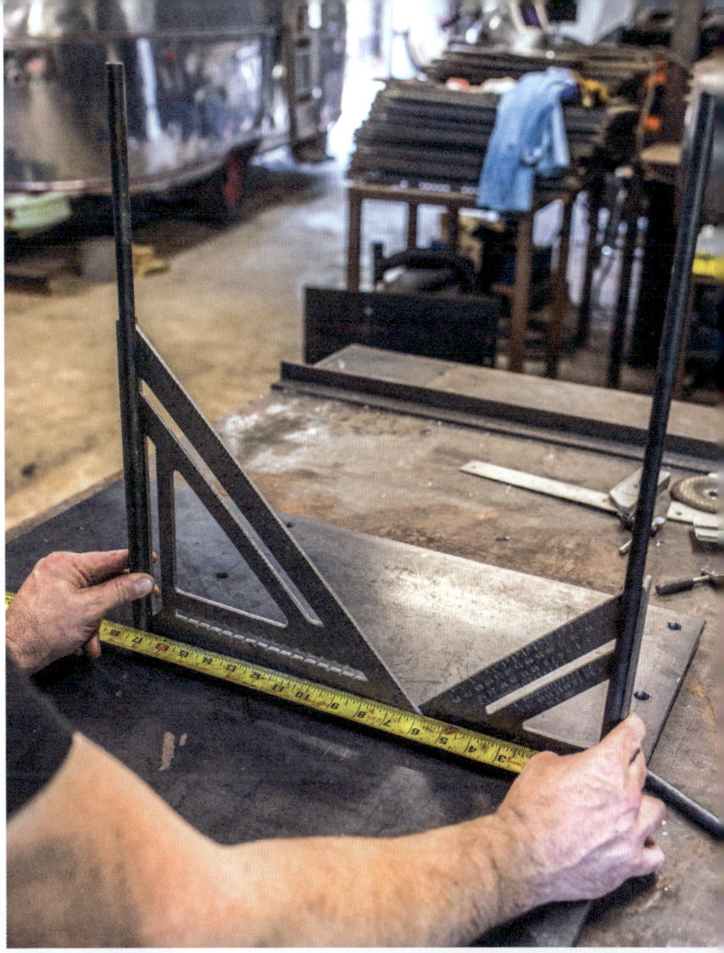

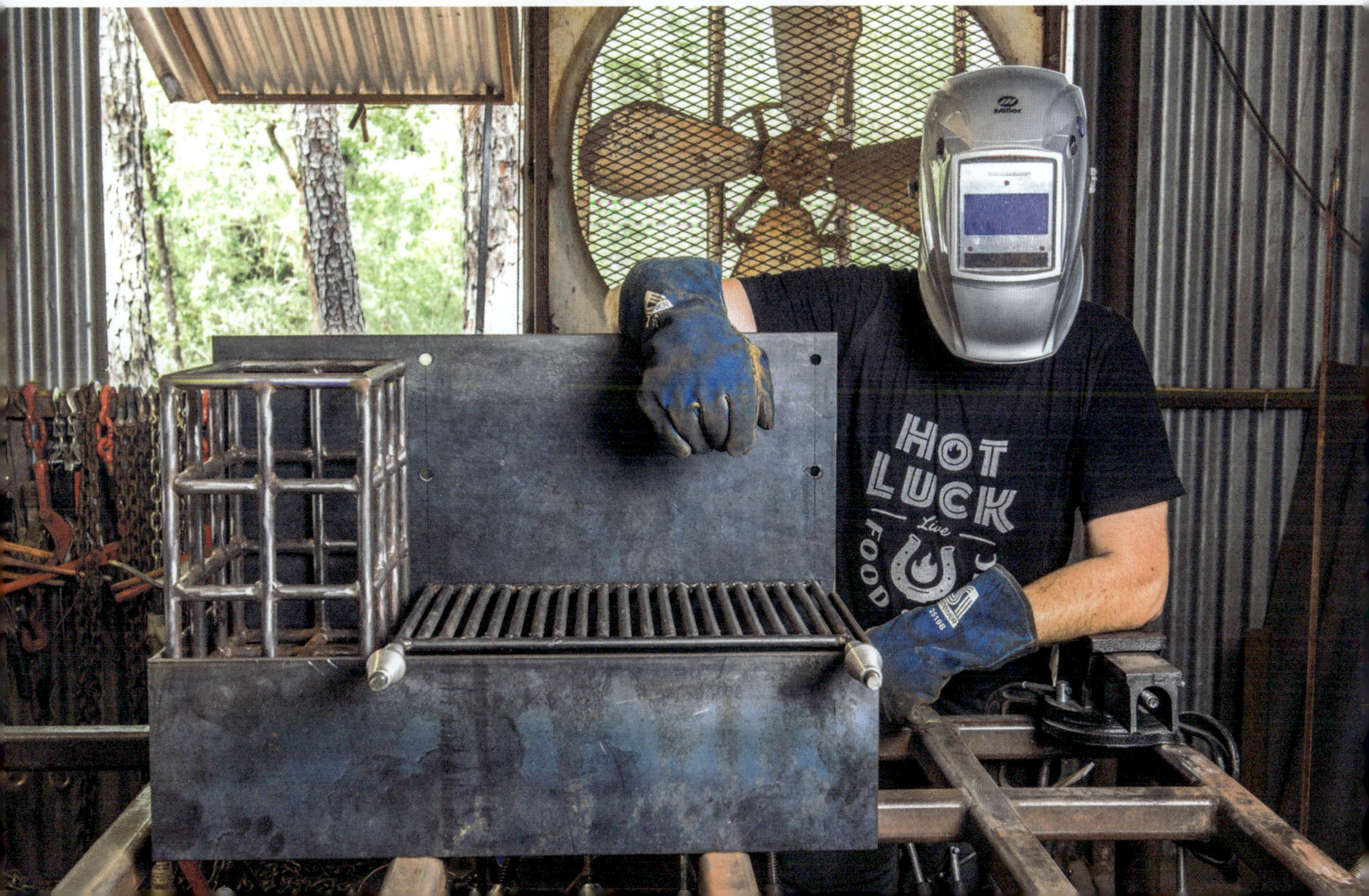
HOT
LUCK
Live
FOOD

Aaron's Instructions

This is a simple build. All in all, it won't take more than 5 hours for a moderately experienced welder if he or she works quickly and efficiently. The key to success is getting things done in the proper order so one step builds on the other. A beginning welder can tackle this, too, though it will take a little longer. Also, I'm giving fairly loose instructions, as this crazy cooker was pretty much improvised on a sketch pad and then built from stuff that was around the shop. Be sure to wear safety googles or a face shield and protective leather gloves as you work and to have a fire extinguisher on hand.

EQUIPMENT AND MATERIALS YOU'LL NEED

- Welder
- Grinder
- Steel ruler or measuring tape and Sharpie, for measuring and marking cuts
- Straight edges and clamps
- Drill press or regular drill (former makes the job much easier)
- 1 sheet steel plate, 4 by 8 feet and 5/16 inch thick (a ¼-inch-thick sheet can be used, but 5/16 inch is better because it retains heat more efficiently and doesn't warp or bow as easily)
- 30 feet ½-inch cold-rolled round steel (for the cooking grate)
- 20 feet ⅝-inch cold-rolled round steel (for the wood cage)
- 2 spring grill handles, ½-inch rod (available online or at hardware stores)

Step 1: Cut the Pieces

1. Get yourself ready for an easy welding assembly. First, using a steel ruler and Sharpie, mark your 5/16-inch steel plate for the rectangles, which will become the back, sides, bottom, and front of the firebox. You'll end up using a little over half of the plate. Before you begin, check the squareness of the plate you're working with because the sheets are not always perfectly square, and you'll need those proper angles.

   I lay out my cutting plan so the side pieces, the front piece, and the back piece all have a factory edge. That is, I mark the cutouts along each side of the sheet, so one edge of each piece uses the clean, well-cut edge from the factory. This way, you'll make fewer cuts and what's left in the middle can be used for the bottom, where the exposed edges don't matter.

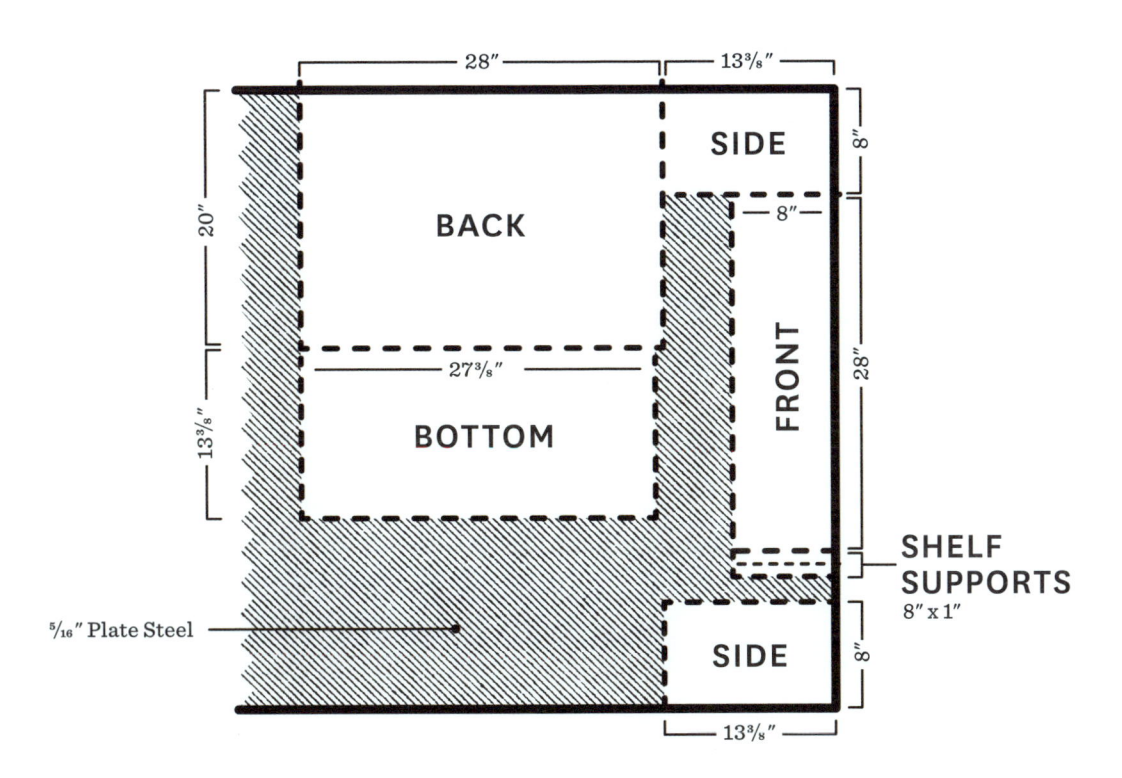

I used the following dimensions, but you should feel free to make whatever size grill you want. Cut the pieces for the firebox from the steel plate:

2 sides • each 13 3/8 by 8 inches

1 back • 28 by 20 inches

1 front • 28 by 8 inches

1 bottom • 27 3/8 by 13 3/8 inches

2 shelf supports • 8 by 1 inches

2. Cut the following pieces for the cooking grate from the 1/2-inch round:

    2 pieces • 21 inches long, for the grate sides

    2 pieces • 16 7/8 inches long, for the grate front and back

    19 pieces • 12 inches long, for the interior grates

3. Cut the following pieces for the wood cage from the 5/8-inch round:

    6 pieces • 6 3/4 inches long, for the top, bottom, and sides

    4 pieces • 13 inches long, for the top, bottom, front, and rear

    10 pieces • 11 3/4 inches long, for the tall vertical pillars and bottom

    15 pieces • 3 1/2 inches long, for the short crossbars

    8 pieces • 3 inches long, for the sides

THE GRILL

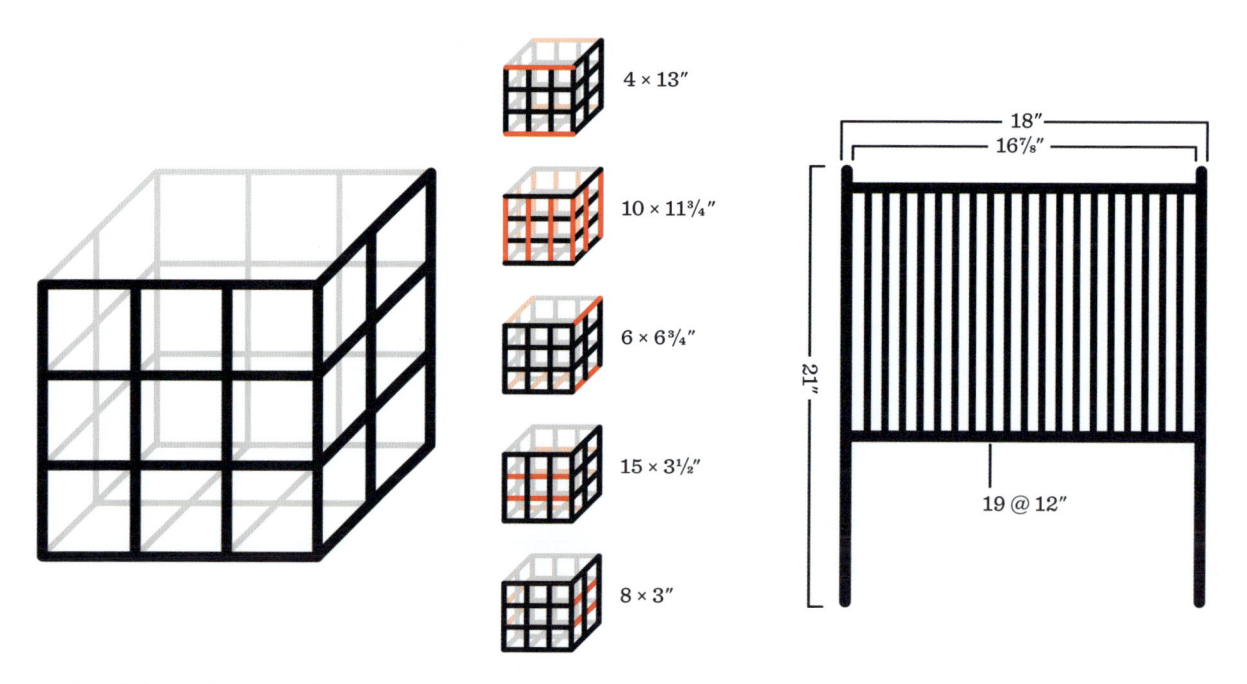

Above left: A side view of the wood cage. Above right: An overhead view of the cooking grate.

Step 2: Build the Components

Firebox • Before assembling the firebox, make the holes you'll need in the back piece, as it's much easier to do this before the box is assembled. These holes are for pegs that will stick out from the back and will allow the grate to be suspended at various heights above the fire.

It's imperative that these holes be even and symmetrical, which means you must mark them and drill them out carefully. I recommend measuring and then clamping a metal ruler or other flat straight edge, followed by a second metal ruler or straight edge ½ inch above it. Use a piece of the ½-inch round and the Sharpie to trace the circle where you need to drill the hole. Make a pair of these horizontal holes a few inches apart at whatever heights you want to be able to lift the grates.

Looking ahead to the next step of building the grates, here is a handy trick: use these first two holes as a jig for the grates, which is better than using the grates as a jig to drill the holes. That's because if something goes wrong with the grate, you can always build it again. But if you screw up the holes, you can't drill new ones. So after you've drilled the holes, take your two 21-inch rods of ½-inch round and place them in the holes—you'll want to grind down those ends a bit and round them off so they fit easily and offer more tolerance when the hibachi heats up—so ½ inch or so of each rod extends through the back. Next, put right angles on the rods to make sure they're straight and then tack in your crosspiece on both sides. All of a sudden, you have the frame for your grate!

FRANKLIN STEAK

Once the holes are drilled, the rest of the firebox is easy. Use right-angle magnets to hold the bottom, sides, front, and back together so the shape is solid and correct, and then use the welder to make little tacks to hold them in place. Finally, make all the welds on the inside so the outside looks really clean.

Cooking Grate • Because you used the holes in the back as the jig for the grates and tacked on the crosspieces (see the previous step), the frame is already done.

From there, draw a line in the middle of the frame and put your first grill grate there, just to mark it. The idea is to start out in the middle and then work your way symmetrically to each side. Don't start on one end and then space everything out from there. If you do that, you'll end up with one gap that fits funny. Just be sure to measure very carefully as you go.

I tacked in that first middle piece and placed a little piece of metal flush next to it, which was spacing for the next one. And after that, I just worked my way down—tack, tack, tack— adding rods of ½-inch round. The tacking is so the grate doesn't warp, because if you put too much weld, the whole thing will bow upward.

Get it together, make sure it's right, and then do your welds on one side. Flip it over, and on the back side, start on the same spot. It's like tuning a drum—there's a counteraction for every action. This is so it's solid, balanced, and doesn't warp.

Now attach your pair of spring handles, and the grate should be ready to go.

Wood Cage • This part is simple. Because your box is already assembled, you should begin making the cage in the bottom of the box so the spacing is correct. I also recommend leaving a wide enough gap between the side of the cage and the edge of the firebox to wedge in a piece of metal or a sheet pan to keep the wind off the fire. If you want, you could even weld a flat piece there. (I didn't, but if I were to build this contraption again, I might do that.)

So, using the ⅝-inch round, start by building your square end pieces in the bottom of the firebox in order to get the spacing and angles correct. Once you've built one square, you can add the vertical rods, using an angle measure to get that perfect 90 degrees. You can then pull the whole thing out and build the rest of the cage outside of the firebox. When you've completed it, place it where you want it in the box and weld it in as lightly or as firmly as you want.

Step 3: Enjoy Your Grill

You're done! Enjoy your own hybrid hibachi, perfect for small fires and versatile cooking. The cage can be used to hold a loose pile of small logs, which will create a continuous source of wood coals for longer cooks. It's easiest to get started by using a charcoal chimney (see page 142). Drag the resulting coals under the grate for heating. Alternatively, the firebox is great for charcoal, wood coals, or binchōtan.

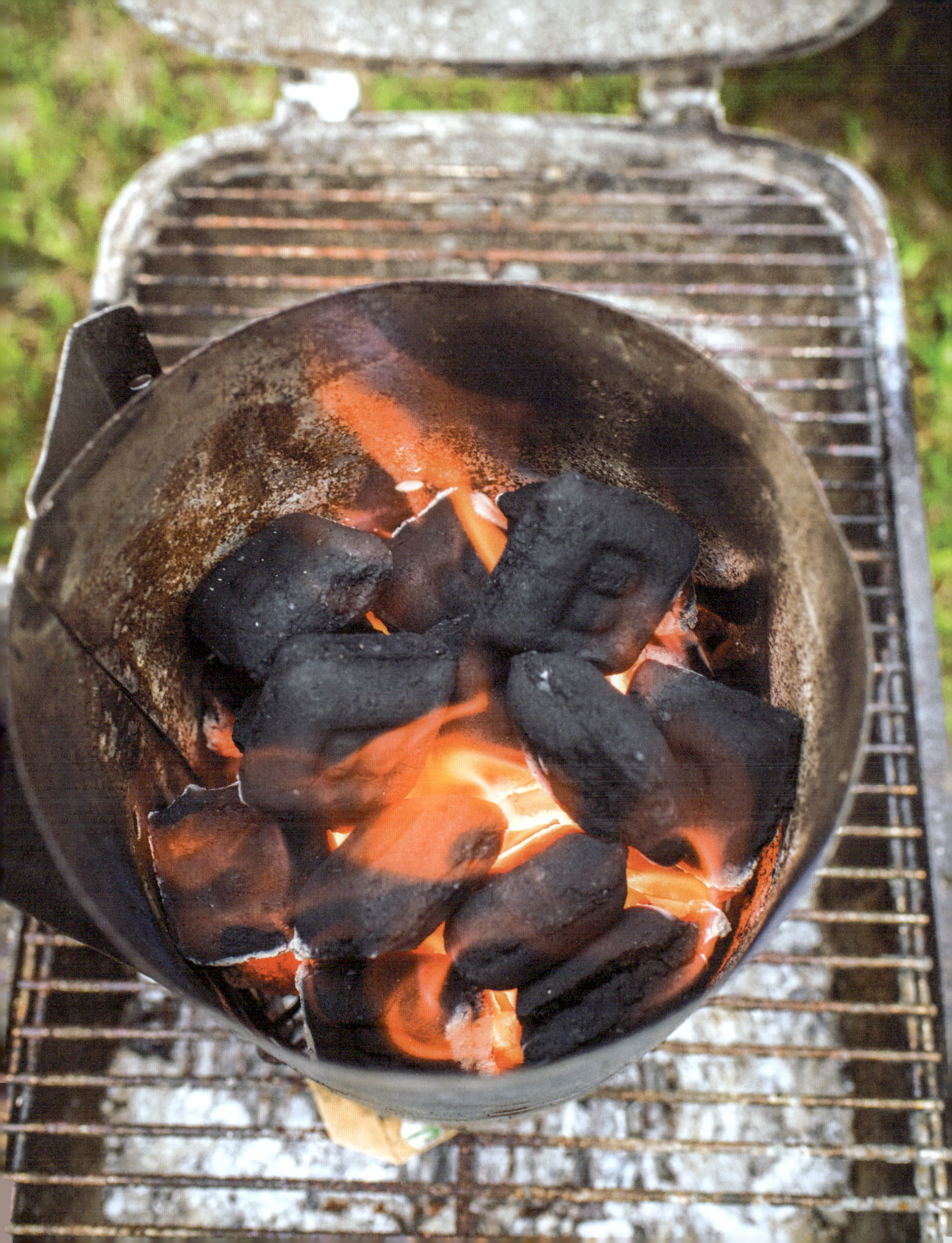

CHAPTER 6

Fuel

When it comes to grilling steak, the fuel source is a seasoning, so you should have some idea about what you want out of your fire when you get started. Do you want a hot fire or a more mellow one? Do you want it to be short and intense or long and slow? Do you want a lot of smoke or just a little? All of these questions will impact the kind of fire you want to create and what you want to burn, which makes understanding your fuel sources critical.

Of course, what we're really talking about here is charcoal and wood. Gas burns clean and adds nothing of itself to the taste of the meat (thank goodness).

Charcoal is amazing stuff, the go-to heat source of the American grill, the flickering fuel of Fourth of July picnics and poolside barbecues. It has many wonderful qualities, which we'll get to in a bit, but wood is fuel for the soul. After all, it powers Franklin BBQ, and the smell of slow-burning oak is the smell of warmth and happiness and dinner. Each fuel has its place and purpose, but whichever one you go with requires learning and practice. This chapter will help get you familiar with both and set you down the road toward mastering your cooking fuel.

Charcoal: Great Bags of Fire!

Every time we grab a bag of charcoal at the store, we fail to consider that we're actually buying an example of one of the most important and oldest human technologies. It's not known exactly when early peoples starting producing charcoal, but it goes back at least tens of thousands of years, if not longer. The earliest example of charcoal being used was over thirty-eight thousand years ago by Cro-Magnons, who adopted it for both drawing on cave walls (they liked to draw beef cattle) and for fire. Around 4000 BCE, charcoal was the catalyst of the Bronze Age: an everyday fire is not hot enough to melt copper, but charcoal along with a forced airflow can reach temperatures in the 2000°F range, the level needed to melt copper.

If you're so inclined, you can do as the ancients did and make your own charcoal, which is not a bad money-saving idea if you have lots of extra wood lying around. Early humans learned to pile wood into a mound and cover it with earth, leaving only slight air intakes on the bottom. They'd light the pile, get it burning, and eventually seal it. Inside, the wood would keep on burning, though slowly and at a relatively low temperature. After several days of smoldering and when the mass had cooled, they'd uncover the mound to expose a pile of dry, crumbled charcoal, much like what we see today when we purchase a bag of lump charcoal. The process isn't too different nowadays; it just takes place in large metal kilns that do the job more efficiently.

If you're scientifically minded, you might wonder what's going on inside that mound or kiln to create charcoal. It starts, of course, with the wood, which at a molecular level is composed of long chains of carbon, hydrogen, and oxygen. When wood is burned, first it dries out, as the free water inside it boils and then disappears as steam. When you hear a fresh piece of poorly seasoned wood hissing in a fire, that's what's happening. Burning along with the water are volatile organic components of wood that, when heated, combine with surrounding oxygen to produce combustion. The products of combustion are light and heat, water, and carbon dioxide. After the wood is completely incinerated, all that's left is the mineral content, which we call ash.

The process of making charcoal involves restricting the combustion so all the carbon doesn't burn away. This is accomplished by limiting the amount of oxygen that reaches the fire. In a fire, the carbon and oxygen molecules in wood combine to become carbon dioxide. If you restrict the oxygen flow, the volatile components and water burn away, leaving mostly pure carbon and minerals, or charcoal.

Charcoal burns much hotter than wood precisely because it's lost all that water, as the energy required to vaporize water is considerable. This is also why charcoal burns without much smoke and without much flame when compared with wood.

The biggest drawback when it comes to charcoal? A yield of charcoal weighs only in the neighborhood of 25 percent of the original wood from which it was made. That is, it takes a lot of wood to make only a little charcoal. An article titled "Peak Wood and the Bronze Age" in the public policy magazine *Pacific Standard* describes how charcoal contributed greatly to the deforestation of the island of Cyprus, a center of early bronze production: "Some 120 pine trees were required to prepare the 6 tons of charcoal needed to produce one copper ingot shaped roughly like a dried ox hide and weighing between 45 and 65 pounds. One ingot, therefore, deforested almost four acres."

The future of charcoal production may lie in looking beyond wood: after all, charcoal can be made from pretty much any organic substance. Some chefs, like Dan Barber of New York's Blue Hill at Stone Barns and Adam Sappington of Country Cat, in Portland, Oregon, fashion charcoal out of animal bones in an effort to reduce waste. They then cook the very meats over those coals. Charcoal made from coconut (see page 128) is big throughout Asia. No matter what the charcoal is made from, however, it's going to give what it does—speed, heat, and consistency. Those are great, but to get the most out of a fire, you have to roll the process back and start with wood.

TYPES OF CHARCOAL, FLAVORS, AND SMOKE

Given how many different brands and types of charcoal exist, choosing what to use can be a bit of a headache. Lump or briquettes? Mesquite or oak? Everyone has his or her preferences, but it's worth remembering that charcoal is nearly pure carbon. That's wood stripped of every substance that made it distinctive. People talk about the unique character of smoke that comes from different charcoals, especially those made from different woods. But unless it's improperly made charcoal that still contains some of the compounds of the wood, the small amount of smoke you get from the coals of various woods will not be terribly dissimilar. There can be differences based on the density and composition of briquettes, of course, but pure lump charcoal is pretty much just charcoal. We'll get to that in a while, when we discuss the different kinds of charcoal you can buy.

Charcoal Briquettes

The charcoal briquette has a somewhat surprising history, going back to camping trips taken by automobile magnate Henry Ford and such buddies as Thomas Edison and Harvey Firestone. More like glamping, these affairs involved a large retinue (including a chef) conveyed in a cavalcade of automobiles, one of which was outfitted as a kitchen. A Michigan real estate agent named Edward Kingsford was invited along in 1919 to discuss timberland with Ford, who needed the wood for Model T construction. Shortly thereafter, Kingsford would broker a huge tract of Michigan forest to Ford.

From top: Thaan-brand Thai-style binchōtan, lump charcoal, charcoal briquettes

Logging the forest and milling the car bodies out of the timber left much behind in terms of sawdust and wood scraps, which Ford, ever thrifty, hated to see go unused. So he decided to employ a technique invented by University of Oregon chemist Orin Stafford to put sawmill waste to use. Stafford found that by combining sawdust with a bit of tar and using cornstarch as a binding agent, he could make a light, portable fuel, which he named "charcoal briquettes." Edison designed a briquette factory next to the sawmill, and Ford was suddenly in the briquette business.

Unfortunately for Ford, the briquette business was not as robust as the car business. He would have to wait some twenty-five years for briquettes to come into fashion. The Great Depression and a world war didn't leave a lot of people in the mood for cooking out. In 1951, another group bought Ford Charcoal and rebranded it Kingsford, after the man who sold Ford the land. But the product did not take off until an event in 1952: the invention of the Weber grill, which soon made backyard cooking a national pastime and created a demand for little bags of charcoal.

Nowadays, there are many brands of briquettes on the market, and they're all made roughly the same way they have been since Orin Stafford first introduced them. However, that process has been refined. The reason some people stay away from briquettes is the additives used along with the pure charcoal. For instance, the recipe used by Kingsford, which still makes the country's best-selling briquettes, includes wood char, mineral char and mineral carbon (both extra heat sources), limestone (to improve the look of the ash), starch (binder), borax (to help the briquettes slip out of their molds during production), and sawdust (to help the briquettes ignite). Although seeing ingredients like limestone and borax might make you balk, they're both naturally occurring minerals. All in all, despite the laundry list of additives, none of them is terribly concerning. But still, it's hard to get away from the thought of cooking on all those substances that have nothing to do with wood, especially when there are other, cleaner options.

Those options are briquettes labeled "all natural," which contain nothing but char and 4 to 5 percent binder made from vegetable starch. If you care about such things, why not use all natural? There's really nothing to lose. And if you're in the common situation of needing to add more charcoal to an already hot coal bed to extend the length of a cook, a fresh briquette that lacks additives is preferable to one full of additives. So we always choose all-natural charcoal.

Some really great all-natural charcoal briquettes are out there. B&B charcoal, based in Texas, makes some of the best around. Stubb's briquettes are very good, too, as are Kingsford Competition all-natural briquettes. Royal Oak is another good-quality, popular brand.

The advantage of briquettes over lump charcoal is precision. If you've practiced and paid attention to your charcoal use, you more or less know exactly how much heat you can get out of one briquette, allowing you to manage your coal bed to whatever the desired temperature and to know how many more briquettes to add when the fire needs more fuel.

The last thing to say about briquettes is to ignore the kind known as "easy lighting" or "self-starting." These arrive saturated with some sort of lighter fluid, so all you have to do is strike a match and throw it onto a pile of them and they'll ignite. The problem is that lighter fluid is petroleum based and gross, which means you definitely don't want it coming anywhere near your food. Lighting a batch of charcoal in a chimney (see page 142) is easy and effective, making lighter fluid–soaked briquettes unnecessary.

Lump Charcoal

When it came to marketing this stuff, maybe they could have found a better word than *lump* to compete against the more suave-sounding *briquette*. Sometimes this charcoal is called "hardwood charcoal" or "charwood," both an improvement on "lump." Whatever it's called, it's a different, simpler form of char than briquettes: the original, basic, ancient form of charcoal, made solely from pure wood burned in a sealed chamber. No need for binders, accelerants, or igniters.

Because it's pure carbon with no additives, lump charcoal should theoretically burn hotter but shorter than briquettes. That said, it's difficult to compare the fires from both types of charcoal because lump is so varied in size and shape. Even if you weighed out the same exact amount of both lump and briquettes and then burned them, you'd probably get different results each time you did the test. If the pieces of lump are big and awkwardly shaped, the resulting coal bed might be hotter, as more air would likely be able to move through the stack. On the other hand, if the pieces are small and include a bunch of dust from the bag, the fire might be cooler because less oxygen can penetrate the mass.

Some claim that lump gives more flavor than briquettes, though in theory this shouldn't be the case. After all, if the charcoal is properly made, there will be little to no actual wood left in the material. So whether the original material was mesquite or oak should make slim difference. In practice, however, sometimes the wood isn't completely carbonized, meaning some wood compounds are left to burn and provide a bit of smoky flavor. (If you truly *want* smoky flavor in your meat, this whole question is moot: just throw a little actual wood on the coals and you'll get as much or as little of the smoke as you need.

Lump charcoal does have a couple of drawbacks, both of which arise in lower-quality products. It's not uncommon to find bits of foreign objects in bags of lump charcoal, such as nails, staples, cords, shards of plastic, and the like. First, you definitely don't want these things to be cooking into your food. Second, their presence suggests the wood you're using may not have been pristine logs in the first place, but rather some sort of reclaimed or treated wood from who knows where. Another issue with lump charcoal is that, because of the irregular shapes of the pieces, it tends to have a lot of useless dust in the bag. That's because lump charcoal can grind down against itself in transit and in the store. This dust is useless and can even have the effect of inhibiting combustion if it gets into you coal bed.

Binchōtan

If you've never splurged on a small package of expensive but amazing Japanese charcoal, or binchōtan, you should consider playing around with it, as it's amazing stuff. For instance, it

THE BOTTOM LINE: LUMP VERSUS BRIQUETTES

This is always the great question. You want a lively, somewhat erratic fire that may get really hot but not last long? Go lump. It's perfect for searing steaks. Or do you want something more mellow and consistent that will burn longer and with some predictability? Go briquettes, which are the best anchor for longer-cooking meats.

Here are a couple of other suggestions to help you get to the heart of this debate. When you choose a brand of charcoal—lump or briquette—stick with it for a few months or even a year before you try something else. Get to know its trajectory and heating curves. Note its behaviors. Does it light easily and come quickly to temperature? Or does it start slowly and then maintain a very hot plateau for a long time? Or maybe it reaches a peak and then comes crashing down quickly? Once you have confidence you understand the way that choice behaves, you can stay with it as your go-to charcoal or endeavor to learn a new one.

Another option in the never-ending debate of lump versus charcoal is to completely ignore the question at hand and change the rules, much like Captain Kirk did when he undermined the Kobayashi Maru test on the original *Star Trek*. Why choose one when you can also mix the two charcoals together? Load a chimney half full with your favorite all-natural briquettes and then fill the other half with your chosen brand of lump hardwood charcoal. This way you get the stamina of briquettes in a dense coal bed. But you also get the flair of lump with its searing highs, and its irregular-shaped pieces will contrast with the briquettes to keep the coal bed well aired without too much ash.

---

clangs like metal when you bang it together. While it has an eerie whitish gray cast like a White Walker, it in fact burns really, really hot and maintains that heat for hours and hours. And if you don't need a 900°F heat source for a full five or six hours, you can submerge the coals in water, let them dry for a day, and use them again.

Made using a process that goes back centuries to the Edo period (or perhaps much longer, as the record isn't clear), binchōtan takes its name from a single artisan, Binchū-ya Chōzaemon, who perfected the process. Today, binchōtan is still made by artisans, as its process requires much more nuance and technique than Western charcoal. The finest is said to come from Kishu in Wakayama Prefecture, an area in the southern part of Japan, south and west of Osaka. The wood used for traditional binchōtan is called *ubame* oak (*Quercus phillyraeoides*), a native Japanese species with heavy, shiny leaves and a diminutive stature. These trees don't grow like twisting, gnarled, massive live oak trees. Rather, their branches are relatively thin and wiry, making them not much of a building material.

The wood is harvested in mountains and brought to nearby stone kilns. The branches are generally crowded upright into the kiln, and a fire is started using the same wood. Then the kiln is mostly sealed up, to keep the temperature

FUEL

lower than what is used to make conventional black charcoal. This slow, methodical burning is monitored by the producers for up to a couple of weeks, as they examine and smell the smoke emerging from the kiln. When they can tell that most of the volatiles have burned off, they increase the heat massively and seal the kiln for a short time, which purifies and protects the carbon left in the wood without destroying it. At the right moment, the kiln is opened and the glowing, almost neon-orange branches are raked out (using *really* long rakes, as it can be over 1800°F inside) and instantly smothered under a mixture of damp sand and ash to cool them down quickly. This dusty ash covers the oak, giving it its distinctive white cast.

The result is a product of almost pure carbon, far purer than our black charcoal. Besides its role as a heat source, binchōtan has many other uses. For example, it's a great water purifier: just drop a small piece of it into a pitcher of water and it will instantly start burbling the water through its negative space, filtering out the impurities that stick to the vast, microscopically porous surface of the charcoal. It can do the same filtering magic for the air in a room.

Because of its long life, you see it used at yakitori grills in Japan, as a handful of pieces can last an entire six-hour service. Also, because they're practically pure carbon, binchōtan coals burn with almost no smoke. Jordan loves nothing more than ducking into a little Tokyo bar or *izakaya*, ordering a draft beer (the Japanese major labels like Asahi and Yebisu taste so much better over there) or a Hibiki with a cube, and then sitting back to watch the cooks grill skewers of everything from pork to chicken skin, closely above the glowing-hot binchōtan coals. There's no smoke, and the meat is so near the heat that the evaporating meat juices are captured and spritz back up onto the meat. It doesn't create flare-ups, just vapors of oils and other compounds seasoning the meat. Of course, fatty beef *will* create flames, so be careful. When cooking beef over binchōtan this way, most chefs use very thin slices that need the ultrahigh, clean heat to sear the outside but leave the inside nice and juicy.

One additional note about binchōtan: It's hard to light, as it takes long, intense heat to get going. The easiest way to do it is to light a chimney half full of regular charcoal and place the binchōtan above that for twenty to thirty minutes. And, as mentioned, if you don't need sustained high heat for five or six hours, you should submerge the binchōtan in water, dry it, and use it another time.

Coconut Charcoal

Charcoal made from coconut shells hails from Southeast Asia. Its fans love it for a number of reasons: It burns hotter than American charcoal and with very little smoke and ash, and it burns for a long time (though not binchōtan long). Some say the vapor it does emit has a sweet smell. Made from the spent hulls of coconuts, it's more eco-friendly than other forms of charcoal, as the process recycles a natural waste product—no trees are cut down. It's more expensive than conventional charcoal, but half the amount gives the same heat for the same length of time.

To make the charcoal, carbonized coconut shells (after about a day of cooking in sealed pits) are ground into a powder, which is mixed with starch (usually from the root of the cassava shrub, also the source of tapioca) and a little water to bind it. Perhaps the cassava starch is what produces the sweet odor. This mixture is extruded into thick-walled tubes and then baked again to remove the water. The result is very dense, heavier than conventional wood char. Like charcoal making everywhere, coconut charcoal doesn't seem to be a particularly highly regulated industry, so quality varies from brand to brand and sometimes even within single brands. When not well made, coconut charcoal can feel messy because it produces a ton of ash while still fetching prices well above conventional wood charcoal. So, if using it, pay attention to its performance and demand better if you think it's producing too much ash and burning uncleanly.

Coconut char is perfect for grills operated by street vendors in places like the Philippines, Malaysia, and Thailand. These cooks, who transport portable grills on the backs of their bicycles and motorbikes, are ready to whip up a fire at any time and grill narrow strips or skewers of meat. Only a small amount of charcoal is needed to fire these grills, which makes dense, hot, long-burning coconut charcoal the perfect solution. Because of the cost and large amount of space required, it's not economical to think about firing the vast cooking surfaces of American-style grills, unless you're grilling a variety of things over a period of an hour and a half to two hours. However, coconut briquettes have been embraced by some American cooks doing long or overnight cooks on their home grills. The lack of ash and the extended cook times make the briquettes ideal for a low-and-slow approach.

Wood: Hug a Tree Today

Enough about charcoal. Even if charcoal has been a species-altering technology (much as the cow was a species-altering animal), using it will never be the equivalent of cooking with wood. When Jordan asked Victor Arguinzoniz, a chef who cooks everything on his menu over wood and whose restaurant, Asador Etxebarri (see page 131) in the Basque Country of Spain, is one of the greatest in the world, to name the most important factor in cooking a steak well (and he makes a great one), his answer was simple: "Use only wood."

You'd have to be blind to miss—as backlash in the wake of molecular gastronomy and the advent of sous vide—that one of the biggest restaurant trends in the last ten years has been the construction of wood-fired hearths. They seem to occupy a central space in every other fashionable restaurant opening these days. Chefs such as Francis Mallmann of Argentina and his rustic, remote mountain hearths and campfire coziness have captured the imagination of a new generation of chefs and diners alike.

Fire has a powerful pull. No other fuel offers the savory, smoky, spicy flavor of wood—not to mention the primal sense of warmth and community, romance, and mental and physical engagement. The smell of sweet wood smoke causes people in the area to snap their heads up when they catch a whiff. The crackle of gently burning wood reminds the ears that this fire is its own living thing. It's also a beacon of civilization and safety. Jordan remembers as a little kid backpacking through the mountains of Washington with his family and feeling terrified by the vastness and loneliness of the peaks, forest, and night sky towering above him. But once his dad or his uncle got that fire crackling, all fear, isolation, and forlornness lifted away, like smoke to the stars. Yet given all the wonderment of fire, most of the time we content ourselves to cooking over charcoal. Why?

As any good scout working on a merit badge knows, a good wood fire is a commitment, and not a small one. Not terribly different from a great affair of the heart, a fire-stoked affair of the hearth brings pleasure but also pain. Indelibly etched in Aaron's brain are thousands of nights spent around a fire. At this point, he has probably spent more time tending fires than doing anything else. The sound of the crackling, the smell of smoke, and that jumpy light are as comforting as cracking open a beer. He's fallen asleep next to fires more times than he can count. (He's not that good at counting, probably because he's also lost so much sleep staying up to make sure the fire keeps going.) He constantly smells like smoke and can't always shower it out of his hair. But he likes to think that cavemen might have been a lot like that, too, except they didn't have shampoo.

An energetic, blazing fire isn't easy to create—it takes planning and time—and can be just as difficult to control. It has a mind of its own and often the muscle to defy you. It can be dangerous and wasteful. It's a commitment of time, attention, and physical engagement. It's an agreement that you and everything you're wearing will smell like smoke until the next shower and washing. It's an acceptance that you're going to get slightly dirty and will have a good bit of cleaning up and ash removal to do. Furthermore, wood can be expensive, and you go through a lot of it in the effort to create and maintain a good coal bed.

But we all know it's worth it—every grimy smear of ash on the brow, every shower you have to take to get the smoke out of your hair, every singed eyelash. Wood fire makes it up to you by creating the most delicious meals and offering memorable experiences that bring people closer to one another and to our own natures.

CHOOSING WOOD

Remember, steak is the ultimate piece of ingredient-driven cuisine, and the fire is a key ingredient, so think of wood as you would any crucial component of a dish. You should choose it with the same care you choose the meat. Follow the same guidelines as you would for smoking: hardwoods over softwoods, good seasoning over green, and sourced from healthy trees over sick.

Hardwoods come from deciduous trees (ones that shed their leaves annually) and produce some sort of nut or fruit. Examples include oak, cherry, maple, hickory, apple, almond, and many more. Softwoods are conifers and are to be avoided. They have needles instead of leaves and include cedar, pine, fir, spruce, and redwood. Hardwoods have a much slower growth rate and much higher density than softwoods and thus cost more. They also have a resistance to fire that makes them slower and more even burning.

Of course, nothing is ever that simple. Some softwoods are harder than hardwoods. Balsa, for instance, is technically a hardwood, but anyone who's done arts and crafts knows that it's way softer than pine. Of course, you never want to cook with pine, as it has highly flammable resins that, when burning, give off a noxious, sooty smoke that's the last thing you want landing on your food.

ASADOR ETXEBARRI

**Plaza de San Juan, 1
48291 Atxondo, Bizkaia
tel: (+34) 946-58-30-42 • asadoretxebarri.com**

It is no surprise that we talk a lot about Spain in this book, seeing as it boasts a legendary carnivorous nature and is home to the greatest steak culture in Europe. Across the country—but especially in the north in Basque Country—are hundreds of little *asadors*, grills that specialize in steak. Unfortunately, the secret is out on the greatest of them, Asador Etxebarri (etch-a-bar-ee), in the small town of Axpe, about an hour outside of San Sebastián in the foothills of the Pyrenees. In the 2018 version of the *The World's 50 Best Restaurants*, Etxebarri clocked in at number 10, which is absurd considering it's open only for lunch except on Saturdays, and there's no fancy cooking, no spherification or gelification or foams or even sous vide. Rather, Etxebarri is one of the most primitive restaurants anywhere—everything is cooked only on wood coals. This is chef Arguinzoniz's way. A quiet guy, he grew up in a farmhouse that lacked electricity, so everything was grilled, everything kissed by smoke. Eventually, he bought an old, run-down restaurant in the center of town and started cooking the same way.

But Arguinzoniz's culinary ambition soon grew, and he began to devise little mesh baskets in which to cook things like tiny eels and caviar over fire. He built a collection of mini-grills, each with a Santa Maria–like raising and lowering cable to control heat. And he purposed two ovens in which to keep a constant supply of wood coals at the ready, one for oak coals and one for coals made out of grape vines. After each service, the grill grates are scoured back to perfectly clean stainless steel. Victor wants no lingering bitterness from char passed on to his ingredients—whether langoustines, tuna, or porcini—all of which are impeccably sourced to display a purity and vibrancy we rarely if ever experience. Seasoning is only salt, olive oil, and delicate smoke. It's not unreasonable to compare Victor's mastery of the grill to Mozart's of the musical note or Serena Williams's genius with the tennis racket. Each dish gets its own little mound of coals, perfectly calibrated to cook with absolute precision. Items emerge from the fire vibrant and fresh, with the line between raw and cooked hard to comprehend. It is as if they still bear some energy, some lingering soul from when they were alive.

The savory finale of each meal (before the smoked ice cream) is a *txuleta*, or rib steak from a superannuated, locally raised dairy cow, sometimes fifteen or eighteen years old at slaughter. Tender, juicy, and intensely beefy, the steak bears only oil and some crunchy crumbles of sea salt. For most who taste it, it's the best steak they've ever consumed.

SEASONING GRILL WOOD

Seasoning is the amount of time a log has had to dry out. It's perhaps even more important in grilling than in smoking. In an offset barbecue pit, if you've got a raging fire of 750°F in your firebox, including a poorly seasoned log every now and then is not going to make a decisive difference. However, if you're grilling and burning basically one log at a time, green wood can drive you crazy. First, the wetter the wood, the worse the smoke. Then, evaporating all that excess water in the wood costs energy and will keep the temperature of your fire down. For complete combustion and the good fine smoke you want, you need well-seasoned wood.

As always, when you go out to the wood pile, you'll find logs of varying weights and shapes. Hopefully, most of them will be cut to pretty much the same size. Pick up several different pieces in your hands. Some will weigh more than others, often considerably so. You'll be surprised that two similar-looking logs can feel so different in heft. The idea is to get a sense of the ranges and choose something in the middle. If the log is too heavy, it's not well seasoned. Leave it on the pile for another few months (or years, depending on the climate). If it's too light, the wood is extremely well seasoned and will go up like a match, which lends an unpredictable and charged quality to any cooking fire. Use that piece in the fireplace in winter or throw it on early in your fire and let it burn down before cooking.

(Note, too, that much of the prepackaged firewood sold in grocery stores is kiln dried, a process that speeds up the seasoning. It's good for getting your living room fireplace hopping, but most of it is overseasoned for grilling purposes. We don't recommend it.)

TYPES OF WOOD

Any hardwood can be great for grilling if you age it long enough. That said, different species of hardwoods tend to display different characteristics. They are subtle, for sure, but if you work with one kind of wood for long enough, you do get to know it. As with charcoal, we recommend that you commit to a type of hardwood for a few months or perhaps a year. Even without trying—you don't need to keep a journal or a spreadsheet detailing your experiences—you'll develop a keen knowledge and sense for the wood.

Alder

Most famous as a vehicle for salmon, alder is hardwood carrying a mellow, slightly sweet profile that goes well with fish. Jordan has cooked with it a bunch in the Pacific Northwest, where his family's from, and knows that alder also sets a good fire and can be used effectively to gently season steak. When camping out in the San Juan Islands in Puget Sound, you can find seasoned alder, build a fire, and grill local oysters over it before throwing on some local coastal-raised beef. The wood has a sweetness that goes well with salt. Put alder with the more delicately flavored cuts like the tenderloin. It's also better with steak that hasn't been dry aged too long, as the funkiness from aging clashes with the sweetness of the wood.

Apple

As you'd expect, this classic fruitwood has a bright, fruity, and somewhat sweet character. It's even more subtle than alder, though, and its flavor might get crushed by beefier cuts. Use it on delicate cuts, like tenderloin, or on thinner cuts that spend less time on the grill.

Cherry

A wonderful and fairly rare fruitwood for cooking, cherry has a delightful floral sweetness that we associate with other fruit trees. But there's something else, a little more depth and richness that allows it to work well for both pork and beef. With beefy steaks, it can handle the heavier, more richly flavored cuts, like New York strip, bavette, and flat iron.

Hickory

A specialty of the Midwest and the South, hickory can be counted on for relatively strong flavors, but also for strong and long burn times, which makes it a great foundation for a fire. Aaron has only good things to say about cooking with hickory; it's his second choice after oak. Hickory may be a little sweeter than oak, but it burns just as consistently. The flavor it imparts to the meat gives a sense of depth and umami, a rich savory note, and an abiding sweetness. It's great for the rich, beefy cuts, like ribeye, porterhouse, and strip.

Mesquite

The controversial wood—some love it, some hate it. More than any other kind of smoke, mesquite can always be recognized. It's usually not Aaron's first choice—it doesn't have that softness or sweetness of oak. Mesquite is a hardwood that is indeed very hard and very dense. *Aged* mesquite is a different story, though—it grills great! It just takes a long time to season properly. Mesquite tends to burn quickly and hot, which is why it's popular for charcoal. (Also because it grows in inhospitable places, often as a pest, choking out grasslands for grazing.) Its massive root system makes it hard to remove, and its thorns can cut through anything, including car tires. It's an ornery wood with an ornery flavor. Used in too great an amount, its harsh, peppery flavor will dominate any ingredient. That's why you don't want to smoke things over it. However, carefully used in short-cooking situations, such as flank or skirt steaks, mesquite can be acceptable.

Oak

May the smell of oak be with you. Even just saying "oak smoke" sounds good. (Aaron likes to joke about coming up with some sort of fragrance line based on oak, like Oak Smoke Joke!) Post oak is the signature wood of Central Texas, and it's the sweetest, richest, cleanest-burning, straight, easy-to-handle wood there is. It's perfect for everything. You can almost never go wrong with any good old oak, however. Red oak, white oak—use anything but green oak. Actually, live oak needs a few years of seasoning before its character is rid of a somewhat intense herbal greenness. Of course, the Central Texas favorite post oak continues to be a blessing. It not only burns beautifully but also offers a lovely balanced flavor. In general, oak brings some undertones of vanilla to a profile steeped in spiciness and sweetness. It's more savory than fruitwoods, but more high-toned than hickory.

Pecan

The pecan is actually a part of the hickory family and closely related to the walnut. The wood has a delicate fruitiness to it, with some hints of nut and spice. It tends to burn long but fairly cool and without too much smoke. In the fall, when the pecan nuts hit the ground, some people even throw spent pecan shells into their

Mesquite

Cherry

Grape Vine

Hickory

Oak

Alder

Apple

Pecan

fires before putting on the steaks to add a spicy, sweet tinge to the smoke.

Grape Vine

Now that nearly every state is producing some sort of wine from grapes, it means nearly everyone has the opportunity to get grape vines for cooking. This is a woody substance, but not from a tree. Using vines is a good way to reproduce some of the flavor of a good steak cooked over fire in places like Tuscany or rural France. Jordan once stayed for a couple of nights in a three-hundred-year-old stone house in the town of Panicale, Umbria, in Italy. The house had a big, old fireplace and was close to a great Italian butcher. He couldn't resist trying to do a *bistecca fiorentina*, the great steak of Tuscany, so he bought a huge, two-and-a-half-inch-thick porterhouse from the butcher and then drove up behind a nearby winery and grabbed a trunkful of old grape vines piled behind a stone barn. Back at the house, he built a roaring fire out of the vines. When the flames died down, he threw on the steak and cooked it until almost burned on the outside. The coals burned out before the steak was done, and it was still raw in the middle. But he didn't mind, as that's the way the Italians eat it anyway. And when you wash it down with some local, tannic Sangiovese, it tastes great.

While it's not easy to find large chunks from thick grape vines (because few are removed each year), vines are pruned of their long canes annually. Most trimmings get stacked up and thrown away. But if you see some or know someone with a winery, don't let them go to waste. Make sure they're well dried, though. They're cut off living plants in the winter, so if you collect them in February or March, bundle them up, and store them through the summer and into fall, they should be ready to go. A handful of dried grape vines thrown on the fire can add a vibrant, peppery spice note. Think of them as seasoning for the fire—add them to another wood, as they are too thin to make a decent fire or create coals on their own.

SOURCING GRILL WOOD

If you want to grill over real wood coals, it's good to buy in bulk and store the wood at your house. If you've got a shed or a covered area, all the better. If you need to stack it on the side of the house, that's fine, but cover it with a tarp in case of showers. You'll want the backlog (no pun intended!) because you'll find yourself going through a lot of wood, and you don't want to have to worry about running out of it.

Finding a good source is necessary. Most areas, even urban ones, are served by a number of firewood delivery services. These are usually companies that are also in the tree trimming and removal business. Much of the time, the landowners just want the wood off their property, so it becomes a free commodity to the sellers. However, wood sellers have to have their own property where they can stack and age it.

Do a little research to find the most honest, reliable companies. For instance, if there's a restaurant you like with a live-fire grill, ask the manager for the source of the wood. Perhaps that firewood vendor would be willing to supply you, too. If people are selling wood on the side of the road, ask how long they've been keeping the wood and what shape the wood is in. For instance, if you live in a rainy area and the wood hasn't been aged long, it may require more aging before it's optimal for using in a cooking fire.

It seems the price of a cord of wood (128 cubic feet, or a stack that's four feet wide and high and eight feet long) has gotten more expensive over the years. We remember a time when it was $75, but in many places now it often runs between $250 and $450. (In Napa, where Jordan lives, it can go over $500 for a delivery—and that doesn't include stacking; a truck drives up and the wood is just dumped in a massive pile in your yard.) And this depends on the type of wood. Softwoods like pine tend to be significantly cheaper than hardwoods. Of course, always spend the extra bucks on the latter.

CUTTING WOOD DOWN TO SIZE

So you've got your firewood delivered and stacked. It's been aged for a few years by the time you bought it, so it's good to go. Now you just need to have it in usable sizes for whatever your grill setup is.

The equipment you'll want is an electric saw and a maul. You could cut your wood down with a chainsaw, but that can be clumsy and dangerous. A better idea is a miter saw (more of a finesse instrument) or chop saw (a bit burlier). These are both saws with circular blades that rotate quickly and can be raised and lowered by hand to cut through whatever's in front of them.

A quick word of warning: These things are dangerous if used carelessly. Always do your wood cutting earlier in the day, and never under the influence of alcohol. Make sure the saw is well anchored and that the log is comfortably and stably resting under the blade. If the wood isn't secure between the base and the side of the saw, there's a real danger it could kick out violently as it is being cut, putting everything at risk. Please be careful!

Firewood usually comes in 16- to 18-inch lengths. For Aaron's signature setup in the PK (see page 148), he likes to cut that down to a 12-inch log, so a whole log fits snugly in the grill. Then the 4- to 6-inch leftover pieces can be used as small logs for making the base fire in the PK or in another grill.

The 6-inch pieces need to be split so they'll burn faster and more evenly. As always, the tool of choice for splitting wood is a maul, not an ax. This is because we are splitting wood along the grain. (An ax is for chopping wood against the grain; a maul is for splitting it with the grain.) The maul is the lovechild of an ax and a sledgehammer. It is much heavier than an ax, and the point is to use its own weight to crack the wood in half. Once the blunt edge finds the grain in the wood, it effortlessly snaps the wood in two. You can get mauls with 32- or 36-inch-long handles, but if all you're doing is splitting little pieces of firewood into smaller sizes and kindling, a 16- or 24-inch handle will be easier to maneuver.

Once you've sourced your fuel—whether it's a quick bag of charcoal you purchased that morning or some perfectly seasoned wood you bought from a reliable source and cut down to the ideal size, it's finally time to get lit—er, get your fire lit. Since you've perhaps gone to the trouble of buying well-sourced meat, dry aging it to perfection, and seasoning your hardwood for a year or two, a lot is riding on the success of this fire. In the next chapter, we're going to put it all together and end up with something extraordinary to eat.

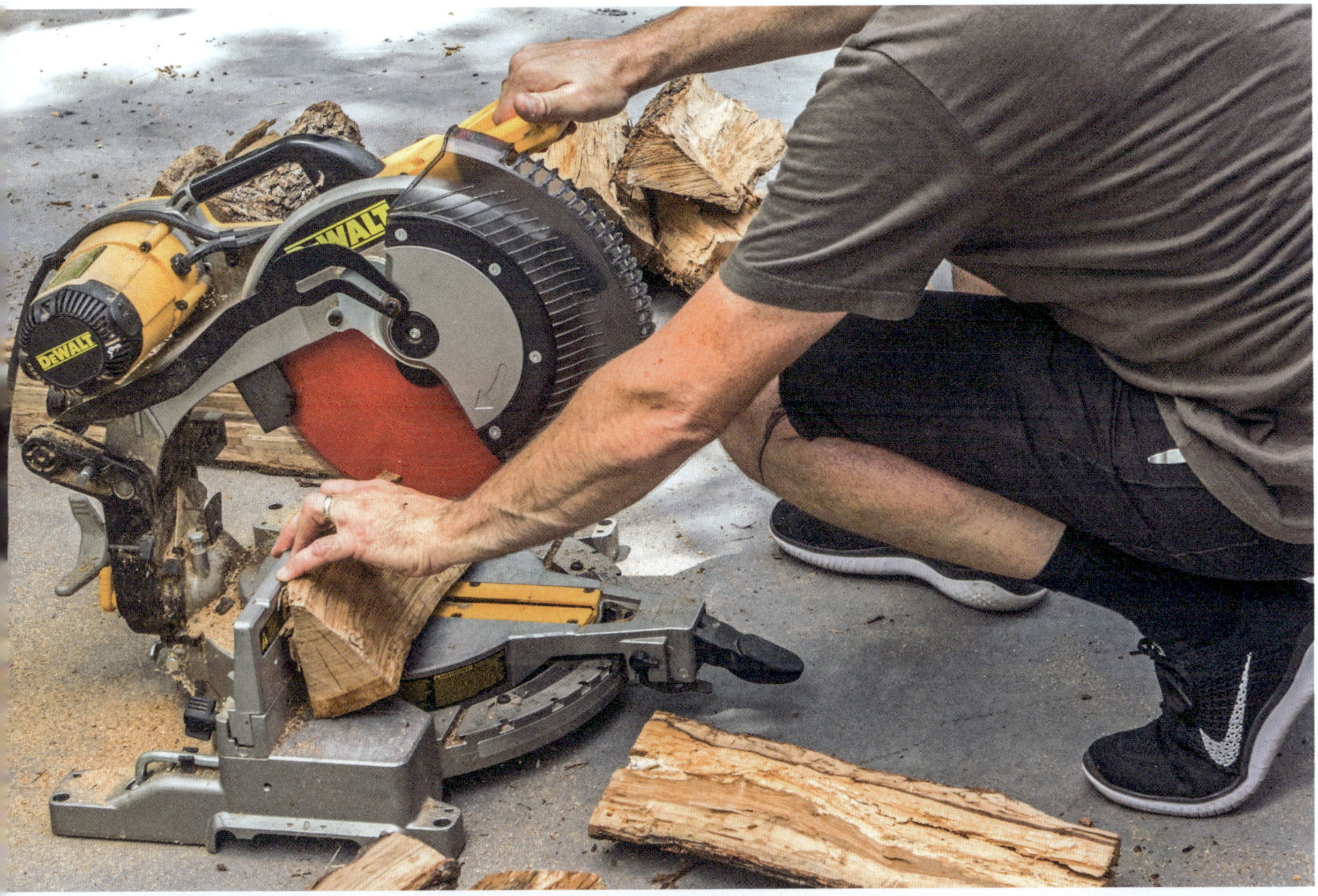
DEWALT
DEWALT

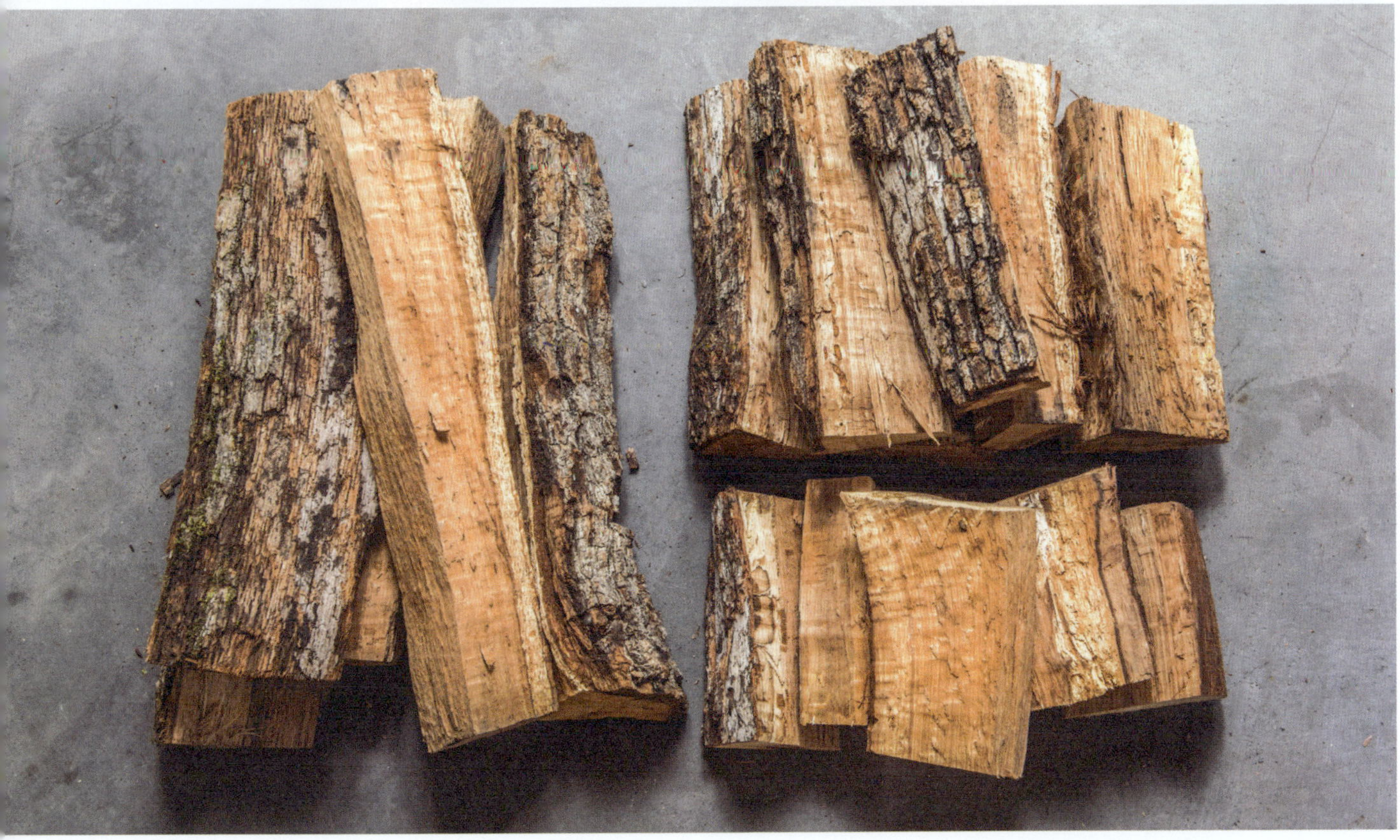

PERF

Part III

STEAK SECTION

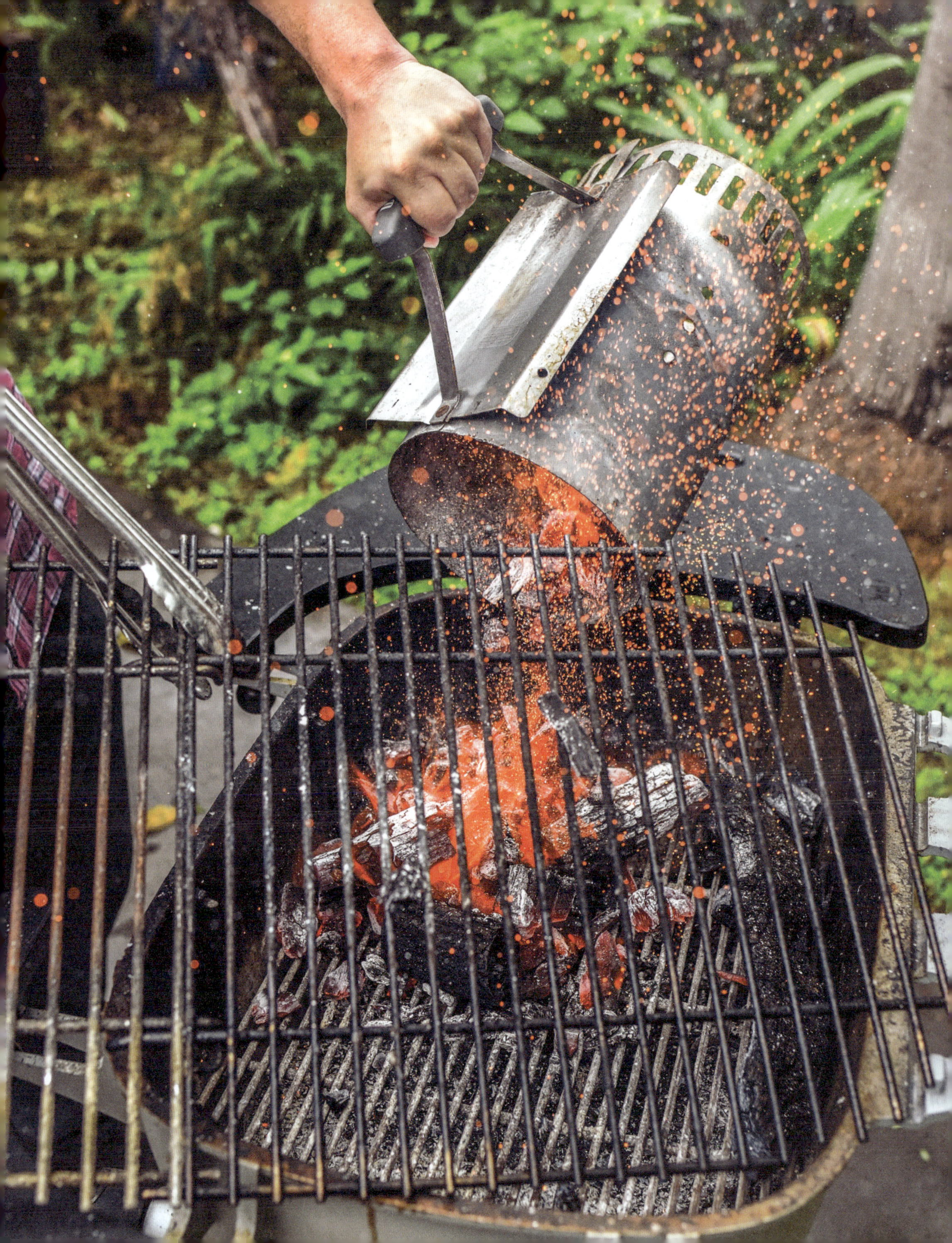

CHAPTER 7

Firing Up

So, okay, after however many dozens of pages, it's finally time for the main event: putting meat to fire. Well, we're almost there. (This kind of reminds us of the last book, where you're not cooking brisket until the third act.) Anyway, this long-winded display isn't intentional (though we do like to yak), but you've got to walk before you run and you've got to have good fuel and meat before you can produce transcendent steak. And you've also got to have some good tools, as they will make the job better, easier, and less painful. What's a surgeon without a scalpel? What's a painter without a brush? So in this chapter, we're going to look at the basic stuff you should have at hand in order to get a fire rip-roaring, manipulate hot coals and sizzling meats, and do it all without hurting yourself or making too much of a mess.

Then we're going to offer some ideas for grill setups and coal-bed alignments. We're basically making the simple act of cooking a steak more complicated. But it's oh, so good!

Equipment

As with cooking almost anything, being prepared when the food hits the fire is an important key to success. Make sure your *mise en place* (prepped ingredients) is perfect, that all the tools you'll need are nearby. These tools are neither expensive nor hard to find, so no excuses on cutting corners.

CHARCOAL CHIMNEY: LET THERE BE FIRE!

You'd think this simple piece of technology would be so common now that everyone with a backyard grill would have to own one, but surprisingly that's not the case. Every year we meet a couple of people who, on seeing a charcoal chimney, say, "Wow, I've got to get one of those!" Go figure.

A chimney is nonnegotiable. Every home griller should have one. They're not only the easiest, cleanest, and most effective way to light charcoal but also a cooking medium in and of themselves. All you need is some newspaper or other dry paper and a bag of your favorite charcoal. Within twenty minutes you'll have a glowing mound of incendiary charcoal hot enough to grill anything you want.

A chimney is just a thin metal cylinder with an insulated handle attached. The cylinder has two chambers. The smaller bottom one is separated from the top one by a perforated sheet or thin steel bars, and the top chamber is open to the sky. Air holes have been cut out around the sides.

Here's how to use it • Turn the chimney upside down so the shorter chamber is facing up. This is where you stuff a couple of sheets of crumpled newspaper, a scrunched-up paper bag, or even a few wads of paper torn out of your bag of charcoal. Don't compact the paper too much, as this is what you're going to light and it needs channels for oxygen to power the flames.

Pro tip • To ensure that the paper burns completely, squirt it with a little cooking oil.

Now turn the chimney right side up and set it down on a hard stone surface or even on top of your charcoal grill. Fill the top with charcoal, as much as you think you'll need. For short, small cooks where you don't need too much heat, maybe you need to fill it only halfway or less. A reverse sear (see page 165) on a thick bone-in ribeye is a good example. If you're grilling a bunch of steaks or need extremely high heat, fill it up.

Light the paper in the bottom. In less than a minute, you'll see plumes of thick, white smoke emanating from the chimney. This is the paper burning and starting to catch the bottommost pieces of charcoal (which create a lot of smoke). Within a few more minutes, the paper will have burned out and you'll see a much smaller trail of smoke coming from the chimney. This means it's lit. In the next few minutes, you'll hear popping and crackling and see sparks starting to shoot out of the top like miniature fireworks. If you don't, add some more paper and relight the chimney.

After about fifteen minutes, you'll see coals glowing orange and turning white with ash, a sign they are really heating up. When they are

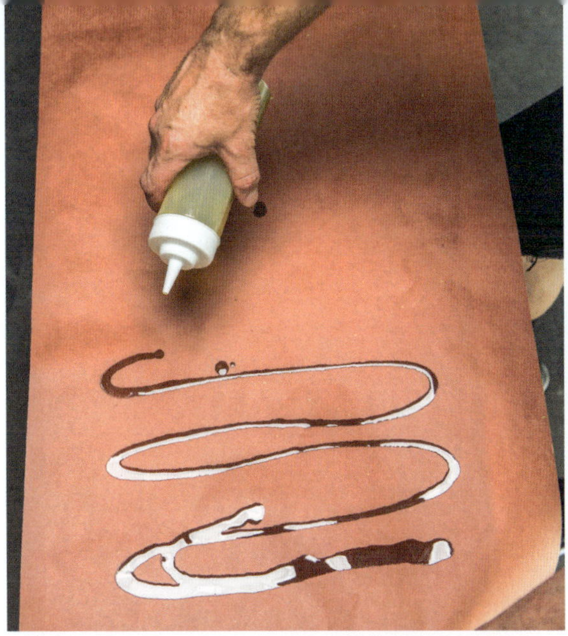
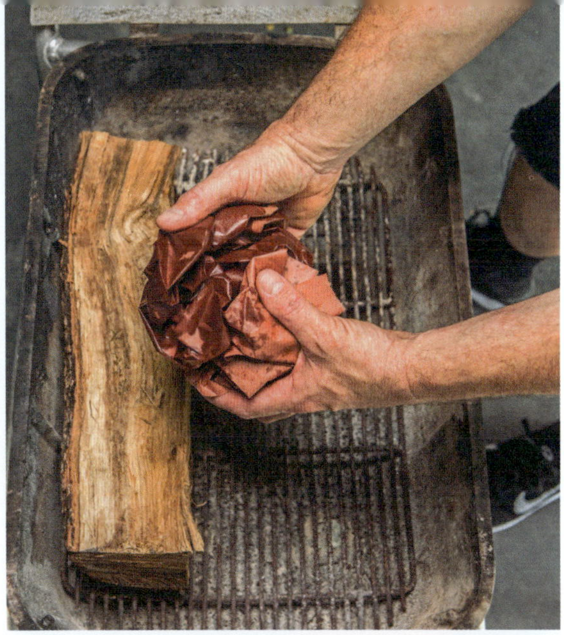
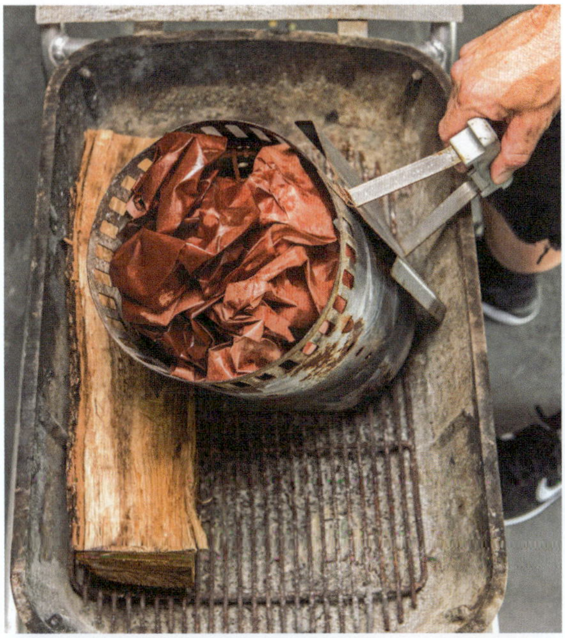
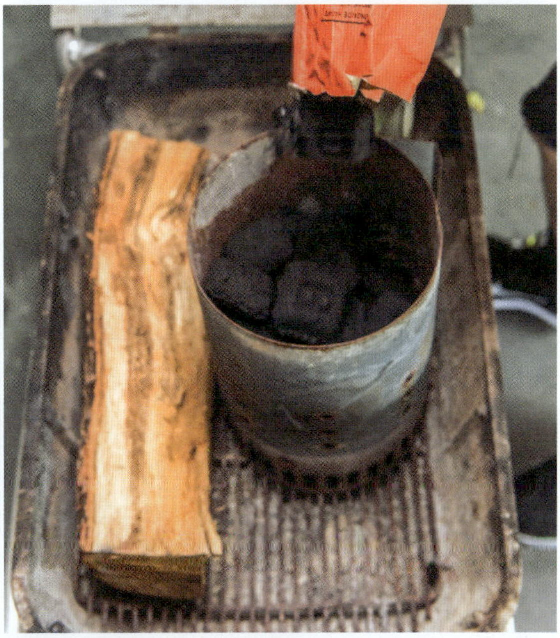
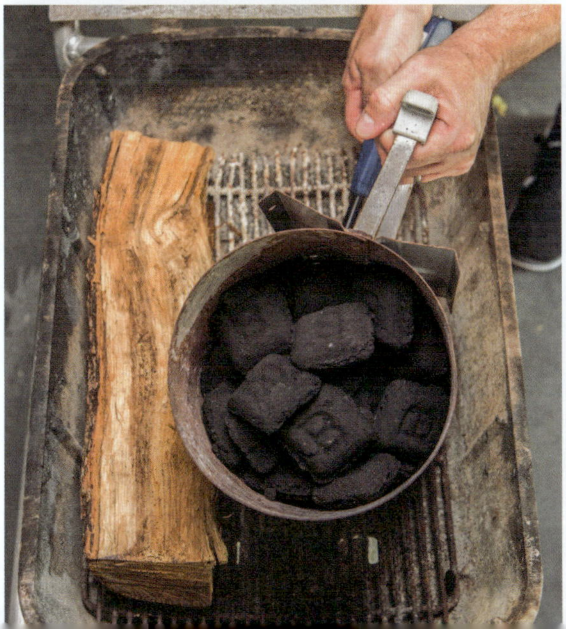
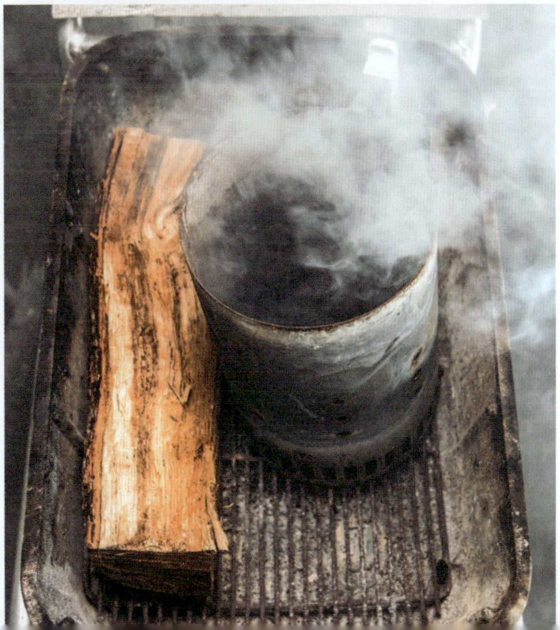

on the cusp of turning from black to white, dump the contents of the chimney into the space on your grill you want to heat. It's that simple.

The reason to have two chimneys on hand is if you need to start with a larger coal bed or need a quick refresh of hot coals. A standard-size large chimney, like the Weber Rapidfire (at fifteen dollars a very good buy; it holds about five pounds of charcoal and has a helper handle to supply more leverage when pouring the coals out), will fill up only about one-third to one-half of the grill space on a PK Grill. So if you're cooking for a lot of people and you need a broader coal bed, you'll want to start with more coals. Lighting consecutive batches of coals in the same chimney won't quite do the trick, as the first batch will have cooked down by fifteen to twenty minutes before the second one is ready to go.

TONGS: WHEN FINGERS ARE NOT ENOUGH

Tongs are as essential to a steak griller as a sword was to a musketeer. Like the sharp-tipped sword of a dueler, they allow you to deal with dangerous elements while keeping your distance. As extensions of our hands, tongs are useful for much more than just flipping meat and vegetables. You'll find yourself using them to convey individual coals or even small chunks of wood from one grill to another. You can poke them through the grates to stir up a dying coal bed to get it roaring again. And you can pick up the entire grate, if need be, to add more charcoal or wood to the fire. Have several pairs of tongs handy at all times; you'll constantly find yourself reaching for them.

We've all probably cooked with ninety-nine-cent tongs from the supermarket—and let us remind you, singed knuckles and burned hands are no fun. Spend a few extra dollars for heavy-duty, well-made tongs.

GRILL BRUSH: SCRAPE THIS

Cleaning the grill is an annoying task and therefore one that doesn't get done nearly as often as it should. The less often, the more annoying, as you quickly find yourself dusted in ash and your hands covered with greasy, sooty streaks. Not only is the task annoying, but it's

FRANKLIN STEAK

also inconvenient. The best time to clean the grill is immediately after you finish cooking on it, when it's still hot and covered with new oils, fats, and crusts. Of course, the moment you take steaks off the grill, you're inevitably concerned with getting everything to the table, not to mention monitoring your steaks as they rest. Cleaning the grill is the last thing on your mind, which means that it often doesn't get cleaned until the next time you use it. That could be the next day, the following weekend, and even weeks or months down the road.

But clean grates are essential to good cooking. First, they help keep food from sticking. Baked-on sugars and proteins create a surface for your meats to bind to when you put them on even a hot grill. Second, sooty or carbonized grates will add a bitterness to whatever you're grilling on them. And last, the thought of picking up traces of old foods cooked on unclean grills is nasty.

A durable grill brush can grind a grill clean with only a few passes. Find one that holds up to continuous use and won't fall apart (leaving dangerous wire bristles behind) or break. We've had the best luck with brushes designed with a trio of brush extensions coming from a single handle. These allow you to press with the greatest force on the grill without breaking the stem.

To get the most out of your grill brush, scrape the grates when they're hot and the coals are reaching their peak. The detritus you scrape off will simply be incinerated by the coals. If you want to spray some water onto the brush to get the benefit of some steam while cleaning, that can help, too. Scrape often, even after cooking one round of meats and before the next.

TROWEL AND STEEL PAIL: THE BUCKET LIST

If you read our first book, you'll remember Aaron's favorite tool for working the big fires in his cookers was a full-size shovel. So you shouldn't be surprised to learn that small fires call for a small shovel and a bucket. These classic garden tools double as useful props on a trip to the beach, but for the home griller, a sturdy little shovel and a durable bucket always come in handy. A trowel or small shovel can be used to shovel out hot coals or for prodding and working the coal bed, lifting the grill grate, and tidying things up. It's also good for scooping ash when you're cleaning out the grill.

A bucket is one of the most useful tools, not just in grilling but in life. Use it to transport coals from a wood-burning fire to a grill, for instance. Dump ash into it when you need to clean out your grills or fireplace. If your needs are few, fill it with ice and beer. And if nothing else, turn it over and sit on it.

SHEET PANS: YOU'RE GOING TO SHEET YOUR PANS

When you're grilling, trekking between kitchen and grill is inevitable. You need trays sturdy enough to hold a load, yet light enough to be easy to carry with one hand while opening doors. Hence, the good old-fashioned sheet pan will always be your friend.

Equip yourself with a few each of half, quarter, and eighth sizes of commercial sheet pans. Their standard one-inch depth is plenty for collecting any juices a finished steak might leave. Also, purchase a couple of cooling racks that fit inside of them. This setup is good not just for carrying steaks in and out of the house but also

FIRING UP

for holding the meat (if you've presalted it) for a day or two in the refrigerator or you simply want to dry it off. Sheet pans are great because they're tough enough that you can actually put them on the grill grates or in the fire (handy for the three-zone cooking setup, facing page) and they'll hold up (even if that will likely render them useless for the kitchen again).

SIZZLE PLATTERS: SIZZLE ME THIS

You've seen them before: thin, small, oval metal plates stacked up fifteen or twenty high in hot restaurant kitchens, typically where jet-blasting flames are firing smoking woks and food comes off fast and furious every couple of minutes. They are really just miniaturized sheet pans, and they have much the same function. But they are handier than your ceramic plates at home, as they can go into hot ovens or onto hot grills without being damaged. And if you somehow manage to damage one, they're only a few bucks each at any restaurant supply store.

KITCHEN TOWELS: THE MOST MASSIVELY USEFUL THING

If you don't already have towels in your home, I'm not sure you should be cooking or serving anyone food. Stock up and always keep a generous supply handy. Let's just remind ourselves of some of the many uses of towels. Dampened, they should be spread out underneath cutting boards to offer stability. They can be used instead of pot holders or gloves to pick up hot things or to protect hands from the fire while manipulating tongs. They clean up messes and spills. They dab the edges of sloppy platters. They can be soaked in cold water to wipe the brow of overheated grill cooks or to clean up the grill itself or any work surface or tool. Find a towel style you like and plan to keep three or four clean ones at the ready.

DIGITAL THERMOMETER: HOT OR NOT?

Because of the short cooking time of steaks and their relatively small size, changes in temperature happen even more rapidly and dramatically than in larger pieces of meat, making a fast and accurate digital thermometer a necessity. Our favorite is still the ThermoWorks Thermapen. It's spendy, running between eighty and one hundred dollars (it goes on sale fairly often), but no other device matches it for speed and precision. When checking the temperatures of ribeyes still sizzling on top of a smoldering coal bed, you don't want to wait seconds to come up with a questionable reading. The Thermapen gives accurate results quickly. It's simply one tool no home chef should be without.

PLASTIC BOTTLE OF COOKING OIL: MAIN SQUEEZE

Surely you already have a bottle of handy cooking oil lingering around your stove. But keeping a plastic, restaurant-style squeeze bottle of cooking oil (Aaron uses grape seed because of its neutral flavor and high smoke point) handy is a low-maintenance, unfussy, easy-cleanup alternative to schlepping around a big glass bottle of oil. Use it to add a sheen to a steak before it goes on the grill, to moisten a paper towel that's about to be used to lubricate the grates before cooking, or to lightly prime the newspaper before lighting the chimney.

Bed Times and Fireside Chats: Setting Up Your Grill and Coals

Okay, *here* is the moment you've been waiting for: prepping your grill and lighting 'er up. At this stage, you have perhaps your biggest decision to make: how to set up the grill. This should always be determined by what you're cooking. For a handy cheat sheet, turn to page 151. But first we encourage you to think about *all* of the variables that go into a successful grill session. Do you have one steak to cook or six? Are they all going to be medium-rare or do some guests want medium and others want rare? Are you also cooking other proteins or vegetables?

Once you've got a sense of everything that's going on the grill, you need to plot out a workflow of when each item is going on, approximately how long it will take to cook, where it's going after it's done, and what's going on next. We're not saying you need to draw Venn diagrams or plot anything out on a computer. But do have a plan.

THE TWO-ZONE SETUP

This is elementary stuff that's been written about hundreds of times before, so we won't belabor it too much. And for those of you who already do a lot of grilling, this won't be anything new. But for those of you who have spent the last couple of decades living in a cave or a city or the Matrix and are just emerging into the world of grilling for the first time, this is the basic configuration you need to know for cooking steaks (and many other things).

You will want to cook any steak significantly thicker than one inch in two ways: quickly and slowly. Quickly uses direct heat radiated by close proximity to a bed of glowing-hot charcoal. Slowly cooks via heat carried by the air circulating around the meat, as in an oven. In the case of a wood or charcoal grill, the quick searing of meat happens via direct grilling, that is, right above a pile of massively hot coals. Slow cooking meat with hot air can also take place on a coal-fired grill, but it needs to happen in a "safe space"—a much cooler spot that makes it hard for the meat to burn or overcook—hence, the classic two-zone setup.

To achieve this, just dump the charcoal from your chimney on one side of the grill. In a rectangular, relatively shallow grill like a PK, this is incredibly easy, as the two sides are well defined. It's a little trickier in a round grill like a Weber; that's why some manufacturers have produced metal separators. And as mentioned previously, this is a pronounced challenge in the Big Green Egg and other kamado cookers: you can put the hot charcoal on one side of the base, but because of the awesome heat retention of the cooker's ceramic walls, if you shut the lid, the whole unit will heat up uniformly. If you *don't* shut the lid, the distance from the coals to the grill allows the heat to spread out, also nullifying the whole point of going with two zones.

THE THREE-ZONE SETUP, GRADUATED AND SPLIT

What could possibly be greater than two zones? Three, of course. Two zones just give you hot and cold. Why not treat yourself to hot, less hot, and cold? With more range, you can achieve greater nuance in the steaks, mimicking a little bit of the flexibility that an adjustable-height Santa Maria grill can offer.

FIRING UP

There are a few ways to achieve the mythical three-zone setup. The first is just an elaboration of the two-zone grill, but in this one, you vary the depth of the coal bed to give you more options. A conventional two-zone configuration calls for coals on one side of the grill and nothing on the other. The graduated three-zone grill involves an inclined coal bed, using more coals on one deep end of the hot zone, fewer in the middle, and then nothing on the other half. This is perhaps easiest with briquettes: just pile your hot charcoal three or four pieces deep on one side, then as you move to the other side, slope the coal bed downward using less and less coal until in the middle the bed is just one briquette deep. This offers you very strong intense heat on the far left, declining all the way to indirect heat on the right.

Another variation, the split three-zone setup, calls for piles of coals on both ends of the grill and zero coals for indirect heat in the middle. This unique setup can be especially effective when cooking larger cuts, say two rib steaks two to three inches thick. You can lay the steaks flat on the grill in the middle, exposing them to heat from either direction. Or you can lay them on their sides. Then, to finish, you have two zones for direct cooking already prepared. For some meaty pyrotechnics, try placing a sheet pan or sizzle plate in the middle between the two coal beds. It will heat up quickly and catch the drippings and vaporize them, allowing their meaty mist to curl back up and infuse the steak, much as happens on a gas grill.

CHARCOAL AND ACCENT LOG (THE FRANKLIN FORMATION)

If you bought this book, you're probably wondering what Aaron's preferred grill setup is. Jordan calls it the Franklin Formation. Aaron calls it stickin' a log in there. It may sound simple, but the Franklin Formation (yes, that's what we're going with) is a terrific hybrid of cooking mediums, leveraging the convenience of charcoal while still tapping into the flavor of real wood. This method works especially well on a PK (see page 111) because of the rectangular shape of the grill, but it could be adapted to a round Weber, too.

First, lay a charcoal bed on one side of the grill. Don't leave the other, the indirect side, empty—oh no, this is when you stick a log in there! In the case of the PK, a log trimmed to twelve inches with a chop saw fits perfectly into the cooker's fourteen-inch width. The presence of the log provides a natural boundary against the coal bed. It also makes the indirect side cooler than if there was nothing filling the space, providing more of a contrast from the direct side and allowing even more nuanced cooking. The best part? The point where the hot charcoal contacts the log becomes a small area of combustion. The slightly burning log provides a bit of wood smoke and perhaps some flickers of flame. But because this is a large, dense, and not-too-seasoned piece of wood, there's no danger of it igniting and creating a conflagration, which is what happens if you toss small wood chunks onto the coal bed to get smoke. You can keep this going for a long time, and all you have to do is regularly replenish your charcoal bed; the piece of hardwood will take its time burning down. And it looks cool!

THE WOOD COAL SETUP

The Franklin Formation is handy because it's convenient, yet still has the allure of a wood fire. But we know there are folks out there who are only interested in the purest, most primal and existential grill setup: 100 percent wood fired.

We get it. Meats grilled over wood taste better than meats cooked over charcoal, pure and simple. Grilling over wood showcases the defining components of physical existence, time and space. First, time: When starting with logs, it takes a long time to develop a good coal bed. And *timing* remains a challenge throughout the cook because wood coals burn faster and don't last nearly as long as charcoal, and catching them at their peak and maintaining them for as long as you need is a difficult proposition.

Next, space: A good wood fire needs space to hold enough wood to provide a consistent source of hot coals. This cycle of constant replenishment of wood and coals is why many restaurant grills sport some sort of reinforced metal cage in which logs are stacked high over a coal bed. As the lowest log starts to burn into coals, cooks rake those newly formed embers out under the grilling surface, allowing the fresh wood in the cage to slide down and keep the process going.

In the home setting, there are a number of ways to accomplish this. For instance, you can make a small wood fire in your grill using wood chunks. But once they get going, they burn up quickly, and if you need a stable coal bed for more than fifteen minutes or so, you'll have to add fresh wood to the coals. Fresh wood also produces a ton of flames and smoke, which might be overwhelming if you've got meat on the grill. So the answer is to do as the restaurants do and burn your wood down to coals at a little distance from where you're cooking the meat. But where?

At home, the best solution is to employ two grills. Trust us, it's actually much easier and cheaper than you imagine. If one grill is primarily going to be used to burn down logs, it needn't be fancy. It could be a light, inexpensive Weber with the grate removed so it can hold three or four standard-size logs. It can be handy to have a second grill anyway, for expanded space on the grates or an alternative shape. (If your primary is a PK, for instance, keep a round Weber on hand for things like pizza or paella.) A quick check on craigslist or another local listing

FIRING UP

site can often land a used Weber kettle for under fifty bucks. Another option is one of those premade firepits. These round, solid-metal pits are made to burn down logs, and they can double as a backyard campfire site to sit around on cool evenings.

With your trusty shovel and bucket to convey said coals to your primary grill space, you're ready to get cooking. You'll have enough coals to grill thick steaks (or rounds of them) over medium to low heat. Enjoy the fragrant whiff of wood smoke and flickering flames. Wood-fired grilling isn't just a cookout, it's a ritual.

Starting a Wood Fire and Building a Coal Bed

On page 142, we showed you how to light a fire if you plan to use charcoal, using our favorite charcoal tool, the chimney starter. Starting a wood fire is a bit trickier. First, make sure you have a few small wood chunks (four to six inches) as well as larger logs. The easiest way to get it all started is to light a handful of charcoal pieces in the renowned chimney and either put the wood chunks on top of them or simply dump the charcoal into your firepit and arrange the small pieces of wood on top. Throw on some crumpled newspaper to accelerate the process (which you can prime with cooking oil or tallow if you'd like).

Once you have a small fire going, put on a couple of larger pieces, and as the fire gets hotter and expands, some even larger pieces. Aaron does indeed like to build his little log cabins over a few glowing charcoal briquettes. And when he doesn't want quite a log cabin–size fire, he builds a tepee with three logs angled over the coals. The point is to have airflow coming in at the base so the heat catches the logs above.

If you just burn down one or two logs and take the coals to fire your grill, there won't be enough to sustain your wood fire. Instead, burn through a round or two of logs to establish a solid and enduring coal bed. (Hey, we said a wood fire takes time.) This is a philosophical, communal, meditative activity that requires an hour or two to ease into. If you're used to barbecuing ribs or brisket, which take even longer, you get it. Hanging out and drinking a beer as burning wood crackles and hisses and the smoke tickles your nose is one of life's great pleasures. The steaks taste better for it, too.

CHEAT SHEET
Grill Setups

The configuration of your grill is the second thing you should consider after what kind of steak you're going to cook, as it will determine what you can and can't do with a fire. There aren't too many variations, but the differences between them are important to note. More detailed accounts of each method were in the previous pages, but we've summarized them for you here.

SETUP	USES
Two zone	The standard setup, good for all steaks thicker than skirts and flanks, or any cut that needs to cook a little longer on the inside without overcooking the outside. The key is to make sure your zones are distinct: one superhot and one much cooler.
Three zone	When you need a bit more nuance, such as the thick tweener cuts between roasts and steaks, like tri-tips and thick-cut bone-in ribeyes.
Franklin Formation	The quick and easy way to cook using two zones with charcoal while getting a steady, even dose of wood smoke and a serious contrast in heat levels.
100 percent wood fire	The best historically, the best today, and the best forever and ever. No combustion-based heat source provides the depth of flavor, the sweet complexity, and the connection to our earthy souls like a coal bed made of real wood.

FIRING UP

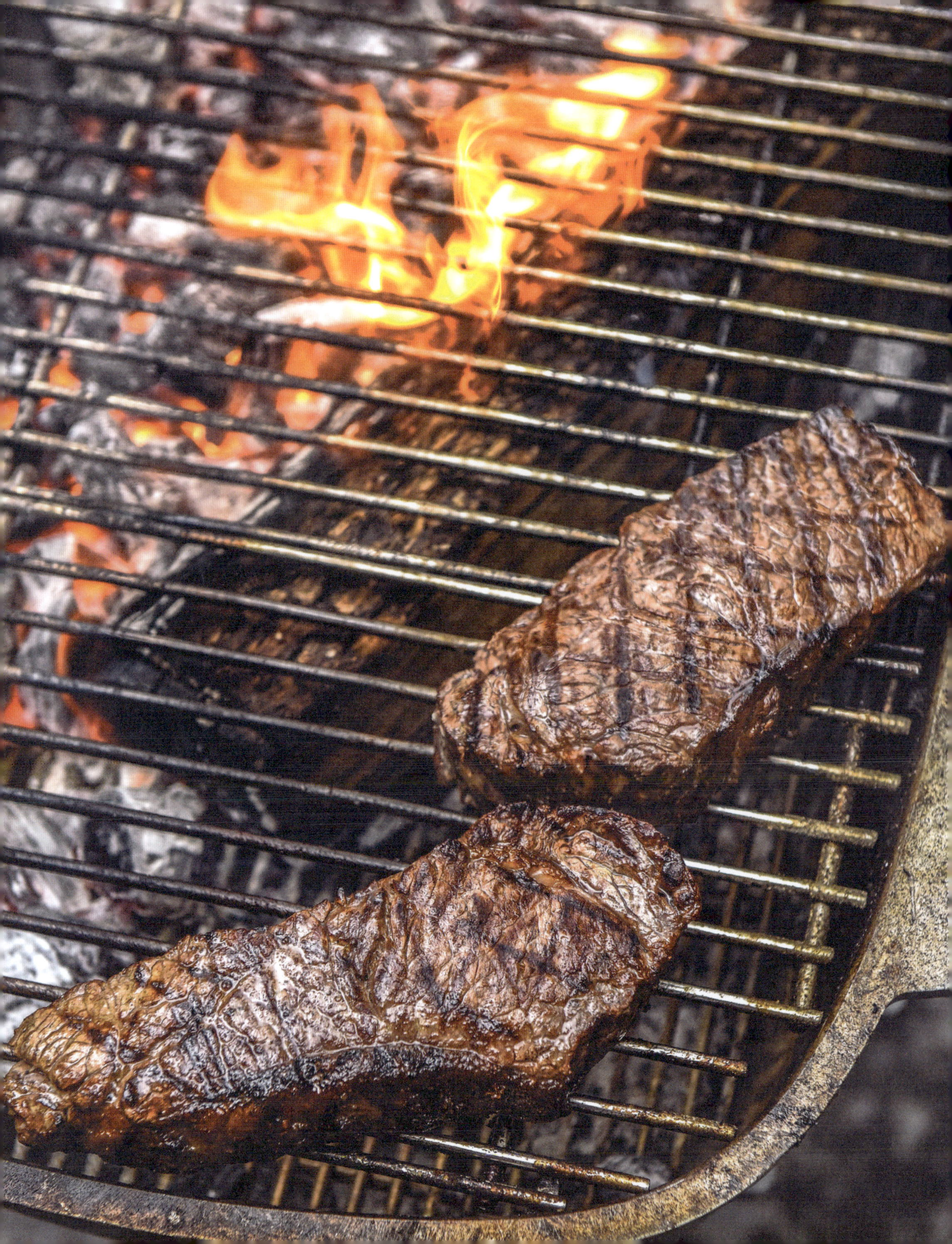

CHAPTER 8

The Cook

The barbecue mantra of "low and slow" has been in Aaron's head ever since he put his first brisket on a cheap offset smoker. And, indeed, he's logged thousands upon thousands of hours since then, many of them sleepily overnight, gently guiding large pieces of meat into transcendent states of tenderness and flavor. The art of barbecue is very much the art of controlling temperature—how to burn a clean, hot fire while at the same time maintaining absolute temperature consistency inside the cook chamber. But there's something appealing about the fast cook, too. In barbecue, the product is the smoke. You're not using the flame. When it comes to grilling stuff—which he loves to do—the flame is the product and you've got to figure out how to get the most of it without burning everything up. It's a completely different challenge.

Indeed, if slow cooking is like steering a canoe on a lake, grilling is like skimming wake on a Jet Ski. And while slow cooking is art, it's much more forgiving than fast cooking. Fast cooking relays different pleasures, but they require skill to coax out. The most flavorful steak on the planet if poorly cooked is lost to the world. Conversely, an exceptionally well cooked but average piece of meat can still be tasty. In other words, the cooking is super important for steak.

Now, truly, at last, everything is lined up. You have your meat: some excellent steaks you've been waiting to cook. Your equipment—sheet pans, towels, tongs, thermometer—is ready. Your grill setup is dialed in, and your fuel source is nearby. It's time to get grilling.

We've taught you *how* to achieve different grill setups, but now it's time to figure out *when* each is appropriate. This depends on factors like the kind of meat (grass fed or grain fed), the cut (lean or fatty), the size (thick or thin), and whether there's a bone or not.

The two primary goals for great steaks are simple: (1) a robust, savory crust across the entire surface of the meat, and (2) a perfect medium-rare finish (though you can customize this to your own taste).

GOAL #1
A Robust, Savory Crust

The crust is one of the things that makes a steak a steak. No other cut of beef can achieve the steak's deep, glistening, reddish brown crust, with its crystallized bits of protein and fat sparkling like gems and its deep, irresistible beefy smell. It's one of the most compelling phenomena in the entire world of food. And this crust comes from complex chemical processes called the Maillard reactions.

Named for the French scientist who discovered them in the early 1900s, the Maillard reactions are often conflated with caramelization. Although both produce complex molecules and both are referred to as browning reactions based on the color they produce in food, they are different. Caramelization involves the simple breakdown of sugars, whereas the Maillard reactions, according to Harold McGee in *On Food and Cooking*, are all about the thousands of new, distinct compounds created when amino acids react with a carbohydrate or sugar molecule in the presence of high heat. The Maillard effect happens not only to meat but to all sorts of things that brown, including bread, coffee beans, and chocolate. Like caramelization, McGee writes, brown color and deep flavor occur, but "Maillard flavors are more complex and meaty than caramelized flavors, because the involvement of the amino acids adds nitrogen and sulfur atoms to the mix . . . and produces new families of molecules and new aromatic dimensions."

That all sounds very sciency, and it is. But the bottom line is, the true glory of steak is not just a result of the cut itself but also, crucially, of how it is cooked: Maillard reactions when applied to the proteins in beef! Even if you boiled a ribeye, god forbid, to perfection, you'd come out with something far less appealing. That's because Maillard reactions don't occur in the presence of water. Until water becomes vapor, its temperature can't exceed its boiling point of 212°F. That's not hot enough for Maillard reactions to occur. High heat accelerates the rate at which reactions take place and hastens the evaporation of water. That means a dry cooking environment is needed, hence baking, grilling, and frying (yes, frying, that is, cooking with oil, is considered a dry technique, as water is anathema to oil).

So, Maillard is good. But how do you encourage it? How can you guarantee you're going to get a great crust on your meat? Making sure you have a dry environment, a dry surface, and high enough heat (but not so high that the meat burns) are the keys. Maillard browning occurs most optimally between 225°F and 355°F, so an insane amount of heat isn't even necessary. High heat only provides speedy browning before the heat has time to penetrate to the interior of the meat.

The most reliable, foolproof method to achieve a great crust is probably to cook the steak in a pan or on a *plancha* (a thick, steel flattop or griddle, whether fired by gas in a restaurant kitchen or placed on the grill over hot coals). This is because metal is a good conductor of heat, but not *too* good. It enables a prolonged exposure of the meat to heat, allowing a great range of Maillard reactions to take place.

Grilling can also achieve a tremendous crust, of course, but it's a little trickier, as the heat is usually much more intense. Glowing red coals can be so hot that browning on the exterior of the steak can happen too rapidly. Before you know it, you've taken the meat out of the realm of Maillard reactions and into the zone of pyrolysis (a fancy word for burning).

The art of steak cooking is finding the right rate of heating to accomplish Maillard browning without blowing right through it to burning before the interior is cooked to the desired doneness. That brings us to. . . .

GOAL #2
Proper Doneness

So let's get the formalities out of the way: Anyone can cook a steak to well-done. Today, most people—in the United States, anyway—consider that to be overdone, so we're not going to spend time talking about overcooking steaks. Most steaks taste best at medium-rare. Meat has little flavor when raw and is tough and bland when overcooked. Mid-rare is the fine line between them.

There are exceptions, of course, especially when it comes to butcher's cuts (see page 68). In some cases, the cut itself and the type of beef should have a say as to how the steak is cooked. Certain cuts or styles may benefit from a little more or a little less time over the fire. And everyone has his or her own tastes.

Heat-to-meat ratios can be a little counter-intuitive. For the least cooked meat you want the hottest fire. That is, a rare steak is cooked very hot because the outside cooks before the heat penetrates to the interior. Medium-rare takes a little more time and a lower flame because you have to slow it down. A well-done steak (perish the thought!) has to cook even slower over an even lower fire. Some people think well-done should be hotter and longer. That will result in a dry, tough piece of meat. Instead, sear it like a rare steak and then finish it over lower heat.

So how do we heat the interior of the steak to our desired doneness without overheating the exterior? The first thing to remember is that the thickness of the steak is more important than the weight. A two-inch-thick steak that weighs three pounds will cook much more slowly than a three-pound steak that's only a half inch thick. Well-marbled or fatty meat takes longer to reach the desired temperature than leaner beef because heat conduction is slower through fat than through protein or water. Even the grain of the meat plays a role in the transfer of heat. If the heat source is applied parallel to the grain, the steak will cook about 10 percent faster than if the heat is applied perpendicular to the grain.

When you really think about it, the exterior of a steak is vastly overcooked—beyond well-done into the realm of desiccation and near carbonization. We mention this only as a reminder that much of the pleasure of eating a great steak comes not from uniform doneness but rather from a contrast of finishes. That crisp, complex, crunchy crust is sublime in part because it's the opposite of the moist, satiny interior. And between these two extremes are intermediate degrees of doneness, including a thin band of gray, well-done meat just inside the crust meat that gets rarer and rarer as you move toward the center. The best steaks are when that band of well-done meat isn't too thick but also isn't nonexistent (it's all about textural complexity, people!).

Sounds pretty tricky, doesn't it? But really, there's one key: work on the interior of the steak slowly. That's why we spent all that time talking about two or three heat zones. Indirect cooking is your friend.

The only other question is how to measure the interior doneness of the steak. We've already waxed poetic about the Thermapen (see page 146), so now's the time to use it! Why leave things up to guesswork when you can be precise with an instant-read thermometer? Just make sure to aim the probe carefully at the center of the steak to get the most accurate reading and to take the temperature at several spots to get a sense of what's going on in there. Remember that the steak will be ten to fifteen degrees cooler next to the bone, so plan accordingly.

The last thing to consider is the concept of carryover. When you pull a steak off the fire, it doesn't stop cooking immediately. All of the heat you've introduced remains in the meat, working its way to the center, and you must account for this residual heat when you estimate doneness. When you're cooking hot and fast, carryover will be more aggressive than when you're cooking low and slow. And then, the amount and forcefulness of the carryover also depends on the mass of meat that was heated and if there's a bone. A thin, wide skirt steak will not carry over too much as the heat will quickly dissipate, while a thick-cut ribeye will hold on to more heat. With the latter, it's good to pull the meat about five to ten degrees lower than the desired temperature and assume it will eventually get to where you want it to be. You probably want some concrete numbers—which is always risky with steak, but here it goes: To reach 132°F, the middle of medium-rare, aim to pull the steak off around 125°F to 128°F. But remember, every piece of meat is different, and feel always trumps temp! After that, let it rest for five minutes before slicing (we know that sounds like a short rest period, but trust us, we've tested; see page 161).

Worth Their Salt

Steak without salt is sacrilege. It just doesn't work. Salt isn't just salty. It enhances the flavor of whatever it's applied to. And when applied in the proper amount, salt should never cause you to say, "Oh, this tastes salty." Instead, you'll say, "Wow, this steak tastes damn good!"

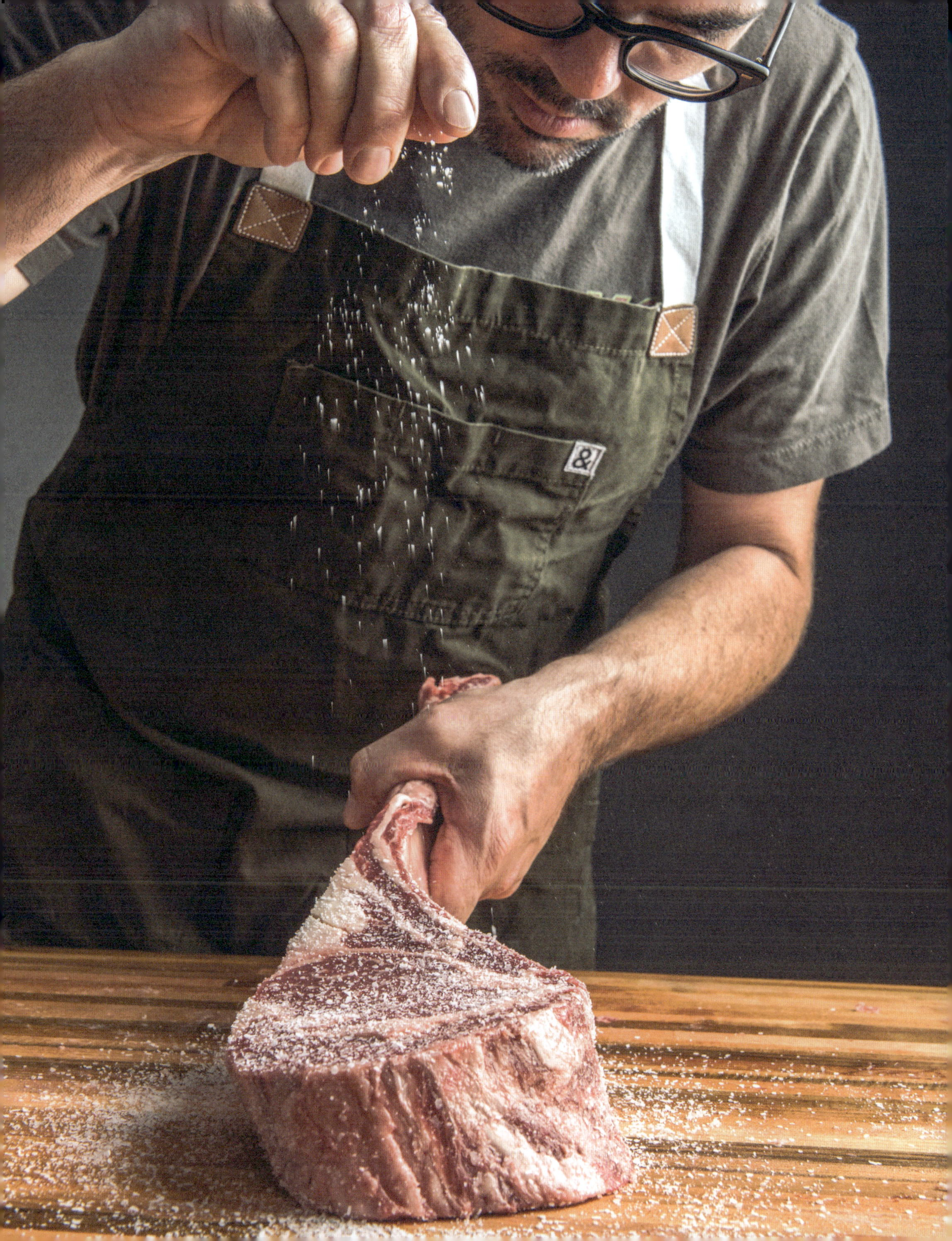

But the question always comes up of *when* to salt. Often people don't think about it until the last minute, and then they rain a downpour of salt onto their steak while the pan is heating up. Unfortunately, this is the worst time to salt the steak.

It's good to salt the meat in advance of cooking it, just not immediately before you heat it. Because there is an electrical attraction between NaCL (sodium chloride) and H_2O molecules when you salt a steak, the first thing that happens is the salt draws moisture out of the meat. This extracted water then dissolves the salt, instantly creating a mini brine. After fifteen to twenty minutes, the meat starts to pull the salty moisture back into its cells. The salt penetrates into the fiber of the meat, traveling deeper into it the longer you wait. People worry that salt will dry out the meat (and over time it will, but meat will also dry out on its own over time), but in fact the opposite is true: it makes the meat juicier.

If you cook the meat only five minutes after you've salted it, you won't have given the steak enough time to pull the moisture back into its cells. There will be a wet slurry of salty water sitting atop the meat, which will slow down the browning of the exterior and speed up the cooking of the interior. Bad! If you start with wet meat and you're hoping to get a nice brown crust, you could end up with an overdone interior by the time you achieve it.

Because we can't help ourselves, and because we love this type of cooking experiment, we trial cooked a number of 1½-inch-thick ribeyes that had been salted at different intervals before cooking: 48 hours, 24 hours, 12 hours, 6 hours, 4 hours, 2 hours, 1 hour, 5 minutes, and just before going on the grill. We sprinkled each steak with a measure of kosher salt equivalent to 1.5 percent of its original weight, which meant a four-hundred-gram steak got hit with six grams of salt. All of the ribeyes were cooked straight out of the 35°F refrigerator (again, if this runs counter to what you've been taught, take a look at page 160) on a *plancha* heated to 350°F until they reached an internal temperature of 127°F.

The results of the test were quite clear: the ones that had been salted longer not only cooked better—more evenly and faster—but tasted better, too. Our favorite was the steak salted 48 hours before we cooked it. On the grill, it quickly formed a deep and even crust (maybe because the exterior had dried a bit). When we looked at a cross section after slicing, there was a pretty dramatic shift between the crusted exterior and the pink interior. Most of the other steaks had a more gradual gradient. The flavor of the 48-hour steak was also the best. The salt had thoroughly penetrated and integrated with the meat, seasoning it inside and out.

The steaks salted between 24 and 48 hours all turned out equally well. The main difference from the 48-hour meat was that more gradual gradient between the well-done exterior and mid-rare interior. They all tasted good and had a good integration of salt and meat, but they were not transcendent like the 48-hour steak was.

The difficulties mounted for the steaks salted for 4 hours and under. Even on the 4-hour steak, there was a wet residue on the surface. When cooked, all of these steaks developed blotchy crusts. Most disappointing (when compared to the longer-salted steaks) was the flavor, which clearly tasted like salt on the outside and unseasoned meat on the inside. There was no integration.

Listen, if you don't have time to plan ahead and end up salting immediately before or during cooking, we're not going to tell you to throw your steaks away. They will still taste good, but you won't end up with that beautiful merging of meat and salt. But if you can remember to salt your meat four hours or more in advance, you'll be golden.

Generally, it's nice to keep at least a couple of different types of salt on hand. Coarsely grained kosher salt is easy to sprinkle with the fingers. A medium-grain sea salt has a great briny flavor and some slightly larger crystals, which are good for an aggressive salt flavor and the occasional crunchy bite.

Even if you've presalted—as long as it wasn't too heavy—a little finishing salt is an effective touch. To this end, every kitchen should have a big bowl handy of lovely, flaky finishing salt. Maldon sea salt, which comes from the southeast coast of England, is not too strongly flavored, is delicately scented with minerals, and either dissolves quickly on the surface of the food or offers a lovely little crunch when encountered by the teeth. Just sprinkle a bit of it or some other comparable salt on top of the steak before it hits the table.

Fats and Oils: Never Cease with the Grease

Another question that often comes up with steak is, do you need to use butter or oil in the pan or on the grill when cooking? The answer is largely a matter of preference and depends on the method of cooking.

On the grill: Many people spray the grates with oil before throwing on the meat. An easier solution is to rub a little cooking oil over the meat before putting it on the grill. You get more thorough coverage of the meat, and the oil acts as a conductor of heat to help the steaks cook more quickly and evenly. Just remember that when preparing the grill, always scrape down the grates with a grill brush before cooking and then put a little oil on a folded paper towel and, using tongs, wipe down the grates.

In the pan: For the same reasons just cited, it's a good idea either to coat the meat with oil or to put a little oil in the pan. An elegant solution is to use the meat's own natural fat. If you have a thick ribeye with a fat cap on one side, place it on its fatty side in a hot pan to render out some of the fat. When you have enough melted fat to cover the pan, turn the steak on its flat side and begin cooking.

What about finishing the steak? Should you use butter or oil at the end? That's a matter of preference, but it never hurts. Butter can be a strong flavor, but it goes well with salt and protein and certainly improves bland meat. For pan-cooked steaks, many chefs toss in a few pats of butter along with garlic and thyme and finish the steak by pan basting the seasoned, melted butter over the meat for a minute or two before plating and cutting. For his part, Jordan loves the Italian practice of dousing the cut meat with a generous drizzle of fine extra-virgin olive oil, which gives it wonderful richness and a hint of flavor. A good olive oil can be sweet, nutty, slightly bitter—all flavors that accent the steak beautifully. And as the juice from the steak runs into the platter and commingles with the oil, you get the most delicious little liquid for dipping meat, bread, whatever into as you mop up the scraps.

Sometimes it all boils down to family tradition (Aaron's father's cold butter baste, for example).

Does Steak Need to be at Room Temperature before Cooking?

For decades—generations, maybe—one of the primary instructions in any steak recipe was to let the meat come to room temperature before cooking. Recipes would usually call for the steaks to be removed from the refrigerator twenty to thirty minutes before cooking to ensure they cooked more evenly and quickly. But we're here to tell you this is baloney. There are *many* reasons why this is bad advice for steak.

Let's start with the obvious: twenty to thirty minutes is a joke. A half hour is not enough time to let the meat warm by two degrees, let alone thirty degrees (the difference between your fridge and room temperature). Actually, it will take several *hours* for a steak to get up to room temperature. Those hours sound great if you're a bacteria or a fly trying to get some of that juicy raw meat! Sorry, we don't mean to be alarmist, and your meat is probably fine if you do let it sit out. If we were talking about a large hunk of meat like a pork roast or a brisket, a few hours at room temperature isn't a bad idea (though the relentlessly cautious USDA would frown), considering how long it takes to cook and the risk of overcooking the outside by the time the inside comes to temperature. But this isn't really relevant when it comes to small cuts like steak.

We're going to go way against common wisdom here and say that *sometimes* you want the steak to be cold when you cook it. This is especially true for a very thin cut, where the trick is keeping the inside at medium-rare while producing a good crust. The colder the meat to begin with, the longer it will take to heat up, giving you the time to brown the exterior properly. Thick steaks (an inch and a half to two and a half inches) are another question. There, the challenge is getting the interior done enough in the relatively short time it takes to build a deep crust.

Basically, unless you want to leave your steak out for hours and hours, you're going to be cooking it with some chill on it from the fridge. Guess what? That's what almost all restaurants do. They can't have raw meat sitting around at room temperature all day, and the chill helps with thin steaks anyway. Whether or not you've tempered your steaks or are cooking them straight from the chill, the point is to be aware of the temperature of the meat when you put it on. As the exterior begins to sizzle, visualize what's happening with the cold meat internally. Understanding the temperature of the meat and cooking accordingly is much more important than having it at a certain temperature before your start.

The Tyranny of Grill Marks and the Myth of the One-Time Flip

In the past, in magazine photos, ads, and television shows, that crosshatched pattern of dark, charred grill marks was the hallmark of a perfectly juicy steak right off the grill. The thinking on that has changed, and nowadays we recoil with horror at the sight of conventional grill marks. Why? Grill marks indicate a delicious Maillardian crust, so why limit that tastiness to just a small portion of the steak's total surface? Go for the all-over crust—that's where the flavor is! Of course, the danger in going for the all-over crust is that the area where the bars of the grill touched the meat becomes not just crust but also bitter, blackened, burned char. So the grill marks can sometimes become a flaw, not a symbol of success.

Combatting this requires denying another steak myth, one that chefs continue to perpetuate today: the one-time flip. That's when you put a steak on the fire or in a pan, you don't turn it for a set number of minutes, and then you turn it only once. Although this is a good way to get dark grill marks, it is not a good way to create a crust. Science has even debunked it. As food-science writer Harold McGee told the *New York Times*, "It's true that frequent flipping cooks the meat more evenly, and also significantly faster: flip every minute instead of once or twice and the meat will be done in a third less time. This works because neither side has time to absorb a lot of heat when facing the fire or to lose heat when facing away. You don't get neat grill marks or the best char this way, but with high enough heat, the surface develops plenty of flavor."

To Rest or Not to Rest?

The advice to rest a piece of meat after it comes off the heat falls into the same category as advice about tempering the meat and flipping it only once: it's old-school, it's the way both of us were taught to do it, and its importance might be greatly exaggerated.

Now, we're not telling you to skip resting and just cut into the meat immediately. But we don't think we need to convince you that it's better to eat hot steak than lukewarm steak!

We tested the question of resting on five steaks, each weighed before and after cooking as well

---

FROZEN

A few years ago, the food magazine *Cook's Illustrated* published a piece that began, "Rather than follow the convention of thawing frozen steaks before grilling them, we discovered that we could get steaks that were just as juicy by cooking them straight from the freezer." Not surprisingly, given how catchy notions spread on the Internet, that content was seized and amplified by various webzines, producing articles with titles like "Want the Best Steak of Your Life? Don't Thaw the Steaks before Cooking Them" and "Why You Should Never Thaw Frozen Steaks before Cooking Them."

Even we, anti-tempering evangelists that we are, were dubious of this advice. But we tested it out (yay, science!), taking a frozen steak and throwing it on a hot grill to get a sear and then finishing it in the oven at 275°F, just as the magazine directed. And, yes, it worked. Eventually. The steak took quite a while in the oven to cook to medium-rare. Visually, it appeared okay. And the internal temperature signaled that it was cooked properly. But then, when we tasted the meat, we were not impressed. The texture was tough and chewy, the flavor muted and dull. In short, it tasted like a steak that had been frozen just moments before. Yes, you can cook a steak this way. But why would you do that to a good piece of meat?

as after resting and after cutting. The steaks were rested for 0, 5, 10, 15, and 20 minutes. The results were telling and clear. The steak that was unrested lost three times the amount (by percentage) of liquid than the rested steaks lost—no good. The steak that rested for 20 minutes lost the least amount of juice. But—and here's where we get sciency again—the amount lost wasn't statistically much more than the steak rested for 5 minutes. So our advice is, for normal steaks more than one inch thick, between 3 and 5 minutes should be sufficient. Thicker pieces of meat need more time to rest—closer to 15 minutes or even more. These you can keep warm by loosely covering with a piece of aluminum foil. Steaks that have been reverse seared are cooked so gently that the temperature is quite uniform and the juices are well distributed, so 1 to 2 minutes off the heat is sufficient. If you can touch it, you should slice it.

Choose Your Own Adventure, Steak-Cook Edition

How you cook your steak obviously depends on what steak you are cooking, and we'll get into that, don't worry (see page 172). But for now, we're going to use thick-cut (one inch and above) steaks like ribeyes or strips as a control group to help you decide which method is right for you.

HOT AND FAST

This is the basic way to cook a steak—starting hot and just going for it. It's obvious, and you can do it on the stove top or on a grill.

On the stove top, you can set up only two zones: the high heat of a cast-iron or steel pan over the burner and a preheated oven at 250°F. On the grill, you can set up two or three zones, depending on your needs (sometimes that third zone is great for slow cooking a steak).

Pros

This is hands-down the easiest way to cook a steak. It requires almost no forethought or preparation to execute. This makes it effective when you've done no planning or preparation and just want a steak and want it now. Sometimes this happens.

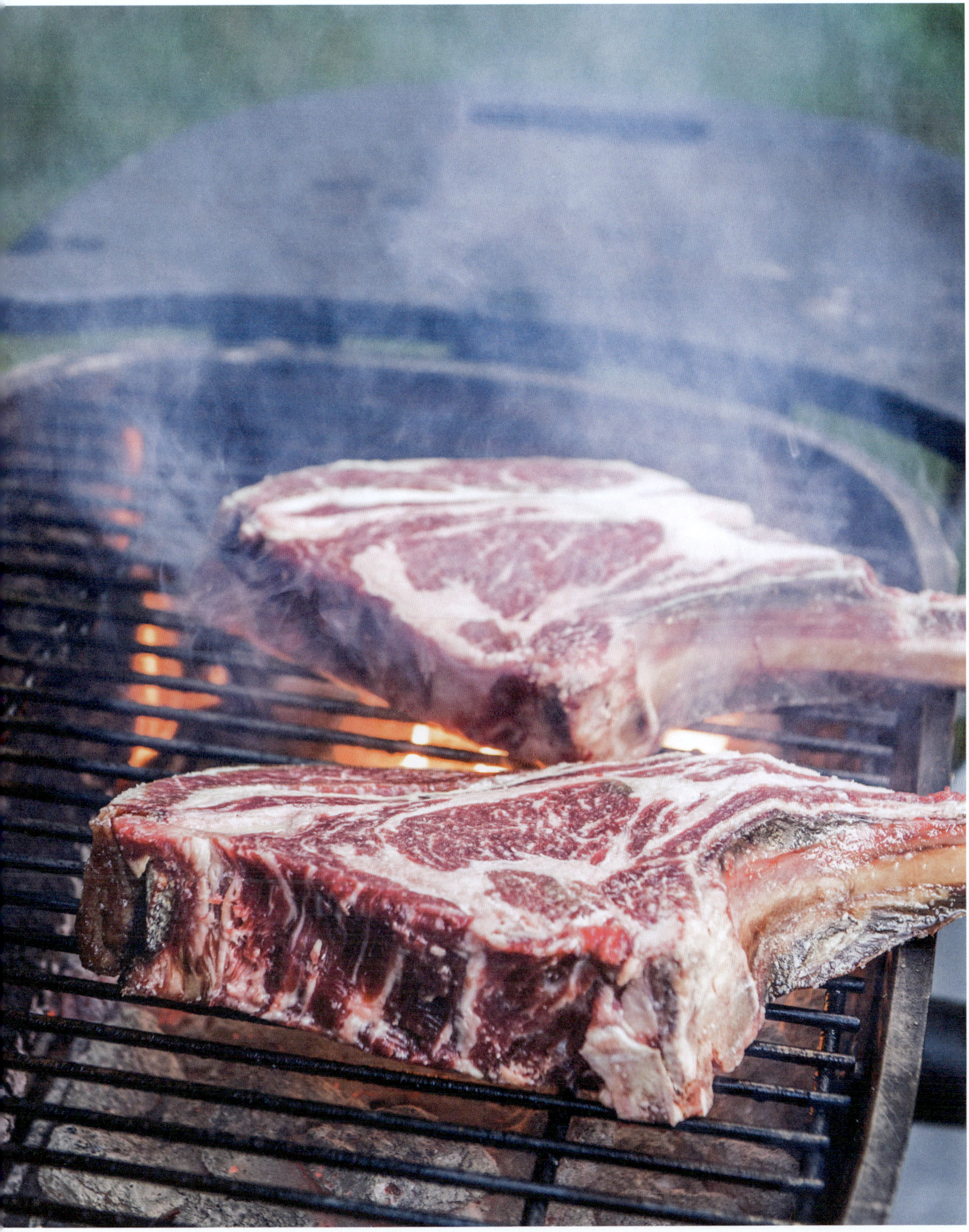

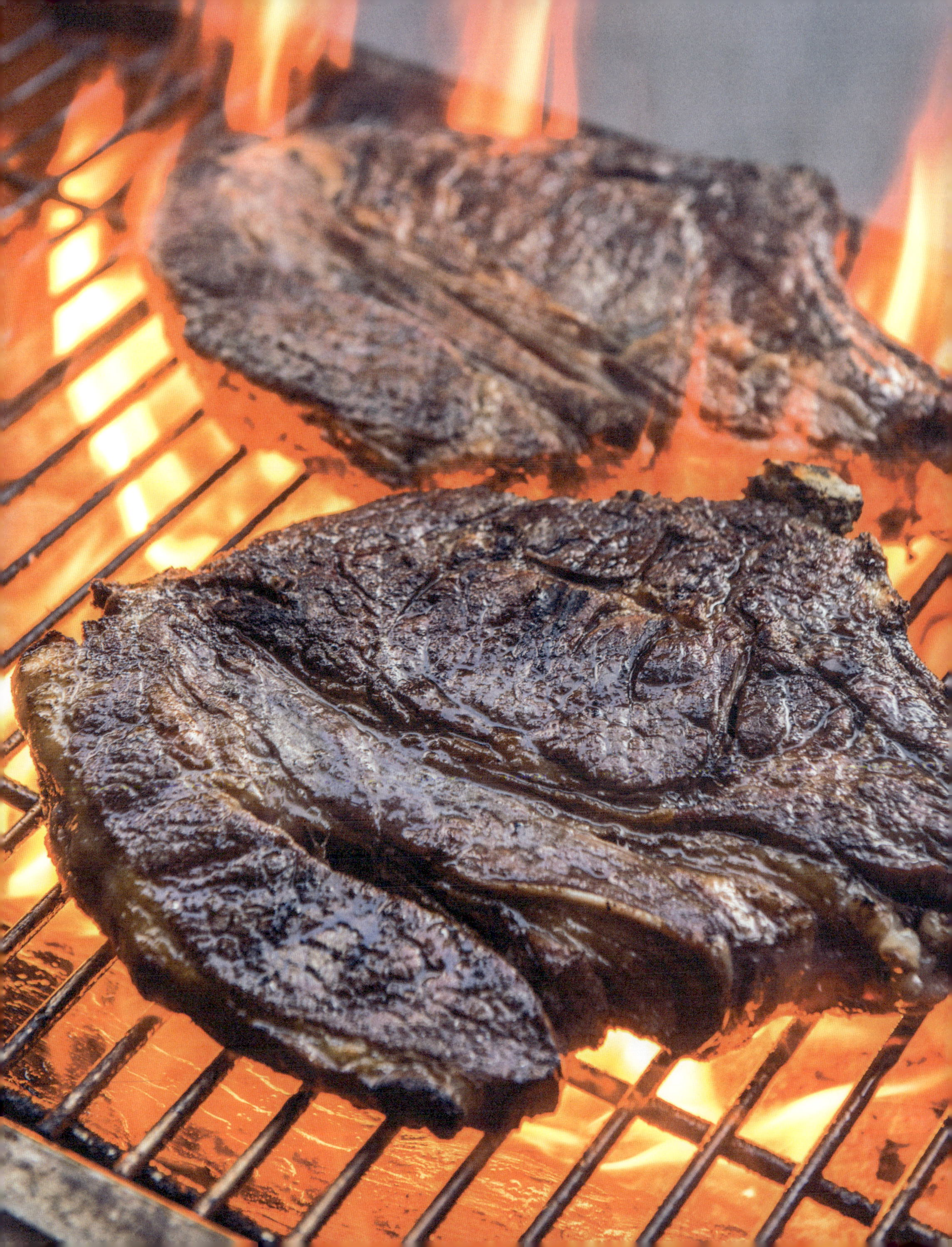

Cons

You run the greatest risk of overcooking the meat. By searing and browning the outside first, you're introducing a lot of heat to the steak right off the bat, and it's hard to go back once the thing is heated.

How to Do It

1. Ideally at least 4 hours before the cook, season the steaks generously with salt and keep them, uncovered, in the fridge. If you're cooking on the stove top, preheat the oven to 250°F and heat a cast-iron or steel skillet over high heat. If you're grilling, build a nice, glowing-hot coal bed in your grill using one of the grill setups on pages 147 to 150. The target temperature is 400°F for the direct-heat zone and around 250°F for the indirect-heat zone. Thoroughly dry the surface of the meat with paper towels and lightly apply some neutral oil with a high smoke point (like grape seed oil).

2. When the pan reaches 350°F to 400°F (a few drops of water flicked onto the surface should evaporate in 2 to 3 seconds) or the grill fire reaches its target temperatures, add the meat to the skillet or grill (do *not* cover the grill). Move the meat regularly and flip every 30 to 60 seconds to develop a nice brown crust. The color you want is a nice dark brown with orange and red tones to it. Don't let it blacken. If it does, take it off immediately!

3. When the crust has been achieved, move the meat to the cooler zone. This will be after 3 to 5 minutes per side (depending on the temperature of both the beef and the fire), or if you're moving the meat and flipping often, a total of about 10 minutes. Indoors, this would mean transferring the steak to the oven (transfer the meat to a sheet pan if you don't want the exterior to keep cooking) to finish in the preheated oven. On the grill, this would mean moving the steak onto the cool side of the two-zone setup.

4. Using a digital thermometer, keep track of the internal temperature of the meat and pull it when it is 10 degrees shy of your desired doneness temperature. Depending on the thickness of the steaks, this can take anywhere from 6 to 12 minutes.

5. Let the meat rest for a few minutes on the counter away from a breeze to allow the temperature to equalize throughout the interior. If you don't want the meat to cool too quickly or you're working in a cold room, cover it with aluminum foil. Slice (against the grain) and serve.

REVERSE SEAR

The term *reverse sear* was coined sometime in the last fifteen years, but in northern Spain they just call it "how we've always been cooking steak for as long as we can remember." And the grill cooks of northern Spain know what they're doing when it comes to steak (see page 131).

Pros

The reverse sear is the most foolproof and practical way to cook a thick steak perfectly, and is especially popular in restaurant kitchens. When you cook the interior slowly and methodically, it ends up consistent. You don't have the thick band of overcooked meat that conventional hot-and-fast cooking often leaves. By slow cooking the meat first, you dry off the surface, so the Maillard reactions will happen faster and more fully than with a steak with some moisture. What's more, you end up with seemingly impossible tenderness. That's because slow cooking allows native enzymes in the steak to go to work

THE COOK

breaking down some of the muscle fiber, leaving a wonderfully silky texture.

Cons

There are two reasons why this isn't the most convenient method. The first is effort. It's not hard to preheat an oven and a pan in a kitchen. But getting your grill set up properly (if you're using a baffle) takes a little effort and forethought, and making sure the cool zone is holding a low temperature (200°F to 225°F is ideal) takes skill and experience.

The other major cost of the reverse sear is time. It just takes longer to cook your steak this way. A big piece of meat can take hours to get to doneness; then, you have to rest the meat for quite a while before searing. If you have plenty of time, though, you can cook your steak at a superlow temp (sometimes Aaron goes as low as 170°F), ensuring a beautifully precise cook. Your time is well served by the superiority of the meat, and patience and time become much easier if you have a cold beer in hand and some good company!

How to Do It

1. Ideally at least 4 hours before the cook, season the steaks generously with salt and keep them, uncovered, in the fridge. If you're cooking on the stovetop, preheat the oven to 200°F. If you're grilling, build a small- to moderate-size coal bed in your grill using one of the grill setups on pages 147 to 150. The target temperature is around 200°F for the indirect-heat zone. You'll build the fire back up to blazing hot for the sear later. Thoroughly dry the surface of the meat with paper towels.

Important Note • When doing the reverse sear on a grill, it's important to protect the meat from the high heat of the coal bed. Even given the rectangular shape of the PK Grill, one edge of the steaks will be closer to the coals than the other, and there's a risk of overcooking that side. Therefore, in order to truly protect the cooler side from the coals, there are a couple of solutions. You can put a piece of metal between the two sides of the grill as a baffle. This is where a small sheet pan or sizzle plate comes in handy. Or you can throw a small stainless-steel bowl on the grate over the steaks, protecting them from the direct radiative heat.

Another Important Note • To reverse sear on a closed grill, the heat must be kept low. It's very easy to overload the grill. Even one extra piping-hot briquette can make a huge difference in temperature. For this, you have to know your cooker and how much fuel is required to take it to 200°F for what will be *at least* a 20-minute cook, sometimes much longer. For a well-insulated cooker like a PK, that might be, say, six or seven briquettes. For a Big Green Egg, it may be fewer. For a thin, steel Weber, it may take a few more. The point is, be careful. If it's too high, the steaks may dry out on the outside before reaching the desired internal temperature.

2. Remove the steaks from the refrigerator. If cooking in the oven, place the steaks on a rack set over a pan (this is so the meat isn't in contact with the metal of the pan). Alternatively, add the steaks to the indirect-heat side of the grill and *cover* the grill. Because you'll be grilling with the lid closed, it's important to keep track of the heat level, making sure it remains at the target temperature. If the coal bed proves too large and the temperature keeps creeping up, open the lid frequently to let heat escape. Do not move or flip the steaks.

3. Using a digital thermometer, keep track of the internal temperature of the meat and pull it when it is at least 10 degrees shy of your desired doneness temperature. Depending on the thickness of the steaks, this can take anywhere from 20 to 45 minutes—or hours for a giant, bone-in steak. But give it time, as the low temperature allows the meat to cook evenly all the way through. When the steaks are finished with this stage, they won't look appealing; they'll be in good shape for the final cooking in the next step, however. Incidentally, when they've reached that desired internal temperature, you can pull them from the fire and let them hang out for 30 to 60 minutes while you build up heat for the next step. (Actually, you could rest them up to 3 hours—it's important to rest before searing.)

4. If cooking on the stove top, preheat a cast-iron or steel skillet over high heat until it's blazing hot (400°F to 500°F, or when a drop of water will instantly vaporize). Make sure the meat is dry, then rub it with a little oil before adding it to the skillet. On a grill, you'll need to build up your fire in the direct-heat zone. After pulling the steaks, keep the lid open and rustle the coals to get them glowing hot again or add more lit coals if needed. Coat the steaks with a little neutral oil (like grape seed oil), then put them to the fire. Move the meat regularly and flip every 30 seconds or so to develop a nice brown crust. The color you want is a nice dark brown with ocher and red tones to it. This should take 1 to 2 minutes per side, regardless of the thickness of the steaks.

5. Let rest briefly—only a minute or two, as slow cooking allows for even temperature distribution throughout the meat, which is usually the goal of resting. Slice (against the grain) and serve.

STEAK ON THE COALS

If the reverse sear seems overly complicated to you, here's an approach that couldn't be simpler. Go caveman style and ditch the grill and the grates and forget about the two zones. Nothing could be more basic and primitive than this: just throw the steak on the coals. If that sounds crazy, it sort of is. But it's also a leap of faith—kind of like when Tony Robbins gets people to walk barefoot over hot coals as a self-confidence exercise. But with this, instead of having (ideally) perfectly unseared, uncooked feet, you get perfectly seared and cooked steak. And it can really boost your steak confidence!

Yes, there's sensible theory behind just throwing your steaks onto coals that are over 1000°F. When the steak is in direct contact with hot coals, it is indeed conducting that heat. However, meat, which is 75 percent water, and fat are not good heat conductors, so the steak cooks relatively slowly. In addition, because the meat sits right on the hot coals, there is no room for air and, therefore, no fire, as flames can't exist without oxygen. The result is that meat can be seared and cooked even when thrown into the fire.

Pros

There's an appeal in this most primal, basic, simple way to cook meat. Cavemen might have even had more sophisticated methods. So some people love this technique for its simplicity and for the smoky, charry way it makes the steaks taste. It's also impresses guests and saves on cleanup time—no scrubbing down the grill.

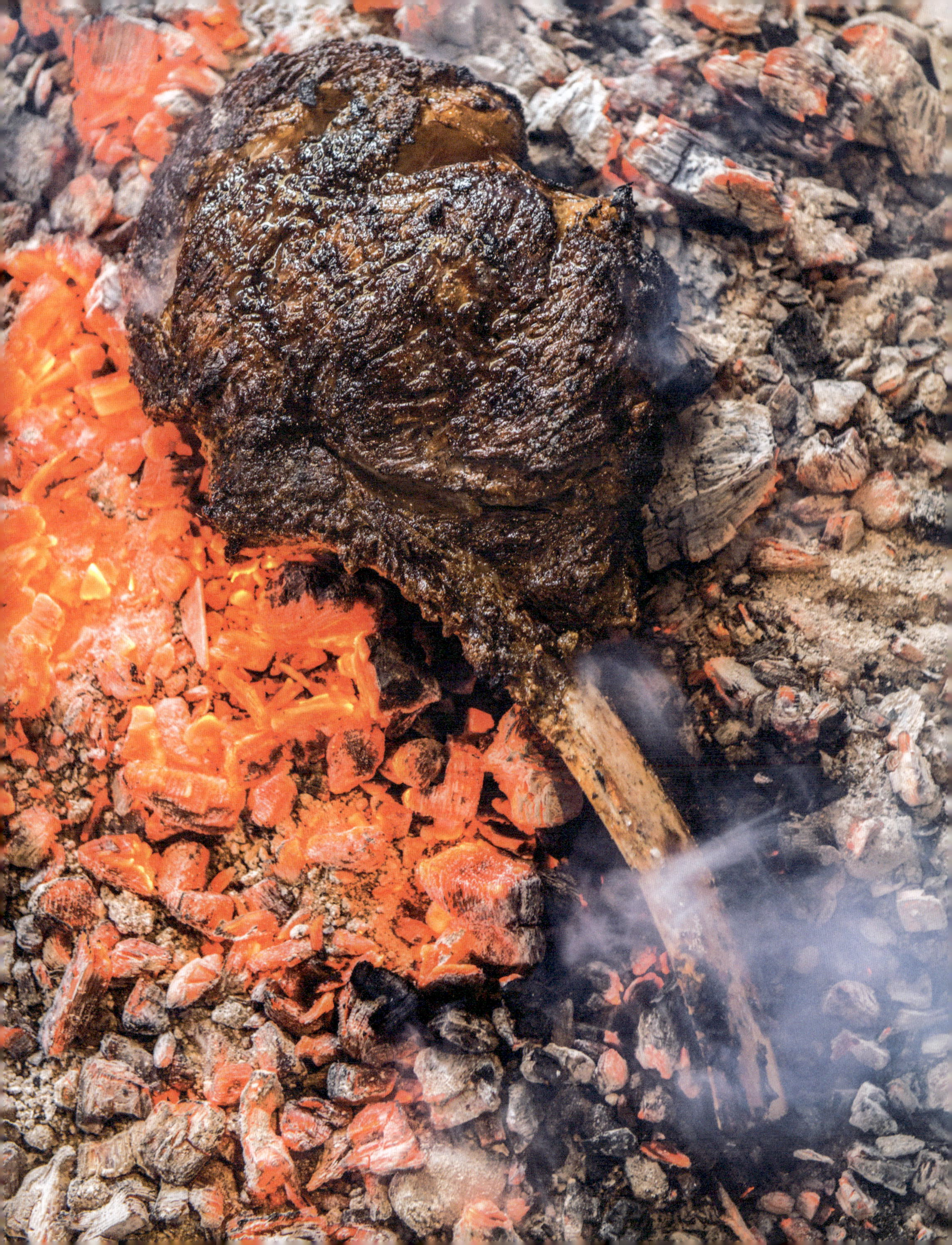

Cons

Often the taste of coal-cooked meat has a somewhat charred, earthy, ashy note that may even include a few bitter bites here and there. Nothing is wrong with this, and, like we said, some people enjoy it. But we happen not to love it. Also, the exterior doesn't cook terribly evenly, meaning it's downright difficult if not impossible to achieve that lovely all-over Maillardian crust.

How to Do It

1. Ideally at least 4 hours before the cook, season the steaks generously with salt. If working with steaks an inch thick, it's a good idea to temper them for at least an hour or so, to bring up the internal temperature, as they'll cook quickly on the coals. And if your steak is more than 1½ inches thick, before throwing it on the fire, you may want to reverse sear it (see steps 1 through 3, pages 166 to 167) in a 200°F oven to 15 degrees below your desired temperature. This step is optional.

2. Build a nice, glowing-hot coal bed using lump hardwood charcoal or real wood coals. Do not use briquettes because of their impurities. The coal bed must be large enough so that when you turn the steaks in step 4, you can turn them onto fresh coals. It's better than returning them to the same coals.

3. When the coals are at peak heat—glowing orange, not emitting flames, and covered lightly with ash—blow (or fan) all of the ash off of them. They will have reached anywhere from 900°F to 1100°F, so be careful and don't burn yourself!

4. When you're ready to cook, don't oil the steaks first, as that introduces a flammable substance. Dry them with paper towels and then, using tongs, nestle the steak into a flat bed of coals, trying not to leave any major air gaps. Cook without disturbing for 3 to 5 minutes on the first side (this depends, of course, on the thickness of the steak), then flip the steaks onto a fresh section of coals. If you smell burning meat (not searing but burning), you know it's time to flip. Cook the second side for another 3 to 5 minutes.

5. Using a digital thermometer, keep track of the internal temperature of the meat and pull it when it is about 15 degrees of your desired doneness temperature. There may be some small coals or a little ash clinging to the steak. This is not a problem. Simply brush them off with the tongs.

6. Let the meat rest for a few minutes on the counter away from a breeze to allow the temperature to equalize throughout the interior. If you don't want the meat to cool too quickly or you're working in a cold room, cover it with aluminum foil. Slice (against the grain) and serve.

BLAST FURNACE STEAK

Here's another technique that has surfaced in the last several years, bubbling up from the ranks of steak obsessives who are always trying to find new ways to blast their meat with ever-increasing amounts of heat. The tradition of cooking steaks with brutally, almost comically high heat is not a new one. In the Midwest and Mid-Atlantic, the old term *Pittsburgh rare* exists for a steak that has been heavily charred on the outside but remains rare or, more likely, raw on the inside. This comes from the fact that steel workers in Pittsburgh were known to throw steaks into the iron-smelting furnaces that operated at over 2000°F. The story goes that they rarely had much time for lunch and needed high-energy food for their grueling work. The steak would go into the furnace (sometimes slapped onto the side wall), would be turned after a number of seconds,

THE COOK

169

cooked a little longer, and then removed. This is just a slightly more extreme version of Aaron cooking steaks on a shovel in the 700°F coals of his offset smoker's firebox, which he used to do occasionally for dinner when he'd be up all night on a long cook and the brisket wouldn't be coming off for twelve hours.

In the event that you don't keep a roaring blast furnace or lit firebox regularly going at home, the way that's become popular to blaze steaks with potent flames is to cook them directly over the charcoal chimney. It's true that the chimney works by insulating and concentrating the heat of a few coals to get a larger amount lit. As you know, when it comes to temperature, the chimney gives off wisps of powerful red and blue fire and brings coals to a brilliant, glowing orange state. Why not harness that heat for searing steak?

This technique works best with steaks less than an inch thick. Any thicker and there's simply not enough time to cook the interior before the exterior carbonizes. It's great with thin, tougher cuts that are better with rare interiors, such as flank and outside skirt.

Pros

Superheated coals concentrated in the chimney cook the outside of the steak in a jiffy before too much heat can work its way to the interior, making it perfect for a high-contrast sear along with rare meat in the center. Also, you don't have to set up the grill and cleanup is minimal.

Cons

Try this technique at your own risk. Some people love it, but in our experience, the risks of ending up with a bitter, overcharred steak is high.

THICKNESS VERSUS WEIGHT

Despite what you may have heard, when deciding how long to cook your steaks, thickness has a much greater impact on the cooking time than weight. A two-pound steak that's only one inch thick will cook considerably faster than a one-pound steak that is two inches thick.

- The intuitive sense would be to cook thinner cuts, like skirt steaks or even thinly cut T-bones or ribeyes, over lower heat because they are more delicate. And conversely, to cook thick cuts over massive high heat because they can take it. In fact, the opposite is true. It's better to cook thin cuts very quickly over high heat.

- With thin cuts, you don't have to be concerned about the level of doneness inside, as the heat used to cook the outside will quickly penetrate to the heart of the meat. Thick cuts do better with reverse sear, hot and fast on the stove top, and two- and three-zone setups. Thinner cuts do better with direct sear, direct on coals, and blast furnace.

How to Do It

1. Ideally at least 4 hours before the cook, season the steaks generously with salt and keep them, uncovered, in the fridge. If your steaks are more than ¾ inch thick, before throwing them on the fire, you may want to reverse sear them (see steps 1 through 3, pages 166 to 167) in a 200°F oven to 15 degrees below your desired doneness temperature.

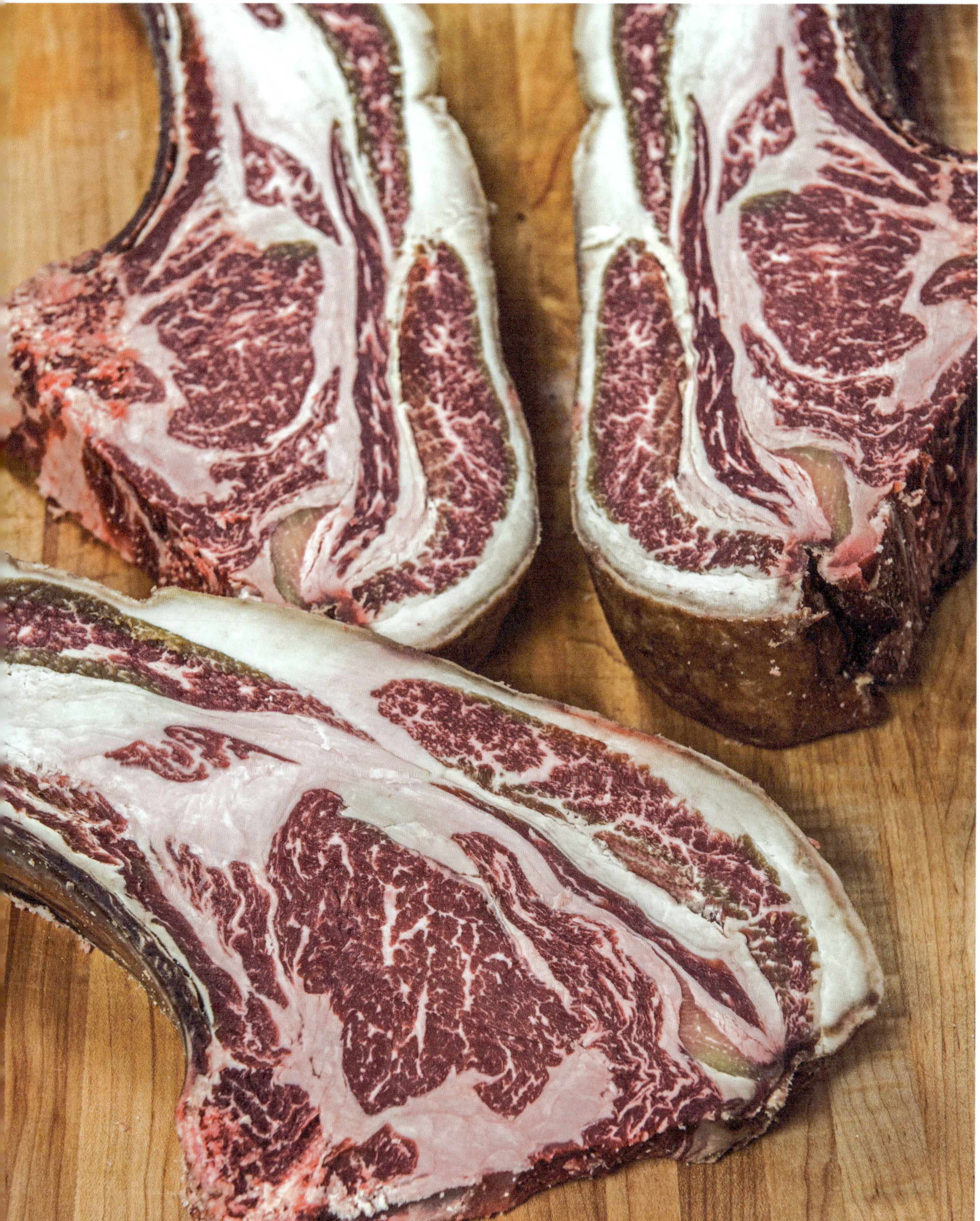

2. Heat a charcoal chimney following the instructions on page 142. Thoroughly dry the surface of the meat with paper towels and lightly apply some neutral oil with a high smoke point (like grape seed oil).

3. When the charcoal is glowing hot and emitting tongues of orange flame, put a thick metal grate over the top of the chimney and put the steak on the grate. Make sure the whole setup thing is steady and not out of balance. The charcoal heat will instantly start sizzling the surface of the steak, and flames may leap up to lick the meat. Flip and move the steak often so no side starts to burn until you get a nice all-over deep brown crust. About 1½ minutes per side should do it.

4. Let the meat rest for only a minute or two or, for a thinner steak, slice immediately (against the grain) on a cutting board that captures the juices, then serve.

The Steak-Cut Decision Tree

You now know literally everything you could possibly know about every permutation of grill setups and cooking methods that will yield a perfect steak. But the one thing we have not discussed is which setups and methods are most appropriate for each cut and type of steak. You didn't think we'd forget that important variable, did you?

- **Grass-fed and other very lean steaks** • Despite the fact that the great grass-fed beef producers like Alderspring and First Light make wonderfully marbled meat, most grass-fed beef you'll find will be leaner than grain fed and will thus require a more attentive style of cooking. The extra fat and marbling in grain fed serves to insulate the leaner sections, as the fat conducts heat more slowly and absorbs the heat first, melting and extending the cooking process. With less fat, grass-fed meat cooks about 30 percent faster. Grass-fed cattle also move more over the course of their whole lives than grain-fed cattle do, so their muscles have worked more and thus can be tougher.

  Tough grass-fed steaks come from too much high heat, which causes the muscle fibers to tense and squeeze out their moisture. And without much fat content to slow things down, the meat can turn tough in an instant. So sear the exteriors of the steaks hot, but then finish at temperatures up to fifty degrees lower than for grain-fed meat, and only to the rarer side of medium-rare or even to rare or bloody; carryover cooking after removal from the heat is more extreme in grass-fed steaks. This is how the French and Italians tend to eat their steaks, which are usually much leaner than American beef. Hot and fast and reverse sear work great, but avoid direct on the coals and blast furnace.

- **Fatty cuts** • Fat is forgiving when it comes to cooking steaks. It begins melting at a lower temperature than water boils, buffering and lubricating the flesh. In general, fatty steaks can be cooked faster and longer than lean ones, though you will still want to pay close attention to temperatures and doneness. For instance, a well-marbled ribeye can take longer and more extreme heat than a typically lean tenderloin, which needs to be cooked more gently. All methods will work well, so use the thickness of the steak to determine which one. Thicker steaks will demand reverse sear or hot and fast with oven finishing, while thinner steaks can't take on-the-coals or blast-furnace heat.

- **Dry-aged meat** • There is no special method for cooking dry-aged steaks. The process is pretty much in line with standard steak cooking. However, there are a couple of factors you may want to consider. One is flavor. Dry-aged meat has a particular funky flavor, which can be powerful or mild depending on the length and intensity of the aging process. To preserve and highlight the flavor of age, many people who dry age meat prefer to cook it in as neutral a way as possible—in a pan with a little neutral oil or butter. The thinking is that the smoke and charcoal seasoning from the grill can overpower the flavor of an already estimable piece of meat.

As far as cooking dry-aged meat, just remember that a well-aged steak (forty-five days or more) may have lost 20 to 30 percent of its water volume. That doesn't mean it will dry out in the pan or on the grill (that extra water in an unaged steak typically evaporates during cooking). But it does mean that it's a denser piece, with only protein and fat to conduct the heat, which means a slower process. Our recommendation is to be patient and cook rather slowly to let the heat move evenly through the interior. The meat will also be more tender thanks to the enzymatic action during aging, so don't go above rare to medium-rare, as the steak already is at its textural peak. Try cast iron on the stove top for the full-on unadulterated flavor of dry aging. But if you're interested in the pairing of smoke and dry-age funk, try Aaron's Franklin Formation (see page 148).

For more specific guidance on how to cook various cuts and styles of steak, refer to the How to Cook Steak flow chart on pages 214 and 215.

THE COOK

173

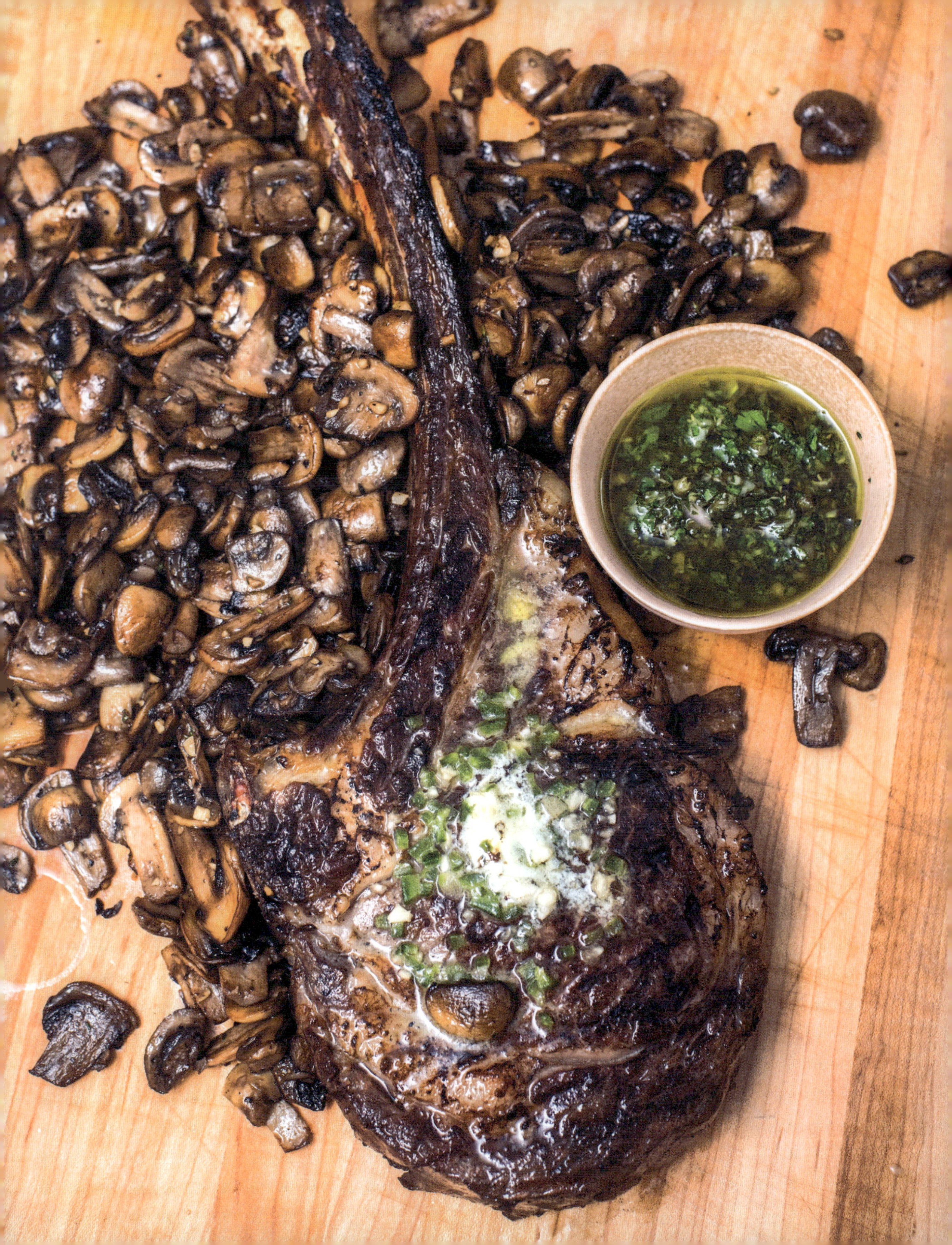

CHAPTER 9

Sides, Sauces, and Drinks

As a kid, Aaron's favorite meals were definitely when his dad would cook steaks at home. But for some reason, the things that really stick out in his mind about those meals was eating iceberg lettuce drenched in ranch dressing and a baked potato with the insides saturated with butter and salt. The steaks were always good, but he remembers loving the sides just as much.

It's a weird thing that way. No one would ever dispute the idea that the most important part of a steak dinner is the steak. Yet many of us carry a surprising fondness and longing for the nonmeat dishes we ate alongside the steak. And if some of us dig deeply enough into our memories, we may even have a revelation that the sides were our favorite part of the meal.

To this day, Jordan doesn't want to eat steak if he can't have a simple green salad with vinaigrette beside it (or at least a crunchy, tangy Caesar salad before it). Something about the interplay between the rich, fatty steak and the cutting acidity and crunch of the salad makes the combination nonnegotiable. Potatoes are a fixture in his memory, too, though he doesn't so much remember baked ones as he does the classic French pairing of crispy, golden fries and steak at such Parisian bistros as Le Severo (see facing page), where Jordan also recalls ordering a second side of sautéed chanterelle mushrooms (see page 180) because the first one was so good.

Steak is a wonderful canvas for fresh produce at its peak. Jordan wistfully recalls the childhood pleasures of charcoal-grilled steaks beside butter-slathered summer corn on the cob, with the sweet corn the perfect foil for the salty, savory steak. Aaron thinks about all the times he's had a fresh tomato salad with succulent bavette, their juices commingling on the plate.

Why, when you have all of this great, expensive meat, are sides so important—so desirable? Maybe the meat is more intense than we realize and our perceived appetites for it exceed our actual physical needs. Maybe the sides stand as buffers, foils, and interveners to keep us from eating more meat than we need.

One thing Jordan and Aaron agree on is that at home they *always* prefer a steak-centric meal with the simplest of side dishes. After all, a steak is delicious on its own, and much of the appeal of cooking steaks is that they don't require much prep or work. This isn't Thanksgiving, where we have to burden the table with elaborate sides to compensate for, ahem, innate deficiencies (we're looking at you, roast turkey).

We desire clean, punchy flavors and textures that both complement and contrast with the steak. A simple salad, potatoes, grilled vegetables—that is how a good meal comes together!

When it comes to sauces, the steak you're serving is hopefully so flavorful that no condiment is needed. (Same goes for barbecue, folks.) But sometimes, even if the steak is good, a little lubrication or complementary flavor is welcome. It might be a drizzle of soy sauce, a pat of garlic butter, or a spoonful of a classic béarnaise. But the one sauce Aaron turns to again and again is a salsa verde that can be an ongoing part of your pantry with little effort.

The following recipes for sides might seem comically simple to you. That's because they are! But they're also the things we never get tired of, so please don't be insulted by their inclusion here. They're almost like condiments themselves, the very basic things we eat with steak.

LE SEVERO

**8 rue des Plantes
75014 Paris, France
tel: (+33) 01-45-40-40-91 • lesevero.fr**

If you are in Paris and in the mood for a quintessential *steak-frites* experience, make the short trek out to the sleepy, residential 14th arrondissement to the diminutive bistro Le Severo. Actually, the steak at this quaint, old-school room is not quintessential, as that would suggest a shabby cut of meat. Rather, the steak at Le Severo, run by former butcher William Bernet, is superb: well-selected *côte de boeuf* (thick-cut bone-in ribeye for two) aged between three and five weeks (or shell out for the more-expensive one-hundred-day aged cuts). Other offerings are usually the *faux-filet* (strip steak) and the *onglet* (our hanger).

There is only one cook in the kitchen, yet he turns out immaculate steaks. The French tend to take their steaks *bleu*, which is seared on the outside but raw on the inside. If you prefer a rare medium-rare (as cooked as you'll be able to get), order it *saignant*. The steaks come with reliably crispy, golden *frites*. And don't skip the punchy *salade verte* and a plate of sautéed *girolles* (chanterelle mushrooms). Much of the lengthy wine list is written on chalkboards across one wall, and the wines are usually excellent—pithy, soulful bottles from small, hardworking producers. And this small, hardworking restaurant has only ten tables, so be sure to reserve yours several days in advance.

SIDES, SAUCES, AND DRINKS

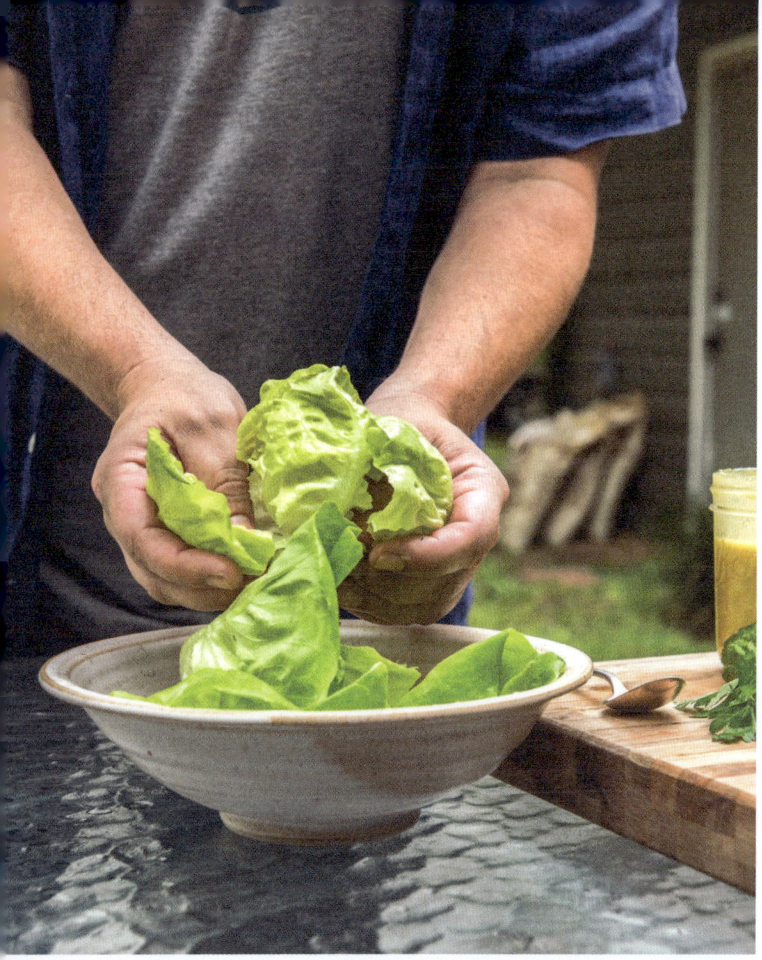
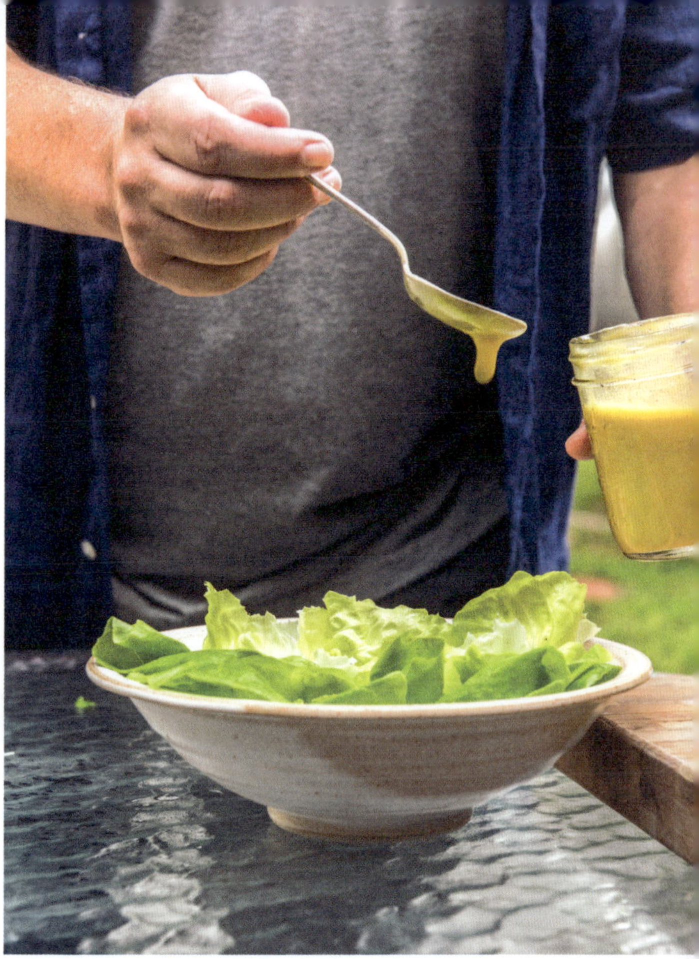
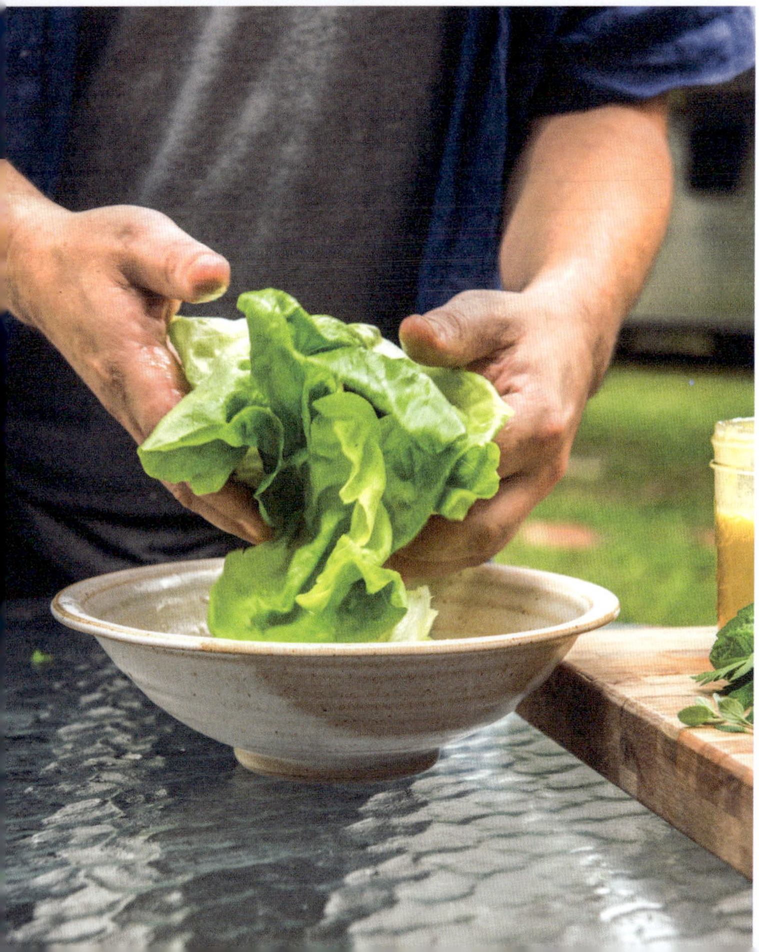
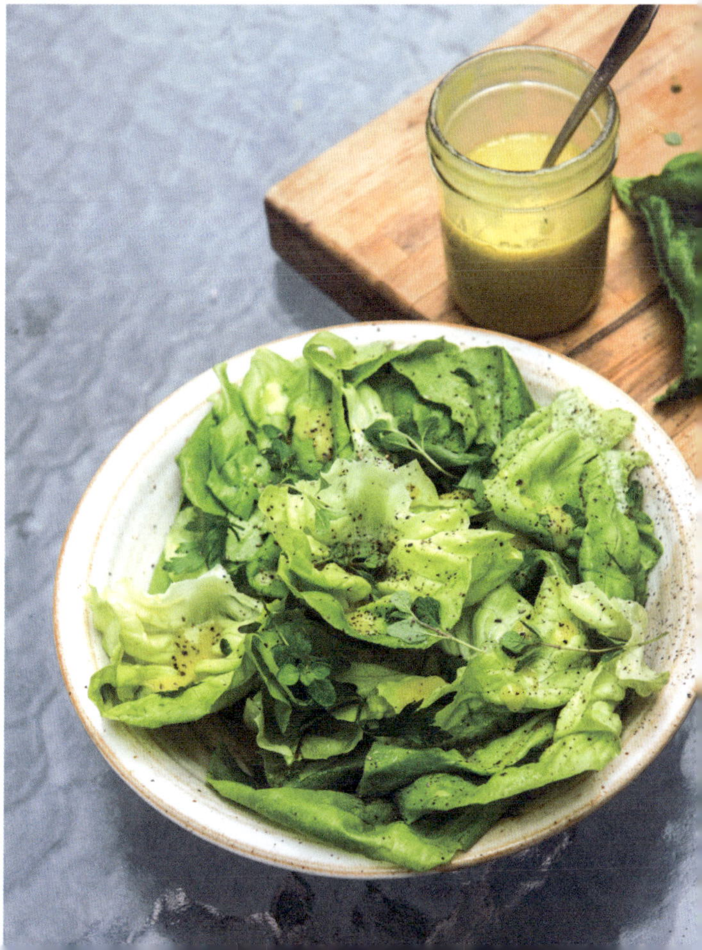

Green Salad with Garlic Vinaigrette

Jordan is a salad fanatic. He goes almost as crazy about finding perfect little heads of crisp baby lettuces—Little Gem, butter, oak leaf—as he does for well-marbled meat. The simple, unadorned green salad—*salade verte*, as the French say—is a remarkable creation unto itself and a brilliant accompaniment to steak. You've probably had the two together countless times, even if you didn't bother to appreciate the brilliance of the pairing. It's all about contrast: the lightness and crispness of the lettuce is a counterpoint to the rich density of the meat, while the tang of vinegar, garlic, and oil keeps the mouth fresh after a heavy bite.

The salad should be both crunchy and silky and be lightly coated with some sort of vinegar-based dressing. Whole leaves from a butter lettuce, their spherical shape intact, or the crunchy interior leaves of a romaine work especially well, but anything fresh and crisp does the trick. A mix of greens is wonderful, too: combine a head each of butter and romaine with the bitter notes of frisée or other chicory. You can serve a few handfuls of the mix and keep the rest in a plastic bag in the refrigerator for the next couple of nights. Adding whole herb leaves—parsley, basil, lovage, mint—is also never a bad idea.

Feel free to embellish your vinaigrette. Finely minced shallot adds a little sweetness and complexity, while herbs such as dried dill contribute a bright, verdant flavor.

SERVES 4 TO 6

1 head butter lettuce, leaves separated

2 cups frisée or chicory leaves (optional)

1 cup mixed fresh herbs (such as parsley, basil, lovage, and mint; optional)

1 tablespoon fresh lemon juice

1 tablespoon champagne vinegar

2 cloves garlic, minced or pressed

1 tablespoon minced shallot (optional)

¼ cup extra-virgin olive oil

1 tablespoon Dijon mustard (not whole grain)

Generous pinch of kosher salt

Small pinch of sugar

Rinse all of the greens carefully and spin them dry in a salad spinner. Chill the leaves in the fridge until ready to serve.

In a small Mason jar with a lid, combine the lemon juice, vinegar, garlic, and shallot and let sit for 10 minutes. Add the oil, mustard, salt, and sugar, cap tightly, and shake vigorously until the vinaigrette emulsifies and is thick and creamy.

Transfer the greens to a large bowl, drizzle with a couple tablespoons of the vinaigrette, and toss until the leaves are lightly and evenly coated, adding more vinaigrette if needed. (Start with a small amount of vinaigrette, as you can always add more. If dressing has pooled in the bottom of the bowl, you've overdressed the salad.) Serve right away.

Garlicky Sautéed Mushrooms

Jordan grew up eating mushrooms alongside steak because that's what his mother always cooked. Scents are powerful agents of memory, so for him the smell of sautéing mushrooms with garlic, butter, salt, and a generous dusting of cracked black pepper is almost inseparable from that of steak. Where did this great pairing come from? His mother says that she does it because her mother did. So where did Grandma get this technique? "It's probably from France," Jordan's mom says. "She took a lot from French cooking." Indeed, Julia Child has a recipe in *Mastering the Art of French Cooking* for *sauté de boeuf à la parisienne* that pairs steak and mushrooms. It calls for whipping cream, Madeira, and beef stock. This dish is infinitely more simple.

Mushrooms are almost a meat substitute. Just like a steak, they brown when they are cooked, lose some water, and develop a dense, savory texture. They're also chock-full of umami, which make them an excellent complement to steak. The mushrooms' function is the opposite of the role of an acidic salad. Instead of acting as a counterpoint, they enhance the steak by doubling down on richness and umami while also adding an earthy flavor.

SERVES 4

2 cups sliced brown cremini mushrooms (5 to 6 ounces), see Note

1 tablespoon unsalted butter

2 cloves garlic, minced or pressed

1 tablespoon extra-virgin olive oil

3 or 4 thyme sprigs

Flaky sea salt and freshly ground black pepper

1 tablespoon chopped fresh flat-leaf parsley

Note • Always buy whole mushrooms and cut them yourself. Baskets of chopped or sliced mushrooms have often been sitting around dehydrating for days in store produce departments. The easiest way to slice a mushroom is to cut a narrow sliver off the bulb to create a flat surface and then lay the mushroom on that flat surface and cut it into as many slices as you please.

Put the butter and the garlic in a cold sauté pan and turn on the heat to medium. Starting off this way allows the garlic to relax and steam a little as the butter releases moisture, keeping the garlic from browning too quickly. As the butter melts, drizzle in the oil. When the butter has melted and mixed with the oil and the garlic is beginning to crackle, add the mushrooms and toss or stir to coat them with the fat. Add the thyme sprigs, turn down the heat to medium-low, and gently sauté the mushrooms until they've reduced by one-third to one-half, about 10 minutes.

Season to taste with salt and with several generous twists of the pepper mill, then remove the long thyme stems and sprinkle with the parsley. Serve a spoonful of mushrooms on top of or just alongside each steak.

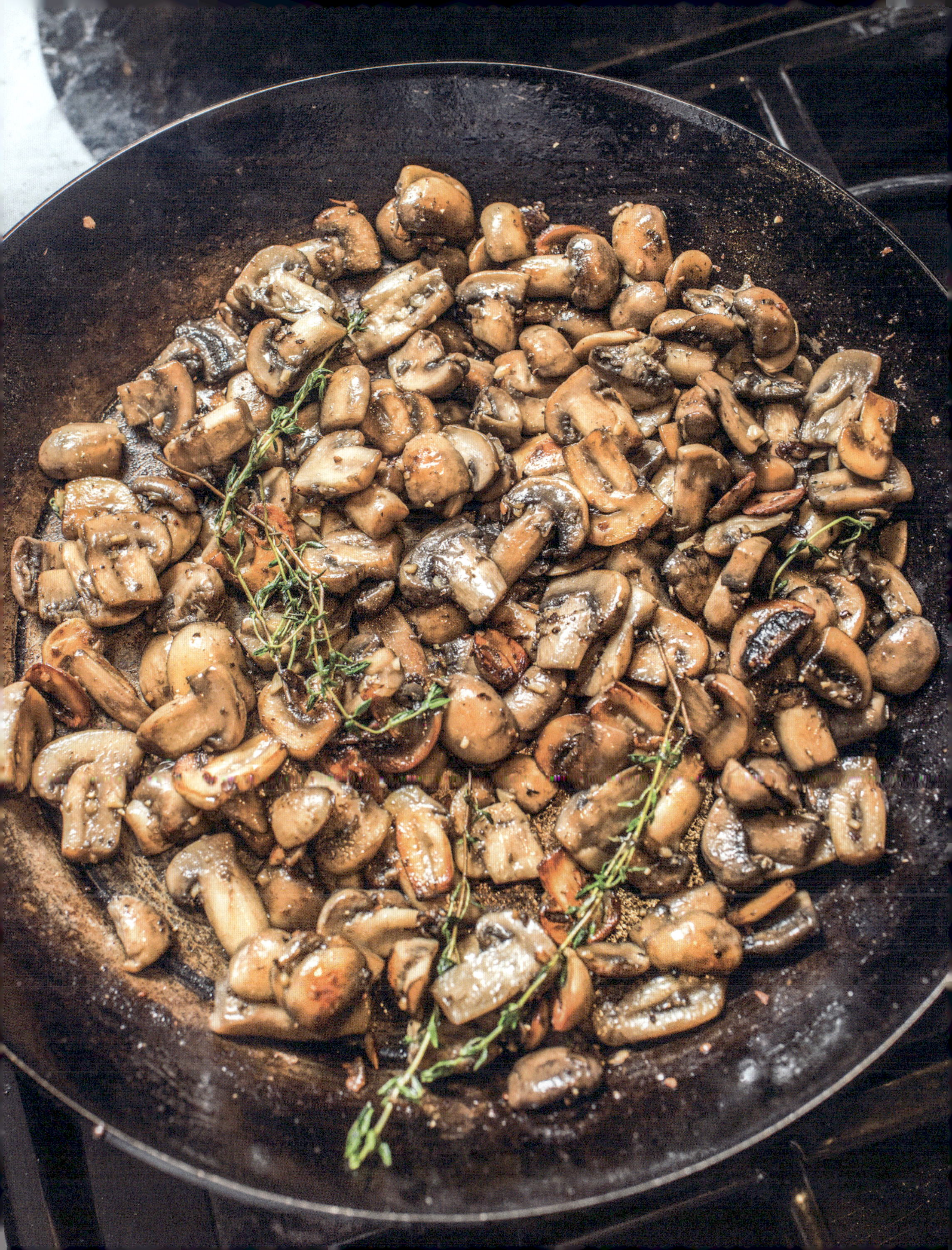

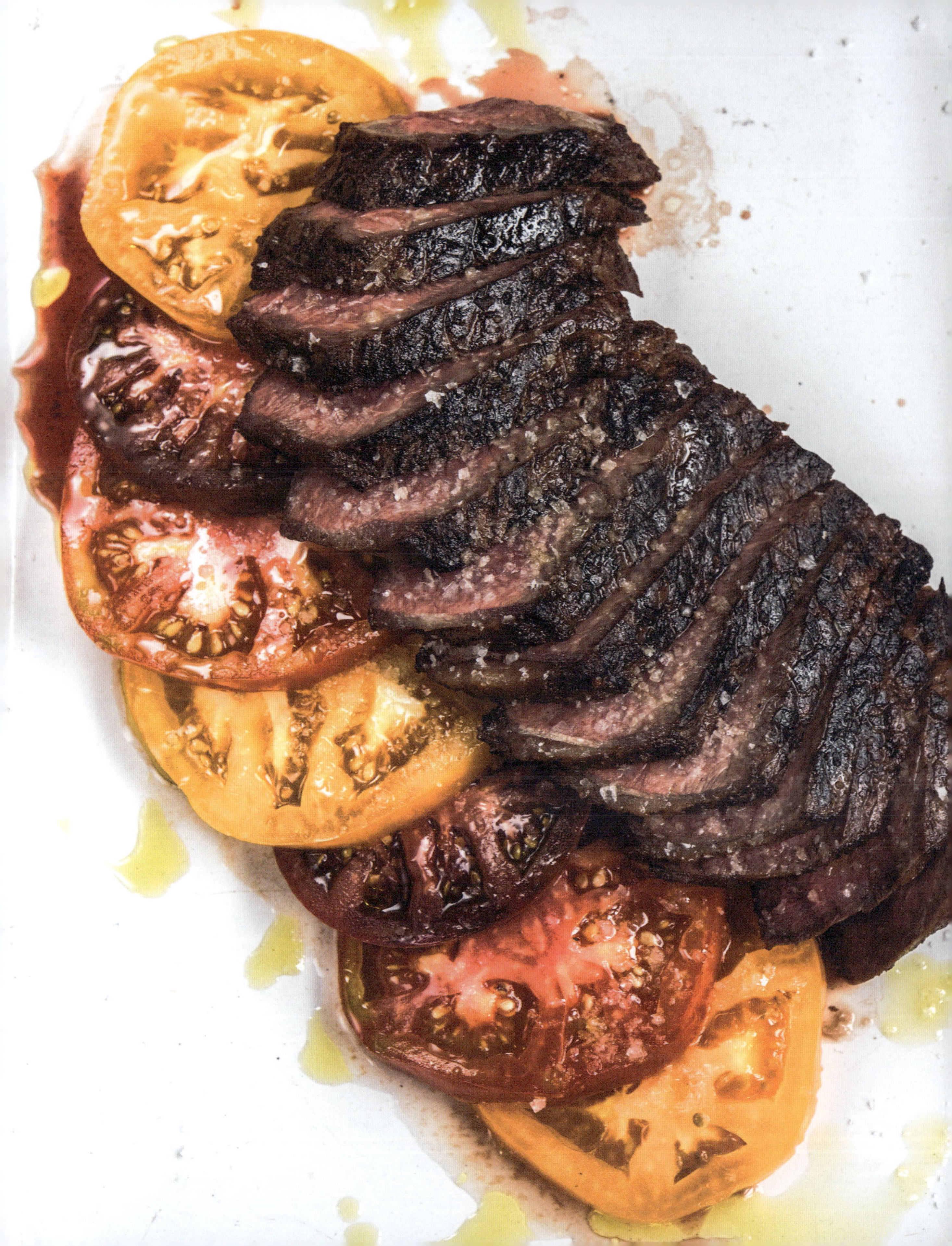

Raw Tomatoes

This is not a joke! Nothing, you say, is sillier than offering a recipe for raw tomatoes, just the way nature made 'em. True. Instead, consider the inclusion of this concept as a recipe to remind you that nothing—nothing!—is more delicious with a juicy, well-seared steak than a few thick slices of sweet in-season tomatoes.

Served underneath a steak, the tomatoes add sweetness, succulence, acidity, and flavor. If the meat you're cooking is exceptional, the tomatoes will only heighten the experience. And if the meat you're cooking is meh, well, they'll supply some of the flavor and succulence missing from the experience. On the plate, steak and tomato juices mix together, forming a delicious sauce for anything that touches it. Do this only in summer when tomatoes are at their peak!

SERVES 4 TO 6

2 or 3 large tomatoes, in different colors (red, orange, and yellow make for a nice look)

Flaky sea salt and freshly ground black pepper

Extra-virgin olive oil, for drizzling

Rice wine vinegar, for drizzling

Cut the tomatoes into ¼- or ½-inch-thick slices and arrange them on the individual plates or the platter (if serving family style) on which you'll be serving the meat. Just before serving, sprinkle with a little salt and a few grinds of black pepper. Place the steak, sliced or whole, on top of the tomatoes and drizzle generously with the oil and vinegar.

SIDES, SAUCES, AND DRINKS

Twice-Baked Potato

Even though the Home Frites recipe on page 187 managed to avoid double cooking the potatoes, they can't escape it here. If you're not up for making fries, but still desire that sacred combination of meat and potatoes, the only answer is the classic twice-baked potato. The double-baking process provides great versatility—one bake to cook it, the other to bring it together.

SERVES 4

4 large russet potatoes

Sea salt

4 tablespoons unsalted butter, at room temperature

½ cup sour cream

1 cup grated white Cheddar cheese

6 slices bacon, cooked, cooled, and coarsely chopped

½ cup finely chopped fresh chives

Preheat the oven to 375°F. Rinse and dry the potatoes, then lightly coat them with salt (this is to give their skin a little extra flavor). Place the potatoes on a sheet pan and bake until they are tender to the touch, about 1 hour. Remove from the oven and let cool for a bit.

Meanwhile, in a bowl, combine the butter, sour cream, and Cheddar (or any cheese you prefer; Gruyère and Havarti also work well). Set aside.

When the potatoes have cooled somewhat but are still warm to the touch, cut off the top one-fourth of each. One at a time, scrape the warm flesh from the small top slices into the bowl with the butter mixture and discard the skins. Using a small knife, carefully slice between the flesh and the skin of the remaining large portion of each potato, gently loosening the flesh and being careful not to slice through the skin. Scoop out the warm flesh into the bowl holding the butter mixture; the heat of the potato flesh will begin to melt the other ingredients. Reserve the empty skins.

Now, grab an old-school potato masher. Aaron prefers the kind with a flat mashing plate with square cutouts rather than the type with a rounded wire base. (In the 1950s and 1960s, Flint manufactured hands down the best potato mashers, but these gems are getting really hard to find, perhaps because Aaron bought them all off of eBay.) Mash the potato mixture until all of the ingredients are fully integrated. Add the bacon and chives and stir with a spoon until thoroughly mixed. Season with salt.

Scoop the potato mixture back into the empty potato skins, piling it well above the tops, and place the stuffed potatoes on the same sheet pan. Set the stuffed potatoes aside at room temperature for up to 1 hour.

Preheat the oven to 350°F. Bake the potatoes until heated through, about 20 minutes. Then, turn on the broiler and broil the potatoes until the tops are browned, shifting them around as needed to brown them evenly. Serve hot.

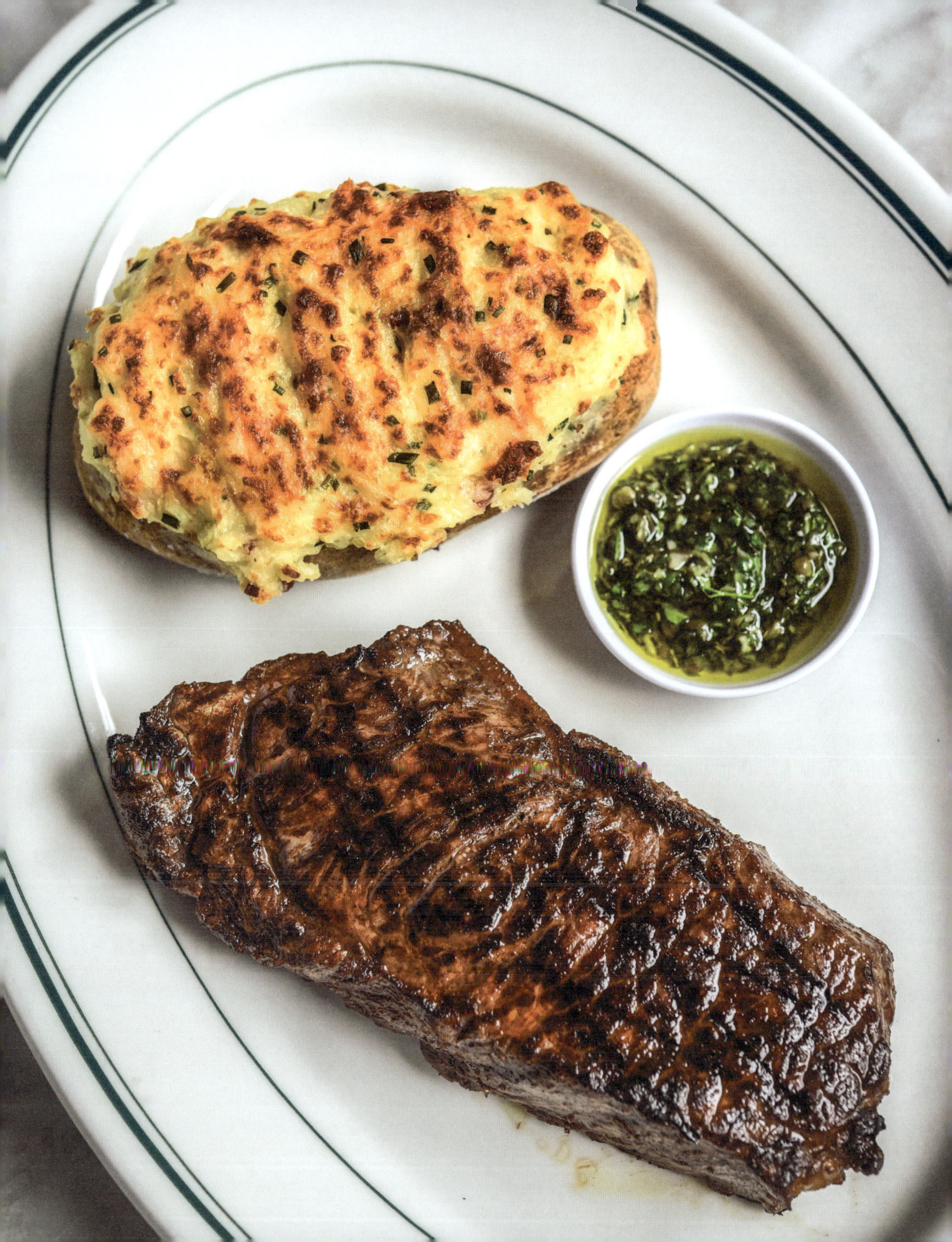

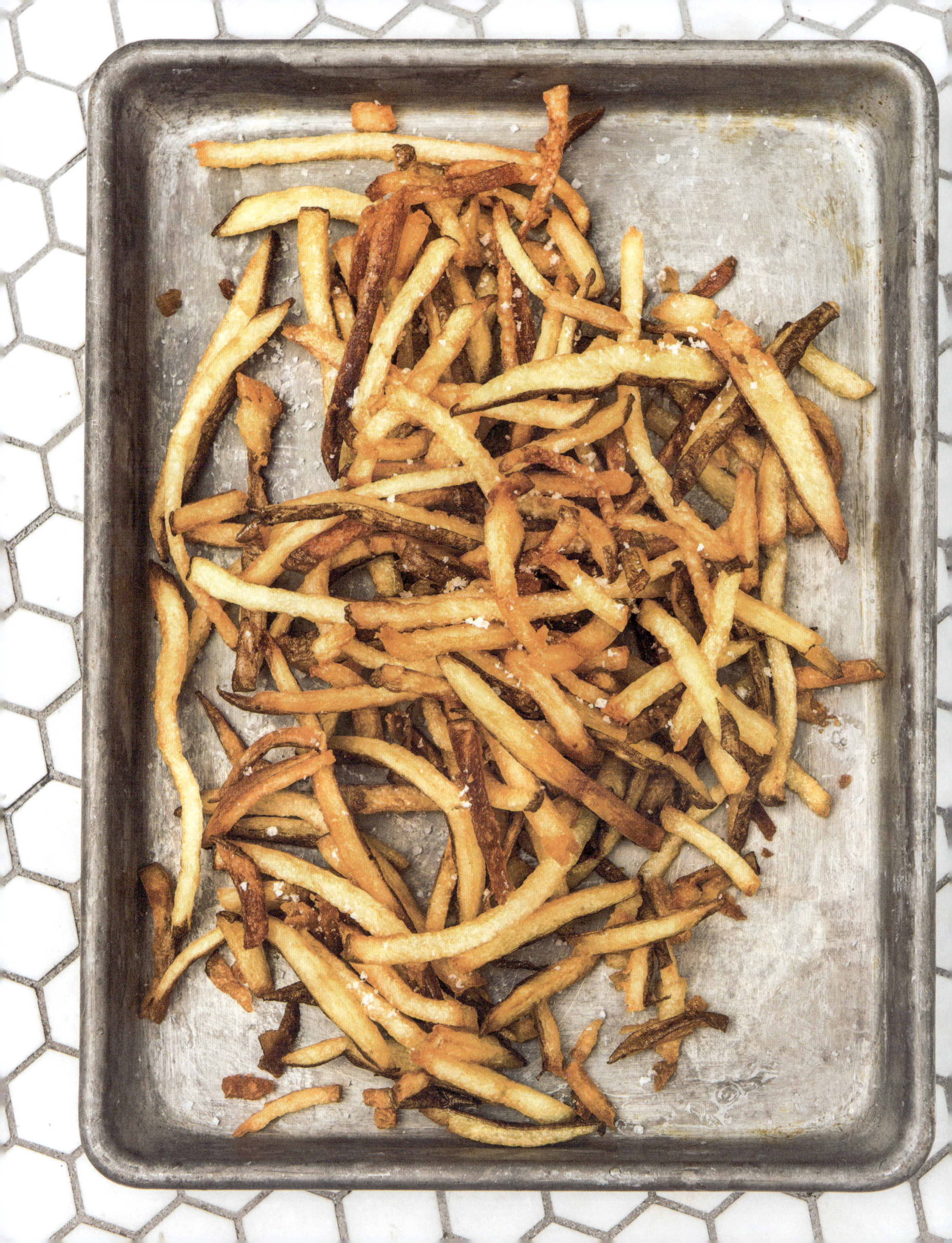

Home Frites

Whether you like French food or not, the French really got one thing right. The ubiquitous French bistro dish *steak-frites* is an all-timer, an iconic pairing of two foods that never gets old. What makes it work? Again, contrast and complement. The crunch of well-cooked fries provides a counterpoint to dense but chewy steak. The sweetness of the oil and the starchy potato complement the beefiness of the meat. Salt is the liaison. Most of us would love to be able to replicate this at home, but the fries are the stumbling block.

Have you ever looked into the preparation of French fries? For such a seemingly simple food, most fries are the result of a multiday and labor-intensive process. The procedure (or some variation of it) that many people claim makes the best fries involves several steps: The potatoes are cut and soaked in water for from a couple of hours up to a day, drained and dried, cooked in oil at a fairly low temperature, drained well, and frozen. Then, when the order comes in, the frozen fries are dropped into hot oil and fried at a high temperature until brown. This lengthy process is one reason why so few people bother to make them at home. Well, that and the fact that most people avoid the hassle of deep-frying. Thus, fries are a treat when you go out to restaurants.

However, it doesn't have to be this way. That lengthy process is common in a restaurant kitchen where fries have to be on the table—or handed through a drive-through window—within minutes of an order being placed. If you have a little more time, which home cooks do, you can make absolutely delicious, crunchy, satisfying French fries at home with little effort.

Some people call this method "cold oil" fries. The other remarkable thing about this technique is that the fries reputedly absorb one-third less oil than the standard twice-cooked ones do. You can choose whatever oil or fat you want to cook the fries in with little guilt. That's not just because the fries absorb less but also because the relatively low cooking temperature of 300°F doesn't damage the oil in the same way that high-temperature frying does. Peanut, vegetable, and coconut oil all work. Animal fats like lard, duck fat, tallow, and ghee (clarified butter) also work well. They're full of healthy fats, have a high smoke point, and leave a nice flavor.

It takes about forty-five minutes to cook these fries. Prep time is only what it takes to slice the potatoes. You can cook them as well-done as you like, and fries, unlike steak, are best when cooked to well-done. They should be crunchy and stiff. Flaccid fries are a farce.

SERVES 2 TO 4

continued

SIDES, SAUCES, AND DRINKS

Home Frites, continued

2 to 4 russet potatoes (depending on how many fries you desire)

Cooking oil or rendered fat (such as canola oil, coconut oil, vegetable oil, peanut oil, duck fat, lard, tallow, or ghee), for deep-frying

Kosher salt

Have ready a large bowl filled with cold water. Peeling the potatoes is optional. Slice the potatoes into batons ¼ thick and 2 to 3 inches long. As they are cut, submerge them in the water. Let the potatoes soak for at least 15 minutes or up to 4 hours.

Line a bowl with paper towels and set it near the stove top. Drain the potato batons and pat them dry, then put them in a heavy pot and pour in enough oil or rendered fat just to cover them. Turn on the heat to medium-low. A few minutes into the cook, as the oil starts to heat up, use a heat-resistant spatula or a wooden utensil to move the potatoes gently around in the pot, dislodging any that might be trying to stick to the bottom. Do this again a few minutes later. As the potatoes begin to cook more deeply, they begin to soften, and, if you move them around too much, they will break, leaving little half fries that are still delicious but less impressive.

Eventually the pot will come to a boil. Adjust the heat to maintain a medium boil—not too fast and not too slow. Every 5 minutes, check on the fries. When they start floating, after 30 to 40 minutes total, they can be scooped out of the pot. Look at their color to gauge doneness, too. We prefer a nice tawny brown.

Turn off the heat and, using a slotted spoon, transfer the fries to the paper towel–lined bowl to drain briefly. Toss the fries a bit and then remove the paper towel. Sprinkle with salt, toss some more, and serve immediately.

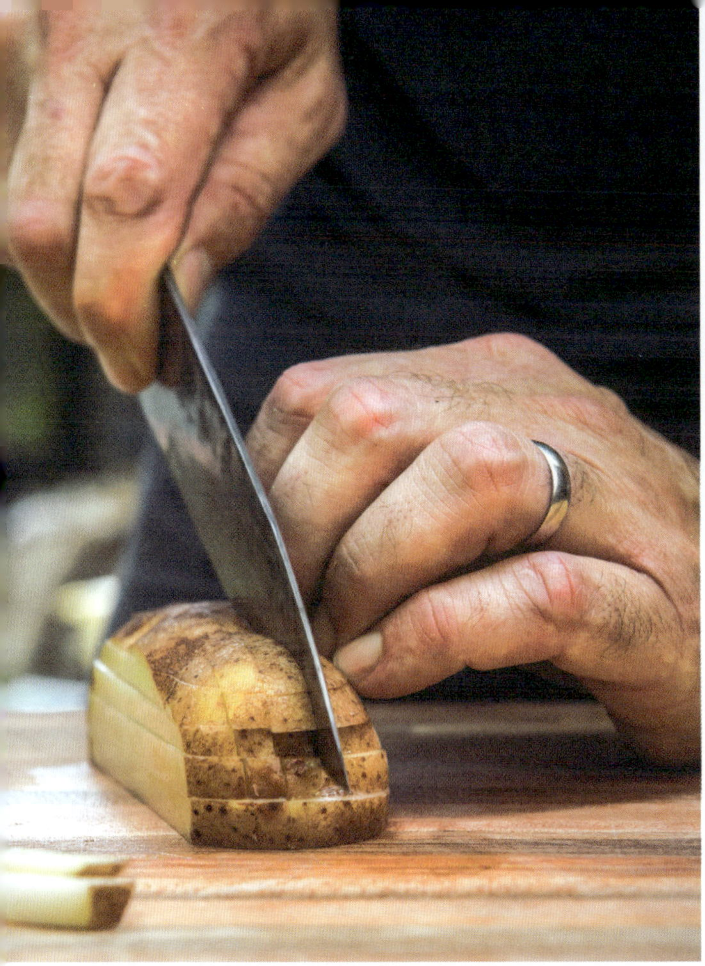

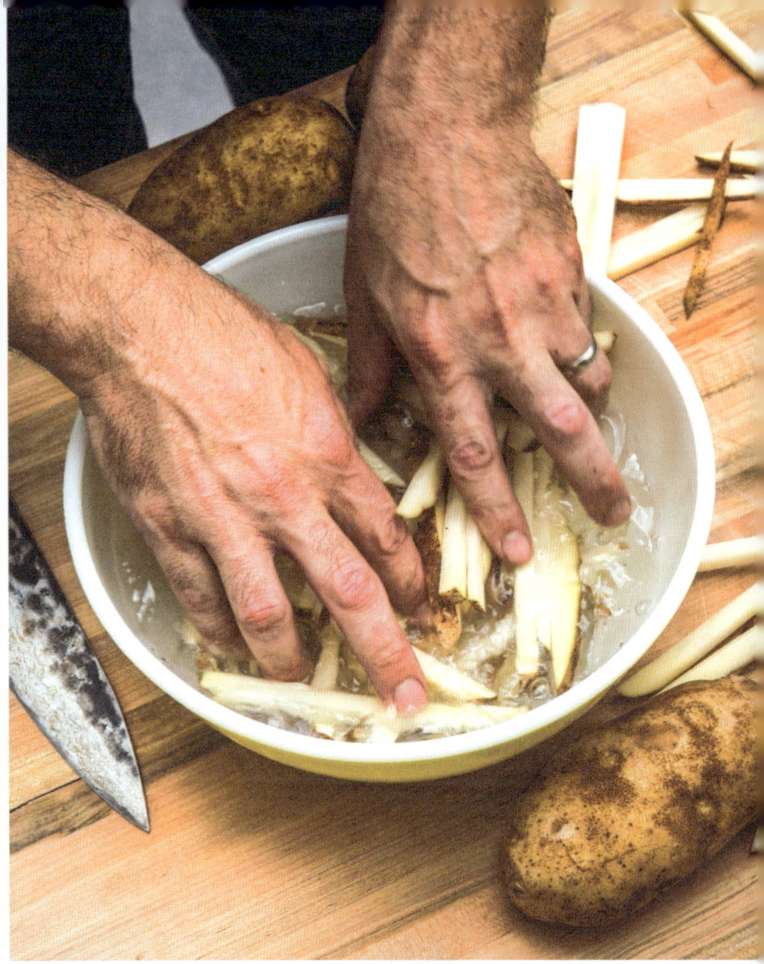

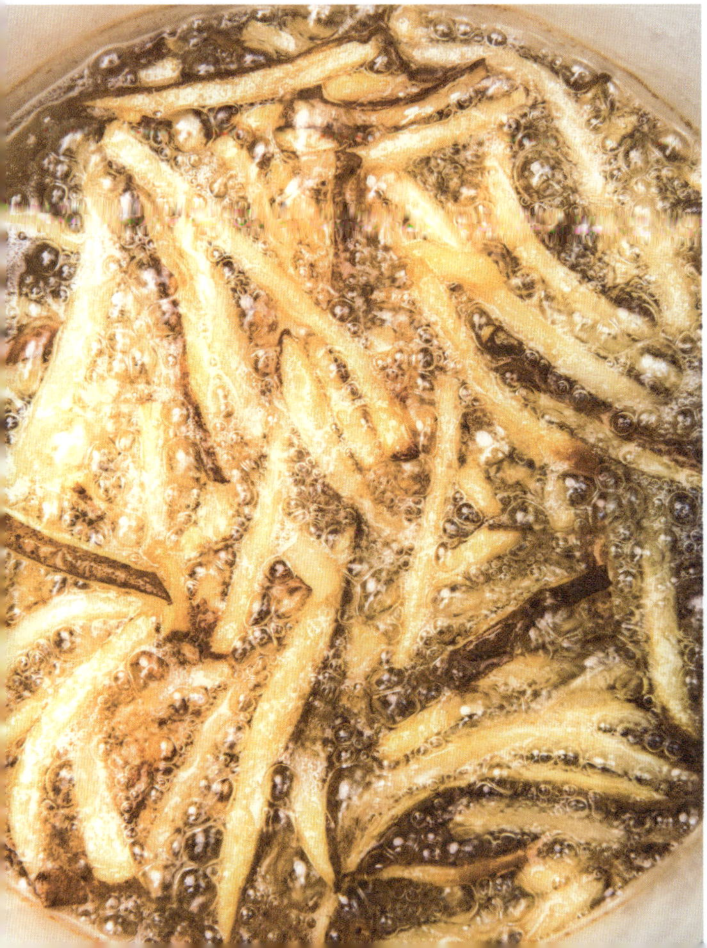

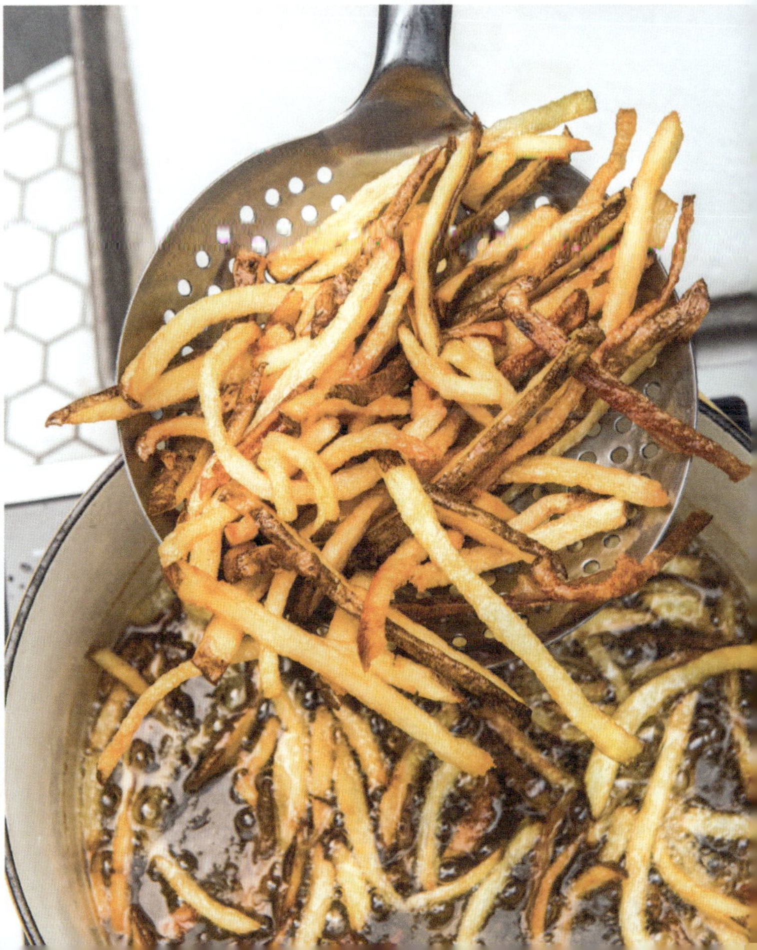

Grilled Vegetables

The art of grilling vegetables can take two paths. One, you can do them gently over slow-fading coals. This is a good way to tenderize thick, stemmy vegetables like broccoli, cauliflower, or asparagus that need a little more time. The other path is the opposite: cook them superhot and fast. This is how Aaron likes to do them—over the superheated chimney with the blast furnace method (see page 169). His method takes very little time and offers a bit of char and some toothsome, semicrunchy bites. It almost mimics the Japanese binchōtan method if you don't have any of that expensive charcoal on hand.

To go the low-and-slow method, use the coal bed after you've cooked the steaks and they are resting. All you need to do is turn the vegetables until they are tender.

To do the blast-furnace method, use a cheap metal cooling rack like the ones you can buy at restaurant supply stores and put it on top of a charcoal-filled chimney at peak heat.

We've included specific vegetables here, but feel free to choose other market-fresh options, such as cauliflower florets, whole green or spring onions, quartered red or yellow onions, whole asparagus spears, whole ramps, halved Belgian endive, halved escarole, quartered radicchio, halved carrots, and more.

SERVES 4

12 broccolini stalks, tough ends removed

20 green beans, stems trimmed

16 sugar snap peas

2 tablespoons extra-virgin olive oil, plus more for tossing

Kosher salt and freshly ground black pepper

Few dashes of fresh lemon juice

In separate bowls, toss the broccolini, green beans, and snap peas with the oil and a little salt, coating evenly.

If using the low-and-slow method, when the grill is hot, arrange the vegetables on the grates (or in a grill basket) over the fire. Depending on the intensity of the heat, either let them go for a while or stand by and move them around and flip them so no side gets burned. They are ready when they are just tender and lightly charred in a few spots.

If using the blast-furnace method, pile on about 4 broccolini at a time and cook for no more than 30 seconds on one side, then turn them all over and do the other side. Cook the stems directly over the hottest coals and leave the crowns just beyond the flames to protect them from the searing heat. Next, cook the green beans briefly before they blister too much and then follow with the snap peas, moving them both around with the tongs so they don't burn. After you remove the vegetables, they'll continue to cook a little, thanks to the carryover heat.

Before serving, toss the vegetables with a little more oil, if needed, and with the lemon juice and salt and pepper to taste.

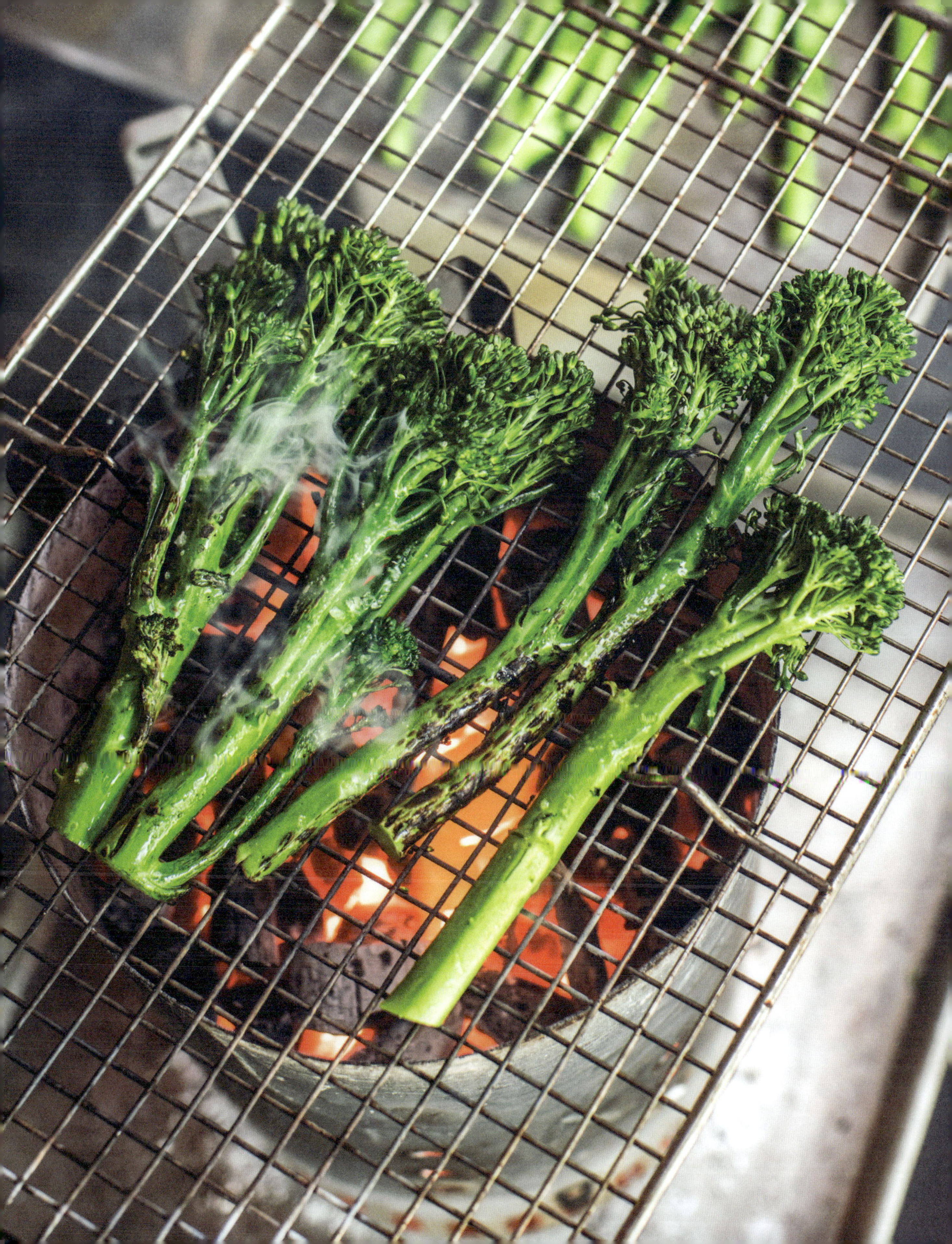

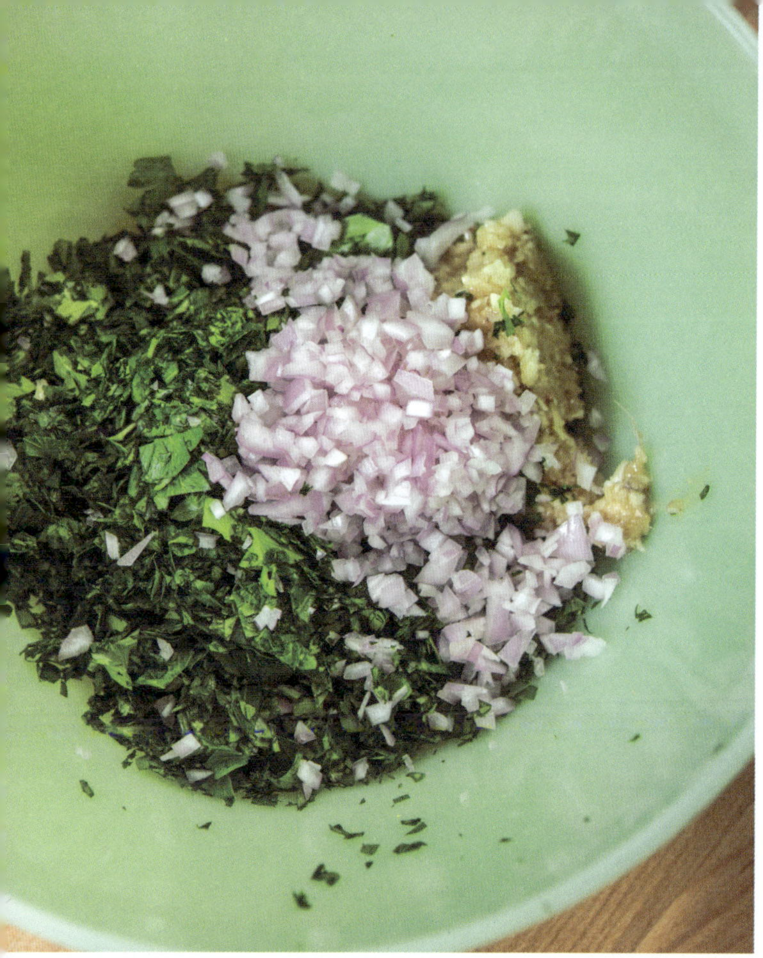
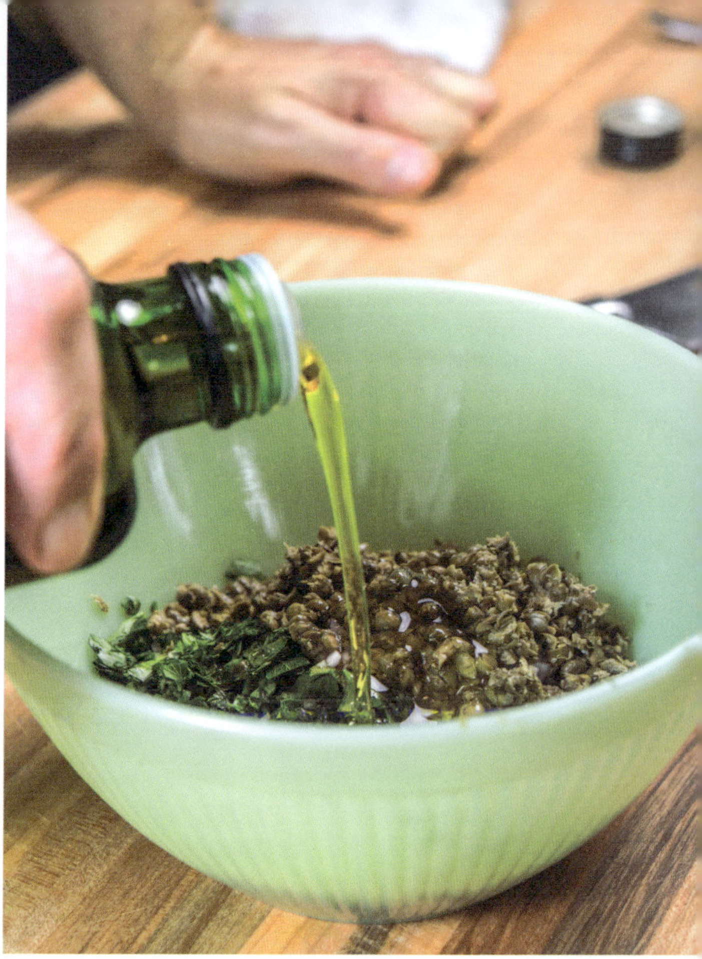
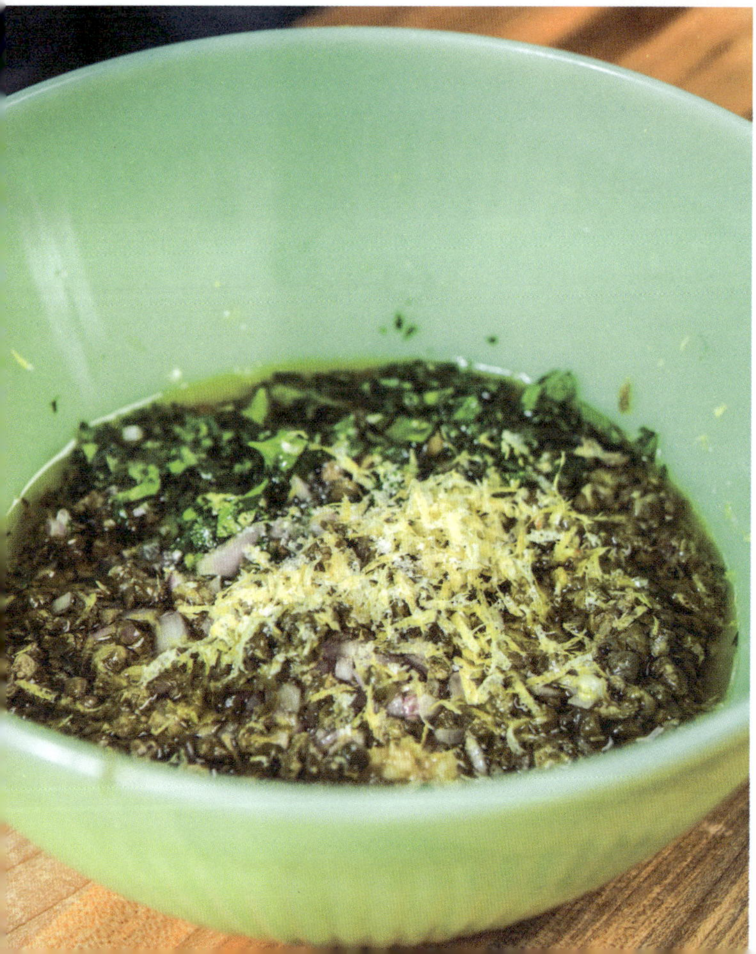
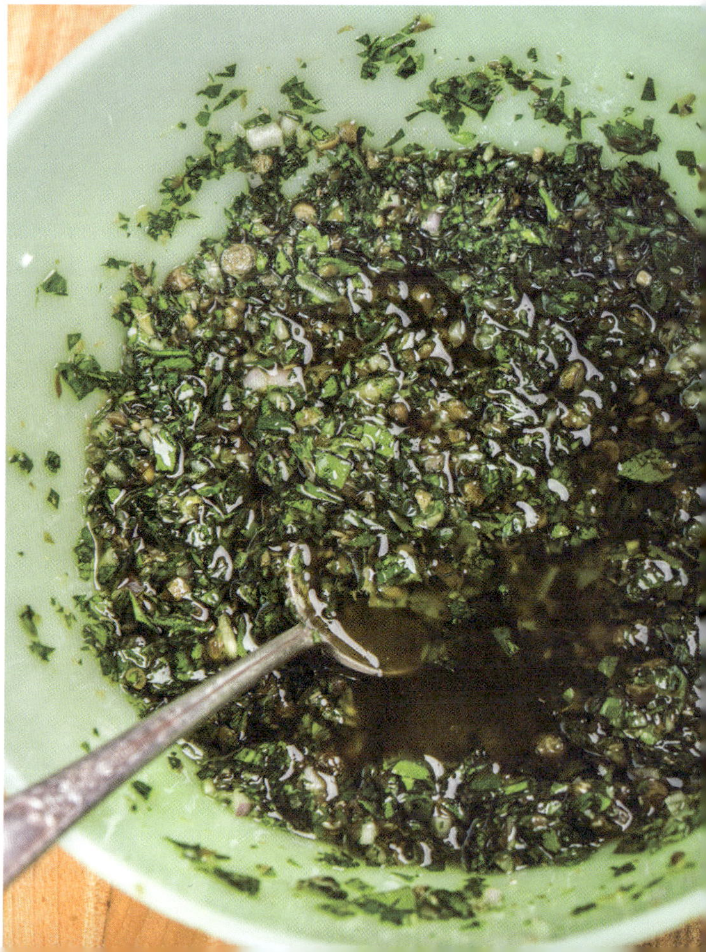

Salsa Verde

Steak has made the career of many a sauce. A.1., *chimichurri*, béarnaise, au poivre—where would any of these be without having been given a star turn next to steak? But the greatest of them all is salsa verde. Back in the day, its friends and family just called it "green sauce," but then it got famous and went upscale, changing its name to something a little more elegant, much as Archibald Leach became Cary Grant.

Three qualities make salsa verde the champion sauce. One, it is versatile. Yes, its intense flavor, tanginess, and umami richness mean it can go toe-to-toe with steak, and we're convinced it's better with a smoky grilled steak than with one cooked in a pan. But it is equally awesome with fish, grilled birds, even pasta. Two, it's improvisational. We'll give you a recipe here, but consider it just a starting point. Salsa verde can be adapted to fit your taste, so long as you don't leave out the two foundational ingredients (and the source of its umami and punch): anchovy and garlic. Three, it lasts and can evolve. Aaron keeps a running jar of it in his fridge, refreshing it every time he has some extra of a new green. Whatever you've got—mint, rosemary, radish tops—can be thrown into the mix. Salsa verde will just evolve over time and will always be there for you when you need it.

MAKES ABOUT 2 CUPS

2 bunches flat-leaf parsley

4 cloves garlic

3 olive oil–packed anchovy fillets

1 teaspoon fine sea salt

¼ cup well-drained small capers

1 cup extra-virgin olive oil

1 teaspoon honey

1 teaspoon rice vinegar

1 lemon

Pick the leaves from the parsley stems and discard the stems. You should have about 2 cups. Using a chef's knife and a cutting board, finely mince the parsley, then transfer to a bowl.

Using the flat side of the chef's knife, smash the garlic on the cutting board and sprinkle with the salt. Chop and flatten the garlic and salt together until a paste forms. Next, chop the anchovies into the paste, then smear and scrape the mixture back and forth on the cutting board until the ingredients are evenly distributed and you have a fine paste. Scoop the paste into the bowl with the parsley. Finely chop the capers and transfer them to the bowl.

Add the oil, honey, and vinegar to the bowl and stir to mix well. Finally, using a fine-rasp grater, grate the zest from the lemon directly into the bowl, then stir to mix.

Make the sauce several hours, but preferably a full day, ahead of serving to allow the flavors to blend. To store, transfer to a jar, cap tightly, and refrigerate for up to 2 months. Bring the sauce to room temperature before serving.

SIDES, SAUCES, AND DRINKS

Charred Jalapeño–Anchovy Compound Butter

Tried-and-true companions for steak, compound butters never get old. They're nothing more than a highly effective way to add a lovely jolt of additional flavor and a little silky fat to the meat. The concept is simple: take room-temperature butter and mix in some punchy flavors. Popular compound butter additions include anchovies, mushrooms, or herbs, but really anything goes.

Here, we found that the umami-rich combo of anchovy and garlic provides a perfect base for the jalapeño. Blackening the chile adds nuance and brings out its flavor. Don't worry about too much chile heat, as jalapeños today tend to be pretty tame. If you want real heat, sub in a serrano or habanero chile.

This recipe is geared to make two good-size dollops of compound butter, but it scales easily for larger amounts, and it's not a bad idea to make more if you like it. Wrapped tightly, the butter will keep in the fridge for a few weeks or in the freezer for up to three months. And while it's tasty on steaks, it's also delicious melted on corn on the cob, grilled chicken, and roasted fish.

MAKES ENOUGH FOR 2 STEAKS

- 2 tablespoons unsalted butter
- 1 large jalapeño chile
- ½ teaspoon minced garlic
- 1 teaspoon anchovy paste

Allow the butter to come to room temperature on the countertop while preparing the other ingredients. To char the jalapeño, if you've got a hot grill going, simply grill the jalapeño on all sides until blackened all over. If cooking indoors, hold and turn the chile with insulated tongs or a skewer over a medium stove-top gas flame until blackened all over. Allow the charred jalapeño to cool.

When the chile has cooled, cut it in half lengthwise, remove and discard the stem and seeds, and mince finely. By now, the butter should be easily spreadable. If not, let it continue to warm until it is soft enough. In a small bowl, combine the butter, jalapeño, garlic, and anchovy paste and mix well.

Lay a square of plastic wrap or aluminum foil on a work surface (plastic wrap is easier to use). Use a rubber spatula to get all of the seasoned butter onto the square, shaping it into a rough log, and then use the plastic wrap or foil to roll and shape the butter into a uniform log. Wrap the butter in the plastic wrap or foil and refrigerate until firm and chilled.

To use, cut the desired amount off the log and leave it to melt on top of a steak hot off the grill.

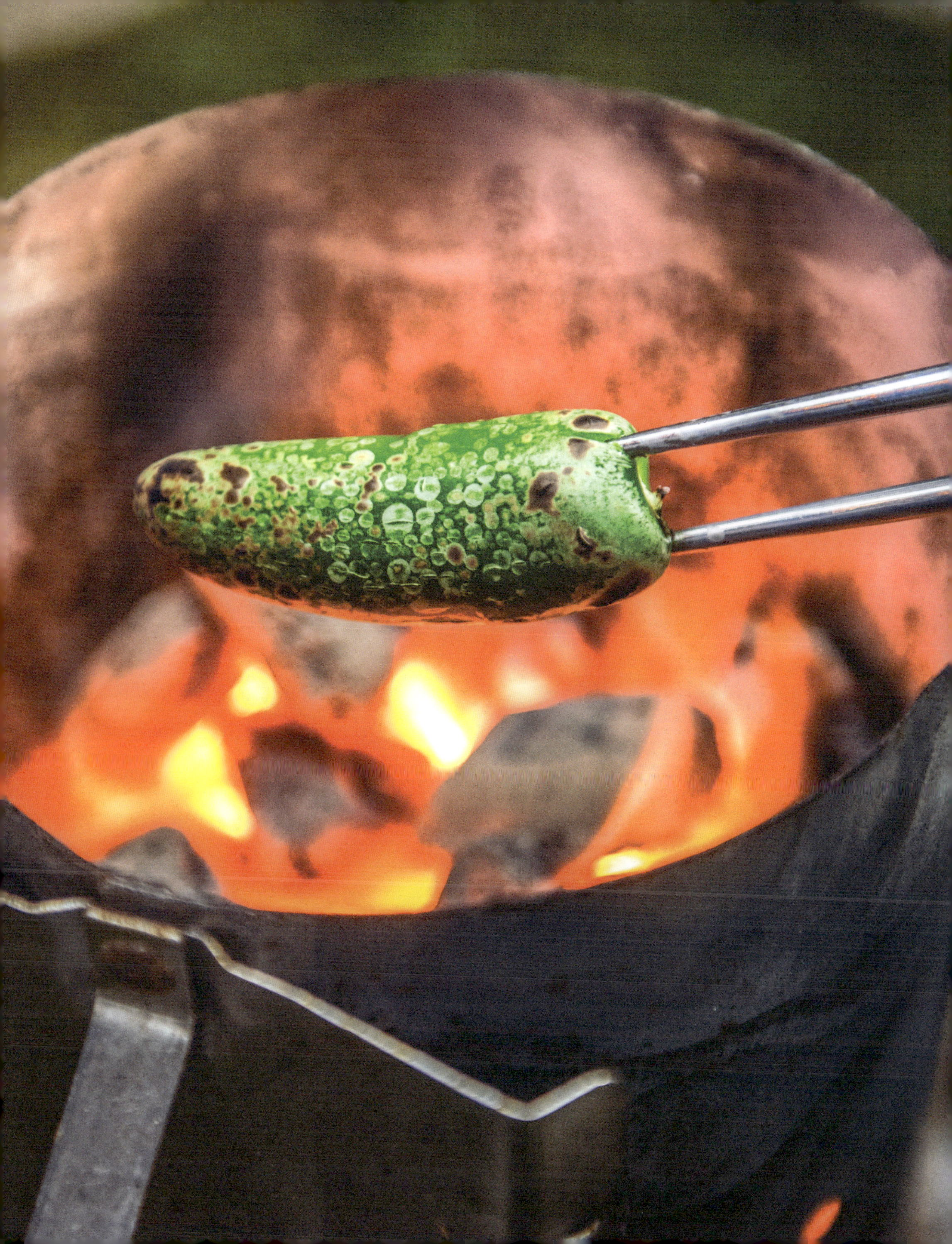

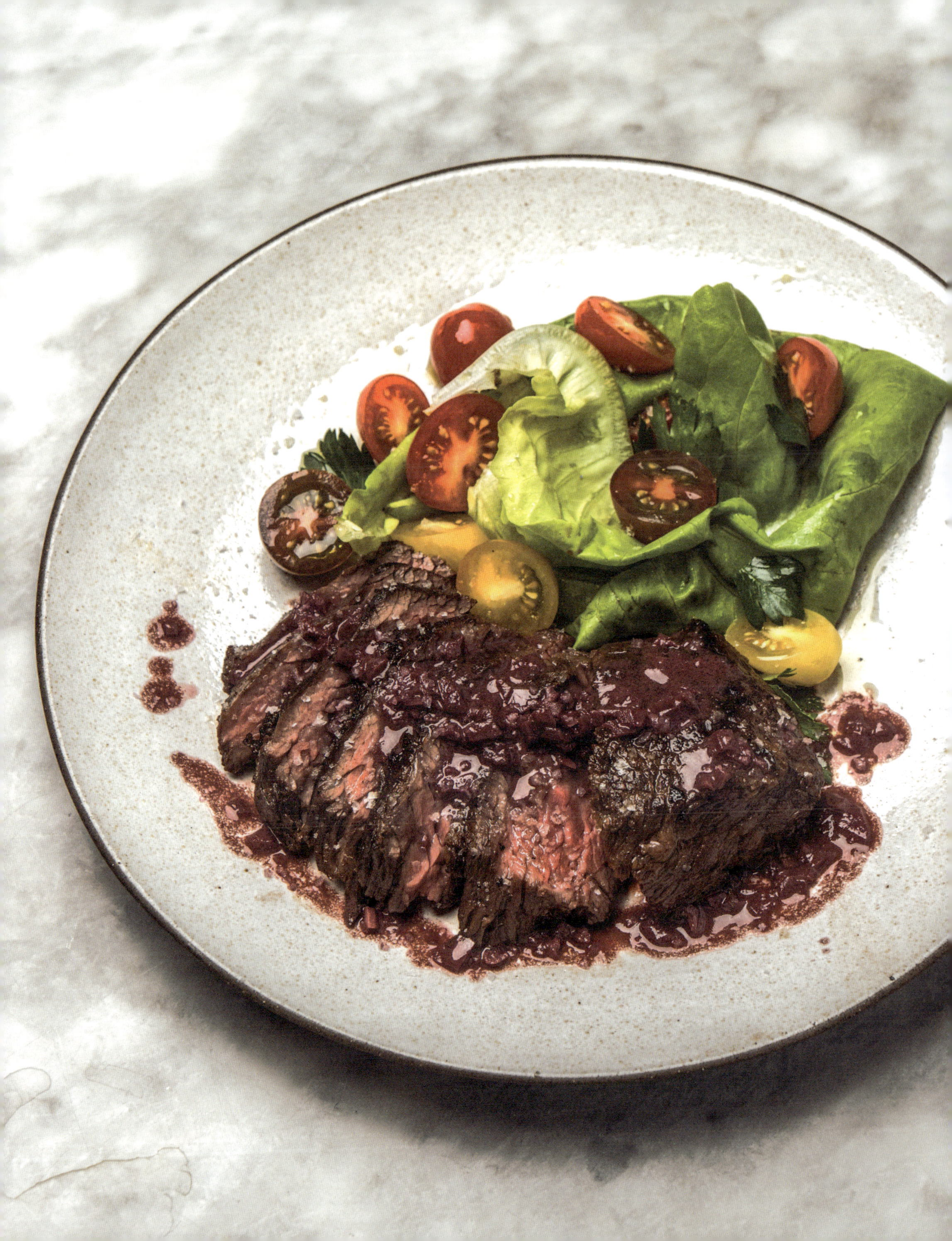

Perky Red Wine Sauce

Just as any baseball pitcher has to have a fastball, any steak cook worth his or her beans should have a classic red wine sauce in the repertoire. It's very "French bistro," and who doesn't love a little taste of Paris? Recipes for a rich, complex Gallic red wine sauce—aka *sauce bordelaise*—tend to get slightly wonky, requiring lots of prep and ingredients like demi-glace and bone marrow. There's no need to go to all that trouble when you can craft a simpler, yet scrumptious red wine sauce in just a few minutes. This version is especially delicious because the unusual addition of lemon juice gives it an acid perkiness that contrasts beautifully with rich meat.

As for the red wine, it doesn't matter what you use as long as it's dry. And smooth (not whole grain) Dijon mustard makes for the most appealing texture.

This recipe is a framework that you can adapt to your circumstances. If you're grilling steaks over coals and want a red wine sauce, then follow the directions here. If you're cooking a steak in a pan on the stove, make the sauce in the same pan (after tossing out all of the fat) and start by sautéing the onions so you can stir up any delicious browned bits stuck to the pan bottom. Also, there's room to add other ingredients. Chopped mushrooms would be a natural in this; just cook them while simmering the wine. Want it to be richer? Throw in a splash of heavy cream. Want even more savory flavor? Toss in a rosemary branch with the thyme.

All those variations will help any pitcher succeed, but mastering the fastball is nonnegotiable.

— MAKES ENOUGH FOR 2 STEAKS —

- 2 cups red wine
- 1 yellow onion, chopped
- 2 cloves garlic, minced
- 8 thyme sprigs
- 2 tablespoons fresh lemon juice
- 2 tablespoons Dijon mustard (not whole grain)
- 2 tablespoons cold unsalted butter, cut into a few pieces
- Kosher salt and freshly ground black pepper
- 1 tablespoon chopped fresh flat-leaf parsley (optional)

In a small saucepan, combine the wine, onion, garlic, and thyme and bring to a low boil over medium heat. Simmer until the wine has reduced by half. Turn off the heat, and when the wine has stopped bubbling, pull out and discard the thyme sprigs. Add the lemon juice and mustard and whisk until blended. Whisk in the butter until it melts and the sauce thickens slightly, then season to taste with salt and pepper.

Plate the steaks and spoon the sauce over the top, or spoon the sauce onto individual plates and lay the steaks on top. Sprinkle with the parsley and serve.

SIDES, SAUCES, AND DRINKS

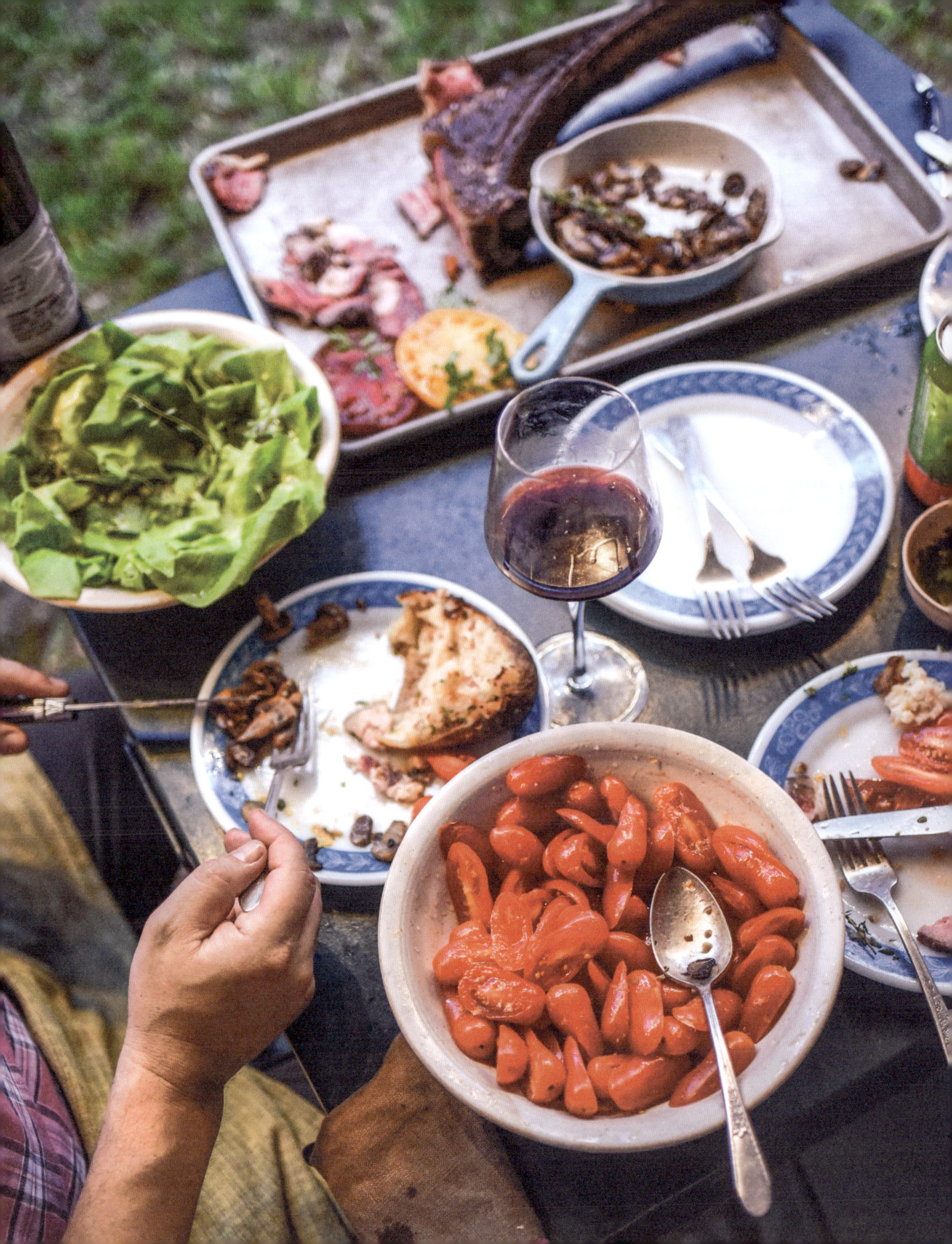

Drinking Steak

What to drink with a steak is as important a question as what sides to serve with it or who to eat it with or even which college to send your kids to. That is to say, it's important. Why? Because can you imagine only drinking a glass of water with a steak? If you're going to put steak on the menu, it needs to be matched in level and intensity on the beverage front. The balance and harmony of the meal demand it.

Aaron physically can't grill anything without a beer in his hand (or it waiting impatiently for him on the table nearby), and he often carries the style of beer he's drinking into dinner with the steaks. At his house, it's almost guaranteed to be an Austin beer like Live Oak Pilz in a can. Jordan has had many memorable bottles of wine with steak and seemingly none of them was bad. But there was that one frigid winter night a couple years ago, where the heat in the house wasn't working and he, his wife, Christie, and a couple of friends were staying up late huddled around the fireplace for any shred of warmth. Around midnight, hunger returned, and Jordan threw a steak over a little grate in the fire and opened up one of his favorite Italian reds, a Barolo Monvigliero from Fratelli Alessandria in Verduno. When the sizzling, slightly smoky steak came out of the fire, it was perfect with the heady dark cherry flavors of the wine. Talk about staying warm. . . .

The good news is that steak is versatile with beverages. It doesn't work with everything—put away the margaritas and daiquiris, for example, or the Sauvignon Blanc—but it does open its big, steaky arms wide in embrace of a vast number of possibilities. And to be clear, we're talking *adult* beverages here. Let's look at the major categories.

BEER

To quote Homer Simpson, "Ah, good ol' trustworthy beer. My love for you will never die." According to Aaron, beer is what to drink with steak. Remember that old restaurant chain Steak and Ale? They got at least one thing correct! And all styles work pretty darn well. If you're doing it right, you've been drinking beers through the entire steak-cooking process, so it just makes sense to continue on into the meal. Aaron prefers light, crisp beers in general, about the same ones that go with barbecue, unless it's wintertime. That's a different scene.

Not a big fan of superhoppy beers like huge IPAs or really bitter pale ales, he stays away from them in general, which works here because they're not that good with steak. They don't actually go with many foods, but sharp and tart hops particularly grate against the flavor of beef. If you like extreme hoppiness, consider adding a sauce or condiment to the steak. A pungent, herbal salsa verde or *chimichurri* sauce will help bridge the gap.

Steak calls for beers that show the flavor of the grain, whether it's a creamy, sweet, oaty flavor or a roasty, toasty malt. Provided they're well made, some lighter beer styles will work with steak. A nice, malty Kölsch, for instance, could be good with a leaner, thinner steak. A pilsner with substance is always good no matter what, but it's also great with steak, especially on a hot summer night. A classic brown ale works in fall or winter.

Dark beers are classic with steak, as they've got all this creamy richness that plays right into the silky texture of the meat, as well as that roasty, toasty quality that picks up the char. Look for porters, stouts, and bocks that aren't too extreme in alcohol or hops.

SIDES, SAUCES, AND DRINKS

AARON'S FAVORITE STEAK BEERS

Live Oak Pilz • One of the best beers around, this is a go-to pilsner that's also great with steak. Live Oak is an Austin, Texas, brewery that makes clean, perfectly balanced beers in largely classic styles. This one has a nice grainy feel and a modest hoppiness that give it a little edge.

Double Mountain Kölsch • A great Oregon brewery, Double Mountain makes this crispy ale all year long. It's unfiltered, so there's a nice creaminess to it, and it has a bit more hoppy character than you'd find in a straight-up German Kölsch. It's great with a steak, especially when you want the meat to really take center stage.

Anchor Steam Beer • From Anchor Brewing Company in San Francisco, this is just one of the great all-around beers that never gets old. It's right down the middle—not too light, not too heavy, not too sweet, not too bitter. The body is perfect to put with beef, but it's still crisp and refreshing, too.

WINE

Red wine was seemingly invented for steak. Indeed, it's not hard to imagine the ancient Romans or the Celts tucking into their rich hunks of fire-roasted aurochs while quaffing some lustrous red tapped straight from the barrel. For Jordan, steak can almost be an excuse to crack some lusty bottle of red wine, as few other foods have the chutzpah to go with some of today's richer reds. He's been writing about wine for years, and his wife is a former sommelier who now is a wine professor at the Culinary Institute of America in Napa Valley, so he's constantly surrounded by wine, except when he's with Aaron, when he's constantly surrounded by beer. But beef and red wine is one of the greatest matches on Earth, and he never gets tired of putting the two together.

The affinity between red wine and beef is no accident, and chemistry explains why they work so well. When you eat a bite of steak, it laces the mouth with molecules of fat and protein that cling to receptor cells on the sides and the roof as well as the tongue. This is how we taste steak and why, as its flavor lingers on the mouth, it bestows our minds and bodies with a sense of well-being and nourishment at the intake of nutrients like protein and fat.

Let's take one second to look into red wine. Wine contains compounds called tannins, which are organic, antioxidative substances that occur in tree bark and wood as well as in the skins, seeds, and stems of grapes (and also in tea leaves). The reason red wines—and not many whites—contain tannin is that the color and substance of the reds come from steeping the juices of the grapes with their skins (and occasionally stems) during fermentation. During this process, tannins are extracted from the skins, much in the same way the color and flavor of tea comes from steeping a tea bag in hot water. And like tea, if you steep wine too long, it becomes bitter and astringent. But if the winemaker does the job well, the level of tannins in the wine will be just right, and the wine will be robust, substantial, and structured rather than bitter or astringent. Tannins contribute mightily to the sense of body in a red wine.

Chemically, tannins also bind to protein and fat molecules, like the ones that are clinging to the inside of our mouths after a particularly succulent bite of steak. So when you have that sip of red wine, it's literally coursing through the mouth, grabbing ahold of the loitering steak molecules and stripping them off of your tongue. The result of this theft is not an immediate sense of loss, as the delicious flavor of a fruity and savory red wine replaces the flavor of meat. Rather, the result is a sense of revitalization. Wine has cleansed the palate and refreshed it, prepping it for the next bite of delicious steak. In this way, for better or worse, red wine helps us consume more steak and makes it more pleasurable, so that instead of the buildup of proteins and fat become boring and ponderous, our mouths are continually revived, allowing the pleasure of eating steak to be experienced again and again. The binding of tannins also makes the wine taste silkier.

Pretty much any red wine fulfills this function. Cabernet Sauvignon, the world's most popular wine grape, also happens to be one of the most tannic of all reds, which only supports the popularity of beef. California Cabernet is even more tannic than Cabernet from Bordeaux, France, the most famous region for the production of the wine. But in most California Cabs, you might not sense the tannin as acutely as you do in Bordeaux wines (which historically have been known for astringency in their youth, a prime reason these wines were aged, as tannins fall out of the wine over time, making it smoother and softer) because the warmth and brightness of sun-drenched California vineyards ripen the tannins to a greater degree, making the wines thick and chewy. Plus, the wooden barrels in which these wines are aged contribute a toasty, charred flavor that echoes the Maillardian sear on the exterior of the meat. This is why California Cabs have become a classic accompaniment to a good, American-style charcoal-grilled ribeye. The more sumptuous the steak is, the greater its affinity for big, tannin-rich reds.

Of course, reds other than Cabernet Sauvignon work well, too. Syrah, Merlot, Cabernet Franc, Tempranillo, and Sangiovese are all fairly tannic wines that will be just as good. Lighter, less tannic wines like Pinot Noir and Gamay also make great partners.

Red wine is not wine's only answer to steak, though. In many cases, white wine can also be a match. White wine lacks the tannin of red, but it still has great acidity. The acids in wine also cut through fat and refresh the mouth. (Red wines have acid too, just not usually as much as whites.) The reasons whites are less popular than reds with steak are body and flavor. Much as lighter, hoppier beers like pilsners aren't classic steak pairings, white wines lack the body and substance to stand up to steaks and their flavors tend toward herbaceousness and green fruits. One exception to this is Chardonnay, especially in its greatest incarnation in the white wine of Burgundy. Dallas steak chef John Tesar of Knife (see page 84) has shown how the pairing of white Burgundy and well-aged steak is the most remarkable combination. What makes this match so magically delicious? We have no idea, but it's amazing.

SAKE

The idea of pairing sake and steak might seem unexpected to Americans, but after visiting Japan in early 2018, Jordan was converted to the joys of *izakaya* beef paired with light, transparent sake. It wasn't an easy conversion, and

SIDES, SAUCES, AND DRINKS

to get it, you have to try to let your mind get into a particularly Japanese sensibility, paying attention to smaller, subtler details referencing texture, art, and nature.

Japan is, of course, the land of Wagyu cattle—the world's most outrageously decadent and marbled beef—and is where steak is consumed in bite-size cubes that are as rich as entire ribeyes in the United States. Drinking sake with those steak cubes is a common activity in Japanese steak houses and *izakayas*, which are essentially mellow drinking spots with short menus of simple dishes. Classic Japanese steak from rich, fatty Wagyu cattle might seem the perfect candidate to pair with Cabernet Sauvignon. And it does work well. But sake is pretty much the opposite of Cabernet

WINE AND STEAK, MATING FOR LIFE

Here is a rundown of some great steak and wine pairings from the wine regions of the world.

France • Several of the world's greatest steak wines—Bordeaux, Loire Valley (Cabernet Franc), Burgundy (Pinot Noir), and northern Rhône (Syrah)—are French. But to choose one, it would have to be northern Rhône Syrah. Just can't escape that pithy dark red and purple fruit, wild gamy notes, and moderate tannins are perfect with a juicy cut of steak. Almost any Syrah would do, but a moderately priced, easily sourced one like Saint Joseph Rouge from Domaine Faury is nearly ideal.

Italy • Many Italian wines are remarkable, but because the heart of Italian steak culture is in Tuscany, the compulsion is strong to go with a Sangiovese-based wine, native to the area. Something strong but not too heavy or oaky will do the trick, showing bright cherry fruit and lots of juicy acid to counter the fat in the steak. Try the Rosso di Montalcino from Le Ragnaie.

Spain • The greatest steak country in the world also has, unsurprisingly, tons of fantastic red wine, lots of it big and burly to go with the flavor bomb that is Spanish beef. But you don't want the wine to overpower the meat, which is possible, so something with a little grace and restraint is in order. With a great steak from an older cow, try a wine from great steak lovers, Olivier and Katia Rivière, whose Gabaxo, from Rioja, is made from Tempranillo and Garnacha.

California • In some ways a fusion of Spain, Italy, and France, California brings together a longstanding red wine tradition, a climate where it's almost always possible to grill steaks outside, and a great local meat scene. The variety of reds and of vineyards in California makes choosing difficult. But Napa Valley is king for a reason. There's a young guy making killer wines up on Diamond Mountain who also happens to be passionate about steak. His name is Ketan Mody and his wine projects, Beta and Jasud, are focused on handmade and hand-grown Cabernet Sauvignon from rocky, wild sites on Diamond Mountain and Mount Veeder. You can't find better steak wines than these, and it helps that Mody himself is a steak fanatic.

Sauvignon. Made from water and white rice, it has no tannin, no color, and its flavor is much subtler than that of a big red wine. Great sake is usually appreciated as much for its delicacy and grace as we respect wines and beers for their robustness and power.

So it's easy to see why people pair sake with the delicate tastes of fish and vegetables. But steak? Well, sake comes in many styles, some of which are not as delicate and finessed as the styles we usually see here in the States. Also, we have to remember that while the flavor of Japanese steak is reliably and intensely beefy, the texture can be quite different from American beef because of the amount and qualities of the fat. Wagyu steak offers that melt-in-the-mouth feeling thanks to a higher concentration of oleic acid. The graceful explosion of juicy, lithe fat in a bite of Wagyu is the real entry point for a sake pairing, as sake has a parallel silkiness.

A typical sake can be fine with steak, but a couple of styles really stand out. The first category—which is one really growing in popularity among sake aficionados—has two variations, *kimoto* and *yamahai*. These styles use native, wild bacteria in the fermentation. They bring an unpredictable and slightly earthy, wild, and umami note—it's subtle, but noticeable—that makes a wonderful pairing with the savoriness of meat.

Another category with great affinity for beef is *nama-zake*. The Japanese word *nama* means "fresh" or "raw," and that's exactly what a *nama-zake* is—unpasteurized, unadulterated sake. As with milk, beer, eggs, and so many other products, pasteurization is a process that neutralizes some enzymes and kills unwanted bacteria, ensuring a long and stable shelf life. But because many of these bacteria and enzymes influence the overall character of the brew, there are trade-offs. Most sakes in Japan are pasteurized twice, which means they have been literally stripped of these defining elements. A great *nama-zake* will have a robust, vibrant, and complex flavor and mouthfeel. It may lack some of the delicacy and finesse of other styles, but that's simply because it remains in possession of all of its parts. Alongside a juicy, well-crusted steak, it will hold its own, providing umami-rich flavors and creamy texture to clean the palate.

Seeking out individual bottles of sake can be a tough task. It's better to know a few good importers whose products can be trusted, because they select great breweries and then take care of the (inevitably fragile bottles) throughout the importation process. Look for the names of these importers on the backs of the bottles: MTC, the sake division of mega Japanese product importer Mutual Trading Company, based in Los Angeles; Vine Connections, based in Sausalito, an unusual company specializing in South American wine and artful, high-end sakes; JFC, another big importer of Japanese products with a huge and rich sake book; World Sake Imports, based in Honolulu, which has a small but brilliantly chosen selection; and New York's Joto Sake, a reliable importer of fascinating and high-quality product.

SPIRITS

Sorry, gin, but without question, the best spirits to pair with steak are whiskey and mezcal. Yes, we celebrate and revel in the venerable tradition of martinis and steaks. However, the association of the two isn't exactly a pairing. Martini consumption ought to come before and leading up to the steak. A martini is cold, clean, and crisp, a seemingly sensible way to transition out of the prescribed rationality of the workday into the carnal pleasures of dinner and beyond. But

COTE

**16 West 22nd Street
New York, New York
tel: (212) 401-7986 • cotenyc.com**

New York has a venerable and well-documented steak house culture, so to write another tribute to Peter Luger or Keens or Sparks seems unnecessary. It's more fun to talk about a new shrine to beef that has emerged in recent years: Cote. We've all had Korean barbecue, but Cote fashions itself as a Korean steak house, a detail emphasizing the focus on high-quality, dry-aged meat.

That focus is instantly apparent on looking at the menu, which features large, color images of the best cuts, from marinated short rib to hanger to ribeye to "Cote steak" (chuck flap). All beef is Prime or higher and dry aged in the basement aging room a minimum of a week, with cuts aged from 45 to over 100 days available on request (we even tasted some at 220 days). As in Korean barbecue, Cote's steak is cooked by staff on a little glowing grill set into the tabletop and is accessorized with all manner of tangy, fermented Korean goodness, such as soy stew (anchovy broth with zucchini, tofu, and potato), kimchi stew, and *banchan* (a collection of umami-rich side dishes). All of the accompaniments make for deliciously zesty contrast with the unctuous beef that's coming right off the grill to your plate. Although the sexy vibe of this Flatiron District hot spot is both modern and Western, the flavors don't hold back on Korean funk. It's a wonderfully satisfying experience.

Another thing Cote gets right is the beverage program. The inclusion of slurpy frosé tells you that the place doesn't take itself too seriously, but the creative cocktails are complex and well balanced. And the lengthy, well selected wine list—dedicated to small, rarefied producers—balances perfectly with the Korean elements. Cote is a unique and delicious experience that should be on the radar of any true steak lover.

the two should remain separate because the martini (and we're talking gin here; vodka is just flavorless booze, so don't bother with it) is the opposite of a steak. It's cool and bright, slick and herbal, almost giving the feeling of disinfecting the mouth. Steak is dark and warm and juicy and chewy and bloody. If you're a spirits drinker first and foremost, have the martini(s) in advance and change gears with the steak.

Whiskey is the classic pairing for a reason. Sweet woodiness from barrel aging echoes the toasty savoriness of the steak's grilled crust and smoky overtones. The sweetness from the grain of whiskey connects to the subtly caramelized sweetness of the Maillardian crust. And whiskey's rounded, soft texture plays to the juicy explosion of well-marbled meat on the tongue. When it comes to choosing whiskeys to pair with steak, anything goes. But the sweeter-tasting profiles of American whiskeys do seem to make the best matches, whether it's the corn-based softness of bourbon or the spicy savor of rye. (And let's not forget that most American cattle are fed grain in their last months, making the pairing even more intuitive.)

Other whiskeys work well, too, but warrant some discernment. For instance, single-malt Scotch whisky can be great with a steak, but not all styles. Heavily peated single malts, such as the famous ones from the islands of Islay or Skye, are often so powerfully briny and flavored with iodine or seaweed that they can overwhelm the inherent sweetness in a good piece of beef. The more approachable Speyside styles work better. Scotch has a drier and more austere character than the typical American whiskey, highlighting the grain over the wood. Because single-malt scotch has such a fiercely unique expression of character, the old classic blended scotches (Johnny Walker, Chivas, and the like) are good compromises for steak. These whiskeys blend dozens of different scotches together to form some sort of a composite expression of Scotland as a whole. The best of them will balance subtle smoky notes against a range of grain and oak flavors to come up with something tasty, if not fervently expressive of any particular place or intention.

Japanese whisky can also be very good with steak. Like sake, most Japanese whisky prizes finesse and balance over other qualities. Although their cues come from Scotland, Japanese malts are gentle brushes with silk compared with the cudgel of many single-malt scotches. They tend to ride the line between savory and sweet and powerful and subtle. This deft balancing act they perform make them good for, let's say, ordinary steaks. If you're going for a big-impact steak—starting with a superthick cut, heavy smoke and seasoning, and a big, dense crust— a Japanese whisky might be overwhelmed. However, thinner cuts seasoned simply and carefully can be perfect with a Japanese malt.

When it comes to agave-based spirits, mezcal, because of its smokiness, makes a more interesting steak match than tequila. And we're just talking straight up here, not in a margarita or any other cocktail that diffuses the flavor of the spirit. Tequila can work adequately with a steak, but its general notes of pear and herbs tend not to complement beef. When you age tequila—when it becomes *reposado* or *añejo* style—it takes on more of the character of whiskey and will match with steak a little better. In contrast, premium mezcal, which is made with agave cooked in an underground pit, possesses a native smokiness that harmonizes beautifully with grilled steak. If you throw in a side of grilled Padrón peppers and onions, the pairing will be perfect.

SIDES, SAUCES, AND DRINKS

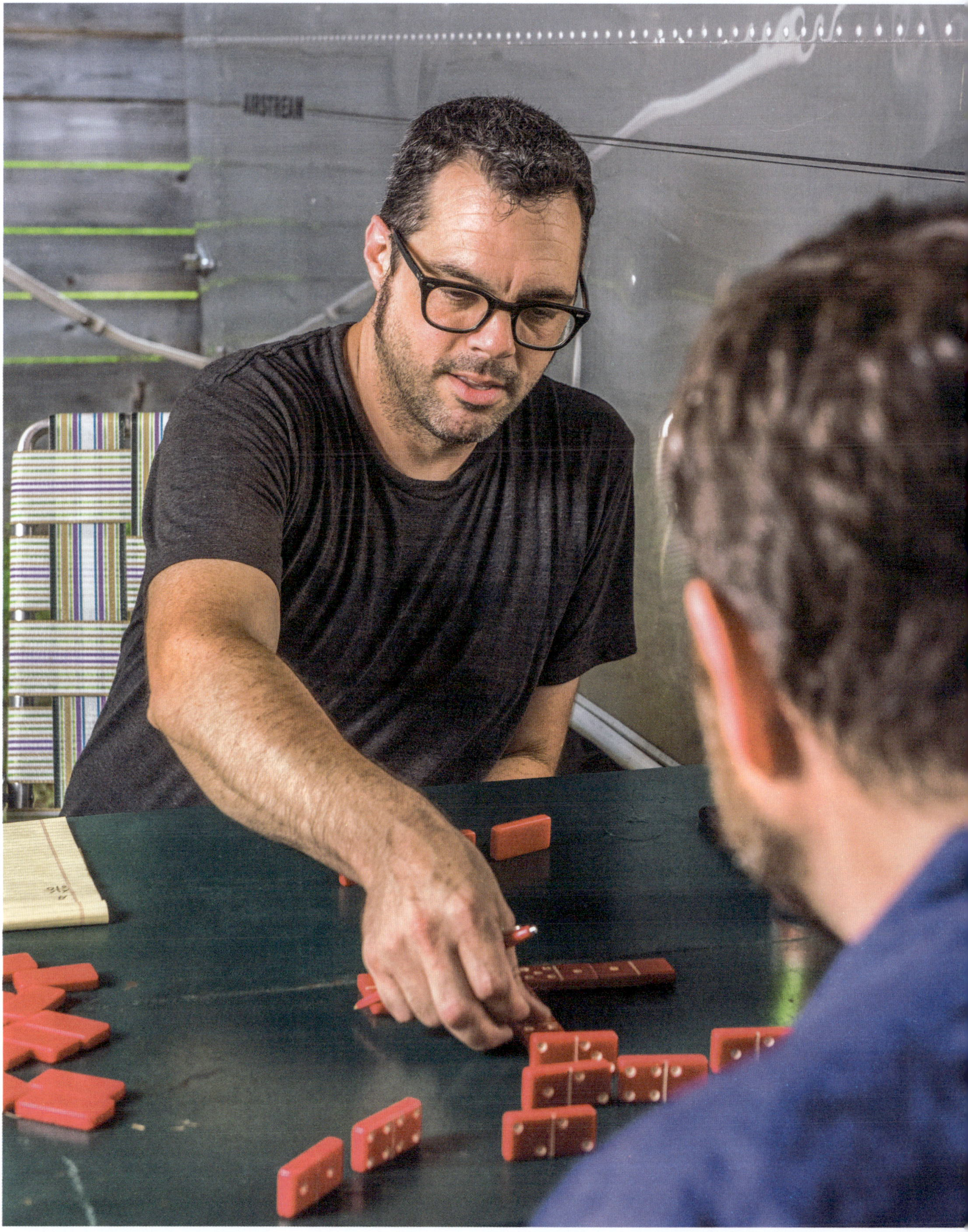
AIRSTREAM

Resources

The Best Mail-Order Meat

Here are a few reliable places to order some of the best steaks in the country.

Alderspring Ranch • alderspring.com

Betsy Ross • Best to message on Facebook

Carter Country • cartercountrymeats.com

Creekstone Farms • creekstonefarms.com

Crowd Cow • crowdcow.com

Flannery Beef • flannerybeef.com

Heritage Foods • heritagefoods.com

Holy Grail Steak Co. • holygrailsteak.com

Joyce Farms • joyce-farms.com

Snake River Farms • snakeriverfarms.com

Great Grills

Korin Konro Hibachi • korin.com

Lodge Sportsman Grill Hibachi • lodgemfg.com

PK • pkgrills.com

Santa Maria Grill • santamariagrills.com

Weber Original Kettle • weber.com

Sweet Steak Knives

Laguiole on Aubrac • laguiole-en-aubrac.fr

New West Knifeworks • newwestknifeworks.com

Opinel • opinel-usa.com

Acknowledgments

Together, we'd like to thank a number of people without whom this book would not have been possible. On the book-team side, it starts with our dear literary agent, David Hale Smith, who will never turn down even an average steak and is as good in the boardroom as he is at the table. Next, we want to thank Aaron Wehner and Ten Speed Press for making this book happen. We were gifted with unbelievable support and effort from a team of massively talented people, beginning with our editor and good friend Emily Timberlake, who got us over the finish line with her energy, creativity, and humor. Having Elizabeth "Betsy" Stromberg, book designer and part-time art director extraordinaire, on the job ensured the book would look wonderful. Sharon Silva proved way more than a copy editor: her meticulousness, knowledge of food and cooking, and good taste greatly improved the final product.

Thanks also to Emma Campion, Serena Sigona, Karen Levy, and Ken Della Penta for making this book better.

Of course, we bow down to the great Wyatt McSpadden, who besides being at the very top of the photography game, gracing our work with his brilliant eye and camera technique, also knows so much about everything that he truly impacts the content of the text as well. He's always on hand for a good pep talk, a good laugh, and a good hug, too. Thanks, Wyatt, you're the best. You know who's also the best? Jeff Stockton, Wyatt's photo assistant, who was at most of the shoots, and Jeff's moustache, which was also at most of the shoots.

We are indebted to Bryan Butler and Ben Runkle of Salt & Time in Austin, Texas. Their generosity with their knowledge and time was a huge asset to this book. We are also grateful to a couple of real—and really great—chefs, Adam Perry Lang and John Tesar, who shared their insights on beef aging and on cutting and cooking steaks and who have been so supportive in general. Another real chef, Matthew Van Orden, was instrumental at photo shoots, helping prepare all of the dishes from the book, keeping things clean, and teaching us some stuff along the way.

We considered ourselves lucky to have one Bryan Butler (the butcher) in the book. But in the end were we blessed with an unexpected boon: another Bryan Butler, this one the remarkable illustrator whose images brought clarity and artistic variety to these pages. Thanks, BBs!

Thanks to Joey Machado of B&B Charcoal, for keeping us well fueled throughout the year as we test cooked. And thanks to Scott Moody of PK, our favorite grill maker, for all of his support on this book and over the years.

And last but not least, as large a thank-you as we can muster to Alfonso Terrazas and his team at Creekstone Farms, which supplied most of our beef during test cooks and aging experiments. The quality of the beef we had to work with was simply astounding, and the generosity Alfonso and everyone at Creekstone showed us was, well, also simply astounding.

From Aaron

Man, there are so many people to thank for helping make this book possible, I could write a book just about that! First and foremost, I say a crazy big thank-you to my wife, Stacy, who has been there every step of the way. She does what's needed, from making sure the house is presentable to finding me a fresh pair of jeans to take to an event, checking my underwear, and all the time giving me crap for everything. But seriously, because I get all the attention, no one has any idea of how essential Stacy is to everything we do. She works so hard, and there would be no *Franklin Steak*, *Franklin Barbecue*, or even Aaron Franklin as you know him without her. Thank you so much, Stacy.

Thanks to my coauthor, Jordan Mackay, who is not only a great writer, and a great friend, but also insanely passionate about food and the craft of cooking with fire. His excitement and talent have proven to be the perfect counterbalance for these projects. Thank you, Jordan! I'm looking forward to the next. . . .

Then, I've got to thank all of the people involved with Franklin BBQ and related enterprises. They keep the ship sailing smoothly while I run around doing things like this book. There are a few people I lean on most. Andy Risner, my right-hand guy at the restaurant, is just so reliable, so good to work with, and such a supertalented cook. Alex Gantos, my left-hand guy, keeps all other ships sailing smoothly. I'm fortunate to have found two highly skilled and reliable people I can really trust. Big thanks also to Miki and Julie at the restaurant for working so hard, keeping things organized, making guests happy, lending a helping hand when I need it, and always having smiling faces.

Last, much thanks to my mom and dad, who, in the process of feeding me and keeping me alive, introduced me to steaks at an early age. My dad has been grilling T-bones my entire life, and working on this book showed me how much that's meant to me.

From Jordan

First and foremost, thanks to Aaron Franklin, great friend and compadre in meat books, whose endless reservoirs of humor and goodwill—not to mention his extraordinary expertise in so many areas—make him an absolute joy to work with, and yes, even when his schedule is almost impossibly busy.

I must offer infinite gratitude to (and for) my wife, Christie Dufault, who doesn't love steak nearly as much as I do and prefers to eat plants, but nevertheless tolerated years of endless steak talk as well as a great deal of beef cooking and grilling. It's over now, Honu. Perhaps.

I've got to offer a similar note to Aaron's wife, Stacy, who has become a great friend over the years, but who also allowed me to be a constant presence in her house and in her social and family life for long stretches while I was in town working on the book.

Beyond those crucial people, I want to acknowledge many of the experts we consulted and who offered outstanding ideas,

ACKNOWLEDGMENTS

explanations, and often beautiful meat to try: Clifford Pollard and Kevin Cimino of Cream Co., who are going to change the meat world; Bryan and Katie Flannery of Flannery Beef, who shared lots of honest information and, more important, were such a pleasure to hang out with; John McLaughlin of McLaughlin Farm, who not only was a wonderful source for everything Highland cattle but also remained a warm and encouraging voice in my inbox throughout the writing; Jason Ross of First Light Farm sent amazing meat, as did Joe Heitzeberg of Crowd Cow and Cameron Hughes of Holy Grail.

Others joined me on or facilitated my research into all things steak. Toshio Ueno guided me around Japan's beefy side and taught me a lot about sake along the way. Sancho Rodriguez went above and beyond in helping schedule and coordinate a week of steak eating in Basque Country, which proved a revelation. Thanks, too, to José Gordón of El Capricho, who floored me as much with his incredible passion and dedication as he did with his beef and cooking. My dear friend David Feldstein has been a frequent presence on the steak trail with me and shares the passion of exemplary beef and wine. Alyson Careaga, another dear friend, has been a constant source of encouragement and help, generously lending her immense talents and energy whenever I needed them. Ted and Andrea Vance were with me on some of the steak tour and survived far more beef than they're used to eating. A shout-out as well to serious steakthusiast and great friend Ashley Santoro, who traveled far to eat steak with me. And a most profound and humble thanks to steak (and tartare) seeker numero uno Talitha Whidbee, with whom I have eaten more steaks than anyone over the years and who has given me so much along the way.

Last, I want to acknowledge the great writer Mark Schatzker, whose original book *Steak* was an inspiration and a guide and is an absolute must-read if you want to understand beef and steak at much greater depths than what you'll find here (it's also a brilliantly fun read). Connecting with Mark was an important moment for me in the writing of this book, as he shared his thoughts and opinions and helped me make some invaluable associations. Also, please read his life-changing book about nutrition and flavor, *The Dorito Effect*.

Index

A

AG, 15
AGW (A Greener World) label, 44
Akaushi cattle, 12, 36
alder, 132, 134
Aldersping Ranch, 24, 31, 172, 207
American Grassfed Association, 44
Anchor Brewing Company, 200
anchovies
    Charred Jalapeño–Anchovy Compound Butter, 194
    Salsa Verde, 193
Angus beef, 11, 13, 35–36
antibiotics, 46
APL, 83, 85, 96
apple wood, 132, 134
Arguinzoniz, Victor, 129, 131
Asador Etxebarri, 129, 131
aurochs, 6–7, 8, 10

B

bacon
    Twice-Baked Potato, 184
Barber, Dan, 123
Bateau, 34
bavette, 70–71, 77
beef
    age and, 23–25, 26–27
    branded, 35–36, 38
    flavor of, 9–10, 16, 18, 23–25, 41–42
    grading of, 38–39, 41, 54
    grain-fed, 16, 21–23
    grain-finished, 23
    grass-fed, 16, 18–21, 24, 25, 26–27, 42, 44, 172
    history of, 6–9
    imported, 46
    local, 30
    organic, 44
    pasture raised, 44, 46
    safety, 38
    See also cattle; dry aging; steaks; wet aging
beer, 199–200
Bernet, William, 177

Bern's Steak House, 43, 66
beta-carotene, 16
beverages, 199–203, 205
Big Green Egg (BGE), 107–8
binchōtan, 124, 126–28
Black Belly, 26
Blue Hill at Stone Barns, 123
bottles, plastic, 146
Brahman cattle, 11
branded beef, 35–36, 38
buckets, 145
Butcher and Larder, 50
butchers
    in America vs. Europe, 75
    buying from, 31, 33, 35, 54–55
    competitions for, 52
    local, 50
    thrift and, 52–53
Butler, Bryan, 31, 50, 52–55, 59, 69–70, 72, 73, 75
butter
    Charred Jalapeño–Anchovy Compound Butter, 194
    finishing steaks with, 159–60

C

Caesar, Julius, 6–7
Cargill, 22, 36
Carter, RC, 26, 27
Carter Country Meats, 26–27, 207
cast-iron pans, 100–102
cattle
    antibiotics and, 46
    breeds, 10–14, 35–36
    feed for, 16, 18–23
    history of, 6–9
    hormones and, 46
    temperament of, 14
Char-Broil, 112
charcoal
    advantages and disadvantages of, 123
    grills using, 108–13
    history of, 122
    lighting, 142, 144
    making, 122–23
    types of, 123–29

charcoal chimneys, 142, 144
Chateaubriand, 66–67
cheese
    Twice-Baked Potato, 184
cherry wood, 133, 134
Child, Julia, 180
chine, 57
Choice beef, 38, 39, 41, 54
Chop Butchery & Charcuterie, 50
chuck steak, 57, 71
Clove and Hoof, 29, 50
coconut charcoal, 128–29
complexus, 59, 63, 68
cooking methods
    blast furnace, 169–70, 172
    on the coals, 167, 169
    by cut and type of steak, 76–77, 172–73
    hot and fast, 162, 165
    with oven, 102
    reverse sear, 165–67
    slow vs. fast, 153–54
    sous vide, 104–5, 107
    stove-top, 100–102
    See also grilling
COOL (Country of Origin Labeling), 46
Cordier, Olivier, 31, 33
Coss, Tom, 34
Cote, 204
côte de boeuf, 57, 59, 60
Country Cat, 123
cowboy steak, 57
Cream Co., 25, 27
Creekstone Farms, 11, 23, 36, 84, 207
Crowd Cow, 33, 35, 207
culotte steak, 57

D

Dai Due, 29
dark cutter, 57
Delmonico's, 67
Delmonico steak, 57, 59
Double Mountain, 200
drinks, 199–203, 205

dry aging
 benefits of, 81–82, 86–87
 challenges of, 87
 cooking methods and, 172–73
 definition of, 57
 history of, 86
 at home, 88, 90–91, 93–95
 length of, 94
 mold and, 96
 popularity of, 81
 process of, 85–87
 thirty-month rule for, 27

E

Edison, Thomas, 123, 125
El Capricho, 24, 26, 34, 62–63
Elzinga, Glenn, 24, 31
Erickson, Renee, 34
Etxebarri, Asador, 129, 131

F

The Fatted Calf, 29
filet mignon, 57, 66
Firestone, Harvey, 123
First Light, 13, 172
flank steak, 73, 77
Flannery, Bryan, 14, 33, 39, 41, 85
Flannery, Katie, 14, 33, 85
Flannery Beef, 14, 33, 85, 207
flat iron, 71–72, 77
Fleisher's, 50
Ford, Henry, 123, 125
44 Farms, 11, 84
4505 Meats, 29
Franklin, Stacy, 100
Franklin Formation, 148, 151
frenching, 57, 59
Fresh From OK, 13

G

garlic
 Garlicky Sautéed Mushrooms, 180
 Green Salad with Garlic Vinaigrette, 179
gas grills, 102, 104, 122
Gordón, José, 24, 26, 62–63

grain-fed beef, 16, 21–23
grain-finished beef, 23
grape vines, 134, 135
grass-fed beef, 16, 18–21, 24, 25, 26–27, 42, 44, 172
A Greener World, 44
Green Salad with Garlic Vinaigrette, 179
grill brushes, 144–45
grilling
 equipment for, 102, 104, 107–16, 142, 144–46, 207
 setups for, 147–50, 151
 starting fire for, 142, 144, 150
 See also individual grills
grill marks, 160–61
Gwen Butcher Shop, 50

H

hanger steak, 69–70, 77
HeartBrand Beef, 12, 23, 36, 84
Heitzeberg, Joe, 33, 35
Hereford cattle, 13, 14, 36
Heritage Foods, 207
hibachis, 110, 207
 hybrid, 114–19
hickory, 133, 134
Highland cattle, 13, 14
Holstein cattle, 7, 13–14
Holy Grail Steak, 207
hormones, 46

J

Jalapeño-Anchovy Compound Butter, Charred, 194
James, Paul, 112
JBS, 22
JFC, 203
Joto Sake, 203
Joyce Farms, 207
Jureskog, Johan, 15

K

kamado cookers, 107–8
Kansas City strip, 67–68
Kingsford, Edward, 123, 125
Knife, 82, 84, 96, 201
knives, 207

Kobe beef, 36, 42
Kosmidis, John, 82, 85, 88, 90

L

Lang, Adam Perry, 83, 85, 96
Lee's, 29
Legako, Jerrad, 9, 10, 13
Le Severo, 176, 177
Live Oak, 200
Ljungquist, Klas, 15
longissimus dorsi, 59, 65, 67, 68
Long Meadow Ranch, 18–19
Lowry, Ethan, 33, 35
lump charcoal, 124, 126, 127

M

Maillard reactions, 86, 154–55, 160, 165
mail-order meat, 30–31, 207
Mallmann, Francis, 129
marbling, 41–42, 45, 57
McCann's Local Meats, 50
McGee, Harold, 38, 85, 86, 96, 154, 161
McLaughlin, John, 14
The Meat Hook, 50
Meigs, Hilton, 112
mesquite, 133, 134
mezcal, 203, 205
Miyachiku, 37
Mody, Ketan, 202
mold, 96
Moody, Scott, 113
MTC, 203
Mushrooms, Garlicky Sautéed, 180

N

National, 22
New York strip, 67–68
Niman Ranch, 36

O

oak, 133, 134
oil, finishing steaks with, 159–60
Olivier's, 29, 31, 33, 75

Omaha Steaks, 30
Oregon Country Beef, 36
The Organic Butcher, 50
organic meat, 44
oven, finishing with, 102

P

Parker, Robert, 33
pasture-raised beef, 44, 46
pecan wood, 133, 134, 135
pepper steak, 57
PK Grill, 111–13, 207
Pollard, Cliff, 25
Porter, Valerie, 9
porterhouse, 65–66, 76
Porter Road, 50
potatoes
    Home Frites, 187–88
    Twice-Baked Potato, 184
primal cuts, 57
Prime beef, 38, 39, 41, 54
Prime Foods Distributor, 82, 85
prime rib, 59
"Product of the USA," 46
Publix, 35
Purely Meat Co., 50

R

Rancher's Reserve, 36, 38
resting, 161–62
reverse sear, 165–67
ribeye, 59–60, 68, 76
rib roast, 59
Rivière, Olivier and Katia, 202
Ross, Betsy, 20–21, 207
Runkle, Ben, 31, 50, 52–55, 69, 75

S

safety, 38
Safeway, 36, 38
sake, 201–3
Salad, Green, with Garlic Vinaigrette, 179
Salsa Verde, 193
salt, 156, 158–59
Salt & Time, 29, 31, 50, 52–53, 72, 75
Santa Maria grills, 108, 109, 110, 207

Sappington, Adam, 123
Schatzker, Mark, 42
Scotch, 205
seam butchery, 75
Select beef, 38, 39, 41
sheet pans, 145–46
shovels, 145
Singer, Nate, 26–27
sizzle platters, 146
skirt, 72–73, 77
Smith, Steve, 13
Smith & Wollensky, 82
Snake River Farms, 12, 207
sous vide, 104–5, 107
spinalis dorsi, 59, 60, 63, 68, 91, 93
Stafford, Orin, 125
standing rib roast, 59
Steak Cookoff Association, 113
steaks
    bone-in vs. boneless, 60
    with butter, 159–60
    buying, 25, 29–31, 45, 207
    color of, 45
    crust of, 154–55
    cuts, 56–57, 59–60, 65–74, 76–77
    doneness of, 155–56
    flipping, 160–61
    frozen, 161
    labeling of, 42, 44, 46
    marbling in, 41–42, 45
    with oil, 159–60
    resting, 161–62
    salting, 156, 158–59
    temperature of, before cooking, 160
    thickness of, 170
    See also beef; cooking methods; *individual cuts*
strip, 65, 67–68, 76
subprimals, 57

T

tannins, 200–201
Taylor's Market, 50
T-bone, 65–66, 76
tenderloin, 65, 66–67, 69, 76
tequila, 205
Tesar, John, 82, 84, 96, 201
thermometers, 146
Thornhill, Taylor, 34

three-zone setup, 147–48, 151
tomahawk steak, 57, 60
Tomatoes, Raw, 183
tongs, 144
towels, 146
tri-tip, 73–74
trowels, 145
two-zone setup, 147, 151
Tyson, 22, 35

U

USDA grades, 38–39, 41

V

Vegetables, Grilled, 190
Vine Connections, 203

W

Wagyu beef, 11–13, 16, 23–24, 36, 37, 202–3
wet aging, 38, 86
whiskey, 203, 205
Williams, Allen, 16, 18
wine
    pairing steak and, 200–201, 202
    Perky Red Wine Sauce, 197
wood
    advantages and disadvantages of, 129–30, 151
    choosing, 130
    cutting, 130
    fire, starting, 150
    seasoning, 132
    setup for grilling with, 149–50
    sourcing, 135–36
    types of, 132–35
World Butchery Challenge, 52
World Sake Imports, 203

How to

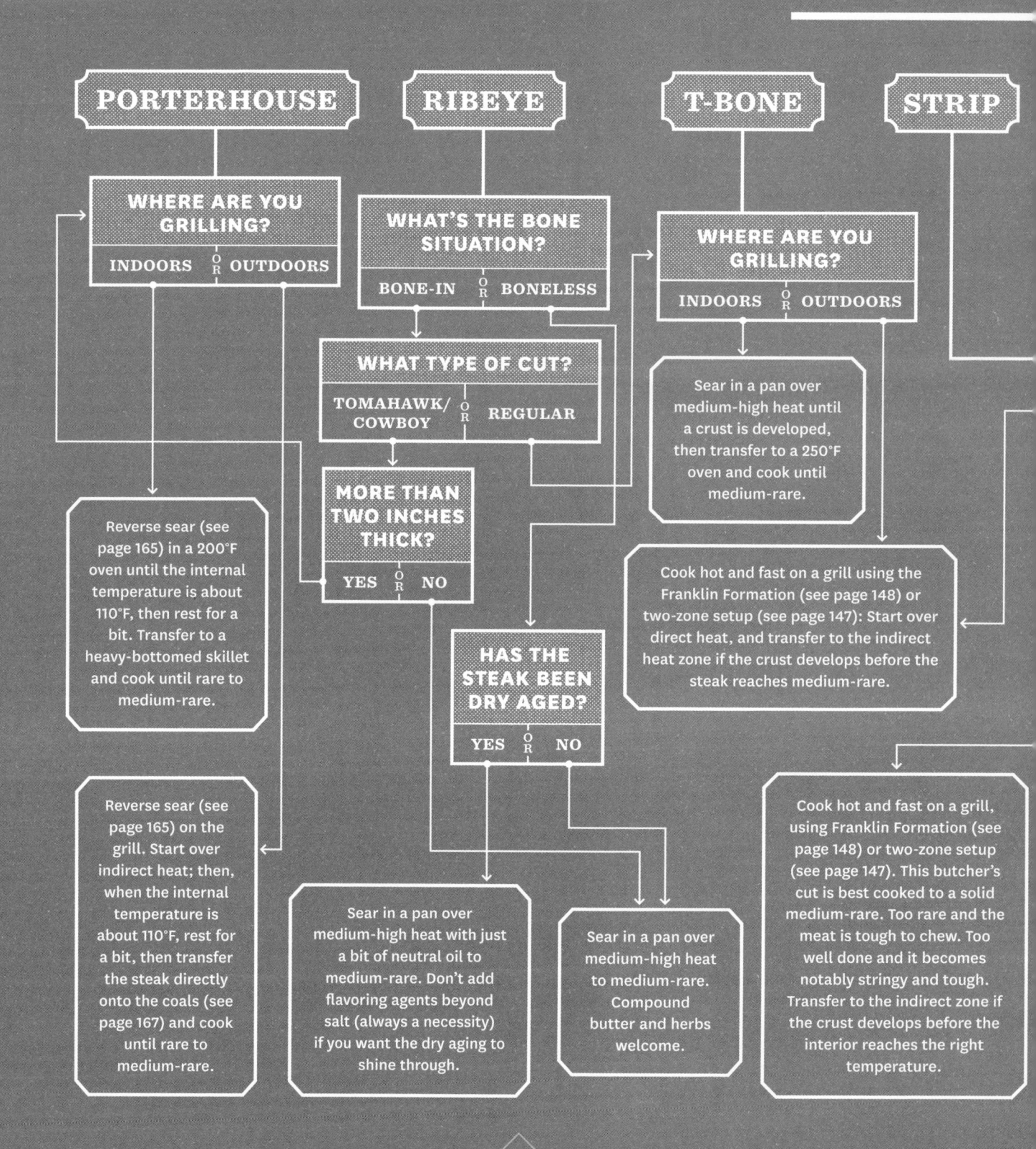

PORTERHOUSE

WHERE ARE YOU GRILLING?
INDOORS OR OUTDOORS

- **Indoors:** Reverse sear (see page 165) in a 200°F oven until the internal temperature is about 110°F, then rest for a bit. Transfer to a heavy-bottomed skillet and cook until rare to medium-rare.

- **Outdoors:** Reverse sear (see page 165) on the grill. Start over indirect heat; then, when the internal temperature is about 110°F, rest for a bit, then transfer the steak directly onto the coals (see page 167) and cook until rare to medium-rare.

RIBEYE

WHAT'S THE BONE SITUATION?
BONE-IN OR BONELESS

WHAT TYPE OF CUT?
TOMAHAWK/COWBOY OR REGULAR

MORE THAN TWO INCHES THICK?
YES OR NO

HAS THE STEAK BEEN DRY AGED?
YES OR NO

- **Dry aged:** Sear in a pan over medium-high heat with just a bit of neutral oil to medium-rare. Don't add flavoring agents beyond salt (always a necessity) if you want the dry aging to shine through.

- **Not dry aged:** Sear in a pan over medium-high heat to medium-rare. Compound butter and herbs welcome.

T-BONE

WHERE ARE YOU GRILLING?
INDOORS OR OUTDOORS

- **Indoors:** Sear in a pan over medium-high heat until a crust is developed, then transfer to a 250°F oven and cook until medium-rare.

- **Outdoors:** Cook hot and fast on a grill using the Franklin Formation (see page 148) or two-zone setup (see page 147): Start over direct heat, and transfer to the indirect heat zone if the crust develops before the steak reaches medium-rare.

STRIP

Cook hot and fast on a grill, using Franklin Formation (see page 148) or two-zone setup (see page 147). This butcher's cut is best cooked to a solid medium-rare. Too rare and the meat is tough to chew. Too well done and it becomes notably stringy and tough. Transfer to the indirect zone if the crust develops before the interior reaches the right temperature.

Cook Steak

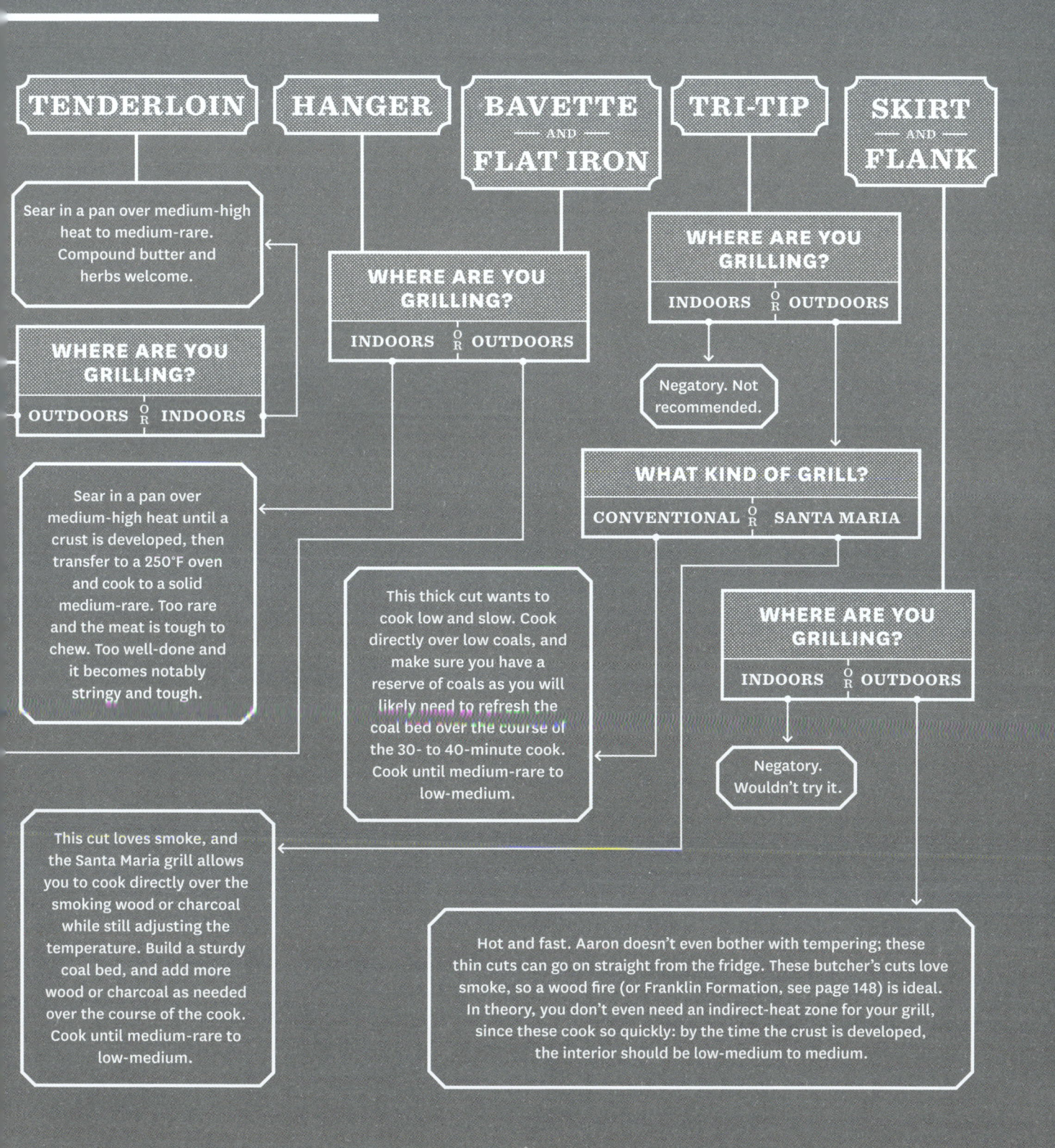

TENDERLOIN

Sear in a pan over medium-high heat to medium-rare. Compound butter and herbs welcome.

HANGER

WHERE ARE YOU GRILLING?
OUTDOORS **or** INDOORS

Sear in a pan over medium-high heat until a crust is developed, then transfer to a 250°F oven and cook to a solid medium-rare. Too rare and the meat is tough to chew. Too well-done and it becomes notably stringy and tough.

BAVETTE AND FLAT IRON

WHERE ARE YOU GRILLING?
INDOORS **or** OUTDOORS

This thick cut wants to cook low and slow. Cook directly over low coals, and make sure you have a reserve of coals as you will likely need to refresh the coal bed over the course of the 30- to 40-minute cook. Cook until medium-rare to low-medium.

TRI-TIP

WHERE ARE YOU GRILLING?
INDOORS **or** OUTDOORS

Negatory. Not recommended.

WHAT KIND OF GRILL?
CONVENTIONAL **or** SANTA MARIA

This cut loves smoke, and the Santa Maria grill allows you to cook directly over the smoking wood or charcoal while still adjusting the temperature. Build a sturdy coal bed, and add more wood or charcoal as needed over the course of the cook. Cook until medium-rare to low-medium.

SKIRT AND FLANK

WHERE ARE YOU GRILLING?
INDOORS **or** OUTDOORS

Negatory. Wouldn't try it.

Hot and fast. Aaron doesn't even bother with tempering; these thin cuts can go on straight from the fridge. These butcher's cuts love smoke, so a wood fire (or Franklin Formation, see page 148) is ideal. In theory, you don't even need an indirect-heat zone for your grill, since these cook so quickly: by the time the crust is developed, the interior should be low-medium to medium.

Ten Speed Press
An imprint of the Crown Publishing Group
A division of Penguin Random House LLC
1745 Broadway
New York, NY 10019
tenspeed.com
penguinrandomhouse.com

2025 Ten Speed Press/Publishers Trade Paperback Box Edition
Text copyright © 2019 by Hasenpfeffer LLC
Photographs copyright © 2019 by Wyatt McSpadden
Illustrations copyright © 2019 by Bryan B. Butler

Penguin Random House values and supports copyright. Copyright fuels creativity, encourages diverse voices, promotes free speech, and creates a vibrant culture. Thank you for buying an authorized edition of this book and for complying with copyright laws by not reproducing, scanning, or distributing any part of it in any form without permission. You are supporting writers and allowing Penguin Random House to continue to publish books for every reader. Please note that no part of this book may be used or reproduced in any manner for the purpose of training artificial intelligence technologies or systems.

Ten Speed Press and the Ten Speed Press colophon are registered trademarks of Penguin Random House LLC.

ISBN 978-0-399-58096-3
Ebook ISBN 978-0-399-58097-0
Box set ISBN 978-0-593-83963-8

Originally published in hardcover in the United States by Ten Speed Press, an imprint of the Crown Publishing Group, a division of Penguin Random House, LLC, in 2019.

The photograph on page 53 appears courtesy of Bryan Butler and Ben Runkle.
Illustration on page 8 by iStock.com/clu.

Design by Betsy Stromberg

Manufactured in China

10 9 8 7 6 5 4 3 2 1

First Paperback Box Edition

The authorized representative in the EU for product safety and compliance is Penguin Random House Ireland, Morrison Chambers, 32 Nassau Street, Dublin D02 YH68, Ireland, https://eu-contact.penguin.ie.

FRANKLIN BARBECUE

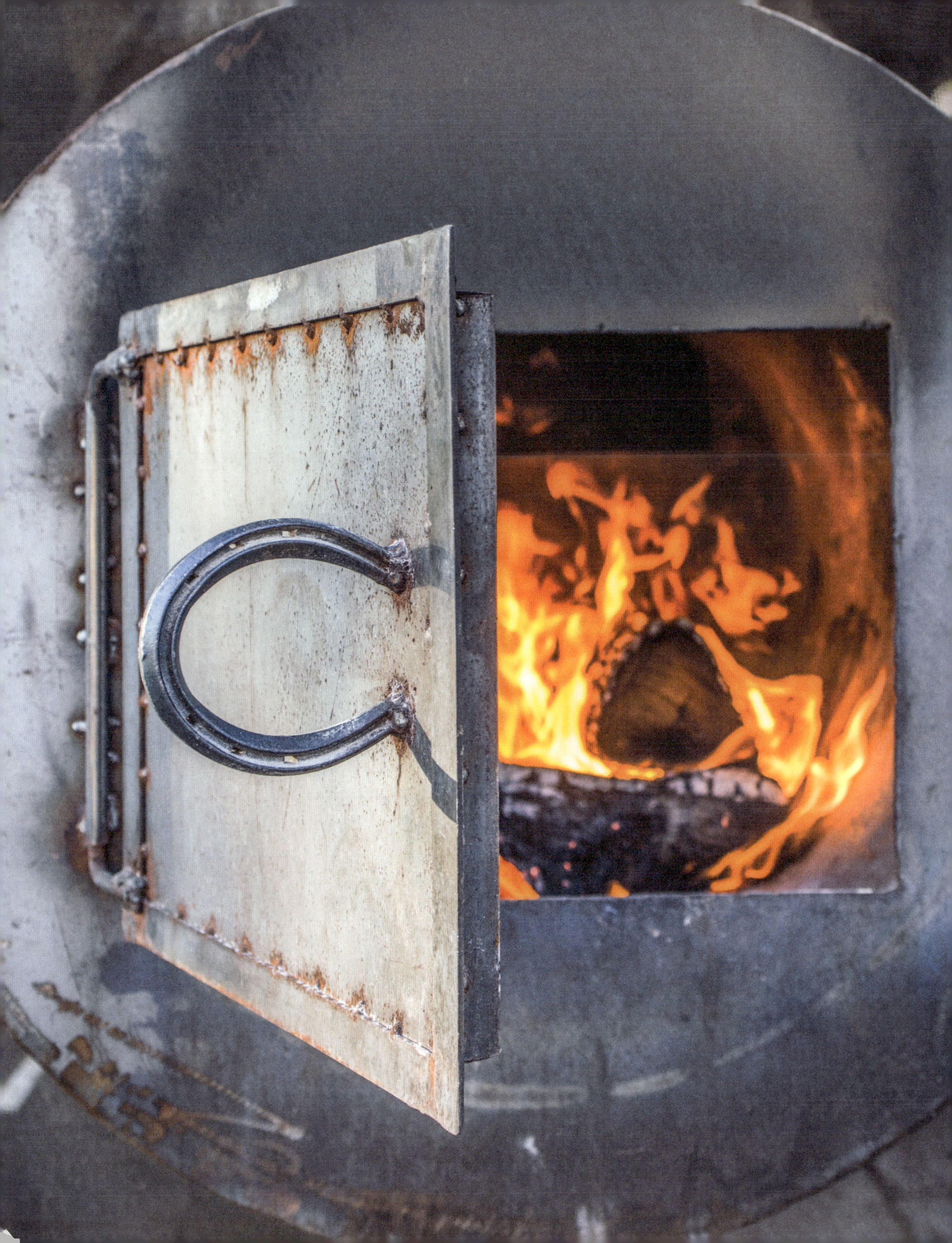

FRANKLIN
BARBECUE

• A MEAT-SMOKING MANIFESTO •

AARON FRANKLIN
and
JORDAN MACKAY

Photography by Wyatt McSpadden

TEN SPEED PRESS
Berkeley

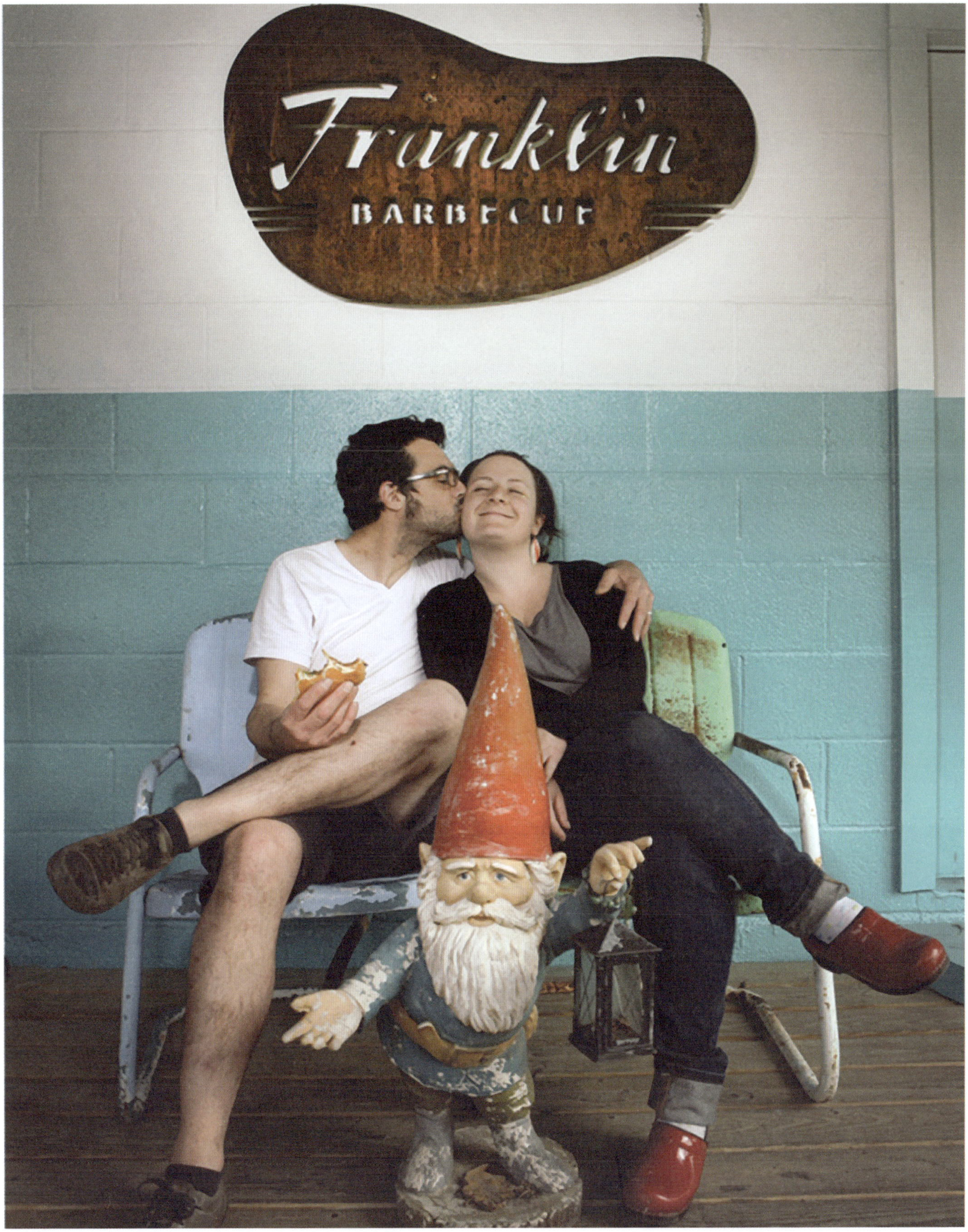
Franklin
BARBECUE

DEDICATION

*To my wonderful wife, Stacy,
our beautiful daughter, Vivian,
and our little dog too!*

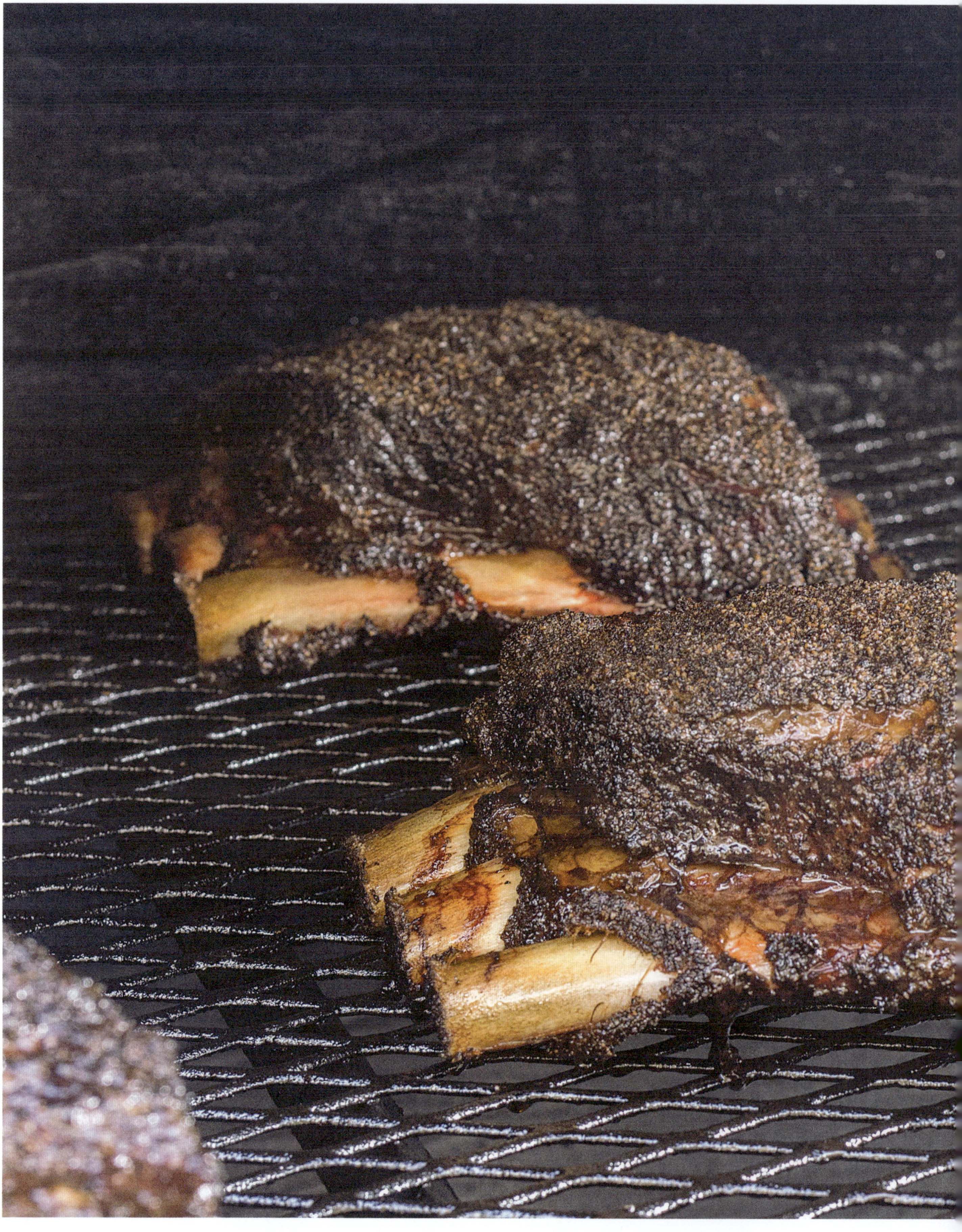

• **Contents**

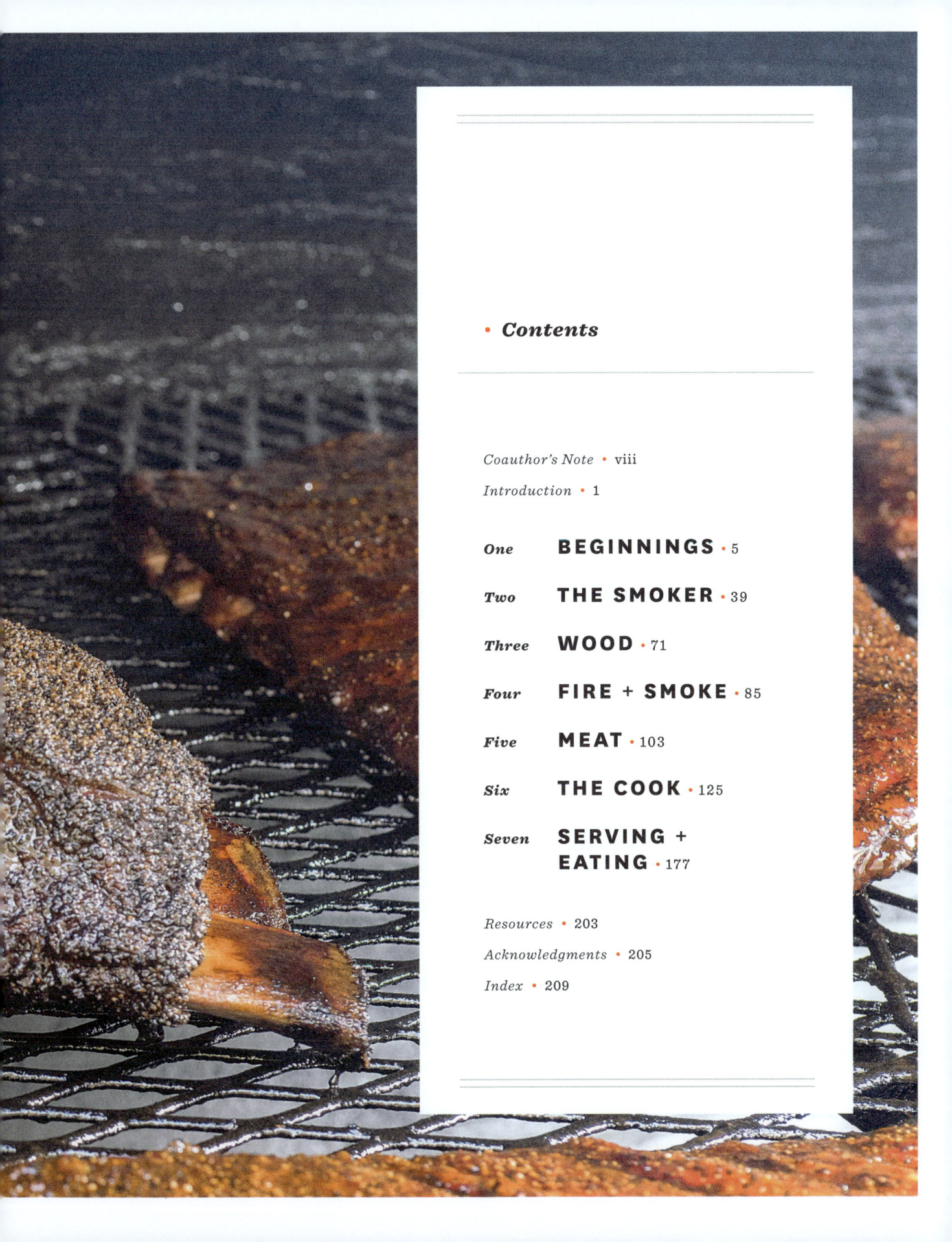

Coauthor's Note • viii

Introduction • 1

One **BEGINNINGS** • 5

Two **THE SMOKER** • 39

Three **WOOD** • 71

Four **FIRE + SMOKE** • 85

Five **MEAT** • 103

Six **THE COOK** • 125

Seven **SERVING + EATING** • 177

Resources • 203

Acknowledgments • 205

Index • 209

Coauthor's Note

The first question people always asked when they heard I was working on a book with Aaron Franklin—the man whose Austin restaurant is as famous for its incredibly long lines as it is for its food—was, "Is it really that good? Is the barbecue that much better than everyone else's?" And, I always answered, Yep, pretty much.

The second question was always the same too. "What does he do that's so different from everyone else?" And my answer to that was always the same too: Not that much.

So what is the secret? That's what everyone really wants to know. It's true that Aaron uses more expensive and higher grade meat than almost everyone else. It's also true that he has a talent for designing and tinkering with his smokers to get the optimal smoking action he desires. And, yes, he has an almost demented attention to detail when it comes to cooking meat—every log on the fire, every rib, every brisket is treated individually and given discreet consideration as it cooks and becomes barbecue. But I can't answer the original question by describing any specific maneuvers or secret techniques I learned while working with Aaron. What I can say after having spent hours and hours cooking with him at all times of day and night is that the reason his food is so successful seems to lie in his personality, his work ethic, and his remarkable talent for comprehending how things work.

During our time together, I jokingly referred to the latter as his ability to "think like smoke." When he constructs a smoker, burns wood in a firebox, and puts meat in the cooker, Aaron appears—in his own completely intuitive form of consideration—to calculate the way heat and smoke will curl and bounce around the insides of the smoker, around the meat, and ultimately swirl out of the stack in his desired perfect "vortices." He understands how it all works, and consequently he wraps and pulls his meats at just the right moment. It's impressive.

But even more impressive—and what I most admire about the man and what I think is his greatest asset and the greatest secret of his success—is the absolute, utter commitment he has to the customers who truly humble him every day by waiting for hours in line for his food. His obsessive dedication to the happiness and satisfaction of every person who eats at Franklin Barbecue is awe inspiring, especially given how easy it would be for him to kick back, drink some beers, and rest on his smoky laurels. I've never met anyone who, while running an overwhelmingly popular restaurant, welding, working on books, and filming television shows, also tries so hard to make sure people get what they want. And these people—diners, media, fans, amateur pitmasters—want a lot from him. He sleeps very little, and I hope he can keep it up.

Some folks may also wonder how a writer best known for his writing on wine ended up in Austin working with a modern barbecue master. Besides the fact that I grew up in Austin and went to school there (though I now live in San Francisco), wine and barbecue share several qualities that deserve observation. Both are best when made "low and slow," with wine being one of the few products that goes even lower and slower than great barbecue. With both barbecue and wine, you're never exactly sure how it's going to turn out until it's done and you open it up. Both rely on a combination of good-quality natural ingredients and the technique and skill of an experienced practitioner. Thanks to local, natural ingredients—be they beef or pork, hickory or oak, Pinot Noir or Riesling—and the techniques that have been developed to transform them, expressive, distinctive, and regional styles have arisen in both the barbecue and the wine world. In short, at their best, both wine and barbecue have some sort of *terroir* (a great French term): give me a taste of your barbecue or a swallow of your wine, and I'll tell you who you are.

That said, very little wine was consumed during the making of this book. And happily so. While wine is wonderful, immersion in the far-more-relaxed culture of barbecue was refreshing and inspiring (though the day often starts way too early). Yes, we drank a lot of beer.

Now that I'm in, I don't think I'll ever be able to leave the barbecue world. I'm in too deep; the compulsion is there now. I'm going to continue working on keeping my fires steady, get better at knowing when to pull the ribs, and practice getting my rubs more evenly spread. And whenever I get back to Austin, I'll be putting in a few hours waiting in line at Franklin Barbecue because, yes, it's just that good.

• ***Jordan Mackay***

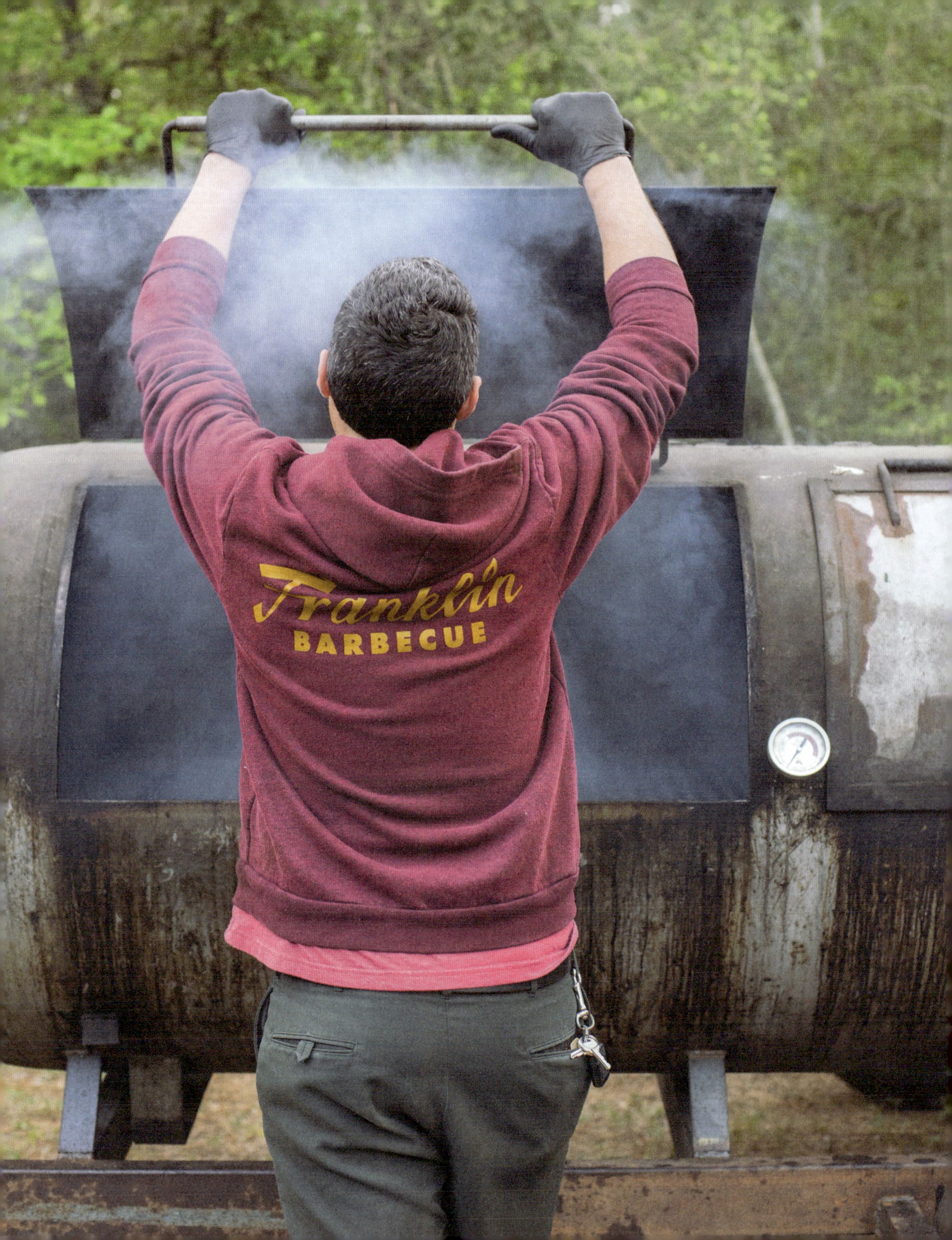
Franklin
BARBECUE

• *Introduction*

The notion of putting everything I know about barbecue into a book is a daunting one. Not because I know so much—I'm still learning—but because of the nature of barbecue itself. It's because the printed word—definitive, exacting, permanent—is in many ways antithetical to the process of cooking barbecue, which is, for lack of a better word, loosey-goosey.

So many people want to have a recipe, but with all of the variables in barbecue—wood, quality of fire, meat selection, type of cooker, weather, and so on—there is no "magic" recipe. It just doesn't operate with absolutes of temperature, time, and measurement. In fact, there are no rights or wrongs in barbecue (well, that may be a stretch), no "just one way," and certainly no simple "black and white." You're much better off with general knowledge of what you want and an arsenal of tricks to have up your sleeve.

So unlike most books that you may flip through a few times and then place on the shelf to display with the others, I hope this one will live a good portion of its life out in the field, be it in the kitchen or out by the smoker. These recipes aren't really recipes but more of an idea of how I go about cooking barbecue and some guidelines.

Now, this book is not a survey of barbecue traditions across the country. While I've been all over the United States and have eaten lots of great barbecue, there's really only one tradition that I know intimately: my own. My style is steeped in the tradition of Central Texas, but it's also got some wrinkles that I discovered along the way. So, with the greatest respect to all of the other styles around the country, in this book, all I discuss is what we do. Yes, I am wedded to the tradition of great Central Texas barbecue and the principles it holds—brisket, oak, open flame—but I'm also always willing to try something new or look into new designs that might make things cook faster and better. And my hope is that by being hyperdetailed and specific about my techniques, I will help you in your cooking and in your ability to develop your own style too. At Franklin Barbecue, the only thing we've got is the dedication to make the best food we can and to keep it consistently the same every day (which itself is the biggest challenge). It's that dedication that keeps us evolving as cooks and constantly thinking about new ways to do old things.

You'll notice that there's a serious thread of do-it-yourself running through this book. That's because one of the words with which I've been known to describe myself is *cheap*. For large stretches of my life, I didn't have the cash to buy things I wanted, so I often just figured out how to make them myself. In the process, I sometimes discovered how to make them better or at least how to tailor them to my own needs. However, while I participate in DIY culture and continue to build stuff all of the time, it's by no means necessary to take this approach in order to benefit from this book. I say, use whatever equipment you've got on hand; ideally, the information I present here will help you make the best of it.

Most barbecue books I've looked at are organized around the major food groups: beef, pork, poultry, and so on. (At least, those are *my* food groups.) In this book, which isn't heavily focused on recipes, I've taken a different approach. It's a more elemental and theoretical breakdown of the barbecue process. In each chapter, I drill down into some fairly technical information with regard to how the process of barbecue works. It can get a little geeky, but I hope that in a way the geekiness keeps you engaged. I include this information because I myself love the technical details. Understanding how something works is the first step toward successfully replicating and improving it.

The first chapter is an extended telling of my own story. I include it at this length not for the purpose of vanity, but the opposite—so that everyone can see how you don't have to have much money, history, training, or even time to become proficient at barbecue. I really just want to show how a love for barbecue coupled with enthusiasm can equal really good-tasting smoked meat. If I can do this, you can too.

The second chapter is all about the smoker. In Texas, this piece of equipment might be called a smoker, cooker, and pit all in the same sentence, but whatever you call it, barbecue practitioners have no end of fascination with these clunky steel constructions. Everyone who designs and builds his or her own smoker does something a little bit different, always looking for that tweak that will improve its performance. In this chapter, I talk about various kinds of smokers and various modifications you can make to improve the performance of an inexpensive off-the-rack smoker you might buy at an outdoors store. I also give a very basic template for how to build your own smoker from scratch. It's by no means a blueprint but rather intended to give you an idea of what to think about if you undertake such a project. While smoker construction sounds—and is—fairly ambitious, I can tell you that I've built very heavy smokers in my backyard with a cheap welder, rope, and a tree branch to hoist pieces up.

Chapter three is about wood. Wood is our sole fuel, but it's also arguably the most important seasoning in the food. Without wood, barbecue wouldn't be barbecue, so we have to take the wood we use as seriously as we would any ingredient in any dish. Just as you wouldn't sauté meats and vegetables in rancid butter, you want to use good-quality firewood in pristine condition whenever possible. In this chapter, you'll learn all about seasoning, splitting, buying, and judging wood for barbecue. After reading it, you'll definitely be wanting your own little woodpile in the backyard. Just keep it dry.

It's no big leap from wood to fire and smoke, the subjects of chapter four. Most people don't realize there are gradations of smoke and fire. But a good fire and the fine smoke it produces are two of the most fundamental elements to producing superior Central Texas barbecue. In this chapter, I get into the nitty-gritty of what good smoke and fire mean and how to produce them in various conditions. It's a bit sciencey, but it also tends to be pretty interesting, so hopefully you'll get a lot out of it.

INTRODUCTION

Chapter five is about meat. One of things I do differently from most other barbecue joints is use a higher grade of meat. It makes things more expensive for everyone (including me), but I think it's worth it not only for the quality of the end product but also for the quality of life of the humans eating it and of the noble animals that were sacrificed to bring us this food. You'll learn here what certain grades of meat mean, where they come from on the animal, and how to go about selecting the best meat for your cooking.

Chapter six is a doozy. It's the one where I finally get into the actual cooking of the meat. If you buy this book and just want to dive right in, you could start here, though I recommend going back at some time to read all of the other stuff. This is the chapter where I do things like suggest temperatures and times for your cook, even though ultimately you have to figure out the fine details of these things for your own kind of cooker, your own conditions, and ultimately your own taste. But I do talk about other important stuff like trimming meats, rubbing, and wrapping—all the techniques that will help your meat turn out great. The bulk of this chapter is devoted to brisket and ribs, which are the two most popular meats, and cooked using the two basic methods of cooking we do. All of our other fare basically follows these methods, so to learn how to cook brisket and ribs in a smoker is to learn how to cook just about anything.

Lastly, we talk a little bit about sides, sauces, serving, drinking, and all of the stuff that goes hand in hand with enjoying the fruits of your labor. In Central Texas, sides and sauces are always considered secondary to the meat, if indeed necessary at all. So I don't place a huge emphasis on them, even though I will admit that our beans are really good. More important is brisket slicing technique, which is something I go into detail about here. It's hard to train people to cut brisket really well, but once you practice and repeat it, you'll be glad to have good skill in this area, since there's nothing worse than hacking up something you just spent a day coddling. And at last, beer, like day and night, is a fact of life for the pitmaster, and it's something I think about a lot! So I talk a little about what I like and what I think works best with barbecue, though beer in general gets a big fat *Yes*.

Hopefully, while you read this book, you'll find yourself chomping at the bit to get out there and throw a few racks of ribs or a big, honking brisket onto your smoker. And all I can say is, Go for it! The key to my own development—and it will be to yours—is repetition. Just as with anything, the more you do it, the better you'll get. In barbecue that's especially true, particularly if you pay close attention along the way to what you did during the cooking process and when you did it, and then you note the final results and think about how to make the next cook better. That's what I did, and my barbecue improved steadily along the way. And I didn't even have a resource like this book.

Ultimately, that's the best advice I can give. Do, and do some more. Drink beer, but not so much that you lose track of what you're doing. And pay attention. Sweat the details and you'll end up producing barbecue that would make the most seasoned of pitmasters proud.

BEGINNINGS

• ***Chapter One***

It's 2 a.m. on a foggy, cold February night. I have just arrived at work and am looking everywhere for the tamper for the espresso machine. It's not where it should be, and I'm slightly annoyed. Here at Franklin Barbecue, often the very first thing new kitchen employees are trained to do is pull a good espresso shot. Very important. We have a two-group classic La Marzocco Linea espresso machine taking up good real estate back in the kitchen, and it pulls beautiful shots. Espresso is not on the menu, though, and we don't serve it to customers. It's just for us. But it's what you need when your day starts at 2 a.m.

Having no luck finding the tamper, I improvise and pull the shot anyway using the bottom of a hot sauce bottle. Good enough. Warm espresso cup cradled in my hand, I step outside into the bracing 28°F night. We're in the middle of one of the massive cold fronts that swoop down through the Midwest from Canada and plunge Austin—and all of Central Texas—into subfreezing weather. This happens several times a year. It can be tricky when it comes to barbecue, as dealing with the changing weather is one of the supreme challenges of cooking good, consistent meat. Weather this cold affects temperatures, cooking times, and the way our smokers draw. But I'll talk a lot more about that later on.

We have many different shifts at Franklin Barbecue: cooking the ribs, putting the briskets on, meat and sides prep, pulling the briskets off, cutting lunch, and more. The 2 a.m. shift is the rib shift, and I work it a couple of times a week. When I arrive, I say good night to the late-night guy who's been tending the briskets—which went on yesterday morning around 10 a.m. and were pulled starting around 1 a.m. this morning—and get about my business.

Yes, it's the middle of the night—but there's a lot to do before dawn, before another person shows up to work, which won't be until 6:30 a.m. But first, I spend a moment with my steaming cup of espresso, which I take outside where I'll tend the fires. I pause to smell that beautiful mingling of crema with the ubiquitous but still sweet smell of the smoke from the multiple oak fires I have going right now.

Here's what I need to accomplish between now and 9 a.m.: trim and season sixty racks of ribs and get them on the smokers; get the giant cauldron of beans started while warming and breaking up the brisket trimmings from the day before, which will be added to those beans; assess and feed all of the fires we've got going; trim and season about twenty giant turkey breasts; constantly keep all of the cookers at about 275°F, taking into account the temperature variations that occur due to the whims of wood fires crackling in freezing cold weather; chat with Melissa, the pie woman, who makes all of our desserts; accept and possibly put away the thousands of pounds of meat—a day's supply— we'll receive from the delivery guys at 6:30 a.m. (though, annoyingly, they usually don't show up on time); carry shovelfuls of coals from the smoker (which we affectionately call Muchacho) to smoker Number Two to start the fires for the turkey breasts and (later) the sausages; get the turkey basting sauce together; check on and moisten the ribs multiple times; pull sixty giant sheets of foil to wrap the ribs; spray, sauce, and wrap the ribs; and get Rusty Shackleford up to temperature for tomorrow's briskets. Even though it's the wee hours of the morning and not a single person is around, I often find myself literally running from the kitchen out the back door to check temperatures and load the fires and running back in to handle my duties in the kitchen. Of course, I give myself a short break here or there for an espresso or, in this cold weather, an Americano, which allows for longer sipping. You can balance these coffees on the top of the firebox or on the handles of the heavy smoker doors and let the heat of the cookers keep them warm.

By now, it's been light for a couple of hours, though I may not have noticed the actual moment the sky changed. Also by now, the line is beginning to form and stretch around the side of the restaurant. On weekdays the first people usually show up by 8 a.m. On Saturdays it can be as early as 6 a.m.

By 9 a.m., I've completed most of the duties of my shift. I'm starving by now and can take a brief breather. It's Austin, so we eat a lot of breakfast tacos. I'll either put together some brisket breakfast tacos here at the restaurant or head out to Mi Madre's a mile away for some classic ones. I'll eat and maybe spend some time answering emails before checking in with my staff, which has been gradually arriving. I'll go over the day's preorders and consult with the person who's cutting the meat today (if it's not me). All kinds of demands will be hitting me now just about running the restaurant. And then, it's 11 a.m., and the mayhem begins. We open the doors, the line starts moving, and for the next four hours we'll serve over 1,500 pounds of brisket, all of those sixty racks of ribs, twenty turkey breasts, and 500 to 800 sausage links, not to mention gallons of beans, coleslaw, and iced tea and a lot of beer. I stick around for a good part of the day, putting out fires, checking food, busing tables, and greeting guests, which will be a mix of locals and people from all over the world. Today they waited in the cold, but much more often they may be waiting in the 90°F to 100°F temperatures that we see a lot of around here.

A DAY IN THE LIFE AT FRANKLIN

12 a.m.
Briskets are pulled off the smoker to rest.

2 a.m.
Espresso! Start prepping for rib shift; trim and rub the beef ribs and build fires.

2 to 3 a.m.
Beef ribs on! Time to trim and rub the pork ribs.

3 to 4 a.m.
Pork ribs on! Continue to watch the fires.

4 to 5 a.m.
Prep turkey; set up mise en place.

5 to 6 a.m.
Turkeys on! Another espresso. Spritz and sauce the ribs; set up warmers.

6 to 7 a.m.
Wrap ribs; set up for line outside; start to rub tomorrow's briskets.

7 to 8 a.m.
Wrap turkey! Make sides; continue to rub tomorrow's briskets; start sorting cooked briskets; set up front of house; put up deliveries.

8 to 10 a.m.
Start checking the line; start pulling ribs. Cook sausage. Finish beef ribs and turkeys.

10 to 11 a.m.
Put food on warmers; put tomorrow's briskets on the smoker; cut any pre-orders.

11 a.m. to 3 p.m.
Lunch! Trim briskets for the next day. Do pork butts; cook potatoes; prep in kitchen; watch fires; dishes.

3 to 6 p.m.
Finish lunch service; clean; continue to trim briskets.

6 p.m. to 12 a.m.
Make sauce; tend briskets; kitchen prep.

Rinse and repeat!

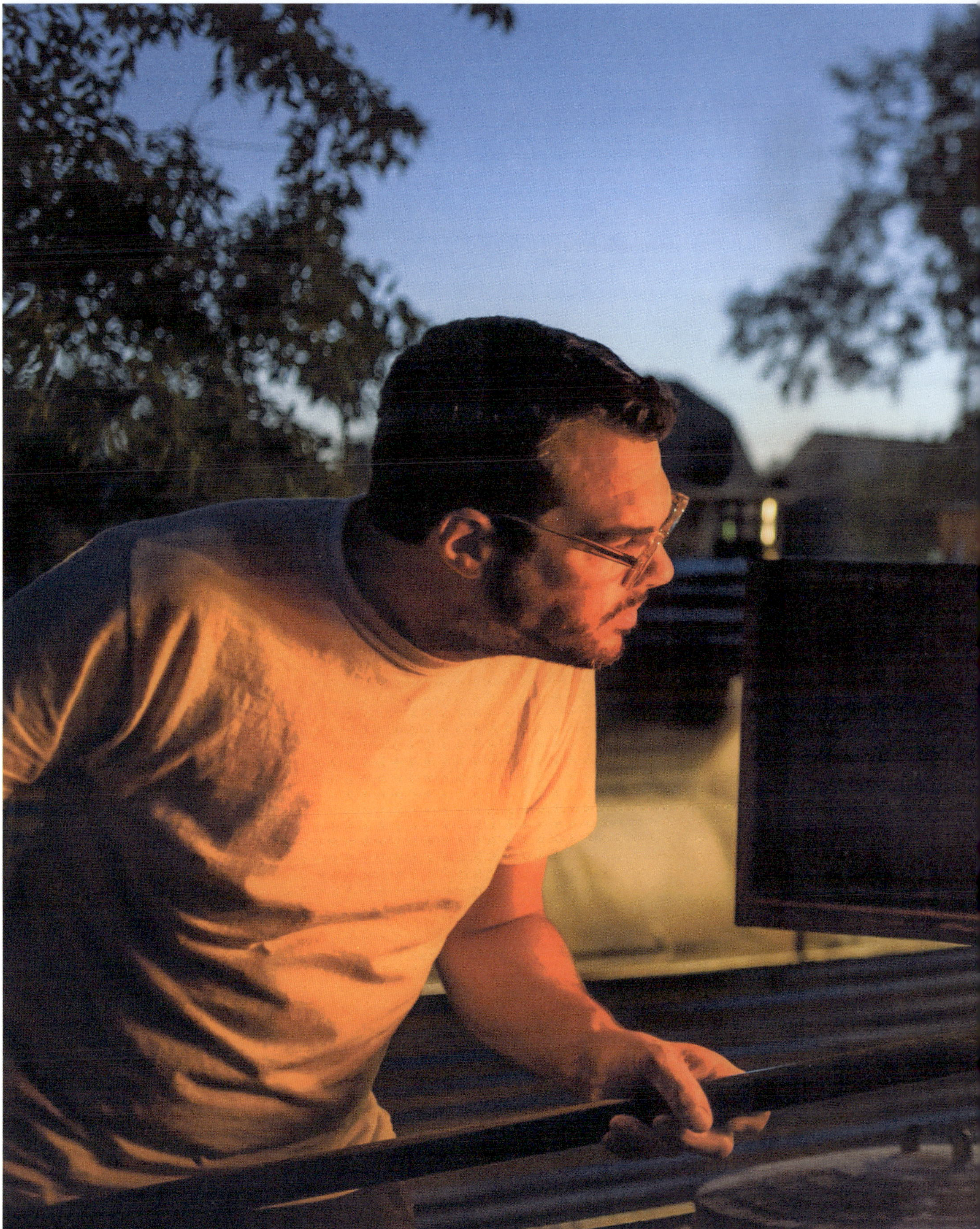

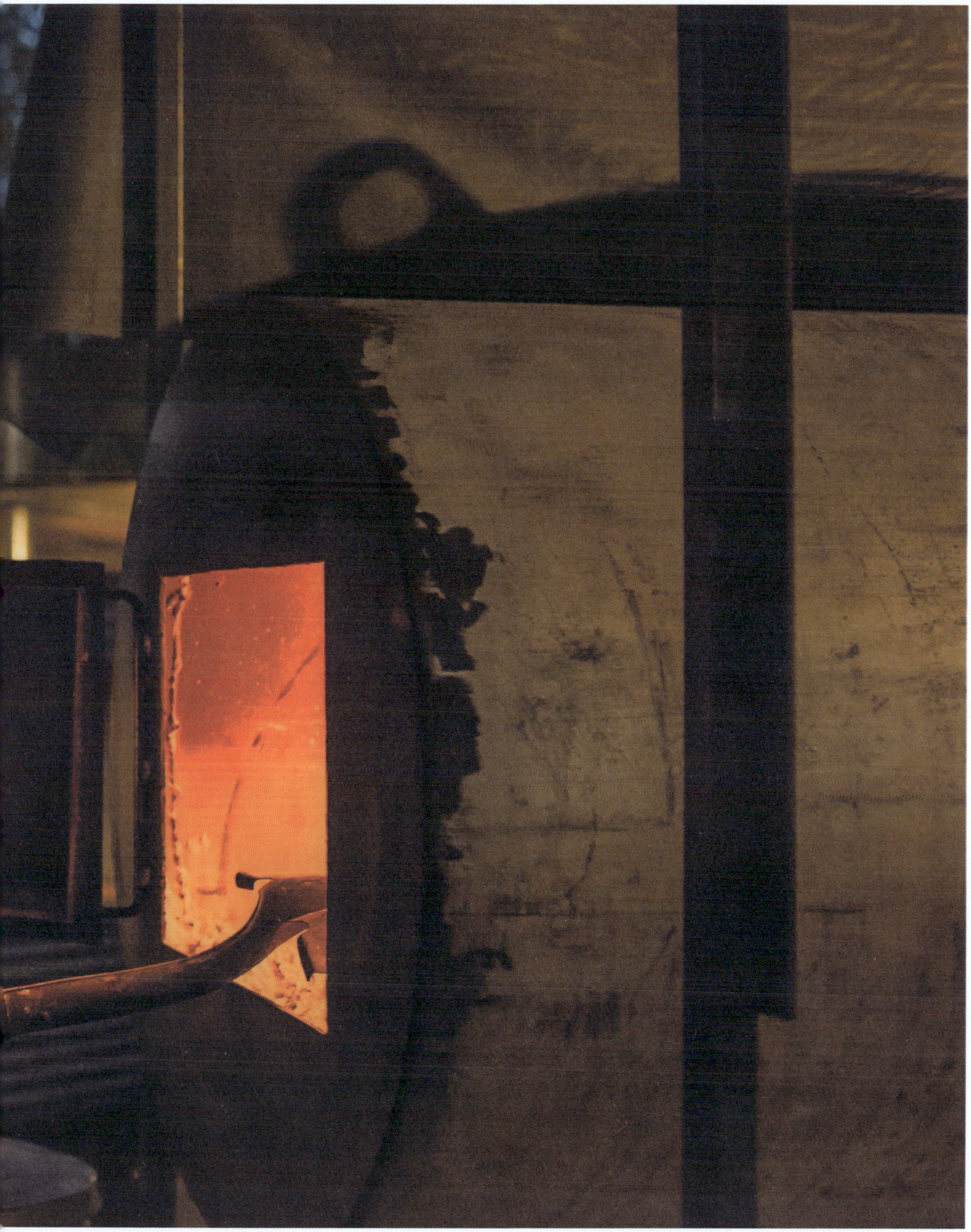

They all have in common that they waited anywhere from three to five hours to eat the meat that I've been blessed enough to be able to prepare for them.

After lunch, I'll probably run errands around town or have some meetings. Or I might just go home and fall asleep for a while before dinner. Bedtime is usually between 9 and 10 o'clock, before it starts all over again.

EARLY DAYS

A lot of people might tell their backstory for the sake of storytelling—for the sake of entertainment. And that's good and valuable in its own right. But when I look back on my barbecue life, I can see that where all this came from is absolutely integral to what it eventually became. What I mean is, I didn't learn how to cook barbecue just to master a craft. Its evolution in me is a true expression of who I am and where I came from. Specific places, specific times of life and states of mind, and specific people all contributed greatly to what Stacy and I and our restaurant have come to be. You'll be surprised that when we started we had absolutely nothing—no resources, no knowledge, no image of what we wanted to become. All I had were my own two hands, a work ethic, a positive attitude, a sense of humor, and a fine lady to help it all come together.

Barbecue to me is about more than just the smoke and the meat, more than trying to cook better with more flavor and more consistency (though those things are definitely important). Barbecue is also about a culture that I love. It's about the smell of smoke and meat browning and the sound of a wood fire crackling. It's about time, the slow passage of hours. It's about the people that I hang out with, but also about the solitude of the long, solo cook. For me, it's about the look and feel and construction of not only smokers but also of buildings, cars, guitars, and other beautiful, artfully designed things. It's about service and about people relaxing and having a good time. It's about the connection I feel to a vast, time-honored cooking tradition and to all of the people practicing it across Texas and across the country every single day.

. . .

In 1996, when I moved to Austin from Bryan–College Station, Texas (100 miles northeast of Austin), it was never my intention to open a barbecue restaurant. In fact, I wasn't even into barbecue. I was nineteen years old and into rock 'n' roll. Barbecue wasn't something I even really thought about much.

It's true that when I was little, around eleven years old, my parents did own a barbecue joint in Bryan for a while. It was a cool old place with a classic brick pit from the 1920s, a fire on the floor (in barbecue, *pit* is an interchangeable term for *smoker* or *cooker* and may be an actual pit or might be something that stands on legs or wheels aboveground)—the kind of joint that just reeks of character (and that you can still find in small towns across Texas).

It did make an impression on me, but not necessarily on how I cook. Rather, it just sank into my psyche and came to kind of nestle there, associating barbecue for me with the good things in life—with family and friends and that certain sense of well-being that you have when you're a kid in a good place. Even though it didn't really occur to me until long after, I think the sense of nostalgia that I carry from my parents' restaurant

BEGINNINGS

sits at the heart of the passion for barbecue that I later found in myself.

But equally important was the music store that my grandparents owned. I spent a lot of time there and worked there throughout my teenage years. I did a little bit of everything—selling instruments, setting up PA systems, giving guitar lessons, repairing guitars and amps. I developed my passion for music there but also for something else: for taking things apart and fixing them—for tinkering, for disassembling objects and seeing firsthand how they work.

You might not think that that approach to things has much application to preparing great barbecue, but it does. Understanding how things are put together and how they work is the first step toward improving them. The more you do it, the better you get at it, and if you don't have any fear of getting a little dirty or of prying something open and examining how it functions, you start to develop the confidence that you can fix most anything and even make it run better than it did before. And that's basically the approach I've taken my whole barbecue career and am still taking today, working daily to improve my smokers and my restaurant in general to make it more efficient, more consistent, and more durable.

But back then, after I graduated from high school, all I wanted to do was play music. So I went to Austin and had a good time working odd jobs and playing in a couple of bands. We'd play rock shows, go on tours in vans, that kind of thing—24-inch kick drums, Marshall stacks, fists in the air, Pabst Blue Ribbon. I realize now that even playing music fed into my later endeavors. It may not seem like it, but there are many similarities between playing in a band at a show and putting on a barbecue.

• • •

My love of barbecue—my insane obsession with it—started to crop up about the same time I met Stacy, now my wife and collaborator (enabler?) in everything. It is a good thing she's patient and accepting of me because she had to tolerate a lot of barbecue talk for a long time. I'm not sure where barbecue came from exactly. It's not like it all just hit me one day. No, it was more like the way winter turns to spring slowly until one day you look up and it's green everywhere. That's how barbecue started for me, as just a little interest, before it became a full-on infatuation and ultimately, unpredictably, my life.

The whole thing really started rolling when we got our first little cooker, a New Braunfels Hondo Classic smoker, for $99 from Academy, an outdoors and recreation store here in Austin.

It's a classic offset smoker in the Texas style, with a firebox that connects to a cooking chamber on one end and a smokestack on the other. It's so cheap because it's made economically and with very thin, inexpensive metal that's not designed to last or even hold heat or smoke very well. Why did I get it? I went out to get a grill for our first place together, but I bought a smoker instead. I guess if you live in Texas long enough, barbecue starts to penetrate your consciousness. And when you get that hankering, you get a smoker, and this was what was available to me at the time.

I have a love of design and architecture overall, but especially of a certain roadside style of Americana from the 1940s, 1950s, and 1960s, which in my mind is really represented in barbecue culture. In 2003, *Texas Monthly*, our state magazine, released its second full issue devoted to barbecue (the first came out long before, in 1997), and that's when things started to hit home for me. The first time I saw Wyatt McSpadden's photos of these great old barbecue temples in Central Texas towns, I thought, *Wow, that is so cool!* I'd never been to the places Wyatt was shooting, but his photos made me think of my parents' place back when I was a little kid, and I realized that barbecue just triggered all sorts of great feelings.

Now I realize that it was about more than just the meat; it was about the character and resonance of barbecue culture. You don't go to those places just for the meat. To walk past the open fires into the smoke-blackened halls of Smitty's in Lockhart is practically a religious experience. You wouldn't want to eat barbecue—even if it was the greatest in the world—at a restaurant that felt like some sterile white box. It wouldn't taste the same without the visuals, the smells, the smoke on the walls, the memorabilia, the pit guy lifting up the smoker lid and a plume of smoke coming out.

My relationship with Stacy was one of the main reasons I gave up the touring musician lifestyle. She supported all of my obsessions—music, carpentry, and, eventually, barbecue—but the band would go out on these tours, and I'd find that I just missed her and missed being home. I thought maybe I should just come home and get a job, but that's also when barbecue started to become a persistent presence in my mind. Stacy is from Texas too (Amarillo, way up in the Panhandle, to be exact). She wasn't *as* in love with barbecue as I was, but like me she enjoyed throwing parties and was always game to put on a cookout together. Believe it or not, a series

BEGINNINGS

of casual cookouts ended up being my only real training before we opened the trailer that would eventually turn into our restaurant. So each one of those backyard parties with friends remains pretty vivid in my mind, especially as they were often tied to a particular residence we had at the time. Austin is full of funky neighborhoods and funky old rent houses, and we moved around a lot.

I cooked my very first brisket in 2002 at one of those backyard cookouts. (For those of you who are keeping track, we opened the Franklin Barbecue trailer in 2009, which means, yes, I had been cooking brisket for only seven years when we first started.) At the time we lived in a little three-plex. My band had done an in-store performance at a record shop, and we had maybe a third of a keg of Lone Star left over. So I told everyone, "Hey, I'm cooking a brisket. If anybody wants to come over tomorrow, we'll finish off this keg and eat it."

I had just gotten my New Braunfels cooker, and this would be my maiden voyage with any kind of smoker. It could hold two briskets, if they were stuffed in there, with each brisket capable of serving maybe ten people. I picked up the brisket on sale at H-E-B—our big chain of Texas grocery stores—for $0.99 a pound. It was prefrozen, commodity, probably Select-grade meat. And I had no idea what to do with it because I'd never cooked anything on an offset cooker. In fact, I'd never shown any particular aptitude for cooking with fire. Negative talent, probably. So, I went online to try to figure out how to make a brisket. Let's just say the Web in 2002 was not as robust as it is today. I called my dad and asked him how to smoke a brisket, and he said something vague like "Just cook it until it's done."

About fifteen of us—the band and some friends—convened the next day. My brisket was flavorless—tough and dry—but everyone was terribly nice about it. They all said it was good. Maybe they really thought that, but I knew it was not true. In hindsight, I didn't wrap it, and I pulled it off right when it was at 165°F internal temperature, smack in the middle of the stall. (We'll talk much more about that later, but at the time I didn't even know what that was.) That was my first brisket: $0.99 a pound on a cheap cooker I'd bought for $99.

Shortly after, Stacy and I moved to Bryan–College Station with the plan to save some money and eventually move to Philadelphia, a city I adore, for a while. Only, we were so miserable to be back in a small town that we found ourselves driving to Austin all the time for work, to be with our friends, and to play music. But it was in Bryan that I did my second cook.

We had a small two-bedroom wood-frame house from the 1950s. It had a pretty nice little backyard. So we had a few people over on a Sunday, just like everyone does. I was itching pretty badly to smoke another brisket, which, again, I purchased on sale for an incredibly low price, and I cooked it on the same little cooker. I still didn't know what I was doing, but I do believe this one turned out slightly better.

I also decided to take things to the next level by making a bunch of barbecue sauces. As a test, I also bought a bunch of crappy commercial ones. We composed a grid and asked everyone to pick their favorite sauces and to offer some tasting notes. I didn't realize it at the time, but I was clearly behaving in a way that suggested I might think of doing this in some kind of official capacity. The sauce test was pretty much the moment when I learned to stop asking for opinions and to listen to my own judgment. People chose the worst ones as their favorites. I believe Kraft actually won. The few commercial ones that I really liked didn't place very high, while the couple I made from scratch placed somewhere in the middle. As it was, our experiment of living in Bryan to save money didn't last long. We missed our friends and our lives in Austin and were spending lots of our time there anyway. Ultimately, we gave up the Philly idea and decided to head back to Austin, where our futures clearly lay.

. . .

Still, Stacy and I were incredibly poor, and when I say poor, I mean well below the poverty line. The kind of poor where you're writing your rent check before you get your paycheck and just hoping it works out. After your paycheck goes through, you realize you have $8 to last you a week before you get your next one. I remember going down to H-E-B to cash in a jar full of change so I could go out and buy a little barbecue.

But we weren't terribly stressed about this. Austin was like that back then. It was a good time and a simpler one. You could pass on jobs to friends, just as you could houses or apartments. You could live cheaply off minimum wage and tips. It was a city full of people like me—people not doing the stereotypical thing of going to college just to get out and find a job, but trying to figure out and do something they really enjoy, like playing music for not much money. People like to say that Austin was a town full of slackers, and I guess on the surface I could have fallen under that category. But I was never a slack worker. I've always had various jobs and always worked hard. I just can't easily work for other people or do work that I don't care for.

Stacy had a job—she waited tables. She was the breadwinner for years, though I always had something I was doing, something to bring in some money. For years, I did random stuff—more often than not, I worked for free on projects for friends. Someone would ask me for help, and I'd think, *Well, I don't have a job right now, so, sure, I'll help you build that.* There were times when Stacy was definitely frustrated with me.

And, yes, in those years, my interest in barbecue was still percolating—it was kind of a constant buzz in the back of my mind. I did a small tour with my friend Big Jeff Keyton, a terrific local musician, and his band, and on those long drives we realized that both of us were really into barbecue. So he started taking me out on occasional day trips to visit local barbecue joints—heading 30 miles south down to Lockhart for Smitty's and Kreuz, or 20 miles farther to Luling's City Market, and especially 40 miles northeast to Taylor to the great Louie Mueller. I'd save and save to scrounge together a few bucks just to be able to go out and taste some barbecue.

I remember that first morsel at Louie Mueller. The place has great counter service— really nice and friendly—and the staff traditionally cuts customers a little taste of beef when they get through the line and up to the counter to order. When I got to the front of the line, Bobby Mueller gave me one bite that turned out to be a whole end cut. I don't know why he gave me that gigantic piece. My eyes must have been bulging, and I might have cried a little bit, but it was so, so good. Sooooooo good! And it started to change me.

It was maybe another year before my next cook, in 2004. This cook signaled another small step in my development, as I prepared the sides as well as the meat, and learned I could put it all together myself. A friend wanted to have a party and said, "Hey, I'll buy the briskets if you want to cook them."

BEGINNINGS

I said, "Hell yeah," because any chance I could get to learn how to cook these things was a boon. And so I cooked the briskets in the front yard of our house and took them to his house while they were resting. And I remember that was the first time people recognized me and said, "Man, that's Aaron, the barbecue guy."

For that party, I had saved up my money and bought a $20 knife. Friggin' sad. I saved up $20! But it's true. I had gone to Ace Mart and bought a cheap Dexter-Russell knife. Still have it. It's at the restaurant, though we don't use it anymore. It just goes to show that you don't need fancy equipment to do most any task in barbecue.

Our next residence was an incredibly dumpy house. There was no real backyard, as the house was on a quarter lot and it took up almost the whole property. It was a one-bedroom, 480-square-foot house, probably around $500 a month in rent. We had one barbecue while we lived there. That was the fifth cook, and the year was 2005.

I had played a show somewhere that night, packed up my drums and left the show early, and got back to the house feeling very gung-ho. The prospect of cooking a brisket was just the most exhilarating thing. Months had gone by, with me trying to scrape together enough cash to put this one puny barbecue on. And, man, I was so excited. I remember firing up that little New Braunfels cooker. I had bought two briskets from H-E-B on sale for $0.99 a pound. I recall feeling like a badass walking out of H-E-B with a shopping cart filled with a whopping two briskets.

I got home from that show probably around 2:30 a.m. I remember just sitting in this small hammock in our tiny, 10-foot-wide backyard, getting the fire going. Our place was at a four-way stop, and there was this streetlamp that would cast its light down into our yard. I just stared at it, thinking it was the coolest thing to see that smoke start wafting up into the night. I was so stoked.

I dozed outside on the hammock while tending the fire. By the next morning, things were going smoothly. I'd pulled the briskets and we were getting the yard ready. Just when it all seemed perfect and twenty to thirty people were about to show up, go figure, the plumbing backed up. A root had cracked a pipe from the toilet, and there was sewage floating up into the yard. Gross! The owner of the house was in prison, so we couldn't really call anyone. And I had bought all of this food with what was, as usual, my last few dollars, so we couldn't call it off. It was a Sunday, and I remember finding a piece of plywood and just covering up the swamp. Stacy and I were looking at each other saying, *Oh my God, oh my God, oh my God. The bathroom doesn't work. This is terrible!*

But, somehow, no one noticed, except that we couldn't use the house's one bathroom. I remember not being really happy with the brisket. For one thing, I may not have realized that cooking two briskets at the same time would alter the process. But I might have also been disappointed that I wasn't improving by leaps and bounds every time I managed to cook a brisket. Now I know that progress doesn't always flow in a steady stream. You have to give yourself some slack, because learning how to make barbecue takes time, and not everything's going to be a big success.

Not that this was by any means a failure. The brisket just wasn't appreciably better than what I'd done the last time. (Of course, what do you expect when you take months and months off in between cooks?) And I didn't know if my sauce would come out really bad, so I bought a gallon of some really crappy stuff that I could doctor up

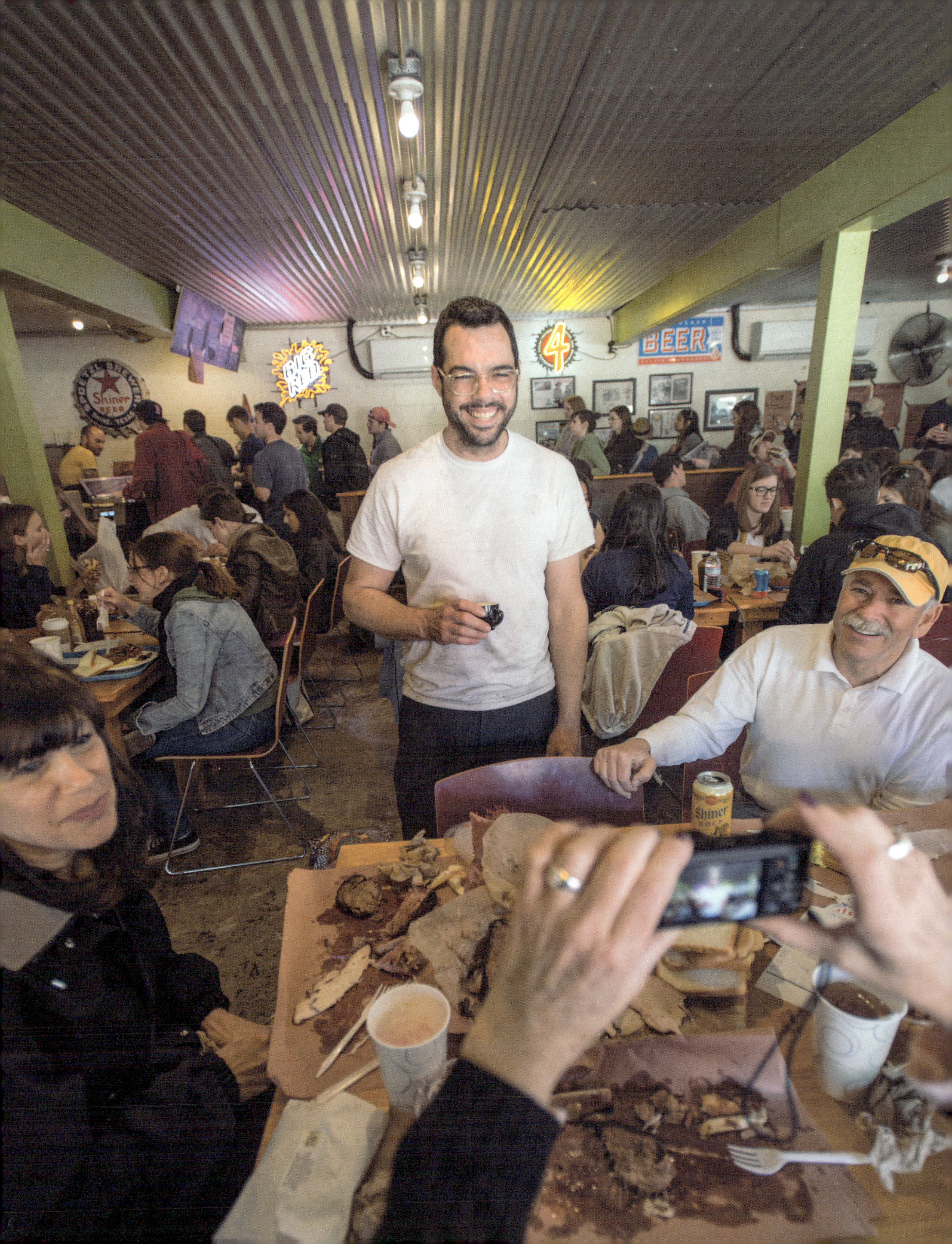

just in case my own efforts were inedible. But my sauce was fine, and everyone seemed to have a great time. The next day I fixed the pipe. We got out of that house pretty darn quick.

• • •

I was still working various jobs that didn't pay too well. I worked at a van place, fitting out and customizing vans. I worked in various restaurants. But there were two jobs that ended up having the greatest impact on me: at a coffee shop called Little City, where I worked in the back making sandwiches and doing maintenance, and where I started developing my love of coffee; and the Austin barbecue joint of John Mueller, grandson of the legendary Louie Mueller.

Somewhere around that fifth cook—yes, the one with the septic disaster—I caught myself daydreaming about opening my own barbecue place. (Of course, now that I have my own restaurant, bathroom disasters are an ever-looming threat!) I'd hardly ever been that excited about anything other than music. So I started applying to a bunch of Austin barbecue joints, some of them several times. I wanted to work at a place that barbecued with a real fire, not gas ovens, and there weren't many of these in Austin at the time. I wanted to learn barbecue from the inside out; I want to live it.

I got the job at Mueller and worked a lot, even though I was making only $6 or so an hour. I was constantly observing and soaking up whatever lessons I could. (I should interrupt myself here and offer a little backstory for anyone who doesn't know John Mueller. Here is how *Texas Monthly* describes him: "If there's a dark prince of Texas barbecue, it's probably John Mueller, the famously irascible, hugely talented, at times erratic master of meat who left his family's legendary joint—Louie Mueller Barbecue, in Taylor—and set out on his own in 2001." That place is the one I worked at. It developed a big following, but for various reasons he closed it in 2006 and disappeared from the scene for a while. He opened a new place in 2011 with his sister, but a fallout there led to him departing again. Now he has his own place once more. He and I appeared on the cover of *Texas Monthly* together in 2012.) When I worked at John Mueller's, I didn't cook anything. But I got good at chopping cabbage and onions. I could cut 50 pounds of onions without shedding a tear. I started rubbing briskets in the afternoons and watched how John handled the meats. I ended up getting to cut the brisket for the customers, which turned out to be a valuable skill. Often at night, the owner would leave, and I would just be left there on my own, which was great. People would come in, and I'd greet them warmly, take their order, and cut their meat for them. At those times, I would sort of treat that place with care and a friendly spirit as if it were my own. That kind of amiable, hospitable spirit is important, something that we've always emphasized at Franklin Barbecue.

It helped that I love cutting brisket, and I love talking to people. To this day, people who used to eat at that defunct restaurant still come into Franklin every now and then and remember me from when I was working behind the counter. Even more than I care to admit, that short-term job probably led to much of what I do now. But it wasn't because I received any mentoring. It was because I found myself doing something I really loved. Eventually, when I could see that writing on the wall that its days were numbered, I quit.

• • •

LEGENDARY CENTRAL TEXAS BARBECUE

Before I ever cooked a brisket, I was taking day trips out to visit the various pillars of Central Texas barbecue. In those days, there wasn't really any good barbecue in Austin; it all lived in the small towns outside of the city in every direction. There are barbecue joints everywhere in Central Texas, but there have always been a few places that have stood above the rest. It's worthwhile to visit these temples because in their old buildings and time-honored ways, they provide a window into barbecue history, not to mention a taste. These days quality can be up and down, but they all do something really well, and when they're on, the food can be as good as it gets.

SMITTY'S MARKET, LOCKHART • Just 30 miles southeast of Austin, Lockhart is a historic barbecue town, and Smitty's is a glorious living relic of the way things used to be. The building itself is a must-see place that all barbecue fans should visit. You enter through the back and walk right past a roaring fire literally at your feet, even if it's 100°F outside. • **FAVE DISH:** the best sausage!

KREUZ MARKET, LOCKHART • Just down the street from Smitty's is the massive redbrick food hall known as Kreuz. Smitty's used to be called Kreuz, but due to a familial disagreement, one sibling took the name while the other kept the original building. So here you have a new building, but with the original name and techniques. Mutton-chopped, soft-spoken Roy Perez is the pitmaster and a barbecue celebrity. It's always heartening to stop in and see him tending his pits. No forks or sauce here, following the old ways. Lots of good food is on offer, but the true specialties are the smoked-to-perfection pork chop and the snappy, spicy sausage links. • **FAVE DISHES:** end-cut prime rib, pork chop, jalapeño-cheese sausage.

CITY MARKET, LULING • Luling is a little town 15 miles past Lockhart and is home to yet another Central Texas barbecue great: City Market. Under the pitmastership (yes, I just coined that term) of hard hat–sporting Joe Capello, City Market is one cool spot. You enter a little smoke-filled room in the back of the restaurant where the meat is cut. Then you step back out into the dining room to find a table. There's great people-watching at City Market, and the sausage and ribs are great! • **FAVE DISHES:** sausage, crackers, cheddar cheese, great sauce.

LOUIE MUELLER BARBECUE, TAYLOR • An hour to Austin's northeast is the little town of Taylor, which is probably most famous for the epic Louie Mueller Barbecue. Founded as a grocery store in 1946, with barbecue coming a few years later, the building itself is a beautiful shrine, with smoke-blackened walls and heavenly light streaming in through the fog. The food here has had its ups and downs over the years, but when it's good, there's almost nothing better. And it's been on a hot streak for a while. While the dipping sauce is sort of thin and watery, the meat's so good it doesn't need it, led by super-peppery brisket and a beef rib that will blow you away. Do not miss this place. • **FAVE DISH:** beef rib.

SOUTHSIDE MARKET, ELGIN • Elgin is the sausage capital of Central Texas in large part because of the Southside Market. Started in 1882, this place oozes amazing tradition, much in the same way its famous Hot Guts sausages ooze deliciously meaty juices. In the past Hot Guts were spicier than they are today, but they're still darn good. Just a 30 minute drive from downtown Austin, this place is always worth a visit. • **FAVE DISH:** sausage, obviously.

BEGINNINGS

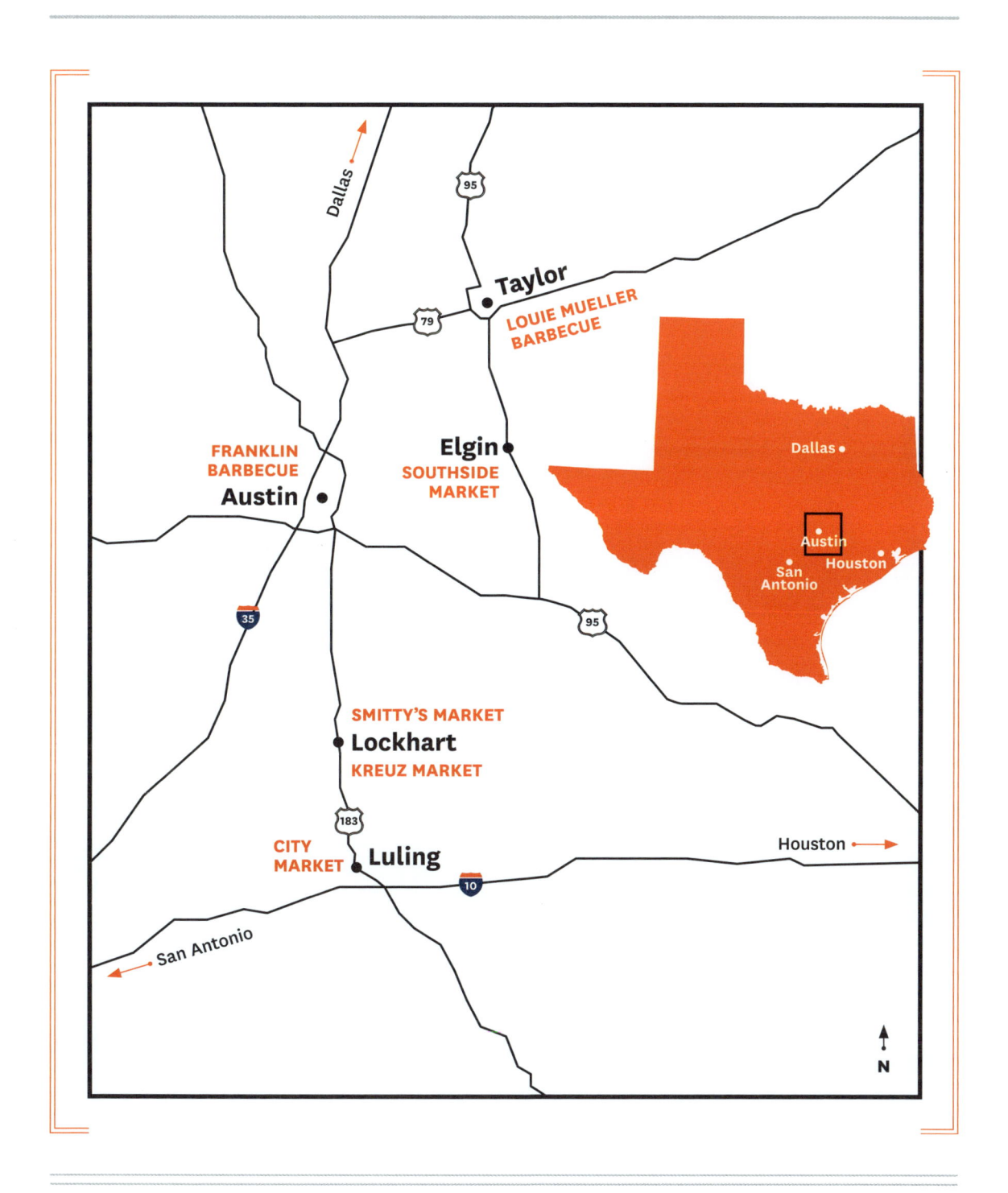

It was now 2007, and I had it in my head that I wanted just a lazy little lunchtime spot that I could design, decorate, and cook for on my own. I was trying as hard as I could to figure out some way to get my hands on or make a cooker that was big enough to cook multiple briskets. I had a dream but no real idea of how to get there except for sheer desire.

More and more, I saw entertaining as practicing for the big time when I would have my own place. I'd be calculating in my head, *This is the time I'd put the meat on; this is the amount of time I'd have to make the sides.* I knew I wanted my restaurant to be as authentic and old-school as possible, with a personal touch—*I'll never cut the brisket in advance and put it out for people to pick at. I'm going to slice each and every piece individually for each customer because that is how it's done.*

Looking back on it now, I know I probably seemed naïve. And I was. But I'm also proud that we made it happen with just ourselves and the help of our friends and family. Sure, I was poor. But barbecue has never been a rich man's pleasure. It's always been a culture of thrift. It's a poor, rural cuisine based on the leanest, throwaway cuts of the animal being cooked until edible with a fuel that can be picked up off the ground (at least it used to be).

And that's what I loved about it. How many other things can you start from nothing? There aren't a lot. In barbecue, you sell something that you bought and prepared on the same day, which gives you a little bit of positive cash flow to buy the next day's raw ingredients. You add value to the ingredients through cooking, and then do it all over again. That's how this entire thing has happened and is in fact still happening. This restaurant has not accrued one cent of debt. And that's because you can build something out of nothing if you're just willing to work at it.

And that's where all of this isn't that different from playing in a rock 'n' roll band. I didn't know it at the time, but it's all kind of the same. You get in a van, you hit the road, and you play and play and play as much as you can to get better and earn a little money. That's punk rock. That's DIY. That's the spirit. You make something with your own two hands. I run the restaurant the same way I'd run a band. It's the same thing, just a different venue.

ALMOST THERE

When it came time to rent a new house, I definitely, without question, had cookouts on the brain. So we went with a place with a huge backyard, almost a third of an acre. I was looking at this backyard and seeing barbecues. Like a party house. It was still inexpensive, but it was a step up.

Our next cook was on the Fourth of July. We'd always had barbecues on Sundays because Stacy and I worked on Saturday nights. That meant I'd be out pretty much all night on Saturday, get home at 2 a.m., and start cooking for the next day. People would come at 5 p.m. the following evening, and we'd start serving at 7 p.m. But we scheduled this Fourth of July barbecue for a Saturday instead of a Sunday because of the holiday weekend. What a mistake. People drink a lot more on Saturdays and stay too late. Still, I was feeling good about the brisket; it was definitely improving from one cook to the next. Lesson learned: don't have barbecues on a Saturday night, because you're just asking for trouble.

I still had the one, original New Braunfels (which, by the way, is still around; I loaned it to a friend with the instruction that he could never get rid of it without asking me, as it's a sentimental piece with serious mojo, even though it's just a crappy little cooker that's probably rusted out on the bottom by now). But after we had gotten rid of the last guests—wiping the sweat off our brows and feeling lucky that we'd dodged a bullet at this rowdy party—I went online. We had dial-up Internet on one of those old clear iMac computers. Pretty much every day I looked on Craigslist under the searches "Free" and "BBQ." I'd check the Free section for anything that I could possibly use to make a smoker: old refrigerators, old water tanks, an old oven that was getting thrown away. I even tried to figure out a way to turn an old bathtub into a smoker (real classy!). Anything of substance that was free and I thought might come in handy, I considered.

That night I typed in "BBQ." To my surprise, as it had never happened before, a listing for a cooker came up, the second or third item in the list. The ad said something that amounted to "free smoker, used twice, stinks at bbq, come get this piece of junk."

And I went out of my head. I yelled to Stacy, "Oh my God, I've got to go get this thing! Somebody's probably already got it!" I ran to the truck. It was late at night. As I drove I could imagine the scenario: someone had a disastrous experience cooking some meat earlier that day, got so frustrated that they wheeled it out to the driveway, went inside and put the thing up on Craigslist that very night, and swore to themselves that they'd never do it again.

I've hardly been that excited about anything in my whole life. Thoughts raced in my head as I drove: *Must get there as fast as possible. It's heavy, how will I get it in the truck? I don't care, I'll push it home if I have to. How could somebody put something that valuable ($100) on the street? What if somebody's already grabbed it?!*

I remember turning onto the corner, heart pounding. Then I saw something—just a little black dot at the end of the street. It's getting bigger, it's getting bigger, and there it was. I probably started sobbing in the truck. I rolled up, turned off my headlights so as not to disturb the neighborhood, and took a look at the smoker. A New Braunfels Hondo. *Oh my God, it's just like the one I have! I can double my capacity!* Now I'll have two really crappy cookers that aren't worth anything. But I can do four—count them, four— briskets. That doubles my capacity and thus the number of people I can feed. I had certainly come to realize that cooking briskets on these things was hard because of their thin, heat-leaking construction and other inefficiencies. Later I'd have the opportunity to transcend those ills with better cookers. So I wheeled the thing into the street. It rattled loudly, like a shopping cart on a cracked parking lot, and I loaded it up myself. It was heavy, and a full-size truck is pretty high up there. But I got it in and drove off with what until then was my greatest-ever find.

. . .

Something changed in me when I got that second smoker—something clicked, and I started to feel as if maybe owning my own place wasn't so crazy or far-fetched after all. So I decided to start saving up some money in earnest. I was doing good, making about $11 in tips a day at Little City. Stacy worked every Friday night waiting tables. At that time, on Fridays I'd spend the money I'd saved up all week at Half Price Books, just a few dollars on whatever cool cookbooks I could find, as well as books on architecture, anything barbecue of course, roadside stuff—especially Route 66 Americana—1950s design, and old diners. I was gathering information and inspiration like so many nuts packed into a squirrel's cheeks.

After procuring the new smoker, we had our next Sunday-night cook. I think we hosted seventy-five people or so, and to accommodate them all, we collected tables and chairs from Craigslist that we mixed and matched out in the yard (thank you, Free) and strung Christmas lights overhead. I moved an old, cheesy 1960s-style bar from our living room outside and set it up to cut brisket on. I borrowed a friend's little tiny cooker to add to my two and did a record five briskets that night. The food turned out pretty good, and it was one of the most fun barbecues we ever had—and the first one where something novel happened that also helped me along the way. There I was, drinking, cutting brisket in the dark. It was kind of like a block party, way bigger than we thought it was going to be. A line of hungry people extended around the yard, and we ran out of food. Little did we know that we were really ramping up here. Big party, lots of food, major service operation. I had designed a little service area just as I'd do it in a restaurant, really paying attention to *mise en place*, ergonomics, and flow. And the meat seemed to be getting a little better. I was learning how to cook multiple briskets at the same time, learning that each one required its own attention and own program. The idea that so much of this was about attention to detail was really becoming a massive part of the way I looked at barbecue.

Toward the end of that night, Big Jeff, my great friend who's been a part of my barbecue journey since close to the beginning, came up and said, "Hey, I got this for you," and handed me a manila envelope. In it was a roll of ones, fives, and maybe some tens.

"What's this?"

"I took donations for you tonight," he said, taking a slug of whiskey. "You need it."

I didn't know he'd been asking people for money, and I got a little choked up because it was the most thoughtful thing. Throwing that cook probably cost us the equivalent of our rent. The money he raised might not have completely covered our expenses, but it helped a lot. I just couldn't believe it, because I'd worked so hard and had so much fun and then at the end of the night I got paid, which I never expected. It was like playing the best show of your life and then getting paid and realizing the venue gave you some extra and thinking, *Man, we can stay in a hotel tonight!*

I shut the bedroom door and sat on the bed and counted the money and thought to myself, *Wow, maybe I can do this*. And that was the first time it ever truly seemed real to me.

THE FINAL PIECE

I was really conquering something that had felt unattainable. It must be like when people finally run their first marathon. I was on cloud nine by the end of that last cook. This was the first time we had a barbecue where I cut everything to order and had a stack of plates on the table and could ask people if they wanted lean or fatty, just like at a real restaurant. This is what

BEGINNINGS

I still do every day when I cut lunch. I honestly believe that one of the reasons our restaurant is successful is because we take the time to talk to people, to get to know them and what they want to eat—same as if we were hosting them in our own backyard.

Not long after that fifth cook, in 2006, I volunteered to remodel a house for the brother-in-law of my best friend, Benji (who today is an essential part of the restaurant—Benji is the GM, "the Dude"). I'd never remodeled a house in my life, never even really worked on a house. I was just kind of handy with tools, and I'd done some maintenance. On restaurants. Nevertheless, I knew I could figure it out, and I worked on that house day and night.

My final pay was maybe around $6,000 and change. When I deposited it, the bank probably thought I was doing something illegal, because my account had never seen more than $300. It was the most money I'd ever had in my entire life. What did I do with it? I bought a barbecue pit (what we call a smoker in Texas), the one that is today known simply as Number One. How I got it is yet another story of luck, thrift, and perseverance.

I invested $5,000 of the money I'd made into a new house that Benji bought and where Stacy and I would be living with him. That left $1,000 or so for my next big purchase.

Number One was the very same smoker that John Mueller was cooking on when I worked for him. It was made from a 500-gallon tank procured from the side of the highway (to put that in perspective, my New Braunfels smoker had a capacity of maybe thirty gallons. As I saw coming, Mueller's restaurant had failed, and Stacy's old boss had taken over the space and gotten the smoker.

When I found out they had it, I asked them if they wanted to sell it. They said they were going to but mentioned that they thought it was worth about $5,000. *No way*, I thought, *no way*. I told them I thought it was worth about $1,000. Obviously we were far from a deal, but they said they'd get in touch when they were ready to part with it.

That cooker never left my mind, but I went on working my various jobs, doing my thing. And one day, as was my habit, I was searching Craigslist and saw a listing for a cooker. It was the same one. So I connected with the guys and they said, "Sorry, we forgot to call you."

That thing was in terrible condition, but they were holding their price. I countered that it was way too much, as I'd seen it in action a year previously and it was just an ordinary smoker with many flaws. Again, no deal, but I said that if no one bought it, I'd take it.

They called back a little later and agreed to sell it to me for my offer of $1,000. And I thought, *Oh my God, another one!* I was dancing around like a new contestant on *The Price Is Right*, because the price was right. I said, "I'll be there in five minutes," cash in hand.

This thing was huge—14 feet long, solid metal, mounted on a trailer you could pull with a truck. I figured I could put twelve briskets in there—enough to serve more than a hundred people. After all, that's all Mueller cooked with for that whole restaurant.

It didn't look anything like it does now. It had three little doors; a real crappy axle; a solid piece of pipe, probably 3 inches in diameter; two plates to make a cradle for the smoke chamber to sit on; a 500-gallon tank; and then other plates with spindles welded onto them for the legs and tires.

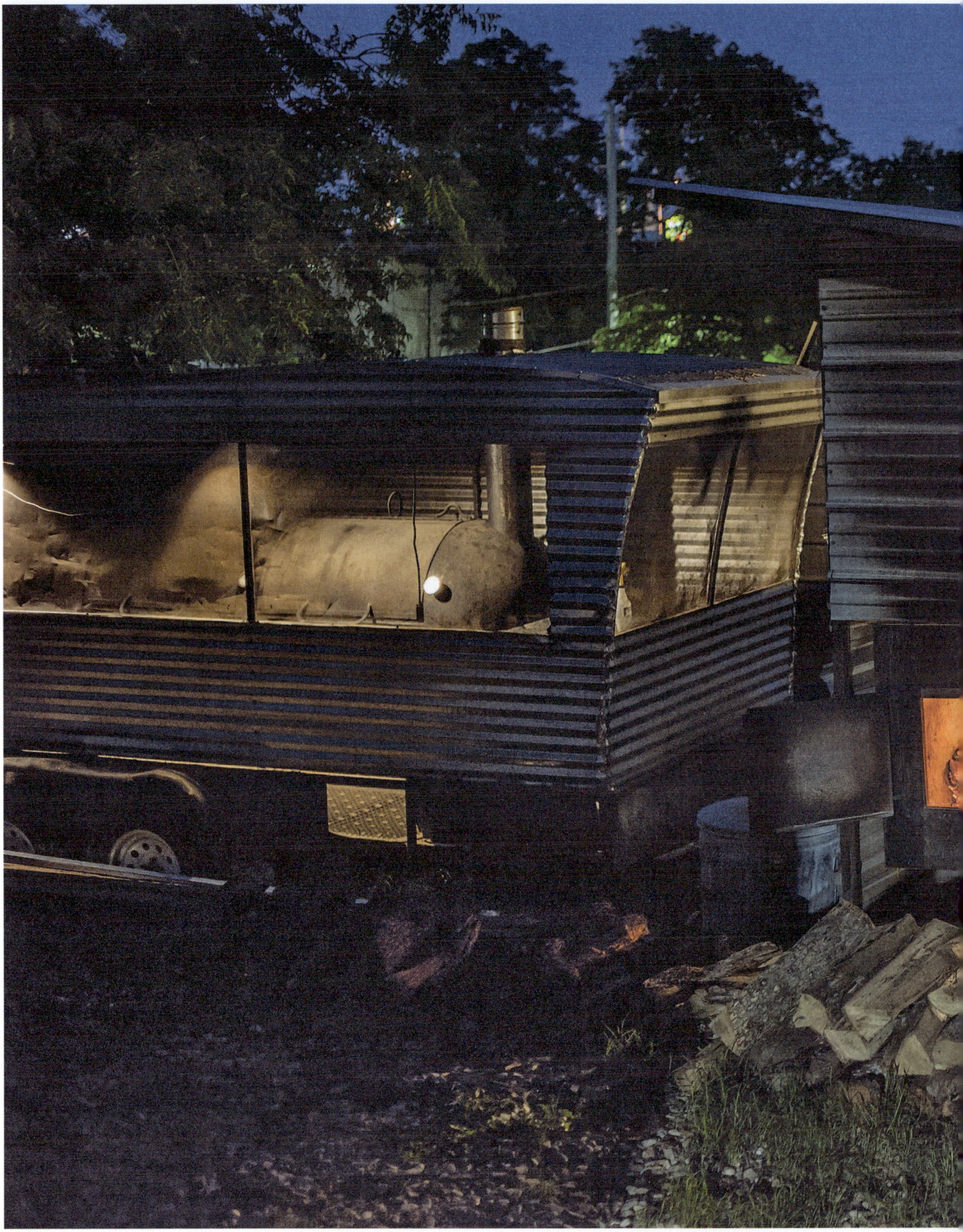

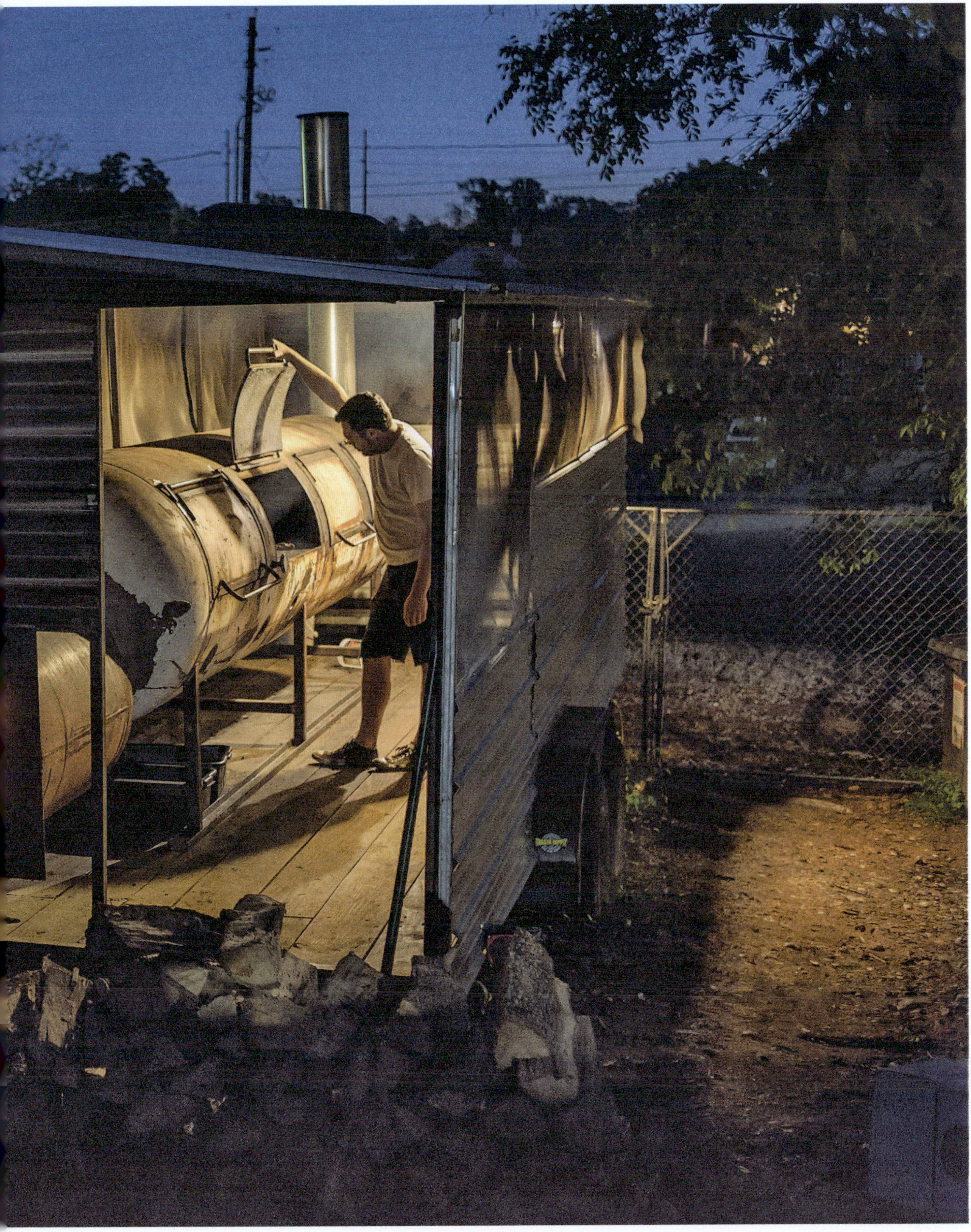

It had one flat tire, and its other tire was from a car. In chapter two I'll explain all of the things that make a good smoker good and what I look for in all of the smokers I buy or build. But for now, suffice it to say, when I bought it, Number One needed some work.

When I got it home, I saw what a disaster it really was. Inside, undrained grease had accumulated all of the way up to the grate, about 18 inches deep. There were still crusts of burned meat stuck to the grates. The thing hadn't been touched in well over a year, and it stank. Opening the firebox, I found it was almost completely full of ash that had hardened and become as tough as concrete. (At the restaurant we clean out the firebox constantly.) It never had a grease drain on it, so the grease oozed into the firebox, which by then had piled up layers of ash, coals, wood chunks, and then a steady trickle of animal fat. It was all rancid and hardened, like sedimentary rock with little pockets of fossil fuels dripping out.

So I went to Home Depot and bought a cheap grinder with a wire wheel (a brush with bristles for removing corrosion and gunk), a grinding disk (for grinding through metal and rust), a rock hammer (for chipping stone), and a $3 pair of goggles. Then I started the excavation, Shawshanking my way through that whole firebox, which is about 40 inches long. It's got this little back door, and eventually I crawled inside the cooker like a miner to access the back end. Chipping away at this ashy concrete, I would encounter disgusting little pockets of rancid fat. Every day for a couple of weeks, I'd grit my teeth and force myself to go back in there. It was gross, but where else would I get a huge cooker for $1,000?

Finally I got it all cleaned out. It was summertime—the sweaty months of June or July—and Stacy was at work. I think it was a Friday night, and I bought a gallon jug of vegetable oil and a spray bottle and a wheelbarrow full of wood for $25. Treating the cooker like a cast-iron skillet, I sprayed it all over inside and out, rubbed it down with towels, and got it looking like new. That was love. Then I packed the thing full of wood and built a raging fire to burn it out, season the smoker, incinerate any remnants of the cleaning process, and seal up the pores in the metal that I'd exposed through cleaning. That was probably a 500°F or 600°F inferno with flames coming out the door. I let it slow down a bit, choked off the fire with the door, and then went to H-E-B to find whatever was on sale. I just didn't want to waste the fire. What was on sale was pork ribs, which became the first rack of ribs I ever cooked in my life.

After that, Number One sat around for quite a while. I would have loved to fire it up again, but what business did I have hosting a huge barbecue when Stacy was really paying the bills? She and I were both working a lot, only she was working for money, and I was working on houses for friends with some vague faith that it would all pay off. In the meantime, the friends I was working for were covering my expenses, and I was amassing a good collection of tools that would eventually come in handy when it came time to open my own joint.

We did smoke a couple of delicious turkeys for Thanksgiving one year. But other than that, Number One just sat in the driveway. We were working and trying to save money, because by now I was fully committed to opening a place. I spent most of my time mapping out the process of somehow opening a place someday. But money had gotten a bit tight, because apparently one guy (me) building a house takes a really long time.

    Consequently it had been about a year since we'd last had a barbecue, and I was really jonesing at this point to have the mother of all barbecues. Eventually, we took some money and really did it up. If I thought I was a badass the last time I walked out of H-E-B with two briskets, think about how I felt pushing out a cart carrying six! Total baller. We had sawhorses in the backyard that we used to support a sheet of plywood for the cutting table. We really thought out the flow of service, with everything I needed to cut the brisket easily at hand, all the sides and garnishes lined up after the brisket station, drinks in the back of a defunct 1966 Chevy truck whose bed we filled with ice.

    We even made little handbills to pass out to friends with directions to our place. I stayed up all night working on the meat; making potato salad, coleslaw, and beans; and keeping the fires. The previous day Stacy had said, "People are really going to show up today. I think this is going to be bigger than you expect."

A WORD ON TEXAS BARBECUE

Making barbecue from pig is not as common in Texas as it is in many other states. The other major barbecue styles in the United States are largely pork-derived. Kansas City is famous for pork ribs and burnt ends, Memphis for its wet (sauced) and dry (rubbed) pork ribs, and North Carolina for its whole hog barbecue and pulled pork.

Texas is mostly associated with beef, though we cook our share of pork too. But really, the state is notable for its diversity. Most folks who travel through Texas for the first time are surprised by what they see. People, especially if they're from other continents, expect the state to look like the desert backdrop of a Road Runner cartoon. But when you live here, you know that this massive state has a diverse landscape, from the lush bayou of the east, to the plains of the panhandle, to the coastal flats of the south, to the Road Runner–esque desert mountains of West Texas. Texas barbecue is just as diverse as its terrain and, indeed, is heavily influenced by that terrain. Classic West Texas style, sometimes known as "cowboy style," involves simply slow-cooking meat directly over mesquite coals. (Mesquite is one of the few trees that grow plentifully out there.) Bordering Mexico, South Texas boasts a barbecue influenced by Mexican *barbacoa*, which is all about smoking goat and lamb and cow heads wrapped in leaves and buried in a pit in the ground. East Texas is next to Arkansas and Louisiana and takes its cues from the cooking style of the Deep South, so you see more pork here, and the wood of choice is hickory and pecan. Central Texas barbecue, which is the style I mainly adhere to, is all about slow cooking in offset smokers on post oak, which grows plentifully in a large part of Central Texas. Meats are brisket and ribs, and every restaurant tends to have its signature sausage recipe too, thanks to the large German and Czech heritage around here, which is also why we have a *kolache* culture in many small towns in these parts.

Which is best? They're all delicious, of course, so long as the person cooking knows what he or she is doing.

I didn't agree, but then on the day of, we started to get call after call from people all planning to come, asking if they could bring friends. It suddenly hit us that we were in big trouble, so we ran out and rented some tables and chairs. We strung lights and hung flood lamps from the huge pecan trees in our backyard. Plugged in a stereo. Made sure we had enough ice to chill the beer that people were asked to bring.

Before I knew it, there were 130 people ambling into the backyard. I got distracted and kind of overcooked the brisket—or so I thought. In fact, it turned out incredibly, the best I'd ever made up to this point, and I took note: brisket needs to cook a lot longer than you'd think to get tender. The guests all formed a line that wrapped around the backyard and down the driveway, and I was there at the cutting board cutting for each and every one of them.

And that's when I hit some sort of stride on this barbecue thing. Something just clicked and it felt so incredibly natural, so good. And it must have seemed that way to others too, because they kept asking me, "So when are you going to open up a place?"

I said, "I don't know, but I really want to someday." Little did I know that, encouraged by the success of this massive party, it was going to be sooner than I thought.

THE TRAILER

In 2008, the now-overgrown food truck scene in Austin was just getting started. Stacy and I knew—had known for some time—that we wanted to open a barbecue restaurant of our own. The only question was how: we were still poor, still just working to get by.

Then Stacy found the trailer. It was posted to Craigslist, a 1971 Aristocrat Lo-Liner. I've been talking a lot about my love of Americana, roadside attractions, and the like—well, this trailer fit the mold *perfectly*.

Now, I hadn't really intended to join the "mobile kitchen" movement—but hey, the Artistocrat cost $300, and we figured we should make a go of it.

"It's a piece of junk," Stacy said, looking up from the computer.

I said, "That's great. That's all we can afford."

Stacy was right; the trailer didn't look like much. But I was already envisioning its future as a mini-restaurant: parked somewhere, with Stacy and me inside, her taking orders and running the register, me cutting meat to order and running out back to check on the smokers when necessary. If we set up some picnic benches out front, people could enjoy their barbecue on-site. It could be perfect.

So we drove out to the property where this trailer was marooned, welded to a boat dock. Inside, it had old beer cozies from the Yellow Rose, a local gentleman's club, and a couple of active wasp nests. The thing needed to go to the dump, but instead it was going to our house. The trailer was in such bad condition that I didn't feel comfortable towing it home, so we actually paid to have the thing brought to our house on a platform truck.

It sat in our backyard, resting on bricks, for a long time. We were still busy, working on other things, and I was trying to decide what to do with it. I sat in it quite a bit, drank beers in there while trying to visualize how it could eventually be configured.

One of the things I was doing at the time was helping my friend Travis Kizer renovate

BEGINNINGS

and build out his coffee roastery. He had this place, an old, late 1940s–early 1950s derelict gas station in the heart of Austin on the access road to Interstate 35, not far from the University of Texas campus, not far from where we lived. We'd work on it every night (because we had other work during the day) sometimes until 3 or 4 in the morning. I was really into it, because Travis is one of the best people I know and because I love old gas stations. (It was thrilling to discover that this one, underneath all sorts of horrible paint and ruin, was a Texaco station from 1951. These stations, which were masterworks of art deco, were designed by Walter Dorwin Teague, who also designed some of the popular Kodak Brownie camera models. But I digress . . .)

I remember one night sitting on the tailgate of Travis's truck, drinking a beer, talking about roadside America, since we were right on the side of a highway. He said, "You've got that trailer at your place, right?"

"Yeah, had it for a while. I just want to open up a barbecue truck so bad." I was just too busy, too short of funds, and didn't know how to get the thing started.

Then Travis said, "You should renovate that thing and just park it here. If you ever make money, you can give me some rent."

I looked at him and said, "Are you serious? Has the beer gotten to you?"

I called Stacy at about 4 a.m. on my way home, even though I was only two minutes away. "Stacy! Guess what? I got a place for the trailer!"

I couldn't sleep a wink that night, my mind was exploding with ideas. Somehow, Travis offering a space was the equivalent of the light turning green for me. It had been yellow, but now it was green. I suppose I was waiting for it to happen when it was naturally meant to happen. And, amazingly, it's analogous to the very nature of barbecue: you never know exactly what's going to happen. You know how you want it to turn out, but you can't force it, and you can't make it happen on your schedule or in your time frame . . . you can only guide it. Same thing with a little dream of opening a place: I knew it was going to happen and what it was going to look like, but it would be ready only when it was ready. After this moment, I threw myself into getting the barbecue trailer going with greater energy than I'd ever thrown into anything.

I called my mom the next day. "I think I've got a place for the trailer."

"Oh, that's nice, sweetie."

"No, seriously! I have a place!" Yes, it was going to be inside a chain-link fence behind a run-down building with no sign, on the side of a major interstate between a strip club and an adult bookstore. But we had a place!

My grandmother had died recently and left my parents some money. They knew my ambitions well and decided to help me out. As they got money, they would transfer it to my account, and I'd go buy a counter or a sink. I was so grateful.

We started gutting the trailer, and every day I'd take it apart, cut holes, install things. We continued to scour Craigslist for everything we possibly could. We found a used sink, a cash register, a food warmer, a refrigerator, a little stove. Just the cheapest things I could find. Our backyard, littered with junk, looked like Sanford and Son.

So, piece by piece, I started to put it all together. And the trailer was beautifully designed, if I do say so myself. It was outfitted like the cabin of a boat or a submarine—the most ergonomic, tight-fitting, efficient use of tiny space you could imagine.

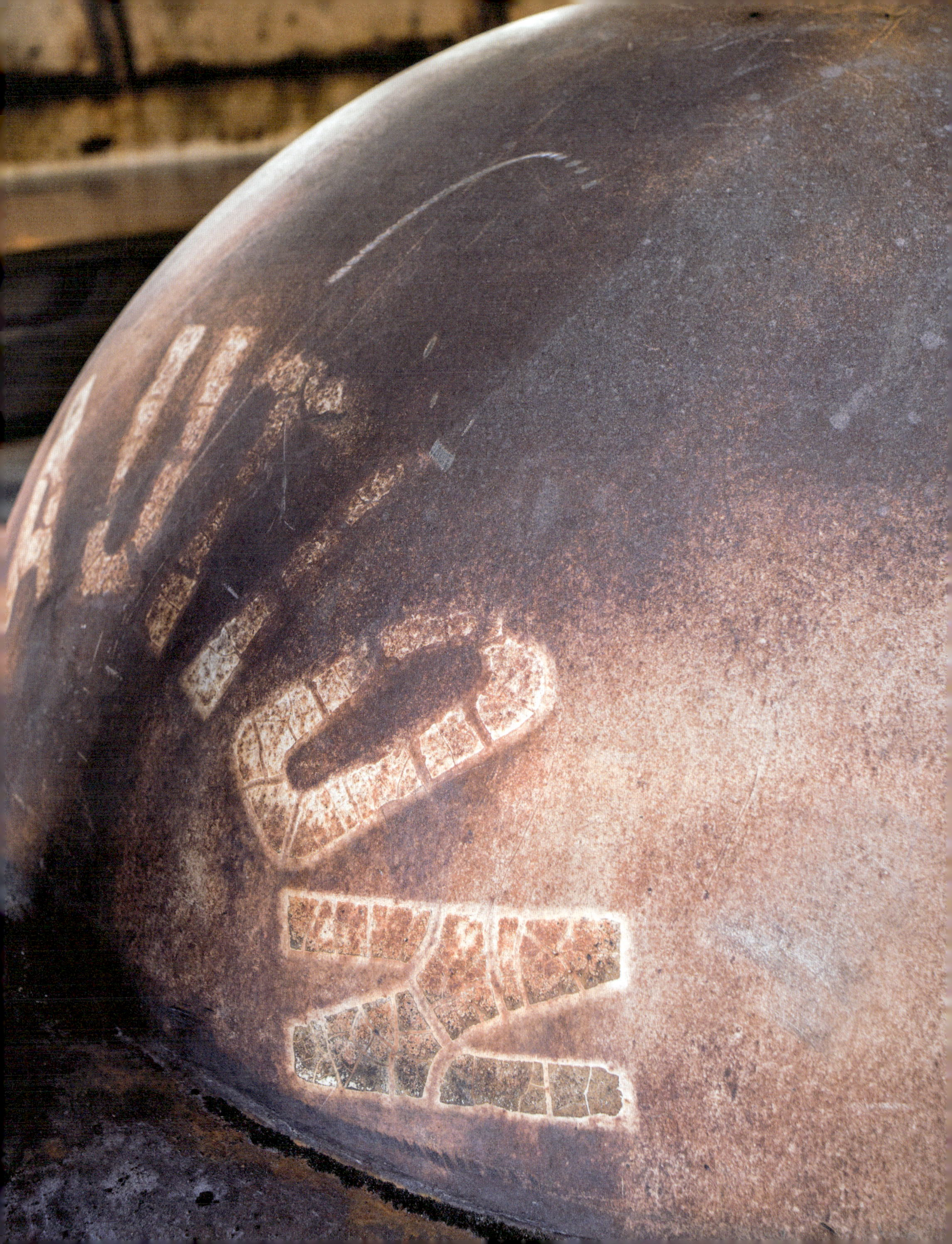

BEGINNINGS

Everything inside was either from Craigslist or scavenged. I started pulling out pieces of wood and other bits of shelving and metal I'd saved from my various construction jobs. (I'd been working these for a couple of years now, always with the trailer in mind. If we tore off the panel from a kitchen door or a good piece of wood, I'd save it. The backyard looked like it belonged to hoarders.)

The food truck permit we were getting stipulated that all of our food had to be served from the trailer, and all the sides we served had to be made in the trailer—I couldn't make stuff in our home kitchen and just bring it over. So we wired up the whole thing for electricity. I converted a little old stove to propane. Overhead and down below, I built tight, round-edged shelves for spices, plates, cups, lids, bus tubs, side dishes, bread, butcher paper. There was a neat little pocket for a slide-in trash can I could pull out with my foot when I needed to sweep something off the cutting board. I installed an 11-foot countertop, measured precisely for my dimensions: I took into account how far beneath it my toes would hit the baseboard, and I lowered the counters from standard 36-inch serving height to compensate for both the 1½-inch cutting block and the towel beneath it.

In December 2009, we put a used marquee up by the I-35 frontage road that said **FRANKLIN BBQ OPEN**. We'd festooned the freshly outfitted and ready-for-business camper and the trailer housing Number One with white, orange, and red lantern lights for as festive a vibe as you could muster in such a weird location.

It was cold—in the mid-40s, overcast—and I was a bundle of nerves. My stomach was in knots. It was heartening then that my first customers were Big Jeff Keyton and his wife, Sarah. There were probably twenty-five customers that day, and they were all friends. But it was a good day. And every day thereafter got a little bit better, although the weather wasn't great and we were heading into the holidays. As it got busier and busier, I could see how tough it was going to be. Benji came around and helped as much as he could. And Stacy worked with me on the weekends, when she wasn't at her other job.

At first, everything was cooked on Number One. The briskets were pretty darn good right out of the gate. The ribs were a little shaky. The pulled pork was fine. This was when I really started learning. I kind of thought I had a handle on things before I opened the trailer, but I quickly realized that I did not. It's when you start doing something multiple times a day, every day, that you really start to get better.

Early on, it was a real cool vibe. I could put a brisket on after lunch and watch it until 8 or 9 o'clock at night while drinking a beer. In the evenings, I'd fire up a huge pot of potatoes, which I'd peel for an hour and half each day, dicing them all by hand because it was cheaper to buy cases of whole potatoes. After I shut down, I still had the fires going. I'd of course have to run various errands, get dinner, go home. But I'd always rush back, throw a log on, wait by the fires for a little while. At some point in the night, I'd get the fires going and then head home to sleep for a few hours before speeding back to stoke up the fires again and finish things off.

But it was pretty insane in there when it got busy. (At that time, a long line was ten people.) During the week, when I was all alone, I had to bounce between cutting, register, and fire. I'd be waiting inside my little camper for someone to show up. I'd open the window and ask what they wanted. I'd cut the meat and scoop the sides. Then I'd wash my hands, take their money and give them their change, wash my hands again, and go back to serve the next customer. The trailer with Number One in it was positioned such that I could look out and read the gauges. When I saw the temperature starting to dip, I'd ask the customer to excuse me and I'd go out to throw a new log on the fire.

Within a month or so, as we got busier, I got a guy to help out a few days a week. That's how fast things were moving. Quickly, the stove inside became too small for cooking the amount of beans and sauce we needed. We outgrew that and had to start using a turkey fryer. At first, I would pick up one or two briskets every morning, but we started having them delivered instead. We had no place to put them, however. We couldn't use a commissary kitchen, because I had to be there watching fires. You can't leave and then transport things, because you can't be in two places at once, which has been a common theme for the last four years.

I also needed additional space to cook more and more meat, and I had to figure out how to find enough space on the cooker for all the meats that had to be smoked. That's how we created the little systems we have now of cooking the briskets all day and getting them off to rest in time to get the ribs going for that day's service. Even then I didn't have the room. Of course, that all became ancient history the day after we got our first review.

The review was by Daniel Vaughn, who then had a barbecue blog called *Full Custom Gospel BBQ*. He went around Texas and the country rating barbecue joints. It's worked out well for him. Now he's the barbecue editor for *Texas Monthly* magazine. The review was stunning. "It's been a while since I've found an honest 'sugar cookie' on my brisket," he wrote, "but as I waited for my order to be filled, owner and pitmaster Aaron Franklin handed me a preview morsel from the fatty end of the brisket and the flavor was transcendent. If I lived in Austin, I would go here every day if I could be guaranteed a bite like that one."

That came out at the end of January, only our second month, and that's when people started showing up before we opened. Every time I hear the song "Alex Chilton" by the Replacements (big fan), I think of this. It was a Saturday morning, beautiful, and "Alex Chilton" came on. I was drinking a coffee and the line was down the fence getting close to I-35. And we were so exhausted, but I just remember that moment, looking at this line thinking, *What have we done? This is the craziest thing ever. When is this going to stop?* Well, it hasn't yet.

By the time the South by Southwest music festival, Austin's most insane week of the year, rolled around in March, we were already rocking and rolling, serving at capacity to a line most of the time. Lines were stretching around the corner, and the wait was longer than an hour. I realized, *Oh my goodness, I'm going to need another smoker*, and somehow I found some time over six months to build Number Two, which joined Number One in producing our meat. In June 2010, Stacy quit her job to come work with me. (First two weeks: pretty rough trying to figure out how to work together. After that it got smoother.) By that fall, we just couldn't handle the traffic out of our little makeshift restaurant in a parking lot. So we started looking for a real space. And that's when we found the restaurant.

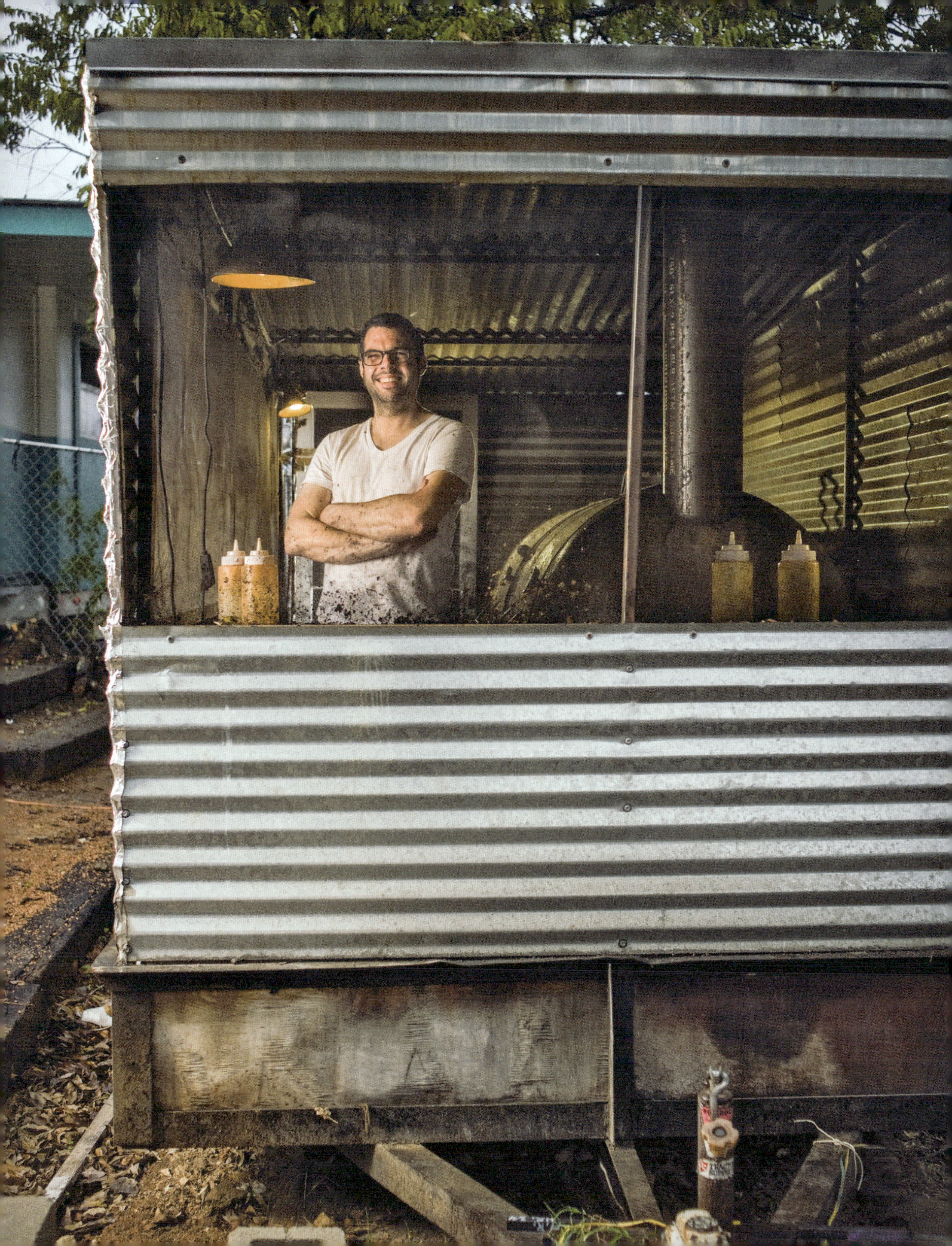

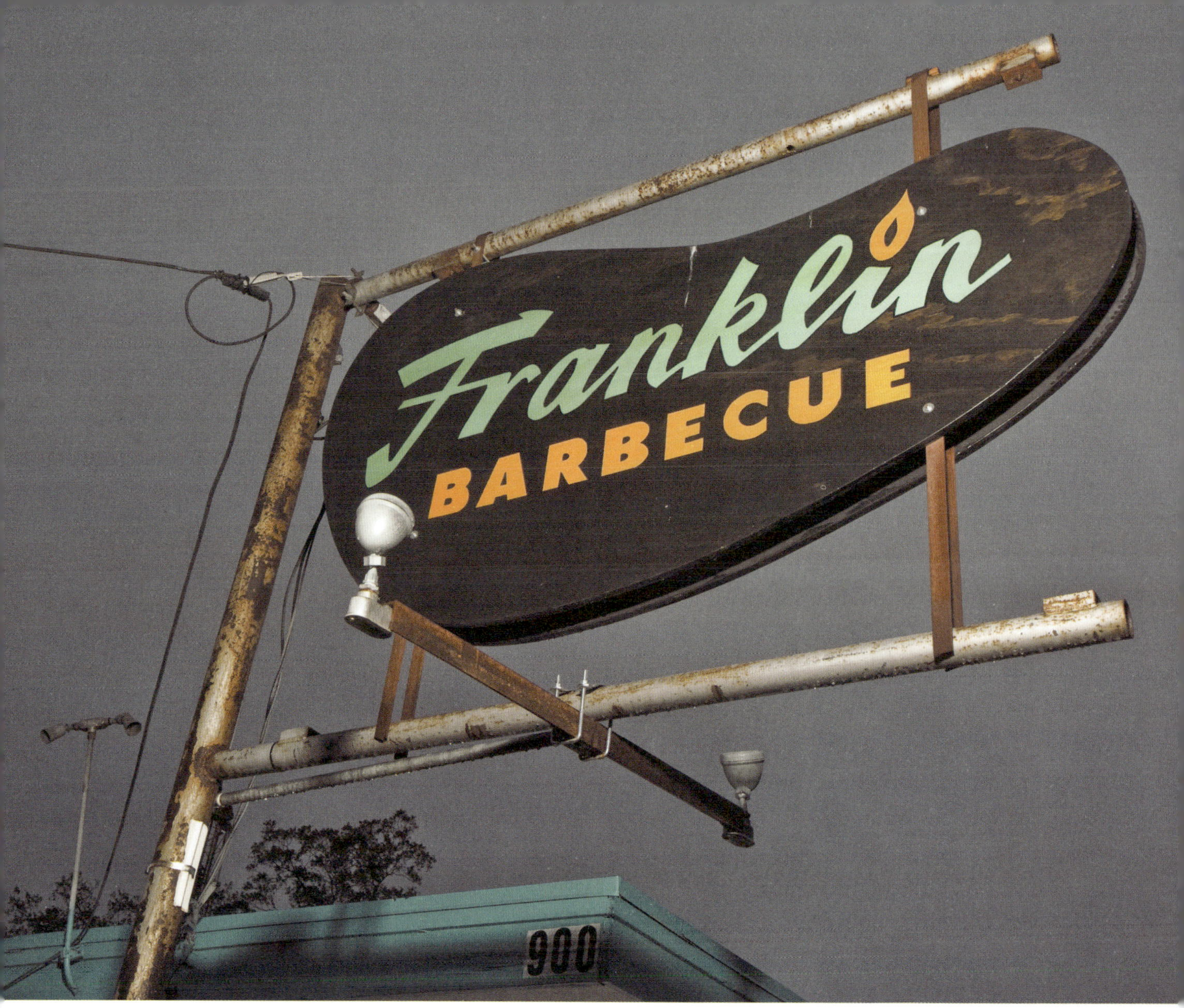
Franklin
BARBECUE
900
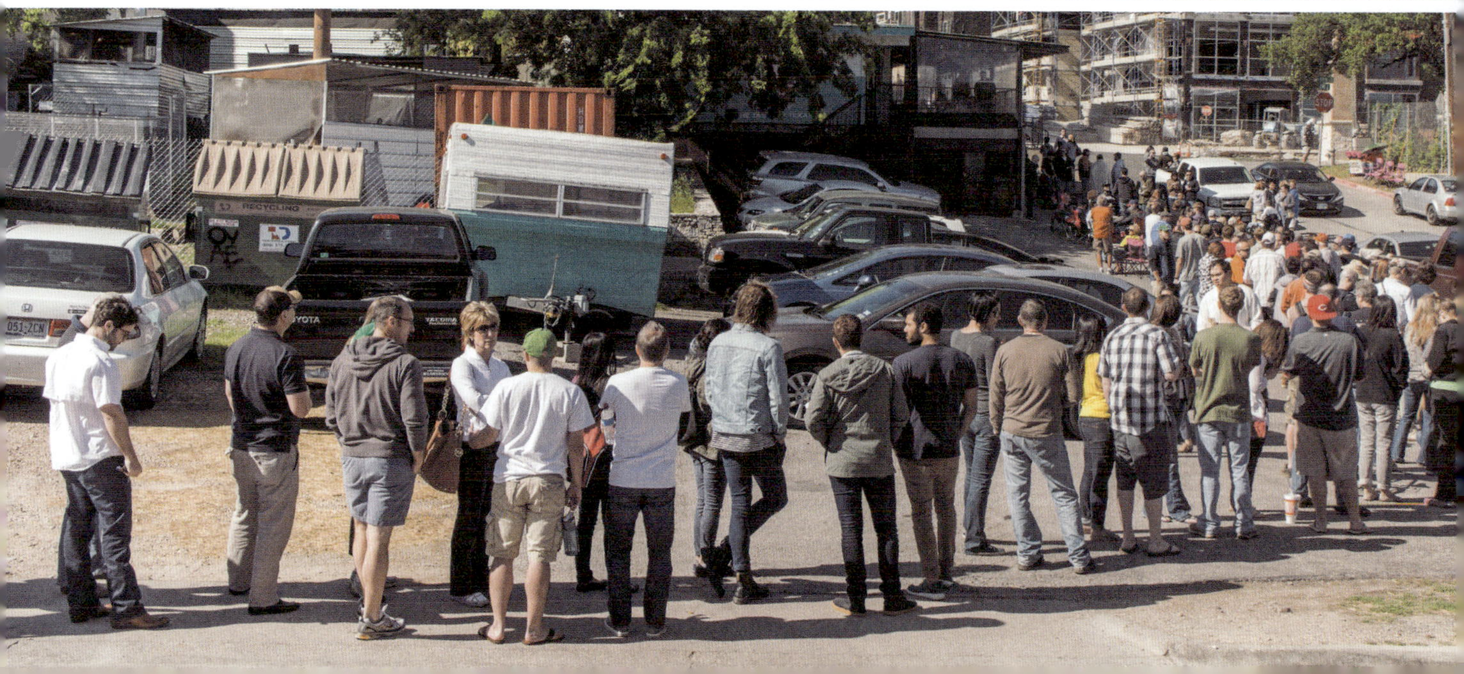

BEGINNINGS

FRANKLIN BARBECUE: THE RESTAURANT

In a lot of ways, our restaurant-opening story is similar to all the other restaurant stories out there. So I won't spend too much time telling it. After running the trailer for about eleven months, we just couldn't handle the amount of business anymore, and we knew that we needed to look for a real place.

We started looking at spaces, but there was one barbecue place that I'd been scoping out for a long time. It was clearly failing, and coincidentally went out of business right about the same time we were looking for a place. I had a commercial real estate buddy get in touch with the owner; he said the last tenants hadn't paid rent in a while.

The guy who owned the business ended up quitting. I think he'd been doing one cook a week and then cutting cold brisket and microwaving it for individual plates. After he left we walked in, and I'm surprised that we didn't get E. coli just from inhaling the smell of this place when we opened the door. The cutting board still had bits of meat on it, the knife was sitting where the previous guy had left it, and there was an apron hanging on the light switch. You could tell that one day he was cutting lunch and just said "screw this" and left. The utilities had been shut off for weeks, but he had chickens in the fridge. There were crumbs all over the counter from his cookies and all of the sinks were full of standing water.

For us, the timing couldn't have been better. We signed the lease on the restaurant almost a year to the day after we opened the trailer. It took three months to build it. Benji and I and Braun and Stacy, we gutted it all, worked our fingers to the bone, did all the carpentry ourselves. When we opened for business in this location on East 11th Street on the first day of SXSW (a famous Austin music, film, and interactive conference/festival), some of our more devoted fans slept outside overnight, determined to be the first in line.

Since then, we've sold out of meat every single day of our existence. We get visitors from all over the world; if you stand in line on any given day, you might meet some kids from Japan who are in the middle of a Texas road trip, a family from Colorado who drove all through the night to get in line at 9 a.m., or some students from the nearby University of Texas who decided to claim a bit of brisket before their afternoon classes. We even got a visit from the President of the United States. In the summer of 2014, we renovated for the first time since opening and built a smokehouse to make things run more efficiently. So far, so good. Since opening the trailer in 2009, it's been an eventful and exhausting haul to get this far. And I don't regret one second of it.

WHY DO BARBECUE JOINTS KEEP THESE ODD HOURS? IT'S HISTORY.

Yes, I realize that my restaurant is technically open for only about four hours a day. People ask sometimes, "Why aren't you open longer?" or "Why don't you open for dinner?"

To answer the first question, we're open for only those short hours because we close when we run out of meat. And we run out every day because supply is less than demand—for the simple reason that we don't have enough real estate on the smokers. Between briskets and ribs, not to mention pork butts, turkeys, and sausages, the smokers are running at pretty much max capacity twenty-four hours a day. In the summer of 2014, we added a new smoker to the lineup, which increased our capacity slightly. But each of our smokers is incredibly heavy and over 20 feet long. I don't want to sound as though I'm making excuses, but the bottom line is that "increasing production" isn't as easy as it might sound.

As for that second question, why we don't open for dinner: it's a good one, and one I often ask myself. After all, there are things about a dinner service that make sense. For instance, I (or whoever is cooking them that day) wouldn't have to get to work at 2 a.m. to put on the day's ribs. If we were open for dinner instead of lunch, technically, I'd have to get to work at only 10 or 11 a.m. to get the ribs going. What a nice, relaxing day!

But barbecue in Central Texas is traditionally a midday—or even morning—meal. For instance, the excellent Snow's BBQ of Lexington, Texas, an hour east of Austin, is famously open from 8 a.m. until *they* run out of meat, which can often be 10:30 or 11 that morning. So be prepared to eat barbecue for breakfast if you go out there. Smitty's Market in Lockhart (a half hour south of Austin) is open from 7 a.m. to 6 p.m. during the week, which are pretty classic hours.

To understand why Central Texas barbecue joints aren't open for dinner, you have to understand the history. They didn't start out as restaurants. Rather, they began as meat markets and grocery stores. People often describe the Central Texas style as "meat market" style. The style takes its cue from the large number of German and Czech immigrants who came to this part of the state, as described by Robert F. Moss in his scholarly book, *Barbecue: The History of an American Institution*. They arrived in the mid to late nineteenth century and became farmers, craftsmen, and merchants, bringing with them many traditions, including butchery, sausage making, and smoking meat. A number of these immigrants opened meat markets. In those days, meat markets were butcher shops, where vendors would break down whole animals and sell the meat. Lacking refrigeration, the butchers would preserve the less popular cuts of meat by smoking them or grinding them up for sausages, which they'd then sell as a ready-made meal on butcher paper, just as we still do today. These places weren't restaurants, so they didn't even offer silverware, sides, or sauce, just pickles and onions, a tradition some of the more famous places in Lockhart upheld until fairly recently.

The cotton industry boomed in Central Texas in the latter part of the 1800s, and before automated harvesting, migrant cotton pickers would swarm through the area for work. According to Moss, "an estimated 600,000 workers were needed for the 1938 crop . . . and many went to local grocery stores and meat markets for takeout barbecue and sausages." Given the hours agricultural hands worked in the Texas summer, they'd come in to eat barbecue throughout standard market hours, from 7 a.m. to 6 p.m. Over time, with barbecue proving so popular and supermarkets taking over the niches of the little specialty stores, the meat markets evolved into restaurants, which they remain today, though we tend to keep some semblance of the traditional hours while we serve up this cuisine whose history in these parts goes back 150 years.

But I have another theory as to why barbecue has continued as lunchtime fare: it's just too rich and heavy to eat at night. I wouldn't really want to eat it for dinner, letting it sit ponderously in my stomach as I go to bed (and I go to bed early). Rather, it's much better to eat in the middle of the day, when you've still got a lot of moving around and digesting to do.

THE SMOKER

- **Chapter Two**

At the restaurant, occasionally we show our most enthusiastic guests around the backyard where we cook the meat. Now, in most restaurants, people who are invited into the kitchen by the chef usually don't make a big point about seeing the stoves or inquire about every last detail of the ovens. Yet, here at Franklin Barbecue, every single person who comes back wants to know about the smokers—how long have I had them, which ones did I make myself, what are the differences among them. What is it about the barbecue smoker that inspires such curiosity and scrutiny?

I'm not sure I can answer that question, except that meat smokers, whether they're little backyard fixtures or massive hunks of welded steel sitting on the back of a trailer, are where the magic happens. It's the slowest, least-guarded magic trick in the world, yet it never fails to amaze people how a raw hunk of meat can be transformed into juicy deliciousness by such a simple apparatus. Thanks, thermodynamics!

With so few ingredients and tools needed to make superlative Central Texas–style barbecue, each one is obviously of crucial importance. Yet, of course, every choice you make is fraught with its own complexities. What kind of smoker to buy or build and in what dimensions are puzzling questions that make for hours of agonizing inquiry for anyone interested in barbecuing.

Although I occasionally find myself having to cook on other people's smokers and using styles of cooker I'm not accustomed to (usually when I'm invited to cook at various events around the country), for the most part I just stick to what I know: the classic horizontal offset smoker.

Now, an experienced pitmaster should be able to produce good results on any cooker, but obviously the best chances for success are when you're working with tools you're comfortable with and that have delivered good results in the past.

To learn how to smoke meat in the Central Texas style, you don't need to spend several thousand dollars on a fancy custom rig or even build your own. Although the quality of materials and construction of a smoker are indeed important to producing large quantities of great meat over a long period with high levels of consistency, many beginners will want to start off with a smaller investment in time and money. Whether you're an aspiring professional pitmaster or just someone who likes to cook at home, this chapter is intended to teach you how to buy the best cooker for your needs, some useful hacks to make it work better, some tips on how to care for it, and for other DIY fanatics like me, even some thoughts on how to weld one yourself. I'm not into bells and whistles and am certainly into getting a good deal, so I'm the last person who'll tell you to run out and buy the biggest, most expensive cooker you can get your hands on.

Does equipment really matter? Yes and no. Any barbecue situation is about simply knowing how to deal with and get the best results from the conditions you've got. I've got six cookers at the restaurant right now. They're all pretty much identical, yet they all cook differently, changing throughout the season. In some weather conditions, one will be more consistent or provide a more thorough, even temperature and smoke, while another might cook more slowly or unevenly than usual.

I graduated to these smokers because I needed more capacity. We were having backyard barbecues for an ever-expanding bunch of guests, and I needed to be able to cook more than one or two briskets at a time. If you've read the previous chapter of this book, you'll know that I started off with an entry-level New Braunfels smoker that I bought on sale for $100 at an outdoors store here in Austin. Its weaknesses were . . . well, it had mostly weaknesses. Its strengths were that it was cheap and that it used real wood: the first and primary requirement for making proper Texas barbecue. Was it a great-quality smoker? No, but then neither was I, and as you'd expect, the barbecue I produced from it wasn't that good either.

But you've got to crawl before you can walk, and even though I didn't know what I was doing on that thing at the time, I suppose I learned something from every cook I did on it.

It wasn't until a little further down the road when I started building my own smokers that my cooking got more dialed in. (And, by the way, it's still getting there. I've always got a lot to learn.) Built in early 2014, the sixth cooker I added to the restaurant—Nikki Six, it's called—is so far the best of them all. Little tweaks here and there (and I mean little) to the design seem to have had a sizable impact, and meats on Nikki Six finish faster and just as well as on my veteran cookers like Muchacho and Rusty Shackleford.

So why the offset smoker? For one thing, it's what we do here in Central Texas: old-school barbecue, as opposed to the smokehouses of Carolina or the gas-fired commercial smokers you find almost everywhere. I've been surrounded with this kind of barbecuing my entire life. Two, I love the offset cooker because it's such a simple, primal vessel for smoking meat. Three, it's ideal for cooking with a wood fire, which is a huge key to the great flavors we're after. (That's why one of the monikers of these types of cookers is "stick burner.") It's just a massively simple device for converting fire and air into smoke and heat, which are focused on a path in a chamber and then allowed to exit through an exhaust pipe on the opposite end of the cooker from the firebox. The only moving parts are a few doors on hinges. Couldn't be more fundamental.

However, a basic sailboat is a simple and primal vessel too, yet it still requires competent handling to both avoid disaster and ensure a graceful and elegant ride.

As with a sailboat, much of the expertise in handling a smoker comes in dealing with the elements. In this case, it has to do with the wood you choose, the airflow to the fire, and the weather of the day. But when you've set yourself up well and the fire is effortlessly crackling, a clear, blue smoke is swirling out of the stack, and your meat is gradually browning to perfection, there are few better feelings in the world.

PROPERTIES AND TYPES OF WOOD SMOKERS

I hold no science or other higher learning degrees of any kind. But I do think it's important to understand something about the tools you're using. Knowing how they work will help you use them more effectively.

Basically, people will make barbecue cookers out of almost anything. I've seen them built from everything from old water heaters to filing cabinets. To qualify as a smoker, all you need is a place to hold a fire and a place to put the meat so it cooks in the smoke (rather than over direct heat). In the sections that follow, I outline the different types of smokers, and the basic way they function.

Barbecue Pits

The fact that people still call barbecue cookers "pits" suggests the origin of this style of cooking: a fire contained in a hole in the ground. In Central Texas, the fire might still be slightly dug into the ground, as it is at Smitty's (see page 18 and the photo below), where the "pits" are big brick boxes taking smoke and heat up through an opening from an adjacent wood fire that burns in a shallow indented pit in the floor of the restaurant.

This is smoke collecting at its most basic. You could just as easily dig a hole in the ground, build a fire in it, construct a cinder-block structure next to it and a chimney at the other end, and smoke something successfully, if you could get convection to pull the heat and smoke in. All basic offset cookers are advancements of that ancient concept.

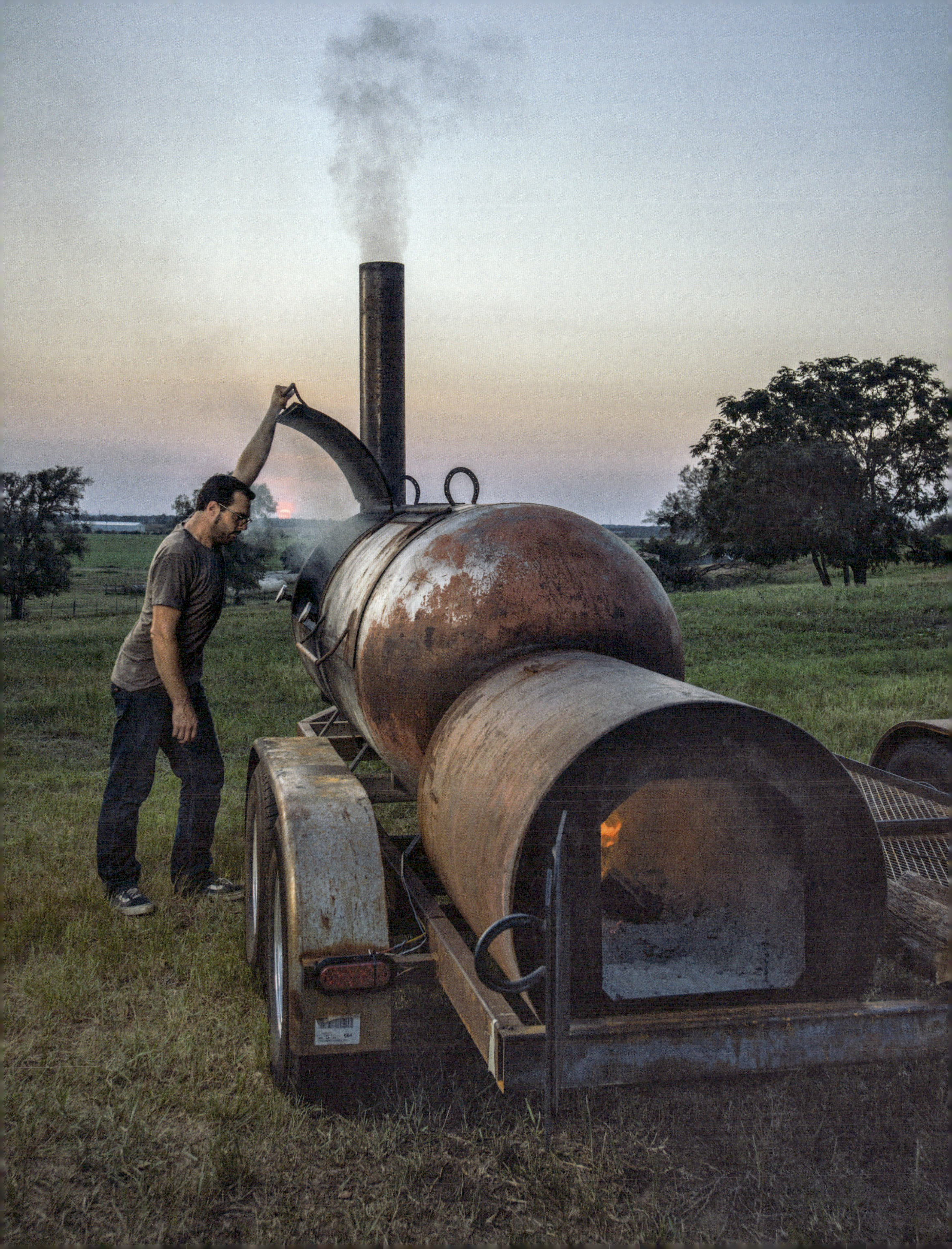

Offset Cookers

The style of "pit" I use likely originates from a different tradition, one that's welding intensive. Offset smokers, like the ones at Franklin, owe their popularity to the deep connection in Texas between the oil and barbecue industries. You'll often hear of the supposed affinity oilmen had for smoked meat, what with so many people finding work in Texas oilfields during the twentieth century. Oil extraction and refinement require a lot of metalwork, and so it's quite common to see barbecue smokers cut from old oil drums or welded from sections of heavy steel pipe. There are stories that in down times for the oil industry, bosses had their welders build barbecue pits to keep them busy.

My smokers don't come from oil drums or pipeline but from used propane tanks. We take long 1,000-gallon propane tanks and cut four doors, each up to 3 feet long, along the length of them to make our cook chambers. At one end, we attach a smaller tank of 250 gallons, cut in half, for the firebox, and at the other end, we affix a tall, wide smokestack made from pipe. Clearly, acquiring and welding a 1,000-gallon tank isn't practical for most home cooks, so I've suggested a couple of tips for adapting your own, appropriately sized smoker in the section "Modifying a Cheap Store-Bought Smoker" (page 62).

Reverse Flow Smokers and Tuning Plate Smokers

The offset smokers I build are as simple as they come. However, there are many tricked-out versions of offset smokers that are available to home cooks. One example is the reverse flow smoker. In the reverse flow, the smokestack is located on the same side of the rig as the firebox, with the intent that the heat and smoke will travel to the far end of the smoker under a plate beneath the grates and, unable to escape there, will be pulled back to the smokestack, thus making a complete tour of the cook chamber and smoking the meat more efficiently and evenly.

Another option is an offset smoker outfitted with what are called tuning plates: heavy metal plates suspended in the bottom of the cook chamber to balance the differences in temperature that inevitably occur along the length of the chamber. Typically, the plates are laid snugly next to one another at the firebox end to form a buffer against the powerful direct heat coming from the fire. Farther away from the fire, small gaps are left between the plates to allow more heat to rise into the chamber holding the meat.

I don't really care too much for either design, but that's maybe because I've learned to cook my way on a simple, unmodified cooker. I don't feel that I get my preferred amount of convection pulling heat and smoke through the cooker with the reverse flow, and frankly, it just changes the dynamic I'm used to. As for tuning plates, I haven't worried about those things at all, instead just relying on knowing my smoker and using experience to cook on it properly. A lot of people believe in plates and reverse flow, but my feeling is that I don't want anything restricting airflow in the smoker. Ultimately, you need to figure out what works best for your style of cooking and follow that road with confidence.

The So-Called Cheap Offset Cooker

If you read around, you'll find that a good deal of antipathy exists for what is called the cheap offset smoker. This is the kind of horizontal smoker with a low price tag that sits chained up outside a Home Depot. Of course, that's exactly what I started with—my New Braunfels Hondo was nothing if not a cheap offset.

I began with one of those because I didn't know any better and because that's all the money I could scrounge together. But the cheap offset smoker is in many ways set up for failure, especially for people who are just learning. It is inconsistent and porous and because the metal

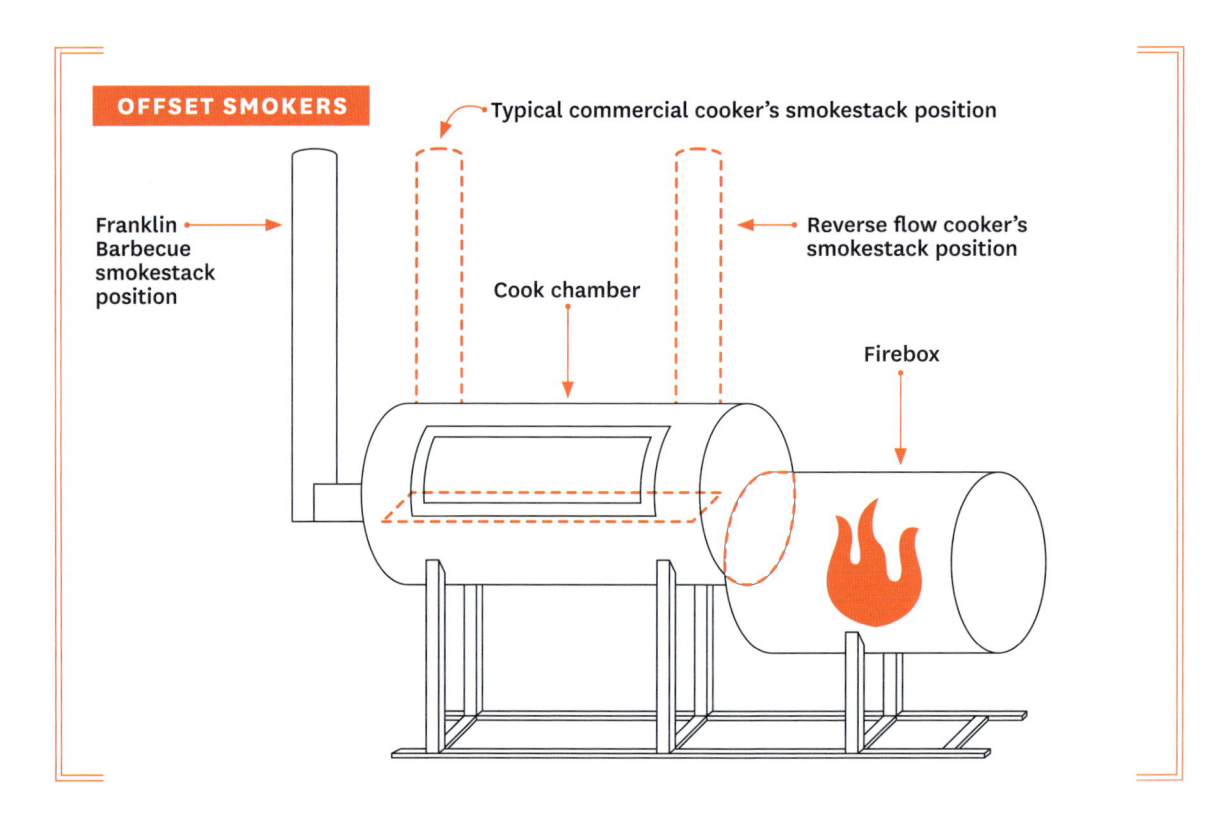

OFFSET SMOKERS

- Franklin Barbecue smokestack position
- Typical commercial cooker's smokestack position
- Reverse flow cooker's smokestack position
- Cook chamber
- Firebox

is so thin, it doesn't retain heat well. When I picked up my second cheap smoker, which was abandoned at the curb and advertised in the Free section of Craigslist, I couldn't believe my good fortune. Today I can easily imagine its owner screwing up yet another brisket and simply wanting the thing out of sight. And, no, owning two cheap smokers does not improve your odds of success. But I do think that my cooking inevitably got slightly better as I continued to cook on them. So if a cheap offset smoker is all you can afford—and you'll know it's a "cheap" one not only because of the price tag but also because of its use of very thin metal and rickety design (see "What to Look for When Buying a Smoker," page 49)—I say buy it. A cheap offset is better than no smoker at all, and you can always modify it a bit to somewhat mitigate its feebleness. You might not be able to achieve greatness, but you'll be able to learn, as I did.

Upright Drum Smoker

The only smoker that is more basic than the offset is the upright drum smoker. This design uses a single barrel or drum with the fire built at the bottom and the heat and smoke rising vertically through a shelf or series of shelves containing your meat. Since what you are cooking will be sitting above the heat source, it's necessary to position it high above the fire. Also, since you can't burn wood, which produces flames that will burn the meat, you'll be relying on charcoal and wood chips, which don't give the same flavor as burning wood.

This is a similar technique to what you'd use if you were smoking on a basic Weber kettle grill or on a Big Green Egg or other *kamado*-style cooker. You place the coals on one side and the meat on the other, cover, and get the smoke and heat you need. Again, the drawbacks are relying on smoke from smoldering—not burning—wood and the difficulty of regulating temperature and airflow. Big Green Eggs and company are a better choice than a flimsy Weber kettle, because their thick ceramic sides allow them to stabilize and hold a temperature more efficiently, which is what you need for long cooks. They're basically naturally fired outdoor ovens with smoke.

UPRIGHT DRUM SMOKER

- Removable cooking grates
- Firebox

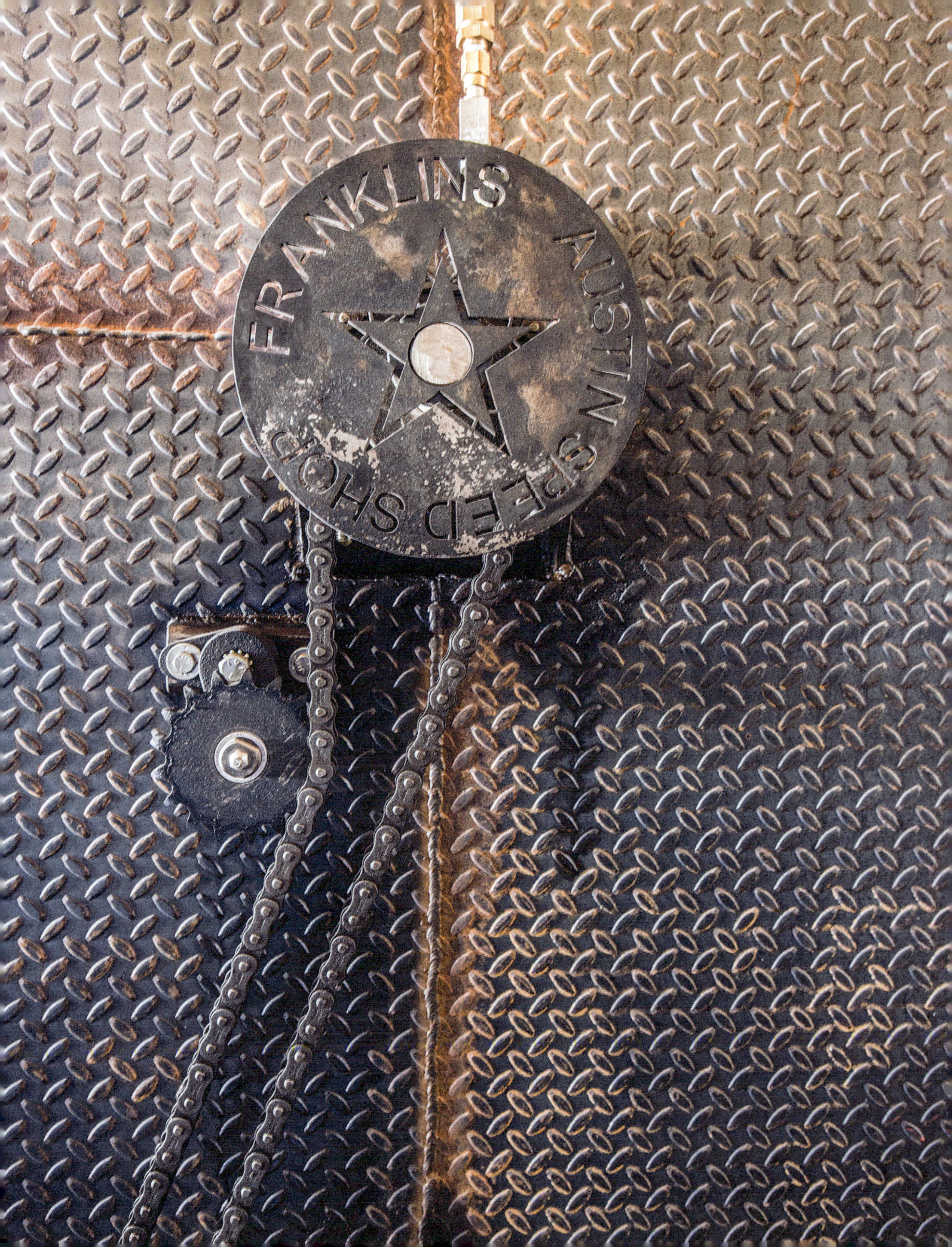
FRANKLINS AUSTIN SPEED SHOP

THE COOKERS OF FRANKLIN BARBECUE

I've gone through quite a number of smokers in my day, but here's the roster we're playing right now at the restaurant.

NUMBER TWO • This smoker, which I built during the heyday of the barbecue truck, now sits on a trailer in my driveway and gets pulled out occasionally for a mobile cook. It is made of a 500-gallon tank, has an insulated firebox with an 8-inch stack, and is the model all my 1,000-gallon smokers are based on. It is my favorite!

MUCHACHO • Built just after we moved into the restaurant space to satisfy still-rising demand for barbecue, I made Muchacho in my standard design of a 1,000-gallon propane tank, with a firebox made from a 250-gallon tank cut in half and insulated with a 24-inch liner. We use him for brisket, ribs, and turkey.

RUSTY SHACKLEFORD, AKA SHORTY • Demand continued to rise and rise, so a couple of months after Muchacho, I built Rusty with the same design. Rusty has since been renamed "Shorty" because we had to take 20 inches off him to fit him into the new covered smokehouse we built in the summer of 2014. Shorty helps us out with brisket, beef ribs, turkey, pork butts, and sausage.

MC5 • The line kept growing, so I just kept building smokers. A good, solid cooker, MC5 is my least favorite mostly because the grate is ¾ inch lower. That's the way it goes—every cooker is different, even if it basically looks the same. MC5 does its service with briskets and ribs.

NIKKI SIX • My favorite 1,000-gallon cooker! Nikki cooks ribs and briskets faster and better than all of the others.

BETHESDA • The most ambitious cooker I've ever built, Bethesda is a big, bad mama. She is a rotisserie, which means she has sturdy racks that rotate around, cooking ribs and briskets more evenly and in less space than in long, horizontal smokers. Bethesda can handle seventy-two racks of ribs at once, cooking them evenly and deliciously, and unlike all commercial rotisseries (which rely on gas for heat), Bethesda is completely wood fired. My favorite part? Some badass local dudes who design motors for drag racers built the motor that drives her.

HOW SMOKERS WORK

With any new smoker I see, the most important consideration is airflow. It's the airflow that dictates how evenly, quickly, and effectively the smoker cooks.

You probably understand the principles of airflow intuitively, but it always helps to be able to visualize the mechanics. It's fairly basic thermodynamics. Cooler air is drawn in through the firebox door by the fire, which is ravenously consuming oxygen to keep itself going. With the cool air pulled into the fire from one direction, the rapidly expanding hot air is pushed off from the fire in the opposite direction—into the cook chamber. We know that, due to the expansion of gases when heated, hot air rises because it is less dense than cool air. (Scientists would tell you that what's happening is that cooler air is falling because it is denser and thus more affected by gravity.) Anyway, this movement of air is convection.

For offset cookers, the action of the fire is not the only force driving the movement, however. The smokestack is another part of the engine, working in tandem with the fire. Thanks to something called the stack or chimney effect, columns have a way of focusing the energies of convection. As the hot air is sucked into the cook chamber, an imbalance of air pressure from the cooler air outside can create tremendous airflow that will in turn create convection inside the cooker, and, when everything's right, the heat and smoke will move continuously and vigorously from the fire out through the

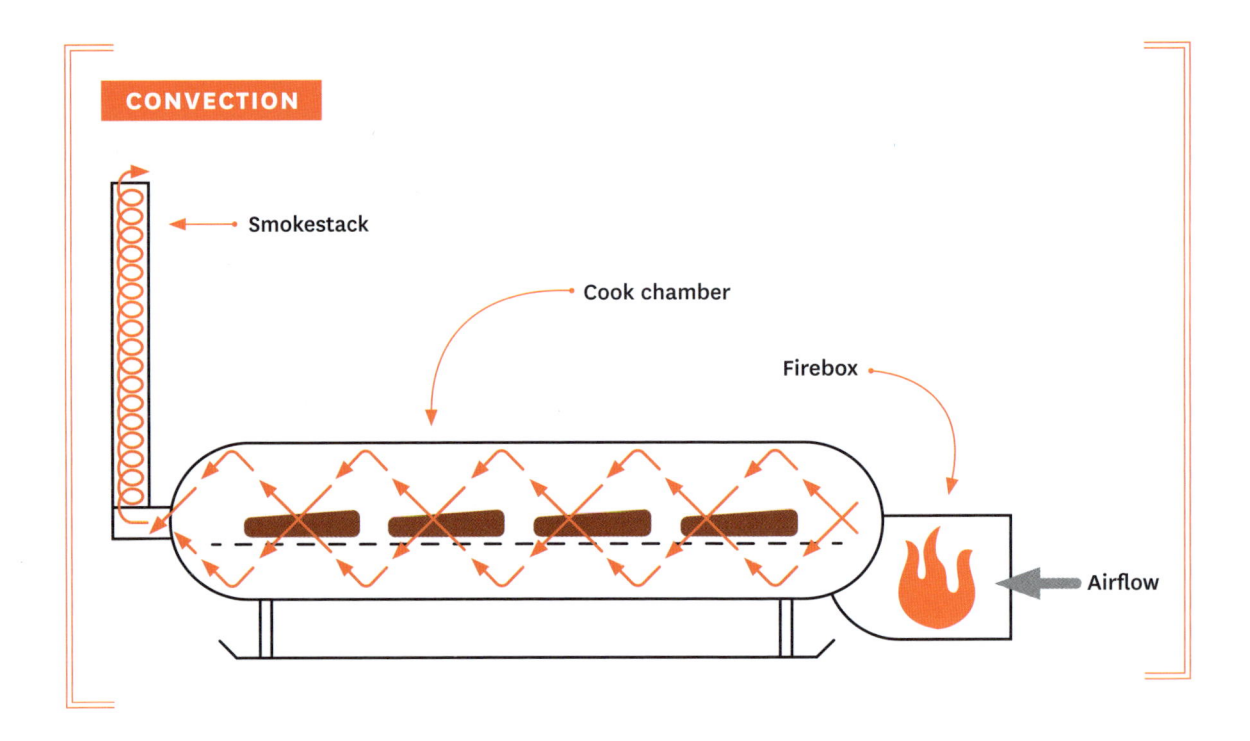

CONVECTION

Smokestack · Cook chamber · Firebox · Airflow

stack. Hot air that's moving cooks things faster and more evenly than stale warm air (which is continuously being cooled by the thing being cooked), thus crucially speeding up cooking times. The smokestack is an essential part of getting the hot air flowing.

Smokestacks and chimneys need to have the right proportions with regard to the cook chamber and firebox so they vent the heat and smoke properly. Too tall a smokestack and the cooler outside air will exert more pressure on the dwindling heat, which will back your smoker up and ultimately extinguish your fire. Too big an opening on the cook chamber will cause the smoke and heat to evacuate too quickly and you won't have enough heat or smoke for cooking.

A science book covering combustion and convection might have formulas that describe all of this and might lead you to a reasonable ratio of firebox volume to cook chamber volume to smokestack height and diameter. But when I'm building a smoker, I just tend to eyeball it. I can offer some advice, however: longer smokestacks tend to pull harder. And it's easier to make a stack shorter than it is to make it longer (I've done both). In other words, you can always dampen a stack that works too well, but it's much harder to make a stack "pull harder." The best thing to do is to get a measure of your smoker's draw and be willing to lengthen the stack somewhat if you think it might help or shorten it if you think things are getting bogged down. There's no better way to discover this than by simply learning your cooker.

Ultimately, repetition is the key to cooking well on any cooker, but especially a standard offset cooker. Experience, patience, and attention are going to be the keys to successful cooks. I've talked to many people who've screwed up a brisket because they left the cooker for too long, weren't watching their temperatures, fell asleep, and so on. Heck, I've done the same things myself. There's nothing worse than ruining a big expensive piece of meat into which you've already put hours.

But the more you use your cooker, the better you'll understand its airflow, the needs of its fire, the draw out through the smokestack, the high and low temperature points within the cook chamber, and more. And as you get to know this simple machine, your cooking will get better and better.

Of course, at the end of the day, if you're buying a new smoker, you still want something that makes your job as easy as possible. Yes, practice *does* make perfect, but better still would be to buy or build a smoker that sets you up for success. I've worked with many of the varieties of commercial offset cookers out there and can offer you the following tips when you're looking to make your next smoker purchase.

WHAT TO LOOK FOR WHEN BUYING A SMOKER

Because barbecue is so popular these days, you'll find a huge variety of smokers in a wide range of prices on the market. In some cases you get what you pay for; in others not so much. As with any significant purchase, you should avoid an impulse buy and take a while to consider a number of factors before you choose. Some of these factors may seem obvious, but I think it's good to be reminded of them, if nothing else than for the sake of due diligence.

Do You Have a Place to Put It?

This may seem like a foolishly basic point, but it's worth considering. People can become infatuated with barbecues the way kids get about puppies. They want one real bad, but after a month of scooping up poop and having to walk the animal twice a day, suddenly they're foisting those chores off on their parents. Likewise with great barbecue. After having tasty brisket somewhere, people become inspired, and in the excitement of the moment, they rush out to the store to buy a smoker. It's when they get it home that they realize it takes up a third of their yard or that they'll have to stow it in the garage behind all of that other stuff. They'll have to clean it and take care of it too. Suddenly it's wasting away. Don't let your cooker become a neglected puppy!

My advice is to figure out exactly where you're going to put it before you buy it. Some of these smokers have a big footprint, so take a measurement and really visualize the space. Also consider that you'll need to access the firebox with enough space to throw in another piece of wood. You'll want to be able to get around this thing. And it must be freestanding, not leaning up against a wooden fence or a side of the house. (That's obvious, I know, but every year some three thousand homes burn down because of barbecue and grill fires, according to the National Fire Protection Association.)

And if it's a smaller backyard cooker, it's better not to stow it in the back of the garden shed or garage. Chances are that you'll use it less often than you would if it's placed in plain sight and you see it every day. Consider these simple things before laying down your money.

What and How Much Do You Plan on Cooking?

I was so excited when I got my first smoker. It could hold one, maybe two briskets comfortably—enough to serve ten to twenty people. But it wasn't long after my first cook that I was invited to cook for a friend's birthday and then a wedding party, and then our backyard barbecues started to expand. In effect, I'd outgrown my smoker after just a couple of cooks. So you need to think about how you'll use your cooker, especially if you're planning to buy something that costs more than a couple of hundred dollars.

For how many people will you usually be cooking? If it's just you and a couple of friends, you might not need too much space on the grill. But if you often daydream about being referred to as "the barbecue guy" and cooking for big parties, you'll probably want to start off with something that can handle more volume.

Volume is important, because the slow part of "low and slow" cooking is very real. It's not like a steak, where you can just throw another one on and it's done in 5 to 10 minutes. In fact, with barbecue you get significantly less than what you started with. Over 12 hours, 25 pounds of brisket gradually becomes 15, and you can't "throw another one on" when your cousin decides to invite her neighbors. Slowness and capacity have continuously challenged us at the restaurant—how to find enough grill space to do the volume we want to do when we need it done. As it is, our smokers are in use 24 hours a day. We are literally at maximum capacity. So, if you're firing up the smoker for a big party and doing a couple of briskets, you have to remember that those things will occupy the entire surface of a small smoker

TO INSULATE YOUR FIREBOX OR NOT

Some fireboxes are insulated, using everything from multiple layers of metal, fire bricks, and fiberglass insulation to mineral wool. Ultimately, the question of whether to have an insulated firebox or not depends on the nature of the cooker you use and where you're cooking.

The main reason to insulate your firebox is to improve heat retention. Once up to temperature, an insulated firebox will hold its temperature much better than an uninsulated one, even if you'll be going in and out of the cook chamber a bit, which always costs you heat. Other advantages to insulation are much more efficient fires and therefore lower fuel costs. (My first smoker, Number One, doesn't have an insulated firebox, and it uses almost twice as much wood as Number Two, which does.)

Insulated fireboxes are a must for people who live in cold climates and want to cook in winter. You'll want a well-insulated firebox so you're not constantly battling to keep your temperatures up.

There are corollary disadvantages too. If the firebox is insulated with rock or with an extra layer of metal, the cooker will be heavier and consequently more difficult to move around. If logistics are a concern, this is something to think about. Also, too much insulation can generate too much heat for a smaller cooker. If the firebox is too well insulated, it will keep its coals warm for really long periods, hardly requiring wood fuel to keep its temperature up. This way, without smoke, the cooker is basically an oven. We do want a smoker to exhaust its fuel at a fast-enough rate that we can keep adding wood to maintain a continuous supply of smoke. A certain amount of inefficiency can be a good thing. It's important to be able to balance the power of the heat source with the cooking vessel—a giant bonfire is counterproductive if you're just trying to scramble a single egg.

That sense of proportion is why I think an insulated firebox is really important for a large-scale cooker, but not as critical on a smaller one, as long as the smaller one is still constructed out of reasonably thick ¼- or ⅜-inch steel. For really long cooks in which you've got anywhere from five to twenty-five briskets going, you're going to need that steady, powerful source of heat from an insulated box. If you're just doing one or a handful of briskets, you can manage fine without.

My large cookers' fireboxes are two concentric cylinders with a small pocket of air between them. They're round instead of the more common square firebox because the round firebox allows me to build up a nice deep bed of coals at the base of the circle. Wood stacked across the arc of the circle gets natural airflow between it and the coal bed. I also like the way the flames rise in the round firebox and are forced to curl around the edges. I feel (no hard science here) this helps create a certain amount of vorticity that propels the air, heat, and smoke with great velocity and chaos into the cook chamber.

for 12 to 18 hours. You won't have a chance to cook anything else on there before the party starts, so it had better be enough.

Speaking of brisket, before you buy your smoker, take a look at how big a full 12-pound brisket measures and then think about how many you can get on the cooker you're looking at. And you don't want the meat smushed up against the edges either. It needs to have space around it for airflow. Now visualize a couple of racks of ribs, which can measure between 12 and 18 inches in length. Also consider height, such as the stature of a whole turkey, which you will quite likely want to smoke some Thanksgiving.

Quality of the Build

Now you're in a hardware or outdoors shop looking at the various models of offset smokers they have. As with anything you're buying—a car, a jacket, a puppy—you're going to want to consider the quality of the materials and workmanship. If you've never bought a smoker before, how will you know what's good or not? First and foremost, trust your instincts: you'll be surprised to what degree rickety construction—and, likewise, really good craftsmanship—will stand out to even unpracticed eyes. But there are also some other details to consider.

If you're cooking with wood—and, after all, that is what we're talking about here—there are some important qualities you should be looking for. Wood fires are more inconsistent and variable than those fueled by gas, charcoal, or electricity. Therefore, heat retention is key, and good heat retention is a feature of thicker metal. At the low end of the price spectrum, you'll definitely see a number of cookers whose cook chamber and firebox are built out of thin, stamped sheet metal. You'll want to avoid those, as the heat will spike or escape quickly, leading to terribly uneven cooking. Likewise, it will be hard to achieve and hold decent temperatures in colder weather. Thicker metal is more expensive and unwieldy to transport, but it will save a ton of aggravation during your cooks. Acceptably thick metal will run anywhere from $1/8$ to $3/8$ inch thick. You'll know metal that's too thin, because it's not much thicker than sheet metal.

Durability is also a significant question. If you buy a new smoker, season it, modify it, and spend months discovering its inner habits and quirks, you won't be too happy if its doors don't fit, its screws buckle, or it burns through in a year or two. Of course, this is a particular worry with cookers made of thinner metal. Rust is an inevitability with anything made from metal, but thin fireboxes can rust through within a couple of years of moderate usage. Best to look for a solid, well-constructed or insulated firebox. Especially with cookers made of thinner metal, good maintenance means dealing with rust as it occurs: take a wire brush, sandpaper, or steel wool and scour rust out when you see it pop up.

Along the same lines, you need to examine the quality of the closures, seals, and of the insulation, if there is any (see "To Insulate Your Firebox or Not," page 51). Doors lacking seals or outfitted with flimsy ones will leak heat and smoke copiously, which makes a cook uncontrollable and unpredictable. Seals should be tight and completely cover the gap between the door and the body of the cooker, usually from the outside. If at the store you see a smoker with a door that seems to fit so perfectly and snugly that you're convinced it's well sealed, don't be convinced. Just wait until you get it home and get it fired up at 300°F for 10 hours. You'll see even thicker metals twist and shift when heated, and suddenly a seemingly well-made smoker of dainty metal becomes a contorted, ill-fitting heat sieve.

DETAILS AND ACCESSORIES

Good, simple offset smokers have few moving parts, but the ones they do sport should be of good quality and soundly integrated.

Thermometers are important. While making good barbecue requires touch and instinct, I refer to temperature gauges dozens of times every hour. I'd go as far as saying that great barbecue is impossible without them. So, two things that you want to look for in your prospective smoker are thermometer placement and quality. The gauge should be located down at grill height. If it's not, but rather placed up at the top of the chamber, make sure that it won't be too hard to install a new thermometer yourself, as I discuss later in this chapter.

Also, check to make sure that it's a good-quality, heavy-duty thermometer. The probe will be sitting for long periods of time in a hot environment filled with soot, tar, smoke, and grease. Chances are the included thermometer won't be of the greatest pedigree, so make sure that you can replace it with one of your own purchased down the road.

A baffle is a device (such as a wall or screen) that is used to control the flow of something (such as a fluid, light, or sound). In a cooker, it's a plate used to redirect heat and smoke as they enter the cook chamber from the firebox. It's often welded right above the opening between these two spaces, so it redirects the heat from the fire down and disperses it into the cooker, instead of letting it rise up and out through the top. It also adds to that chaotic effect, getting heat and air bouncing around, reducing unevenness in the cooking. I think it's important to have one of these in pretty much every offset smoker design.

I use the firebox door to control airflow to the fire (more on that in the fire chapter), but a damper on the smokestack can be a handy tool to further control the rate of draw. It's also handy for closing off the stack if your smoker's not going to be in use for a while, to keep the critters out. However, if you do leave a smoker completely closed up, it can eventually get moldy inside. So, if you're not going to be using it for a long time, always leave it cracked.

Other things to consider include the handles of the cooker and firebox doors. Are they made of a less conductive material so that you can grab them without melting the skin on your hands? Are they sturdy and well attached?

Finally, is there an outlet for drippings? Over a 12-hour or longer cook, a brisket might lose half its weight. Most of that is just going to drip down into the bottom of the cooker in the form of grease and rendered fat which, incidentally, is a fire hazard. You'll want to get it out of there rather than just letting it pile up and turn rancid. It's much easier to have some sort of drain or valve to let it pour out than to have to remove the grates, lean in, and scoop it out by hand. I'd look for a cooker that has a drip pan, a place for a drip pan in the bottom, or a drain at one end from which grease can run out.

BUILDING A SMOKER

I started our business back in the trailer with a smoker that I bought from someone else. But since then, for the barbecue we sell at the restaurant, we haven't cooked on a smoker that I didn't build or design myself.

Building a smoker might sound like a daunting task, but if you have the right tools and some common sense, it's not as hard as you might think. It helps to be drawn to taking things apart, tinkering, and building stuff, which I am. Since I was kid, I've liked deconstructing things just to figure out how they work. If I didn't know how to use a tool, I just taught myself. It's that simple. And building a smoker can be too.

You'll need elementary metalworking skills. If you read that last sentence and thought, *Yeah right, buddy*, just skip ahead to "Modifying a Cheap Store-Bought Smoker" on page 62, where there are some more entry-level projects laid out. But welding big, stupid hunks of metal is not as hard as it might look. Welding complicated, delicate things like jet engines—now that's another story. But I started welding when my parents gave me a rig, and I basically taught myself. The more I welded, the better—and faster—I got.

Building smokers got a lot easier for me when I rented a basic workshop space in a small industrial park on the outskirts of Austin and stopped doing it in the sweltering heat and uneven ground of my backyard. Now it's just the sweltering heat of the shop. But it was indeed the backyard where I started the hot, grimy activity of welding together large pieces of heavy steel. It also got easier when I procured an old, 1970s Komatsu forklift. But by then we were well into business at the restaurant, and I needed to add cooking capacity and speed as quickly as possible. I spent many, many brutal days cooking from 2 a.m. at the restaurant, working through lunch, then heading off to weld for a few hours before grabbing a quick bite to eat and collapsing.

In this section of the book, I want to take you through some of the basic decisions and processes you'll want to consider if you go the route of building your own smoker. This is by no means a manual, and I'm offering no schematics or measurements. Indeed, I never started with any of those myself for any of the many smokers I've built. Rather, I've just employed my eyeballs and good judgment when designing and figuring out proportions. As I said, it's not rocket science—just effort, commitment, and a small degree of handiness.

Speaking of which, here's a look at some tools you'll need. I own these tools because I do a lot of welding. But if you don't see yourself getting grimy and breathing slag on a regular basis and still want to try your hand on a one-time project, I'm sure you can find hardware shops that will rent the tools for the few days that you'll need them.

Welder • I recommend a MIG welder over a stick, which, in my opinion, is not as easy to use. A MIG you can just plug in and go. A 140-amp wire-feed MIG should be sufficient for light jobs and plugs into a standard home outlet.

Welding helmet • I have an auto-darkening one; it's neat.

Angle (disc) grinder • I have a big one and a smaller one from DeWalt. You use these to grind down your welds, smooth sharp and jagged edges, cut thinner pieces of metal, and the like.

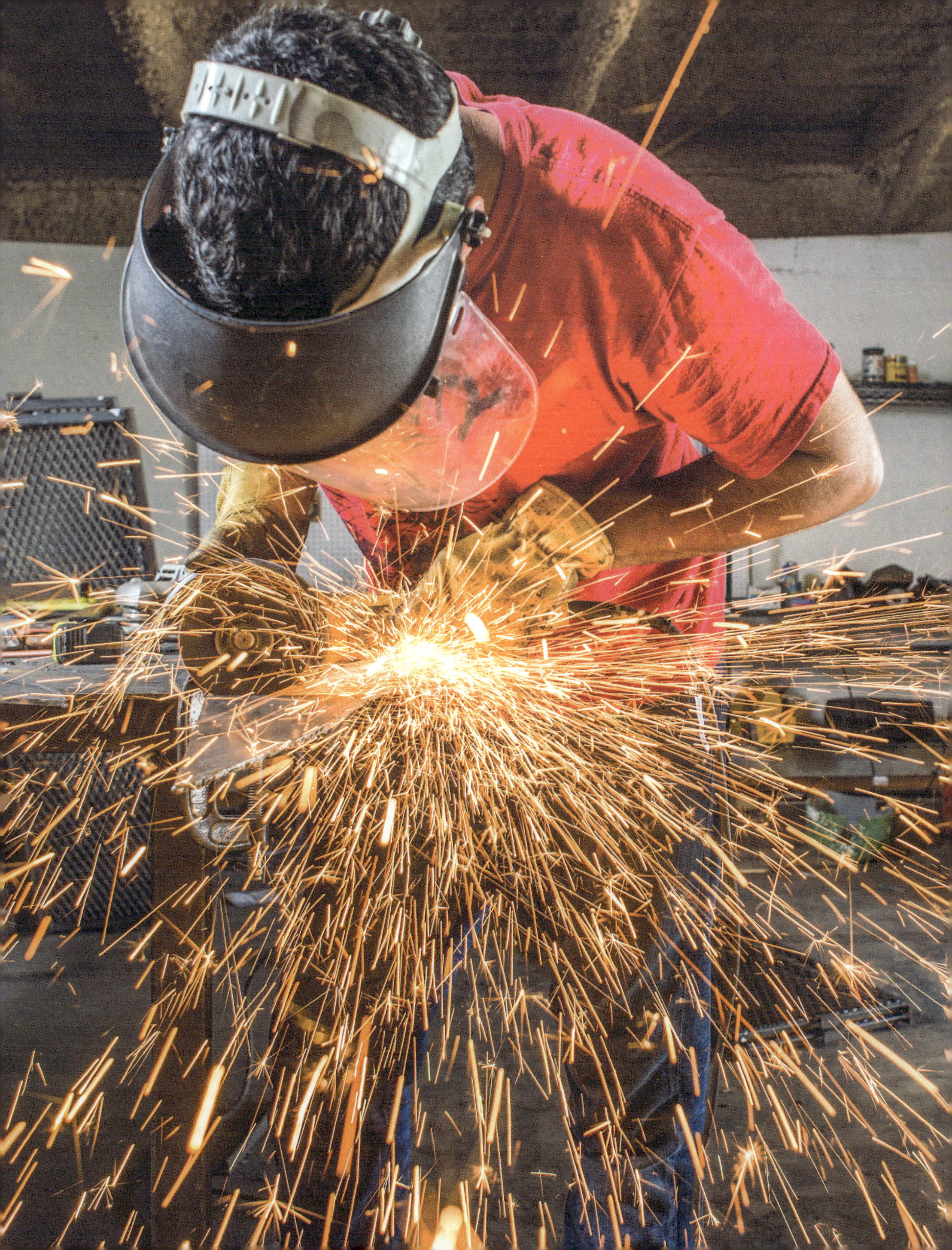

Dry-cut metal saw • This speeds up cutting of thinner metal rods, pipes, and tubes, but you could also get by without one.

Assorted measuring tools and clamps • These are what you'd need for any building project: levels, measuring tape, soapstone pencil (for marking steel), magnetic welding angles, gloves, and a range of vice clamps for holding pieces together before you apply the weld.

Choose Your Material for the Body and Firebox

A simple horizontal offset smoker is really just two cylinders welded together with legs and a smokestack or some fundamental variation of that. Most homemade smokers I've seen are made of scrap metal, a detail that brings the satisfaction of creating something for cheap or for free with your own ingenuity, which, as you can tell from chapter one, is what I'm all about.

The first thing you'll need to do is figure out what you want to make your main body out of. As noted earlier, I use old propane tanks for my big smokers. These are 1,000-gallon tanks that are 16 feet long. The fireboxes are made from a 250-gallon tank, cut in half. I like propane tanks for their ready-made cylindrical shapes, their rounded ends, and their heavy but manageable 5/16-inch steel walls.

Before I proceed, I must offer a disclaimer: I am in no way recommending you procure and cut into a used propane tank. In industrial zones you can often find whole yards full of used propane tanks just sitting there, rusting in the dirt. They sit because they're difficult to recycle, as some propane outfits won't sell them for scrap because there's a chance they'll blow up upon deconstruction. It's said that working propane tanks are never completely empty and that even the metal used to fashion them is porous and can absorb potentially explosive propane traces. Resale of used propane tanks might be illegal in your area, or you may find that some shops will refuse to sell them because of liability. I've been stymied on many occasions, yet I've also found businesses that will gladly sell.

So, now that my disclaimer is out of the way, I will say that these propane graveyards often have used tanks with open or busted valves that would almost certainly not have any gas left in them. Also, before using the tanks, people often fill them with water and lots of dish soap to force out any remaining gas and the stinky mercaptans added to propane to give it an odor (so we will notice when there's a leak).

Alternatives to propane tanks include finding two pieces of used big steel pipe from a discount store or a scrap metal operation and fusing them together. Diameters of 20 or 24 inches will work well for this purpose. Or you can always buy plate steel and have a machine shop roll it for you to a length and diameter of your choosing.

Typically, if your firebox is insulated, it doesn't have to be quite as big as an uninsulated firebox.

Notes on Building the Stand

Once I've determined the dimensions of the smoker's body and firebox, I set out to making the legs and the stand. For smaller smokers I'd use 1-inch square steel tubing that comes in 12-foot lengths. For bigger ones, I've used 2-inch square steel tubing. Determine and cut the lengths of tube for the two pieces that make up the base. These look like skis. I prefer these to freestanding legs on casters because they offer more reinforcement. I choose a length a couple of inches longer on each side than the entire assembly is going to be, including the cook chamber and firebox. Position these parallel to each other as far apart as the diameter of the pipe or tank and weld a couple of crossbars in between them (see **"A" ON FIGURE 1**, page 58).

Next, build the leg assemblies. For this, consider what is a comfortable height for the actual grill that will hold the meat. After all, this will be your cooker, so you might as well design it to fit your own body. I'm 5 feet 10, and for me, the ideal (waist) height is 36 inches off the ground (see **"B" ON FIGURE 1**, page 58).

There's no need to get fancy when shaping the ends of the legs that will attach to the tank. Cutting a 45° angle on these ends will allow it to fit the cylinder pretty closely, and you can fill in the gaps through welding.

After you've cut and fused the leg pieces together and perhaps reinforced them with their own crossbar, you can weld them to the base skids to create the whole stand. Then you've got to lower your tank or pipe onto the stand. I can do this easily with a forklift now, but in the old days of backyard builds, I'd have to use ropes and pulleys and a tree branch to lift the metal cylinder onto the shafts of the legs. Once that's done, however, all the parts are easy to fuse together. By this point it's starting to take shape, though you will probably want to attach tires or casters for easier movement of something that will end up weighing several hundred pounds. I recommend good, strong casters. Estimate how much your assembly will weigh and buy casters that are rated appropriately.

The most important thing in building the stand is this: Don't cut corners. Don't have flimsy welds; use strong-enough materials.

Cutting the Doors

Figure out how many doors you'll need to be able to access every section of your cooking area. Doors are pretty easy to design and cut. Things to remember about the cook chamber doors is that they should extend right down to the height of the grill itself (which should be located at the midpoint of the circle) and extend up close to the apex of the circle (see **"C" ON FIGURE 1**, page 58). Make sure to give yourself room to work. When you need to reach in there to place or turn heavy pieces of meat, you'll realize that the cook chamber doors need to be fairly wide and pretty much span the entire length of the chamber.

One tip I can offer: don't cut the entire piece of the door completely out after marking it on the side of the cylinder. Rather, I leave the corners just barely attached. That allows me to weld on the hinges before cutting out the last connecting bits of the door, saving a lot of trouble in trying to realign what ends up being a very heavy piece of metal.

For the firebox, just weld a piece of plate metal to cover the end of the cylinder and mark a pretty good-size door, one that's long enough to get decent-size logs in and then to be able to shift those around with a shovel or poker.

I spend way too much time making my own hinges from steel rods and tubes. A much easier solution is to buy some heavy-duty ones at a welding supply store.

The final step is to weld the strips of flat bar trim to the edges of the doors so they overlap the sides of the cook chamber and firebox (see **"D" ON FIGURE 1**, below), making a snug fit to ensure very little heat and smoke escape and cold air doesn't get pulled in.

Attaching the Firebox and Smokestack

If your firebox and cook chamber are both made out of pipe or other cylindrical metal, when you attach them, the opening will resemble a football, an oval-shaped aperture existing in the zone where the two circles of pipe overlap each other. The bigger the opening, the more heat you'll get flowing directly into the cook chamber. You'll need to install a small plate (see page 53) to prevent grease from entering the firebox. Try to position the top of firebox to meet the cook chamber at grate level; that should give you a good-size aperture (see **"E" ON FIGURE 1**, below). Remember, grate level should be waist high for you, the eventual pitmaster. Fireboxes that are set too low won't draw as well.

You'll see lots of commercial cookers with the smokestack coming out of the top of the cook chamber at the opposite end from the firebox. But I do things differently: my chimneys are attached at about grate level, which means I weld it to the side of the cook chamber rather than the top (see **"F" ON FIGURE 1**, below). This is because I want the smoke and heat to flow across the meat thoroughly and evenly rather than be on a rush

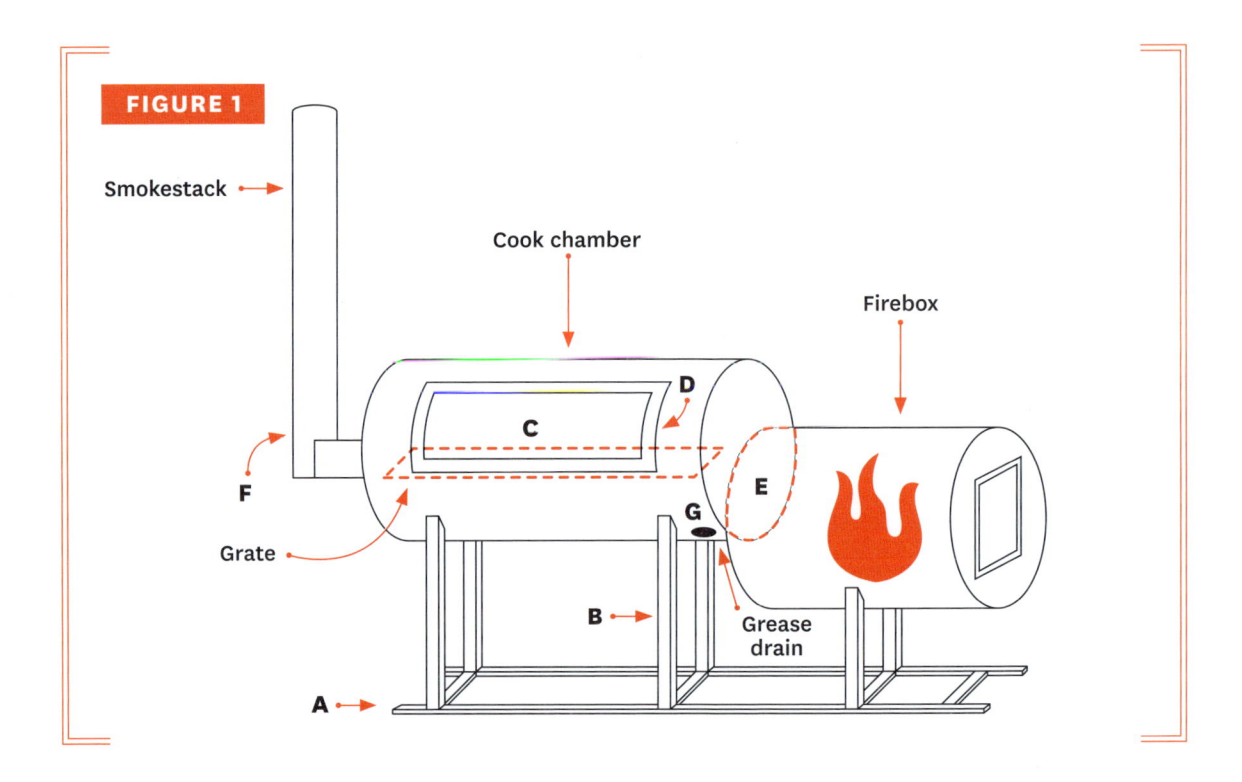

FIGURE 1

Smokestack
Cook chamber
Firebox
F
D
C
E
G
Grate
B
Grease drain
A

THE SMOKER

to rise out of the cooker. You can attach the stack any way you prefer. You can buy prefabricated 90° exhaust elbows. I tend to buy a pipe, cut a piece out of one end, and fabricate an assembly that allows it to attach to the farthest end of the cook chamber at the midpoint. And, in general, I prefer pretty wide and tall smokestacks. I wouldn't go any smaller than a 4-inch diameter, and I like them to be as long as possible, between 3 and 4 feet for a smaller backyard smoker. I usually just determine the length in 6-inch increments. Better to have too much draw than too little. You can always install a damper to regulate airflow if you feel it's pulling too hard once you've fired the thing up.

Last Things

Once you've got all of this built and cut, it's quite easy to go in and install the brackets that will support the grates that hold the meat. Naturally, you'll want to install several brackets for good support, since the grates will have to be in pieces to facilitate easy placement and removal. I cut the brackets out of what's called angle iron, which you can find at any metal shop. For the grates, I buy steel raised expanded metal. I put a frame on the outside of each grate, like a window screen, for structural integrity and because it makes the grate much easier to take in and out when we clean. Make sure that you construct your "screens" small enough that they can be inserted and removed through the width of your cook chamber door.

Above the opening between the firebox and cooker, below the grate inside the chamber, I like to add a small plate to deflect the direct heat that will enter from the firebox. This small but crucial step will buffer some of that intense heat and allow you to use more of that cooking surface on the end close to the firebox.

Last but not least, don't forget to make a hole in the cook chamber, at the end closest to the firebox (see **"G" ON FIGURE 1**, left), from which grease can drain (into a bucket that you'll place underneath).

Burn It Out

Before using any new smoker, be it store-bought or homemade, it's crucial to burn it out with a hot fire to seal up the pores of the metal and incinerate any remains and by-products—oil, grease, metal shavings, and any other gunk—of the manufacturing process. I build as big a fire as I can and let it go for an hour or so. Then treat your smoker like a cast-iron skillet and season it by rubbing vegetable oil, tallow, or lard into the metal.

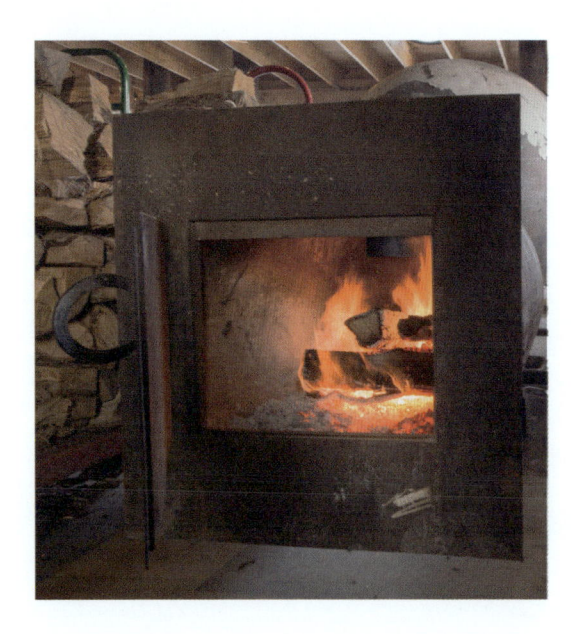

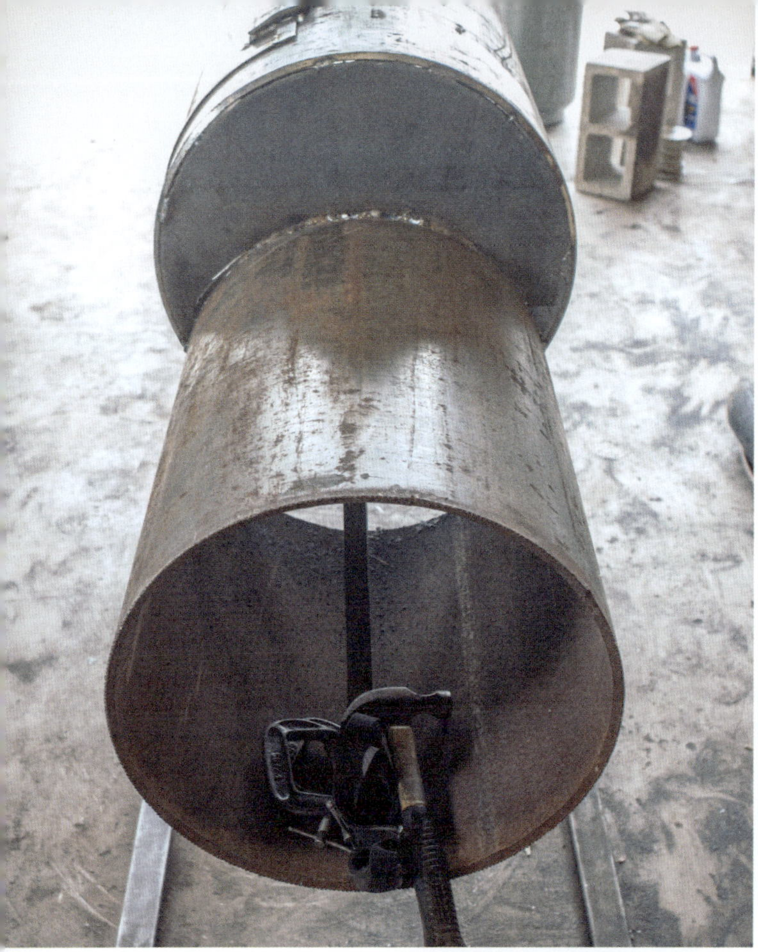
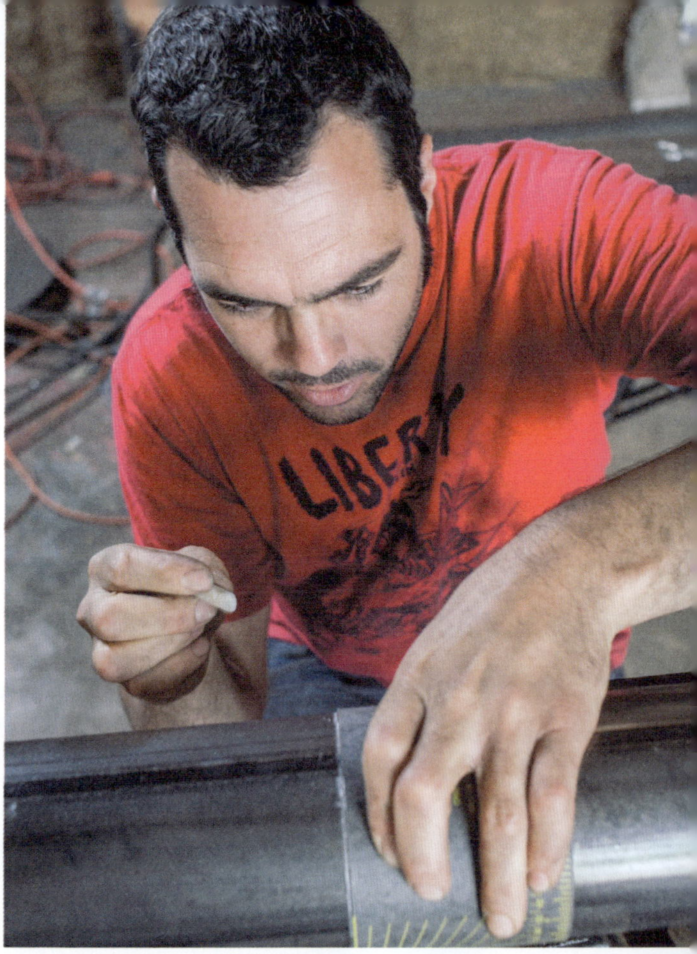
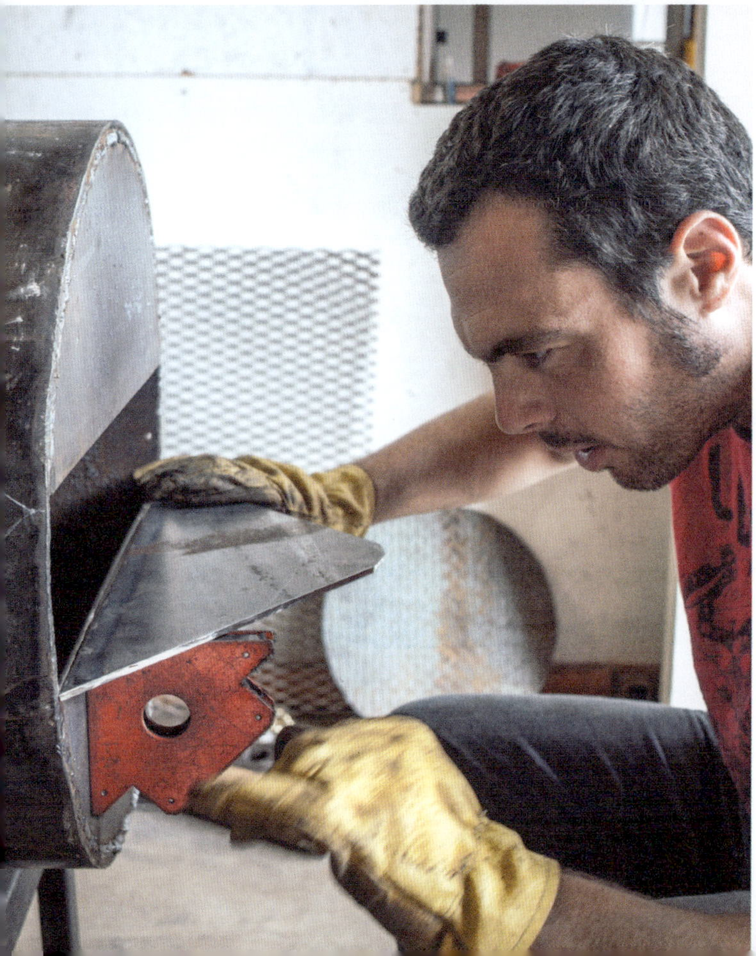
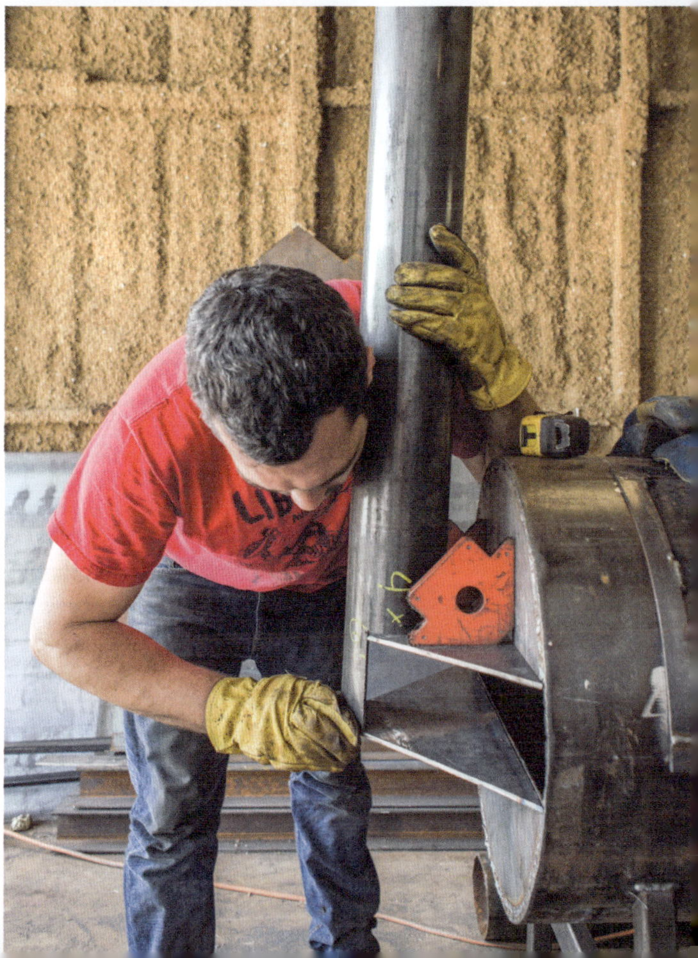

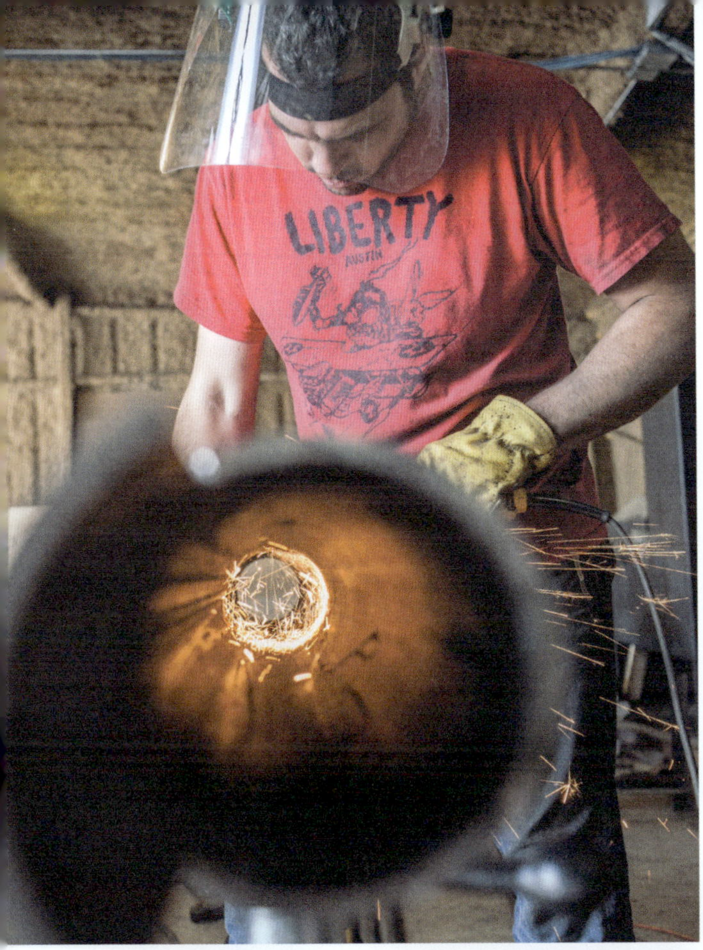
LIBERTY
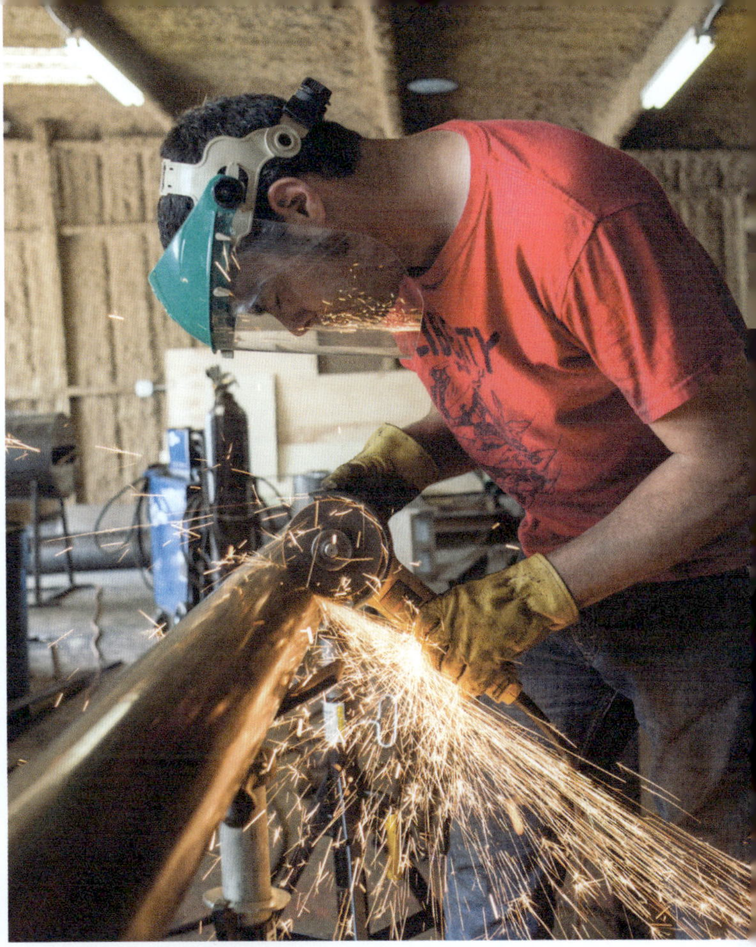
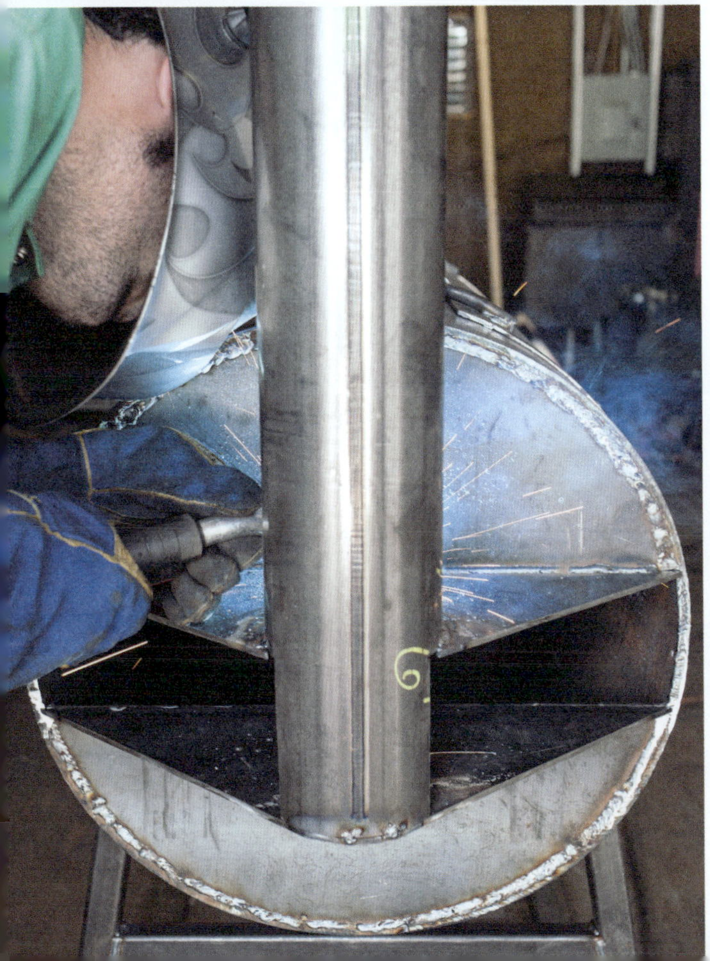
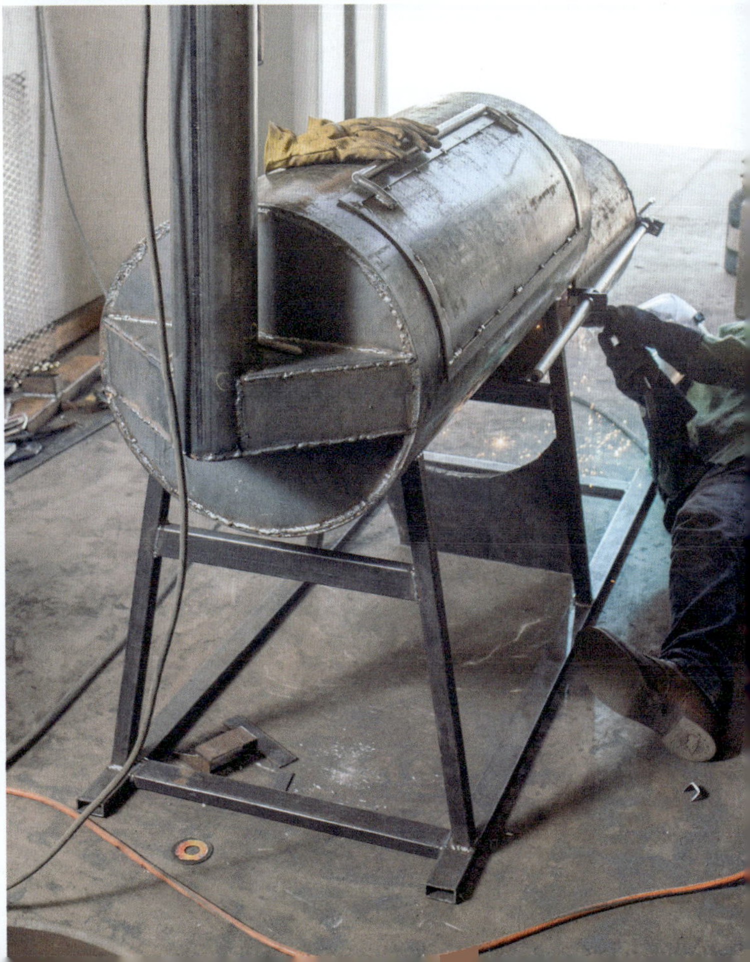

MODIFYING A CHEAP STORE-BOUGHT SMOKER

Building a smoker from scratch is, even for the most bullish barbecue enthusiast, a big—and perhaps impractical—endeavor. Even I didn't start out by building a smoker from the ground up. But that doesn't mean you're stuck using whatever smoker you can buy in a traditional outdoors or cookware store. I've found that with some relatively simple modifications (okay, I know, this *is* coming from the guy who just admitted to owning a forklift and welding for fun), you can improve practically any smoker you buy.

Installing a Proper Temperature Gauge

One of the easiest and most essential modifications you can make is to install a decent thermometer in a smoker that doesn't have one or replace or reposition the thermometer that comes preinstalled in many entry-level smokers.

Knowing your cooking temperature and keeping it consistent are two of the most important factors in barbecue. If they even have a temperature gauge, most inexpensive smokers position it, stupidly, at the top. Perhaps this convenience is meant for lazy people who want to be able to read it without bending over, but it's a useless placement for reading the temperature at the cooking surface where the meat is. Because heat rises, the temperature of the area near the top of the smoker is going to be higher than the temperature down where the meat is, which is obviously the only place that matters. In addition, smoker companies save money by using inferior thermometers, which only compounds the problems of bad placement. You'll want to throw down a few bucks for a higher-quality thermometer. After that, the work is easy and takes only a few minutes, yet moves you significantly down the road toward improving your homemade barbecue.

Equipment

- Thermometer: There are many of these on the market, at varying prices. Without question, my favorite is the Tel-Tru Barbecue Thermometer BQ300, which costs between $40 and $50. I recommend one that has a 2.5- to 4-inch stem and is made out of high-quality stainless steel, shatter-proof glass and plastic, and paint that won't fade over time. Tel-Tru makes a variety of models, and if you order on the Internet, you

THE SMOKER

might also want to throw in the Thermometer Installation Kit to ensure that you've got everything you need.

- Drill with a hole-saw attachment capable of drilling through light metal.

Steps

1. • First, determine exactly where to drill the hole. The temperature gauge should be positioned between the meat and the heat, right at meat level. This means the hole you're going to drill will be near the edge of the lid, close to where the lid meets the grill top, about 1 1/2 inches from the bottom edge of the smoker's lid because that's about where the center of a piece of meat would be. To determine the distance from the firebox opening, measure the length of a hypothetical 10- to 12-pound brisket, which is generally somewhere between 15 and 22 inches long. It's easy enough to measure this out inside the smoker and then eyeball it on the lid, where the hole needs to be drilled. On the outside of the lid, mark off with a pencil or a Sharpie where you're going to drill the hole (see **"A" ON FIGURE 2**, page 67).

2. • Next, select the right-size hole saw. If you use a Tel-Tru, the website tells you the size of the hole you'll need for each model. Otherwise, you can measure the back of the temperature gauge to figure out the diameter of the hole needed to allow the gauge to fit securely.

3. • Finally, time to drill. Easy enough. All it takes is a steady hand. Now, insert the temperature gauge and screw it in from the back, making sure it fits snugly but not too tight. Adjust the dial for easy reading but make sure not to turn it by the gauge, which can throw off calibration.

Extending the Stack

When I cook on other people's smokers, one of the biggest challenges is bad airflow. Smoke may be billowing out the chimney, but often too slowly and without enough force. The solution for this is to extend the smokestack upward, which will increase the draw.

In the discussion on building a cooker (see page 53), I mentioned that I like to position the smokestack to leave from the midpoint of the back of the cook chamber, not the top, because it pulls the heat more evenly across the surface of the meat. Many store-bought smokers have the stack connecting at the top of the chamber, creating exactly this problem. The solution for this is to lengthen the smokestack *inside* the cooking chamber down to within a couple of inches of grate level.

In a pinch, to extend the smokestack upward, I've been known to collect empty soup cans, cut out the bottoms, and pinch them onto the smokestack to gain several inches or a foot. But, for a longer-term solution, you can get thin flexible sheet metal and a few screws or clamps and simply wrap it around the stack to increase the length. Likewise, extending the smokestack down to grate level is not hard.

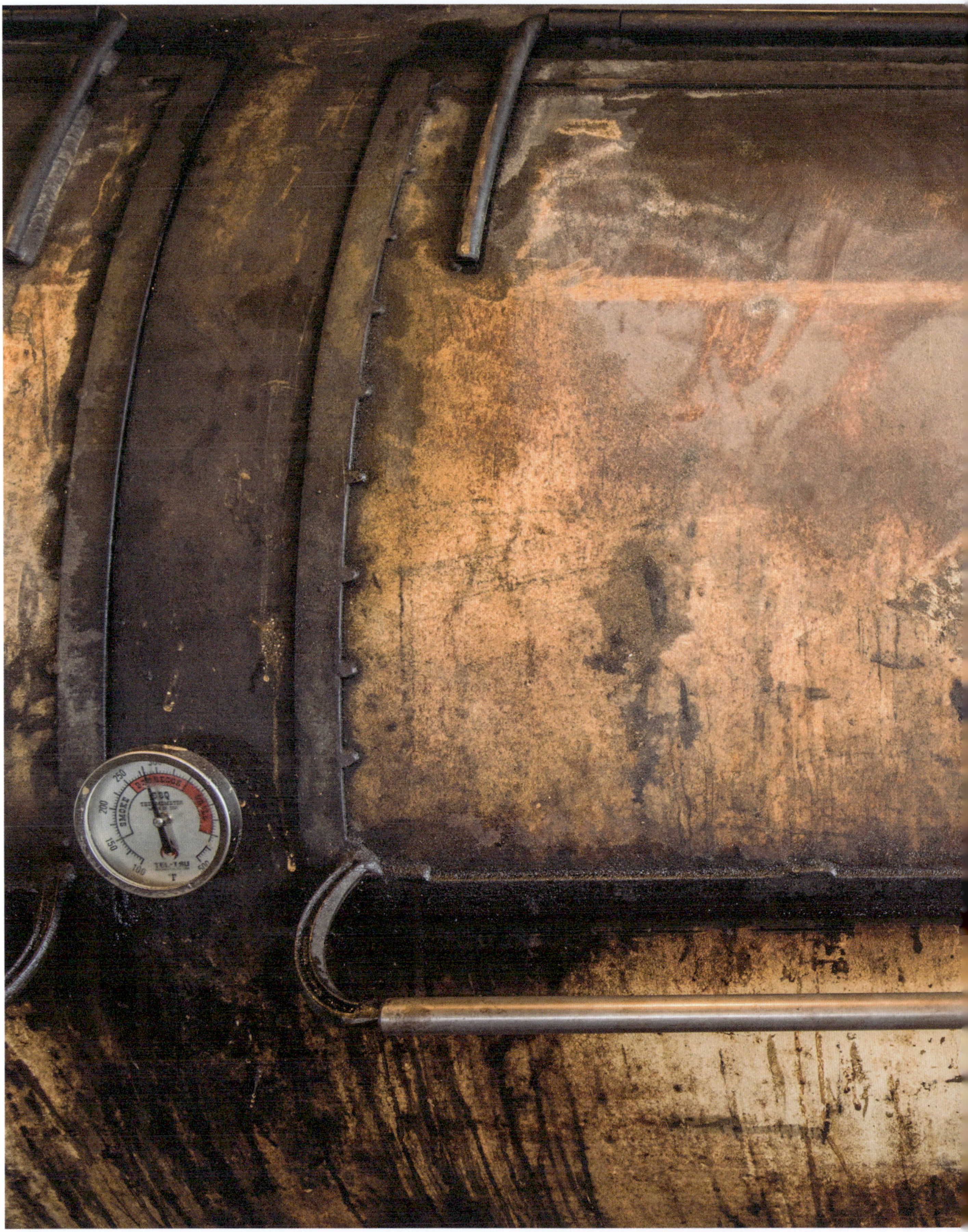

SMOKE
BBQ
TEL-TRU
100
150
200
250

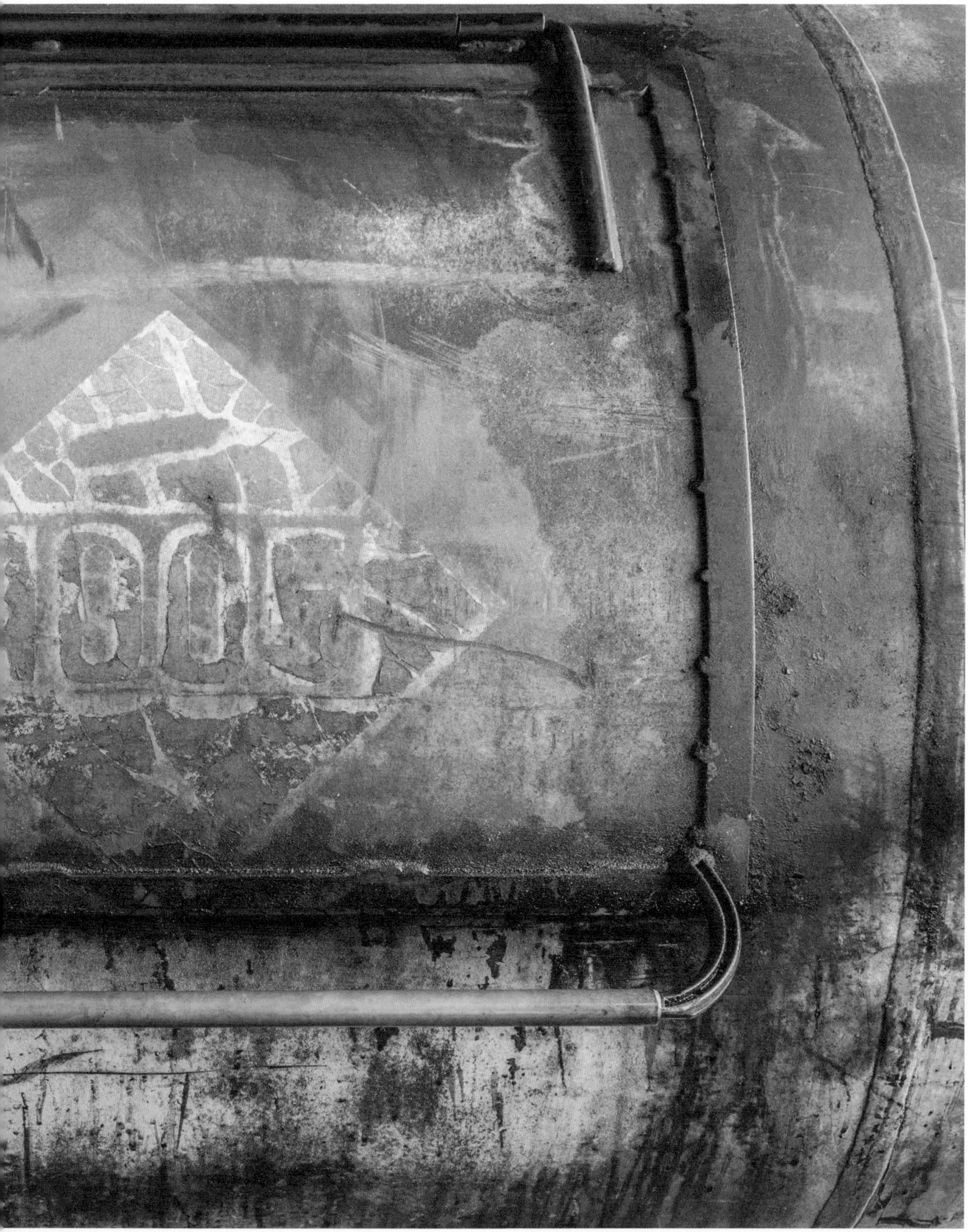

Equipment

- Flexible aluminum or steel hose, a foot or two, at the diameter of your smokestack (hose usually comes in 1-inch-diameter increments)
- Hose clamp to match the diameter of the hose
- Screwdriver
- Clippers to cut the metal

Steps

1. The smokestack will likely protrude slightly into the interior of your cook chamber. Measure the diameter to determine the width of steel hose you'll need to buy.

2. After procuring a short length of tubing, attach it with the clamp around the edge of the smokestack, tightening the screws of the clamp.

3. Measure the length you'll need to extend the smokestack within an inch or two of grill height and cut off the rest of the hose. This should extend the smokestack inside the cook chamber to reorient airflow closer to the grill (see **"B" ON FIGURE 2**, right).

Heat Buffer Plate

The flow of heat from the firebox into the cook chamber is largely a good thing, except for on the side closest to the firebox, where the heat will be much greater than on the far side. And if you've got a smoker packed with meat, which retards airflow, heat has an even tougher time getting over to the far end of the chamber, creating a frustrating disparity between ends of the cook chamber.

One solution to this problem is to install a baffle (buffer plate) above the opening to the firebox, extending at a downward angle into the cooking chamber (see **"C" ON FIGURE 2**, right). In a pinch, I've even jammed an old license plate into that opening. But with more time and space, it wouldn't be hard to cut a piece of thick metal from something lying around.

Water Pan

I'm of the mind that you should always use a water pan while cooking on an offset smoker, so this isn't a modification so much as a technique. It adds humidity (which is constantly being whisked out by convection) to the cooking environment, which is important to your success, as it helps hasten the cooking process while slowing the drying process of meat. But if the smoker you bought doesn't have a built-in place for a water pan (and it probably doesn't), you could buy a small, 4- or 6-inch-deep, narrow steam table pan at a restaurant supply store (although really, any small metal container will do), place it on the grate nearest to the firebox, and keep it filled with water while doing a cook (see **"D" ON FIGURE 2**, right).

THE SMOKER

FIGURE 2

Water pan

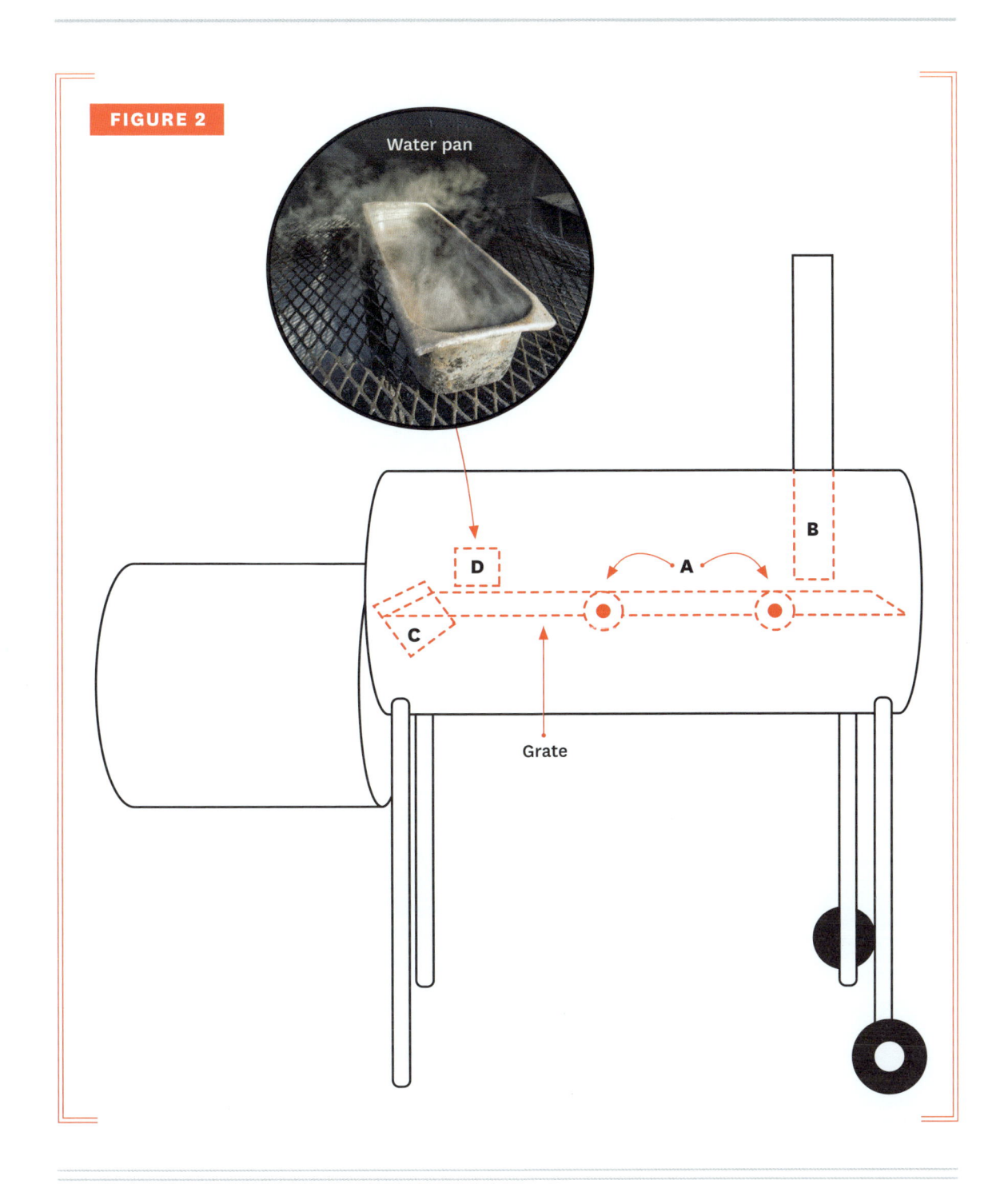

Grate

CARE AND MAINTENANCE

Taking good care of your cooker is crucial for both its own longevity and for the quality of what comes out of it. At the restaurant, we clean the smokers once a week, on the day we're closed to the public, and we periodically take one off duty to perform maintenance and adjustment.

Home cookers will not be running 24 hours a day as ours do, so there will be far less wear and tear. But time always takes its toll, so here are some ways to care for your smoker.

First, as mentioned earlier, make sure to burn out a new smoker. Get a vigorous wood fire going and let it rage for a good 45 minutes or an hour—as long as it takes. This is also a good thing to do if you haven't used your cooker in a long time and don't clean it regularly and the inside is covered with rancid grease or mold. The process is roughly the same as any modern, self-cleaning oven.

After burning it out, you should treat it like a cast-iron skillet. Wipe away any smoke or ash and then apply oil to the surface. I like to use tallow, which is beef fat from our brisket cooks. But any sort of vegetable oil will work just as well. You want to season the metal with the oil, as it helps form a protective layer that slows down the onset of rust.

As for regular maintenance on our cookers, once a week we use shovels to clean the bottoms thoroughly of any grease or burnt bits that have fallen down there. We take a wire brush to the grates and then hose the whole thing off. If you're cooking on your smoker only periodically, you'll want to do this after each use.

Another thing you'll want to do after each use is to shovel the ashes out of the firebox and dispose of them. (Use a shovel, don't hose it out. Do not get water in the firebox.) Leaving them in there, especially on smokers made of thin-gauge metal, greatly accelerates the rate of rust. And once your firebox has rusted out, it's hard to repair.

LAST THOUGHTS

Building, modifying, and thinking about smokers is a big part of what I and any serious barbecue cook does. We're always looking at our cookers and thinking of ways to make them more efficient, cook more evenly, and—for the restaurant—cook faster. That said, once you get one that's in great tune, you'll know it. Then the trick is to use it over and over, every time taking note of its cooler and hotter zones, the way it cooks in different weather conditions, and always trying to get a sense of the way heat and smoke are flowing through there when the door is closed. The more you work with a smoker, the more you'll understand it. That's when you might get the hankering to modify one you've bought. And after you've reached the limits of what homemade modifications can offer, that's when you might consider building your own. In any case, you end up having a pretty intimate relationship with your smoker. You should know it well and hopefully spend many happy hours together.

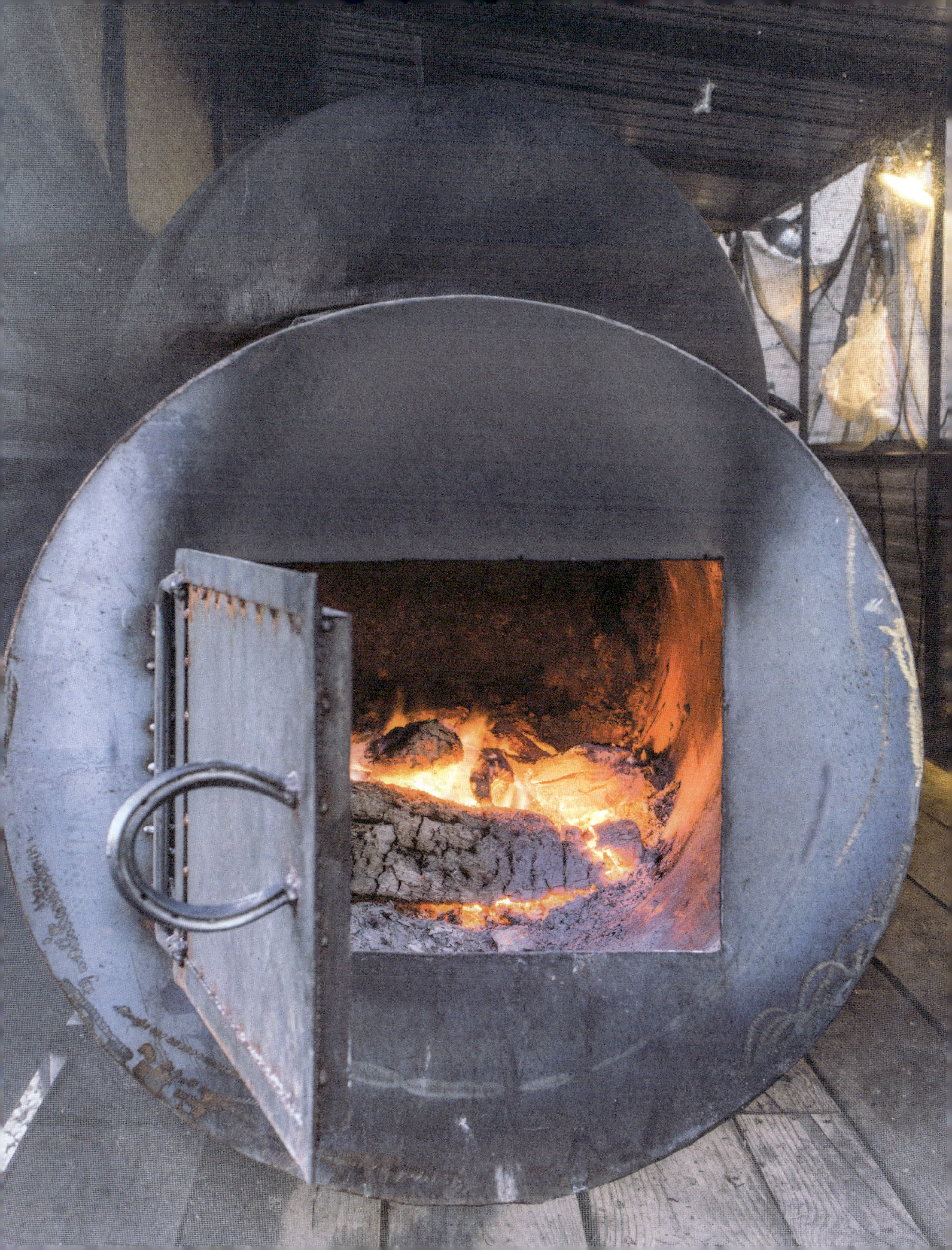

WOOD

• **Chapter Three**

Wood is king in Central Texas barbecue. We like to cook with a full-on wood fire. That is, we always like to see a flame in our smokers, convinced that this gives us the sweetest smoke. In the age of gas-fired restaurant smokers, this is not as common a thing as you might guess. But there's an art to burning wood for barbecue.

When I was just starting out and cooking barbecue out of a trailer parked on the I-35 access road not far from the University of Texas, I didn't have as good a sense for firewood as I do now. A significant yet overlooked factor in a restaurant's ability to produce good barbecue is a consistent, reliable source of quality firewood. At our little trailer restaurant, I did not have this.

In those days, I'd buy my wood from here and there and scour Craigslist for people selling firewood from their yards, deer leases, ranches, and rental properties. I'd pretty much accept what they brought me. After all, I was already pulling close to twenty-hour days, cooking all of the meat and making all of the sides by hand. It was a lot of work, and it left me little time to cultivate wood sources, even though I was probably going through about a third of a cord (128 cubic feet—in other words, *a lot*) per week.

In retrospect, I realize that I mostly lucked out with my wood sources in those early days.

I know this because, well, one time I *didn't* luck out and was delivered really green wood. I'll never forget that experience. This was about a month into our year in the trailer. Up until then, all of the logs I'd been cooking with had been relatively dry and well seasoned. But one day I got a big delivery of wood that was really green—a term used to describe wood from a tree that was recently alive—probably from a living tree that had been cut down to clear land and then sold without giving it any time to season. I just stacked it up to use later in the week.

The day I got into that wood, I had trouble getting the fire to go. All through lunch, I was completely frustrated, as I struggled to stoke the fire while simultaneously trying to cut meat for customers. I'd have to say to the person at the window, "gimme a second," and I'd run outside to look at the fire, throw a log on, and then rush back to keep cutting meat. All day, I ended up fiddling with it, trying to get the fire to work.

I was splitting the wood into smaller and smaller pieces so it would burn faster. But it was fresh, so incredibly fresh.

Up until then, I'd used only stuff that was pretty dry, and I didn't realize how nice that was. You could throw a piece of wood on, it would catch, and you would see the temperature get hotter for about 10 minutes and then cool off when the wood was spent. The green wood didn't want to catch at all. But as I found out at the end of that fateful day, not catching wasn't the green wood's only problem.

It all started around 4 p.m. the previous day, when I needed to get the briskets going. I warily watched the fire as it putzed around, haphazardly burning. I put another log on and hung out for a while, staring into and poking at the fire, trying to get a sense of its character. Finally, dead tired and having been there all friggin' day, at 10:30 p.m. I thought to myself, *Man, I've got to go home! It's okay to leave it. Going to be back here in a couple of hours anyway.* But another part of my mind cast a shadow of doubt on that, unsure whether it would manage to sustain itself while I was gone.

But part of doing barbecue is that you've got to be able to walk away. You've got to train yourself to know your fire and know your wood. If you just stand there, staring at the fire the whole time, you'll go crazy. So I convinced myself that it would be okay and went home to catch a couple of hours of sleep.

In those days, I had a different process for making briskets than we do today: I'd set a fire, put the briskets on, and let them go for about six hours of smoke time, then I'd return at the crack of dawn (before it, actually) and revive the fire and finish them off. But this time, when I came back to finish them off, I found that I didn't need to. The green wood had more than done the job for me. Too much so.

Given that it was wood that I'd had so much trouble lighting, I naïvely didn't realize that eventually it was going to light, and that when it did, that sucker was going to burn hot and big. When I came back the next morning, I'd burned up everything. Little toasty pucks of badly burned meat—barely edible, just barely salvageable—were all that was left. And I had a line to feed, so I served them. But everyone ate for free that day—I didn't charge a soul.

That's the day I learned my lesson about green wood and also had drilled into me why it's so important to know your wood and to have a good idea of what you're going to get when you put a log on the fire. That skill clearly comes with experience, but hopefully sharing what I know will help you avoid what happened to me that day long ago.

PROPERTIES AND TYPES OF WOOD

Chefs may value their stoves and their ovens, but they aren't an essential flavor of their dishes. How many other cuisines are there in which the heat source is a vital part of the dish?

Wood is important for two functions: providing heat and supplying smoke. The two are obviously connected but different. When you're cooking, moments will arise when you want more heat (but not necessarily more smoke), and there will be times when you're after extra smoke (but not necessarily more heat). Having a sense of your wood supply will allow you to approach your woodpile like a chef approaches his spice

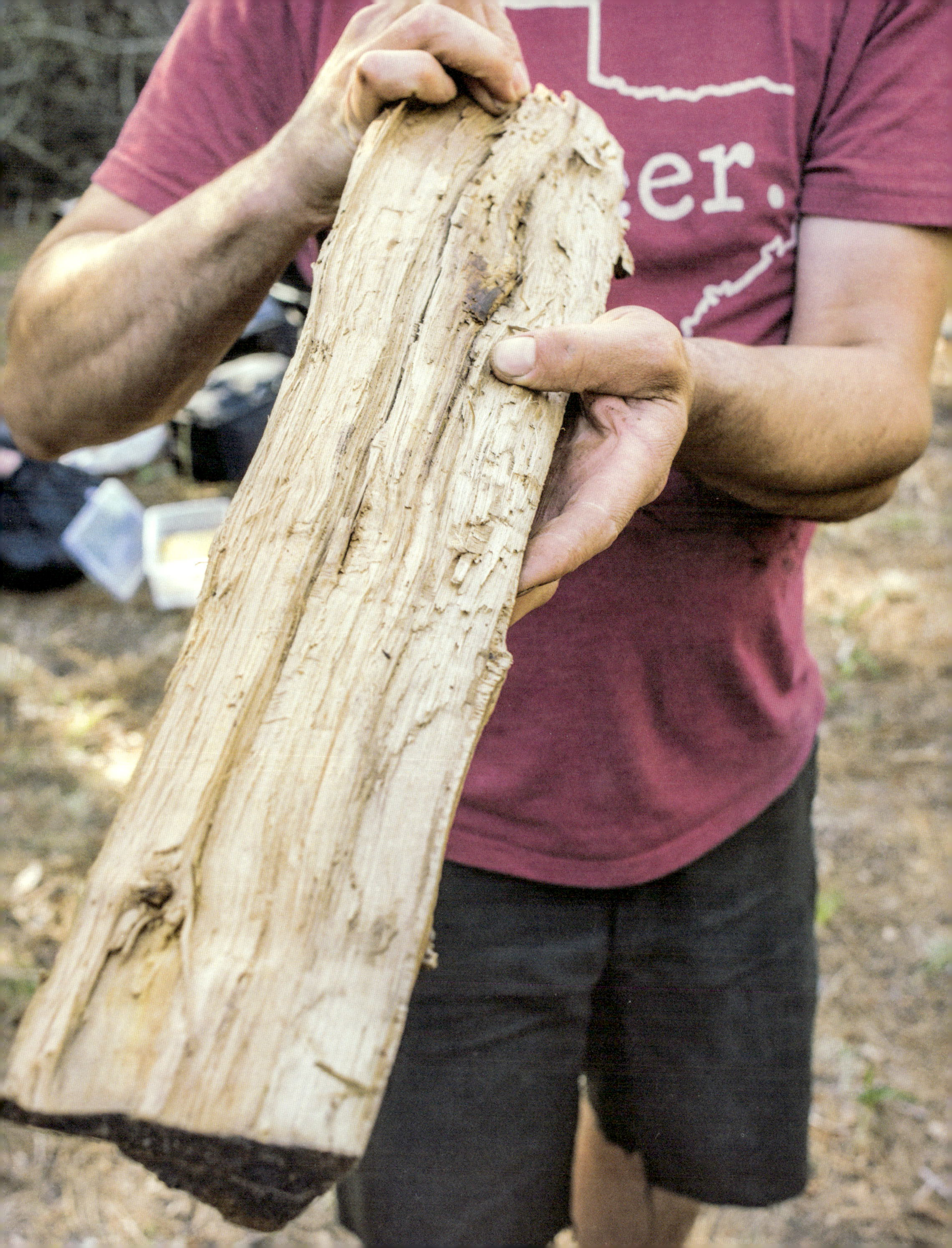

rack. Well, maybe not with that much precision, but you'll see that an experienced pitmaster will have more control over cooking temperature and smoke absorption than a lot of people would believe.

Since we're going to be using so much wood, I find it empowering to have some idea about its makeup. Thanks to one of my favorite books, Harold McGee's indispensable *On Food and Cooking*, I know that all wood is composed mostly of three organic compounds: cellulose, hemicellulose, and lignin. They give the cell walls of wood its structure. Green plants are made up of cellulose, but in wood, the high percentage of lignin provides the girders that reinforce the cellulose and hemicellulose cells and gives wood its tensile strength. It also provides many of the more flavorful compounds of smoke (which is why we barbecuers care about it at all) and also burns hotter than cellulose.

Lignin content in wood varies and is pertinent to the discussion of woods for barbecue. Yet it's good to note that solidity is not what distinguishes hardwoods from soft. That distinction has to do with how the two plants reproduce: hardwoods produce seeds with covering (for example, a fruit or a nut), while softwoods like cedar and pine release their seeds uncovered. (However, it is true that on average most hardwoods are in fact harder [denser] than most softwoods. Yet wood geeks will point out that balsa—a notably soft and flexible wood—is technically a hardwood, making the whole discussion moot.)

Smoking meat is much better when done with hardwoods. They burn slower and with less heat than softwoods, and they tend to have less resin than softwoods do (which burns into a nasty soot). Incidentally, mesquite, a hardwood, has much higher lignin content than oak, which causes it to burn hotter and faster and also have a much more pungent and distinct smoke, which some people really go for.

Along those lines, all different woods burn slightly differently and supply unique things to any smoked food. Up in the Pacific Northwest, folks use alder planks, which contribute delicate flavor to salmon. East Texas and much of the barbecue along the Eastern Seaboard rely heavily on hickory, while great swaths of Texas favor mesquite. But in this state we've also got pecan and various fruitwoods. The long and short of it is that most people use what's plentiful locally.

In Central Texas, we're lucky to have access to a lot of oak. Having played around with other woods, though, I feel lucky to be located in the middle of the Texas oak belt, since, for my style of barbecue, I feel oak is just about perfect.

Of course, there are many other hardwoods you can cook with. Each has its own contribution to make to a meat—and you should choose whatever wood is readily available where you live and that you like. Like I said, at the restaurant, all we use is oak (although the odd, unintentional log of something else might slip in occasionally). That said, I've had the opportunity to experience cooking with several other kinds of wood, and here are a few of my opinions on them.

Oak

How can you not love oak? The very symbol of strength and persistence, it's meant so much to humanity during our brief existence on this planet. Great to build with, it's created a lot of shelters and sturdy sailing vessels that for centuries got people around the planet. It produces wine barrels, furniture, and those little shellacked coasters to put your drink on, and here in Austin tremendous live oak trees with huge, undulating branches are great for kids to climb on and provide tons of shade during our long, hot summers. And, of course, we love the fires oak makes and the sweet smoke it produces.

There are some six hundred species of oak. But the one I'm most concerned with is *Quercus stellata*, what we call post oak. A relatively small oak, post oak is classified as a white oak and, according the USDA Forest Service, "is a medium-sized tree abundant throughout the Southeastern and South Central United States where it forms pure stands in the prairie transition area." Central Texas could fall into that definition, as it transitions from the wetter forests of East Texas to the desert of West Texas. The Texas Native Plants Database adds that it occurs in "all areas of Texas except the High Plains and Trans-Pecos" and remarks that it's "a shrub or tree ranging from 20 to 75 feet tall with stout limbs and a dense rounded canopy, it grows in dry, gravelly, sandy soils and rocky ridges." Those stout limbs are classified as "very resistant to decay." That and the fact that it doesn't grow too big made it popular for use as fence posts, hence the name. But it also seems to me the perfect wood for cooking brisket.

Oak is one of the mildest woods. It burns beautifully—not too fast, not too slow. It gives fairly even and predictable moderate heat, meaning that I can control the fire pretty accurately. And it gives a mellow, smoky flavor whose presence is obvious yet at the same time sort of hovers in the background, letting the flavor of the meat itself take center stage.

Red oak and live oak are also commonly used, but both seem to have a stronger flavor and burn slower than post. Blackjack oak, *Q. marilandica*, grows in and around the groves of post oak here in Central Texas, especially toward East Texas, and is notable for the dark ring in its core. We occasionally burn a log here and there when it comes mixed in with the post oak, but I'm not a big fan. For one thing, the post oak tends to rot from the outside in. The blackjack oak tends to decay from the inside out because it is softer in the middle, which means you're not burning pristine wood when you throw it on the fire.

Hickory

The Texas Native Plants Database recognizes many different kinds of hickory growing in Texas, most of them in East Texas, where hickory is probably the dominant wood for smoking, as it is nationwide. Hickory is a bit more powerful than oak, but I like it because it burns long and clean. The taste is strong and smoky, with a hint of sweetness. I think it's best for heavier meats like beef, but people use it all the time for chicken and pork, which can be good too. In my experience, it burns about the same as oak.

Pecan

Actually a member of the hickory family, pecan is also plentiful throughout East and Central Texas. It doesn't burn as hot as oak, but its gentle, sweet flavor is delicious. Nor does it burn as long as oak, so I like to use it for short cooks. Fish, chicken, and especially pork take to its mildness.

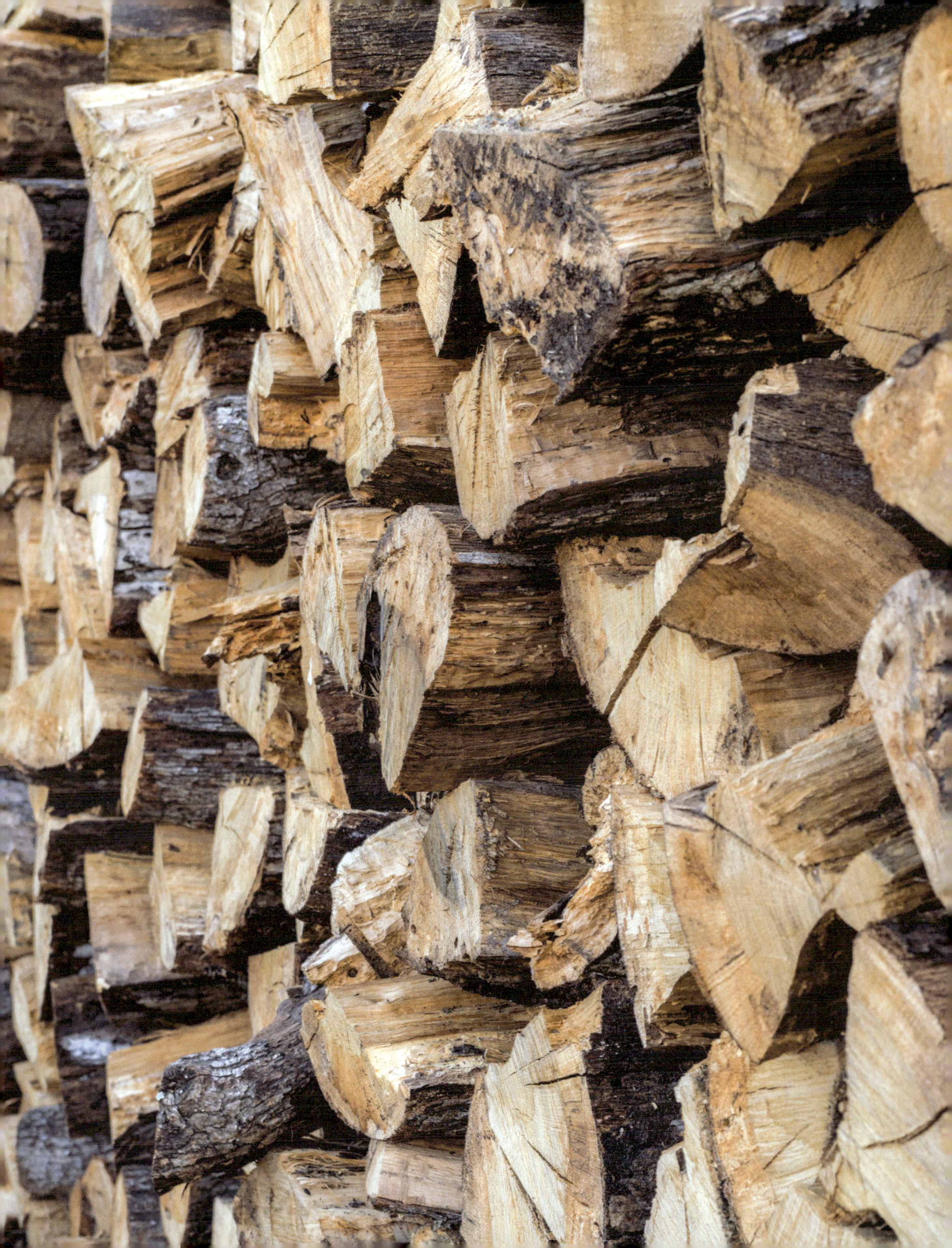

Apple, Cherry, Peach, and Other Fruitwoods

The fruitwoods are a terrific family of quality fuels. They tend to have a gentle, rounded sweetness and extremely subtle flavor impact. Because of this subtlety, these woods wouldn't do a lot for a brisket, as it's such a huge, bulky, and powerful piece of meat. But they can be really nice for fish, chicken, and pork, which might get overpowered by a bolder wood. I think fruitwoods are best when they're a little greener—barely seasoned—as they deliver a denser smoke. Because of their relatively short cook time and mild flavor, fruitwoods are better for direct cooking than long smoking.

Mesquite

Mesquite is generally a strong-flavored wood. It burns hot and fast, but becomes more transparent the more it cooks. For this reason I like to use it best when it is burned down to coals, for direct grilling. Beyond that, it's used so ubiquitously as hardwood charcoal and on steak-house grills that its heavy flavor now seems somewhat generic. If mesquite is at all green or has some sugar left in it, it's overly aggressive for my tastes. But if it's really dry and heavily seasoned, it doesn't have its characteristic smell and it's more acceptably neutral, though it still burns fast. That said, if you're looking for some quick, smoky flavor when grilling a steak, it's a convenient and effective wood.

SOURCING WOOD

As you know from chapter one, Craigslist has been a constant in my life. But as with any classified-ad marketplace, it's also full of charlatans, scammers, and cheats. Some of them sell wood. Plenty of firewood is available for sale on Austin's Craigslist site and probably where you live too. Folks are always needing to clear land or cut down old, inconvenient, and dangerous trees and then want to profit from it.

Over my years of buying wood, I was lucky enough to find Rod Moline through Craigslist. It was totally random, but since then, thanks to his knowledge, honesty, and reliability, he has become known simply as Rod, the Wood Guy around Franklin Barbecue. Supplying firewood is not his full-time job, however, but rather a weekend offshoot of his projects in clearing and organizing some of his land outside of Austin. But he's taken it upon himself to help organize other suppliers for us, which we really appreciate. While Rod still brings us a good bit of wood, he also got us connected with Joan Barganier, who has made selling and distributing firewood her full-time job.

For unfortunate and disturbing reasons, the availability of oak right now is high. This is because of the prolonged and dangerous drought that has been drying up Texas. The drought started in 2010, and at the time of writing, it's still going. It has been called among the five worst in the past five hundred years, according to the state climatologist. In a few short years, the desiccated soil has led to the deaths of between three hundred million and five hundred million trees across the state. And that's left a lot of landowners with thousands of dead trees across their property.

"These dead trees present a real hazard to property owners," Rod says. "They're instant fuel for raging prairie fires and they become housing for all kinds of pests, from rodents to snakes to insects."

Land needs to be cleared of dead trees quickly, only it's not possible to clear it fast enough. There's too much land and too many dead trees. A lot of ranchers will just drag the dead trees together and create massive bonfires to get rid of them. It was seeing such measures that led Joan to get into the business. "I just hated to see all that good wood going to waste," she says. "It seemed foolish to just burn it when there are plenty of people out there who want firewood." So she became entrepreneurial.

I rely on my wood suppliers not only to cut up the trees and split the logs into the sizes I can use but also to bring me good, sound wood, which requires an understanding of what I need and a sense of responsibility on the part of the supplier. They know I need high-quality logs, because part of them are going into the food.

"The drought is also influencing the quality of the wood right now," Rod says, "because these trees are not dying a natural death. They're already stressed when they die and vulnerable to beetle infestation and more."

Rod and Joan bring me the best wood they have. There are variances, of course—not every log is perfect. But for the most part, I need it cut and split to my specifications: clean, not too green, not too dry or overseasoned, not powdery and dead, and certainly not rotting or waterlogged or misshapened. I want logs with energy and some life to them that have some heft and density to give me a great burst of heat and smoke.

I'm lucky to have Rod and the other sources he finds for me. A lot of bad wood guys lurk out there behind the innocuous-seeming listings of Craigslist. People are always trying to cheat you—not everybody, of course, but in my experience about 90 percent of the people who come through here selling wood are shady (no pun intended). Indeed, I still have numbers stored in my phone labeled Bad Wood Guy #1, Bad Wood Guy #2, Guy with Messed Up Oak, and so on. This is so that every now and then, when one of those numbers rings and the fellow at the other end says, "Hey, I've got wood for you," I can instantly know that it's a scammer on the line and can tell him no thanks, that we're in good shape.

Usually, the scam involves overcharging you for the amount delivered. A cord of wood is a neatly stacked block of logs measuring 4 feet wide by 4 feet high by 8 feet long. It amounts to 128 cubic feet of wood. A true cord is a lot of wood but can be difficult to estimate since most people, including us, don't buy our wood in 4-foot-long logs.

People drive up all the time claiming they have a cord of wood, yet when you look at it, you know it's not even close. They deliberately stack it inconsistently or throw it in a big pile so that it can't really be measured. And then they'll try to charge you extra to stack it. They'll fluff it up when they stack it so it looks like more than it is, or they'll split it poorly.

My advice is be wary when people are selling "a truckload" or "a trailer full" of wood. Don't agree to buy it over the phone before you've had a chance to look at it. And when you do look at it, inspect it closely. Don't pull up only the top few logs to assess their greenness or general condition. Poke around and make sure they're not hiding a lot of bad wood just below the surface.

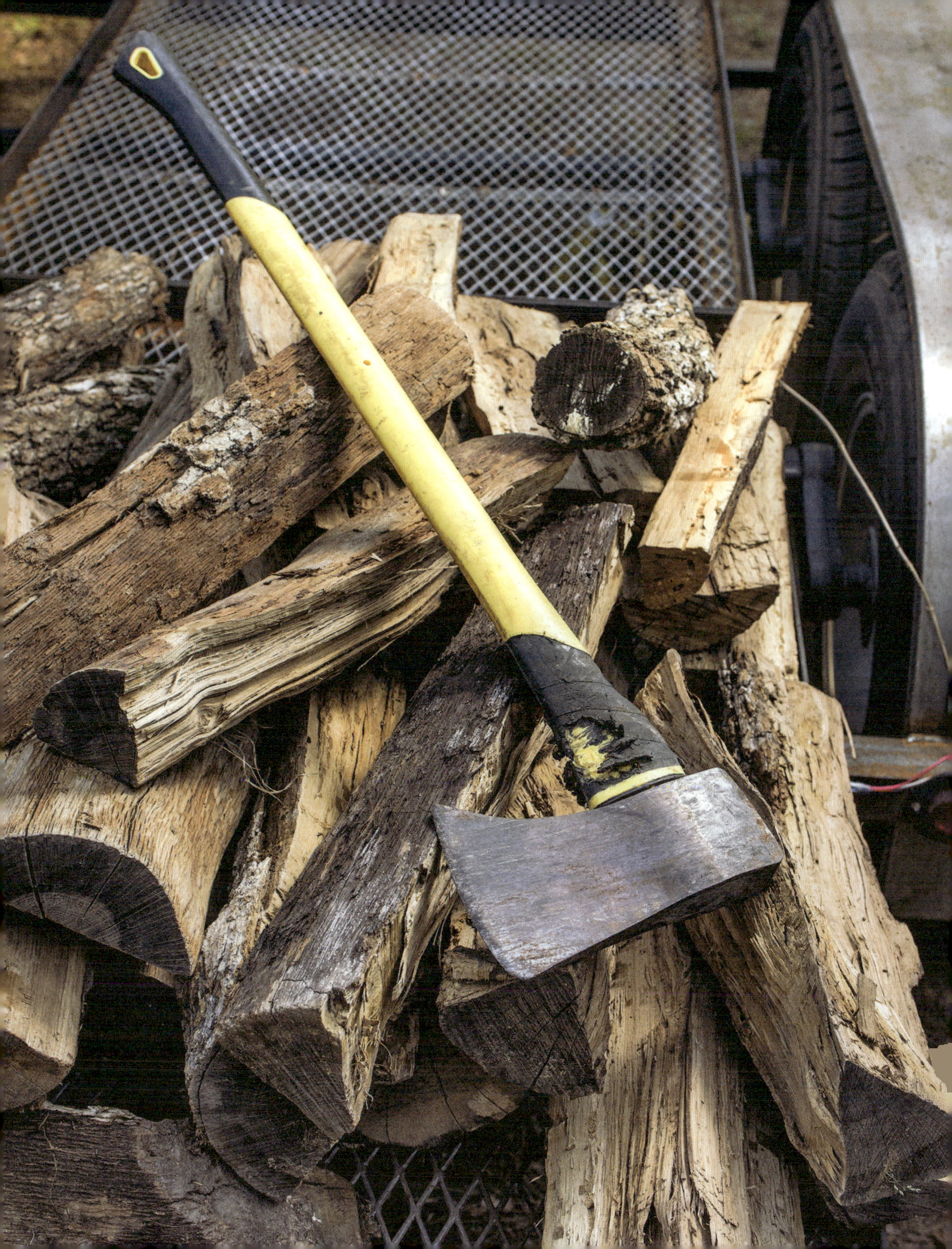

Another thing to watch out for is people selling what's known as a "face cord." A lot of people on Craigslist will advertise a cord when it's actually a face cord. As just noted, a full cord measures 8 by 4 by 4 feet. A face cord shares the first two dimensions but is only 16 to 18 inches deep. Don't pay for a full cord if what you are getting is a face cord.

HOW TO BUY WOOD FROM A STORE

It's convenient that modern supermarkets carry firewood. Or is it? Much of the wood you see in bags or boxes in the grocery aisle between charcoal and cat litter is not suitable for barbecue. One reason is that a lot of it is kiln dried, meaning that even the most pyro-challenged among us will have no trouble starting a fire with it, but the pieces will burn so fast and with so little smoke that you won't get anywhere when you cook with them. Other times, supermarket firewood comes in a bag, so you can't pick up a log to feel whether it's been kiln dried or not.

To tell if a log has been kiln dried, measure by weight in your hand: if the log feels unnaturally light in your hand, then it's going to burn like gasoline. You're better off checking Craigslist or the classifieds for someone selling firewood that you can pick up and feel. Chances are with a little calling and driving around, you'll find someone you like and trust who can become a regular source.

SEASONING WOOD

My perfect piece of wood to use in a smoker would come from a nice straight post oak tree that was cut down alive, split into firewood—for the size of our fireboxes, we like pieces 16 to 18 inches in length and with diameters no smaller than 3 inches and no bigger than 6 inches—and then seasoned for a year or so until the moisture content is about 20 percent. Of course, I never use my perfect piece of firewood.

That's because I don't have access to it. For one thing, I don't cut down trees for barbecue, as there's just too much dead wood already around Central Texas for me to need or want to do that. Two, being located smack in the middle of Austin and operating a young business without a big property, even if I had a lot of freshly cut wood, we don't have room to store a year's worth of it. At least not like the eye-catching stacks you find outside of the major places in Lockhart. Kreuz's infinite-seeming, all-you-can-burn wood yard out back is a thing I envy greatly. That's because it's stack after stack—worth a trip just to marvel at, if you've never been to Lockhart; *you've never been to Lockhart?*—of perfectly cured wood.

Ah, maybe someday... For now, I work with a mishmash of stuff: some of it is green, some is dry, a tiny bit is blackjack oak, most is post oak. With each wood delivery, we're never sure exactly what we're going to get. On one hand, this is frustrating, as even I sometimes discover that a recent delivery of wood is unusably green. On the other hand, I think the diversity of wood we use has probably made us better pitmasters. We've had to learn how to construct better fires and how to get the most from somewhat green wood.

WOOD

Green wood comes from a tree that was recently alive. Living trees are full of water, which is retained in the wood after it's been felled or died of its own natural causes. The weight difference due to the water content in similar-size logs can been startling: up to 5 or 6 pounds in the dimensions we use.

Green wood presents many problems to the pitmaster. The high moisture content makes it inefficient and harder to burn. The demands of heating the water in wood steals some of the heat needed to properly burn the wood, and when heated, the evaporating water cools the combustible gases, making it harder to burn them successfully. The result is a heavier, dirtier smoke than can be useful in very small doses, but it's hardly what you want to build the flavor of your meat around.

On the other hand, wood that's too dry will burn so quickly that it may elevate the temperature of the fire beyond desirable levels and can also break down smoke into lighter, flavorless vapors that don't do you any good.

Hence, the desirability of wood that retains about 20 percent moisture. How do you recognize such a piece? That becomes a question of feel. Locate some properly seasoned wood—that is, wood that has been left to dry out for a certain period of time to lose some of its moisture—and some green wood and compare them. The weight difference and feeling of density will be obvious. Some other clues that a piece of wood is properly seasoned is if the bark is loose or falling off; if it has noticeable cracks or splinters in the grain; and if when you tap it, the sound is deeper and more full-bodied than the short, dull thud you'd hear from a green log.

Once you've got what you think is a good piece of seasoned wood, I recommend you burn it alongside a green piece, either in your smoker or just in your fireplace. Take note of the difference in rate of burn, amount of smoke, and the nature of the smoke.

One of the goals of the pitmaster is to control as many variables as possible during your cooks, which is why many of you might be tempted to start with fresh-cut wood and season it yourself. But be forewarned, seasoning takes time—from months to years, depending on your conditions (temperature, humidity, and the like).

Some general tips on seasoning? Don't start with very long logs. The path by which water works itself out of the grain of the wood is the same as the one the live tree used to transport fluids up and down its trunk and branches—by the grain of the wood. So chop them down to manageable lengths, and the wood will dry out faster. Surface area is also important, so if you leave logs in full rounds, seasoning will take longer. Best to split them into the very smallest size of wood you eventually want to use (see below). Stack the wood loosely enough to get airflow between the logs and make sure the ends of the logs are exposed to the air.

Warmer temperatures have a big impact on drying. If we get a load of green wood in the spring, I can stack it in a sunny place in the yard, and due to Central Texas heat, it can be dry enough to use in just a few weeks. But because we are in the middle of a city, we don't have the space to do this to any reasonable degree. That stack of wood that I just spent three months drying will get used in less than a week.

If you've got a backyard, I recommend you start your own pile of wood, just to make sure that you've always got some well-seasoned logs on hand. Cover it loosely with a tarp to keep the rain off (covering it too tightly can result in trapped moisture, which can rot the wood), though occasional rains will generally just run off the wood rather than into it. If you're in a wet place like Seattle, consider keeping the wood in a shed or in the basement. High humidity will slow the drying process.

HOW TO SPLIT WOOD

At Franklin Barbecue, we buy wood that has already been split for us. But depending on your wood source at home, you may need to do it yourself someday. And we often still have to split larger logs down into more manageable sizes. I suppose the first question to answer in this section is, why split wood in the first place? Well, for one thing, it makes it easier to fit it in our smokers and to carry and stack.

But one of the most important reasons to split wood is because, as I mentioned above, it facilitates proper drying and seasoning.

After wood is cut from a tree, moisture trapped in the wood will begin to drip away, moving parallel to the grain, or toward the cut ends of the round log. The longer the log, the farther this water has to travel, so chopping logs into shorter lengths means the water will leave the wood more quickly. Once we have chopped the logs into shorter lengths, we also split them through the diameter into smaller pieces, to expose more surface area and further speed up the drying process.

HOW MUCH WOOD DO YOU NEED?

You might wonder how much wood you should have on hand to cook a brisket. I wish I could tell you. Unfortunately, so much of barbecue is dependent on context, equipment, wood, and conditions that to give you any sort of estimate would possibly be to lead you astray. The best I can suggest is that you should have more than you think you'll need. Having too much wood is never a problem. Running out of wood is a huge one. So make space and get a good woodpile going in your yard, garage, shed, wherever. Keep 100 to 150 logs on hand. You won't use that many on a single cook. But if that cook goes well, there will certainly be another. And another.

WOOD

This may seem like an elementary topic, but at the restaurant I make sure anyone who's going to be tending the pits and feeding wood into the fire knows how to properly split wood. Failure to know this can result in injury, which is bad for the individual and bad for the restaurant. As I've explained, our wood is delivered to us already split into sizes that we can use, but sometimes one of the logs is too big and needs to be split into more manageably sized pieces.

The first thing to remember is that the process is called *splitting wood* for a reason. We're not chopping it and we're not cutting it. We're splitting it—splintering it along its grain. That's why we don't use an axe, which is best for chopping, but a maul, which is best for splitting. Anyone with a barbecue and a woodpile should own a maul.

A maul is sort of the love child of a sledgehammer and an axe. On one end of the head, it's blunt like a hammer; on the other, it's wedge shaped like an axe though lacking a sharpened blade. A maul, which typically comes in 6-, 8-, 10-, and 12-pound weights, is also much heavier than an axe and uses that weight to splinter the wood apart as opposed to slicing it. One of the advantages of mauls is that they don't need to be sharpened. Because of that, they're safer than axes. You generally don't need a particularly heavy maul to split the kinds of smaller pieces you'll be using for barbecue. The heaviest ones are more difficult to control and will tire you out if you've got a lot of logs to do. So for spot work, it is best to choose a lighter maul.

The rest is pretty simple. You probably should have a chopping block, though at the restaurant we just prop logs up on the ground. We're not splitting heavy, full rounds that much, but rather just halving splits that are too big for the size of the fire we've got going. Make sure you've got your feet spread apart enough to provide a stable anchor for your body. Always remember to focus your eyes on exactly the spot you want to hit and never take them off that spot as you raise the maul overhead and prepare to bring it down. When swinging it down, don't swing it in a long arc, as if you were tracing the edge of a circle, but rather bring it straight down to the contact point. You don't have to put a lot of force into it; the idea is to let gravity and the weight of the head do most of the work. Your job is to guide it and not hurt yourself. But I've seen people hurt themselves by being off balance and incautious, so take splitting wood seriously.

FIRE + SMOKE

• ***Chapter Four***

It's hardly glamorous, but the tool I probably use the most at the restaurant is not a carving knife or a boning knife or a fancy digital thermometer. The tool you'll find most often in my hands when doing a cooking shift is a shovel. At all times, there's one shovel propped outside the firebox of each of our six cookers. It's an essential tool. I don't like the heavy shovels that last forever; I like the light ones you can throw around real easy. That's because, let's face it, I'm using it nearly constantly, and the heavier the shovel, the harder it is on the old body.

Shovels are our high-precision, state-of-the-art tools for tending our fires—the implements we use to constantly groom and tune our fires to optimally produce the smoke we want. The fire and smoke are what set barbecue apart from other forms of cooking. And cooking solely on wood fires is what sets great barbecue apart from the bad or the merely good.

Managing a fire is the most important aspect of the pitmaster's job. It's the crucial factor that determines the success or failure of your endeavor (not to mention hours and hours of time and hundreds or thousands of dollars' worth of meat). We pitmasters are more thermal engineers than we are cooks. Igniting, coaxing, cajoling, molding, suppressing, and enabling fire is the essence of our work. You hardly need to be a scientist to be good at this, but it does help to have some of the characteristics of a good scientist: observational acuity, and an analytical sensibility. But you also need some of the qualities of an outdoorsman: experience, patience, calm, an ability to listen and intuit. And, of course, some of a chef's talents come in handy: an understanding of how meats absorb heat and smoke to gain flavor and color.

But ultimately it all comes down to the fire. Anyone can light a fire and burn wood and cook meat. But doing it well, on demand, over and over again in whatever conditions are present—this is what truly able pitmasters do. It's fine to know how to burn a fire, but knowing why it's working or not and being able to sense what's going on inside the firebox are what makes the process all the more successful and repeatable. As the authors of *Modernist Cuisine* (another of my favorite books) write, "creating and controlling smoke may be a lost art these days . . . a return to first principles can help recover that primeval understanding of why and when wood smolders and burns. You need that knowledge to create quality smoke. And if you also understand some of the basic chemistry of smoke, you gain control over its effect on flavor and appearance."

HOW WOOD BURNS

But before you get that sought-after smoke, you need fire. And in order to get a fire, you need fuel. In general, barbecue, as practiced today, can use many forms of fuel. Gas, electricity, and charcoal are popular in most modern barbecue restaurants because they run with timers and computers and are more convenient and efficient. But in my mind there is no substitute for good, old-fashioned wood.

The negatives of using wood? Well, it's hard to control. Getting and sustaining the temperature needed to properly smoke a brisket is not easy and requires technique, experience, and stamina. Once you've managed to achieve the optimal temperature, level of smoke, and airflow, keeping it there for the 12 or so hours needed to cook a brisket is another challenge completely. The positives of using wood lie almost entirely in the quality of the smoke it produces, which imparts beautifully complex and savory flavor to the meat, something not really replicable with any other method. But to get the wood to produce that really fine smoke, you need a high-quality fire.

So you probably remember from elementary school the model of the fire triangle, which illustrates the three elements that a fire requires: heat, fuel, and oxygen. Fire, as we know it, with crackling flames and a homey warm glow, is basically the molecular unraveling of wood caused by heat in the presence of oxygen. Once it gets going, a chain reaction forms that sustains the release of heat through combustion. But when wood burns, several things are going on simultaneously.

When a heat source is applied to wood, the first thing that happens is drying. Even wood we consider really dry still has about 20 percent moisture. Drying happens as the wood's surface temperature approaches 212°F and water contained inside starts to boil and evaporate. Evaporation also creates a cooling effect, which is why it's so hard to burn green (wet) wood. But once that liquid has largely disappeared, the wood heats much more rapidly.

When wood is heated enough so that all of its moisture has evaporated and it is effectively dried, the heat turns its attention to the structure of the wood itself. At 500°F to 600°F, the heat starts dissolving the bonds between the molecules of cellulose and hemicellulose cells. This releases water vapor, then organic gases (the beginning of smoke).

Finally, as the temperature continues to rise, combustion occurs. The dancing blue, orange, yellow, or red flame you can see (what many of us commonly think of as "fire") is actually the ignition of oxygen and the gases (smoke) released by the wood, a process known as secondary combustion. (Primary combustion, in case you're curious, is the name we give to the direct burning of the solid material—so, the smoldering embers of the wood itself.) As these gases depart, the wood is being reduced to solid fuel—charcoal and, ultimately, ash. Along this journey, at various temperatures, different compounds—among them carbon monoxide (CO), methane (CH4), and about a hundred others—are released and create the complex mixture we call smoke.

So if wood plus heat yields smoke plus charcoal, you can suddenly see why I'm not so keen on cooking over just charcoal. When you do that, you get plenty of heat, sure, but since the charcoal is already in its elemental state, you don't get smoke (which is a by-product of the process of converting heat, wood, and oxygen *into* charcoal). With only charcoal in an offset cooker, what you're basically creating is an oven—great for roasts but not for smoked brisket. Any healthy fire in your smoker needs to have a good bed of coals (glowing embers from the already-burnt wood—that is to say, primary combustion), which supplies heat and helps burn any new wood you add to the chamber, and live fire (secondary combustion), which releases the smoke.

To create the kind of smoke you want, you must keep the fire within an optimal range of combustion temperatures, which is done by regulating both the release of heat and the release of smoke. You are able to manage the fire because you have control over all three components of the fire triangle—heat, fuel, and oxygen—though the tools available are rustic. You can manipulate oxygen with the firebox door and/or a smokestack damper (if you have one). Fuel and heat are controlled by the choice of logs put on the fire and management of the coal bed that you've created from burning logs (as well as airflow).

What's important to remember is that not all fires are created equal and that the manner in which your wood burns is just as important as the fact that it's simply burning. Next, I will address some of the key factors in starting and maintaining the kind of fire that will give you the heat and smoke to cook successfully.

> **THE REALITIES OF YOUR BACKYARD SMOKER**
>
> If you're working with a little backyard one-brisket smoker like I started on, you probably won't have room in your firebox to build the necessary-size wood structure completely out of logs. If your heart is set on starting your fire *just* with wood, then I suggest cutting your logs into even smaller pieces (perhaps 9 to 12 inches long and 4 to 6 inches wide, or whatever fits comfortably inside your firebox) and stacking them in a miniature structure with tinder and kindling.
>
> But to be honest, it can be frustrating to start a roaring fire in such a small space with so few logs. So I propose a little cheat: use a "chimney" charcoal starter (one of those metal cylinders with an attached handle and a charcoal grate inside) to get fifteen to twenty charcoal briquettes rip-roaring hot and then dump them into the firebox. You will have created a quick and easy coal bed to give you the temperatures needed to get wood burning. Just lay your logs down on the bed of charcoal, then you can get the honest-to-goodness, smoke-producing wood fire going. Keep adding wood, as needed, to get your cook chamber up to the desired temperature. (For more on that, see page 95.)

HOW TO BUILD A FIRE

At the restaurant, our smokers are fired up pretty much all of the time, so we have plenty of glowing beds of hot coals that we can shovel into a smoker that's been taken out of service briefly (for cleaning, modification, or the like). That's the easy way to start a fire: we just shovel in a glowing-hot base of coals and throw a few logs on top of that. But starting one from scratch isn't so hard either. When lighting up a cold smoker, I want the fire to start quickly and vigorously, because when cooking something that will take hours and hours, there's never any time to waste.

First, start with well-seasoned dry wood (see page 80) that's going to catch quickly. I choose slim, straight pieces of wood that are noticeably light and dry and split them into skinny pieces like kindling. As with so many aspects of handling a smoker, the primary concern is airflow. Inside the firebox, I build a little crosshatched structure with them, almost as if I were building a cabin with Lincoln Logs. I start with two wedge-shaped larger pieces on either side to create a base, and then I put three smaller pieces, about 2 inches in diameter, on top of the those, and then one more layer of three small pieces or three logs, spaced about 2 inches apart and positioned crosswise in the firebox. Next, I place two logs perpendicular to the first two logs, creating a square. Then I stack one more layer of two logs directly over and parallel to the first ones I laid down. In the structure, the curved shape of my preferred firebox comes into play. Because the logs on the base stretch across the arc of the circle, they allow airflow underneath them too. (If I were forced to work with a flat firebox, I would do the same.)

Now you need some tinder and possibly kindling. For tinder (dry, flammable things to help get a fire going), I usually employ a used piece of butcher paper in which we had wrapped a brisket. It's saturated with fat and grease and goes up like a torch. If I don't have a brisket wrapping, I'll take butcher paper (newspaper will work too) and coat it with vegetable oil. The point is that I've only ever put organic substances in my firebox—no lighter fluid or any other chemical. Splinter a few thin, dry slivers off of a dry log for kindling (larger pieces of tinder to catch from the paper and continue to grow the fire). Now simply crumple up the butcher paper and place it in the middle of your little structure. Place the kindling inside the structure atop the tinder and give it a light.

FIRE + SMOKE

MY BASIC PHILOSOPHY OF FIRES

My general philosophy of fires may sound a little hippie-dippie or like some sort of flaky cop-out. But it's really not. It works. It's simple, but I find myself having to remind my cooks of this all the time: Let wood burn at its natural pace. You don't want to force it do something that it doesn't naturally want to do. You don't need to pump air into it, you don't need to choke it off, you don't need anything but the wood, heat, and air that nature provides you. Your job as a pitmaster is to find the size and shape of the fire you need to sustain your temperatures with good smoke and then do your best to keep it there. This usually doesn't require anything more than adding wood in the right manner and making sure that there's plenty of air.

SMOKE

There have been few moments during the last five or six years when I have not smelled like smoke. Even if I'm away from the restaurant for a day or two and have taken multiple showers, that smoky smell can still creep up. The scent of burning wood has been with me so long and so pervasively that I can't even really smell it anymore.

That ability of smoke to coat and penetrate almost anything, and then to persist there for a while, is almost magical. Magical too is smoke's value to us as an ancient tool for preserving food (besides its drying qualities, it imparts antimicrobials and antioxidants to meat that prevent spoilage; this method has been used for thousands of years) and its ability to make things taste good.

How can something without a form have such a powerful impact on everything it comes into contact with? That question has long fascinated me. And although people love the taste of smoked foods, few who aren't avid barbecuers give much thought to the fact that not all smoke is created equal. You can have good smoke, bad smoke, and too much smoke. This point should be obvious, of course, since whenever you see dark, nasty smoke billowing from something that shouldn't be burning, such as a building or a tire, you are reminded that there are lots of kinds of smoke that you don't want anywhere near your mouth. Much of the craft of barbecue depends on making sure that only good smoke in the correct amount comes in contact with the meat. So what is good smoke?

TROUBLESHOOTING FOR TRICKY CONDITIONS

Weather can present two big challenges to getting a good fire going: cold and wet. The solution to the latter is to start with well-seasoned wood. If it is raining outside, and thus extremely humid, logs that are especially dry can be helpful in getting a fire started. Windy conditions can likewise cause problems. If you can move your cooker, shield the firebox door from the predominant wind and keep it mostly shut while you get the fire going. Once you get it going, you can anchor it with a couple of big logs, which will bring up the heat and get you started on creating that big, deep coal bed that will ensure a good fire.

Well, just like everything else in barbecue, it's simple and complicated. Smoke itself is a complicated thing, containing, as *Modernist Cuisine* handily explains, all three states of matter: solid particles of soot and droplets of liquid suspended in a vapor of air and chemicals. Two of these three forms are visible, the book says, with soot turning smoke dark gray and black, and droplets of tars, oils, water, and other condensates appearing as a gentle blue. Those parts are important, but it's the other part that concerns me even more. "The components of smoke that are in the vapor state, on the other hand," the book notes, "cannot be seen at all—yet it's the vapor that does all the heavy lifting of smoking. Contrary to what you might have heard, the invisible gases in smoke contain nearly all the compounds that color, preserve, and flavor smoked food. Although they're typically just 10% of the volume of smoke, these gases do more than 90% of the work."

The particles of smoke—solids and liquids—that might attach themselves to the surface of the food can contribute some flavor and texture to the meat's exterior. But it's the gaseous elements of smoke that actually penetrate into the interior of the meat itself, giving it the deep, rich flavor that you want to be integrated into every bite.

Getting your fire to the state in which it's producing good smoke most of the time is one of the most crucial aspects of barbecuing with wood. But because we lack the technical instruments and clinical environments that the scientists who analyze the components of smoke use to do their research, we've got to rely on our eyes and nose to determine when our fire is a good one.

Good Smoke/Bad Smoke

People who don't pay close attention or who don't eat smoked foods very often might not notice the distinction between good and bad smoke. They are probably hardwired, as we all are, to respond positively to the generic flavor of smoke—that little caveman or cavewoman in all of us that over hundreds of thousands of years associates the smell and flavor of wood smoke with sustenance, home, and well-being.

But if you're attuned to it, you can easily tell the difference between meat that has absorbed good smoke and meat that has absorbed bad smoke. And once you get it, there's no going back.

Something with bad smoke might taste good the instant you put it in your mouth, but then you'll notice that there is an acrid taste to it that verges on a bitter aftertaste. You may notice a sneaky, biting acidity that jangles on your tongue and that the smoke sits more on the exterior of the meat than inside it. There's no sweetness. Once you get past your initial inherent programming to feel pleasure from smoked meat, you find a caustic, corrosive harshness. And it lingers bitingly in your mouth long after you've finished it.

Good smoke is the opposite. It's lighter and finer. Whereas the bad smoke has an ashy monotone, good smoke offers complexity. The impact is powerful yet strangely delicate at the same time. There's an ineffable sweetness and a level of finesse that penetrates every bite. That's good smoke.

Good Smoke

Getting good flavors out of smoke depends on two things: the wood being burned and the temperature at which it's created. It's very easy to cook meat with bad smoke. In fact, that's what most people do. Not only at home but also at restaurants all over. We get chefs coming through all the time on research trips for the barbecue place they plan to open in their own cities. They want to know our methods, our ingredients, our recipes. And, for the most part, we share that stuff.

What they don't know is that the secret they were looking for by coming to Franklin Barbecue was right there in front of them and wasn't a secret at all. It's all about good smoke. But good smoke requires real wood fires, and real wood fires require space and a level of mindfulness and commitment.

We've already talked about the compounds and flavors of different woods that give slightly different flavors in different smokes. But the difference in character between the smoke that comes from apple versus pecan versus hickory is minuscule compared to the differences between good and bad smoke. So let's concentrate on that.

At the most basic level, good smoke has to do with the efficiency of your fire—the more efficient it is, and the more complete its combustion, the better the quality of your smoke. But what do I mean by "complete" combustion? Here's where things get a bit technical again. Complete combustion happens when there is enough oxygen present to convert *all* of the fuel (specifically, those hydrocarbons I mentioned earlier) into just two by-products: carbon dioxide (CO_2) and water (H_2O). For our purposes, complete combustion is more of a theoretical aspiration. For one thing, it is impossible to achieve complete combustion outside of a laboratory setting, because there is never enough oxygen present in the air to convert the fuel completely. But this is actually good news for us pitmasters, since in complete combustion, there isn't *any* smoke at all—just water vapor and carbon dioxide gas. So really, our goal is to get something *close* to complete combustion, so that our smoke is clean with few by-products, but not all the way there.

On the other end of the spectrum, if you have very *incomplete* combustion, then you'll end up with tons of unwanted by-products in your smoke, such as creosote and impure carbon in the form of soot. Soot in your brisket—not so tasty.

So now the question is, how do we control the level of combustion? The short answer is we need to control the temperature, which in turn is affected by the amount of fuel, the moisture content of the fuel, and the amount of oxygen.

Remember, moisture content directly affects the temperature of the fire. Greener, wetter wood will cool a fire, resulting in lower temperatures and incomplete combustion. That's why the burning of wet wood issues nasty smoke. A fire composed primarily of well-seasoned wood is of prime importance.

Likewise, insufficient oxygen to the fire causes incomplete combustion, which results in that thick, dark smoke. When this is happening, some of the more noxious components in wood are being formed or released without being burned off or broken down into smaller, less offensive particles. You will note that you don't need to have flames to have this kind of poor combustion. Some of the nastiest smoke comes from wood that's smoldering—burning without

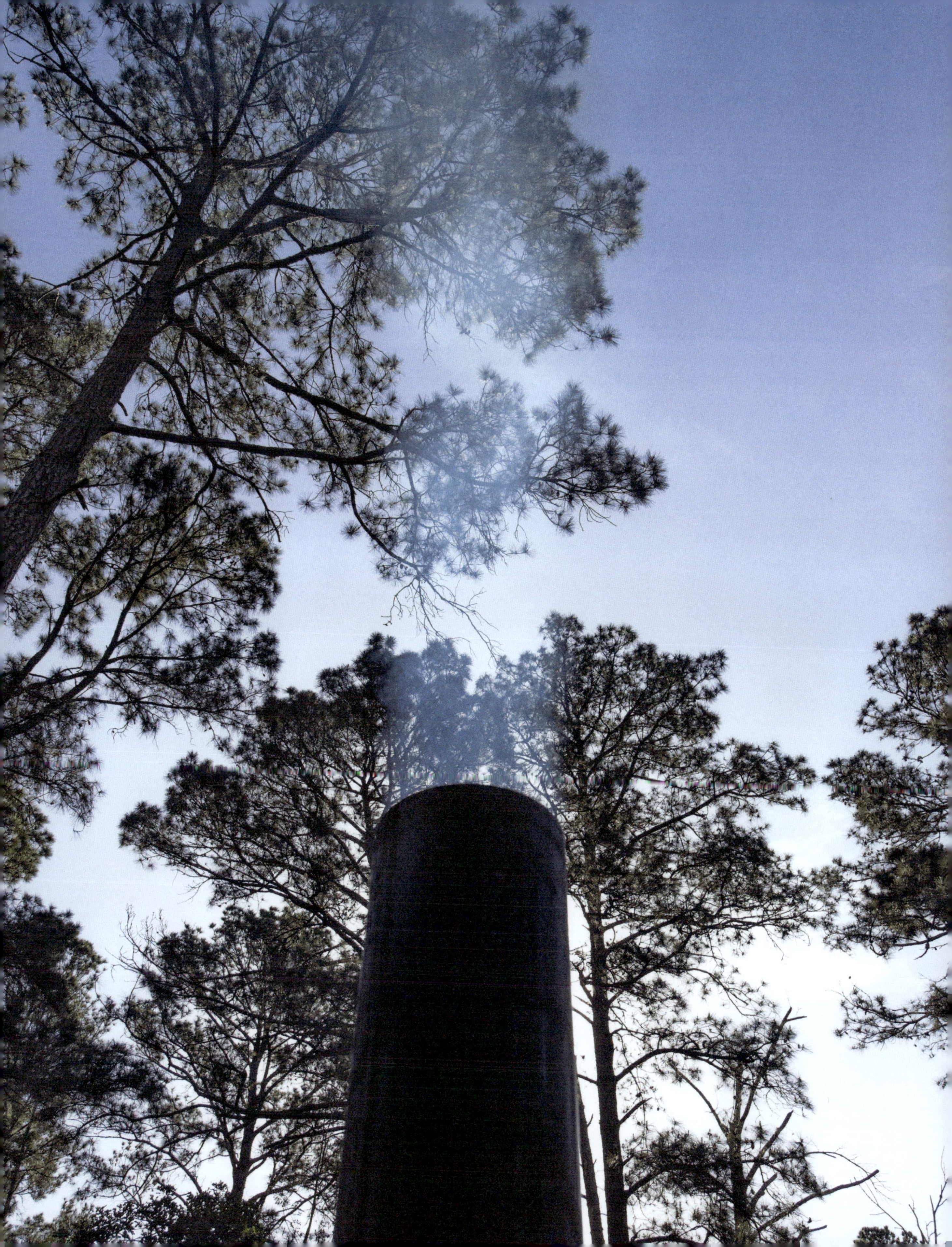

flame. This is a sign of low oxygen levels (since, as you'll recall, secondary combustion—those dancing flames—is a result of oxygen igniting gases released from the wood).

As you increase the airflow to the fire, though, it becomes happier and perkier. When the fire starts to burn more efficiently, more heat is produced. With the rise in temperature, production of the more off-putting compounds wanes and the more desirable gases start to emerge. At these temperatures, the hemicellulose and cellulose are breaking down, releasing compounds (carbonyls, phenols, cresols, vanillin, and many more) that start to flavor and color the meat. As the temperature continues to rise, the lignin starts to break down and even more flavorful by-products are released, including the ones that produce flavors of vanilla, peat smoke, caramel, nuts, and spice—the complex mixture of flavors and aromas that we know as good smoke. A hot fire likewise incinerates many of the nasty volatile compounds that were being released at lower temperatures. Books like *Modernist Cuisine* and McGee's *On Food and Cooking* agree that, to get the sweetest smoke, the best temperature for your fire is between 570°F and 750°F. Above that, the wood is releasing only the lightest and most subtle elements of the smoke, with the heavier particles being incinerated. Good flavor can come in this stage too, but with less impact. Truth told, I don't measure the temperature of the fire itself. I'm more concerned with the temperature of the smoke chamber at the level where the meat sits. Having active flame at all times is important, though. The temperatures at which burning wood instigates visible flames are also the temperatures at which desirable smoke is issued. Another indication is the color of the smoke itself.

It takes some work and practice to produce and maintain a fire that undergoes near-complete combustion. But it's really important to do so, because if you're subjecting a piece of meat to hours and hours of smoke exposure, you want it to be the good stuff. This is why, in my opinion, classic Central Texas–style barbecue is so good. The whole art is predicated on making a fire with near-complete combustion and generating hours and hours of the pure, sweet good smoke. The gas and electric smokers that so many restaurants use these days don't rely on wood to create their heat. Rather, the wood is there only to supply smoke, and it's often smoldering or choked off. Obviously this is not a strategy based around good fires, and thus these cookers and any others that inhibit airflow end up producing a lesser, more acrid smoke, which is why I don't care for them. We've seen these kinds of cookers take over mainstream barbecue, especially as enthusiasm for it has bloomed in major metropolitan areas where it's not as easy (for practical and legal reasons) to burn so much wood. But in recent years, it's also been heartening to see a small trend back to the original, purist form that I practice.

The Color of Smoke

I love to watch smokestacks—not only to see the energy with which the smoke is pumping out the stack but also to gauge the color of the smoke. Simply observing what kind of smoke is coming out of your stack can tell you a lot about the kind of fire you've got and how the meat's cooking.

You'll note that a fresh fire will produce a range of different qualities of smoke as it gets going. At first, the smoke will be thick and gray for a while. Then it becomes white, as the growing combustion reaction craves more oxygen and heat. After a little more time, the fire will hit a groove, and you'll notice that the smoke turns a thin, light gray with even a bluish tint. Then it might even be so faint that it's clear, only noticeable by the rippling in the air. It's kind of like getting up in the morning: you start off dense, slow, and foggy, and as you wake up, you become clearheaded and quick.

The color of smoke is determined by the size of the particles that compose it, and the size of the particles appear to be directly related to the fullness of combustion. So the more incomplete the combustion, the bigger the size of the particles. Large particles actually absorb light and appear black to gray. Slightly smaller ones look white. And even smaller ones reflect only the blue wavelengths of the spectrum and create blue smoke. You can witness blue smoke erupting from such other places as the tailpipe of a motorcycle, but when it comes from a barbecue chimney, it's a thing of beauty, considered the most desirable of smoke phases and the key indicator that your fire is burning properly. Then again, sometimes the smoke that issues from my stacks has no color at all, just clear ripples in the air. This is that step beyond blue—that light, clean, delicate smoke. Given our long cook times, I'm happy to have a certain amount of that to go along with the various other smokes that are perpetually hitting the meat.

GROWING THE FIRE AND GETTING GOOD SMOKE

While all of this technical talk about smoke and fire is interesting, actually accomplishing it isn't as hard as it sounds. As I said before, once you introduce fire to wood, it's just a matter of the fire finding its own rhythm and burning the way it wants to burn. For beginners, the best thing you can do at your early stages of barbecue is watch your fires and become familiar with the way they go.

Burn Seasoned Wood

You can eventually get good smoke with green wood, but you'll have to go through a lot of dirtier smoke to get there. The best smoke comes from well-seasoned dry wood that will burn vigorously and fairly quickly. You go through more wood this way (and have to keep a watchful eye on the smoker), but the results are worth it.

Heat That Cooker Up

Cold surfaces keep the temperature of the fire down, which results in dirtier smoke. So once you get your fire going, give your cooker time to absorb the heat thoroughly throughout the firebox and the cook chamber. I build a new fire in a cold smoker and let it go for anywhere from 30 minutes to an hour before I throw any meat on. You want everything to be solidly in its proper temperature zone before you upset the conditions by adding a mass of cold meat.

Don't Rush the Fire

Remember, always let the fire burn at its natural pace. And that means letting it find its groove. I've seen the analogy of a truck used for a smoker. The firebox is the engine for a big heavy truck. If you stomp on the gas and get it revved up, it will gradually accrue more and more speed and force. You do it too quickly and suddenly you find yourself barreling down the road at breakneck pace, which forces you to crush the brake to slow down or stop. The result is a very unsmooth ride and a great waste of energy. The same thing goes for a fire. Instead of piling on wood and building a huge, raging fire that you then have to choke back, I prefer to gradually grow a fire to ease into where you want it to be. It may take a little longer, but it's ultimately a much more graceful and sustainable ride.

Have a Strong Coal Bed

Once the fire gets going and has broken down a few logs into a nice bed of glowing embers, you've got your foundation. This goes part and parcel with warming up your smoker properly, but developing that foundation of coals is key to holding a stable temperature, which is a key to a successful cook. Having a nice, deep bed of coals will also allow new logs to start combusting quickly, minimizing the release of bad smoke.

Preheat the Wood

This is a technique that I use in cold weather. In warm weather, there's no need. But cold wood—and especially cold, green wood—can take a while to get going and might pump out volumes of dirty smoke before it really takes off. You can reduce this time by warming the wood before you add it to the fire. Once you have that primary fire started, before you've added your meat to the smoker, just stack a few pieces of wood on top of the firebox and let them hang out there for a while warming up their little toesies before they jump in. Then, when the meat's on and you need to add more wood, the logs will be ready to combust much more rapidly.

Cook with the Fire Door Open

To say "cook with the fire door open" is like saying "look both ways before crossing the street"—almost a cliché and such a basic truism that it almost doesn't need to be said. Then again, lots of pedestrians are hit by cars every year, and lots of firebox doors are left closed. If the conditions are good, there's no reason not to allow the maximum airflow your fire needs. Adjust its temperature by the amount of fuel you put in it, but let that fuel burn as cleanly as possible. A healthy fire will gulp that air up and turn it into thorough combustion and the kind of smoke you want on your meat. Of course, there are times when you might want to close that door a little bit, however. For instance, in rain, cold, or really windy weather, the elements might affect your fire in a negative way.

Many people think that if your fire has gotten too big and hot, closing the fire door is a way to suppress it, at the cost of producing some dirtier smoke. It would have to be DEFCON 1 ("Nuclear war is imminent") for me to consider closing the door. Sure, sometimes you get too much of a rager, with dangerously spiking temperatures. But in those instances it's much better to just open up the cook chamber doors and let the heat out quickly and completely (or shovel some coal towards the back of the cooker, or both) than to slowly choke down the fire.

TUNING THE FIRE

Now that your fire is built, your coal bed is full and self-sustaining, your smoker has warmed to the right temperature, and wispy blue smoke is swirling from the stack, you're ready to put the meat on. We'll talk more about the meat in chapter five. But once you've put it on, you're not going to do much with it for a long time. What you will be doing is constantly checking your temperatures and maintaining the fire. The most important pieces of equipment during this stage are your handy shovel, a thermometer to follow the temperatures in the cooker, and an ice chest full of cold beer.

Yes, this part is the long slog of barbecue, but it's also the time to pull up a lawn chair, pop a beer, chat with friends, or, if you're alone (as I often am on long cooks), simply reflect on life. You'll learn to keep a near-constant eye on the fire, smokestack, and cooker temperature gauges. Generally, just looking at one of those will give you an indication of what's going on. And periodically, you'll get up to throw a log on or adjust the fire.

The goal at this stage is consistency. You want to keep your temperatures within the zone in which you've decided to cook (see chapter six for more on that). Inevitably they will rise and fall a bit, but get too far off course, and you can either damage your meat or you'll find that it's taking hours longer than you planned, which can be a problem if you have people waiting to eat.

It's also important to remember that you have more control than you think. Even a chef in a modern kitchen will see a lag in time between when he or she turns up the dial in an oven versus when the food actually sees that heat. You will see that happen in a good smoker much more quickly. Smokers look clunky, heavy, and dull, but a well-built one will respond quickly to your adjustments. When I rummage through the woodpile looking for a piece that might give me another 10 degrees of heat and then I throw that small, dry piece on the fire, it might catch instantly. And when it does, thanks to that good airflow, that heat that the wood has just created will be whisked into the cook chamber within seconds. Because of that, I do feel I have the ability to control the temperature in the cook chamber almost in increments of degrees. (It's just holding them there that's the challenge.)

Skill at this part of managing a cook comes largely from experience. You have to know your wood, your smoker, and the weather conditions. Below I'm going to offer some of my techniques for managing the fire, but the best advice is to develop your own methods depending on your equipment.

CHOOSING WOOD AND MAINTAINING THE FIRE

Wood choice depends on what you want at any given time. And my favored techniques tend to change and evolve over time. Lately, I've preferred to use smaller pieces of wood. These offer more precision, more consistency, and a tighter control of the fire. Using smaller pieces means that I have to put more individual pieces in the firebox, of course, but I avoid the problem of really big spikes. The choir of smaller voices keeps a steady chatter going, maintaining the desired temperature, instead of the up-and-down, up-and-down bellowing that comes from larger pieces. The trade-off is that it's higher-maintenance cooking, which means you'll have to keep up with the fire more frequently instead of just setting a large piece of wood and walking away.

FIRE AS CHESS

Your fire is always evolving. So while it's good to take stock of it at any given moment, you also have to look at where it's heading. Think of it like a game of chess. Your opponent is inconsistent temperatures. Your pieces are your logs and your shovel. The board is the fire itself. You study the board, think about where you want to get, consider what the opposition is likely to do, and then plot your moves.

Here's an example: The temperature gauge may show that the cooker's humming along at a nice 275°F. But you see that the main log that's been burning is about to break down. It needs to be replaced. But if you put another big one in there, you're going to lose heat and smoke as the log heats up and starts to burn. So instead of that one, you might opt to put in two smaller ones. Or you might decide to use a small piece that's going to catch quickly and give a bump of heat, then follow that immediately with a larger, denser piece that's going to anchor the fire for another 30 minutes.

Here's another situation: I might stoke the fire a little bit with the shovel because I need about 5 degrees of temperature, but I don't want to put a new piece on because I'm about to open up the smoke chamber to flip the ribs, and I don't want to inhale a bunch of smoke. So I'm creating clean heat (poking at the embers, stimulating primary combustion) instead of smoky heat.

Of course, there are an infinite number of scenarios, and your plans and plays will be evolving constantly.

The key is to be both analytical and prepared for where your fire is heading. There are many different paths to get to the same end. But it's good to have the flexibility that's offered by a decent-size wood supply. Having a number of logs of various shapes, sizes, densities, and dryness gives you a lot of options for keeping your fire on track.

THE MAGICAL SHOVEL

An arsenal of different wood sizes is helpful, but even easier is just altering the structure of the fire itself. For this, never forget your trusty shovel. It's the number one way to keep air flowing over and into the fire. Use the shovel to slide logs or coals forward toward the cooker if you need more heat, or to pull them back toward the door if you want to slow down the fire by letting heat escape through the backside. When I put a new log on, I'll often use the edge of the head of the shovel to carve out a little channel in the coal bed, creating a pathway for the air under the log so that it lights faster. On a cold day, I'll spread coals toward the back to preheat the air hitting the fire.

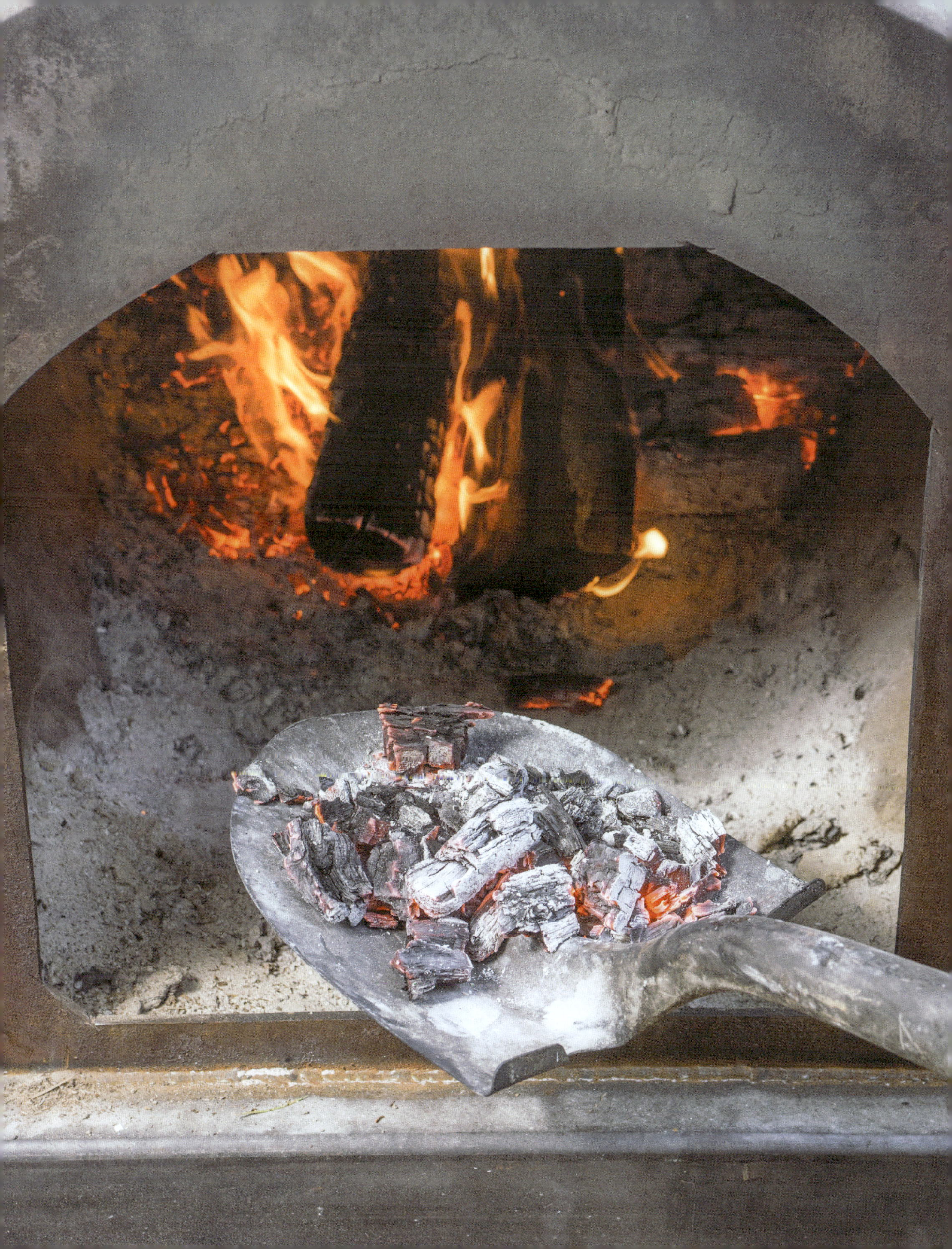

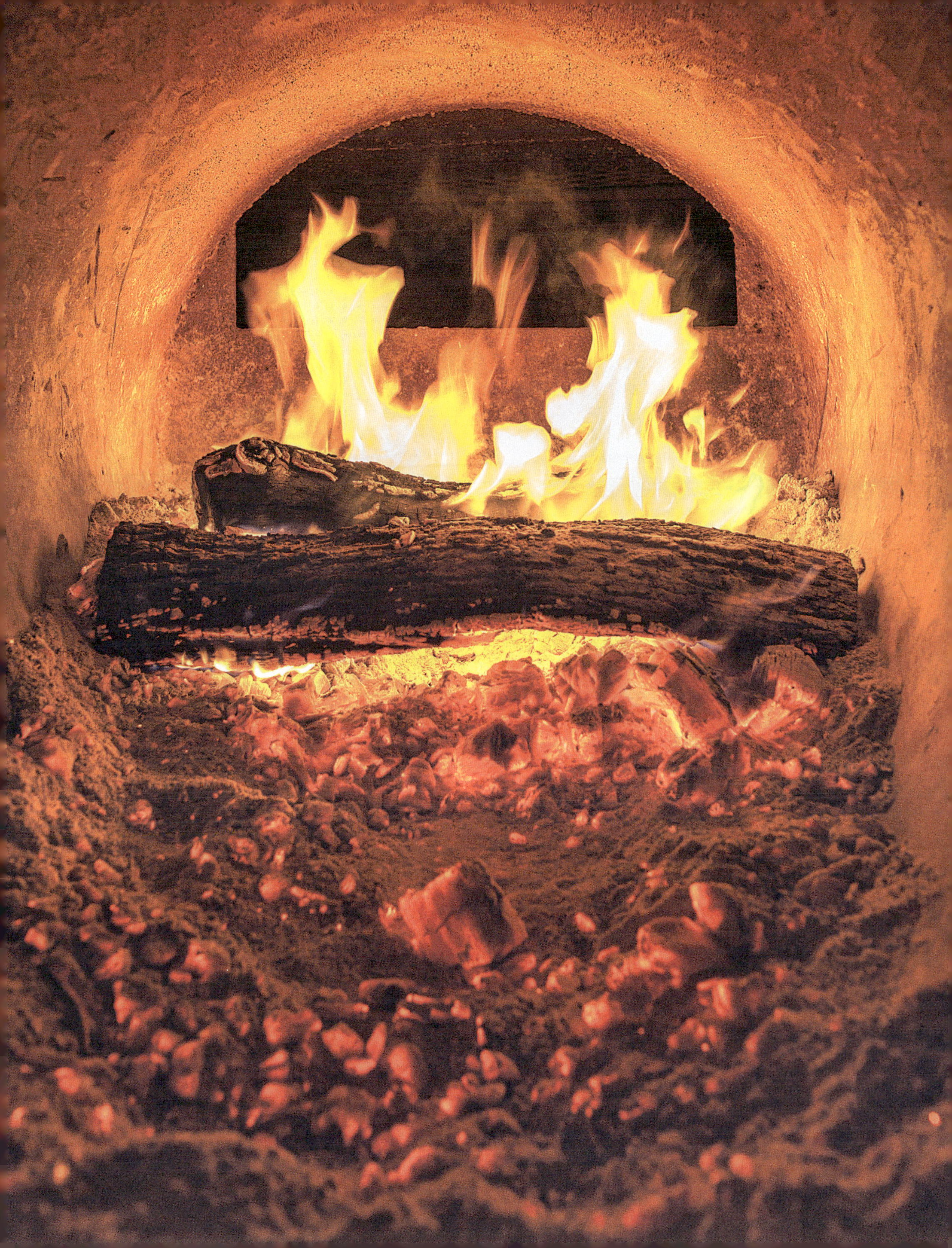

USING GREEN WOOD

It's been well documented that I use a fair bit of green wood when I cook. For the record: that's because of necessity, not design. If I had a big lot stacked high with perfectly seasoned wood, I'd use that all of the time. But instead I have to take what I can get, which sometimes includes a delivery of green wood. So here's how I use it.

Greener wood offers heavier smoke. And I cook with so much light smoke that every now and then I want to get a dose of some of the denser, low-temperature smoke that comes from green wood.

However, for the most part this is not the smoke I'm after. Thus, the most common way I'd use green wood is for heat, not for smoke. If I had a stack of really green wood, and I needed to step away from the cooker to run some errands, I'd consider using it *after* I'd wrapped the meats (see page 154), at which point the briskets continue cooking without absorbing tons of smoke flavor. At that stage I might put on the green wood and close the firebox door a bit. It would smolder but provide enough temperature to keep the meats cooking, and the wrapping would prevent them from taking on the smoke.

. . .

Good smoke is an indispensable element of great-tasting barbecue. In this chapter, I presented some key techniques and the thinking behind them, but there's really no substitute for just getting in there with your own fires. Remember to be mindful at all times—of your wood, of the fire, of the airflow—and you should come out fine.

MEAT

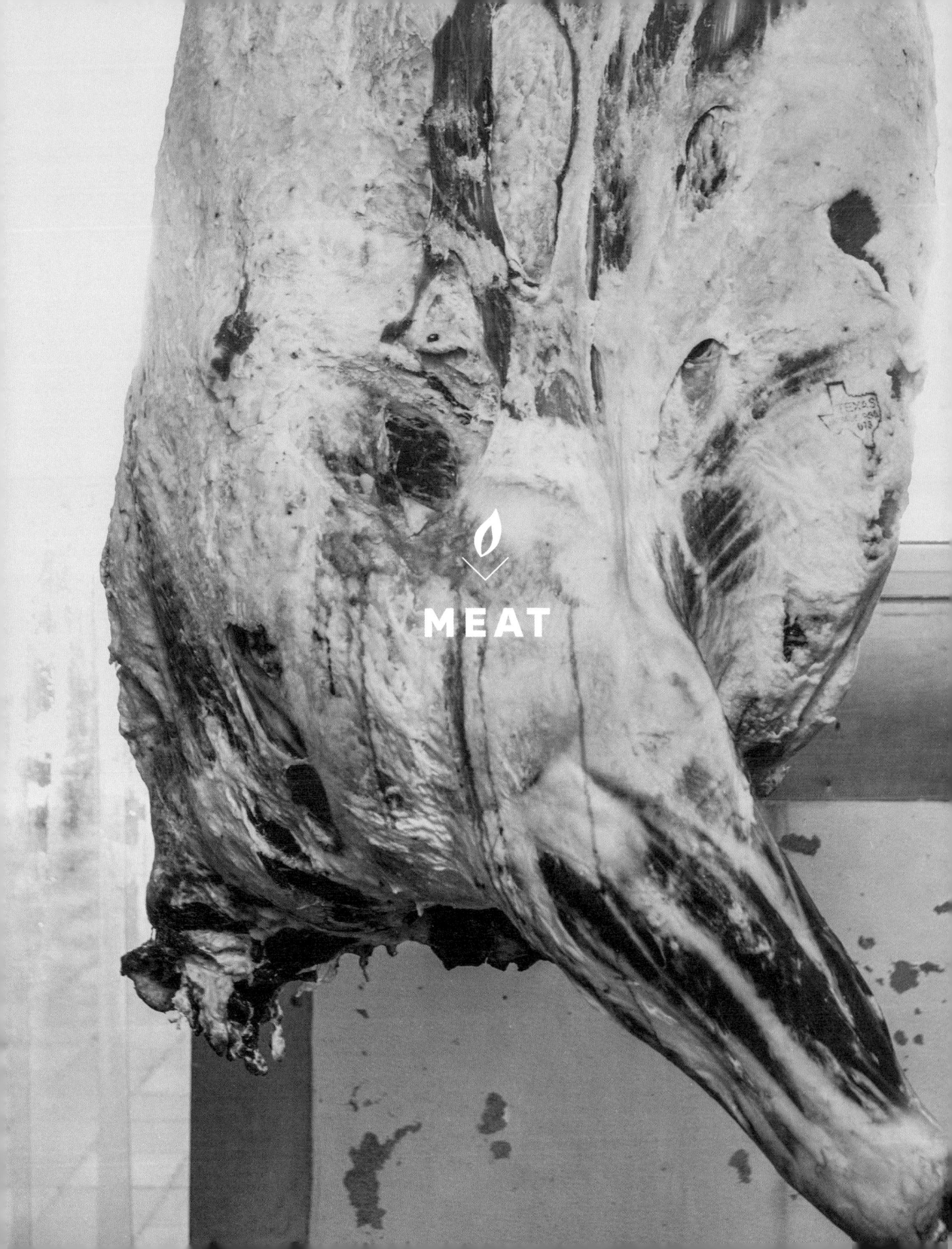

- **Chapter Five**

As someone who makes his living selling enormous quantities of cooked meat—we're talking 2,000 pounds on our busiest days—meat quality is something I care deeply about. High-quality meat is by far our number one expense. Unfortunately, by far my number one headache is also the work it takes to secure the consistent supply of meat at the quality level we require. When things are going well, our supply of well-butchered, ethically raised meat is something I don't have to think about too much. But when things go wrong, they can make for the worst times in this line of work. I'll never forget our one epic month of brisket drama.

In 2013, the meat plant that supplies our briskets caught on fire and had to shut down for about a month. Luckily, we had just taken delivery of a couple of pallets—about three hundred briskets. But we saw the trouble on the horizon and tried to ration our meat accordingly. We were slightly stingy for a couple of weeks, cutting it close as to how much we cooked to get through a day, and more careful than ever about how we cut our meat and what we might throw away. But our stocks on hand dwindled and dwindled and eventually our supply ran out.

Within about two days of having used up the last of the meat in our own walk-in, I exhausted the entire supply of all-natural (hormone- and antibiotic-free) brisket in the state of Texas. For a few days, we had to dip down and use an entirely different grade of brisket, the crappy commodity stuff that's widely available everywhere (and that most barbecue joints use). This truly was the last resort, because our commitment to high-quality, ethically raised meat is something I never want to compromise. Indeed, before we even took this step, the idea of closing the restaurant until we got our beef back did enter my mind, but that was impossible. We have customers who may have organized their trips and planned months ahead to eat at our restaurant, not to mention employees who need to work. The show, as they say, must go on, so we had to figure out a way to cook the second-rate briskets.

And it was tough. Yes, the meat, but also those few days! It was probably the hardest period we've ever had. Trying to nurse that meat into something our customers would still rave about was almost impossible. The briskets were so incredibly lean and tough. We resorted to techniques we never do: mopping with oil, butter, onions, and garlic to add moisture, richness, and fat; wrapping them with foil (the dreaded so-called Texas crutch) to try to seal in what little juiciness they had. It felt as if I were running a different restaurant for those days. And unfortunately, a food writer happened to come in at the time, resulting in the only bad review we've ever received. All of this was the result of some guy at the meat processing plant leaving a tool on a conveyor belt and burning down part of the factory.

The whole time I was feeling pretty crappy about the quality of our product, not to mention the welfare of the animals the meat came from. I worked maniacally to source more, better brisket. The benefit of having one source for all of my briskets is the convenience of dealing with one vendor who knows exactly what I want. The risk—well, the risk is obvious. If something breaks down, there's nowhere else to go to pick up the slack. You can't just order one hundred cases of brisket (five hundred to six hundred pieces) from a purveyor you don't normally use, because they don't keep that much extra product in their supply chain.

We were scrambling. Within a day, calling in every favor I had, I exhausted all of the briskets in Austin. We were working every meat supplier we could find. I went through San Antonio. I went through Dallas. Trucks were showing up at 2 in the morning with briskets from Oklahoma. One day, I had to drive two hours out of town to meet a semi on the side of a highway behind a truck stop to pick up meat, because the driver couldn't go any farther off of his scheduled route to meet me. After that strange transaction, I hauled ass back to the restaurant, rubbed the briskets down, and threw them on the smoker. I barely got them cooked on time.

Finally, our usual supplier came back online, just in time for the *Texas Monthly* barbecue festival—an annual festival showcasing the magazine's Top 50 barbecue joints—at which we were scheduled to cook for thousands of people. It was a huge honor, since the magazine had just named us the number one barbecue joint in the state, but I'll admit I was *stressed*. Our deliveries had only just started arriving again, which meant the meat was completely fresh because we were starting from scratch. When the briskets arrived, I discovered that they had been butchered so quickly and carelessly that only two of them looked what I'd call acceptable, and we needed eighty. Normally, we like some postmortem wet aging on the briskets (see page 111) because it tenderizes them and deepens the flavor. These were from animals that had been alive a mere three days before we were preparing them. Thus, we unfortunately appeared with brisket that was clearly not on top of its game.

That's what happens when you run a place that deals with as much volume as we do. Supply will no doubt never stop being an issue. If I was shopping every couple of weekends for a brisket or a few racks of ribs, as the average home barbecue cook does, it would be much different. I'm sure I'd enjoy the process of procuring meat. But we go through so much meat and have such rigid standards about it that simply getting as much meat of as high a quality as I want is a constant challenge.

Some people get all excited about their brines, rubs, injections, and all of the other various treatments they subject meat to. We don't have that option, because at Franklin, we don't do much. We keep things simple, secure in the knowledge that it's the smoke and the cooking methods that are the keys to our success. And meat quality is at the heart of that.

We serve brisket, pork ribs, sausage, pulled pork, and turkey breasts on a daily basis. And once a week, on Saturdays, we also sell beef ribs. Now, just as with wood and fire, I do think it's important to have some understanding of what you're cooking and where it comes from.

BRISKET

It's true that a bumper sticker on my truck reads, **BRISKET IS MY SPIRIT ANIMAL**. If Texas barbecue has one emblematic cut, it's the brisket. It's the longest to cook, the hardest to perfect, and the one meat by which every Texas pitmaster is ultimately judged. If your brisket is tough, dry, or flavorless, you're going to hear about it.

As long-standing and venerable as the tradition of Texas barbecue is, brisket, surprisingly, wasn't always the main attraction it is today. It's a relatively recent phenomenon, which probably hit its stride in the 1970s. That's when what we call "boxed beef" became widespread. Before the advent of boxed beef, cows were pretty much slaughtered locally or shipped as whole carcasses—what the industry calls "hanging beef." In those days, Central Texas barbecue joints were really just meat markets where shop owners would break down whole animals and sell the most desirable parts for people to cook at home. The leftovers they would cook up themselves. This would most likely include the brisket—a tough, ornery piece of meat—but was hardly restricted to it.

When IBP (Iowa Beef Processors, now Tyson Fresh Meats) introduced boxed beef and pork in the 1960s, it was the beginning of a revolution. Rather than shipping whole carcasses, IBP started breaking down steers into their constituent cuts at a central processing plant and then vacuum-sealing each cut individually. This accomplished a number of things. Vacuum-packing allowed the meats to remain sanitary for longer (something that was previously accomplished by just shipping the animal carcass whole, which made it slower to decay). Vacuum-packing also reduced the cost of shipping because it meant processors could leave unwanted trimmings, fat, and bones behind. And for customers, boxed beef allowed them to order and receive precisely what they wanted to cook without the hassle of having to break down a huge hunk of meat and figure out what do with the less desirable parts. Most people would consider brisket a less desirable cut. But what it had working in its favor was that it was extremely cheap relative to steaks and loins, and, in the right hands, it could become something magical.

Today, brisket has become Texas's sacred cow, to the point that Texas A&M University's meat science department offers Camp Brisket for the meat and barbecue curious, an intensive two-day investigation into everything having to do with this holy piece of meat. One of the founders of Camp Brisket, Dr. Jeff Savell, has become my go-to guy whenever I have a meat-science question.

What Is the Brisket?

Brisket is the pectoral muscle of a steer and is roughly comparable to a human's pectorals, which gird the chest. (It's a bit larger, though—okay, a lot larger. A brisket used in Texas barbecue might weigh anywhere from 8 to 16 pounds.) If you imagine the cow standing on its hind legs, it's the big muscle stretching across the chest and right under the neck. A steer has two briskets, one on each side. Large, dense muscles, briskets are worked heavily in their role supporting a majority of the animal's enormous weight. Although briskets often come with a robust fat cap, inside they are fairly lean and sinewy, dense with connective tissue that enables the muscle to do heavy lifting.

"You've heard that phrase *eating high on the hog*?" says Dr. Savell. "Well that saying comes from the fact that meat from higher on a standing hog or steer is softer. Anything that is on the back is the most tender, anything down on the front end is tougher, and on the legs even tougher. It's not that the muscles are any different in the way they function from other muscles in the body; it's that they have more connective tissue to help harness that movement." In other words, the more work a given part of the cow has to do to walk, run, or just support its weight standing, the tougher the meat. It makes sense then that the cow's legs (shanks) are toughest and its back (tenderloin) is most tender, with brisket falling in between.

A single brisket is actually comprised of two distinct muscles, the deep pectoral (pectoralis profundus) and the superficial pectoral (pectoralis superficialis). Colloquially, these are called the "flat" and the "point." The flat is the lean, broad, rectangular thinner muscle that is the major part of the brisket. The point, or supraspinatus muscle (commonly known as the rotator cuff on humans), is an almost pyramid-shaped mound of muscle connected to one end of the flat. The point has more marbling and connective tissue than the flat and becomes very tender and juicy with long cooking. One of the challenges of brisket is that the point rides right on top of the flat, but its meat is of vastly different consistency and has a completely different grain. They're separate but connected.

Brisket would be an even greater challenge to eat if not for the massive layer of fat, called the fat cap, that covers one entire side of it. Its gradual rendering over long cooking times adds flavor and keeps the meat moist. Try to grill, sauté, or otherwise flash-cook and you'll be unhappy—left with tough, sinewy muscle and a pretty much impermeable layer of fat. But cook it slowly, at perfect fat-melting temperature, and that fat cap liquefies and imbues the muscle with its delicious flavor and texture.

"We did a study of the tenderness of forty major muscles of the cow when cooked in the same manner, over direct heat like a steak," notes Dr. Savell. "And the brisket was thirty-ninth in tenderness. But the fact that in Texas barbecue, you're taking one of the worst pieces of the animal and converting it into one of the best is a miracle itself." Amen.

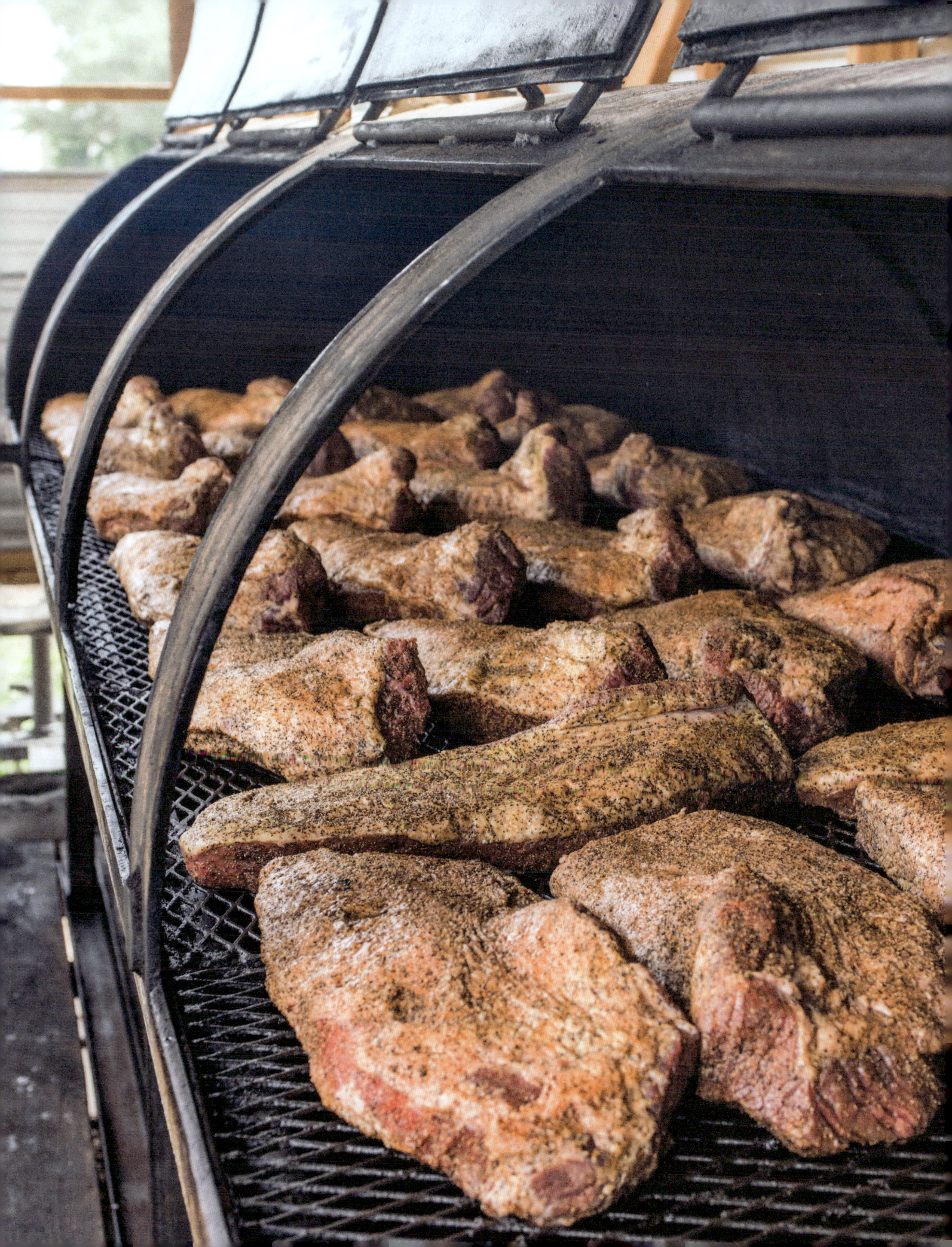

How to Buy a Brisket

There are many things to look out for when buying a brisket, and knowing the difference between different grades and breeds will help you choose the right meat for your cook.

Grades

In my early days of cooking brisket, I could occasionally buy very low grades of meat on sale for $0.99 a pound. Those days are long gone, but brisket is still one of the cheaper cuts you'll find. For a long time, cheap, low-grade brisket was probably what everyone was cooking. But, over the years, with the increased attention that brisket is getting, the grade of the meat has come into sharper focus and can affect the way you buy meat, the way you should cook it, and what you can expect of it when done.

When you get beef from a USDA-inspected facility, it usually comes with one of three grades: Prime, Choice, or Select. Prime is the best grade, Choice and Select a little lower down the ladder. There are lower grades still, but we won't mess with those. The grades are composite scores issued by highly trained meat inspectors based largely on degree of marbling—tenderness, juiciness, and flavor. Marbling, or intramuscular fat, by definition from Dr. Savell, is "the intermingling or dispersion of fat within the lean." It's easy to see the marbling—little wavy strands of white within the lean, red meat. Marbling is very, very important for brisket.

Prime beef is defined as being from young (nine to thirty months in age), well-fed beef with abundant marbling. Choice is considered good

THE FLUCTUATING PRICE OF MEAT

In the barbecue business we deal with many vagaries—temperature, humidity, and wood quality, to name a few. But one of the most inconsistent factors we deal with is also one of the most important: meat. Barbecue is supposed to be a relatively inexpensive food, but these days it's hard to keep meat costs down. Meat has always been a luxury item for mankind, but now many, many factors affect our costs. For one, meat is in greater demand worldwide than it ever has been. This point has been made a lot in the news, but as growing populations like that of China attain new affluence, they want to enjoy more meat, just as we all do. Of course, with limited production, this means a much more competitive global marketplace and escalating beef prices. There are, of course, other factors too. For instance, drought in Texas and other southern and midwestern states has taken its toll on cattle farming, as the price of grain and water has gone up. Escalating fuel prices also affect meat prices, as the meat has to be shipped to me everyday across several states. Yet despite these rising costs, barbecue seems to be steadily rising in popularity. This is a good thing for me, but (hey!) it also means more competition and higher prices for meat.

quality but lower in marbling than Prime. And Select beef, according to the USDA, is very uniform in quality and normally leaner than the higher grades. "It is fairly tender," the USDA says, "but, because it has less marbling, it may lack some of the juiciness and flavor of the higher grades."

All grades of brisket are used in the professional barbecue world; everyone has his or her preferred grade. The most popular around the state of Texas is probably Choice, because it's relatively affordable and in the hands of an able pitmaster can still produce fairly juicy brisket. I use Prime grade, which is by far the most expensive, but its marbling is important to the style of brisket I'm going for, which pushes tenderness and moistness to the extreme. In many grocery stores, you'll be fortunate to find Choice or Prime, but it's worth putting in some effort to try to track one of them down. This is especially true if you're just beginning, as there's a larger margin for error with fattier grades. Then again, the errors are more painful with more expensive beef.

What's most important to me is that the beef we use comes from ethically treated cattle who are raised and slaughtered in a peaceful, comfortable environment. I have visited the plant and talk frequently with the company that supplies our meat, so I do have confidence that we're getting what we pay for. And we pay a lot for it: it's more expensive to raise cattle in an ethical way, and that cost is reflected in the price of beef. Looking at what goes into industrial-farmed cattle and how they're treated, our decision to spend more on better quality and better treatment is an easy one to make. But the supply for this kind of beef is much smaller than the market for conventionally raised animals, which is why we occasionally run into issues.

Breeds and Brands

The breed we use is Angus, which is well respected but also quite common in American beef. You may see packages labeled "Certified Angus Beef." But if your meat doesn't have that stamp, that doesn't mean it's not Angus beef. It still might be Angus, so that's a distinction that you really needn't worry about. The CAB (Certified Angus Beef) brand was started by the American Angus Association in 1978 and is just one—admittedly very big—seller of Angus beef. It has stringent standards, in that the beef CAB sells must bear a grade of either Prime or top-tier Choice. That makes it pretty reliable and popular among chefs. But there are other brands that both raise Angus breed cattle and maintain high standards, even though they don't have the CAB seal, including Niman Ranch (California), Creekstone (Kansas), and Meyer Natural Angus (Montana). If you're going to be doing a lot of barbecuing, I suggest that you take a little time to research the brands available in your area to find one or two that work well for you and then stick with them. You don't have to own a restaurant to value things like consistency and reliability. If you're investing 12 hours into cooking a brisket, you want some assurances that the product is something that you're comfortable cooking.

Another beef breed you might see occasionally is Wagyu. Its name when translated from Japanese is much less exciting than when you don't know what it means—*wa* means "Japanese" and *gyu* means "cow." Japanese cow, that's all it is. But you probably know that Japan is known for its ultra-marbled beef, such as the famous cows from Kobe. Kobe beef is not produced in the United States, only Japan. But we do have beef that comes from cows bearing Japanese bloodlines, though most of these animals have been interbred with American breeds to help them adapt to local climates and conditions. Still, American Wagyu tends to be extremely well marbled and is a popular brisket on the competitive barbecue scene for its sheer decadence. I've cooked many Wagyus for various special events and always find them extremely moist and tender, if not always delivering the deepest, beefiest flavor that I prefer. Still, they are magically textured, with all of that intramuscular fat melting slowly and turning that piece of beef into a buttery, smooth, melt-in-your-mouth kind of experience. Naturally, Wagyu beef is really expensive, but I've always had great success with the product from Snake River Farms in Idaho.

Choosing the Package

Sometimes at the store you'll find a brisket already broken down into the point and flat cuts to make for smaller, more easily workable pieces for the home cook. Brisket is also one of the premier foods in Jewish cuisine, where it might get turned into corned beef, pastrami, or braised brisket with horseradish and onions. No doubt it became popular in Jewish cooking, as in barbecue, because of its low cost. But this is also in part because brisket is from the forequarters, the only part of the cow that is certified kosher in the United States. Pastrami is yummy, but don't buy your barbecue brisket preseparated. You want the entire thing, untrimmed. It will probably come whole, sealed in a Cryovac package, which is called a "packer-cut" brisket.

You'll likely find briskets that weigh anywhere from 10 to 20 pounds. Deciding on size is just a matter of preference. But don't forget to take into account that larger briskets will take longer to cook, 1 to 1 1/2 hours per pound, depending on the temperature at which you cook. Consider the size of your smoker and what else, if anything, you might want to cook at the same time. Big honkers of briskets take up a lot of space on a small grate.

Pack Dates and Aging

If you go to buy a single brisket at the store and see that they're all individually Cryovac packaged, you're going to have trouble determining the date the brisket was packed. It's not that the processors are trying to keep it a secret from you. It's just that they put the pack date on the whole case, not on each individual brisket. Your best bet is to ask your grocer about the pack date. (And in case you're curious, the slaughter date will likely be no more than two days prior to the pack date.)

Of course, if the brisket has been flash frozen, the pack date doesn't really matter, since meat won't age when frozen. All the brisket we use has never been frozen. Freezing breaks down the fibers in the meat somewhat, and you'll end up with a mushier product. Always look for fresh meat, though you might not be able to avoid frozen at big-box stores. If you see a lot of blood in the Cryovac-packed brisket, or if it feels overly floppy, it's likely been frozen. If in question, it never hurts to ask the grocer.

The question on aging and briskets is an open one. According to Dr. Savell, the research is conclusive that aging tenderizes and boosts flavor in ribs and loins (steaks). But he says that official research has not been conducted on brisket. Yet unofficial research is being

MEAT

> ### DRY AGING VERSUS WET AGING
>
> Dry aging refers to beef that has been hung or placed on a rack to dry, whereas wet aging refers to beef that is aged in a vacuum-sealed bag (which helps it retain moisture). If you encounter someone trying to sell you a brisket that's been dry aged, avoid it, if your intent is barbecue. I had to cook dry-aged briskets once, and they were very unpleasant. They've lost so much moisture by the time you cook them that it's already a dicey proposition. Then you have to cut off all of the outside meat and fat that is crusty and dry. By the time you're finished, the cut is so small that it looks like a squirrel brisket. Then a long cook in the smoker further removes so much fat and moisture that you end up with a dried piece of driftwood. Don't ever waste your money on dry-aged brisket.

conducted all of the time. Even though the USDA doesn't suggest there's any benefit to aging briskets, I think there is. In competition barbecue, I've heard of people holding on to a brisket for forty days or so from the packing date, pushing it as far as they possibly can. I wouldn't take it quite that far, but I do keep my briskets anywhere from fourteen to twenty-one days after the packing date before cooking them.

Flexibility

If you've got a number of vacuum-sealed, packer-cut briskets in front of you at the store, how do you choose which one to buy? Some people will start enthusiastically telling you about the importance of a brisket's flexibility. But we're not talking about Mary Lou Retton on the uneven bars here. So instead of talking about meat's *flexibility*, I tend to use the more fun word *floppiness*.

The idea is that a brisket with more marbling and softer fat will have more give. So if you press on it gently, pick it up, and sort of toss it around in your hands for a few seconds, you might find one brisket that's floppier than the others, and that's the one that you'll want to buy.

I give some credence to this idea. If the briskets are not frozen yet still hard as a rock, that stiffness may not disappear entirely during cooking. Stiffness may be due to the hardness of the fat. Huge amounts of hard fat are undesirable, though some is unavoidable. Plus, vacuum-packing is snug and the plastic these briskets are wrapped in is tough, so it's not always easy to get a sense of flop value just by handling a brisket at the store. But if you're about to drop anywhere from $40 to $100 on a piece of meat, it doesn't hurt to be thorough.

Fat and Grass

Speaking of fat, I really do try to avoid briskets that sport heavy, compacted layers of rock-hard fat on the outside. In my experience, this kind of fat is a hallmark of a cow that's been raised industrially on grain and fed all kinds of growth hormones and antibiotics to be brought quickly and unhealthily up to a slaughtering weight. I find much less of this fat on briskets from cows that have been more humanely raised. Tender, white fat is something I really like to see.

If that fat is not white but has a yellowish tint, that might be a sign that the animal was grass-fed. Grass-fed beef is a growing movement, and in general I support it, but not for brisket meant for the barbecue. An animal that's been raised entirely in the pasture will have a much more diverse diet than one raised primarily on grain. That diet will be reflected in the diverse organic compounds found in the meat and fat, resulting in a stronger flavor and aroma when the meat is cooked. A grass-fed steak can be an interesting and rewarding eating experience. A grass-fed brisket cannot. Trust me, I've done it. The long, slow cooking of a huge, fatty piece of grass-fed muscle brings out too much of that funky, herbaceous, beastly flavor. It's not an enjoyable meal.

A lot of the animals we use are pasture raised for the first part of their lives and then transitioned onto a grain and corn diet for the last part. That seems to produce healthy animals with good flavor and fine, soft fat.

Meat on the Flat

The thinnest strip of meat on the brisket is going to be at the end of the flat, where the muscle starts to taper down. You can see this part through the packaging, and it is a good indicator of the level of marbling and general evenness of the meat. One side of the end of the flat tends to be thicker than the other, so I always look for a flat that has a fairly consistent thickness across the end because it will cook more evenly and slice better. If I don't have a choice and have to use a brisket that tapers off wildly, I'm going to end up trimming that back anyway until I get a more even shape. So if you do have a choice, look for a consistent thickness across the end of the flat.

BEEF RIBS

Almost as iconic in Texas as the brisket, beef ribs are spectacular for both cooking and eating. Incredibly rich, tasty, and delightful, they're also really expensive and take pit space away from our staples like brisket and pork ribs. But they're delicious, so we cook them only on Saturdays. People love them and it's not hard to understand why: they are truly impressive cuts. At Louie Mueller in Taylor, the spot that's probably most

---

LEFT-SIDED BRISKETS

Some people in Texas say that they like to cook only a left-sided brisket—that is, the brisket from the left side of the steer. Their reasoning is that most steers sit on their left side when they're lying down to ruminate or rest. That suggests that they'll have to push harder on their right side to raise the majority of their mass. Therefore, these people contend, the left-sided brisket is less worked and more tender than the brisket on the other side.

For the record, I think this is a joke. In all the thousands of briskets I've cooked, I've found no evidence that the meat from one side of the cow is noticeably more tender than the other. I guess I slightly prefer the shape of left-sided briskets because it's easier to wrap, but it's not really something I pay much attention to and I recommend that you don't worry about it either.

famous for them in Texas, the beef ribs are served as a giant hunk of meat with an enormous, caveman-style bone sticking out one end. The meat is succulent, juicy, and thickly coated in black pepper.

The cuts of ribs on a steer and on a pig have both similarities and differences. Of course, they come from either the top or the bottom of the animal. One major difference is that a steer is much, much bigger than a typical pig, meaning that there are much greater differences between the ribs on one end versus the other. Another difference is in the nature of the meat that attaches to the ribs on the top and bottom of the animal.

The rib cage and shoulder area of the steer is so big that it's divided into three main sections called primals: the chuck, the rib, and the plate. The chuck and rib primals are on the top of the animal and the plate primal is underneath. The division between the chuck and rib is made with a cut between the fifth and sixth ribs. Ribs 1–5, which are on the head end, go with the chuck primal, and ribs 6–12 go with the rib primal. Chuck meat, which is the hardworking shoulders of the steer, is best cut up for braises and stews. Those few ribs on the chuck side are often found cut very thinly and horizontally (with each piece of meat containing multiple round pieces of bone) as flanken- or Korean-style short ribs. Not too many people barbecue chuck ribs.

Back ribs come from the top of the animal, much as baby backs do on pigs. The difference is that the meat that beef back ribs are cut away from is the rib-eye, the most desirable cut on the whole animal. Therefore, butchers cut as close to the bone as possible to preserve as much on the boneless rib-eyes as they can, which can almost always be relied on to leave shiners (see page 116) on the ribs. Obviously, not a lot of meat is left, and it's generally found between the bones, not on top of them. It's tasty though not hugely popular at a lot of barbecue joints.

The real showstopper, the kind of ribs we use, comes from the plate primal. (To situate you, the plate primal sits on the underside of the cow just behind the brisket and in front of the flank.) The plate short ribs are the meatiest, with the meat on top of the bones layered with fat. The meat on these is heavily marbled and also dense with connective tissue, making them richly flavored and ideal for long, slow cooking. Shorter cuts of these are often sold as short ribs. We go for plate ribs 6, 7, and 8—right in the middle of the rib cage—which have the longest, widest, meatiest bones, like brontosaurus ribs. They make spectacular barbecue. Although beef plate ribs are perhaps not the easiest thing for the professional to cook every day, they are fantastic for the home cook.

PORK RIBS

The conventional wisdom has it that Texas barbecue means beef, and the barbecue from most other places is mainly pork. In this case, the conventional wisdom has it wrong. Although there is a strong beef tradition here, Texans have also been smoking pork for a long time. And visiting various barbecue joints across the state will show you that all manner of pork is widely available on menus, from shoulder to ribs to chops. At Franklin Barbecue, we offer pulled pork (not a Texas specialty), but we're even better known for our ribs.

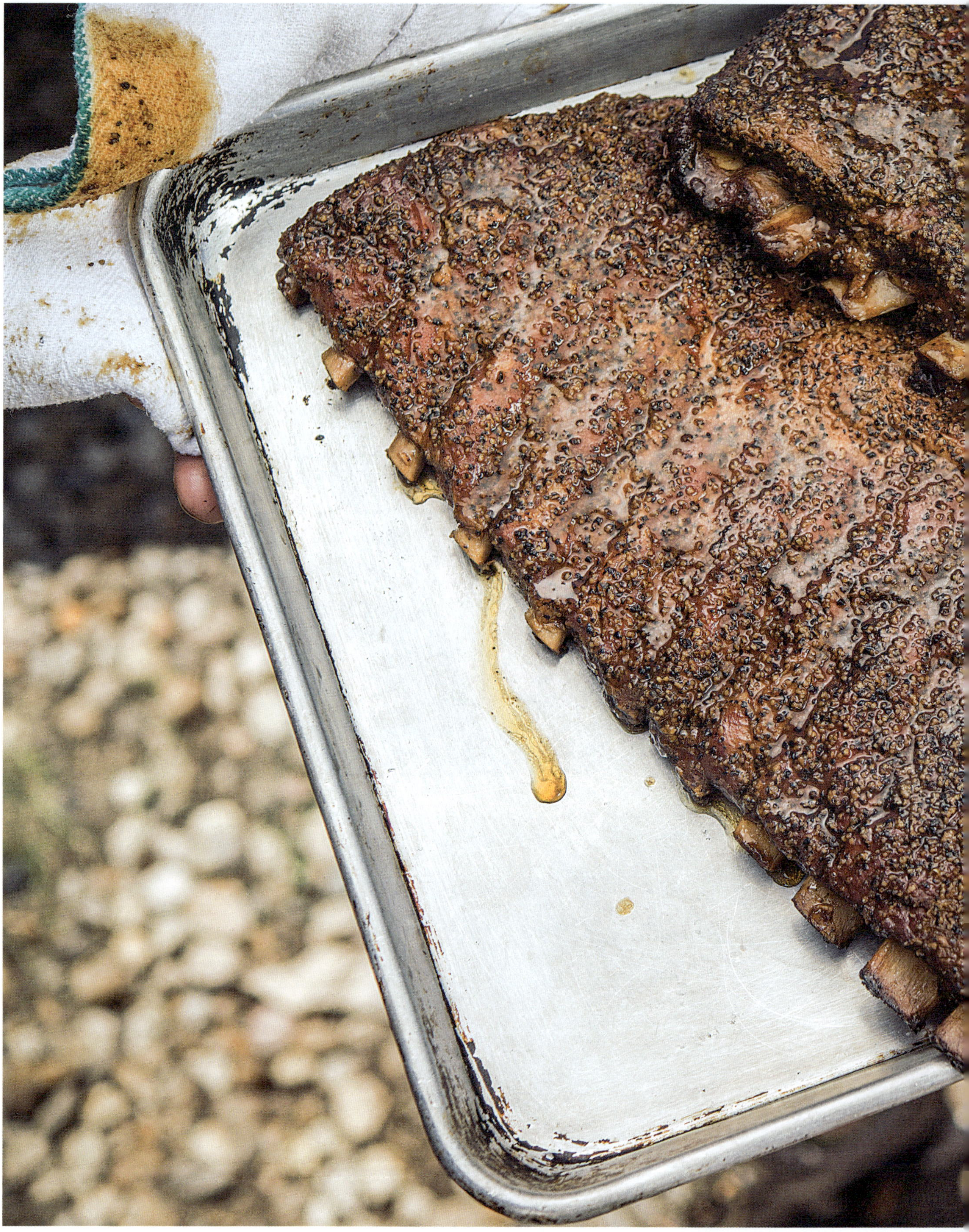

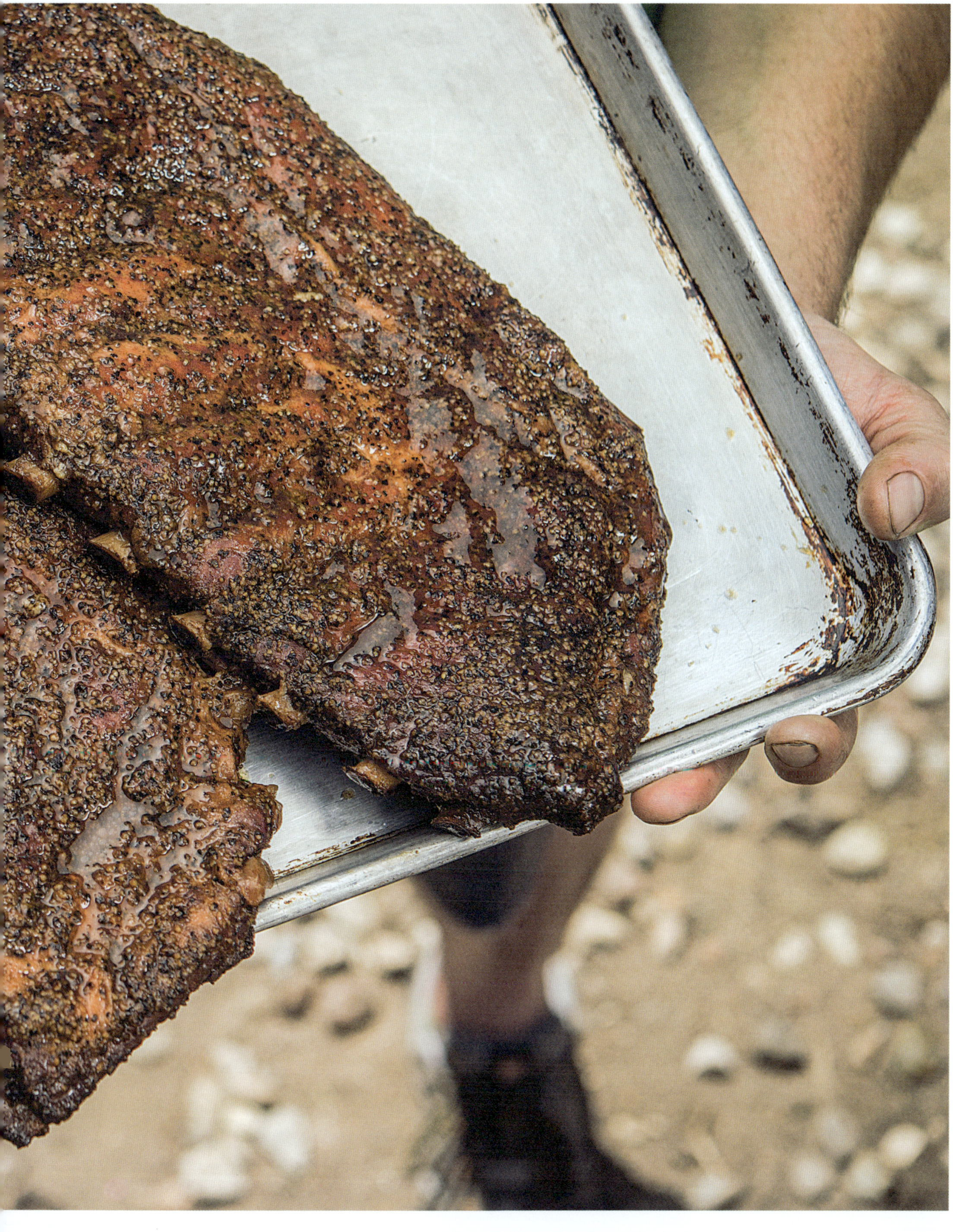

> **SHINERS**
>
> As a beer from Texas, Shiner can be quite desirable. But as a quality on a rack of ribs you're buying, it's something to look out for. On ribs, a *shiner* is the term for a bit of the bone that's showing through on the top of the rack where there should be meat. This happens when overzealous butchers rob the rib of meat in order to give it to another cut (or when a piggy was just too skinny).
>
> Shiners are more likely to be found on spare ribs than on baby backs for the simple reason of the cut spareribs sit next to. Baby back ribs are next to the loin, which is not a highly desirable cut of pork and usually sells for less than the baby back ribs. Therefore, when separating the back ribs from the loin, it actually behooves the butcher to leave a little more meat on the ribs because he's getting more per pound for ribs than for loin. Spare ribs, on the other hand, are taken from the belly. The belly fetches some of the highest prices on the pig. So it tempts butchers to leave as much on the belly as possible when removing it from the rib. And if they remove too much and cut too close to the bone to where you can see the bone on top, that's a shiner. Avoid them and look for meaty ribs.

It wasn't too long ago that baby back ribs blasted into the American consciousness, but even though most people are familiar with the term, they have no idea what it means. Baby backs come from the top of the rib cage. So, if you visualize the ribs of a pig being long and rounded (like us humans' ribs), you can imagine that the baby backs are taken from up near the spine, which is where they get their signature curve. They might just as easily be called back ribs; instead, they get their name not because they come from baby pigs, but because they are smaller than the spare ribs (the longer, bottom half of the rib cage). Attached to the loin, which is a lean cut of meat, baby backs are typically leaner than spares. But their meat is still juicier and fattier than the loin, which is one reason for their popularity. Another reason is a certain boppy commercial jingle for a national restaurant that never seemed to go away.

Baby backs are nice, but for the kind of smoking I do, I prefer spare ribs. Spare ribs—also spelled *spareribs*—come, as noted above, from the bottom of the rib cage. They're not called spare because they're thin or left over or not as good as strike ribs or kept in the trunk in case your main ribs get a flat. According to *Merriam-Webster*, the word *sparerib* is "from Low German *ribbesper*—pickled pork ribs roasted on a spit." More important, they're the opposite end of the rib cage from baby backs. That places them down at the belly, to which they're connected. (I shouldn't need to remind anyone of the glorious fattiness of the pork belly—just remember that that's where bacon comes from.) Spare ribs also connect to the breastbone. Usually coming thirteen to a rack, spare ribs are straighter, have more bone, and have more fat and connective tissue than the baby backs. It's that last reason that makes them particularly appealing for long, slow smoking. The meat is juicier and richer down on the belly, which translates to robust flavor and fall-away tender meat.

I use a bone-off spare ribs, which I'll explain more in the section about trimming ribs in the next chapter (see page 161). Put simply, the ribs are separated from the breastbone, and the rib tips are not cut off, giving the rack a vaguely rectangular shape with fairly even consistency, which makes the ribs good for cooking in large numbers every day, which we do, starting at 2 a.m.

How to Choose Spare Ribs

When buying pork spare ribs, I look for as much marbling as possible. Like briskets, the ribs may come prepackaged, but you can always get a good look at the meat, which should show lots of wispy threads of marbling throughout the pinkish red meat. You should be able to see the square ends of the bones, where they've been sawn from the baby backs on one side. The other side ends in soft cartilage where the breastbone was. Sometimes you'll see this section of the slab taken off in the "St. Louis cut." That section, composed of meat and cartilage and connective tissue, can be cooked up into rib tips, which make tasty little snacks. Or you can leave this delicious end on the rack itself, as I do, because it provides good eating and actually cooks better when it's part of the whole.

The Solution Problem

Most of the prepackaged ribs you'll find at the major store chains and in big grocery stores will have been what they call "enhanced." Always be suspicious of words like that, which are designed to make you think you're getting something better without telling you exactly what has been done to it. In this case, they're not trumpeting the word *enhanced* but rather printing it in very small letters, if at all. The enhancement in question is the common practice of big meat packers to inject solutions consisting mainly of water and salt into the pork and poultry they sell. Other components of the brine might include sodium phosphates and sugar. They might offer all sorts of reasons for this, but they all pretty much mean that it's an industrial solution to the industrial problem of mass-producing and mass-distributing pork. "Enhancement" adds artificial moisture to pork that's otherwise dried out, extends its shelf life, reduces the amount of liquid that seeps from meat that's been sitting around for a while, and, most insidiously, makes meat more profitable by adding weight to something you're buying by the pound. I never buy solution-injected products.

Now it can be tricky to identify these products, as that's exactly what packers don't want to happen. It's also possible that your local supermarket won't carry anything but solution-injected pork. Look for terms like *enhanced, improved, injected, marinated,* or *basted,* then, as with any food product, look at the list of ingredients. If it includes more than one thing, you're holding a piece of meat that's been "enhanced."

If you do find yourself unavoidably trapped into cooking with some of this stuff, be aware that it's going to have unnaturally large amounts of water already in it, making it more likely to steam than roast or fry. And also be careful about oversalting, as these cuts are basically prebrined. But my best advice is to find a meat market that will sell you pork that has not been messed with.

Breed

Breed has much more of an impact on pork than it does on beef, and you've probably heard a lot about heritage pork over the last few years. There are dozens of different heritage breeds available these days. As the term suggests, these were pigs raised in different places (and thus different conditions), but always outdoors. Heritage pork comes from farm animals who often forage and dig for their own food. Because they live outdoors, they exercise and develop a healthy layer of fat to combat the cold. In addition, their meat tends to be darker and more flavorful.

Heritage breeds were once the standard, but after World War II, things began to change. Consolidation and vertical integration led to more industrial pig farming, which also meant focusing on a few breeds designed to live indoors and on muscle rather than fat. As we all know, fat usually means flavor. Purveyors decided to develop a strategy to market pork as a health-conscious, lean alternative to poultry. Remember "the other white meat" days? Eventually people started to notice the declining genetic diversity in American pigs, and a movement began to popularize heritage breeds.

The pork ribs we use are from pigs of a hybrid heritage breed, a combination of the Chester White and Duroc breeds. The mix yields great marbling, tenderness, and juiciness—perfect for smoked ribs. Plenty of information about heritage breeds exists online, but my major recommendation is to look for ribs from heritage breeds. That's where you'll find that beautiful, richly colored, heavily marbled meat that is a bit more delicate but has so much flavor.

PORK BUTT

Pulled pork is something that you hardly ever used to find in Texas, but these days it is becoming more and more popular. Why? I'd hazard that Texans have traveled more and experienced the wonders of pulled pork from Tennessee and the Southeast, and they have been inspired. We've also had a lot of people move to Texas from other parts of the country, and they may have brought their pulled pork skills with them.

My inspiration came from a really good meal I had in Memphis once when I was on tour. I'd never had pulled pork before, and it really just struck me. In hindsight, maybe this place wasn't so great. I've been back several times since then and it didn't seem as good. But at the time it blew my mind. When we got back from the tour, I went right home and bought some pork butts to cook.

The pork butt is the most misleading of food names (along with Rocky Mountain oysters, headcheese, and geoduck). At least the *pork* part of the name is legit. It has nothing to do with the rear end of the pig and everything to do with the shoulder, which, in fact, it is.

A whole pork shoulder may come divided into two parts. These are the lower and the upper cuts, which are almost always divided. The top is known as the Boston butt or simply pork butt, while the lower is known as the picnic or the picnic ham. (Just to make matters even more confusing, picnic ham does not refer to the ham you know and love. That ham comes from the butt—well, the hind leg, or haunch, of the pig.) In pulled pork circles, there is always debate about whether the butt or the picnic makes for the better preparation. The pork butt, coming from higher up, has more connective tissue and less bone, thus is more tender and meaty. Some say the picnic is more flavorful, and it definitely has more bone and is prone to larger pockets of fat that won't dissolve with long cooking. I always use the pork butt.

Whichever cut you use, make sure to take the skin off, if that's how it's presented at the store. While pig skin is edible, it's tough as a football when barbecued and will absolutely block both smoke and rub from flavoring the meat. There will be a shoulder blade bone in the pork butt, which I advise leaving in. Taking it out can cause the meat to cook more unevenly, and it is much, much easier to remove when the meat's done cooking.

SAUSAGE

Sausage is a work in progress at Franklin Barbecue. Don't get me wrong: I love sausage and eat a sausage wrap practically every day. But a critic once dinged us (her only complaint) because we don't make our sausage in-house. Instead, we've had someone else make it for us to our recipe. There's a reason for this. Primarily, it's that sausage making is very labor-intensive, and we've had our hands full dealing with just the day-to-day running of an insanely busy restaurant. But making our own sausage in-house is something I've always planned on getting around to (in fact, I've been working on it while writing this book).

Sausage doesn't have the glamour that brisket and ribs do. But here in Central Texas, which was settled early on by German and Czech settlers with rich sausage-making traditions, it's taken very seriously. A lot of people really pride themselves on their sausage, and rightly so. I don't care how good your brisket and ribs are, when you nail sausage, it's a thing of beauty. But nailing it isn't easy, and that's why it's been an evolution here at Franklin. That said, I've done lots of research, and performed plenty of sausage-making experiments, so I can talk about it a little.

Generally speaking, sausage is an excellent and efficient product of whole-animal butchery—a way to use up the bits and scraps that wouldn't otherwise get cooked and served (I'm looking at you, intestines). In its purer forms, sausage is just meat and fat that is ground together, seasoned, and stuffed into casings. So why do people get so squeamish about it? Commercial sausage manufacturers—the ones who throw salivary glands, nostrils, and eyeballs into the mix—are the ones to blame. Buy a random hot dog or chorizo and who knows what's in it? But I digress.

At Franklin Barbecue we take a more old-school approach, which means we treat our sausage as an efficient use of all of our brisket and rib trimmings. We trim quite severely, and to toss that stuff in the trash is basically to throw money away, especially since we use Prime brisket and all-natural heritage pork. Even so, sausage making is a labor-intensive (and consequently costly) endeavor. The trimmings themselves have to be trimmed (separating the lean from the fat), then there's the tricky task (craft, really) of stuffing and tying off the individual sausages.

Coming up with a sausage recipe isn't terribly difficult—it's hard to get wrong, really—but variations in the meats you're working with can make following an exact recipe a difficult proposition. And because sausage is largely

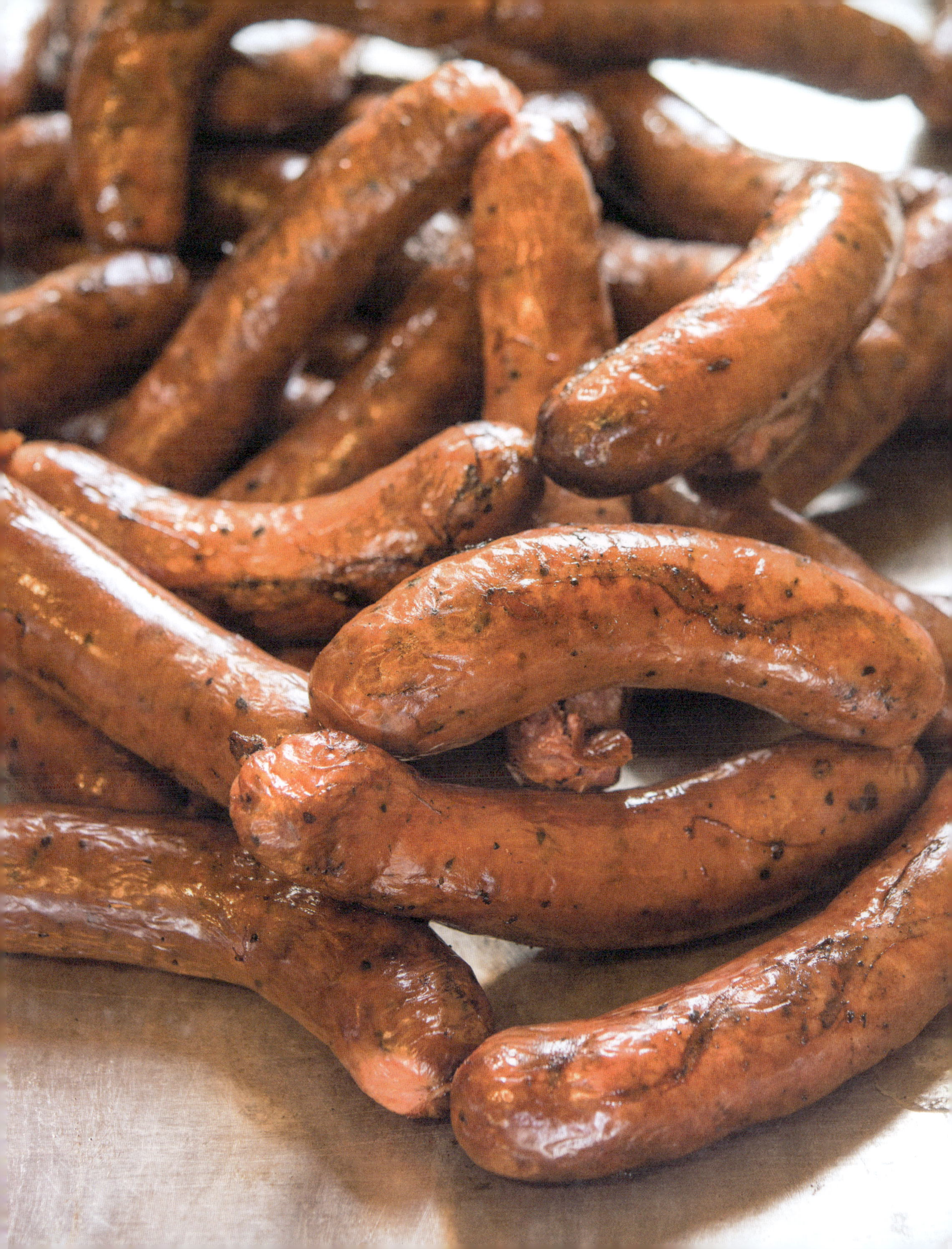

composed of scraps, what you have available to put in it might vary. Having a restaurant that produces a consistent volume of scrap meat makes it easier for me to have a consistent mix. But for home cooks, feel free to play around with your own mixtures and to discover what works best for you. The main things to remember are to include enough fat to ensure that the sausage is juicy inside and not to be bashful with seasonings, as you want the flavors to really pop.

Generally speaking, a good rule to follow for sausage is 70 percent lean, 30 percent fat. At Franklin we get there by mixing about 60 percent Prime-grade brisket, about 10 percent pork (mostly from the pork butt), about 27 percent raw brisket fat, and around 3 percent all-natural beef hearts for depth of meaty flavor. When coming up with your recipe, you must consider both the amount of fat you want to grind into your stuffing and the fat content of your meat. For instance, because we use Prime-grade brisket, I add less pure fat than someone who is using Select. Meat from a heritage pig like a Duroc or Berkshire is going to have more fat than meat from a conventional pig. It's something you have to judge for yourself.

Seasoning a sausage is a measure of balance. The spices are there to enhance the meat and the savory appeal of each bite. It's important not to overspice, as you don't want to drown out the flavor of the meat. When you're tweaking your recipe at home, season, then break off a small nub of the filling mixture, shape it into a patty, and grill it. Taste the cooked sample for seasoning and add more if you need to.

Sausage Casings

The biggest challenge when it comes to making sausage is finding the perfect casing. I'm a perfectionist, and perfect sausage is an elusive thing. A perfect sausage is one that's been cooked and looks smooth and glistening on the outside. When you bite into it, your teeth meet a little resistance before the casing breaks with a snappy pop and all that delicious flavor bursts onto your tongue. A great bite of sausage is a textural, flavor, and even aural experience.

How do you get the perfect casing? It's incredibly hard, because the casing is the one variable in sausage production that we at Franklin Barbecue don't have full control over. Casings, which are made from hog intestines, are never uniform and tend to have varying dimensions, textures, and lengths. (Note that you *can* buy synthetic sausage casings—they're more prevalent, actually—but I always say you should go for the real thing.)

We use a 30- to 32-millimeter-diameter casing made from pretty young hogs. For small batches, you can buy them packed in salt, then rehydrate and clean them in water to get the salt off. (When bought in bulk, sausage casings usually come in a bucket of solution.)

But the real issue is that all of the casings come from commodity pigs. It's seemingly impossible to get casings that are all natural, made from animals that were well treated and raised cleanly and sustainably. Here, we are filling the casings with all-natural pork, really high-grade beef, and all-natural beef hearts from ethically raised cows, and they could be coming from anywhere—China, Mexico—where we have no inkling of how they were produced. This means that we can't claim all-natural sausage, because we aren't at all sure. Almost all pork casings are supplied by DeWied, a big corporation that describes itself on its website as "one of the largest selectors of hog casings worldwide." That alone suggests that the casings can and probably do come from anywhere, and that DeWied does not have much control over the original animal. It's a problem for which I still don't have a solution.

TURKEY

Honestly, I don't have much to say on the subject of turkey. But I do have a recipe for smoked turkey breasts in this book, and chances are if you own a smoker, you'll cook a bird in it at some point in your life. So my advice is simple: don't buy turkeys that come prebrined or preinjected, because you'll have no control over the saltiness or moisture content of the meat (not to mention the random chemicals manufacturers might decide to squirt up in it). As I suggest earlier in this chapter with regard to pork, read the packaging or consult with your local meat purveyor to find unadulterated, natural, or organic birds if possible. Heritage breeds are cool, but they're usually very expensive and more unpredictable to cook than the conventional, untreated turkeys we cook here at the restaurant. They're delicious, however, and turkey on a smoker is always a good thing.

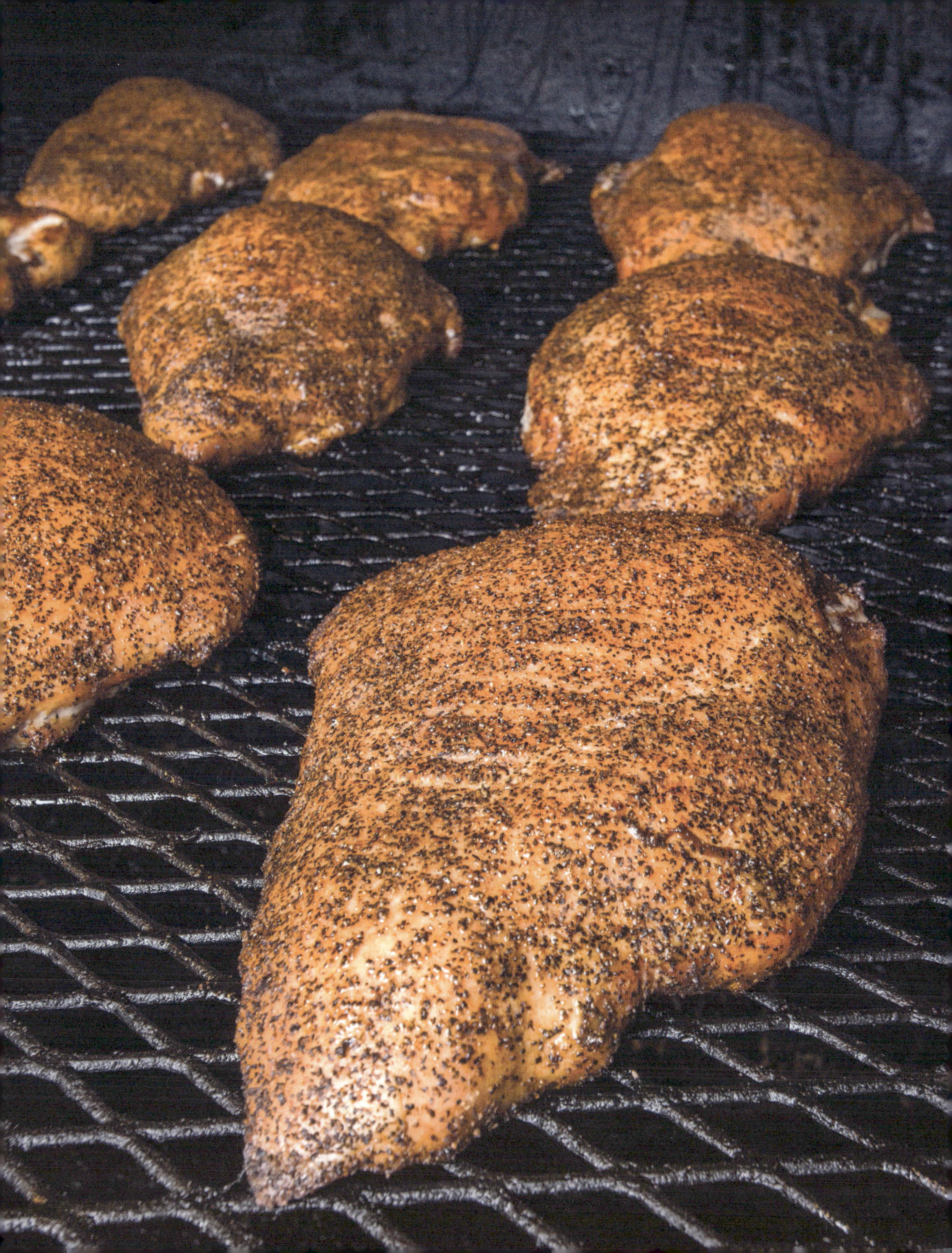

THE COOK

• **_Chapter Six_**

At long last, it's finally time to get cooking. You've gotten to know your smoker and you've sourced or seasoned the best wood you can possibly find. You've considered building and tending a fire, generating the good smoke that makes food tasty, and you went to the store and bought some nice meat, whose quality you can really stand behind.

Now it's time to put all of this information to use. Now it's time to put the meat in the cooker!

In this chapter, I'm going to walk you through four separate cooks: brisket, pork ribs, beef ribs, and turkey. You'll notice that the steps for each are quite similar—nearly identical, in fact. And now I've got a confession for you: almost everything we cook in the smoker is done in a comparable way. There's really no secret. Let your meat—whatever it is—smoke at a consistent temperature until it has absorbed enough smoke. Determine this by the color it has turned and by the quality of the bark that has formed on the outside. When it's reached this condition, wrap it and let it keep cooking. It's that simple.

You might balk when you see that there are only four recipes in this chapter. But I swear it's not because I'm being lazy, secretive, or anything like that. I don't include tons and tons of "recipes" here because at the end of the day, the method for smoking pretty much any meat is the same. I can give you rough guidelines for the time it takes to cook things, but, as always with barbecue, it's done when it's done. You can't rush it; you can't cut corners. The trickiest parts are knowing when to wrap and when something's done. Although I can do my best to describe how and under what conditions you should make these decisions, ultimately you just have to cook a few times and learn from your mistakes. So read through this chapter carefully, practice, and take note of what went right and what went wrong. In the end, you'll be able to cook incredible meat with great consistency in all conditions.

AN IMPORTANT BARBECUE FABLE

But before I send you off on your brisket- or rib-cooking way, I want to share one more story—an important one, I think, for anyone who is nervous about screwing up their first brisket cook. Let me preface this by saying that this story has a happy ending. It also touches on many of the topics I've discussed in the preceding chapters, making it a good summation leading into the all-important cook. And there's a moral at the end: even when everything is going against you, never quit and never stop trying!

Braun, our kitchen manager and one of our longest and most trusted pitmasters (and Stacy's cousin), and I were in New York to cook at a big event. There were bands, cooking demos, and renowned chefs from all over the country. This was going to be a big event, so we had to be on top of our game.

We showed up at noon the day before the event to meet the wood supplier, to receive our meat, and to see the cooker arrive. Turns out the cooker they had arranged for us was actually a grill—not gonna work. So I reached out to a buddy of mine on Long Island—we like to call him Long Island Phil—who found us an actual smoker so we could cook all of the meat.

The festival was on an island, so there we were, on the island, waiting for the trucks to bring our stuff. We're waiting and waiting, and they keep telling us the trucks are on their way with our stuff, so we stick around to receive the goods. Eventually the cooker arrives from Long Island Phil. It was a reverse-flow Lang; I think it was a dual 84, a huge cooker. Supposedly this thing was big enough to cook all of the meat they wanted us to prepare, but, alas, it was not. And it was reverse flow, which, you will recall, I do not like because it has this plate running through it to redirect the smoke and heat. It's also got more baffles and levers than I know what to do with.

It's a sunny day, just beautiful, except for the fact that our meat never shows up. We were expecting all of these great briskets to arrive and they do . . . super-duper late. Late and brisket is never a great combination. And then the firewood was supposed to be there. We were supposed to be getting oak that was not kiln dried, which was going to be a feat, because in New York it all has to be kiln dried. Supposedly we were getting some under-the-radar oak, more like what we were accustomed to using at home.

The meat finally shows up at about 7 p.m. We were supposed to start cooking at 6, because we had planned to cook them most of the way, go to bed, and finally finish them off in the morning. By the way, the festival organizers' initial emails said they were expecting us to feed thirty-five hundred people. That's so impossible, I don't even know what to say. But I promised to cook as much of the meat they gave us as I could.

So it's starting to get dark now, well past the time we wanted to begin our work. I'm wandering around looking for the hand-washing facilities (clean hands and sanitary conditions are of extreme importance to me). No luck. No water. No hand-washing facilities. And it turns out . . . no lights! The crew had turned off all the lights and left because no one was cooking overnight except for us and a couple of other guys. So our meat shows up late and by the time we start trimming, it was dark. We're trimming it as fast as we can by moonlight, just hacking the briskets up in the middle of a field in the dark on an island.

THE COOK

Finally at 10 p.m. our firewood shows up. And it's nothing like what we wanted. It is kiln dried, no life to it, and it's also not even close to the amount I'd asked for. It's going to burn fast, hot, and with absolutely no smoke at all. And that's to say nothing about the quantity. We have to do a 15-hour cook and then keep stuff warm. We're looking to burn this pit for 20 to 24 hours. And they bring us a single wheelbarrow full of wood.

So we finally start cooking 4 to 5 hours too late. I spent much of the night playing the part of the barbecue panhandler—calling everyone I knew, bugging them to please bring us more wood. We beg drinking water and even more wood from some other cooks who had turned up. Compared to us, they're like wealthy aristocrats. I remember one group shows up with ten or twelve people to cook a single pig. They have a huge cooler full of beer. They have cars because they live around here. Another team shows up with a car service—a driver in a black van just waiting around for them.

By about 3 a.m., more wood shows up. Braun's getting a little worried because we haven't opened up the lid once (trying to retain every degree of heat due to our limited wood supply). So we open up the lid, and these briskets look horrible. They're splotchy from weird airflow. They've got no color. They're yellowed, and their fat hasn't even started to render. They look as if we'd put them on an hour ago.

Then, of course, a huge storm blows through. Turns out there's a tornado warning; we get word that one has just touched down not far from us in Queens. When the lightning starts, we're standing in water up to our ankles, with water also submerging electrical outlets that are hooked up to a generator. I start thinking this will be the cook that breaks us.

As I stand in a puddle of water, I smell something distinctive that sets off an alarm in my head. "Oh, no," I yell. "Grease fire!"

This Lang cooker is not really meant for this kind of use because of that reverse-flow plate onto which our brisket fat, finally rendering, is dripping. I crack the lid and spy a little tiny flame about the size of a quarter on the plate over the firebox. It's not really much at all. But as soon as I open the lid, it becomes a scene from *Backdraft*. A sheet of fire erupts across the whole cooker. I try to shut the fire down by closing every vent and pipe on the cooker, but it doesn't work. So I just start pulling out briskets in the rain, throwing them to soaking-wet Braun who puts them down, steaming, on our little soaking-wet table. In the back of the cooker a couple of briskets have caught on fire.

Then my buddy and super chef Adam Perry Lang comes running over. Not actually running—I remember it being more like in the movie *Crouching Tiger, Hidden Dragon*: he came skipping over the tops of the tents like a ninja. He pulls this giant knife out of its sheath and uses it to stab and toss each burning brisket from the cooker. The grease fire is out of control now and flames are licking at his arms, which I'm trying to cover with wet towels as he heroically helps pull the briskets off.

Finally we get the last brisket out and shut the lid. The fire goes out. The briskets and the three of us are just sitting there in the rain, thinking about how awful things are. But we still have to serve these fatty, hard-as-a-rock, nowhere-near-done briskets . . . and now the whole place smells like burned arm hair.

We get the meat back on and the fire under control about 4 hours before service. Braun takes a piece of cardboard and goes and sleeps under a tree for about 30 minutes. Then it starts raining again. The only good thing is that it's wetting our balsa wood, which at least slowed down the burn rate and ironically may have helped us not run out.

We're pushing the briskets really hard, just trying to get them done. It's light outside, and I've cranked the cooker to push these briskets through. I can smell that they're cooking too fast, but I have no choice. At last, around 11 a.m., we get some color and wrap them. About a half hour before service, I pull off one brisket that feels about right. I set it on the table. About 20 minutes later I pull another three, then all of the briskets right before the gates are opened.

I unwrap the meat, which has just started to get tender. I can feel from the briskets' form that they just might be okay, despite coming off too soon and not having nearly enough rest time. I slice one end and show it to Braun, as a wave of irrepressible joy shoots through us—it's rendered, it's tender, it actually looks pretty good. There was maybe a bit of a crispy char on the bottoms, but it was definitely better than we ever could have hoped for. Then the gate opens and the hordes of people bum-rush from the gate directly to our tent. There are TV cameras, and they record a literal stampede heading toward the Franklin tent. For the next three hours, we have a long, snaking line to the counter until we run out of meat. Somehow we've pulled it off. Worst. Cook. Ever.

A moral of this incredibly long story of brisket woe? Is it that brisket is more forgiving than you think? Is it to plan even further in advance than you think is more than enough?

No. The moral of the story—and for every cook you ever do—is this: never give up.

Brisket can test you, but you just have to persevere. The other moral is that there are many paths to cooking a good brisket. Things can go wrong—hopelessly, horribly wrong—but at the end of the day, there are multiple ways to pull it together. Also, have a portable espresso maker, which, luckily, I did.

GETTING READY FOR THE ACTUAL COOK

It seems somewhat artificial to divide the book into all of these chapters, as I have, since smoking meat is in many ways inseparable from choosing wood and tending a fire. People ask me what the secret to my success with brisket is, and I always tell them the same thing: attention to detail. In this case, attention to detail means sweating the little things that others may not even notice. It means being vigilant and present throughout a cook that can last 10 to 15 hours or longer. It means paying individual attention to each piece of meat you're cooking and giving it the specific care that it needs.

So on the one hand, barbecue appears relaxing and simple—the kind of cooking that allows you to pull up a lawn chair and prop your feet on your cooler full of beer and settle in for a long, easygoing afternoon. On the other hand, you have to pay regular, if not constant, attention to the fire and to your temperature gauges. So, I guess you could call the required state of the pitmaster a stance of relaxed focus. Enjoy your beers, but don't have so many that your concentration lapses.

SAFETY CONCERNS

I'm a real stickler when it comes to food safety, not only at the restaurant but also wherever it is that I'm cooking. Of course, at the restaurant, one mistake on this front could mean the end of everything we've worked so hard to build. So we don't mess around or cut corners. But at home too, it's just as vital. The last thing you want is anyone getting sick or worse because you were simply lazy about the handling of meats.

Here, I won't go into the science of meat safety. Instead, I'd recommend you go over the information offered at www.foodsafety.gov, which includes a thorough discussion of grilling and barbecuing safety issues. The most common and serious issue is cross contamination, which is what happens when germs from raw meats or tainted items spread to foods that are ready-to-eat. Proper cooking will kill dangerous microbes, but carelessness can allow them to spread onto foods that we're going to put directly into our bodies.

The number one thing you can do to prevent cross contamination is to wash your hands. A lot. When I work a shift, I probably wash my hands twenty-five times or more. And this is thorough washing: with soap under a full stream of warm water for at least twenty seconds. We also put on sterile, disposable, nitrile food-service gloves every time we handle meat (I don't like vinyl). We keep boxes of these in the kitchen and a box at every smoker. Before I open the smoker and handle the meat, I always put on a new sterile glove. This is as ingrained a habit as throwing another piece of wood on the fire.

At home, wearing sterile gloves may seem a bit excessive to you. At the very least you need to train yourself to handle raw meats with only one hand. Your clean hand holds the knife when trimming and holds the shaker when applying rub. It never touches the meat. Your gloved hand flips the meats and turns them as needed. That way you'll never get the knife handle or the spice shaker dirty. And then, of course, wash your hands every time you handle raw meat.

We also thoroughly wash down every knife and cutting board we use to trim and rub the meats, as cutting boards are one of the prime culprits when contamination breaks out. In food safety courses, you're instructed to keep cold foods cold and hot foods hot. We follow that to the letter, never letting cold meats warm up until they're about to be cooked. And after they've been cooked, we hold them at 140°F until they're going to be served.

Lastly, there's one other safety issue I care deeply about: the pitmaster's. If you work around smoke as often as I do, you are going to be smelling a lot of smoke. If you're smelling it, you're inhaling it on some level. So, it's of prime importance to minimize smoke inhalation as much as possible. For me, this means turning my head and holding my breath every time I have to go into a cooker. This is not hard to do, since all you get when you open a smoker is a big face full of smoke anyway, but think about it every time you open the chamber door and consciously try to form this good habit.

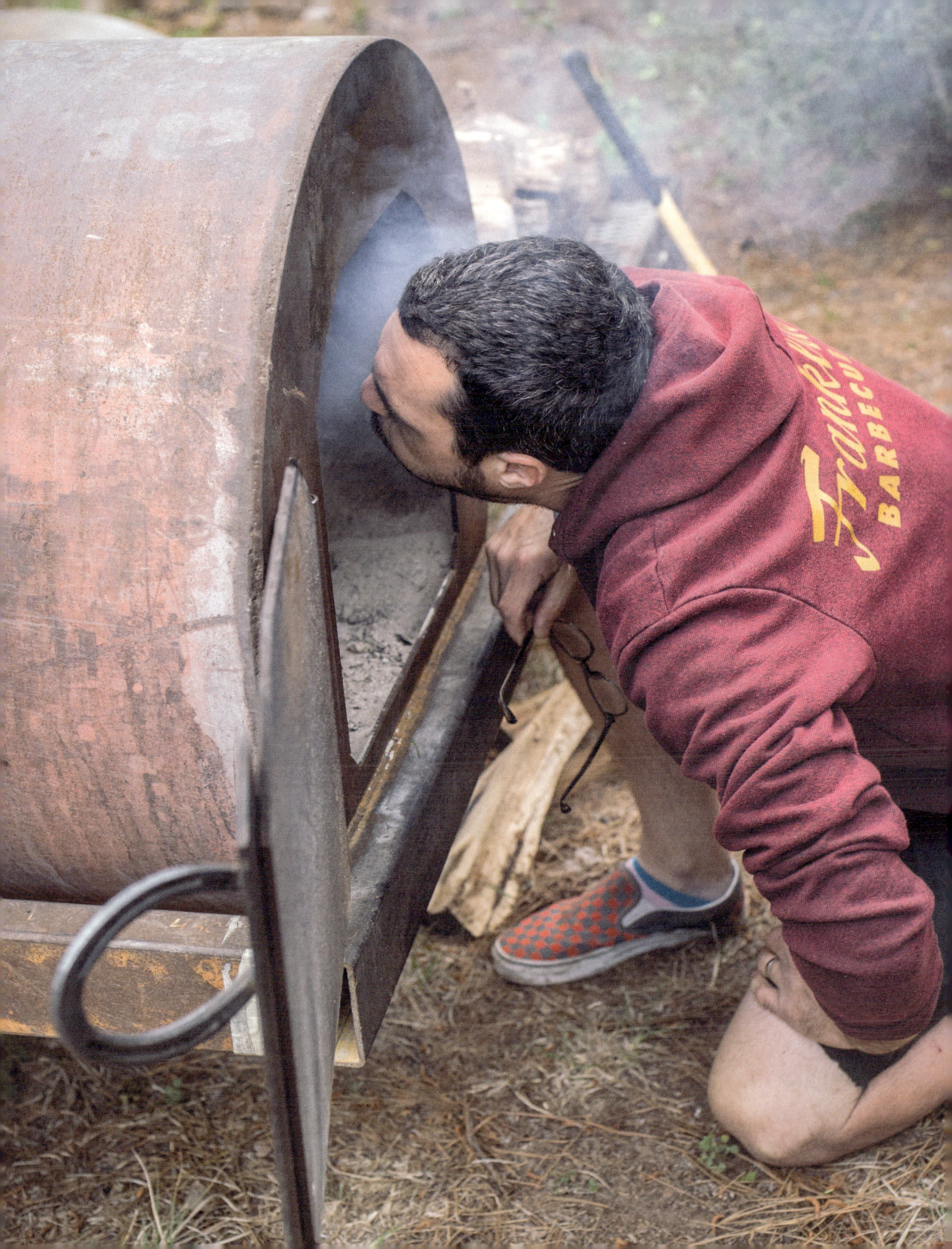

THE COOK

And while the cooking itself is easy, there are several steps along the way that need to be done right. Now, these are steps that all good pitmasters will take, but I have particular methods that I follow every time I cook and that I teach to all of the people who come and work at Franklin Barbecue. On pages 147 to 158, I share precisely how I do it, but you are more than welcome to come up with your own methods too. There are many ways to get to the same, delicious end, but as I said, you've got to have a way and follow it precisely each time.

PRINCIPLES OF SMOKING MEAT

The art of long-smoking meat is about cooking it to an extreme form of tenderness while capturing smoke for flavor. To that end, we want to expose the meat to a constant supply of fresh, good smoke and also keep it at a consistent temperature that will allow it to cook slowly, gradually, without drying out. At the same time we want to generate a flavorful crust or "bark," which is the result of regulating the surface temperature and texture of the meat to facilitate smoke adhesion. Luckily, in a properly controlled cooking environment, all of these processes happen in a well-choreographed procession.

As always, I believe a rudimentary understanding of what's actually happening is a key to success. The more you understand *why* a brisket cooks the way it does, the better you'll be able to control the finished product.

Many of our favorite meats are in fact muscles, which are in turn made up of bundles of fibers that are interwoven with thin wrappers of connective tissue. This connective tissue is largely composed of collagen, a very tough substance. The toughness of muscles is determined by the woven fabric of muscle fiber and collagen. Muscles like brisket, pork shoulder, and ribs have plenty of collagen, making them ornery and tough.

Lucky for us, collagen can be broken down into gelatin, that soft and silky substance that makes sauces thick and glossy. In its melted form, gelatin provides the meat with texture and richness. Our goal, then, is to break down that collagen into supple goodness, which will render the meat tender and flavorful. But the fascinating thing about collagen is that it requires specific conditions to break down in the way we want it to.

At the most basic level, all you need to break down collagen is heat and water, a process called hydrolysis. There's ample water in the meat to fuel this reaction. We supply the heat, which starts to be adequate when the internal temperature of the meat gets above 122°F and happens faster as the temperature increases. The more collagen, the longer a piece of muscle takes to break down (which is why a finer-grained piece of meat is more tender). So that's great, you think to yourself, but then what's the deal with all this "low and slow" stuff? Why not just cook things faster and avoid all of this endless fire tending? That's because of a confounding trait in collagen's nature. Push temperature too hard, and it doesn't break down well. The action is sort of like one of those Chinese finger prisons. You stick a finger from each hand into either end. The faster you try to pull your fingers out, the more it contracts and binds them. Only the very slow and relaxed withdrawal of your fingers allows them to escape the prison. Collagen, when heated quickly, begins to shrink. Just like squeezing out a washcloth, the shrinking of this connective tissue squeezes the moisture right out of the muscle fibers, causing them to be tough and dry. (And if you heat things up *way* too much, all of the moisture will evaporate and hydrolysis will not occur, leaving behind solid collagen and an unfortunate mess of dried-out, chewy muscle fibers—no good.)

This is why even meat submerged in liquid (that is, a braise or stew) can be dry and tough if heated too high and too quickly. But at long, slow cooking temperatures, the collagen slowly melts away, and the fibers of the meat just fall apart. What about all of the moisture that we've lost, you ask? Well, even though the long cooking and shrinking of the collagen has caused the meat to lose water, there is ample gelatin and melted fat to lubricate the meat and make it succulent.

Fat is also important. As Harold McGee explains, "Fat contributes to the apparent tenderness of meat in three ways: fat cells interrupt and weaken the sheet of connective tissue and the mass of muscle fibers; fat melts when heated rather than drying out and stiffening as the fibers do; and it lubricates the tissue, helping to separate fiber from fiber."

Fat is also richness. Fat starts to melt early on in the cooking process, well before the collagen breaks down. Because it's right there, interwoven between strands of collagen and muscle fiber, it brings moistness and a glossy richness, basically basting the meat internally. A good amount of intramuscular fat aids the cooking process immensely, another great argument for using Prime- or Choice-grade beef.

Furthermore, fat contributes flavor. "Meat flavor," McGee writes, "has two aspects: what might be called generic meatiness, and the special aromas that characterize meats from different animals. Meatiness is largely provided by the muscle fibers, character aromas by the fat tissue."

Meanwhile, Back on the Surface . . .

Now that we have a picture of the internal transformations of the meat, let's briefly talk about what's happening outside. Over the course of the time the meat is in the cooker, its color will evolve from a rosy pink to a crusty golden brown to almost black (in the case of brisket), if you do it right. And while it might initially appear burned, this crust, which is called the bark, is not overcooked at all. Rather, it's deeply, deeply smoked and caramelized.

Two different things are occurring on the surface of the meat. One is that the meat is browning due to classic browning reactions, in particular the very famous (at least in cooking circles) Maillard reaction. My barbecue science friends at Texas A&M describe the Maillard reaction as "when the amino acids in foods react with reducing sugars to form the charactcristic brown cooked color of foods." But we laypeople know it as the sweet, irresistible flavors that come from searing steak in a pan, toasting bread in the oven, roasting coffee, or, yes, cooking brisket in a smoker.

But the Maillard reaction flavors are subtle, and of course with brisket we get a great deal of flavor from the smoke (not to mention the rub). For this reason, one of the pitmaster's primary tasks is to expose the meat to smoke and maintain the meat's ability to capture smoke for as long as necessary. This may seem simple: *Just leave the meat on the grate and keep the smoke going, right?* Well, not exactly. If you want the smoke to both adhere to the surface *and* deeply penetrate the meat, the conditions have to be just right.

Smoke is composed of many—as in, hundreds—of chemical compounds, some liquid, some gaseous. As *Modernist Cuisine* describes, "Capturing the flavor of smoke . . . involves two challenges. The first is making sure the flavor compounds you want are gases, not liquid droplets, when they reach the food. That requires keeping tight control of the temperature of the smoke in the chamber. The second challenge is keeping the food just wet enough to allow the volatile organics in those vapors to stick to the food, form a film on the surface, and then diffuse deep inside." In other words, we need to keep the temperature of the cook chamber *just so*, to maximize the amount of gas particles in the smoke. But at the same time, we have to make sure that we don't get things too hot, lest the surface of the meat dry out and the smoke's gas particles have nothing to adhere to. It's a delicate dance.

To achieve the proper bark, we need to have a humid atmosphere inside the smoker. A humid environment both encourages the penetration of smoke and slows the drying of the exterior of the meat, allowing it to smoke for longer. As the meat's exterior dries out, it becomes harder and harder for the smoke to penetrate. Yet it's also difficult for smoke to adhere to the dried crust. That's why it's crucial to keep a water pan in the smoker at all times, which ensures ambient humidity thanks to the slow evaporation of the water.

I also directly moisten the surface of the meat further into the cooking process, using a spray bottle filled with practically anything wet. Common liquids sprayed onto meats are water, vinegar, and apple juice. But it could be wine, marinade, anything. I often spray the surface of the meats in the last half hour to hour before they get wrapped. Your goal is to keep the surface of the meat from getting hard and dried, but you don't want it to be wet either. The surface needs to have a tacky, glistening sheen. That's when you know you've gotten it right.

At a certain point, the meat will have absorbed enough smoke. You'll know when this is happening by looking at the darkness of the bark. I provide color cues for each of the different meats featured later in this chapter (brisket, ribs, turkey), and as with everything else, you'll get better at figuring out the ideal smoke saturation point the more you practice. If you're unsure about the color, you should observe the drying rate: eventually it will become harder and harder to keep the meat moist, even as you spray it. That's when it's time to wrap.

THE BASIC STEPS FOR SMOKING MEAT—ANY MEAT

Before we dive into the recipes themselves I want to explain the fundamental steps of pretty much any and every cook. When I talk about "attention to detail," in many ways, these are the details I'm talking about: how you apply the rub, when you wrap, whether or not you recognize and account for the stall, if and how you maintain the temperature of the cook chamber. These are the elements that are at the heart of all barbecue—and how well you master each technique will decide whether your finished product is pretty good or great.

The Rub

The spice mixtures called rubs are important to barbecue for two reasons. One, they help meat taste and look delicious and they're crucial to the formation of a tasty, crusty bark. Two, they help meat attract and adhere smoke, because smoke is attracted to tacky, uneven surfaces, and rubs typically contain salt, which draws moisture to the surface.

Aside from the presence of salt, what exactly is in the rub is of debatable importance. Although people niggle about their rubs and guard their secret spice mixtures with the zeal of a Colonel Sanders or Coca-Cola, the role of a rub in smoke attraction and bark formation is arguably more important than its composition. Ultimately, the flavor the rub contributes is subtle when compared to all of the other flavors contained in meat and smoke. So, by all means, get a good rub recipe. But even better, come up with a spice mixture that works for you.

Here in Central Texas, the standard issue for German- or Czech-style barbecue is just salt and pepper. On this point, I agree with tradition wholeheartedly! A mixture of salt and pepper is by far the simplest and most magnificent seasoning; it complements the natural flavors of any nice piece of meat. But sometimes you're in the mood for a little something extra. And that's good too. One great thing about Franklin Barbecue is that we haven't been around for a hundred years. We've got no tradition to uphold! No family recipes to stick to for fear of insulting centuries of ancestors. The only thing we've got is the dedication to make the best food we can make and to keep it consistently the same every day (which itself is the biggest challenge). It's that dedication that keeps us evolving as cooks and constantly thinking about new ways to do old things. With a solid foundation of traditional Central Texas barbecue and a desire to keep everything as pure and simple as it should be, we're left with a lot of room to refine our technique and experiment with the five meats we cook every day.

As you build a rub, first think about what it is you are cooking. How do you want it to taste? How long is it going to cook? How big is it? How hot will you cook it? All of these questions play into how I go about making a rub.

Take a brisket, for example: It is large and will take a long time. It will need a good natural bark and will take a lot of flavor from the wood. For that, I like a lot of black pepper. It melts into fat nicely. It provides a coarse surface to promote smoke adhesion and, in my opinion, should be the dominant ingredient for a brisket rub. Next is the salt. Brisket is a huge hunk of meat, so I think it needs a good bit of salt. Since I use good-quality beef, the beef's natural flavors make me want to build a rub that is as transparent as possible, with nothing to conflict with the smoke and confuse the palate. So salt and pepper it is!

That's not to say that playing with seasoning salts, garlic powder, onion powder, or any of the hundreds of other spices and seasonings that are available at most grocery stores would be wrong. I'm just saying that you don't have to have a complicated rub to make great barbecue . . . but sometimes it's fun to add something special.

What follows is a short list of common rub ingredients and some notes on each, where applicable. There are far too many possible ingredients to list, and since each one opens a door to another, I'm just digging in to the more common elements of a basic rub.

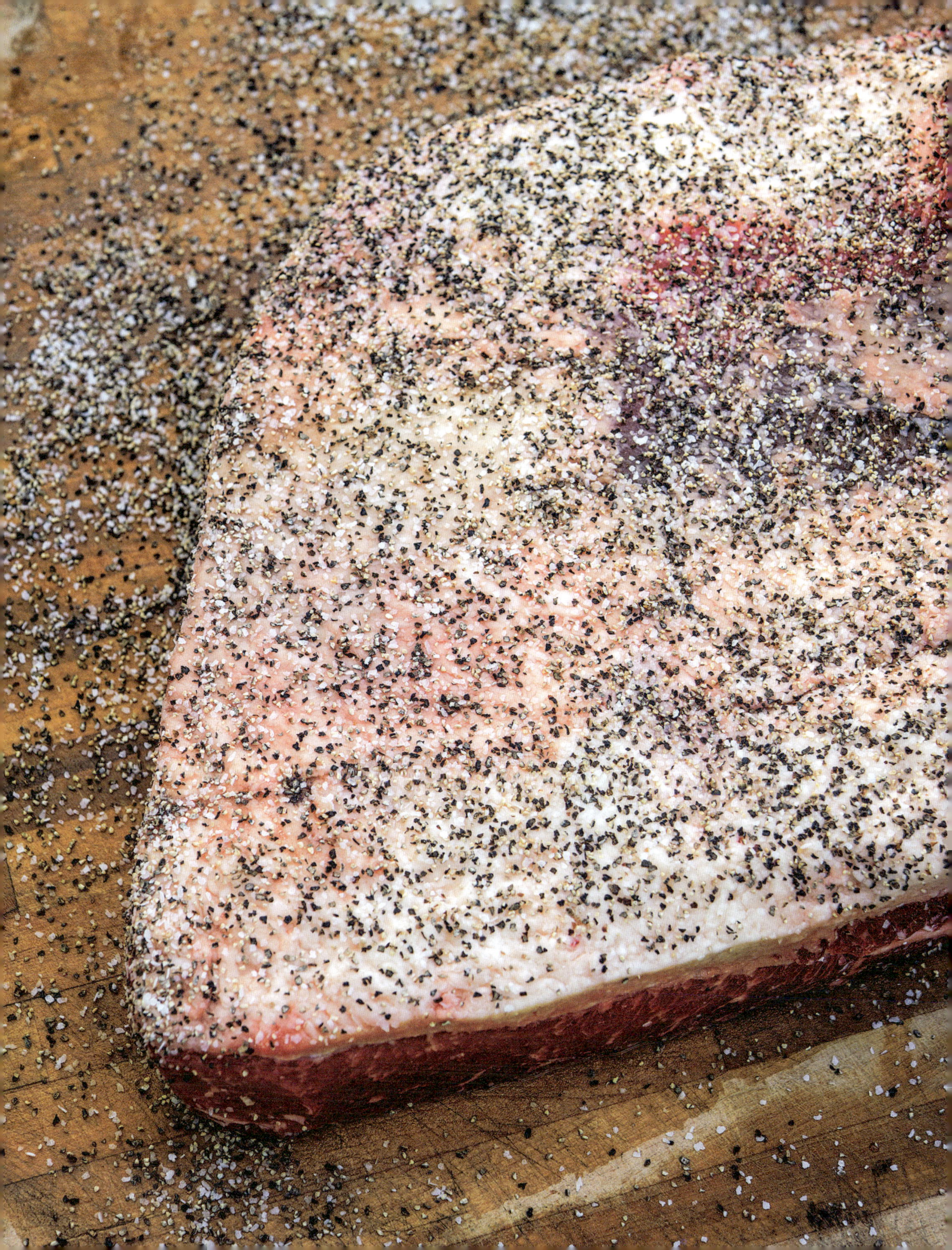

Standard Rub Ingredients

Salt • I use only Morton brand kosher salt. I like it because all the granules are consistently the same size. The thicker the meat, the more salt you'll use. The amount you'll use will always depend on the size of the brisket, so when it comes to quantity, you should trust your instincts. I use roughly 1/4 cup (which is about 2 ounces with Morton brand) per brisket.

Black pepper • I like 16 mesh. The mesh number refers to the size of the pepper particles. The pepper has been sifted through a screen that has 1/16 by 1/16-inch openings. It ends up being the right size to mix with its companion, kosher salt. Really coarse pepper would be 10 mesh, where as the finer stuff is more like 20 or 30 mesh. Most people prefer a fresh grind, but I like pepper that's been ground for at least a few days. I want a lot of pepper for texture and appearance, so the fresh stuff is just too strong. The toned-down older version works best for me. (I'm not talking about going into your mother's spice cabinet and pulling out pepper from the 1970s. But I do like it to have been ground for a few days to a few weeks.)

Seasoning salt • There are many seasoning salts available, and they are typically comprised of all of the usual suspects: salt, sugar, onion, and garlic for flavor and paprika and turmeric mostly for color. You should expect to find countless assortments of ingredients that someone, somewhere thought tasted good on something. Seasoning salt is an easy way to add complex flavors to a rub without having dozens of spices sitting around. Even though I don't think sugar should be involved in a long cook (see "Sugars," right), very small amounts contained in the finished rub don't seem to have an adverse effect on bark formation.

Granulated garlic and granulated onion • Both of these are great! Try to use granulated garlic and granulated onion instead of powdered, as the granulated stuff is close in size to the kosher salt and your 16-mesh black pepper, so texturally it just mixes and disperses much better than a fine powder. Do not try to get fancy and use fresh ingredients. Fresh aromatics don't work for rubs; they're too strong and will completely dominate the meat and they will burn.

Paprika • Big fan! Paprika is made from ground dried chile. It can come from many different countries and in various varieties, such as smoked, sweet, and hot. I like plain ole Hungarian paprika, just to keep it simple. If you cannot find it at your local grocery store, check for it at a gourmet grocery. The more common and cheaper Mexican variety is great for adding color but doesn't add much flavor. The Hungarian is a nice dark red and has a complex flavor that is mild and savory.

Chile powders • Many ground dried chiles don't end up under the paprika header, and since Texas is so far south, most of the chile powders I use are from Mexican peppers. I don't use them in rubs at the restaurant, but they certainly lend a wonderfully "Texasy" flavor to meat if I'm playing around or cooking something for friends. The generic type of chili powder will have a Texas-chili kind of taste and won't specify which chiles are used to make it, but others can be chile specific. Some of my favorites are made from dried poblanos (ancho powder) smoke-dried jalapeños (chipotle powder), or dried cayennes (cayenne pepper).

Sugars • Almost every commercial rub has a high level of sugar. I like sweets plenty, but not on my barbecue. There, I've said it. Sugary rubs burn and turn bitter when exposed to high heat for too long and are a way to cheat the acquisition of bark over a long cook. There are many sugars to choose from, some more processed than others. Use them *all* with caution.

Other (More Questionable) Rub Ingredients

Hickory or mesquite flavor • I use real fire to get my smoke and wood notes, so these seem silly to me.

Beef or chicken flavoring • Useful only if you're seeking a high concentration of flavor. Seems like a cheat to me, but I suppose it could help you get an edge in a competition. I'd much rather use flavorful, high-quality meat than some sort of processed flavoring, however.

Worcestershire powder and soy powder • These are good if you want to bolster the umami quotient, the so-called fifth taste, which is best defined as a sense of savory deliciousness. Umami is said to be caused by glutamic acid and is typically in fermented and aged proteins. Its most common application has been in MSG. Yes, soy and Worcestershire taste good, but many commercial rubs just use MSG for that type of flavor enhancement.

Building the Rub

Every rub I make starts with a base of salt and pepper. Then I add other spices to complement the meat that I am cooking. The goal of any rub is to complement a nice piece of meat, not to obscure a crappy piece of meat. All spices should react well with one another. No one spice should stand out or be too recognizable, so add just enough to taste. It would be a shame to buy a nice piece of meat, spend a ton of time prepping and cooking it, and have it taste like an overzealous mixture of flavors. Restraint is the name of the game when using seasonings other than just salt and pepper.

RUB RECIPES

Brisket and Beef Rib Rub

INGREDIENTS Equal parts 16-mesh ground black pepper and kosher salt.

QUANTITY A rough guideline is that you'll need about ½ cup (4 ounces) of rub, total, for each 12-pound brisket. A 3- to 5-pound rack of beef ribs will require just a bit less rub, maybe ⅓ to ½ cup, total.

Pork Rib and Turkey Rub

INGREDIENTS 2 parts 16-mesh ground black pepper and 1 part kosher salt.

QUANTITY A rough guideline is that you'll need about ¼ cup (2 ounces) rub, total, for each rack of ribs or turkey breast.

Optional Add-ons

GRANULATED GARLIC

GRANULATED ONION

PAPRIKA Add for color and savory aspect.

SEASONING SALT However much you add, subtract the same amount of salt from your rub.

I mix my salt and pepper in a large 16-ounce shaker, which is actually a spice container from a restaurant supply store. It's got a top with three openings: one large opening with a sliding lid for pouring and two sets of different-size circular holes for sprinkling. This is the vessel I use to apply the rub. I start by pouring one layer atop the other as a form of measurement, using my eyes to ensure that the thickness of the layers is equal to the proportions I want. Then I shake them all up until thoroughly mixed. (Remember to close off the lid.)

Applying the Rub

Always apply the rub to meat about 1 hour before cooking and let the meat warm up to room temperature. That will let the seasoning "sweat" into the meat, and the warmer meat will shave off hours of cook time.

The following directions might seem trivial. But again, the devil is in the details. And I'm not joking when I say that every new kitchen employee at Franklin Barbecue gets a lesson in how to properly apply the rub. The goal is to get it evenly distributed with the right concentration over the entire surface of the meat. If you apply the rub more densely or more sparsely in certain areas, patches of the meat will cook unevenly, yielding splotchiness, dry patches, and general mayhem over the course of a multihour cook.

To apply the rub evenly, you've got to keep things loose—in the elbow, in the wrist, and in

THE COOK

the mind, with a relaxed but focused attitude. First, keep the shaker about a foot or two over the surface of the meat, or however high you feel comfortable. (Of course if you're aiming for a specific spot, you can bring the shaker down lower.) Sprinkling it from a height allows it to spread out and apply more evenly than if you're trying to direct it from up close.

Once you start sprinkling the rub, you've got to keep the shaker moving. This is accomplished with two separate but related gestures. With the elbow and forearm, gently get the shaker moving in small circles to get the rub flowing out of it. At the same time, allow the wrist to swivel a bit to keep the granules inside jumping around. Being heavier than pepper, salt tends to quickly congregate at the bottom of the shaker, making for an uneven mix if you don't properly jumble it all up.

Slathers

Slathers are a liquid or paste applied to the meat before the rub goes on. They act as a kind of glue to help rubs stick to the meat and can be anything from yellow mustard to hot sauce to plain ole water. Slathers are also a neat way to sneak in very subtle flavors and can be quite useful in some situations. Things to remember when using a slather:

- Due to the solubility of certain types of smoke, I prefer to use a water-based rather than an oil-based slather.
- Keep a very low sugar content. Too much sugar will harden and can seal off the surface of the meat, inhibiting flavor penetration.
- Apply a very conservative amount, just enough to create a tacky environment for rub and smoke adhesion. Too much and you run the risk of building an impermeable barrier between the meat and the pending flavors. Too heavy a slather can also give you a premature crust that has the potential for flaking off, taking most of the smoke and seasonings with it.

Wrapping

Most of what I cook gets wrapped at some point in the cooking process. Ribs and pork butts get wrapped in foil; brisket gets wrapped in butcher paper.

Wrapping a brisket in foil has been derisively referred to as "the Texas crutch," because it helps a long-cooked brisket turn out better and keep from drying out in the last stage of cooking. Strangely, in the serious barbecue community it's looked down upon almost as cheating, despite the fact that it helps many people make better brisket than they would otherwise. Even some pros use it on a regular basis, so I don't exactly see the evil in it.

The idea is that at a certain point, the meat has absorbed all of the smoke it's going to or all of the smoke it needs, but it's not yet done cooking. This is the moment when I wrap. The meat then continues cooking in a sealed environment until it's done internally. Technically, at this point you could remove the meat from the smoker and continue cooking it in a conventional gas or electric oven, but we just throw it back on the smoker, which is already at the proper temperature. (We don't have oven space for sixty briskets anyway—that's cheating!)

How do you know when to wrap? I judge by color. The meat's already to temperature. It's looking fine; I just want to make sure that I get a really dark color on there. Some of the color will actually wash off as the meat steams in its wrapper, which is why you want to make sure that you have a good, authentic dark color before you wrap. Toward the end of the smoking process—particularly if you're using fairly dirty smoke—it's possible that you're just layering ashy smoke on the outside, so I hit brisket and ribs with a spray of water to gauge the true color of the meat or bark. If the color washes off easily, I'll give the meat more time in the smoke. If it seems dark enough, I'll wrap immediately.

Early on in my career, I found that I liked the way a brisket cooked in butcher paper better than in foil. Whereas foil creates a fairly hermetic pocket, the butcher paper still allows a bit of interchange with the outside environment. Because of this breathing, using butcher paper is a blend of using foil and not wrapping at all, a happy compromise that works really well for me.

There's a time and a place for foil, however. If you have to cook something that's really lean or you need to speed something up, use foil with caution. It's a trick to have up your sleeve. I might wrap a brisket in foil if it's an especially lean one. A lesser grade with little marbling needs every bit of its moisture conserved, so I'd wrap that in foil and probably wrap it quite early. For richer cuts, it's not as important to seal it up as soon, as they have ample moisture, thanks to all of the intramuscular fat of the marbling.

THE COOK

Maintaining Temperature

If I have a favorite temperature—other than 98.6°F and 75°F and sunny—it's got to be 275°F. This is my reference point, my safe place, when it comes to the ideal temperature for a cook.

Now I've said in several places in this book that the pitmaster needs to be flexible, read each situation, and adapt depending on the circumstances. That said, if I'm using equipment other than my own (which I feel very comfortable with), I'll always try to get the temperature of the cook chamber (at grill level, remember—where the meat is actually sitting) to 275°F. It's my default, and you can cook just about everything, from brisket and ribs to sausage and turkey, at this temperature. It's basically right in the middle—not super low, not too high. Some people are more comfortable cooking brisket *really* low and slow, which is around 225°F. But it's not just that that's a little too slow for me (which it is). Keeping things at 275°F is ideal because it allows

COOKING IN WEATHER

One thing that professional pitmasters and home cooks have in common is that at some point or another, we all have to cook in crappy weather. If you're working at a restaurant, you can't just close down because it looks like rain. And if you've planned a backyard fiesta for weeks and guests are showing up at 3 p.m. no matter what, you can't *not* cook because a cold front blows through.

Every kind of atmospheric condition requires its own set of responses, though no matter what you're doing, you're trying to counter factors you can't control. There are no easy answers, but here are a few things I've found.

High wind High wind can wreak havoc with fires and airflow. Although it's good to keep your firebox door open as much as possible, when it's windy, especially if the wind is blowing into your fire, you've got to close the door to shield the fire. Position your cooker so that the firebox door faces away from a prevailing wind that will whip the fire and stoke things up too wildly. In the case of crosswinds, try pushing your fire up in the box, away from the door.

Rain Nothing is worse than cooking in the rain. Both you and your cooker will inevitably be miserable for having to get soaked while trying to keep your temperatures up. Just make sure to keep your wood dry (cover it with a tarp or move it under shelter) and push through it.

Cold Wood selection changes for different weather. I'll be sure to use drier wood that burns hotter on cold days. I'll also probably cook a little hotter than usual to compensate for the low ambient temperature outside. I'll rake the coal bed too, so that it's a little longer than normal and goes all the way to the firebox door. That way, the air crossing it gets preheated before it hits the fire.

Heat You have to be careful on really hot days not to let your temperatures get away from you. I might cook lower—at, say, 265°F instead of 275°F—knowing that the smoker is not fighting the ambient temperature outside.

brisket to form a good bark while still rendering properly on the inside.

This is yet another reason why when I'm on the road, I always take my handy ThermoWorks probe with me. I'll take an onion or a potato, cut it in half, and turn it into a little stand for the thermometer, which I then prop in the cooker because I don't trust other people's gauges. I even take four Tel-Tru temperature gauges in my travel kit and have been known to unscrew the existing thermometers and substitute these just to get a better sense of the hot and cool spots along the cook surface.

Sometimes I might go up from 275°F but not usually higher than 315°F or so. I know people who start it on 350°F and then slow it down as the cook moves along. I don't agree with that. I find it impractical and risky to pull temperatures back if things start cooking too fast. I'd much rather nudge it forward with gradual temperature increases until I find just the right place. Too hot is more dangerous than too low. You can always cook something longer, but you can't unburn it. Also, the slow progression upward along the temperature scale, I believe, allows me to get the depth of flavor and layers of smoke that I'm looking for. Balance is key. At the end of the day, yes, it should taste like smoke and salt and pepper. But you also want to taste the flavor of the beef. And 275°F is the safest way to get there.

Now, to be clear, 275°F is not the word of God for the temperature for brisket, because every brisket is different. If you showed up at Franklin Barbecue on any given day and took the temperature of our smokers at grill level, odds are you'd get a reading of 285°F. But that's on our cookers, cookers we know well, so we can afford to go a bit hotter and faster. Every cooker is different. Every brisket is different. With briskets containing more marbling, you can cook at a lower temperature and still get the rendering you need. But if it's a low-grade, commodity brisket with a lot of hard, waxy fat, you're going to want to cook higher to break that stuff down. The big takeaway? A temp of 275°F is always a good place to start; just pay attention and go up or down as needed.

THE WATER PAN

Always cook with a water pan. If you don't, you'll dry out the meat and it won't cook at a proper rate. You need a very humid environment, as it slows down the rate of moisture evaporation, collagen breakdown, and fat melt so that they all happen in concert. The slower rate of cooking also allows the interior of the meat to keep pace with the cooking of the exterior. Finally, the humid environment helps preserve the moist, tacky surface of the meat, which is desirable to attract smoke.

The Stall

I often get emails that all say the same thing: "I cooked a brisket, and it looked great and tasted great, but it was tough. What did I do wrong?" Inevitably, I'll write back, "Let me guess the temperature you pulled it off at. Was it in the 160°F to 165°F range? You pulled it off during the stall!"

THE COOK

THE STALL

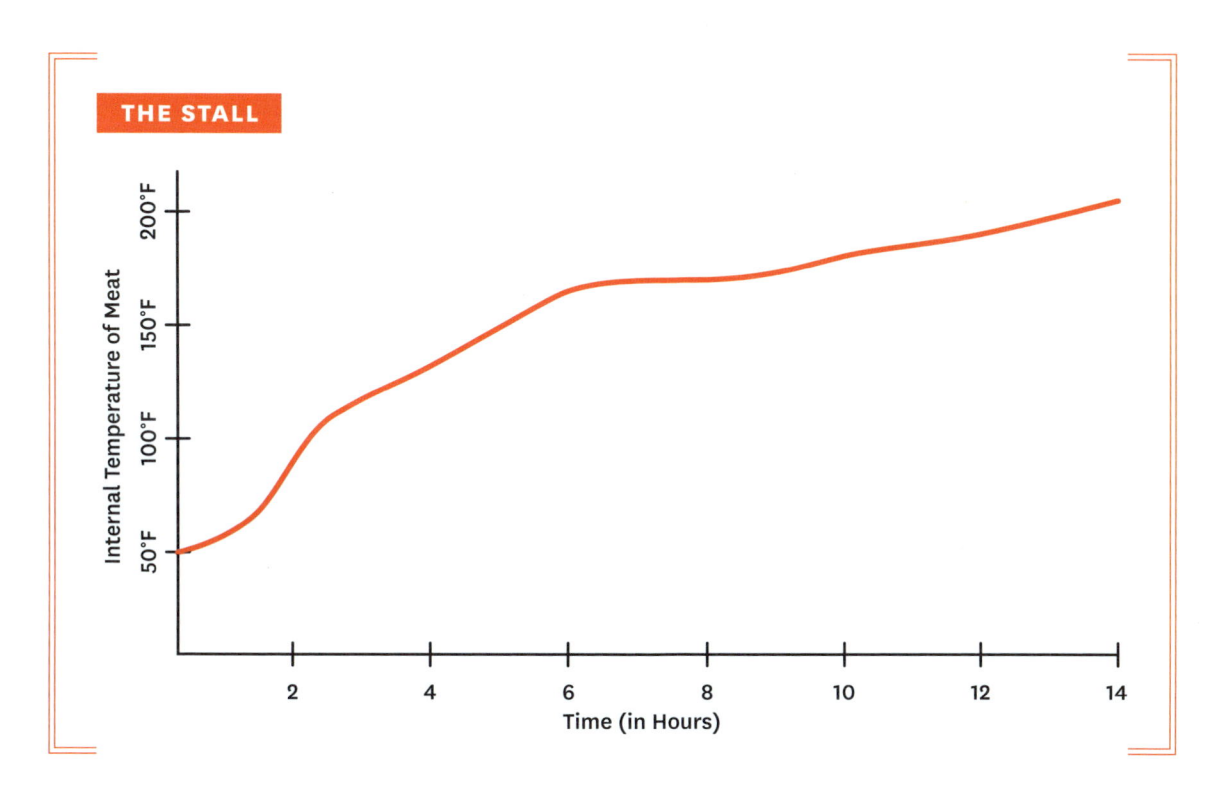

[Chart: Internal Temperature of Meat vs. Time (in Hours). The curve rises from 50°F, climbs to about 160–170°F by hour 6, levels off (the stall) through about hour 8, then rises gradually to just above 200°F by hour 14.]

What is the stall? Similar somewhat to the way a prop plane might stall before restarting its engine and continuing through the air—and far more heart-stopping—a big piece of meat cooking in the smoker hits a patch in its progress where cooking appears to stop. You can chart it with a meat thermometer. At first, the temperature goes up and up, just as anything we cook always does. And then, gosh darn it, it levels off. This is usually between 160°F and 170°F. And it stays leveled off. And it stays. And it stays at the same temperature until you think it's not going to get any higher. This freaks people out. It sure did me when I first encountered it.

What do freaked-out people do with meat that's been stuck at the same temperature for hours? They're not stupid—they pull it off. After all, at 160°F or thereabouts, it easily satisfies the FDA guideline for when beef is done (ahem, 145°F). And then they cut into it only to find the brisket is as tough as a sneaker.

Anyone can be forgiven for doing this, because the stall defies logic. Not only does the meat hold the same low temperatures for hours in an ovenlike environment, sometimes it can actually be observed dropping in temperature. So what gives?

The stall happens as a result of something called "evaporative cooling." It's the same mechanism that allows sweat to cool down the body. Sweat works like this: when moisture sits on the surface of the skin, it's evaporated by heat energy given off by the body. So when the water changes from liquid to gas form, it absorbs a significant amount of heat energy from the skin, creating a cooling effect on the surface it's leaving. Basically, your sweat is sucking up radiant heat from your body, getting converted into gas, and then evaporating away. This happens more easily in a dry heat than a humid one, which is why a hot and dry day feels cooler than a hot and humid one. Your sweat evaporates much more easily when there's less moisture already in the air. In high humidity, it doesn't evaporate well or at all and we feel warmer, even if the actual air temperature is not high.

This is why we often refer to "dry bulb" and "wet bulb" temperatures. Dry bulb measures the actual air temperature, whereas wet bulb measures the temperature of the air but adjusts for the cooling that occurs as moisture dries from a surface. Therefore, wet bulb temperature is lower than dry bulb, except in an environment of 100 percent relative humidity, in which case the two temperatures are the same. (In 100 percent humidity, there's no room in the molecules of air to absorb any more moisture, so there can be no cooling from evaporation.)

Inside a cooker, the piece of meat is sort of sweating too. It's losing moisture to the air in the form of evaporation. Interestingly, air turbulence and humidity have a greater impact on evaporation than actual temperature—and since there's a huge amount of air movement in a smoker (thanks, convection), the evaporation is quite significant. This means that a lot of evaporative cooling is happening, that is, the surface of the meat is cooler than the air around it in the cooker. Therefore a wet bulb thermometer would give a more accurate reading of the temperature than the dry bulb ones everyone uses.

Evaporative cooling of the brisket continues until the humidity inside the cooker rises or until the surface of the meat has no more moisture to give. (This is a big part of the reason why a water pan is so important, as maintaining the humidity means that the stall won't happen too early in the cook.) A stall will happen when the temperature of the meat reaches equilibrium with the wet bulb temperature inside the cooker—to the meat, it can get no hotter in there. Of course, this is not the case. The dry bulb temperature inside the cooker is much warmer. As the humidity inside the smoker decreases because of the vanishing moisture in the meat, so does the wet bulb temperature, and the meat might even experience a temporary reduction in temperature.

Finally, the temperature will resume climbing when the accessible moisture in the meat has evaporated and the meat becomes just a dry hunk. But nobody actually wants that—a sad, dried-out piece of brisket! Here's what you do instead: add some humidity to the equation by wrapping the meat before all of that moisture is gone. And this is what I do: I cook it exposed long enough for it to pick up smoke and lose just the right amount of moisture, then I wrap it to preserve what is left and let the collagen continue to render.

THE SMOKE RING

If you eat at Franklin Barbecue, you might notice that our barbecue doesn't always have that classic pink "smoke ring" underneath the bark that some people love to hold up as the surefire indication of great barbecue. That's because the smoke ring, in fact, has nothing to do with the way great barbecue tastes, how well it was smoked, and so on. In fact, research has shown that smoke isn't even necessarily required to make a smoke ring. That said, it often will occur in meats smoked under certain conditions.

The first thing that you should know is that the smoke ring—and the red color of your steaks and the juice that comes out of rare-cooked meat—has nothing to do with blood. Instead, it's caused by myoglobin, a red-colored protein that carries and stores oxygen in muscle cells. When it's heated, myoglobin loses its pink color and turns the dull, gray color of well-done meat. So rare steaks aren't red because they're still bloody—they're red because the internal temperature has not gotten high enough to turn that myoglobin brown.

It makes sense then that the interior of meat would stay pink. So how is it that the smoke ring on some briskets is on the outside, which presumably gets even hotter than the interior, which has turned gray? The answer involves complicated chemistry, but let's just say that carbon monoxide and nitrogen monoxide in the smoke react with the myoglobin in meat to keep it pink. The depth of the smoke ring indicates how far the smoke has penetrated the meat before it contacts meat whose internal temperature has already risen enough to turn gray.

Thus it's logical that if you start with cold brisket—say, straight from the freezer—you can get a wider smoke ring, as the smoke can penetrate further before the interior of the meat heats up. And, surprise, that's a popular technique in competition barbecue to get that luscious-looking ring.

But smoke rings don't contribute anything whatsoever to flavor or texture, so we're not too concerned with them. And if we were to make an effort to put especially cold briskets on the smoker, it would take them even longer than the 16 hours they already require to finish.

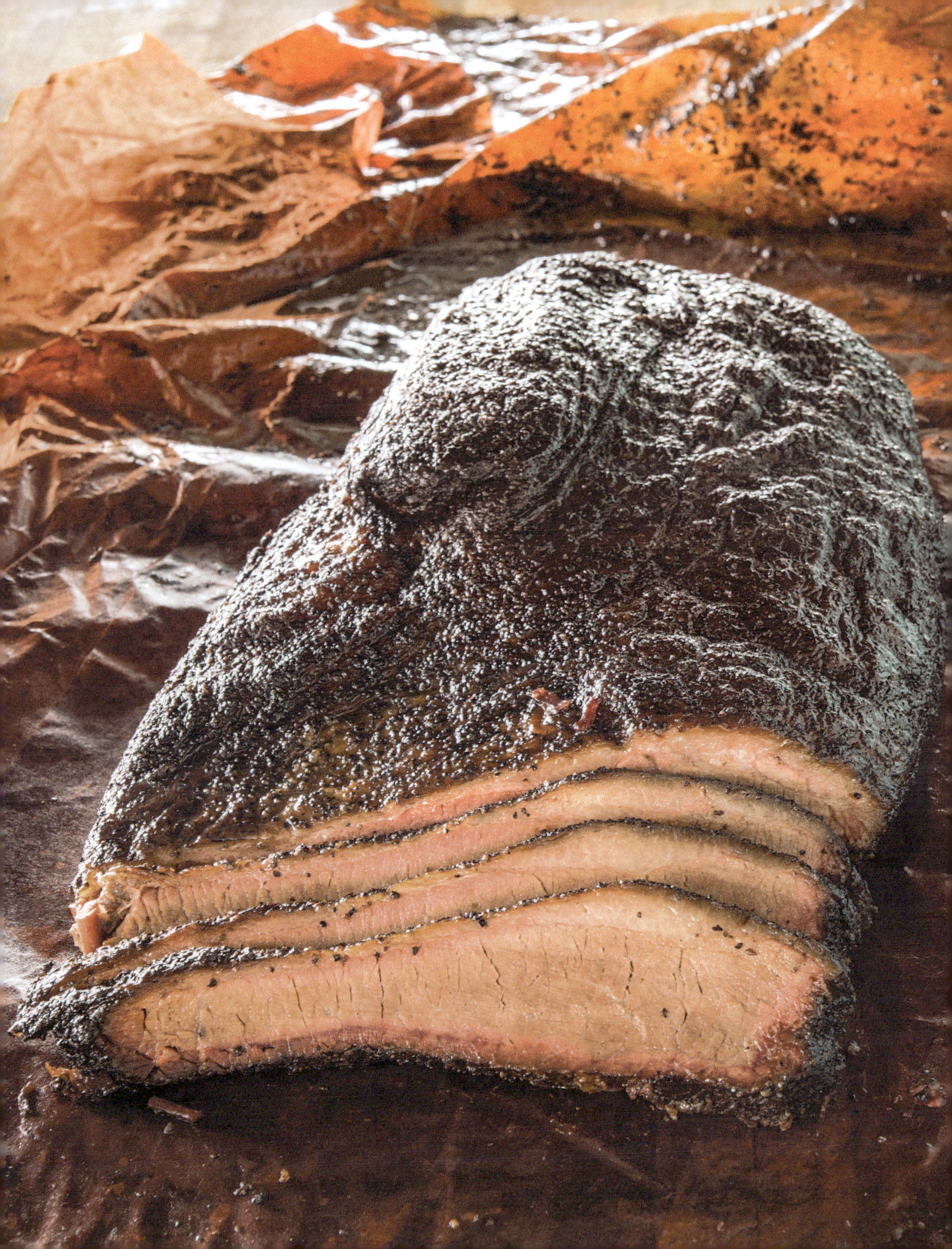

BRISKET

Brisket is a big, dumb hunk of meat, but it turns into something heavenly when done just right. Cooking a brisket intimidates a lot of people, probably because it's a big investment in money and time. If something goes wrong, there's not a lot you can do. Well, I have two things to say to that: Don't mess it up, as it's not that hard. And if it's not perfect, don't fret—you've still got smoky meat to serve, and most people are pretty forgiving about that.

There aren't many steps in making a brisket. First, I'll outline the entire process, then I'll go into greater detail about each part.

Ingredients and Tools

- 1 (12- to 14-pound) brisket, packer cut (see page 110)
- About ½ cup Brisket and Beef Rib Rub (page 137)
- Desired slather ingredients (see page 130), optional
- Spray bottle of water, vinegar, or other liquid
- 2 sheets of 18 by 30-inch unfinished butcher paper
- Seasoned firewood (preferably oak)

Overview

1 • Trim the brisket.

2 • Apply the slather, if using, and the rub (equal parts salt and pepper), then let the brisket warm up to room temperature (1 hour).

3 • In the meantime, start your fire and check that the water pan is full. Get a feel for the wood you will be using—how quickly it burns, how clean the smoke is, and so on. Build a nice coal bed.

4 • When the smoker is reading at the desired temperature (in the 275°F range, depending on preference), place the brisket on the cooker. I prefer fat side up and the brisket point facing toward the fire. Gently close the lid. Maintain a clean fire at or around 275°F for the duration of the 8- to 10-hour cook (timing depends on brisket size and cooker temperature and efficiency).

5 • Keep the lid closed for the first 3 hours. After 3 hours, start periodically (roughly every 20 to 30 minutes) checking the color. Start spritzing occasionally with water or vinegar if the brisket surface starts looking dry.

6 • At 6 hours, the internal temperature should be getting through the stall. Start paying attention to the bark formation and whether the fat cap is rendering. Think about wrapping soon. If the temperature is stalling but you don't have a sufficiently colored bark, or the fat cap is still very hard and solid, consider bumping up the cooker's temperature to push through the stall. When the bark is getting

nice and crusty and the color is looking even, remove the brisket from the cooker, spritz, and wrap it in butcher paper.

7 • Return the wrapped brisket to the cooker and maintain the fire.

8 • About 10 hours in, start "feeling" the brisket with a thin towel. Take note of how it starts to feel soft and pliable under the point and the flat. As the brisket gets closer to doneness, the whole piece will begin to feel tender. If you must, check the internal temperature of the brisket in the middle of the flat. It may read anywhere from 190°F to 203°F when it is done. But keep in mind, feel trumps all. If it's tender, it's done!

9 • Take the brisket out of the smoker and let it rest fully wrapped until the internal temperature comes down to 140°F to 145°F (1 to 2 hours, depending, of course, on the ambient air temperature).

Step 1 TRIM THE BRISKET.

The bad news is that there's an art to trimming a brisket. The good news is that it is not a very hard art to learn. What you should know is that trimming the brisket is really important and does factor in to the way the brisket cooks. Basically, trimming well is an opportunity to set yourself up for an easy, successful cook.

A lot of what I've talked about in this book regards feel. I've said that you should let the fire burn at the rate it wants to. I've talked about envisioning the way smoke flows through a cooker. Well, trimming a brisket falls into that category too. As you prepare to trim, imagine the way smoke and heat will travel across the brisket's surface, borne by airflow. You want to make the surface of the meat streamlined and smooth so that it cooks evenly and thoroughly, removing any odd bits of fat or flesh that might dry out and burn. Basically, you want one harmonious piece of meat. So here's what I do.

First, I put on my nitrile gloves with the idea of keeping one hand clean and one hand that will touch the meat. I will touch the meat only with the dirty hand, while my clean, right hand will handle the knife. The knife I use is a well-sharpened curved, stiff 8-inch boning knife that cuts through the brisket with grace and ease.

It's good to start with a cold brisket, as it's easier to cut into. The brisket will most likely be wrapped in plastic. I put the brisket down on the cutting board, fat side up, and cut through the center of the plastic with my knife, making sure not to touch the meat. Next, I cut open the bag at the end, lift the end of the brisket with my left hand, and use my knife to pull the bag out from under from the brisket. I'll then toss the bag into the trash can that I've conveniently located under or to the side of the table.

Now let's orient ourselves around the brisket. I'm going to call the fat cap side the top of the brisket, because I cook that side up (even though technically it faces downward on the animal). This is the side where the point protrudes upward with a knobby shape. The underside of the brisket, the bottom, is flat.

THE COOK

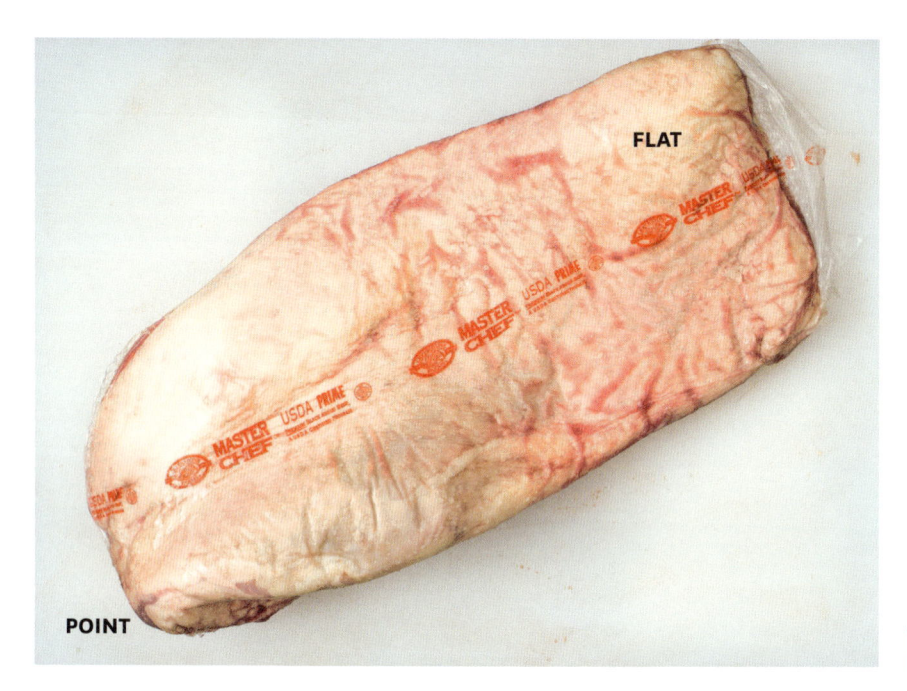

Top of brisket (fat cap side)

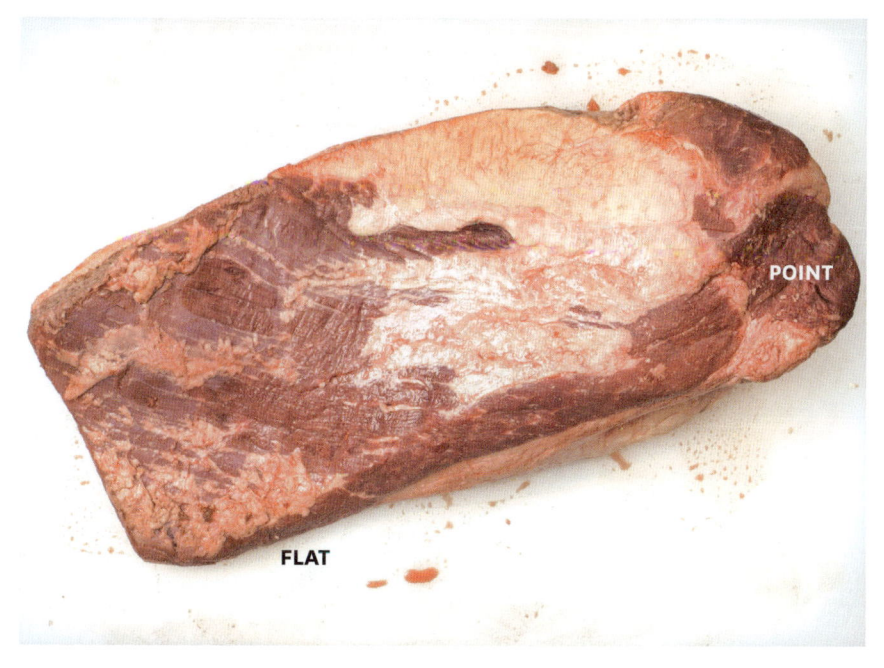

Bottom of brisket

FRANKLIN BARBECUE

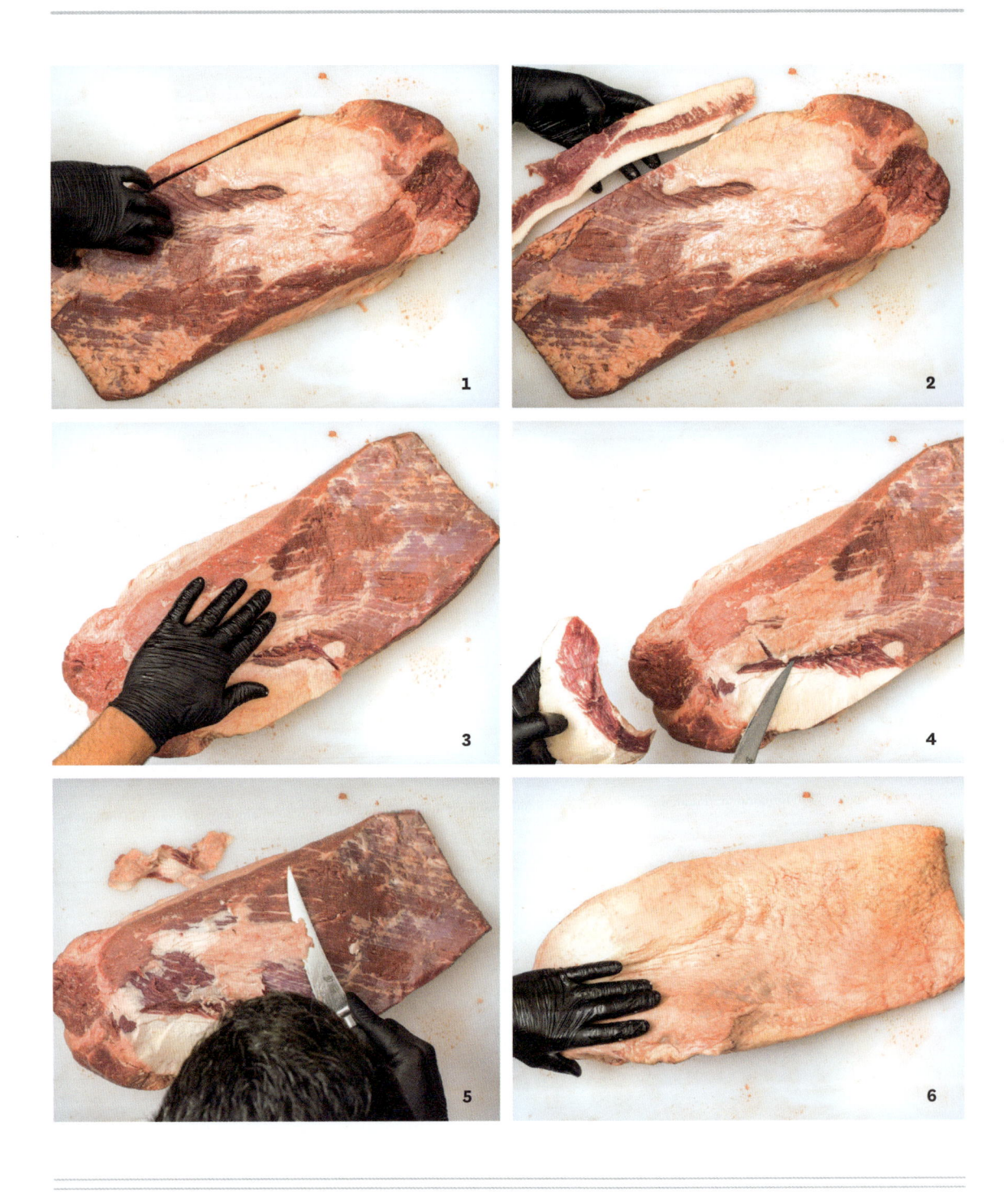

1

2

3

4

5

6

THE COOK

Place the brisket before you on the table, with the point facing down. I first look at the long sides of the brisket, where I like to make smooth, graceful edges. I'll usually trim off a thin strip from the edge, all the way from the top of the point to the end of the flat (see **PHOTO 1**, left). Make a clean, consistent cut, following the line where the seam fat terminates, and you'll have nice sides to the brisket, with meat showing underneath and fat on top.

One thing to understand about my trimming method is that I cut a lot away (see **PHOTO 2**)—more than most, I've been told. That means I'm pretty ruthless, and whereas a lot of people will trim away only fatty bits, I'll cut away both fat and some meat in order to get the shape I want. How do I know what shape I want? I envision the final product after cooking. When looking at the raw hunk of brisket in front of you, try to imagine how it's going to cook down—how the fat cap will reduce into the bark, and how each outward-facing side will render. When you imagine how you're going to slice the cooked brisket, you'll start to see how to trim it. You'll take certain edges and points off, even if they contain some meat, because that surface that you've just revealed will ultimately cook better and offer a better slice of meat.

Take a look at the bottom of the brisket: you'll note a big hunk of fat right where the point and the flat connect. I always think of this big nub almost like a handle you can grip, a fist-size piece that I cut off, because it won't render and won't add anything to the final product. If you make a few entry cuts on one side of it, it's really easy to pull the whole thing back (while cutting it away with the knife) until you can remove the entire chunk and throw it away (see **PHOTOS 3 AND 4**).

Now trim off bigger pieces of fatty membrane that are inevitably clinging to this side (see **PHOTO 5**). This is just a superficial trim, but those thin strands of fat will only disrupt the bark formation as it cooks. Now you're done with the underside. Flip the brisket over so you can get to work on the fat-cap side (see **PHOTO 6**).

Your next step is to trim the fat cap to 1/4- to 1/2-inch thickness. The general goal is to trim it and then to excise any pieces that will burn or cook unevenly. Note where the brisket flops down over the side of the point. Trim this down a bit so that the point will cook more thoroughly (see **PHOTOS 7 AND 8**, page 152). If you don't, the fat that's under the fold won't render and turn to bark.

FRANKLIN BARBECUE

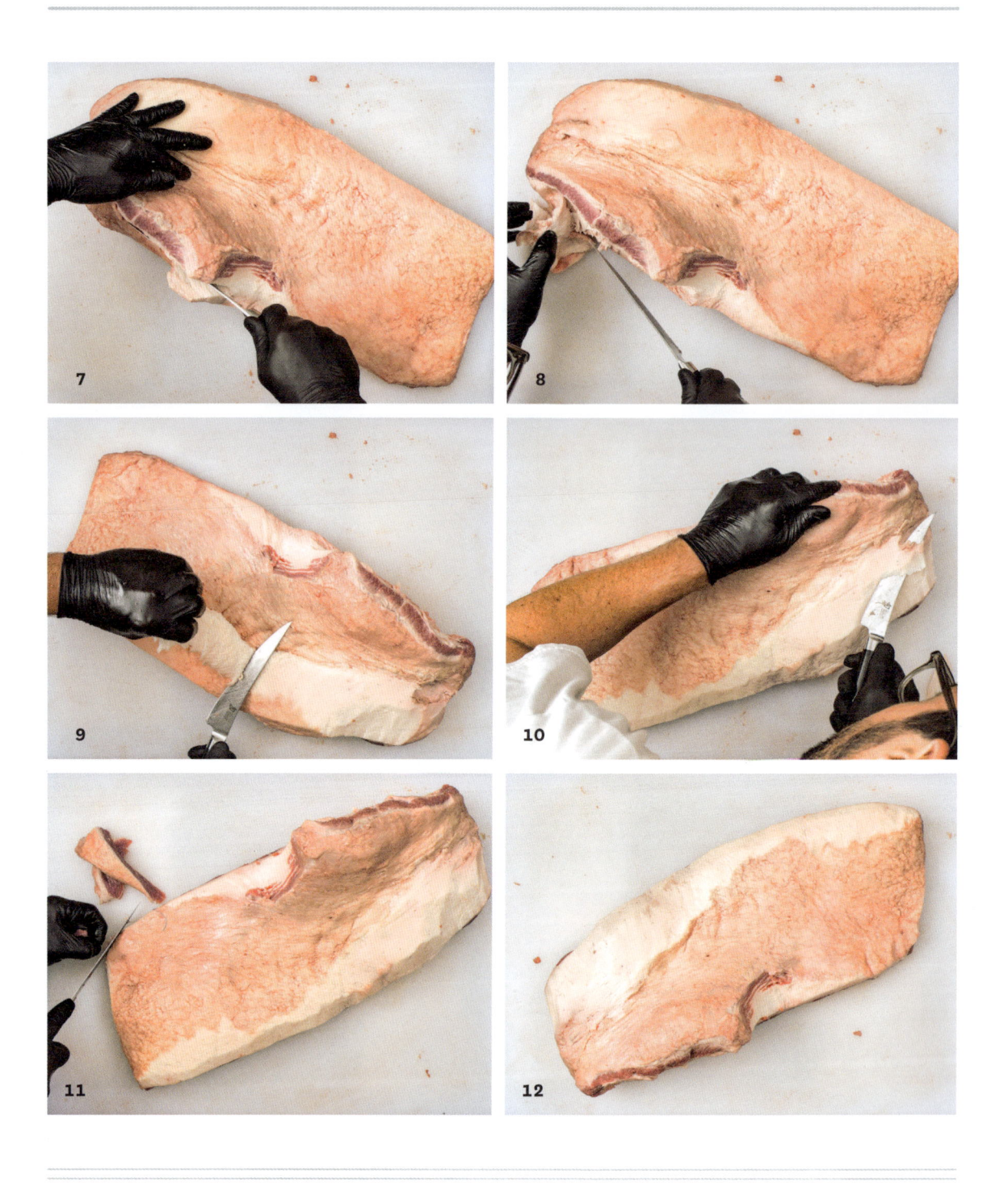

THE COOK

I also like to strip away hard or bad-looking fat that sort of hardens in sheets (affectionately called "Ally Sheety" at the restaurant). I use two general cuts for this. One is a thin horizontal slice up near the point, which I then continue as I peel the slice back while gently cutting underneath it with the knife (see **PHOTOS 9 AND 10**, left). This allows you to cut a long, thin strip off the top. Then I'll go in with shorter slices to get the height I want and a generally smooth surface. You may have to cut away some pretty gnarly chunks of fat. Don't be afraid to do that.

The last step is to round off the edges because corners that stick out might have a tendency to burn and dry out before the rest of the meat (see **PHOTO 11**). You want to remove any little pieces of fat or flesh protruding from the mass, as they can dry out and burn.

Although all of this sounds complicated and precise, it really isn't. Don't get too OCD over this, or you'll find yourself spending 30 minutes doing something that should take no more than 10, and your brisket will warm up and you'll find that your back aches from hunching over it. As I said, turn the brisket into a nice, clean shape with a 1/4-inch fat cap and no bits hanging off the edges (see **PHOTO 12**).

Step 2 APPLY THE SLATHER AND THE RUB.

If you wish to apply a slather, do so before adding the rub. Again, it's your choice whether or not to slather. It can help the rub stick to the surface of the meat, but usually the meat's tacky enough that it's not necessary. Feel free to use water, hot sauce, mustard, whatever you want. I've seen it all.

As I said on page 134, you can get as complicated with the rub as you want—chile powder, cumin, granulated garlic, all the classic spices can be good in there. But in Central Texas the classic formulation is just salt and pepper: equal parts of each. A lot of people tend to go pretty heavy with the rub. I think that's a mistake. I like a fairly light, even coating, so the flavor of the rub doesn't detract from the flavor of the meat.

Mix the salt and pepper in a large shaker. (Use the quantity in the ingredients list on page 147 only as a rough guideline; every brisket is different and you may find you need a little more or less. When in doubt, I think it's better to under- than overseason.) Your goal is to get an even coating of rub on the entire exposed surface of the meat. Then, with the shaker high enough over the brisket to get a good, even mix (1 to 2 feet), get the hand moving and gently shower the rub down on the brisket. To get the rub on the vertical sides of the brisket, I hold my open, flat hand just to the side and use it to deflect the rub onto the meat, gently patting it in every few seconds to get every facet of the brisket covered. Make sure you do both sides and all of the edges: the fat cap and the underside. Now you're ready to throw it in the cooker.

Step 3 START THE FIRE.

Following the instructions beginning on page 88, start your fire and get your smoker preheated to the desired temperature. Again, 275°F is a good starting point. The smoker should also contain a full water pan (see page 66).

Step 4 PLACE THE BRISKET IN THE SMOKER.

Open the door and place your brisket inside. There are two kinds of people in the world: those who cook brisket fat side up and those who cook it fat side down. I'm very much a member of the former group. This is not necessarily because of any sort of orthodox philosophy; it's just my judgment call for the way briskets cook on my smokers. I cook fat side up because I have more top heat than bottom heat. If it were the opposite, I might cook fat side down, as you need to make sure that the fat renders before the bottom gets overdone. Remember this one very important point: every cooker is different, and you need to understand intimately the particulars of your own device.

Find a good place in the middle of your smoker and position the brisket on the grill with the point facing toward the firebox. I orient the brisket this way because the point is covered in a big fat cap and is the most marbled part of the brisket. All that fat will help protect the meat from the brunt of the heat coming directly out of the firebox. I like the middle of the grill because that's where I'm getting the most even temperature. You don't want to put it too close to the firebox opening, as it will likely be too hot there. But you should know what your temp reads up and down your cook surface (if it's long enough) because you've installed gauges to take the temp at grate level (see "Modifying a Cheap Store-Bought Smoker," page 62). With your hands, firm up the brisket and sort of nestle it into its shape, then close the door. Now you're ready to settle in and watch the fire for a long time. This is a good time to open a beer.

Step 5 CHECK . . . OCCASIONALLY.

There's a saying in barbecue that "If you're looking, you ain't cooking." This is very true. Avoid opening the lid to check on the progress of the meat, especially during the first 3 hours of cooking. Every time you open the lid, you're releasing smoke and heat and adding time to your cook. It takes a smoker a while to regain that heat, so it's best just to trust that your meat is cooking. As the meat starts to dry out and darken (around hour 3 or 4), spritz it with your spray bottle once or twice an hour, just to help the bark stay moist and continue to attract smoke.

Step 6 WATCH FOR THE STALL, THEN WRAP.

If you surmise that a brisket will cook in 8 to 10 hours, you can gauge that after about 4 hours, you'll be in the stall (depending on how hot you're cooking), and after about 6 hours, the brisket will be pushing through the stall and starting its eventual climb to doneness. One thing to remember is this: don't wrap during the stall. You'll lose all the momentum if you open

THE COOK

the lid and take out and wrap the brisket while it's trying to sweat off the last of its moisture. Just like an athlete might find it difficult to cool down and then get back up to full speed in a game, so too with a brisket. Better to let it come out of the stall and then wrap.

Conventionally, at home, if you're just cooking one or two briskets, this may be around 6 hours into a cook. But again, this decision should be based on color and bark formation more than any sort of time parameters. I can't really offer an exact accounting for time in a brisket recipe because every smoker, every piece of wood, and every piece of meat is different. Not to mention weather conditions vary. All I can say

is that as the crust of the meat starts to darken into a deep mahogany, almost blackish color, I'll open the lid briefly to spray the meat with a spray bottle. You can fill it with water, marinade, vinegar, apple juice, or whatever you want. I don't think it adds a ton of flavor, but it allows me to spray off any dark, clinging smoke to assess the true color of the meat and also wets the surface to prevent burning. I use the spray bottle to stretch out the smoke gathering and bark formation as long as I need to before I wrap.

When the color is right—that is, when I spray the bark to remove any ash and see that the true color of the bark is dark, nearly black—I pull the meat out and wrap it.

155

To wrap the brisket, I prepare two sheets of my pink butcher paper. It's 18 inches wide and "unfinished," meaning that it has no wax coating. I tear off two sheets each about 30 inches long and place one vertically on the table and the other just overlapping it and veering off at a slight oblique angle. Then I hit the spot where I'm going to lay the brisket on the papers with a quick spray from the bottle.

Next, using towels, I pick up the brisket and lay it down at the bottom of the two sheets of paper, 3 to 4 inches from the base of the sheets. The point is facing up and on the left side. I simply fold the edges of the paper over the brisket, as you'd wrap anything in paper, and then roll the brisket over once, keeping the pocket really nice and neat and as tight as I possibly can. Next, I take the wings of the paper, fold them over again, and once more roll the brisket over, keeping the wrap nice and tight. Now, just a little edge of paper is left, which I fold in a bit and leave. The brisket is in the same position it was when I took it off the smoker, only wrapped tightly in butcher paper.

Step 7 CONTINUE COOKING THE WRAPPED BRISKET.

Put the brisket back in the smoker or even in an oven (set to the same temperature as your cook chamber) to finish cooking. I have to say that I think using an oven is cheating. But realistically, once you wrap the brisket, it's really absorbed all the smoke it's going to. If you want to save wood, or just head inside, finishing the brisket in the oven is a possibility . . . even if I don't really condone it.

Step 8 CHECK FOR DONENESS.

How do you know when the brisket's done? It's a great question, because every brisket is different. Taking the internal temperature is a good indicator of how the cook is going, but is unreliable for calculating doneness. The only true way to know is to use your hands. If the fibers pull apart with the slightest force, it's tender! Too tough to pull? Keep cooking. Crumbly? Overdone.

Of course, I don't want to cut into briskets before we serve them, so I determine doneness by feel. To do this, I pick it up off the grill and test it for pliability. (Yes, hot! I've long since killed all the nerve endings in my fingers. If you can still feel with your fingers, consider wearing gloves.) I'm looking for looseness and some flexibility. If it's pliable and soft in my hands, it's done.

You can also unwrap it a little bit (do so carefully, as the sticky rendered fat can sometimes stick to the paper) and give the brisket a feel. If it's soft and jiggly, you've cooked it perfectly, and you'll find tender, beautifully moist meat inside. Pull it off at this time, because it's done. If you keep cooking it because you're unsure, you're just going to dry it out and make it tough.

Now, if you really have no idea if it's done or not, you can check the temperature. A brisket may be finished cooking in the wide range of 200°F to 210°F. Although I don't recommend using this specific temperature as your guide, I often find that briskets are done at 203°F. Why 203°F? Only because after smoking many thousands of briskets, that temperature seems to come up more often than not. So, if you're really flying blind, that would be my magic number. But, remember, a brisket's done when it's done.

THE COOK

Step 9 REST THE BRISKET, THEN SERVE.

When a piece of meat is cooking, it goes through many changes: it starts as a cool, well-seasoned piece of meat (that can absorb characteristics from its heat source), then its moisture evaporates and it forms a nice crusty bark, and finally it becomes the tender, buttery, glistening end product we've been waiting for. But there's still one last step before we are ready to hunker down and enjoy a meal with our little edible slow-cooked morsel of delightfulness: letting it rest.

You'll probably notice the internal temperate of your brisket will continue to climb after you remove the meat from the cooker—that's called "carry-over." It occurs because of conductive heat. If the outside of the meat is cooked by the heat carried in the air and smoke of the cooker, the inside of the meat is cooked by the heat contained in those outer layers. It takes time for that heat to penetrate to the inside of the meat and do its work there (hence, the long cooking time of brisket). The deep internal temperature of any piece of meat can continue to rise even after it's been removed from the heat source because of this simple effect.

Yet resting after cooking is also incredibly important. It allows meat muscles to relax and reabsorb some of the juices that were squeezed out. If you cut it open right after it's been pulled, you will lose a lot of important liquid, and you will see a great brisket dry up in no time after hours of meticulous cooking.

Judging carry-over and resting times is like trying to predict the future. Carry-over can be tricky on a large piece of meat, as you don't want it to continue cooking so much that it becomes overdone as it rests. The idea is to think about how much momentum the meat has. Did you cook it hot and fast? If you did, carry-over will go further than it will if you were cooking low and slow, in which case there may be very little continuation.

Important to consider is where the meat will rest. On a hot table out in the sun on a Central Texas summer day? Or on a cool marble countertop inside an air-conditioned kitchen with an overachieving ceiling fan? If it's the former, you may not want to cook the meat as long, given the resting conditions. Many factors play into calculating resting time and carry-over. So use your best judgment and remember, just because you pull something at 203°F doesn't mean that that's your actual finished temperature.

Let a brisket rest until the internal temperature is between 140°F and 145°F. At this point you can serve the brisket or continue to let it rest for a couple of hours without losing any of its character. Indeed, a good, solid rest for a couple of hours may actually improve the meat.

After that, it's time to cut and serve the meat. I'm of the mind that cutting brisket properly is of the utmost importance, which is why I've devoted several pages to it (see pages 183 to 188). I suggest you read them before sinking your knife into that beautiful piece of meat you just spent hours preparing.

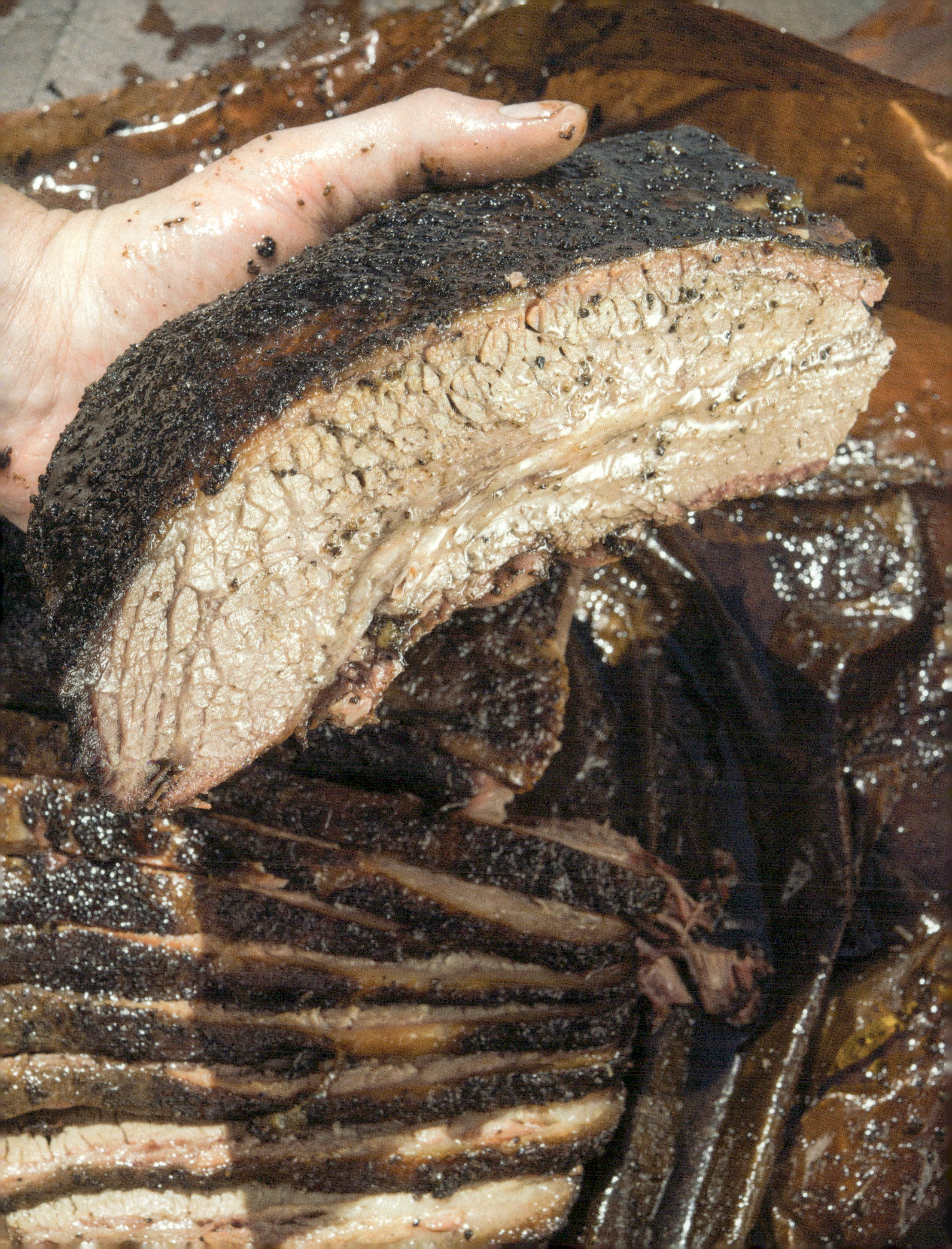

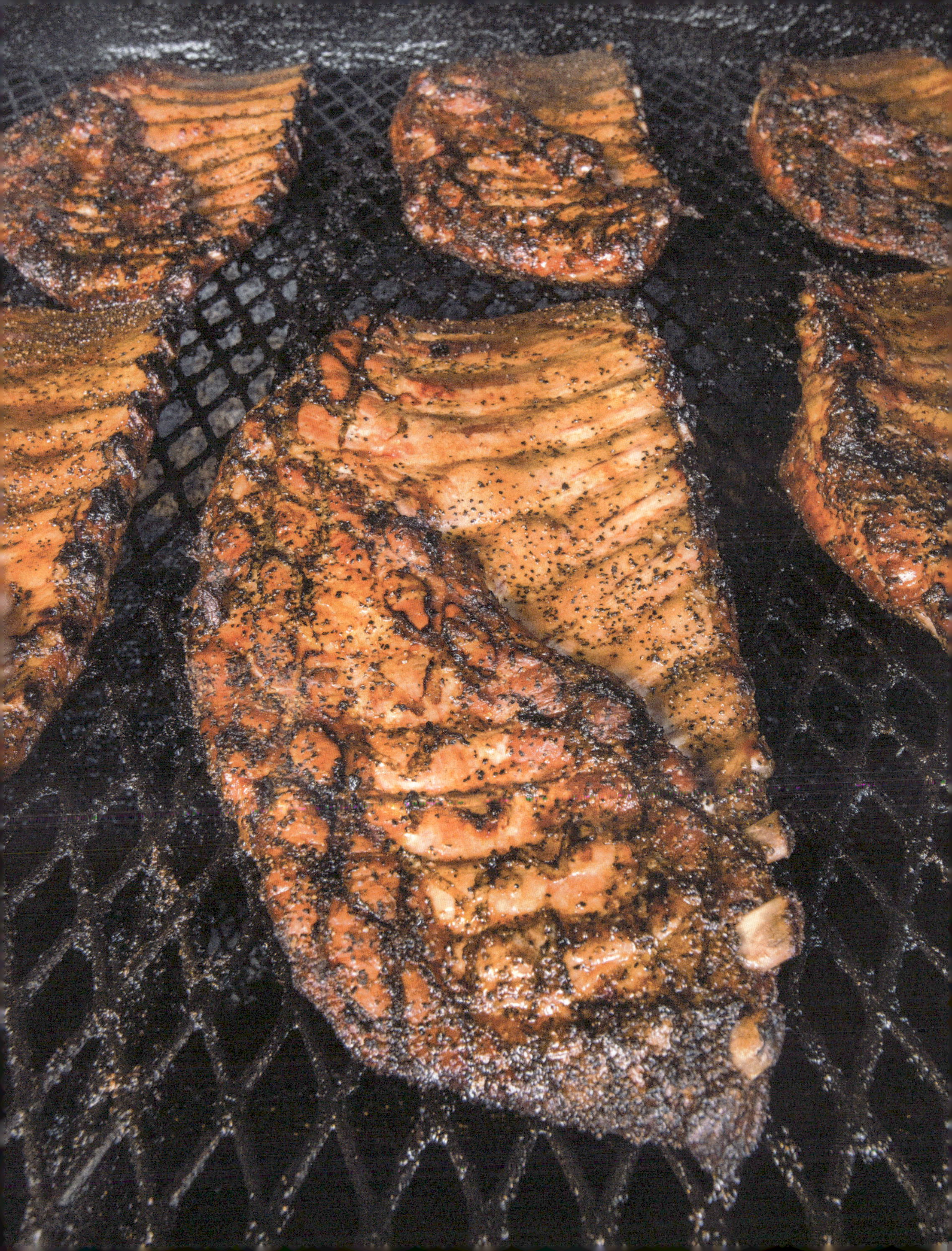

SPARE RIBS

At the restaurant, a rib shift starts at about 1 a.m. That's mighty early. But what's nice about the ribs, unlike briskets, is that one person can see them all the way through. It starts with trimming and rubbing the ribs, and ends with them coming off somewhere between 8:30 and 10 a.m. Then they'll rest and be ready for service when we open the doors at 11.

Ribs are delicate and have a small window of doneness, but once you figure out when to wrap and when they're done, you've basically mastered the art of cooking them.

Ingredients and Tools

- 1 full rack of pork spare ribs
- Oil, fat, water, vinegar, or other liquid, for slather, optional
- About ¼ cup Pork Rib and Turkey Rub (page 137)
- Whatever other rub ingredients you choose (see pages 136–137)
- Spray bottle of water, vinegar, or other liquid
- About ⅓ cup barbecue sauce
- Heavy-duty aluminum foil
- Seasoned firewood (preferably oak or hickory)

Overview

1. Trim the ribs of excess fat, breastbone, and skirt.
2. Apply the slather, if using, and the rub (2 parts black pepper to 1 part salt, plus whatever other rub ingredients you choose).
3. Start the fire and bring the smoker to 275°F.
4. Cook the ribs, meat side up, at 275°F.
5. Occasionally check the color and spritz.
6. When the ribs get to the desired color (after about 3 hours), spray them with vinegar, then coat them lightly on both sides with the sauce.
7. Tear off enough aluminum foil to comfortably wrap the ribs. Spritz the foil, then lightly coat it with the sauce. Place the ribs meat side down on the foil and wrap tightly.
8. Return the ribs, meat side down, to the cooker and cook until tender. (Start checking after about 2 hours.)
9. Let the ribs rest, then serve.

Step 1 TRIM THE RIBS.

If you get a "full spare" of pork ribs, which is what we serve at the restaurant, there's a little trimming to do to get them into optimal cooking shape. It's also possible that you'll see pretrimmed ribs at your store or your butcher.

They might be advertised as St. Louis cut, which means they've already been trimmed and are ready to cook. I like the full spare because we leave more meat on the rack than the St. Louis cut, which is squared off and looks real nice but is a bit smaller than what I prefer.

The good news is that trimming the ribs is easier and requires less time than trimming a brisket. There are just a few simple, automatic cuts that I make on every rack and a few quick snips. At 2 a.m. when I'm trimming the sixty or so racks we cook a day, it takes me only about 20 seconds to trim each rack.

As usual, as a right-hander, I use my left hand to handle the meat and my right hand to hold the knife, which is a German-made chef's knife with a 10-inch blade. I use this heavier knife instead of the lighter boning knife I use for brisket because I usually have to cut through some cartilage when trimming ribs, whereas with the brisket I'm cutting only fat and meat.

Each rack of ribs has two flat faces, one showing the meat and the other showing the bones, which are covered in a thin membrane. And then there are two long edges. One edge is the straight edge of the bones where the processor sawed off the ribs. The other is a slightly arcing, rounded edge where the ribs were connected to the breastbone. One end of the ribs narrows down into a point. This is the small end. The opposite end is much broader. This is where the rack was connected to the breast plate. These are important references for trimming the ribs (see **PHOTO 1**, right).

To begin, I place the ribs meat side down, with the straight edge of the bone side facing me. The narrow, small end will be on my left, and the broad end on my right. With my left hand, I smooth and spread out the whole piece so all of its little imperfect edges are easy to see.

My first cut is to remove the breastbone fragment, if it's still attached. (The ribs we get always have this little bit of the breastbone, connected by cartilage to the rack, but pre-trimmed ones from the store probably won't.) Across from the longest bones is the section that needs to be removed; it's a cartilaginous piece where the rib connects to the breastbone. If your ribs are already trimmed into a St. Louis cut, this part has been removed. But if not, you can see this section, as it's usually covered in a little fat and membrane and separated by an exposed section of meat from the main part of the rack. At about the fourth rib, feel with your hand where the hardness of the rib bones give way to a soft bit of cartilage. Grip the breastbone section with your left hand (if you're right-handed) and, cutting toward yourself with the knife, slide in the knife (see **PHOTO 2**). You'll quickly hit something harder than the meat. This is the cartilage. Find the line it takes in connecting to ribs 1–3 and simply cut through this with a chop by applying pressure to the knife (see **PHOTO 3**). I usually press down on the top of the blade with my left hand to cut through the cartilage. It should sound (and feel) like chopping through fingers in a grisly action movie. Once you've chopped off this section, you can throw it away, use it in stock or beans, or cut the meat off it for sausage making.

The next cut I make is down at that narrow end of the rack. If you feel the end with your hand, you'll notice at the very edge a little baby rib bone surrounded by a thin portion of meat. Using a nice, quick slice, cut out all of this bone, squaring off the end of the rack (see **PHOTO 4**).

THE COOK

rounded end where ribs connected to breastbone

This bone is unattached and you'll end up losing it anyway after the rack is cooked. Plus, the meat it's attached to is so thin that it will burn and might get crusty enough to tear the aluminum foil in which the whole rack will be wrapped. So it's better just to lose this bone now.

We're almost done. With the ribs still meat side down, locate the skirt—a flap of meat hanging off the right side of the rack toward the narrow end. Sometimes butchers will remove the skirt, but often it, or a part of it, is there. Simply slice through it close to the rack to remove it (see **PHOTO 5**, page 163). It's a nice piece of meat and should be used for something, but for the purposes of barbecued ribs, it's likely to burn up when you're cooking it anyway. It will also pull up and away from the rest of the rack when cooking and create a bald patch underneath it, which won't cook as evenly as the rest.

Now I flip the entire rack over to the other face—meat side up, bone side down. Once again I spread or fan out all of the edges flat onto the board so that I can see what the thin, curved edge of the meat looks like. It's always uneven with little shaggy bits sticking out, so I just cut cleanly around the edge, preserving as much meat as possible to create a neat, consistent line on the meat side for even cooking (see **PHOTO 6**, page 163).

Lastly, I feel around on the ribs for any bits of hard or stringy fat that might be hanging off. This is easily removed with a quick slice of the knife (see **PHOTO 7**, left). I also run my fingers across the straight edge of the bones to feel for any sharp or jagged bone ends (see **PHOTO 8**). This is where the processor has used a band saw to separate the ribs, but sometimes it splinters or makes for a prickly edge, which I smooth up with the knife.

THE COOK

You'll notice that a fine, shiny membrane covers the entire bone face side of the rack. There's a debate about whether to remove this or not. Most competition barbecuers do, but most restaurateurs don't. Members of the membrane-off camp say that it hinders smoke absorption into the meat, but I've found that it doesn't make a lick of difference as to how the meat cooks or tastes and, by the end, is barely noticeable at the level of tenderness to which we cook the ribs. So I leave it on, as removing it is both time-consuming and a little bit tricky because the membrane is slick and hard to grip. But if you want to remove it, the technique is to grip it with a paper towel and then slowly peel it off the ribs. You can use the knife to gently loosen it as you peel it back in one long piece. But, again, I don't bother with it. And now you're ready to cook!

Step 2 APPLY THE SLATHER AND THE RUB.

Salt and pepper make a great rub for ribs, but typically we augment this to include "something red." That redness could come from any number of conventional spices, such as paprika, chile powder, or cayenne pepper. My only real goal here is to bring a little bit of reddish hue to the already pink color of the ribs. Once again, you should use the salt and pepper quantities listed in the ingredients list only as rough guidelines; I generally shoot for ¼ cup of rub for each rack of ribs.

Once you've made your rub, you may want to coat the ribs with something to help it stick, though it is not necessary. People slather on oil, fat, water, mustard—anything that will make the surface of the meat tacky so that the rub will adhere to it.

Now, sprinkle on the rub much the same way you would for a brisket or any hunk of meat. Get that wrist and elbow moving and, anywhere from 1 to 2 feet above the ribs, gently shake the rub onto both sides, lightly covering the surface. Again, remember to keep the shaker itself moving in a nice rotation, as the heavier salt crystals tend to sink to the bottom of the mix, making the whole thing uneven when you put it on.

Also remember that it's really easy to apply too much rub, a mistake that a lot of people make. They feel they haven't gotten enough on one section, so they go over that part twice, which then inevitably appears to have a denser layering of rub than the rest of the meat. So they go over the rest again, and suddenly they have too much rub over the entire rack. There are worse things that can happen, but if you're using good meat (which I hope you are), you want the taste of it to be central, with the other flavors of rub and smoke supporting it. So, apply your rub with restraint and consistency the first time, and you're sure to get it right.

Step 3 START THE FIRE.

The process here is the same as for brisket, so turn to page 88 for tips on getting a good fire going. The smoker should contain a full water pan.

Step 4 PLACE THE RIBS IN THE SMOKER.

Now it's time to throw your ribs in the smoker. Ribs are the most finicky things to cook, and temperature matters a lot. They're just really sensitive. As always, use trial and error to find the best temperature for your cooker. But a good place to start is 275°F, which often seems to cook them neither too fast nor too slow. Some recommend cooking them as low as 225°F, but I think that's too cool, and it will take forever for them to be ready. I generally prefer to cook between 275°F and 300°F, depending on the quality of the meat's marbling (leaner meat I cook at a higher temperature). With ribs, temperature matters a lot. Too hot, and you might crisp the edges and dry the ribs out. Too low, and they'll never get tender.

People debate on how to position them on the grate: meat side up or down. I'm a meat-side-up guy because, just as with the briskets, the heat in my smokers is greater above the cook surface than below, so I want to have the part of the ribs with the most fat and meat exposed to that heat so they'll cook evenly. But if your heat is greater below the grate, by all means, cook the ribs meat side down.

The ribs can go for several hours without you needing to open the lid to check on them. Rather, keep track of your fire and your temperature gauge, which is placed to read the temperature of the smoker at grill height.

Step 5 CHECK THE COLOR AND SPRITZ.

About 2 hours in, I take a look to see how the ribs are doing. Hopefully, they're getting the deep color I'm looking for. I cook sixty racks at a time and inspect every one of them to determine how it's cooking. To do this, I take a spray bottle filled with cider vinegar and liberally spray the top of the meat. I don't do this to add flavor but rather to gauge the true color of the ribs and apply moisture. The spray washes off any of the heavier smoke particles that make the ribs look darker than they actually are. Use whatever liquid you want—vinegar, apple juice, orange juice, or water. Or you can dilute a liquid half and half with water.

The color I'm looking for is a deep reddish brown, and I want it to cover the surface fully. The enemy here is splotchiness, which can result from any number of things, but is generally due to some inconsistency in the meat, fat, or rub. This results in the edges becoming dry while the center stays moist, which in turn means there is an uneven surface for smoke penetration. If I see splotches of lighter color on the ribs, I just let them keep going until they've all come to be the same color.

Step 6 ADD THE SAUCE.

When the ribs have achieved that lovely, burnished red color, it's time to give them a little coating of sauce to prepare them for wrapping. I use our straight-up barbecue sauce for this purpose. Feel free to use whatever kind of sauce you want, though I recommend it not be too thick or sugary, which will result in it clumping as it cooks. If you have a thicker sauce, you can dilute it with water, vinegar, apple juice, or white grape juice to get a good, fluid consistency. I put the sauce in a plastic squeeze bottle for easy application. (Note: If it's cold outside, you'll want to warm your sauce, as cold sauce is also prone to clumping and cooling down the meat.)

Before I add the sauce, I hit the ribs again with another couple of sprays from the spray bottle, just to get them wet. This helps the sauce spread evenly when I apply it. Next, I lightly squirt the sauce from the squeeze bottle onto

THE COOK

the ribs, using a back and forth motion. Then I usually spread the sauce out evenly with a (gloved) hand, but you could use a brush. I mist the ribs one more time with the vinegar to help spread out the sauce, and then I close the lid and cook the ribs for about 15 minutes to allow the sauce to set. I flip the ribs over and cook for another 15 minutes to set the sauce on the second side. Now it is time to wrap.

Step 7 WRAP.

I wrap ribs in aluminum foil, not butcher paper. Each rack gets its own little foil packet. There's nothing special about the technique for wrapping ribs; it's pretty much common sense. You'll need a table or other work surface near your cooker. Cut one piece of foil that's a little longer than twice the length of each rack you're going to wrap and stack it on the table. In preparation for wrapping, hit the foil with a few spritzes from your spray bottle and then give it a quick few streaks of sauce from your squeeze bottle.

Use a towel, not tongs, to pull the ribs off the grill gently with your hands. The last thing you want is hard or jagged metal cutting into and shredding all that nice bark and good color you've worked so hard to get. Gently lay the rack, meat side down, on your spritzed and sauced piece of foil. Then spritz and sauce the backside of the ribs. On the ends of the rack, look for any bones that might be sticking out, gently wriggle them free of the meat, and discard them. Jagged bones can easily pierce the foil, allowing all the juices and moisture you're aiming to preserve to leak out.

To wrap, simply fold over the sides of the foil horizontally first and then flip the ribs over again until you've created a neat, tight packet. At this point, you can do as we do at the restaurant and put the ribs back on the smoker to finish cooking for another couple of hours. But, as with the brisket, they're not going to absorb any more smoke once they're wrapped. So, if you're doing this at home, you can also stick them into an oven preheated to 275°F for another 2 hours or so, until they're done.

Step 8 CHECK FOR DONENESS.

The single biggest question mark for a lot of people with regard to cooking ribs is determining when they're done. Unlike briskets, this isn't accomplished with a thermometer for three reasons: the ribs on a rack are of varying thickness and thus will be at different temperatures; the meat is so thin that it's hard to get an accurate reading; and the many bones that are close to the meat will absorb and radiate heat differently from the meat.

The best way to tell when ribs are ready is by feel. This is especially important because these ribs are wrapped in foil, and you don't want to have to go and unwrap every rack to figure out if it's ready or not. It takes practice, but do it a few times, and you'll get the hang of it.

Ribs *can* be overcooked. The meat shouldn't be falling off the bone, which will happen if the ribs cooked too long. The meat will also be dried out. Rather, the meat should be tender and juicy but still require a minimal bit of pull to get it off the bone.

To determine the moment to pull the ribs, I pick up every foil-wrapped rack in my hands with the towel and check its pliability. I grab it with my left hand, placing the tips of my fingers under the ribs in the middle portion. It's these thicker, straighter ribs in the middle that are the last to get done, which is why I check there. Holding a rack in my hand, I let it flex in that hand, allowing it to flop over those fingers with its own weight. If it's too floppy and bendable, it's probably overdone. If it's too stiff, it might need more time. I'm looking for just a nice, easy lever of flexibility that shows that it's perfectly done. There are some ways you can check your work. Some people twist a rib bone in the middle of the rack to see how loose it is. If it starts to break free of the meat, it's ready to eat. Other people might poke into the meat with a toothpick at that midpoint to check the consistency. If it effortlessly punctures the meat with little to no resistance, the meat is done. Generally, you're looking for looseness and a willingness to pull apart without falling apart.

Step 9 LET IT REST, THEN SERVE.

When you've figured out the ribs are done, leave them in their foil packets to rest. You can do this at room temperature for 20 to 30 minutes, and the ribs will still be nice and warm when it's time to serve.

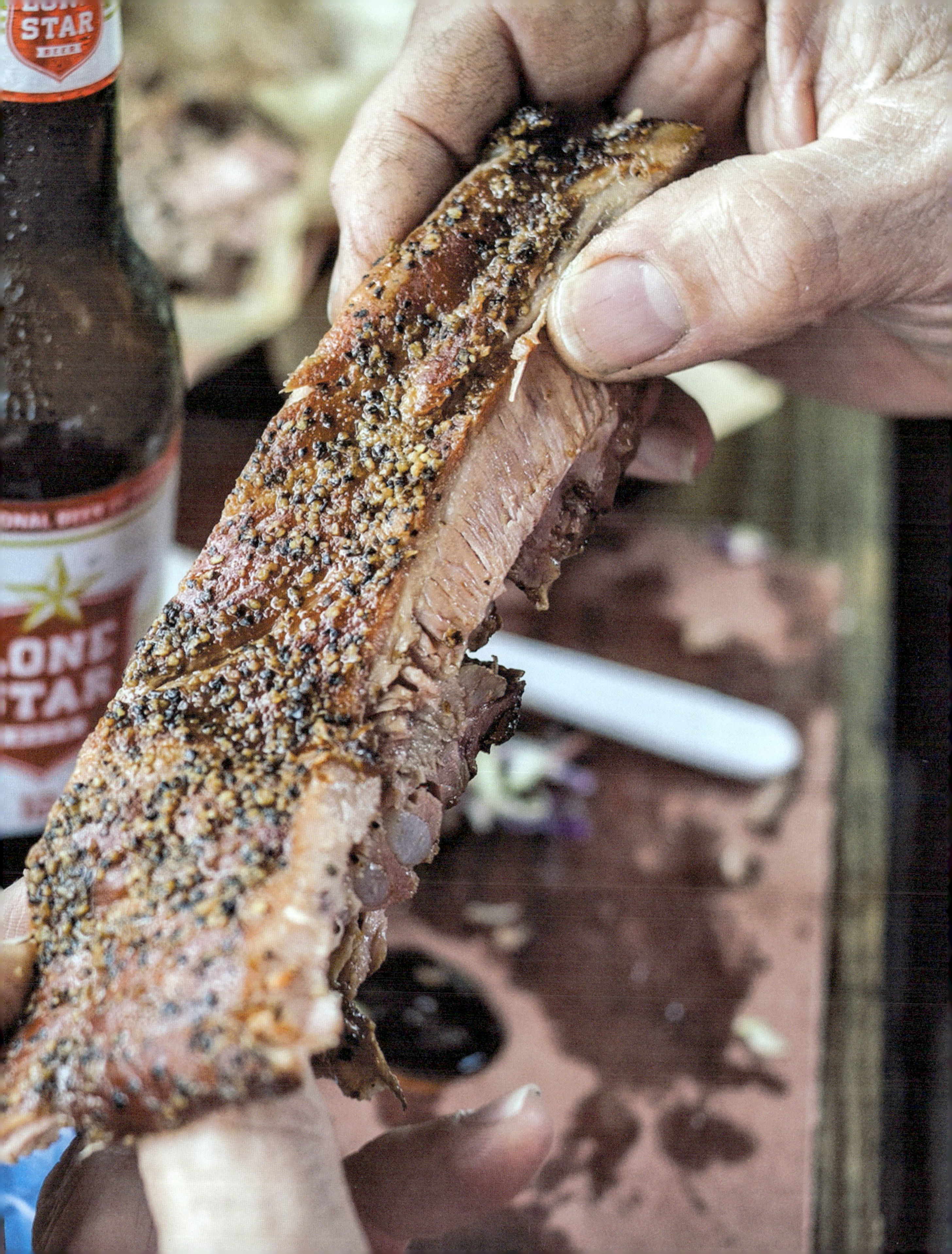
STAR

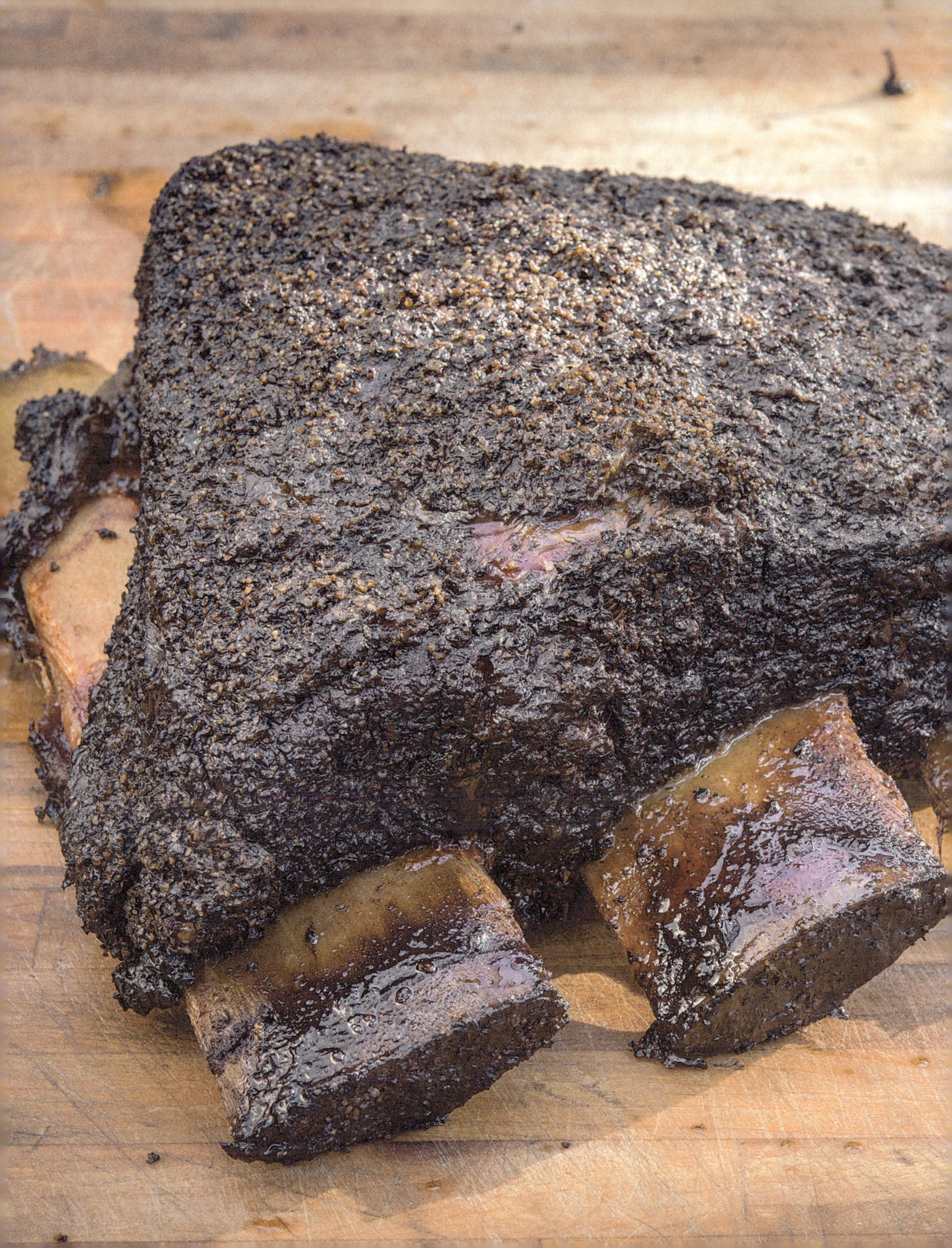

THE COOK

BEEF RIBS

If I had to name my own personal favorite cut of barbecue, it would probably be beef ribs. They are the richest and the most decadent, succulent, and flavorful cut of beef you can put on a smoker. That's also why I don't eat them much—too rich, too hedonistic. We only cook beef ribs on Saturdays at the restaurant: they're a special treat, made all the more special because we do them only once a week.

That said, beef ribs are pretty easy to cook. In this recipe, I include a light slather of hot sauce. We don't cook them this way at the restaurant because not everyone likes spicy food, but it's my preference for sure. I rub heavily because there's so much fat, and the extra rub really melts into it well. Beef ribs don't get wrapped. You'll know they're done when they feel jiggly and soft.

Ingredients and Tools

- 1 (3- to 5-pound) rack of beef short ribs (from the plate, not the chuck)
- 1 tablespoon hot sauce, such as Cajun Chef or Crystal
- About ⅓ cup to ½ cup Brisket and Beef Rib Rub (page 137)
- Spray bottle of water, vinegar, or other liquid
- Seasoned firewood (preferably oak or hickory)

Overview

1. Heat the smoker to 285°F and check that the water pan is full.
2. Trim the ribs if needed.
3. Slather the ribs with a very light coating of hot sauce.
4. Apply the rub (equal parts salt and black pepper).
5. Cook the ribs, meat side up, at 285°F, for about 8 to 9 hours.
6. Spritz during the final 2 to 3 hours.
7. Check for doneness by poking the ribs; when they feel like melted butter (about 203°F between the bones), serve.

Step 1 START THE FIRE.

Following the instructions beginning on page 88, get a fire going and heat the smoker so it's about 285°F at grate level.

Step 2 TRIM THE RIBS.

Beef ribs usually come quite clean and well trimmed, unlike pork ribs and briskets, so there's not much to do. If you see any big chunks or flaps of fat, trim them away. Apart from that, I don't trim beef ribs.

Step 3 APPLY THE SLATHER.

When I'm cooking for myself, I like to slather the ribs with a bit of hot sauce. Of course, you can slather with anything you like—from water to mustard to vinegar. The slather is mainly there to help the rub adhere to the surface of the meat. I just think a little hint of earthy spiciness from a bottle of hot sauce is a fun addition to beef ribs. You can't really taste it in the final product, but it helps build interior layers of flavor.

Step 4 APPLY THE RUB.

Using a shaker, and holding it 1 to 2 feet above the ribs, generously apply the rub—a little heavier than you would on a brisket. This is because, as rich as brisket is, beef ribs are even richer. The extra rub ends up forming a bark that balances out that richness just a little bit. I generally use somewhere around 1/3 to 1/2 cup of rub for each rack of beef ribs.

Step 5 COOK THE RIBS.

Place the ribs, meat side up, in the smoker. As usual, I cook meat side up because I've determined that my smokers have more topside heat and the meat and fat cap can handle that. If you've got more heat coming from below, you might consider going meat side down. Again, it's up to you—the ribs can come out well either way. Cook for 8 to 9 hours, until done.

Step 6 SPRITZ.

During the final 5 hours or so, spritz pretty frequently with water or other liquid to keep the ends from burning.

Step 7 FINISH, THEN SERVE.

Check for doneness by gently inserting a toothpick between two membranes: the one outside the bones and the one that separates the bones from the meat. Inside, the meat should be extremely tender. Alternatively, take an internal temperature reading: the ribs should be done when they reach 203°F. Let them rest for at least 30 minutes before serving. Beef ribs are served on the bone, but great for sharing.

TURKEY BREAST

We're not exactly known for our turkey, but it does come out real nice, and I even know some people for whom it's the favorite of all of the things we cook. That's fine, because it's also the easiest thing to cook. We don't bother with the whole turkey, just as we don't bother with whole cows or pigs. We get nice, plump turkey breasts and try to keep them moist. For this recipe (and in general, in my opinion), it's important to buy turkey breasts that have not been prebrined or injected with any sort of solution. If you're anything like me, you want to be in complete control over what goes into or is sprayed on your bird, and you never know with commercially brined turkey.

Ingredients and Tools

- 1 (3- to 4-pound) skin-on, nonsolution turkey breast
- 1 cup butter
- Heavy-duty aluminum foil
- Seasoned firewood (preferably oak)
- Generous 1/4 cup Pork Ribs and Turkey Rub (page 137)

Overview

1. Start the fire and heat the smoker to 265°F.
2. Trim the turkey breast and apply the rub (2 parts black pepper to 1 part salt).
3. Cook the turkey for 2 1/2 to 3 hours, then wrap.
4. Continue cooking until the internal temperature reaches 160°F (about 1 hour).
5. Let rest for 30 minutes, then serve.

Step 1 START THE FIRE.

Following the instructions beginning on page 88, get a fire going and heat the smoker so it's about 265°F at grate level.

Step 2 TRIM THE BREAST AND APPLY THE RUB.

If the skin is on the turkey breast, remove it. We just tear off the skin and throw it away. I use the same rub for turkey as pork spare ribs, so 2 parts black pepper to 1 part salt. Use your judgement, but I think a bit more than 1/4 cup rub per turkey breast is a good guideline.

Step 3 COOK THE TURKEY UNTIL GOLDEN, THEN WRAP.

Place the turkey, skin side up (meaning, the side that formerly had skin), in the smoker and cook until golden brown (typically 2½ to 3 hours). Remove the turkey from the smoker, place the butter on top of the turkey, and wrap tightly in two layers of heavy-duty aluminum foil, dull side out. The turkey breast ends up braising in quite a lot of melted butter and its own juices and the double layer of foil ensures against leakage. Return the turkey to the cooker, this time flipping it so it's skin side down.

Step 4 FINISH THE COOK.

Continue to cook the turkey breast until the internal temperature registers 160°F. This should take about 1 additional hour.

Step 5 LET REST, THEN SERVE.

Let the turkey rest until the internal temperature drops to 140°F, then slice thinly against the grain and enjoy.

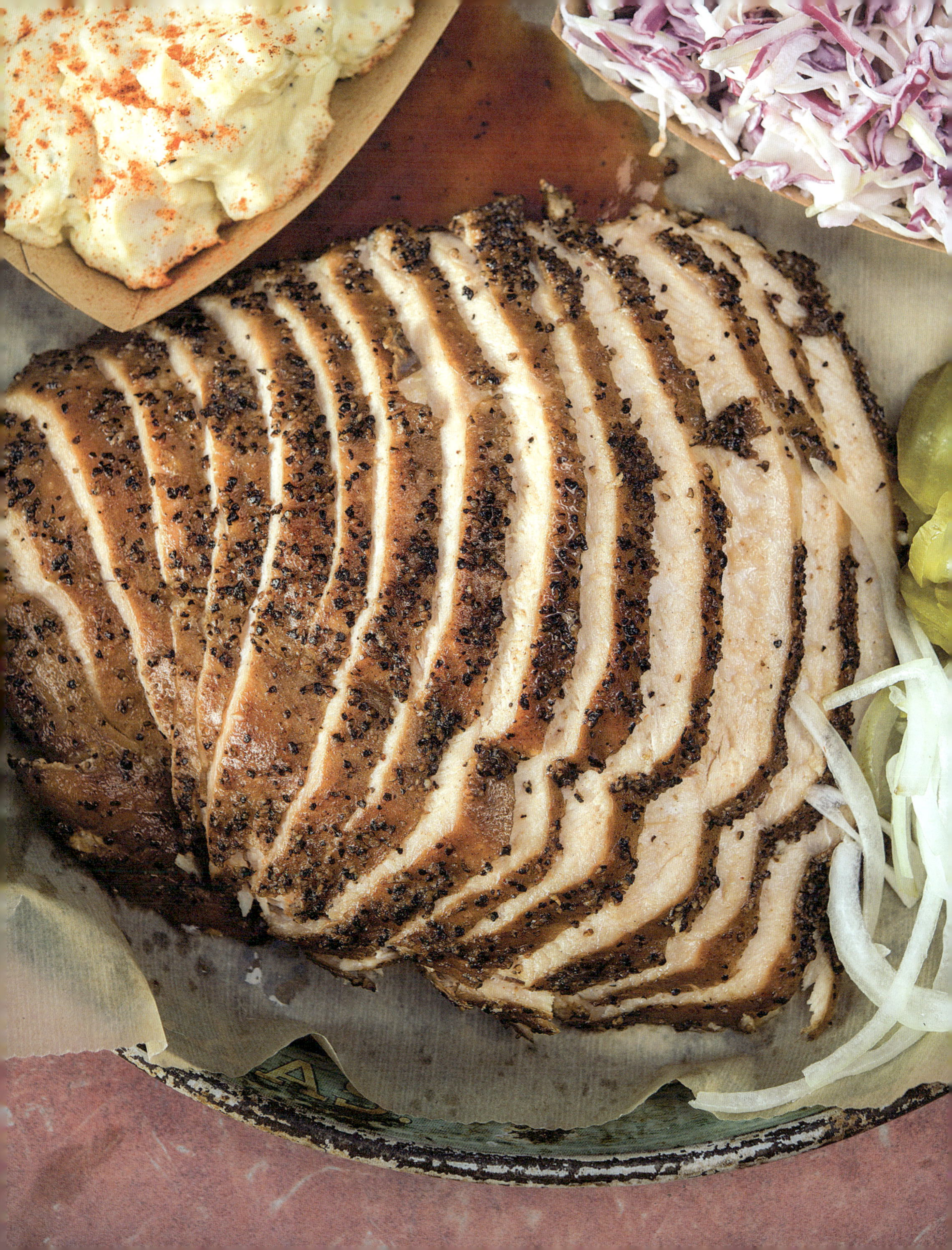

SERVING + EATING

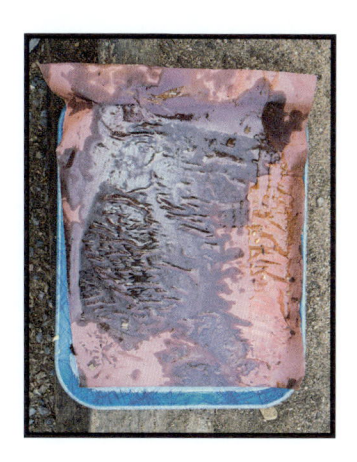

- **Chapter Seven**

Here's my little confession: Since I spend most of my life back in the pits, managing fires and cooking meat, I don't actually eat barbecue all that often. However, in the old days before the restaurant opened, I certainly spent my share of time parked in front of an epic barbecue spread—and I know that having delicious barbecue served to you is much more relaxing than cooking it is.

That said, I believe there's as much an art to cutting, serving, and adorning barbecue as there is to cooking it. At Franklin Barbecue, we put a lot of effort into each one of those things, to make sure that all of our hard labor in preparing the food isn't lost at the most important moment: when a diner sits down to eat. And whether you're running a restaurant or just making barbecue for your friends and family, I urge you to pay close attention to the follow-through, right up to the moment when people are digging into the stuff.

In this chapter, I want to give you a little peek into what goes into serving lunch at the restaurant. Cutting brisket properly is practically as important as cooking it well, so I'm going to go into great detail on how to slice it for maximum efficiency and enjoyment. And no matter what you think about barbecue sauce (here in Central Texas, it's an afterthought), I want you to have the recipes for the sauces we make. The espresso sauce is especially near to my heart, since it combines two of my greatest passions: coffee and barbecue. People tend to have one of two attitudes toward sides, as well. Some have no use for them, believing that all they do is take up room in the stomach that could otherwise be devoted to brisket, ribs, and sausage. Others, however, feel that beans, potato salad, and slaw are an essential part of the barbecue experience. Either way, I offer our humble recipes for those too. Finally, I might rightly be accused of feeling that barbecue is really nothing more than a vehicle to accompany one of my other great passions, beer. At the end, I offer my well-researched conclusions on what styles of beer go best with barbecue.

CUTTING LUNCH

At the restaurant, the position I care about most—and the one I spend the most time on when it comes to hiring—is the person who stands up at the counter, takes the meat order, and cuts the meat. We call that person "the cutter," and it's the hardest job in the restaurant. That's because slicing, serving, and presenting barbecue takes a fair amount of skill. We own a restaurant that feeds hundreds of people every day, so I take serving barbecue very seriously. How the food is presented and how it looks on the tray are both very important to me. These things might be less important to someone cooking at home, but they shouldn't be. Even when I cook at home, I want the food to look good.

Cutting meat is a simple process, so why is cutting lunch so hard? First of all, it's a long, long shift, three to four hours of a constant barrage of hungry people who have waited for up to five hours to get their lunch. Once we open the doors, the line does not stop, so you have to be ready. You can't run off to the restroom or take a coffee break. You have to slice and slice.

And slice and be nice. You're also the first person to interact with the customer, so you have to be friendly, make them feel welcome and at ease. "So, where're you from? Sheboygan? You don't say . . ." Then you might have to help them with their order, as most people don't necessarily know what they want when you ask them, "fatty or lean?" (we'll get to that later), and they don't really have an idea of how much they want by the pound, which is how barbecue is sold.

To cut lunch, you have to know brisket. Every brisket is different (even at Franklin Barbecue, where we work really hard to ensure consistency), and you have to be able to make quick assessments on how each one is going to slice, which sections might be tender, which are especially lean and crumbly. You have to make good, precise cuts, which is not always easy with the kind of super-tender brisket we serve. We want to get every last edible morsel out of a brisket, and bad slicing can end up meaning lost product. You have to make sure that each slice is what it should be and is consistent, that it has the right amount of bark, the right amount of fat, the right amount of meat. There must be no big glob of seam fat and no big crunchy burnt piece off the back of the point. It's almost like a magic trick, requiring quick, agile hands. You hold up a glisteningly perfect piece of brisket with one hand to show the customer—"Does that look good for you?"—while you slide a chunk of burnt edge into the trash with the other.

You have to make it look good. The customer is standing right in front of you watching your every move. You're the one and only connection between that person and all of the people in the back who have helped cook that meat. If a piece of brisket looks off in some way (God forbid!), our first time to see it is the same as the customer's. It has to look great.

Finally, you have to be able to judge supply, constantly being aware of how much brisket and ribs are left versus the length of the line snaking out the door. Before we even open the doors, our staff has gone out to survey the line for how much food each party is planning on ordering. This is because every day we have more people in line than we have food to serve, and we don't want anyone to wait in line too long and not get fed. So we have a "last man standing" placard that goes

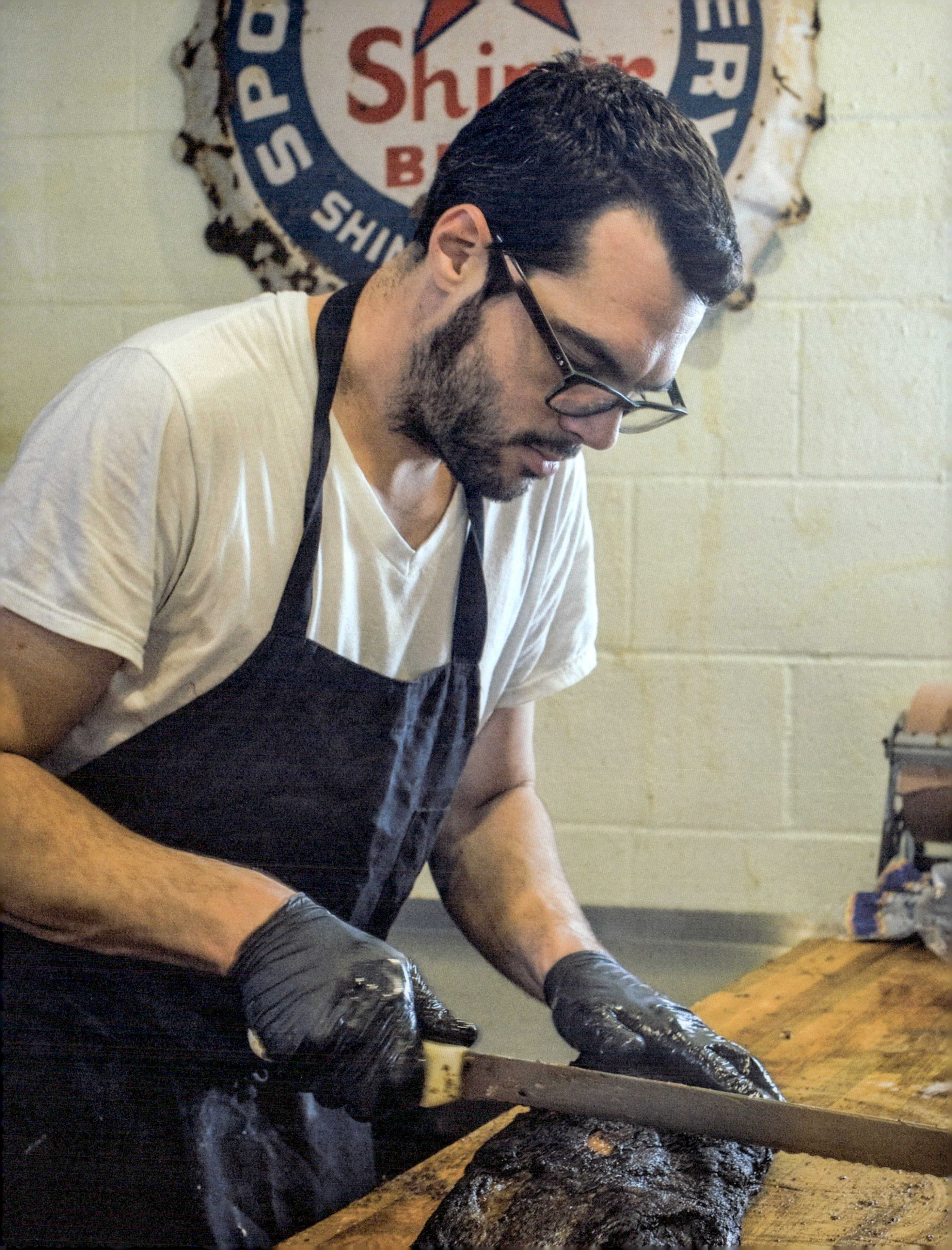

to the last person we guarantee food for. After that person, we leave it up to those people behind him or her to decide if they want to chance it. If you're cutting lunch, you need to be aware of the number of people left waiting to be fed at the end. You have to manage your portions and what parts you might keep, how many bites you are able to give away, and what parts you might be able to stretch depending on the number of people left to feed. (If you mess up either of these things, God help you . . . and the poor folks who waited in line when there was no more brisket.)

The person who cuts lunch must not only have the front-of-the-house skills and charisma of a good bartender or server but also possess the knowledge of how the meat is cooked and the knife skills of a cook. These are not easy people to find. All of this is a way of saying that cutting and serving barbecue is important. Don't concentrate solely on the cooking part of it and let proper service slide once you're almost home. You might have made the best barbecue in the world, but if you screw it up at the slicing table, no one's ever going to know.

HOW TO ORDER BARBECUE AT A RESTAURANT

When you get up to the front of the line at Franklin Barbecue or any Central Texas joint, if you're a first timer, you may not know what you want to order. At our place, someone has probably already polled you in line on what and how much you're going to get, so it shouldn't be difficult. Also, we try to be friendly.

I'll admit this isn't the case everywhere, but I believe that wherever you go, you should get precisely what you want.

If you say you'd like some brisket, at most Central Texas spots, you'll be asked what kind and how much? You'll have noted that they sell by the pound and you'll be thinking to yourself, *How many pounds can I eat?* With such thinking, many people commit themselves to overordering. So, while it's fine to order a pound or a half pound, it's also acceptable to order one slice or two slices or whatever. In this day and age, everyone has a digital scale that can do the calculations, so it makes no difference to us whether you order by weight or by amount.

You'll then be asked what kind of brisket you want, lean or moist? At Franklin, that'll be lean or fatty. If you've read the preceding chapters of this book, you'll know that question refers to whether you want a slice off the leaner flat end of the brisket or the fattier point. It's your call. You're also welcome to ask for a piece that's heavy on bark or even something crispy, if they've got it.

Likewise, you needn't feel the pressure to order ribs by the pound. It's fine to order one rib or two ribs or however many you want. Same goes for pretty much anything else on the menu. Just order any way you want and don't let anyone tell you differently.

When I was really getting into barbecue, before I ever dreamed of having my own restaurant, I had a standard order when I went to visit places around Texas: half a pound of moist brisket and ribs, with a side of potato salad. I'd order a sausage only if it was made in-house, and I'd ask for the barky end piece off the flat of the brisket, if they had it.

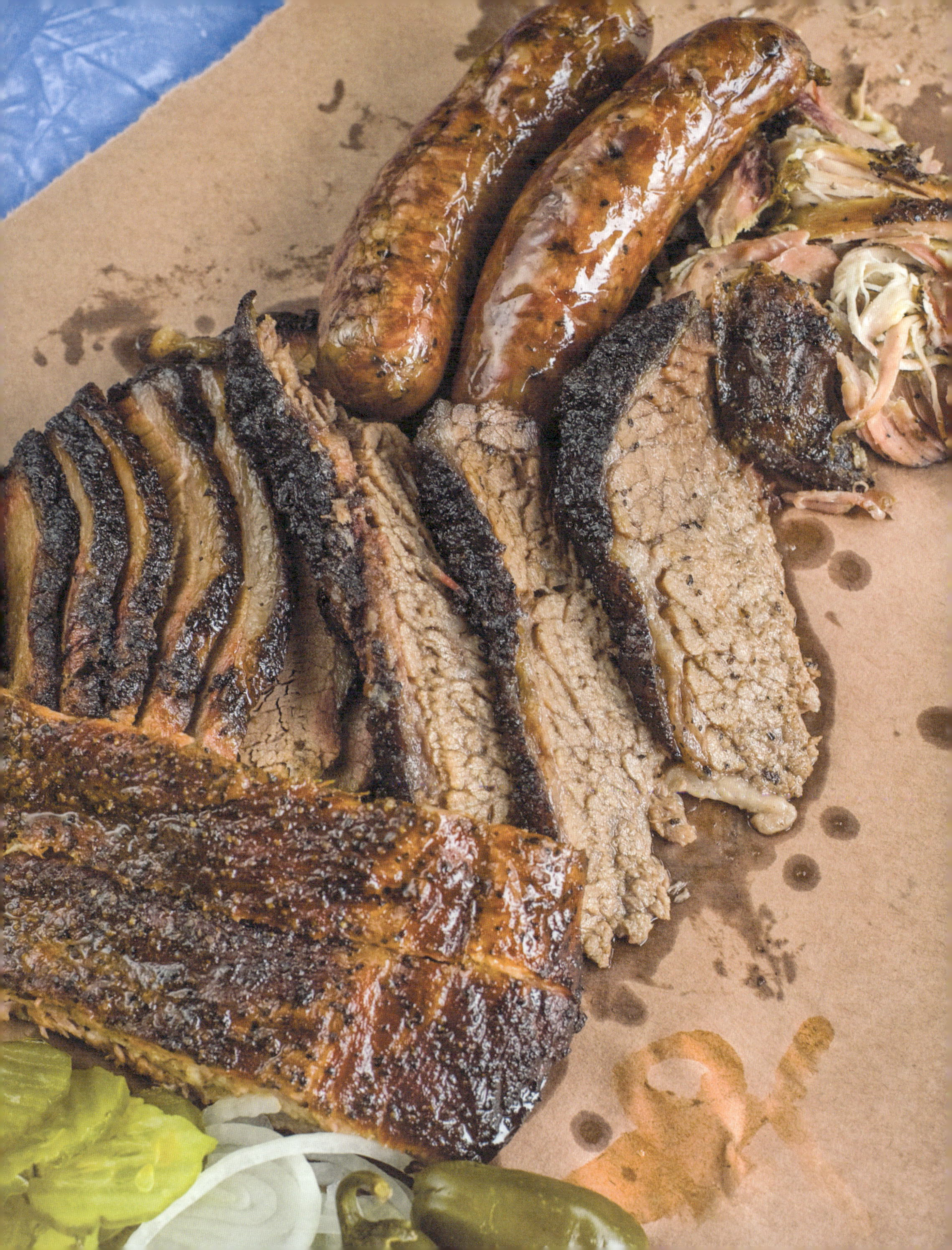

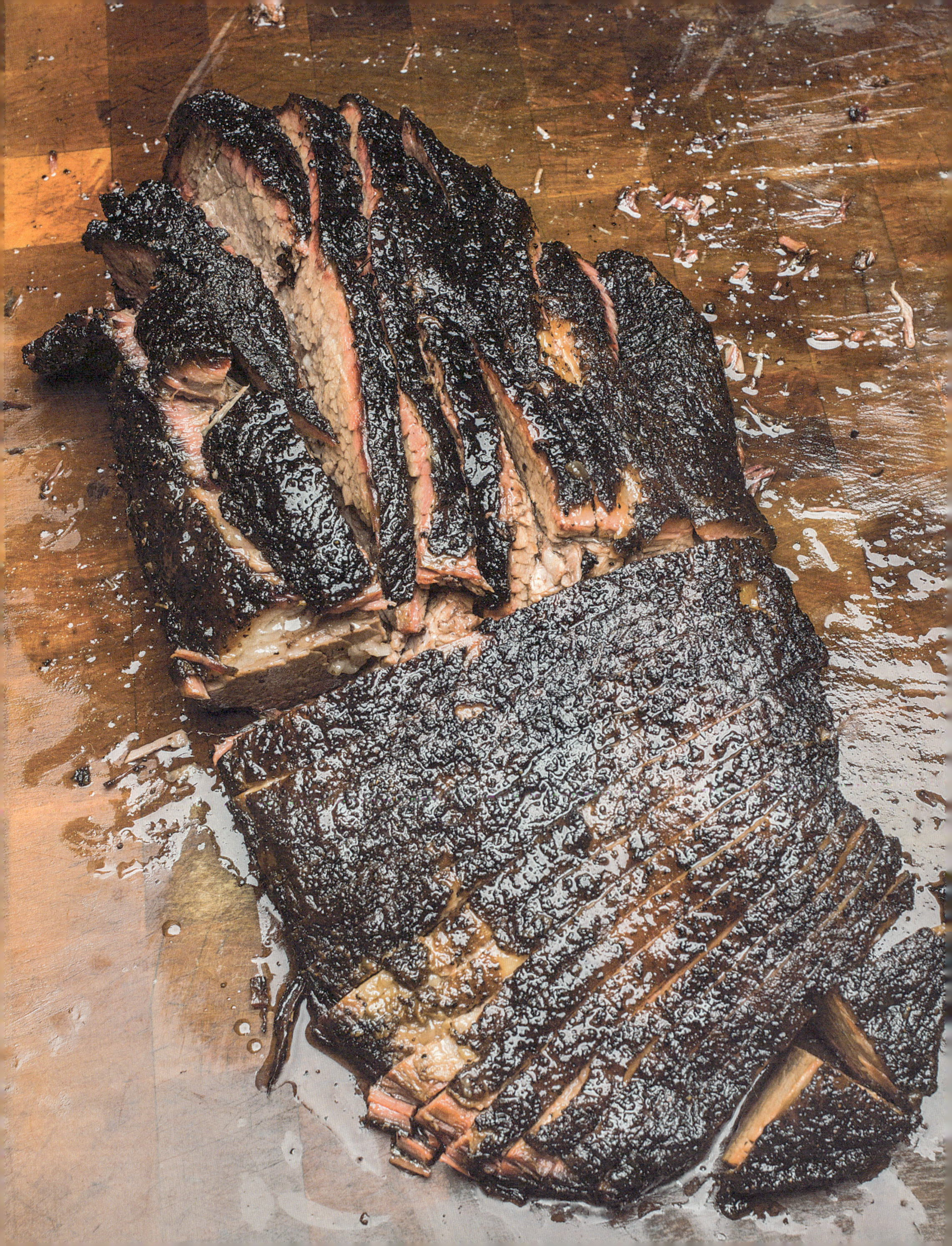

HOW TO SLICE A BRISKET

Everybody has his or her own method for slicing brisket, but there's one thing on which we can all agree: never, ever slice with the grain. That one mistake can turn even a beautifully cooked, moist, and jiggly brisket into brutal strands of chewy fiber. Beyond that one, simple truism, though, there are many ways to do it, and many of them work well.

It's important to know that, just like the way a song is performed can determine a lot about your ability to enjoy it, the way a brisket is sliced will have an impact on the way you perceive that meat. For instance, if you go to a not-so-great barbecue joint, you might find yourself getting a plateful of paper-thin slices. That's a time-honored, wily technique for trying to hide brisket that's way too tough. Likewise, if you get really thick slices, the place might be hiding that the brisket was overcooked and is so overly tender that it lacks any structural integrity (or, it might just mean that somebody rushed through the cutting). If the slices weren't thick, they would fall apart before they got to the plate.

But let's start with the knife. At some places you might see the slicer using an electric knife. While I understand why people might resort to an electric knife—ease, comfort, avoiding the risk of carpal tunnel for people who cut brisket for hours and hours—I can't condone its use. First, it's really slow, taking forever to get through a single slice. Second, you can't feel the blade cutting through the meat, which is important. You receive all sorts of sensory information about the brisket—texture, level of doneness and rendering—from the knife. My favorite knife for slicing isn't fancy at all. It's a serrated, 12-inch Dexter-Russell slicing knife, model S140-12SC. It's the kind with a white plastic handle that you can buy at any restaurant supply store. I like it because the serrations are sharp and well defined but not scalloped. That's going to help you get through the softness of the bark without ripping it to shreds, which is a constant risk.

It's the very anatomy of a brisket that makes it such a challenge to slice well. As you know, the whole packer-cut brisket is made up of two muscles, the flat and the point. And the point sits right on top of the flat, separated by a thin layer of fat. The only problem with this arrangement is that the grain of the meat in the flat runs perpendicular to the grain of the point meat. So if you want your brisket to be sliced into nice, tender pieces, you're going to have to cut each section a little bit differently.

Cutting Brisket, Step by Step

My approach to slicing brisket is based on one simple goal: maximizing the deliciousness of every single piece. To me, the bark holds the most flavor and texture. You can't have a great piece of brisket if it doesn't sport at least a small section of bark, so I try to cut it in a way that ensures every piece a decent bark-to-meat ratio. That's why I don't separate the point from the flat before slicing, the way some people do: the part of the flat sitting directly underneath the point will have no bark. At the restaurant, we may very well not serve some of the meat from this part, as parts of it can be too fat-laden or mushy to be cut into a coherent slice. If it's too fatty, we'll throw it away, and if it's all meat, we may save it to use as chop in the Tipsy Texan sandwich (see page 188), or add it to the beans. Home cooks out there will likely want to save it, even if it doesn't make for great slices.

- You want to wait to cut the brisket until it's cool enough to touch with your hands, maybe an hour or so after you've pulled it from the smoker. Unwrap the brisket and lay it in front of you (see **PHOTO 1**, right). I'm right-handed, so I like to start with the flat on the right and the point on my left.

- Before I do anything, I imagine the line where the point terminates and where the flat dips underneath it (see **PHOTO 2**). You'll know where this is because you'll see the seam of fat that runs between them, and you'll be able to see the point begin to rise up from the flat. You can actually feel the point shift around on top of the flat if you gently move it with your hand. This is the place where I'm going to stop slicing the flat. It's not exactly parallel or symmetrical to the end of the flat (on my right), so I also visualize the way my slices will sort of have to fan out across the arc of the meat if I want them to be even and uniform.

- The first cut I make is called the end cut. It's just the little tapered section on the far end of the flat. It's mostly bark and therefore delicious. A perfect end cut is a good indicator of a well-cooked brisket: this is one of the best pieces you can get! I usually slice the end cut in half and offer the two little nubs as a snack for whoever's at the front of the line at the time (see **PHOTOS 3 AND 4**).

- Now slice the flat. The left hand (for righties) is very important in slicing brisket. If your brisket is really tender, it's your left hand that's going to keep it together as you're running the knife across it. You've got to apply a bit of pressure to hold it together, so don't be shy. I put my left hand very gently on top of the flat to hold it down and hold it together and then I start slicing across the flat. You want to aim for slices that are 1/4 inch thick, the size of a no. 2 pencil, as I like to say. I slice across the flat evenly and gently, cutting it into nice, uniform strips. It's not necessary to be exactly perpendicular to the grain, but rather just cut across it in some way. The flat is never a perfectly even rectangle, so you'll find yourself fanning your angle out a bit. Move the knife smoothly and confidently, sawing gently back and forth. Use the thumb of your nonslicing hand to hold the bark in when necessary, as the serrations of the knife will want to pull some of that bark off (and you don't want this to happen). Stop slicing when you reach the beginning of the point—it's that line you visualized before you started (see **PHOTOS 5 AND 6**).

SERVING + EATING

FRANKLIN BARBECUE

SERVING + EATING

- Now that you've sliced the flat, keeping its slices firmly together (unless you've already served them to a hungry crowd), move the sliced flat out of the way. Sitting in front of you should be the whole, uncut point section of the brisket. Swivel this whole piece 90° (see **PHOTO 7**, left) so its exposed side is now facing you. With your left hand, gently pull back the right side of this piece and you'll find underneath the bark a really jiggly slab of fat with a little meat attached to it. Cut this part away with the knife (see **PHOTOS 8 AND 9**). We throw this slice of mostly fat away.

- Turn the point 180° so that the exposed side where it was connected to the flat is now facing away from you (see **PHOTO 10**). This is where we slice the point in half. It's helpful to cut the whole point in half because it is so soft and moist that it's more manageable to slice this way. After you cut it in half, you can pick up one-half and get that money shot everyone loves of a big chunk of super-tender, moist, dripping brisket (see **PHOTO 11**).

- You'll now be slicing the point against the grain. I like to cut the left half of the point first. Start delicately cutting from the middle out to the edge in slices ⅜ inch thick (the width of a large pencil), or almost twice as thick as you sliced the flat. Place your left hand flat against the bark, gently holding it down as you slice. Keep the slices together as much as possible to prevent the juices from running out across the board (though a lot of juice still will). Also, if you're not going to serve the whole thing at one sitting, the brisket stays juicier and fresher for longer when left intact and unsliced (see **PHOTO 12**).

- If you're going to slice up the whole thing, move the left half of the point (which you have just sliced) out of the way and pick up the right half. Put it in front of you with the sliced side to your right (for righties) and slice it in the same manner as you sliced the other half of the point. When you get to the end, where it's mostly bark, you might find it helpful to push the bark over in front of the knife to make sure that every last possible slice has both some bark and some meat (see **PHOTO 13**, below). It's hard to explain, but when you start cutting it, you'll know what I'm talking about. You'll be left with a thin slice of mostly bark at the end. This is the burnt end, and you can slice it into delicious little snacky-snacks for the hungry hordes who are waiting for you to finish all of this darn slicing!

- If you've cooked the brisket well, the point should stay together, but you might encounter some shreds of beef or little scraps coming from the remnants of the flat underneath it. Take those bits that stay behind along with any little crunchy edges and save them for either the chopped beef or the beans.

- You can judge a great slice and the success of the brisket cook by applying the "pull test." Hold up a slice of brisket between the thumb and index finger of both hands. Now gently pull it apart. The brisket slice should easily break, but it shouldn't fall apart. If it crumbles apart or disintegrates, it's overdone. If it stretches out, it hasn't been cooked long enough.

THE TIPSY TEXAN

At Franklin Barbecue, our menu is mostly traditional Central Texas fare. There is one oddity, however: the Tipsy Texan sandwich, which is essentially a pile of chopped beef, sausage, slaw, and sauce served on a bun. This giant, honking sandwich costs only eight dollars, and considering how much of our prized brisket we use for each one, it's a pretty good deal for the customer (and decidedly *not* cost-effective for the restaurant). I'm not going to lie: I get a little wistful every time I have to chop up some of our beautiful brisket and slap it on a bun. So why do I still keep the Tipsy Texan on the menu? Honestly, I can't really say. But, like the weather or a birthmark, it's just something we have to live with.

The origins of the sandwich date to the earliest days of the Franklin Barbecue trailer. A prominent local bartender, who billed himself as the Tipsy Texan (and still does), would come to eat and, per his request, I'd make him one of these stupid-big sandwiches. In its present-day incarnation, it's a monstrous assemblage of chopped lean brisket mixed with espresso sauce, sausage, slaw, sauce, pickles, and onions, and it probably weighs 1¼ pounds.

In my opinion, the best time to make a Tipsy Texan is when you have extra chips of chopped lean brisket, which we like to mix with Espresso Barbecue Sauce (page 192). But when we don't have chips lying around, our only option is to slice fresh brisket and chop it up—a move that causes many brisket purists to gasp in horror. We top the chopped brisket with a sliced whole sausage, sliced pickles and onions, and finally with about ½ cup of slaw.

What's my final verdict on the Tipsy Texan? Well, it is certainly one of the most delicious and decadent ways to use up leftover brisket—no doubt about it. But it is certainly not the ideal use for pristine brisket. I guess we just keep it around for the sake of tradition. I should also note that *if* you can get your mouth around one and finish it, you might consider a career in professional eating.

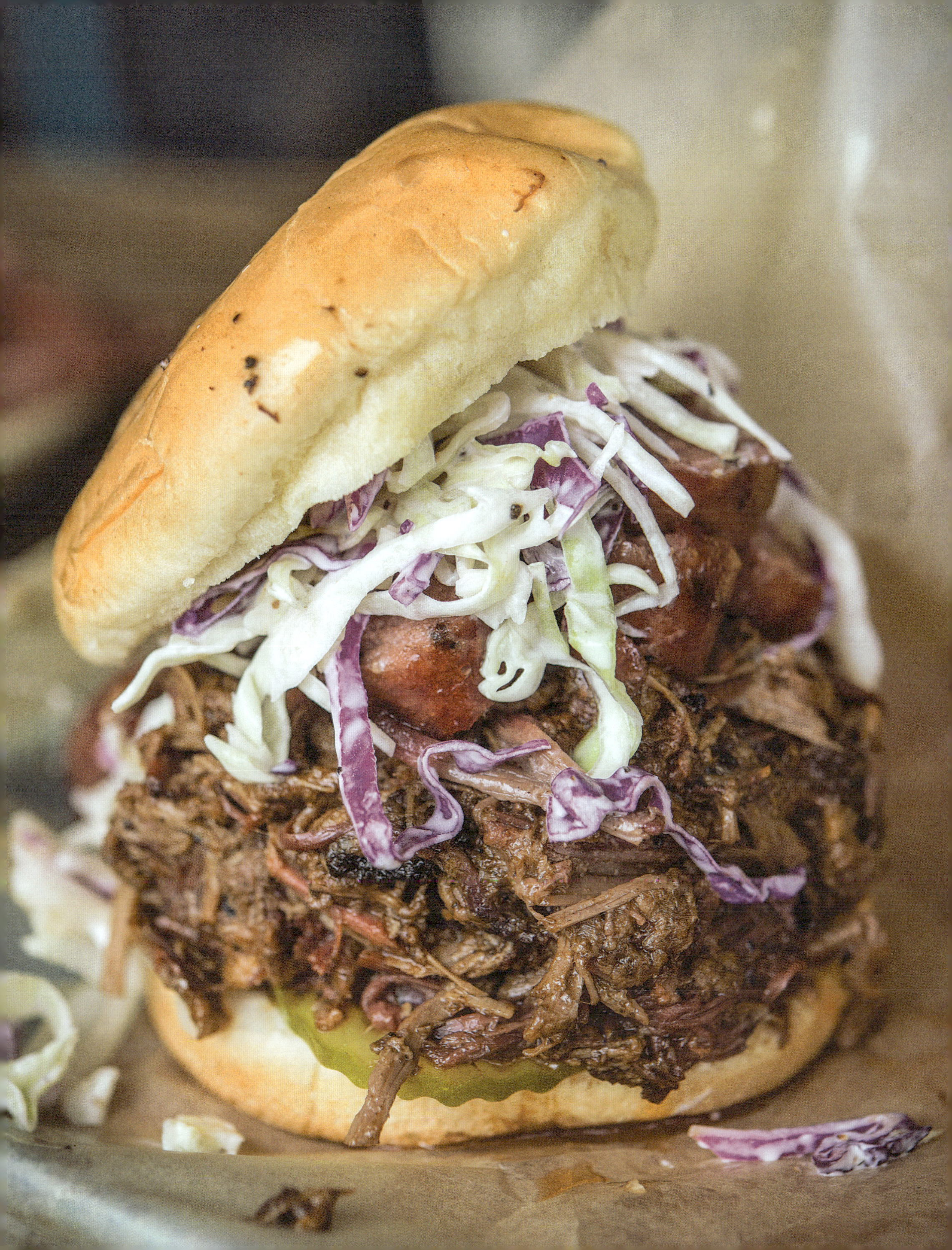

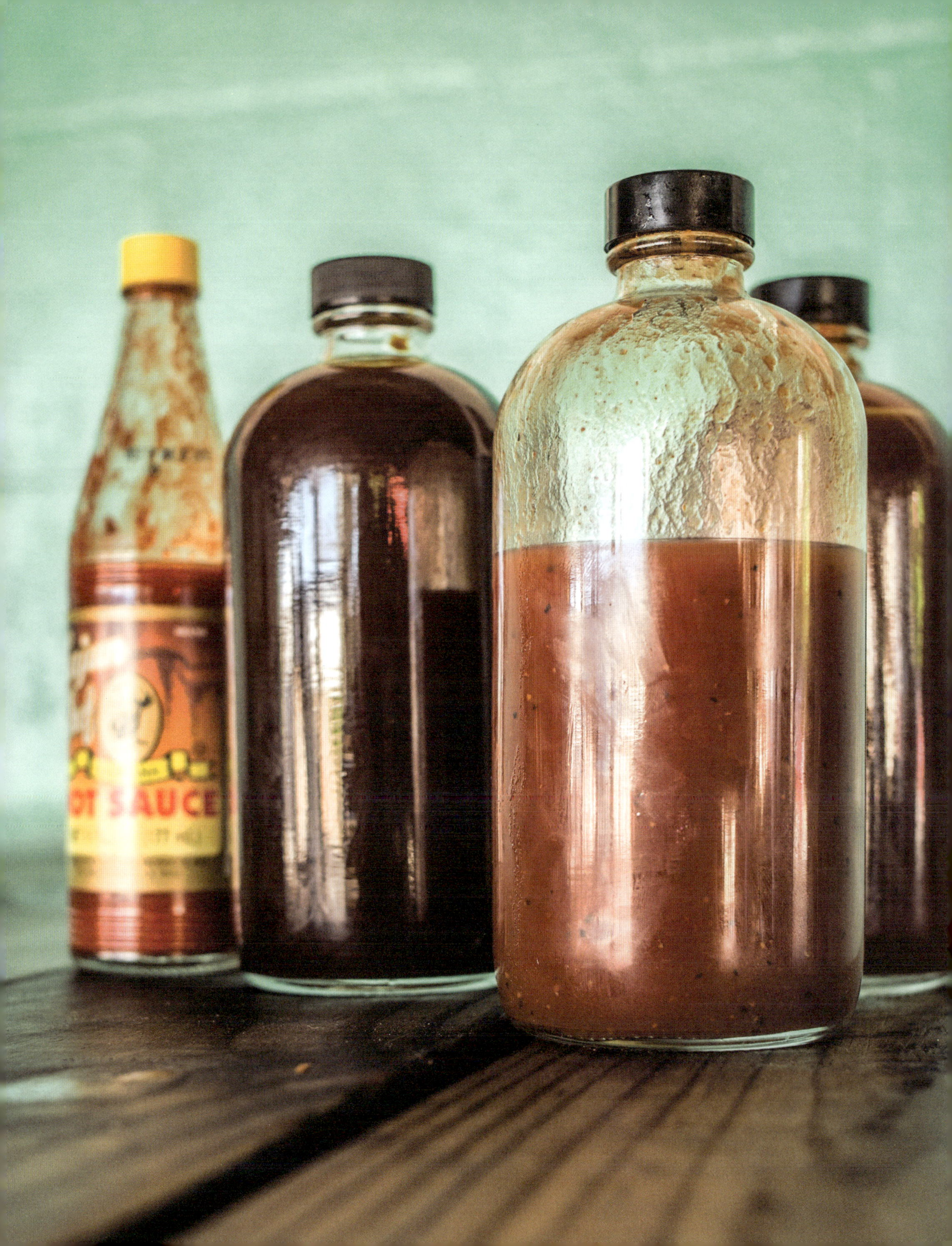

SERVING + EATING

SAUCE

In the rest of the country, sauce is an essential, inseparable component of barbecue. In Central Texas, barbecue sauce is considered optional, at best.

You see, in Central Texas we believe that well-made barbecue has no need for sauce. If the pitmaster has done his or her job, the well-balanced flavors of great beef or pork and sweet oak smoke are complex enough and delicious enough to stand on their own. It's the German-Czech orthodoxy we've inherited, and until recently, there still were places that stayed true to the meat-market origins of the cuisine and didn't offer sauce (or silverware) for their meat. Nowadays, however, pretty much everyone has sauce because diners expect it. And while I truly believe really good barbecue needs no sauce, a little bit can be nice to accentuate the flavors in the meat. But it has to be good sauce.

Bad sauce for me lacks balance—it's too sweet, too thick, too something. And my ultimate hallmark of a bad sauce is a sauce that has liquid smoke in it. Smoke flavoring should come from the meat (and not too much of it, mind you).

Barbecue sauce doesn't make good barbecue, but it can certainly complement good barbecue. There really isn't a Texas-style sauce. Up in the Panhandle, sauce tends to be a bit more midwestern, while in East Texas it tends to have the sweet and ketchupy notes of the Deep South. At Louie Mueller, you get a light, watery sauce with margarine, but if you go to our place, our everyday sauce is a well-balanced ketchup sauce with a little bit of cumin and chile powder going on.

Our sauce is what I'd call Central Texas style in that it's tomato based and balanced between sweet and savory with a bit of acidity. It's really just meant to lubricate already moist meat, to add sweetness that highlights the savory flavor of smoke, and to contribute acidity that helps balance the richness of the fat and protein. I've been working on sauces since the early days of my barbecue cooking endeavor. Stacy ruefully remembers periodically getting home from her restaurant job late at night and me excitedly forcing her to try a spoonful of barbecue sauce the second she walked through the door. That said, I hit on these basic recipes pretty early on and have stuck with them ever since, believing they're the best suited to our style of cooking.

REGULAR BARBECUE SAUCE

This is what I call sweet sauce, even though it's not terribly sweet on the spectrum of barbecue sauces. It's a good, all-purpose sauce. We bottle it, sell it, and put it on the tables in the restaurant. I also mix it with vinegar to sauce the spare ribs when I cook them.

Makes about 3 cups

- 1 3/4 cups ketchup
- 1/2 cup plus 2 tablespoons water
- 1/4 cup plus 1 tablespoon cider vinegar
- 1/4 cup plus 1 tablespoon white vinegar
- 1/4 cup plus 1 1/2 teaspoons brown sugar
- 2 tablespoons plus 1 1/2 teaspoons Worcestershire sauce
- 1 tablespoon chile powder
- 1 tablespoon ground cumin
- 1 1/2 teaspoons kosher salt
- 1 1/2 teaspoons coarse black pepper

Combine all of the ingredients in a saucepan and warm gently over medium heat, stirring occasionally. There is no need to bring the mixture to a boil, as the idea is just to warm it enough to melt and integrate the ingredients. Once you have done that, remove from the heat and let cool. Transfer to a jar, bottle, squeeze bottle, or however you want to store it. Store in the refrigerator for up to 1 month.

ESPRESSO BARBECUE SAUCE

Nowadays various recipes for coffee barbecue sauces are floating around. But when I first came up with mine, it was an original and inspired distillation of my life at the time. I was working at Little City coffee shop, starting to get geeky about coffee and even geekier about barbecue.

An all-nighter on a brisket cook was inevitably accompanied by strong coffee, and it didn't take a genius to notice the affinity that starlight, the sweet roasted aromas of good espresso, and the homey aromas of wood and smoke have for one another. If these smells go so well together in the middle of the night, I thought to myself, their flavors should just as easily merge into a sauce. And the sauce was a way to capture that experience of being awake in the depths of the night watching a fire.

It didn't turn out to be that easy to bring the flavors together. The first time I made the sauce, I used a little Krups espresso machine that a guy I worked with at Little City had given me. And the sauce seemed great to me. Then I tried to refine it, but when I forced a taste of the "improved" version on Stacy, she told me it was nasty and that I needed to hang it up. Then I went back to my original recipe with a few, small tweaks, and it was a go.

It's important to note that there is no substitute for the espresso in this recipe. If you don't have access to an espresso machine, I would take some of the warm sauce to a reputable coffee shop, get them to pull a shot for you, and mix them together there. I know it sounds weird and may even be slightly embarrassing, but the results are worth it. A freshly pulled shot with a good crema brings much more to this recipe than a stale or cold one. I prefer a medium-roast, Central American bean (Guatemala, El Salvador, Costa Rica). The brisket drippings are a matter of taste, but I believe this sauce needs the beefiness to make it taste right.

Makes about 2 cups

- 1½ cups ketchup
- ½ cup white vinegar
- ½ cup cider vinegar
- ¼ cup dark soy sauce
- 1 tablespoon garlic powder
- 1 tablespoon onion powder
- ¼ cup brown sugar
- 3 tablespoons (1½ ounces) freshly pulled espresso
- Brisket drippings, for flavoring

Mix the ketchup, both vinegars, the soy sauce, garlic and onion powders, and sugar together in a saucepan and bring to a simmer over medium heat, stirring occasionally. Remove from the heat, stir in the espresso, and then add the brisket drippings to taste. Let cool, then transfer to a jar, bottle, squeeze bottle, or however you want to store it. Store in the refrigerator for up to 2 weeks.

VINEGAR SAUCE

This is the non-Carolina vinegar sauce that I created to go with my non-Carolina pulled pork. Use whatever hot sauce you like or whatever you've got around. Of course, some are hotter than others, so consider how spicy you want the sauce to be.

Makes about 3 cups

- 1 cup white vinegar
- 1 cup cider vinegar
- 1 cup ketchup
- 1 tablespoon brown sugar
- 2 tablespoons hot sauce
- Dash of Worcestershire sauce
- 2 teaspoons Hungarian paprika
- Kosher salt and coarse black pepper

Combine all of the ingredients, including salt and pepper to taste, in a saucepan and warm gently over medium heat, stirring occasionally. There is no need to bring the mixture to a boil, as the idea is just to warm it enough to melt and integrate the ingredients. Transfer to a jar, bottle, squeeze bottle, or however you want to store it. Store in the refrigerator for up to 1 month.

FIG ANCHO BEER BARBECUE SAUCE

I don't serve this at the restaurant, but I do make fun sauces for some events—and this sauce combines a few of my favorite things.

Makes about 6 cups

- 4 ancho chiles, rehydrated in 4½ cups hot water and the water reserved
- 12 figs, grilled, stemmed, and quartered
- ½ yellow onion, sliced
- 4 tablespoons butter
- 1½ cups brown sugar
- 1 (12-ounce) bottle (1½ cups) stout or porter beer (I prefer Left Hand Brewing's milk stout)
- 1 cup ketchup
- ½ cup white vinegar
- ½ cup cider vinegar
- 6 tablespoons fig preserves
- 1 tablespoon honey
- 1 tablespoon kosher salt
- 1 teaspoon coarse black pepper

In a skillet over medium heat, sauté the chiles, figs, and onion in the butter for about 10 minutes, until the figs and chiles are tender and the onion is translucent. Transfer to a blender and add the sugar, stout, ketchup, both vinegars, the preserves, honey, salt, and pepper. Puree until smooth, adding as much of the reserved chile soaking liquid as needed to reach the desired texture. Store in an airtight container in the refrigerator for up to 2 weeks.

ACCOUTREMENTS: DILL PICKLE SLICES, SLICED ONIONS, AND INDUSTRIAL WHITE BREAD

The German and Czech heritage of Central Texas barbecue is evident not only in the kinds of meats we serve but also in the classic accompaniments for the meats. Not every style of barbecue requires large vats of pickles and sliced onions to be on offer right after you come out of the service line. And although these are add-ons, many people consider them to be highly important to the Texas barbecue experience.

And I don't disagree. The sharpness of dill pickles (sweet pickles or bread-and-butter chips don't work) and of raw white onion is the perfect counter to the unctuousness of good meat (as is beer). Good ole industrial white bread adds a sweet flavor and soft textural touch to the mixture. With brisket, eat these things in combinations and sequences of your own choosing. Some people wrap a slice of brisket in a piece of bread, add a couple of dashes of sauce, and garnish with a few slices of pickle and onion for a delicious sandwich wrap. Others might just pop a couple of pickle morsels and raw onion slivers into their mouth after a particularly good bite of brisket and sausage. Use these tools to your own delight.

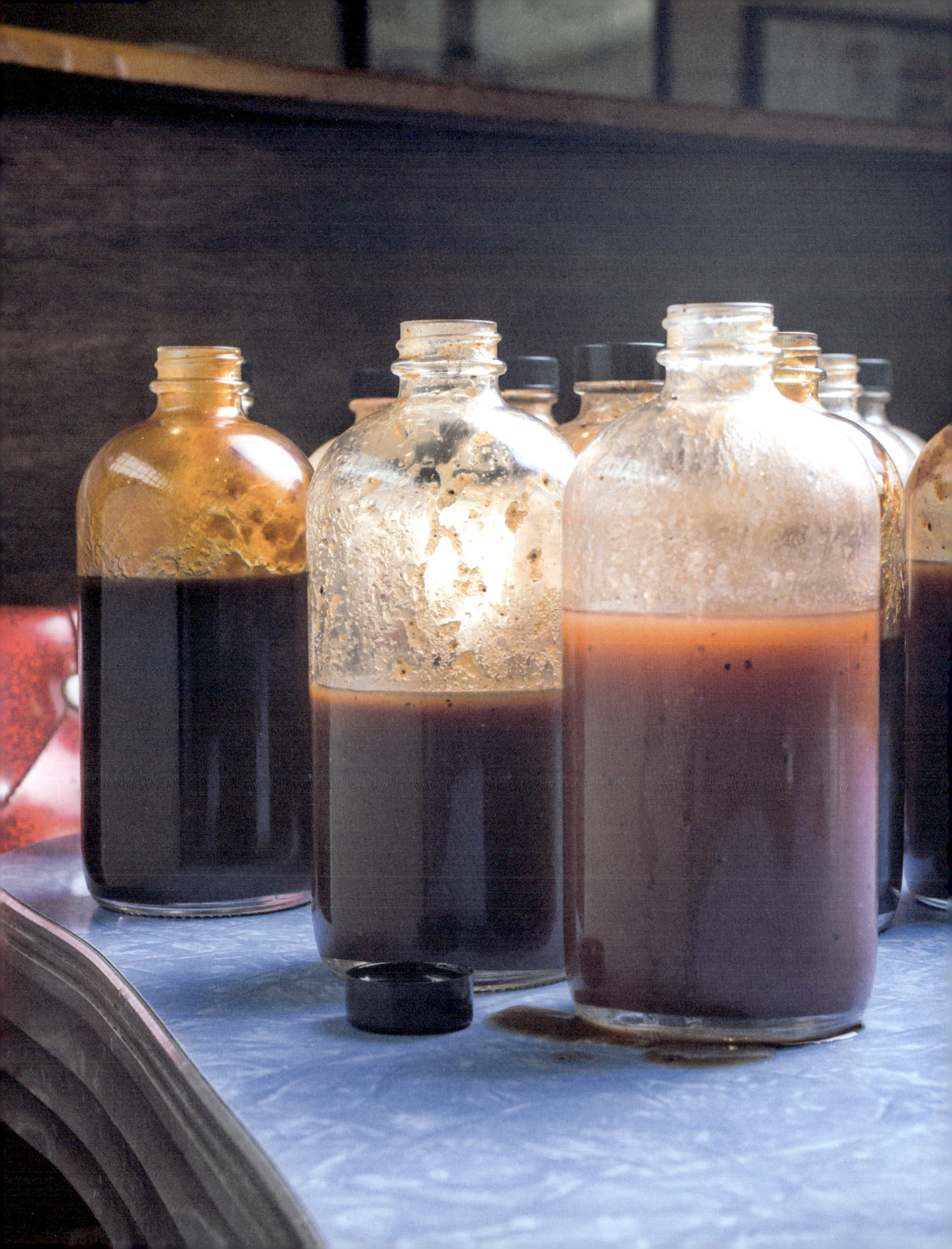

SIDES

In the world of Central Texas barbecue, people treat sides pretty much the same way they treat sauces: they're fine, but you should probably just save the room in your stomach for barbecue. Indeed, the meat-market heritage of Central Texas barbecue doesn't include sides either. But, like sauces, sides have become a staple of the barbecue spread, and today we serve, eat, and enjoy them just the same.

BEANS

We get a lot of requests for our bean recipe. What makes it so popular? Probably the simple fact that it's another way of delivering brisket, which is its second-most important ingredient (arguably).

Makes about 8 cups; serves 8 to 10

- 1 pound dried pinto beans, picked over and rinsed
- ½ cup diced yellow onion
- ½ cup bean seasoning (recipe follows)
- 8 cups water
- 1 cup chopped brisket bark and shredded meat

Combine the beans, onion, bean seasoning, and water in a large pot and let soak for 4 to 6 hours, or for up to overnight, which is what we do in the restaurant.

Add the brisket bark and meat to the soaked beans and bring to a boil. Lower the heat to a slow simmer, cover, and cook for 3 to 4 hours, until the beans are tender.

Bean Seasoning

Makes about 2 cups

- 1 cup chile powder
- ½ cup kosher salt
- ¼ cup coarse black pepper
- 2 tablespoons onion powder
- 2 tablespoons garlic powder
- 1 teaspoon ground cumin

Combine all of the ingredients and mix well. Store in an airtight container.

POTATO SALAD

I spent hours peeling potatoes, drinking beers, and talking to friends when Stacy and I had our little barbecue trailer. I like flavor, so we engineered this salad to have a nice, mustardy bite and lots of pickles in the German-Czech tradition.

Makes about 6 cups; serves 12

- 3 pounds russet potatoes, peeled and cut into 1/2-inch (or smaller) dice
- 1 cup mayonnaise
- 1/2 cup yellow mustard
- 3/4 cup chopped dill pickles
- 1 tablespoon pickle juice
- 1 tablespoon coarse black pepper
- 1 teaspoon kosher salt

Cook the potatoes in a pot of boiling water just until tender. Drain, transfer to a bowl, and let cool. In a small bowl, stir together the mayonnaise, mustard, pickles, pickle juice, pepper, and salt. Add to the cooled potatoes, toss and stir to mix well, cover, and refrigerate immediately. The salad will keep for up to 4 days in the refrigerator. Serve cold.

COLESLAW

Coleslaw serves an important purpose not just as a side, but also as a condiment for barbecue. It offers a crunchy textural contrast to tender meat, and its vinegary zip is a nice counter to the sweet, fatty, and smoky flavors we serve at Franklin. And of course, it's an important component of the Tipsy Texan sandwich (see page 188). This tangy slaw is great alongside all sorts of barbecued meats.

Makes about 2 cups

- 1/2 pound (about 2 cups) shredded cabbage mix
- 1 tablespoon kosher salt
- 1/4 cup sour cream
- 2 tablespoons mayonnaise
- 2 tablespoons cider vinegar
- 2 tablespoons rice vinegar
- 2 1/4 teaspoons coarse black pepper
- 1 1/2 teaspoons dry mustard powder

Place the cabbage in a colander or strainer and sprinkle with the salt. Let the cabbage sit and exude some of its juice while you prepare the dressing. In a large bowl, stir together the sour cream, mayonnaise, cider vinegar, rice vinegar, pepper, and mustard powder. Blot away any excess moisture from the cabbage with a towel, then transfer to the bowl containing the dressing and toss to combine. Cover and refrigerate until ready to serve. Serve cold.

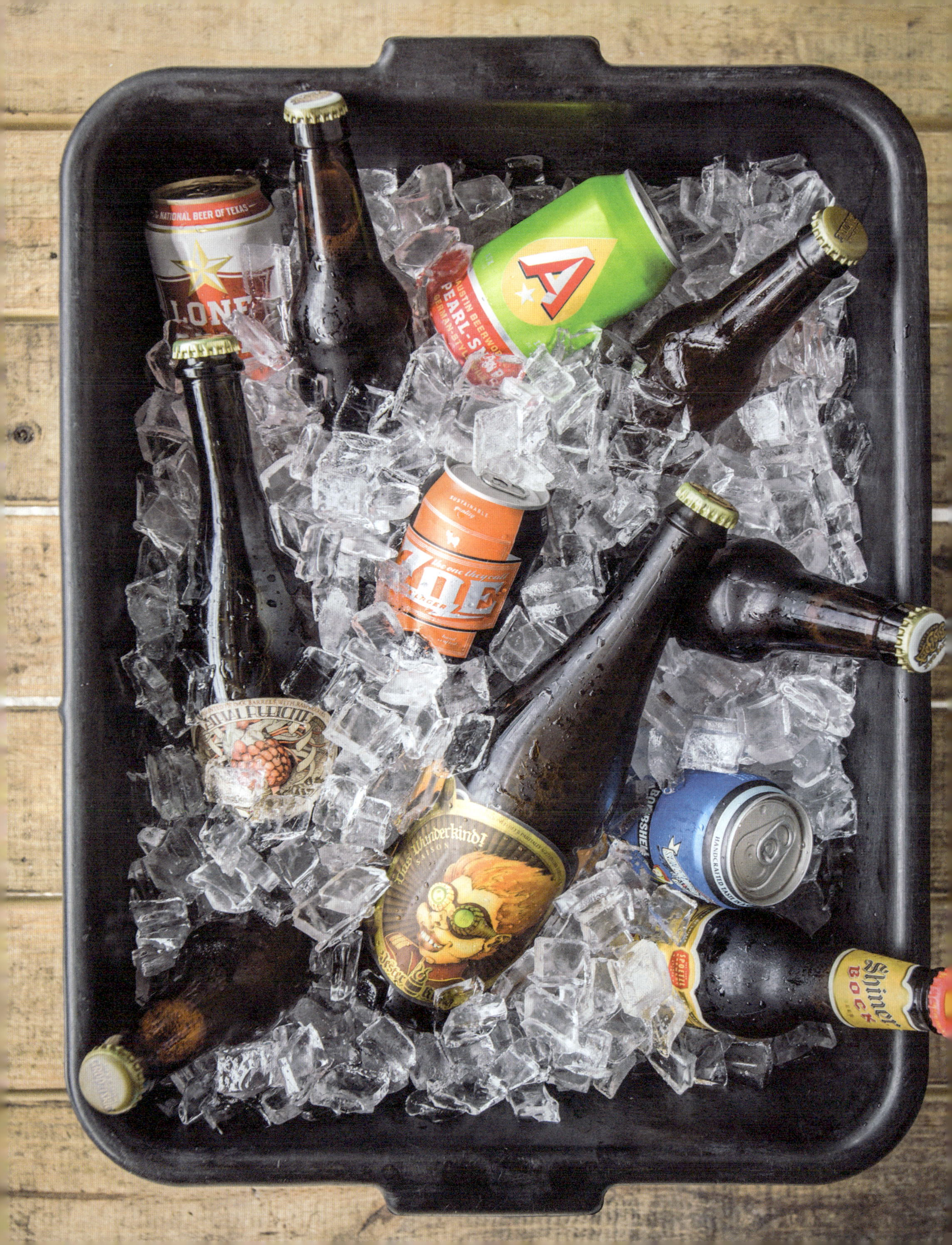
NATIONAL BEER OF TEXAS
ZOE
Das Wunderkind!
Shiner
BOCK

WHAT TO DRINK WITH BARBECUE

I like beer. I like lots of other things too, but I *really* like beer. In fact, it's not at all rare to find one in my hand.

When it comes to pairing beer and barbecue, the first rule is, *yes*! The second rule is, *there are no rules*. That said, I do have my own personal preferences.

Now, I must preface all that's about to follow with the general assertion that I like most beers. But my favorites all share certain characteristics. I'm not into ultra-hoppy beers. They can be exciting for the first half of the beer but end up fatiguing the palate by the end. They also don't pair very well with barbecue—or with a lot of foods, for that matter. I really like more malty beers.

I also really enjoy beers on the lower end of the alcohol scale. This is largely because "sessionability"—a beer's capacity to be consumed comfortably in decent amounts without incurring palate fatigue, slurred speech, motor-skill impairment, and general dufusness—is important to me. I like to drink beer, but I don't like to get drunk, so something not too potent and with a generally balanced and tasteful approach is perfect for me.

Luckily, this seems to be the kind of beer that also turns on lots of Texan brewers, which is one reason I'm so enthusiastic about the brewing scene in this state. Maybe it's only natural that in a hot climate where we drink beer as a form of hydration, mild, sessionable, low-alcohol beers are not hard to find. That doesn't mean that the beers lack flavor or crispness or interest. It just means that it's pleasant to drink more than one of them and to drink them with food.

If I were to name a staple beer for me in life, it would be the Big Bark amber lager from Live Oak Brewing of Austin, one of the best breweries anywhere, if you ask me. Big Bark beer has been on tap at the restaurant since we opened. How perfect is it for barbecue and for me? Well, like Central Texas barbecue, it's has a Czech and German influence—specifically in the form of the Czech and German malts that go into it. It's also got German hops, but not too much—just enough to balance the malt notes. And I like that it has "bark," just like the best part of the brisket, though only in the beer's name. Smooth, balanced, and reddish amber—it's ideal.

But lots of beers are good with barbecue. Even some of the larger-scaled beers like Shiner Bock and Lone Star go real well. Hans' Pils from Real Ale Brewing Company, another Hill Country favorite, is relentlessly refreshing and sessionable. I'm also crazy about the beers from Austin's Hops and Grain brewery. Their Altbier, called Alt-eration, is technically an ale but has a crispness and light hoppiness along with a copper-amber color that makes it not too far off from the style of Big Bark, which is a lager.

Jester King, another local brewery, specializes in sour beers. I'm not always a fan of really tart, sour beers, but a mild sour is delicious, and Jester King makes some good stuff. I think smoke and beer go well together in general, but Ron Extract, one of the founders of Jester King and a serious beer scholar, points out that smoke and sour flavors are a classic combination. "All beer would have originally been smoked," he says, noting that before the days of modern malting techniques, malt was made by drying the grains, after allowing them to steep and start to germinate, over fire, which would have imparted smokiness. He also suggests that most beer in the old days would have been at least slightly sour and funky, since commercial yeast (which is relatively stable and allows for a predictable and notably less funky fermentation taste) had not yet been cultivated. This meant that brewers had to rely on unpredictable wild yeasts to ferment the beer. Wild yeasts are difficult to control and can take fermentations in all sorts of directions, leading to the funky, sour flavors we associate with that style of beer.

If I had to distill my beer-and-barbecue philosophy into a few key points, they'd probably go something like this:

1 • Excessively hoppy beers, such as West Coast–style IPAs, tend to overwhelm the palate. I don't like to pair them with barbecue very much, as their intense grassy, floral flavors seem to conflict with the mellow, smoky-peppery flavors of the meat.

2 • Super-boozy beers and barbecue don't really mix. After drinking a few, you're not really going to be able to appreciate the taste of the barbecue (and if you're mid-cook, you risk losing focus). Session beers in the 5% ABV or lower range are my go-to, as I like to be able to drink a lot of beers without getting drunk.

3 • Czech- and German-style beers are a natural pairing for Central Texas–style barbecue. In warmer weather, I gravitate toward crisp, refreshing styles—think pilsner, Kölsch, or Altbier. In the autumn and winter, I might go for one of the darker styles, like a bock or porter.

4 • Smoked meat loves sour beer! Try a sessionable style like Berliner Weisse, which often clocks in around 3% ABV.

5 • Smoked meat and smoked beer work well together too. In fact, I like this combination so much, I once teamed up with the folks at Thirsty Planet Brewing Company to create the Franklin Barbecue smoked porter (sadly no longer in production), and with Jester King to create a beer with grilled, smoked figs!

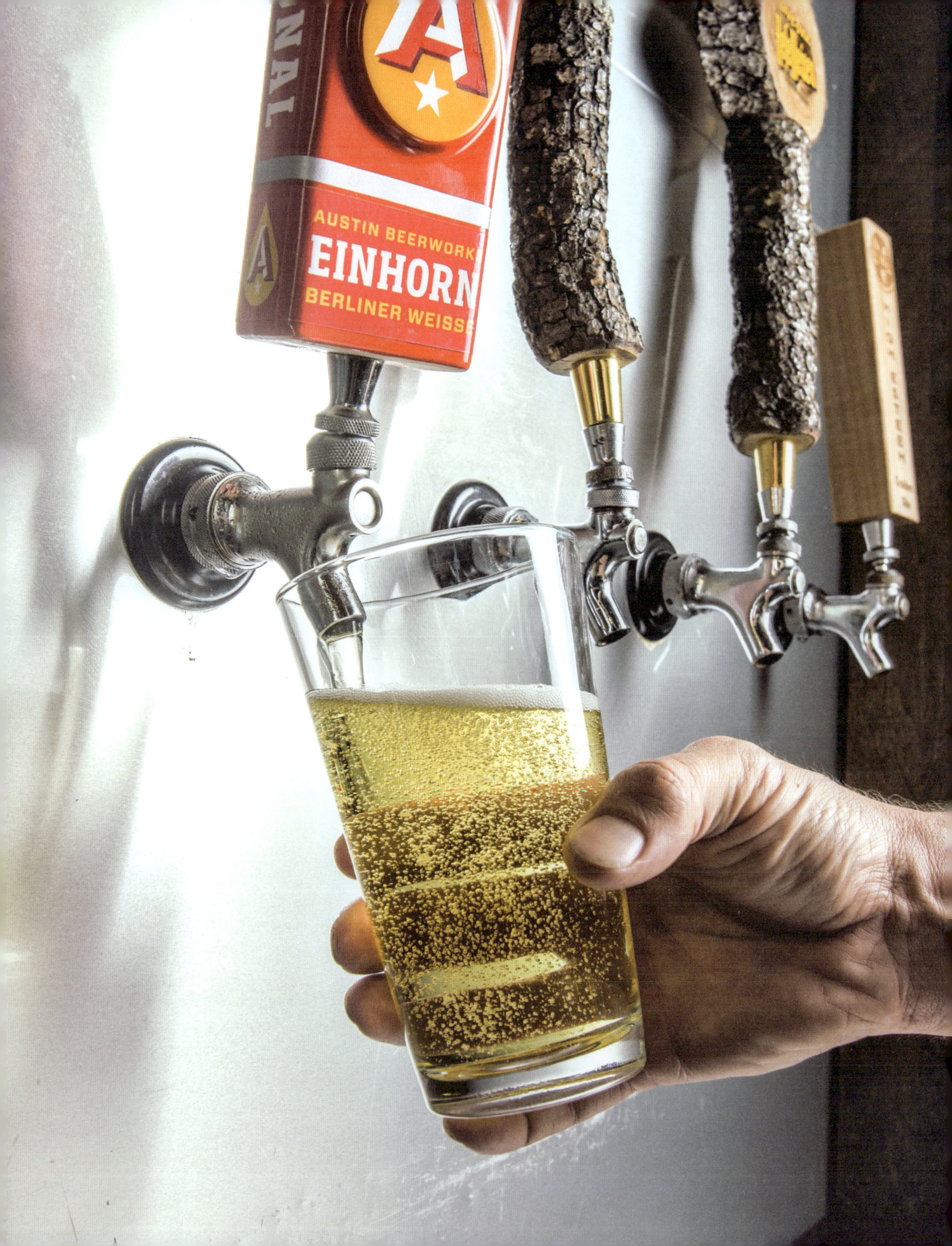
AUSTIN BEERWORK
EINHORN
BERLINER WEISSE

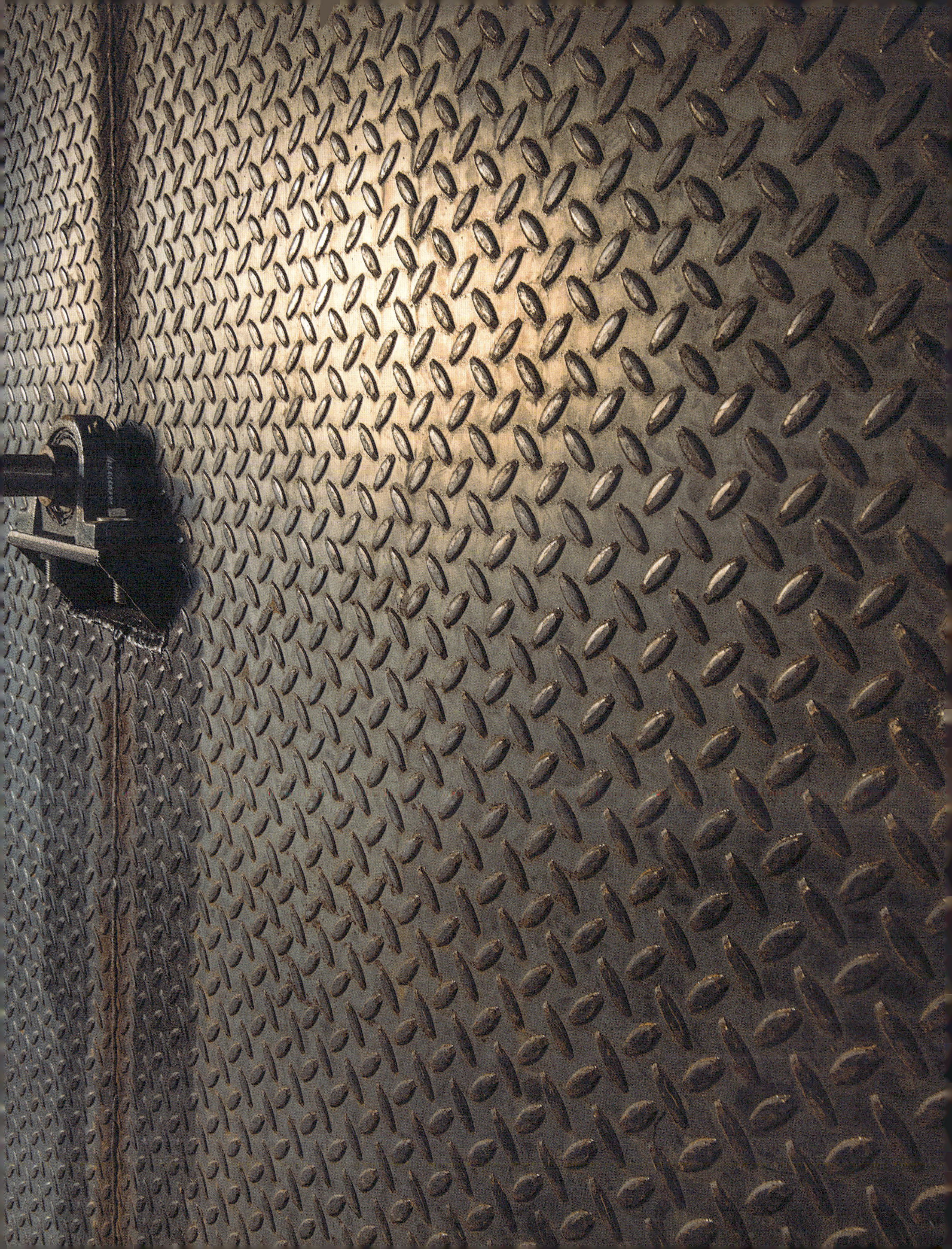

• *Resources*

MAIL-ORDER MEAT

Creekstone Farms
www.creekstonefarms.com

Snake River Farms
www.snakeriverfarms.com

CENTRAL TEXAS BREWERIES

Jester King Brewery
www.jesterkingbrewery.com

Live Oak Brewing Company
www.liveoakbrewing.com

Austin Beerworks
www.austinbeerworks.com

WOOD SOURCES

Craigslist
www.craigslist.org
- There are many online sources for various types of wood chips and chunks, but your best bet for buying whole logs is to find a local source via Craigslist.

BOOKS AND WEBSITES

McGee, Harold. *On Food and Cooking: The Science and Lore of the Kitchen.* New York: Scribner, 1984.

Myhrvold, Nathan, Chris Young, and Maxime Bilet. *Modernist Cuisine: The Art and Science of Cooking.* Bellevue, WA: The Cooking Lab, 2011.

www.amazingribs.com
- An amazing compendium of barbecue knowledge, not just in the Central Texas style, but also for all the different styles of cooking meat.

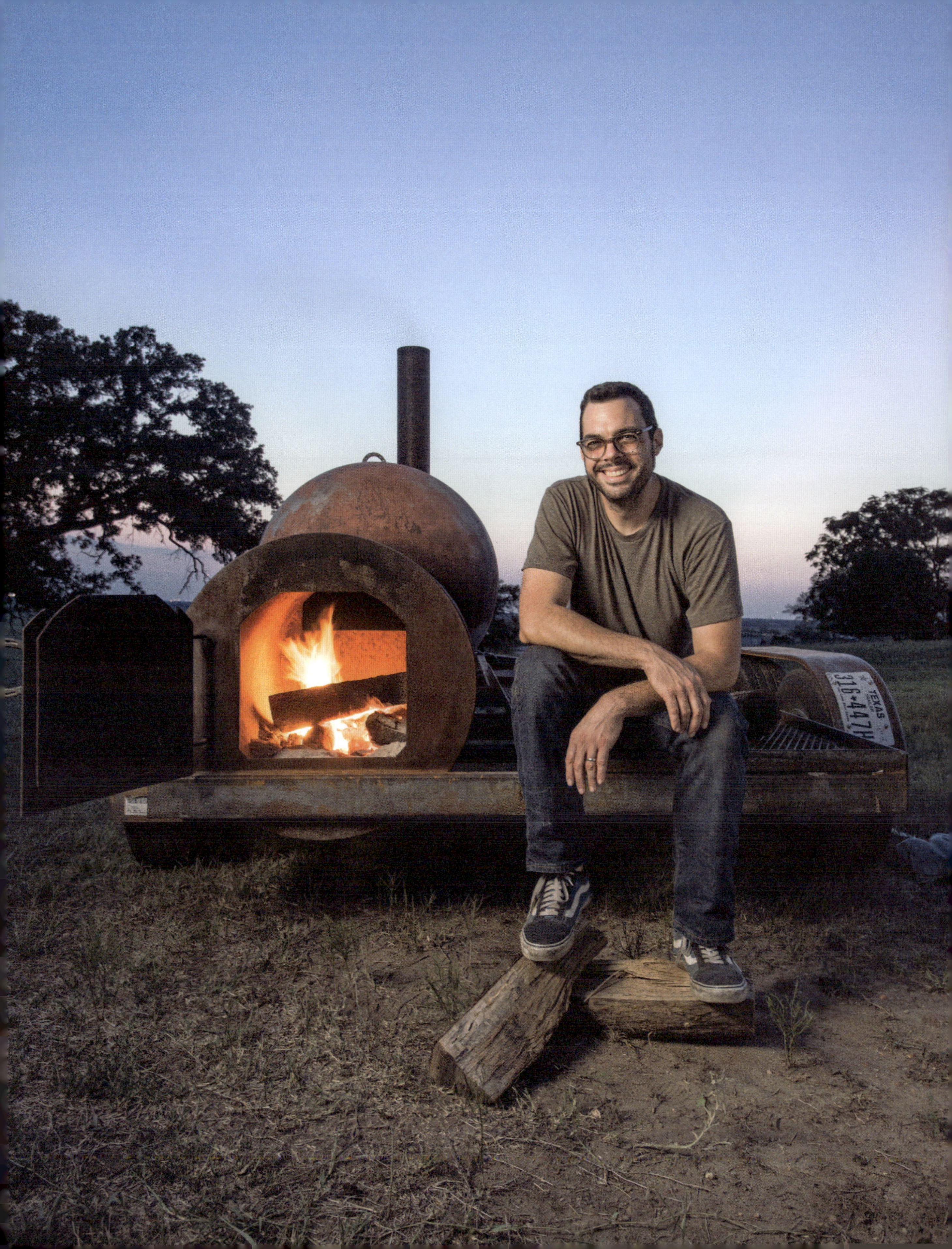
TEXAS
316★447H

• *Acknowledgments*

I poured what I know about barbecue into this book, but this tome and even the restaurant itself wouldn't have been possible without all the collaboration, unfettered support, and hard work of so many people over the years.

First and foremost I thank my wife, Stacy Franklin, the real reason any of this ever happened, and the most vital part of everything I am and do.

Hey, Benji Jacob: Those things don't work on water, unless you've got power! Benji is the third pillar on which Franklin Barbecue stands; he has committed almost as much of himself to this project as Stacy and I have, and has always been unimaginably generous with his hard work, time, and creativity.

Ben and Debbie Franklin, my parents, planted the seeds for this in many, many ways (besides the obvious one). Introducing me to barbecue and restaurant ownership at a young age and helping get things off the ground with some early funds are just two of the ways. Thanks so much.

Thanks to Tommy and Anita Howard, my grandparents. I grew up in their music store, and hanging out with them was a huge influence—without them I wouldn't be the person I am today. Among many other things, they gave me a sense of how to run a family business and an enduring love of music.

Also to my parents-in-law, Helen and Steve Jefferson: Thanks for spending so much time in Austin and always being there to lend a helping hand.

Same to Big Jeff Keyton and Travis Kizer, two guys who believed in me from the get-go, and through gestures big and small have helped me find just a smidge of success in the barbecue world.

Braun Hughes—brisket wizard, workhorse extraordinaire—has been there with me through thick and thin. Braun, besides being part of the family, you keep everything running, and we couldn't do it without you. Thanks, esé. Thanks also to the entire staff at the restaurant and to all the good employees who have ever worked with me. Franklin Barbecue wouldn't be what it is without all the people who have lent a piece of themselves to this project. And that would include

Melissa, the pie woman, often the first person I talk to in a day (when working a rib shift and she comes in at 4 or 5 in the morning to drop off the day's desserts). Also, I thank Rod, the wood guy, for keeping me in the good stuff and saving me from even more headaches. The wood is good. And Dr. Jeff Savell, Meat Science professor of A&M: thanks for bringing barbecue into the academy and giving us all a slight sense of actual sophistication.

When it comes to this book, I've got to recognize David Hale Smith for his hard work and commitment to getting the thing done, as well as for all the other times he's helped me navigate life's pesky fine print. Wyatt McSpadden's photos were totemic for me when I was getting into barbecue, so it was the greatest of honors to have him lend his immense talents to this book. Wyatt's also one of the greatest guys to just hang around and drink a beer with. Thanks to him, his wife, Nancy, and his assistant, Will.

Also, thanks to Jordan Mackay for his words. He somehow managed to make sense of what regularly spills out of my mouth and then spin it into a whole book with things like organization and punctuation. And then Emily Timberlake, our editor at Ten Speed, made sense of his work, while our designer Betsy Stromberg made it all look like a real book. Truly a team effort, so thanks to all the people who made this book a reality.

And, finally, I want to extend my greatest gratitude to all the customers, supporters, and people who've waited hours in line to eat at Franklin Barbecue or at various festivals around the country. I am truly humbled and honored that people consider what we've worked so hard to create to be worthy of their time and energy. Without all of you, honestly, none of this would have ever happened. I hope you'll keep coming back and that you'll enjoy this book.

• *Aaron Franklin*

As work on the book came to a close my wife, Christie Dufault, volunteered that I didn't have to thank her in the acknowledgments because she really doesn't have much to do with barbecue. As someone who sees herself a vegan at heart who is coerced by her husband into all-too-often consuming meat, she sort of had a point. But what she doesn't realize is that she's at the heart of everything I do. It is she that I strive to make proud, and her tolerance of my frequent smoke-tinged trips to Austin, my idiosyncratic work habits, and otherwise self-indulgent way of life allow me to be the sort of writer I want to be. So, sorry, honu, but thanks—for being our anchor and for making me laugh.

I also want to offer gratitude to my mom, Leslie, and to Neal for putting me up all those weeks I was working on the book and for re-arranging their lives so that I could save money by borrowing one of their cars. All that meant a lot. Plus, it was nice to get to spend some time around y'all. Also, I'd be remiss for not mentioning that all that time I was in Austin was likewise made possible by our dear neighbors and great friends Paul and Vanessa Einbund, who looked after Fernie and Thornie.

Thanks also to David Hale Smith for thinking to bring me in on this project and for being there every step of the way. David Black, thanks for getting this deal done; I see great projects in the future. This is my third book at Ten Speed, so I must extend gratitude to Aaron Wehner for continuing to have confidence in me. I also consider myself fortunate to have worked with Emily Timberlake, our wonderful editor. She contributed more than anyone will know. And, of course, muchos gracias to the great Harold McGee, who deigned to look over parts of this book to ensure they made scientific sense.

And, lastly, hail to Aaron Franklin for letting me do this project with him and for squeezing me into his ridiculously busy life (and therefore thanks to Stacy for likewise tolerating my continuous presence). Working on this book has been incredible for me—not just in what I've learned about barbecue, wood, welding, meat, and smoke, but in the general confidence I've gained in myself. Aaron, all that comes directly from your own immense knowledge and your own extraordinary, unshakable confidence. I just wish you could come see my backyard, because only you can figure out how to get that thing you built into it.

• *Jordan Mackay*

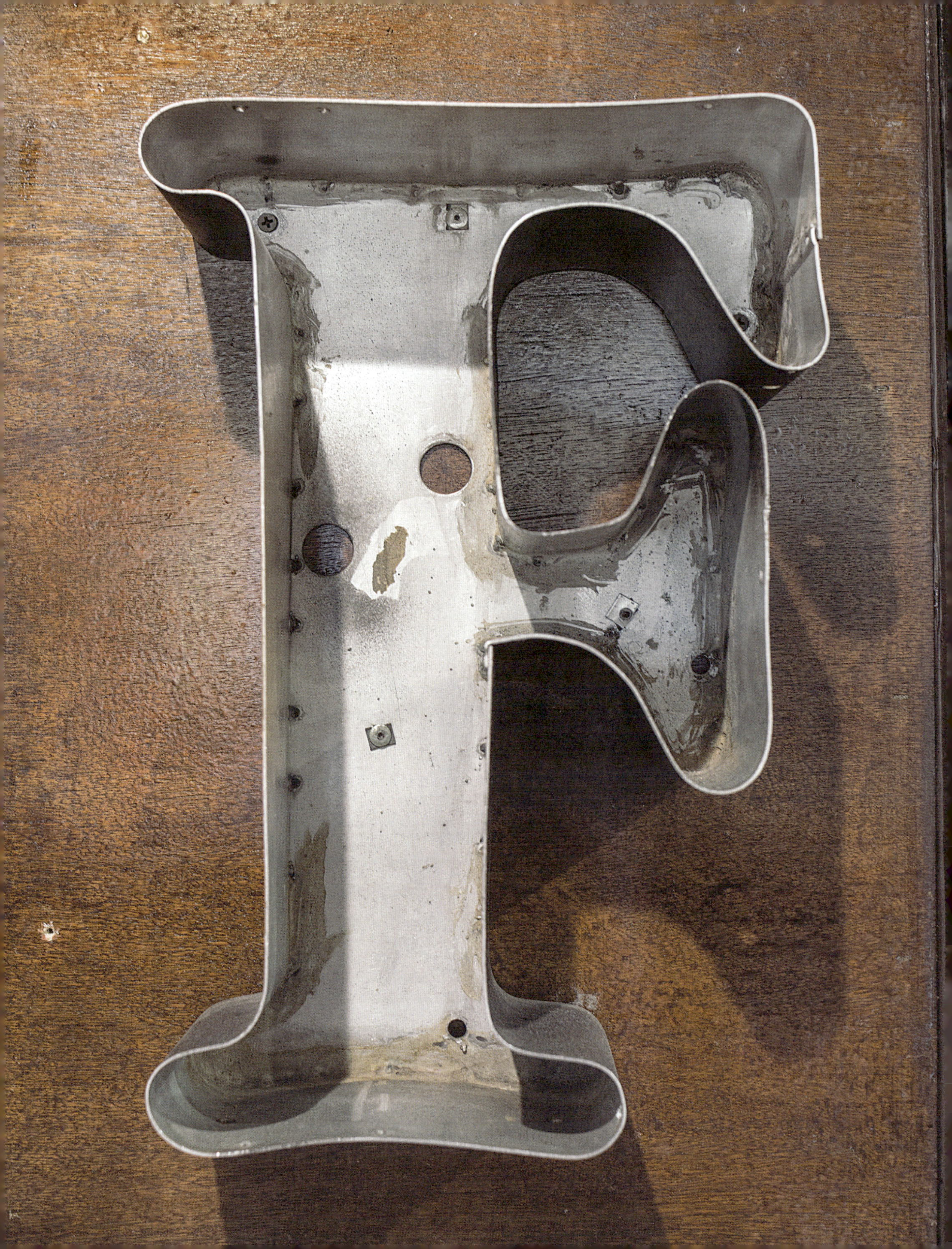

• *Index*

A

Aging, 110–11
Angus beef, 109
Apple wood, 77
Attention to detail, importance of, 128, 133

B

Baffles, 53, 68
Barbecue
    accompaniments for, 194
    culture, 10, 12
    pairing beer and, 199–200
    styles, 27
Barbecue joints
    history of, 36–37
    legendary, 14, 18
    odd hours of, 36–37
    ordering at, 180
Barbecue pits, 10, 41
Barganier, Joan, 77–78
Beans, 196
Bean seasoning, 196
Beef
    boxed vs. hanging, 105
    brands of, 109–10
    breeds of, 109–10
    from ethically treated cattle, 109
    flavoring, 137
    grades of, 108–9
    grass-fed, 111–12
    See also Beef ribs; Brisket
Beef ribs
    cooking, 171–72
    popularity of, 118–19
    shiners on, 113
    trimming, 171
    types of, 113
Beer
    barbecue sauce, fig ancho, 194
    pairing barbecue and, 199–200
Brisket
    aging and, 110–11
    applying slather and rub to, 153
    buying, 108–12
    checking for doneness, 156
    cooking, 147–58
    definition of, 106
    fat and, 106, 111–12
    flat, 106, 112
    flexibility of, 111
    frozen, 110
    grades of, 108–9
    grass-fed, 111–12
    history of, 105–6
    left-sided, 112
    packaging of, 110

Brisket, *continued*
    pack date of, 110
    placing in smoker, 154
    point, 106
    quality of, 103–6
    resting time for, 158
    size of, 106, 110
    slicing, 178, 180, 183–88
    trimming, 148–53
    wrapping, 139–40, 155–56
Buffer plates, 66

C

Camp Brisket, 105–6
Capello, Joe, 18
Casings, 121–22
Charcoal, 87
Cherry wood, 77
Chicken flavoring, 137
Chile powders, 136
City Market, 14, 18
Coal bed, developing, 96
Coleslaw, 197
Collagen, 131–32
Combustion
    completeness of, 92, 94, 95
    primary, 86–87
    secondary, 86, 94
Cook chamber
    material for, 54, 56
    size of, 56
    temperature of, 141–42
Cross contamination, 129

D

Doors
    cutting, 57–58
    opening, 96–97
    seals for, 52–53

E

Espresso barbecue sauce, 192–93
Evaporative cooling, 143–44

F

Face cord, 80
Fat, role of, 132
Fig ancho beer barbecue sauce, 194
Fire
    airflow and, 88, 94, 96–97
    basic philosophy of, 90
    building, 88
    in challenging weather conditions, 90, 141
    chess analogy for, 98
    fuel for, 86
    growing, 95–97
    maintaining, 97–98
    in small backyard smokers, 87
    temperature of, 94, 98
    triangle, 86, 87
    tuning, 97
    See also Smoke
Firebox
    attaching, 58
    insulated, 51
    material for, 54, 56
    size of, 56
Firewood. *See* Wood
Food safety, 129

INDEX

Franklin Barbecue
    cookers of, 39, 40, 47
    hours of, 36–37
    ordering at, 180
    restaurant opening of, 35
    success of, 23, 32, 35
    trailer, 13, 28–29, 31–32
    typical day at, 5–7, 10
Fruitwoods, 77

G

Garlic, granulated, 136

H

Hickory
    flavor, 137
    wood, 75

K

Keyton, Big Jeff, 14, 22, 31
Kindling, 88
Kizer, Travis, 29
Knives, 183
Kobe beef, 109
Kreuz Market, 14, 18

L

Lang, Adam Perry, 127
Lignin, 74
Little City, 17, 21
Louie Mueller Barbecue, 14, 17, 18, 118–19

M

Maillard reaction, 132
Marbling, 108
Mauls, 83
McGee, Harold, 74, 94, 132
McSpadden, Wyatt, 12
Meat
    basic steps for smoking, 133–44
    flavor of, 132
    food safety and, 129
    prices for, 108
    principles of smoking, 131–33
    quality of, 103–6
    temperature of, 142–44, 154–55, 156, 158
    See also individual meats
Mesquite
    flavor, 137
    wood, 74, 77
Moline, Rod, 77–78
Moss, Robert F., 36
Mueller, Bobby, 14
Mueller, John, 17, 23
Myoglobin, 145

O

Oak, 74–75
Onions
    granulated, 136
    sliced, 194

P

Pack dates, 110
Paprika, 136
Peach wood, 77
Pecan wood, 75

Pepper, black, 136
Perez, Roy, 18
Perseverance, importance of, 128
Pickles, 194
Pork
    breeds of, 118
    butt, 118–19
    pulled, 118–19
    solution-injected, 117
    in Texas, 27, 113
    See also Pork ribs
Pork ribs
    applying slather and rub to, 165
    buying, 117
    checking for doneness, 168
    cooking, 161–68
    placing in smoker, 165–66
    resting time for, 168
    sauce for, 166–67
    shiners on, 116
    trimming, 116–17, 161–65
    types of, 116
    wrapping, 167–68
Potato salad, 197

R

Rain, 90, 141
Restaurants. *See* Barbecue joints
Reverse flow smokers, 43, 126
Ribs. *See* Beef ribs; Pork ribs
Rubs
    applying, 138–39
    building, 137–38
    ingredients in, 134, 136–37
    recipes for, 137
    role of, 134

S

Safety concerns, 129
Salt
    kosher, 136
    seasoning, 136
Sandwich, Tipsy Texan, 188
Sauces
    attitudes toward, 191
    espresso barbecue, 192–93
    fig ancho beer barbecue, 194
    regular barbecue, 192
    vinegar, 193
Sausage
    casings, 121–22
    fat and, 121
    making, 119, 121
    seasoning, 121
Savell, Jeff, 106, 108, 110
Shiners, 113, 116
Shovels, 85, 98
Sides, 196–97
Slathers, 139
Smitty's Market, 12, 14, 18, 36
Smoke
    color of, 94–95
    components of, 91, 133
    creation of, 86–87
    good vs. bad, 90–92, 94–97
    inhalation, minimizing, 129
    magic of, 90
Smoke ring, 145
Smokers
    accessories for, 53
    airflow in, 48–49, 58–59, 63, 88
    barbecue pits, 10, 41
    building, 54–59
    burning out new, 59, 68
    buying, 49–53

INDEX

care and maintenance of, 68
developing relationship with, 68
of Franklin Barbecue, 39, 40, 47
location of, 50
modifying cheap store-bought, 62–63, 66–67
offset, 40, 43, 48–49
quality of, 52–53
reverse flow, 43, 126
size of, 50, 52
small backyard, 87
tuning plate, 43
upright drum, 45

Smokestacks
airflow and, 48–49
attaching, 58–59
damper on, 53
extending, 63, 66

Smoking
basic steps for, 133–44
principles of, 131–33

Snow's BBQ, 36
Soy powder, 137
Stall, the, 142–44, 154–55
Sugar, 137

T

Teague, Walter Dorwin, 29
Temperature
ambient outside, 141
of cook chamber, 141–42
dry bulb vs. wet bulb, 144
of fire, 94, 98
gauges, 53, 62–63
of meat, 142–44, 154–55, 156, 158
the stall, 142–44, 154–55
Thermometers, 53, 62–63
Tinder, 88

Tipsy Texan sandwich, 188
Tuning plates, 43
Turkey
buying, 122
cooking, 173–74

V

Vaughn, Daniel, 32
Vinegar sauce, 193

W

Wagyu beef, 109–10
Water pans, 68, 142
Weather conditions, challenging, 90, 141
Welding tools, 54, 56
Wind, 90, 141
Wood
amount of, 82
burning process for, 86–87
buying, 77–78, 80
cord of, 78, 80
green, 71–72, 80–81, 92, 101
importance of, 2
kiln-dried, 80
moisture content of, 80, 81
positives and negatives of, as fuel, 86
preheating, 96
properties of, 72, 74
seasoning, 80–82
size of, 97–98
splitting, 82–83
stacking, 82
from the supermarket, 80
types of, 74–75, 77
Worcestershire powder, 137
Wrapping, 139–40

Ten Speed Press
An imprint of the Crown Publishing Group
A division of Penguin Random House LLC
1745 Broadway
New York, NY 10019
tenspeed.com
penguinrandomhouse.com

2025 Ten Speed Press/Publishers Trade Paperback Box Edition
Text copyright © 2015 by Hasenpfeffer LLC
Photographs copyright © 2015 by Wyatt McSpadden

Penguin Random House values and supports copyright. Copyright fuels creativity, encourages diverse voices, promotes free speech, and creates a vibrant culture. Thank you for buying an authorized edition of this book and for complying with copyright laws by not reproducing, scanning, or distributing any part of it in any form without permission. You are supporting writers and allowing Penguin Random House to continue to publish books for every reader. Please note that no part of this book may be used or reproduced in any manner for the purpose of training artificial intelligence technologies or systems.

Ten Speed Press and the Ten Speed Press colophon are registered trademarks of Penguin Random House LLC.

ISBN 978-0-399-58096-3
Ebook ISBN 978-0-399-58097-0
Box set ISBN 978-0-593-83963-8

Originally published in the United States in hardcover by Ten Speed Press, an imprint of the Crown Publishing Group, a division of Penguin Random House, LLC, in 2015.

Photograph on page iv is copyright © Jeff Stockton. All other photographs are by Wyatt McSpadden.

Design and illustrations by Betsy Stromberg

Manufactured in China

10 9 8 7 6 5 4 3 2 1

First Paperback Box Edition

The authorized representative in the EU for product safety and compliance is Penguin Random House Ireland, Morrison Chambers, 32 Nassau Street, Dublin D02 YH68, Ireland, https://eu-contact.penguin.ie.